Fifth
Edition

APPLIED PSYCHOLOGY IN HUMAN RESOURCE MANAGEMENT

Wayne F. Cascio
Graduate School of Business
University of Colorado—Denver

Prentice Hall, Upper Saddle River, NJ 07458

Acquisitions Editor: *David Shafer*
Associate Editor: *Lisamarie Brassini*
Editorial Assistant: *Chris Stodgill*
Editor-in-Chief: *James C. Boyd*
Marketing Manager: *Stephanie Johnson*
Production Editor: *Maureen Wilson*
Managing Editor: *Dee Josephson*
Manufacturing Buyer: *Kenneth J. Clinton*
Manufacturing Supervisor: *Arnold Vila*
Manufacturing Manager: *Vincent Scelta*
Composition: *Rainbow Graphics, Inc.*
Copyeditor: *Joan Pokorny*

Copyright © 1998, 1991, 1987, 1982, 1978 by Prentice-Hall, Inc.
A Simon & Schuster Company
Upper Saddle River, NJ 07458

Library of Congress Cataloging-in-Publication Data

Cascio, Wayne F.
    Applied psychology in human resource management / Wayne F. Cascio.
  —5th ed.
        p.   cm.
    Rev. ed. of: Applied psychology in personnel management. 4th ed.
1991.
    Includes bibliographical references and indexes.
    ISBN 0-13-834228-8
    1. Personnel management—Psychological aspects.   2. Psychology,
Industrial.   3. Personnel management—United States.   4. Psychology,
Industrial—United States.   I. Cascio, Wayne F.   Applied psychology
in personnel management.   II. Title.
HF5549.C297   1997
658.3′001′9—dc21   97-2914
                                                                CIP

Prentice-Hall International (UK) Limited, *London*
Prentice-Hall of Australia Pty. Limited, *Sydney*
Prentice-Hall Canada, Inc., *Toronto*
Prentice-Hall Hispanoamericana, S.A., *Mexico*
Prentice-Hall of India Private Limited, *New Delhi*
Prentice-Hall of Japan, Inc., *Tokyo*
Simon & Schuster Asia Pte. Ltd., *Singapore*
Editora Prentice-Hall do Brasil, Ltda., *Rio de Janeiro*

Printed in the United States of America
10 9 8 7 6 5 4 3 2

*To My Mother and Dad
whose generosity and self-sacrifice
enabled me to have what they did not*

Brief Contents

Contents

Preface to the Fifth Edition

As in the first four editions of this book, I have tried to create an interdisciplinary-oriented, research-based HR text. My subject matter is personnel psychology—the application of psychological research and theory to human resource problems in organizations. As an applied area of psychology, personnel psychology seeks to make organizations more effective and more satisfying as places to work.

Personnel psychology represents the overlap between psychology and human resource management (HRM). It is a subfield within HRM, excluding, for example, such topics as labor law, organization planning, compensation and benefits, and labor relations. By definition, therefore, this text does not treat all of the areas within the field of HRM comprehensively. Personnel psychology is also a subfield within industrial/organizational (I/O) psychology—the study of human behavior in the work setting. Today, with the tremendous growth of I/O psychology in a variety of directions, HR is appropriately considered only one of many areas to which I/O psychologists have turned their attention.

To be sure, the HR function has changed drastically. Twenty-five years ago it was primarily concerned with housekeeping, file maintenance, and organizational firefighting. Today's top HR manager (Director of Human Resources) often functions as a strategic partner with other top managers of a business. He or she is in on the initial stages of important policy decisions and frequently carries a senior vice-presidential rank. Civil rights legislation, close scrutiny of HR practices of public and private sector organizations by compliance agencies of the federal government, the specter of civil suits or loss of government contracts, the growing administrative complexity of numerous HRM programs are just some of the reasons why the responsibilities of today's HR manager have increased dramatically. HR professionals must, therefore, have a sound understanding of the theory, assumptions, and implications of their policies and procedures, for blatant mistakes in this area can be *very* expensive. The cost in dollars, efficiency, and employee frustration simply cannot be tolerated. In light of the dramatic changes that have characterized the field, I have changed the name of the text to emphasize the interaction of applied psychology and human resource management.

As in the first four editions, I have included material of a decidedly theoretical, statistical, or psychometric nature. No doubt some readers will criticize the book on these grounds and charge that "things just aren't done that way in the real world." Perhaps not, for I agree that some of the ideas and techniques in this book (e.g., decision-theory, experimental and quasi-experimental designs to evaluate HR programs) are probably used by very few organizations. Nevertheless, having consulted with (and having testified either for or against) both public and private sector organizations, I firmly believe that these approaches should be adopted more widely. The book is designed to be forward-looking and progressive, and even though some of the material is presented in a conventional manner with a dose of statistical, psychometric, or psychological theory thrown in, I believe that in the last analysis nothing is more practical.

In writing this book, I have made two assumptions about my readers: (1) that they are familiar with the general problems of HRM or I/O psychology, and (2) that they have some background in fundamental statistics—at least enough to understand statistical procedures on a conceptual level, and preferably enough to compute and interpret tests of significance. As in the earlier editions, my goals are: (1) to challenge the field to advance rather than simply to document past practice, (2) to present a model toward which HR specialists should aim, and (3) to present scientific procedure and fundamental theory so that the serious student can develop a solid foundation upon which to build a broad base of knowledge.

My overall objective is to integrate psychological theory with tools and methods that will enable the student or professional to translate theory into practice effectively. I realize that in the complex and dynamic environment in which we live and work, scientific and technological advances are occurring faster than ever before. Hence, education must be a lifelong affair if one is to avoid what Armer (1970) calls the "Paul Principle": Over time individuals often become uneducated and therefore incompetent at a level at which they once performed quite adequately. If the book projects this one message, then the HR profession will be enriched immeasurably.

The response to the first four editions of this book in psychology departments and in business and professional schools has been particularly gratifying. However, new ideas and research findings in all the areas covered by the book made a fifth edition necessary in order to reflect the state of the art in personnel psychology. In fact, over 50 percent of the references in this fifth edition are new! Year by year the field continues to advance rapidly. Here is a sample of what is new in the fifth edition:

- On a general level, I have added many practical examples of company HRM practices to each chapter of the text, while retaining its research-based character. In addition, each chapter now contains a set of five discussion questions to help students reflect on the implications of what they have read.

- There is extensive treatment of the changing nature of product and service markets, the effects of technology on organizations and people, new forms of organization, and the changing roles of managers and workers.

- We examine the provisions and implications of two recent employment laws—the Civil Rights Act of 1991 and the Family and Medical Leave Act of 1993—as well as the impact of "English-only" rules at work.

- We highlight some of the major rulings (and their implications) of recent civil rights cases decided by the Supreme Court, especially those that concern sexual harassment.

- There is more emphasis on the interpersonal and political nature of the performance appraisal process, on alternative perspectives from which to rate performance, and on practical guidelines for providing feedback.

- Chapter 7 includes new information on construct-oriented evidence of validity, validity generalization, and meta-analysis.

- Chapter 8 includes discussion of sliding bands as a new, alternative model of selection fairness.

- Chapter 9 now includes: (1) a discussion of the implications of shifting from a task-based to a process-based organization of work, as more and more firms reengineer their work processes; (2) a discussion of future- or strategically-oriented job analyses; and (3) examples of scales from the Fleishman Job Analysis Survey designed to measure the ability requirements of jobs.

- I discuss more thoroughly the inextricable links between HR strategy and general business strategy, and present a company example that illustrates the linkage ("How AT&T Global Business Communications Systems Links Its People to Its Business Strategy"). I also explore the effect of mergers, acquisitions, and downsizing on career management systems.

- I split recruitment and initial screening into separate chapters to provide more extensive coverage of these topics. With respect to recruitment, we consider the impact of computers on recruitment ("How Micron Technology, Unisys, and Bristol-Myers Squibb Find Top Students"), recruiting for diversity, recruiting in cyberspace, recruitment tracking ("How Motorola Tracks Résumés"), and new findings in the area of job search ("How Not to Find a New Job").

- Chapter 12 includes new research on letters of recommendation ("How to Get Useful Information from a Reference Check"), plus the latest legal and scientific developments in the use of drug screening, honesty tests, biographical data, and pre-employment interviews. Special sections highlight the practical implications of these developments.

- New developments in the theory and application of cutoff scores are evaluated in Chapter 13, as are advances in utility theory and the strategic context of personnel selection.

- Recent findings regarding personal characteristics that predict success for both males and females as managers, along with novel approaches to the assessment of personality characteristics required for managerial success ("How Microsoft Finds Top Talent"), are considered in Chapter 14.

- Chapter 15 presents the latest findings regarding classification strategies for team jobs.

- Characteristics of effective training practice ("Results of Behavior Modeling Training at Champion International") and new approaches to training-needs identification are discussed in Chapter 16, as are new findings regarding training practices that facilitate positive transfer back to the work setting.

- As in previous editions, Chapter 17 includes the presentation of experimental and quasi-experimental designs to assess training outcomes. However, it now includes a more thorough discussion of some of the practical implications of these designs ("Limitations of Experimental Designs"; "The Hazards of Nonequivalent Designs").

- Finally, Chapter 18 addresses several emerging ethical issues in HRM, such as employee rights to electronic privacy (electronic and voice mail), fair information practice in the information age, workplace investigations, and company codes of ethics. Company illustrations reinforce the importance of these issues ("How Johnson & Johnson's Ethics Code Saved the Tylenol Brand"; "Dun & Bradstreet's Framework for Identifying and Resolving Ethical Issues").

Thanks go to the following people for their helpful comments: Sheldon Zedeck, UC Berkeley;

David Day, Penn State; Paul Greenlaw, Penn State; and Ed Ward, St. Cloud State University.

I would be remiss if I did not acknowledge the moral support and the encouragement (and many times the patience!) of my wife, Dorothy, and son, Joe, throughout the project. Their love and devotion make good times better and bad times a little easier to take.

WAYNE F. CASCIO
Denver, Colorado

1

ORGANIZATIONS, WORK, AND APPLIED PSYCHOLOGY

AT A GLANCE

Human organizations are all around—businesses, hospitals, political parties, military organizations, social clubs, churches, Boy and Girl Scouts, and Little Leagues, just to name a few. Each organization has its own particular set of objectives, and, in order to function effectively, each organization must subdivide its overall task into various jobs. Jobs differ in their requirements. Likewise, people differ in aptitudes, abilities, and interests, and along many other dimensions. Faced with such variability in people and jobs, programs for the efficient use of human resources are essential.

As we move from the Industrial Age to the Information Age, *job* security (the belief that one will retain employment with the same organization until retirement) has become less important to workers than *employment* security (having the kinds of skills that employers in the labor market are willing to pay for).

Hence workplace training and development activities will be top priorities for organizations and their people. Demographic changes in society will make recruitment and personnel selection key considerations for many organizations. Cultural diversity at work will be a major theme as the composition of the work force changes.

Guided by the fundamental assumption that in a free society every individual has a basic and inalienable right to compete for any job for which he or she is qualified, we turn to a consideration of how personnel psychology can contribute to a wiser, more humane use of our human resources. If present market, technological, social, and economic indicators predict future concerns, personnel psychology will play an increasingly significant role in the world of work during the remainder of the 1990s and into the twenty-first century.

THE PERVASIVENESS OF ORGANIZATIONS

Throughout the course of our lives each of us is deeply touched by organizations of one form or another. In the normal course of events, a child will be exposed to a school organization, a church or religious organization, and perhaps a Little League or a Boy or Girl Scout organization, as well as the social organization of the local community. After leaving the school organization the young person may choose to join a military, business, or service organization, and as his or her career unfolds, the person probably will move across several different organizations. The point is simply that our everyday lives are inseparably intertwined with organizational memberships of one form or another.

What common characteristics unite these various activities under the collective label "organization"? The question is not an easy one to answer. Many different definitions of organization have been suggested and each definition reflects the background and theoretical point of view of its author with respect to what is relevant and/or important. Yet certain fundamental elements recur in these definitions.

In general, an organization is a collection of people working together in a division of labor to achieve a common purpose (Schermerhorn, Hunt, and Osborn, 1994). Another useful concept views an organization as a system of inputs, throughputs, and outputs. Inputs (raw materials) are imported from the outside environment, transformed or modified (e.g., every day tons of steel are molded into automobile bodies), and finally exported or sold back into the environment as outputs (finished products). Although there are many inputs to organizations (energy, raw materials, information, etc.), people are the basic ingredients of *all* organizations, and social relationships are the cohesive bonds that tie them together (see Fig. 1–1).

This book is about people as members and resources of organizations and about what personnel psychology can contribute toward helping organizations make the wisest, most humane use of human resources. *Personnel psychology is concerned with individual differences in behavior and job performance, and with measuring and predicting such differences.* In the following sections we will consider some of the sources of these differences.

Differences in Jobs

In examining the world of work, one is immediately awed by the vast array of goods and services that have been and are being produced as a result of organized effort. This great variety ranges from the manufacture of tangible products, such as food, automobiles, plastics, paper, textiles, and glassware, to the provision of less tangible services, such as legal counsel, medical care, police and fire protection, and education. Thousands of jobs are part of our workaday world, and the variety of task and human requirements necessary to carry out this work is staggering. Faced with such variability in jobs and their requirements on the one hand, and with people and their individual patterns of values, aspirations, interests, and abilities on the other, programs for the efficient use of human resources are essential.

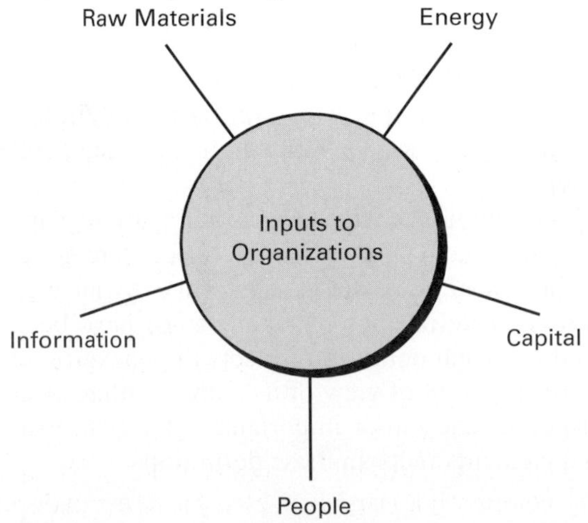

Differences in Performance

People represent substantial investments by firms—as is immediately evident when one stops to consider the costs of recruiting, selecting, placing, and training as many people as there are organizational roles to fill. But psychology's first law is that people are different. People differ in size, weight, and other physical dimensions, as well as in aptitudes, abilities, temperaments, interests, and a myriad of other psychological dimensions. People also differ greatly in the extent to which they are willing and able to commit their energies and resources to the attainment of organizational objectives.

If we observe a group of individuals doing the same kind of work, it will soon be evident that some are more effective workers than others. For example, if we observe a group of carpenters building cabinets, we will notice that some work faster than others, make fewer mistakes than others, and seem to enjoy their work more than others. These observations pose a question of psychological interest. Why? What "people differences" cause these "work differences"? Perhaps these variations in effectiveness are due to differences in abilities. Some of the carpenters may be stronger, have keener eyesight, and have more finely developed motor coordination than others. Perhaps another reason for the observed differences in behavior is motivation. At any given point in time, the strength of forces impelling an individual to put forth effort on a given task, or to reach a certain goal, may vary drastically. In other words, differences in individual performance on any task, or on any job, could be due to differences in ability, motivation, or both. This has clear implications for the optimal use of individual talents in our society.

A Utopian Ideal

In an idealized existence our goal would be to assess each individual's aptitudes, abilities, personality, and interests, to profile these characteristics, and then to

FIGURE 1–1 Inputs to Organizations.

Raw Materials — Energy — Information — Inputs to Organizations — Capital — People place all individuals in jobs perfectly suited to them and to society. Each individual would make the best and wisest possible use of his or her talents, while in the aggregate, society would be making maximal use of its most precious resource.

Alas, this ideal falls far short in practice. The many, and often gross, mismatches between individual capabilities and organizational roles are glaringly obvious even to the most casual observer—history Ph.D.s driving taxicabs for lack of professional work, or young people full of enthusiasm, drive, and intelligence placed on monotonous, routine, dead-end jobs.

Point of View

In any presentation of issues it is well to make explicit underlying assumptions. The assumptions that have influenced the presentation of this book are:

1. In a free society every individual, regardless of race, age, sex, disability, religion, or national origin, has a fundamental and inalienable right to compete for any job for which he or she is qualified.

2. Society can and should do a better job of making the wisest and most humane use of its human resources.

3. Individuals working in the field of human resources, and managers responsible for making employment decisions, must be as technically competent and well informed as possible, since their decisions will materially affect the course of individual livelihoods and lives. Personnel psychology holds considerable potential for improving the caliber of human resource management in organizations. Several recent developments have combined to stimulate this growing awareness on the part of students, practitioners, and professionals. After first describing what personnel psychology is, we will consider the nature of some of these developments.

PERSONNEL PSYCHOLOGY IN PERSPECTIVE

People have always been subjects of inquiry by psychologists, and the behavior of people at work has been the particular subject matter of industrial and organizational psychology. Yet sciences and subdisciplines within sciences are distinguished not so much by the subject matter they study as by the questions they ask. Thus, both the social psychologist and the engineering psychologist are concerned with studying people. The engineering psychologist is concerned

with the design of jobs, workplaces, information systems, and aspects of the work environment. The social psychologist studies power and influence, attitude change, communication in groups, and individual and group social behavior.

Personnel psychology is a subfield within industrial and organizational psychology. It is an applied discipline that focuses on individual differences in behavior and job performance and on methods of measuring and predicting such differences. Some of the major areas of interest of personnel psychologists include job analysis and job evaluation, recruitment, screening, and selection, training and development, and performance appraisal.

Personnel psychology also represents the overlap between psychology and human resource management (HRM). HRM is the attraction, selection, retention, development, and use of human resources in order to achieve both individual and organizational objectives (Cascio, 1998). As a subfield of HRM, personnel psychology excludes, for example, such topics as labor and compensation law, organization theory, industrial medicine, collective bargaining, and employee benefits. Psychologists have already made substantial contributions to the field of HRM; in fact, most of the empirical knowledge available in such areas as motivation, leadership, and personnel selection is due to their work. Throughout the 1990s, dramatic changes in markets, technology, organizational designs, and the respective roles of managers and workers have inspired renewed emphasis and interest in personnel psychology today (Cascio, 1995). The following sections consider each of these in more detail. Figure 1–2 illustrates them graphically.

The Changing Nature of Product and Service Markets

Just as wars—two World Wars, the Korean conflict, Vietnam, and Desert Storm—dominated the geopolitical map of the twentieth century, economics will rule over the twenty-first. The competition that is normal and inevitable among nations increasingly will be played out not in aggression or war, but in the economic sphere. The weapons used will be those of commerce: growth rates, investments, trade blocs, imports and exports (Nelan, 1992).

These changes reflect the impact of globalized product and service markets, coupled with increased domestic competition (largely fueled by deregulation

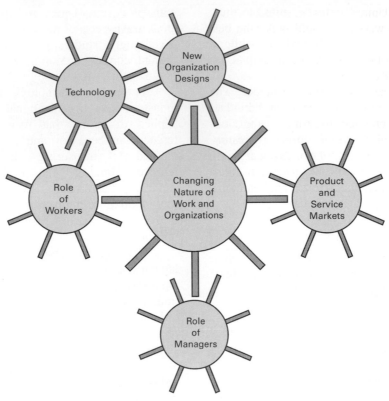

FIGURE 1–2 The Changing Nature of Work and Organizations.

in telecommunications, airlines, and banking) and new business start-ups. By a wide margin, however, global competition is the single most powerful economic fact of life in the 1990s. In the relatively sheltered era of the 1960s only 7 percent of the U.S. economy was exposed to international competition. In the 1980s, that number zoomed past 70 percent, and it will keep climbing (Gwynne, 1992). Today, one in five American jobs is tied directly or indirectly to international trade. Merchandise exports are up more than 40 percent since 1986, and every $1 billion in U.S. merchandise exports generates approximately 20,000 new jobs. For the most part these are good jobs that pay about 22 percent more than average ("Investing in people," 1994).

The results of accelerated global competition have been almost beyond comprehension—free political debate throughout the former Soviet empire, democratic reforms in Central and South America, the integration of the European community, the North American Free Trade Agreement, and an explosion of free market entrepreneurship in Southern China. In short, the free markets and free labor markets that

we in the United States have enjoyed throughout our national history have now become a global passion.

There is no going back. Today firms and workers in America must compete for business with firms and workers in the same industries in England, France, and Germany, in Poland, Hungary, and the former Russian republics, in Mexico, Brazil, Argentina, and Chile, in Japan, Korea, Malaysia, Taiwan, Singapore, Hong Kong, and China, just to name a few of our competitors. However, it takes more than trade agreements, technology, capital investment, and infrastructure to deliver world-class products and services. It also takes the skills, ingenuity, and creativity of a competent, well-trained workforce. Our competitors know this, and they are spending unstintingly to create one.

Impact on Jobs in the United States. As nations around the world transition from wartime to peacetime economies, from industrial societies to information societies, we are witnessing wrenching structural changes in our economy. These changes have impacted most profoundly in terms of jobs

(Cascio, 1993). In the United States, more than 7 million permanent layoffs were announced between 1987 and 1995.

Companies are not downsizing because they are losing money. Fully 81 percent of companies that downsize in a given year were profitable in that year. Rather, downsizings tend to be strategic or structural in nature: to improve productivity, transfers of location, new technological processes, mergers/acquisitions, or plant obsolescence ("1994 AMA"). Jobs aren't being lost *temporarily* because of a recession; rather they are being wiped out *permanently* as a result of new technology, improved machinery, and new ways of organizing work. These changes have had, and will continue to have, dramatic effects on organizations and their people.

Effects of Technology on Organizations and People

Fifty million workers use computers every day, along with other products of the digital age—faxes, modems, cellular phones, and E-mail. This is breaking down departmental barriers, enhancing the sharing of vast amounts of information, creating "virtual offices" for workers on the go, collapsing product development cycles, and changing the ways that organizations service customers and relate to their suppliers and employees. To succeed and prosper in the changing world of work, companies need motivated, technically literate workers.

A caveat is in order here, however. It relates to the common assumption that since production processes have become more sophisticated, high technology can substitute for skill in managing a workforce. Beware of such a "logic trap." On the contrary, high technology actually makes the workforce even more important for success, as Pfeffer (1994) has noted: "This is because more skill may be necessary to operate the more sophisticated and advanced equipment, and with a higher level of investment per employee, interruptions in the process are increasingly expensive. This means that the ability to effectively operate, maintain, and repair equipment—tasks all done by first-line employees—become even more critical" (p. 8). Ideally, therefore, technology will help workers make decisions in organizations that encourage them to do so ("Workplace of the Future," 1993). However, organizations of the future will look very different from organizations of the past, as the next section illustrates.

Changes in the Structure and Design of Organizations

In today's world of fast-moving global markets and fierce competition, the windows of opportunity are often frustratingly brief (Byrne, 1993). The features that dominated industrial society's approach to designing organizations throughout the nineteenth and twentieth centuries—mass production and large organizations—are disappearing. Trends such as the following are accelerating the shift toward new forms of organization for the twenty-first century (Kiechel, 1993):

- Smaller companies that employ fewer people.
- The shift from vertically integrated hierarchies to networks of specialists.
- Technicians, ranging from computer repair persons to radiation therapists, replacing manufacturing operatives as the worker elite.
- Pay tied less to a person's position or tenure in an organization, and more to the market value of his or her skills.
- A change in the paradigm of doing business from making a product to providing a service.
- The redefinition of work itself: growing disappearance of "the job" as a fixed bundle of tasks (see Bridges, 1994), emphasis on constantly changing work required to fulfill the ever-increasing demands of customers. This will require constant learning, more higher-order thinking, and less 9 to 5.

In this emerging world of work, more and more organizations will focus carefully on their core competencies, and outsource everything else. They will be characterized by terms such as "virtual," "boundaryless," and "flexible," with no guarantees to workers or managers.

This approach to organizing is no short-term fad. The fact is, organizations are becoming leaner and leaner, with better and better trained "multispecialists"—those who have in-depth knowledge about a number of different aspects of the business. Eschewing narrow specialists or broad generalists, organizations of the future will come to rely on cross-trained multispecialists in order to get things done. One such group whose roles are changing dramatically is that of managers.

The Changing Role of the Manager

In the traditional hierarchy that used to comprise most bureaucratic organizations, rules were simple. Managers ruled by *command* from the top (essentially one-way communication), used rigid *controls* to ensure that fragmented tasks (grouped into clearly defined jobs) could be coordinated effectively, and partitioned information into neat *compartments*—departments, units, and functions. Information was (and is) power, and, at least in some cases, managers clung to power by hoarding information. This approach to organizing, that is, 3-C logic, was geared to achieve three objectives: stability, predictability, and efficiency.

In today's reengineered, hyper-competitive work environments, the autocratic, top-down command-and-control approach is out of step with the competitive realities that many organizations face. To survive, organizations have to be able to respond quickly to shifting market conditions. In this kind of environment, a key job for all managers, especially top managers, is to articulate a vision of what the organization stands for and what it is trying to accomplish. The next step is to translate that vision into everything that is done, and to use the vision as a benchmark to assess progress over time.

A large and growing number of organizations now recognize that they need to emphasize workplace democracy in order to achieve the vision. This involves breaking down barriers, sharing information, using a collaborative approach to problem solving, and an orientation toward continuous learning and improvement. For many managers, these kinds of skills simply weren't needed in organizations designed and structured under 3-C logic.

Does this imply that we are moving toward a universal model of organizational and leadership effectiveness? Hardly. Contingency theories of leadership such as path-goal theory (House and Mitchell, 1974), normative decision theory (Vroom and Yetton, 1973), or LPC contingency theory (Fiedler, 1967), suggest that an autocratic style is appropriate in some situations. In recent years many organizations (e.g., Eaton Corporation, Levi Strauss & Co.) have instituted formal information-sharing and workplace education programs that reduce or eliminate a key condition that makes autocratic leadership appropriate—workers who lack the information or knowledge needed to make meaningful suggestions or decisions. More often, today's networked, interdependent, culturally-diverse organizations require transformational leadership (Bass, 1985). The ability of leaders to transform followers to bring out their creativity, imagination, and best efforts requires well-developed interpersonal skills, founded on an understanding of human

behavior in organizations. Industrial and organizational psychologists are well-positioned to help managers develop those kinds of skills.

In addition, although by no means universal, much of the work that results in a product, service, or decision is now done in *teams—intact, identifiable social systems (even if small or temporary) whose members have the authority to manage their own task and interpersonal processes as they carry out their work.* Such teams go by a variety of names—autonomous work groups, process teams, and self-managing work teams (see Fig. 1–3). All of this implies a radical reorientation from the traditional view of a manager's work.

In this kind of an environment, workers are acting more like managers, and managers more like workers. The managerial roles of "controllers," "planners," and "inspectors" are being replaced by "coaches," "facilitators," and "mentors" (Wellins, Byham, and Wilson, 1991). This doesn't just happen; it requires good interpersonal skills, continuous learning, and an organizational culture that supports and encourages both.

Flattened hierarchies also mean that there are fewer managers in the first place. The empowered worker will be a defining feature of such organizations.

The Empowered Worker—No Passing Fad

It should be clear by now that we are in the midst of a revolution—a revolution at work. Change isn't coming only from large, high-profile companies doing high-technology work. It has also permeated unglamorous, low-tech work. For example, consider Toronto-based Cadet Uniform Services, which outfits the employees of some of North America's leading corporations (Henkoff, 1994).

Organizations of the 1990s, both large and small, differ dramatically in structure, design, and demographics from those of even a decade ago. Demographically they are far more diverse. They comprise more women at all levels, more multiethnic, multicultural workers, more older workers, workers with disabilities, robots, and contingent workers. Paternalism is out; self-reliance is in. There's constant pressure to do more with less, and steady emphasis on empowerment, cross-training, personal flexibility, self-managed work teams, and continuous learning. Workers today have to be able to adapt to changing circumstances, and be prepared for multiple careers. Personnel psychologists are helping to educate

FIGURE 1–3 Teams Are Now, and Will Continue to Be, Key Features of Organizations.

prospective, current, and former workers to these new realities. In the future, they will be expected to do much more, as we shall see, but first let's consider some organizational responses to these new realities.

Implications for Organizations and Their People

What do these trends imply for the ways that organizations will compete for business? In a world where virtually every factor that affects the production of goods or the delivery of services—capital, equipment, technology, and information—is available to every player in the global economy, the one factor that doesn't routinely move across national borders is a nation's workforce. In the years to come, the quality of the American workforce will be a crucial determinant of our ability to compete and win in world markets.

Human resources can be sources of sustained competitive advantage as long as they meet three basic requirements: (1) they add positive economic benefits to the process of producing goods or delivering services; (2) the skills of the work force are distinguishable from those of competitors (e.g., through education and workplace learning); and (3) such skills are not easily duplicated (Barney, 1991). Human resource systems (the set of interrelated processes designed to attract, develop, and maintain human resources) can either enhance or destroy this potential competitive advantage (Lado and Wilson, 1994).

Perhaps a quote attributed to Albert Einstein, the famous physicist, best captures the position of this book. After the first atomic reaction in 1942, Einstein remarked: "Everything has changed, except our way of thinking" (Workplace, 1993, p. 2). As industrial and organizational psychology in general, and personnel psychology in particular, stands poised on the brink of

---

HRM IN ACTION—CADET UNIFORM SERVICES

Cadet doesn't just hire people to drive trucks, deliver clean uniforms, and pick up dirty ones. Rather, its concept of "customer service representatives" (CSRs) extends much further. They are mini-entrepreneurs who design their own routes, manage their own accounts, and, to a large extent, determine the size of their paychecks.

Cadet ties compensation almost entirely to measures of customer satisfaction. Lose a customer on your watch and your salary sinks. CSR pay is about $40,000 a year, nearly twice the industry average. In practice, Cadet rarely loses a customer; its annual defection rate is less than 1 percent. Employees don't leave either; turnover is a low 7 percent. To a large extent this is because Cadet spends considerable time and effort on selecting employees—those who take pride in their work, are exceedingly neat, and outgoing. In all, 46 different ethnic groups are represented at Cadet.

How has the company done? Its annual growth has averaged 22 percent for the past 20 years, and it boasts double-digit profit margins that exceed the industry norm. Says Quentin Wahl, CEO: "The jobs we do aren't so special—the pay is good, but it's not great. The main thing we have to sell to employees is the culture of the organization" (Henkoff, 1994, p. 122).

---

the twenty-first century, our greatest challenge will be to change the way we think about organizations and their people. The remainder of this book will help you do that.

Trends such as these have intensified the demand for comprehensive training policies that focus training efforts on organizational needs 5 years out or on employees' aspirations. *Job* security (the belief that one will retain employment with the same organization until retirement) has become less important to workers than *employment* security (having the kinds of skills that employers in the labor market are willing to pay for). Demographic changes in society will make recruitment and personnel selection top priorities for many organizations. Cultural diversity at work will be a major theme as the composition of the work force changes. Consider, for example, that more than half of the U.S. workforce now consists of racial and ethnic minorities, immigrants, and women. White, native-born males, though still dominant, are themselves a statistical minority. Women will fill almost two-thirds of the new jobs created during the 1990s, and by the year 2000, nearly half the workforce will be female. The so-called mainstream is now almost as diverse as the society at large. White males will make up only 15 percent of the increase in the work force over the next decade. In short, a diverse work force is not something a company *ought* to have; it's something all companies do have or soon will have.

Demographic changes in the decade ahead will be accompanied by sweeping changes in the nature of work and its impact on workers and society. As Howard (1995) has noted, the following potential problems could surface:

- Insecurity—downsizing, violation of the psychological contract between employer and worker, part-time and temporary work for many, few long-term employment relationships.
- Uncertainty—constant change, multiple reporting relationships, inability to forecast the future.
- Stress—competing demands, long work hours, exhaustion, global competition.
- Social friction—two-tiered society, sharp differences in opportunities based on ability, insufficient work for the low-skilled.

On the other hand, work could provide the following compensations:

- Challenge—endless opportunities for stretching, growing, developing skills, keeping interested.
- Creativity—opportunities to generate novel solutions to emerging problems, self-expression.
- Flexibility—individualized careers and person-organization contracts, personal time and space arrangements, multiple careers.
- Control—empowerment, responsibility for decision making, directing one's life.
- Interrelatedness—global communication, group and team collaboration, end of isolation.

The future world of work will not be a place for the timid, the insecure, or the low-skilled. For those who thrive on challenge, responsibility, and risk-taking, security will come from seizing opportunities to develop new competencies (Hall and Mirvis, 1995). The need for competent HR professionals with broad training in a variety of areas has never been greater.

PLAN OF THE BOOK

In Chapter 2 we will explore what is perhaps the most dominant issue in human resource management today: legal requirements for fair employment practice. In particular, we will emphasize the constitutional basis for civil rights legislation and the judicial interpretation of Title VII of the 1964 Civil Rights Act. The remainder of the book will focus in greater depth on some of the major issues in contemporary personnel psychology. Each chapter will outline the nature of the topic under consideration, survey past practice and research findings, describe present issues and procedures, and, where relevant, indicate future trends and new directions for research.

The goal of Chapters 3 through 5 is to provide the reader with a strategy for viewing the employment decision process and an appreciation of the problems associated with assessing its outcomes. Chapter 3 presents an integrative model in which the major areas of personnel psychology are seen as a network of sequential, interdependent decisions. The model will then provide a structure for the rest of the book, as well as a conceptual framework from which to view the complex process of matching individuals and jobs.

In Chapter 4 we will focus on one of the most persistent and critical problems in the field of personnel psychology, that of developing and applying adequate performance criteria. A thorough understanding and appreciation of the criterion problem is essential, for it is relevant to all other areas of human resource management, especially to performance appraisal.

In Chapter 5 we will examine current methods, issues, and problems associated with the appraisal process. This concludes Part II.

Part III of the book presents fundamental concepts in applied measurement that underlie all employment decisions. Chapters 6 and 7 represent the core of personnel psychology—measurement and validation of individual differences. After comparing and contrasting physical and psychological measurement,

we will consider the requirements of good measurement (reliability and validity) and the practical interpretation and evaluation of measurement procedures. As a capstone to this part of the text, Chapter 8 is devoted entirely to a consideration of the issue of fairness in employment decisions.

Taken together, Chapters 2 through 8 provide a sound basis for a fuller appreciation of the topics covered in the remainder of the book.

In order to provide a job-relevant basis for employment decisions, information on job analysis and on human resource planning is essential. This is the purpose of Chapters 9 and 10, which together make up Part IV of the book. In Chapter 9 we will examine job analysis (the study of the work to be done, the skills needed, and the training required of the individual jobholder). It is the touchstone for all employment decisions. In Chapter 10 we will consider the emerging area of human resource planning. The goal of a human resource planning system is to anticipate future staffing requirements of an organization and, based on an inventory of present employees, to establish action programs (e.g., in recruitment, training, career path planning) to prepare individuals for future jobs. The emphasis of the chapter will be on tying current human resource planning theory to practice.

Part V is concerned with three key tasks that face all organizations: attraction, selection, and placement. In Chapter 11 we consider the theoretical and practical aspects of recruitment and initial screening, emphasizing the nontest techniques in initial screening. Chapters 12 and 13 present current information on employee selection (rank-and-file as well as managerial), and in Chapter 14 we consider some of the knotty problems associated with placing individuals in jobs that best suit them *and* their organizations.

Part VI, Training and Development, focuses on the design, implementation, and evaluation of training and development activities (Chapters 15 and 16). These topics have drawn special attention in HR management, especially in light of the need to develop skills continually in a dynamic business environment. We consider these issues with the conviction that a considerable reservoir of human potential for productivity improvement—managers *and* employees—remains to be tapped.

Finally, Chapter 17 addresses a variety of ethical issues in human resource management. While there are no easy answers to many of these questions, public discussion of them is essential if genuine progress is to be made. Now that we have considered the "big picture," let us begin our treatment by examining the legal environment within which employment decisions are made.

Discussion Questions

1. Why is employment security more important to most workers than job security?

2. How have globalized product and service markets affected organizations and workers?

3. Discuss some of the changes that have occurred in the perceptions that workers and organizations have about each other in light of the massive downsizing that has taken place during the past decade.

4. How does information technology change the roles of managers and workers?

5. Describe some potential problems and opportunities presented by the changing nature of work.

CHAPTER

2

THE LAW AND HUMAN RESOURCE MANAGEMENT

AT A GLANCE

Sweeping civil rights legislation enacted by the federal government during the last three decades, combined with increased motivation on the part of individuals to rectify unfair employment practices, makes the legal aspects of employment one of the most dominant issues in HRM today. All three branches of the federal government have been actively involved in a comprehensive program designed to guarantee equal employment opportunity as a fundamental individual right, regardless of race, age, sex, religion, or national origin.

All aspects of the employment relationship, including initial screening, recruitment, selection, placement, compensation, training, promotion, and performance appraisal, have been addressed by legislative and executive pronouncements and by legal interpretations by the courts. With growing regularity, managers and HRM specialists are being called upon to work with attorneys, the courts, and federal regulatory agencies. It is imperative, therefore, that managers and HRM specialists understand thoroughly their rights as well as their obligations under the law, and that these are translated into everyday practice in accordance with legal guidelines issued by federal regulatory agencies. Affirmative action as a matter of public policy has become a fact of modern organizational life. To ignore it is to risk serious economic, human, and social costs.

Every public opinion poll based on representative national samples drawn between 1950 and the present shows that a majority of Americans, black, brown, and white, support equal employment opportunity (EEO) and reject differential treatment based on race, regardless of its alleged purposes or results. There is agreement about the ends to be achieved, but there is disagreement about the means to be used. EEO has been, and is still, an emotionally charged issue. In the 1960s, dissidents made only slight headway by going "outside the system" and engaging in violence and public demonstrations. In the 1970s and 1980s, however, dissatisfied groups and individuals won substantial redress on many long-overdue issues by working "within the system" and availing themselves of their legal rights. Government also has provided sound legal bases for effecting changes in equal employment opportunity through the sweeping civil rights legislation of the last three decades. The combination of the motivation to rectify perceived inequities and an easily available legal framework for doing so has made the legal aspects of the employment relationship a dominant issue in HR management today.

It is imperative, therefore, that HR specialists understand their rights and obligations in this most delicate area. They must be able to work with their attorneys (and vice versa), for neither can succeed alone. Each has a great deal to contribute in order to identify vulnerable employment policies and practices, to make required adjustments in them, and thus to minimize the likelihood of time-consuming and expensive litigation. For these reasons, HR specialists must become more familiar with the legal system, legal terminology, important laws and court decisions, and underlying legal and scientific issues.

THE LEGAL SYSTEM[1]

Above the complicated network of local, state, and federal laws, the United States Constitution stands as the supreme law of the land. Certain powers and limitations are prescribed to the federal government by the Constitution; those powers not given to the federal government are considered to be reserved for the states. The states in turn have their own constitutions that are subject to, and must remain consistent with, the United States Constitution.

While certain activities are regulated exclusively by the federal government (e.g., interstate commerce), other areas are subject to concurrent regulation by federal and state governments (e.g., equal employment opportunity). It should be emphasized, however, that in the event of a conflict between a state law and the United States Constitution (or the laws enacted by Congress in accordance with it), the federal requirements take precedence. Thus, any state or local law that violates constitutional or federal law is, in effect, unconstitutional. Therefore, it is no defense to argue that one is acting according to such a state or local law.

The legislative branch of government (Congress) enacts laws, called **statutes,** which are considered primary authority. Hence, court decisions and the decisions and guidelines of regulatory agencies are not laws, but interpretations of laws for given situations in which the law is not specific. Nevertheless, these interpretations form a complex fabric of legal opinion and precedent that must be given great deference by the public.

Let us more closely consider the judicial system, one of the three main branches of government (along with the executive and legislative). The judicial power of the United States is vested "in one Supreme Court and in such inferior courts as Congress may from time to time ordain and establish" according to Article III of the Constitution. The system of inferior (i.e., lower) courts includes U.S. District Courts, the federal trial courts in each state. These courts hear cases that fall under federal jurisdiction, usually either cases be-

tween citizens of different states or cases relevant to constitutional or federal law.

Decisions of lower federal courts may be appealed to one of 12 U.S. Courts of Appeals, corresponding to the geographical region or "circuit" in which the case arose. In turn, these decisions may be appealed to the U.S. Supreme Court—not as a matter of right, but only when the Supreme Court feels that the case warrants a decision at the highest level. Generally the Supreme Court will grant **certiorari** (review) when two or more circuit courts have reached different conclusions on the same point of law or when a major question of constitutional interpretation is involved. If a petition for a **writ of certiorari** is denied, then the lower court's decision is binding.

The state court structure parallels the federal court structure, with state district courts on the lowest level, followed by state appellate (review) courts, and finally by a state supreme court. State supreme court decisions may be reviewed by the U.S. Supreme Court in those cases involving a question of federal law, or where the judicial power of the United States extends as defined by the United States Constitution. In all other instances, the state supreme court decision is final.

Equal employment opportunity complaints may take any one of several alternative routes (see Fig. 2–1). By far the simplest and least costly alternative is to arrive at an informal, out-of-court settlement with the employer. Often, however, the employer does not have an established mechanism for dealing with such problems. Or if such a mechanism does exist, employees or other complainants are unaware of it or are not encouraged to use it. So the complainant must choose more formal legal means, such as contacting state and local fair employment practice commissions (where they exist), federal regulatory agencies (e.g., Equal Employment Opportunity Commission, Office of Federal Contract Compliance Programs), or the federal and state district courts. At this stage, however, solutions become time-consuming and expensive. Litigation is a luxury that few can afford. Perhaps the wisest course of action an employer can take is to establish a sound internal complaint system to deal with problems before they escalate to formal legal proceedings.

UNFAIR DISCRIMINATION: WHAT IS IT?

No law has ever attempted to define precisely the term *discrimination.* However, in the employment context it can be viewed broadly as the giving of an unfair ad-

---

[1] Much of the following discussion is drawn from the excellent summaries presented by Seberhagen, McCollum, and Churchill (1972), and Seberhagen (1977).

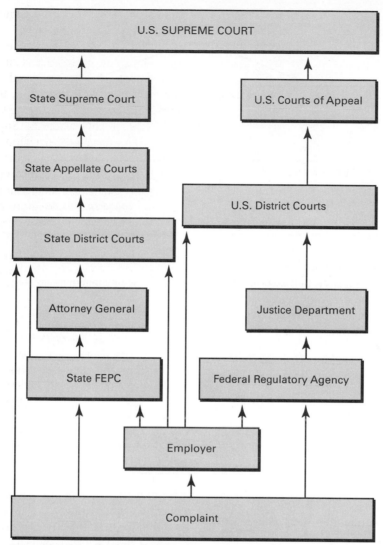

From Seberhagen, L.W., McCollum, M.D., & Churchill, C.D., *Legal aspects of personnel selection in the public service.* International Personnel Management Association, 1972.

FIGURE 2–1 Possible Legal Routes for Complaints Against an Employer's Employment Practices.

vantage (or disadvantage) to the members of a particular group in comparison to the members of other groups. The disadvantage usually results in a denial or restriction of employment opportunities, or in an inequality in the terms or benefits of employment.

It is important to note that whenever there are more candidates than available positions, it is necessary to select some candidates in preference to others. Selection implies exclusion. However, as long as the exclusion is based upon what can be demonstrated to be job-related criteria, that kind of discrimination is

entirely proper. It is only when candidates are excluded on a prohibited basis not related to the job (e.g., age, race, sex, disability) that unlawful and unfair discrimination exists. Despite federal and state laws on these issues, they represent the basis of an enormous volume of court cases, indicating that stereotypes and prejudices do not die quickly or easily. Discrimination is a subtle and complex phenomenon that may assume two broad forms:

1. *Unequal (disparate) treatment* is based upon an *intention to discriminate,* including the intention to *retaliate* against a person who opposes discrimination,

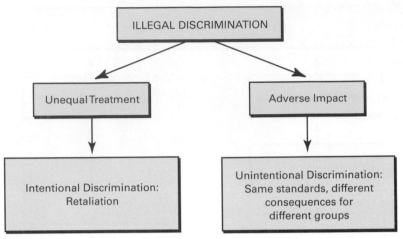

FIGURE 2-2 Major Forms of Illegal Discrimination.

has brought charges, or who has participated in an investigation or hearing. There are three major subtheories of discrimination within the disparate treatment theory.

1. Cases that rely on *direct evidence* of the intention to discriminate. Such cases are proven with direct evidence of:
   - Pure bias based on an open expression of hatred, disrespect, or inequality, knowingly directed against members of a particular group.
   - Blanket exclusionary policies, for example, deliberate exclusion of an individual whose disability (e.g., walking) has nothing to do with the requirements of the job she is applying for (financial analyst).

2. Cases that are proved through *circumstantial evidence* of the intention to discriminate (see *Schwager* v. *Sun Oil Co. of PA,* p. 28), including those that rely on statistical evidence as a method of circumstantially proving the intention to discriminate systematically against classes of individuals.

3. *Mixed-motive* cases (a hybrid theory) that often rely on both direct evidence of the intention to discriminate on some impermissible basis (e.g., sex, race, disability), and proof that the employer's stated legitimate basis for its employment decision is actually just a pretext for illegal discrimination.

   2. ***Adverse impact (unintentional) discrimination*** occurs when identical standards or procedures are applied to everyone, despite the fact that they lead to a substantial difference in employment outcomes (e.g., selection, promotion, layoffs) for the members of a particular group, *and* they are unrelated to success on a job. For example:

- Use of a minimum height requirement of 5′ 8″ for police cadets. That requirement would have an adverse impact on Asians, Hispanics, and women. The policy is neutral on its face, but has an adverse impact. To use it, an employer would need to show that the height requirement is necessary to perform the job. These two forms of illegal discrimination are illustrated graphically in Figure 2–2.

LEGAL FRAMEWORK FOR CIVIL RIGHTS REQUIREMENTS

Employers in the public and private sectors, employment agencies, unions, and joint labor-management committees controlling apprentice programs are subject to the various nondiscrimination **laws.** Government contractors and subcontractors are subject to **executive orders.** Many business organizations are employers as well as government contractors and, therefore, are directly subject *both* to nondiscrimination laws and to executive orders. While it is beyond the scope of this chapter to analyze all the legal requirements pertaining to equal employment opportunity, HR specialists should at least understand the major legal principles as articulated in the following laws of broad scope:

- The United States Constitution—13th and 14th Amendments
- The Civil Rights Acts of 1866 and 1871
- The Equal Pay Act of 1963
- The Civil Rights Act of 1964 (as amended by the Equal Employment Opportunity Act of 1972)

- The Age Discrimination in Employment Act of 1967 (as amended in 1986)
- The Immigration Reform and Control Act of 1986
- The Americans with Disabilities Act of 1990
- Civil Rights Act of 1991
- Family and Medical Leave Act of 1993

In addition, there are laws of limited application. These include:

- Executive Orders 11246, 11375, and 11478
- Rehabilitation Act (1973)
- Uniformed Services Employment and Reemployment Rights Act of 1994

THE UNITED STATES CONSTITUTION— 13th AND 14th AMENDMENTS

The Thirteenth Amendment prohibited slavery and involuntary servitude. Any form of discrimination may be considered an incident of slavery or involuntary servitude, and thus liable to legal action under this Amendment. The Fourteenth Amendment guarantees equal protection of the law for all citizens. Both the Thirteenth and Fourteenth Amendments granted to Congress the constitutional power to enact legislation to enforce their provisions. It is from this source of constitutional power that all subsequent civil right legislation originates.

THE CIVIL RIGHTS ACTS OF 1866 AND 1871

These laws were enacted based on the provisions of the Thirteenth and Fourteenth Amendments. The Civil Rights Act of 1866 grants all citizens the right to make and enforce contracts for employment, and the Civil Rights Act of 1871 grants all citizens the right to sue in federal court if they feel they have been deprived of any rights or privileges guaranteed by the Constitution and laws. Until recently, both of these laws were viewed narrowly as tools for Reconstruction era racial problems. This is no longer so. In *Johnson* v. *Railway Express Agency* (1975), the Supreme Court held that while Section 1981 on its face relates primarily to racial discrimination in the making and enforcement of contracts, it also provides a federal remedy against discrimination in private employment on the basis of race. It is a powerful remedy. The Civil Rights Act of 1991 amended the Civil Rights Act of 1866 so that workers are protected from intentional discrimination in all aspects of employment, not just hiring and promotion. Thus racial harassment is covered by this civil rights law. The Civil Rights Act of 1866 allows for jury trials and for compensatory and punitive damages[2] for victims of *intentional* racial and ethnic discrimination, and it covers both large and small employers, even those with fewer than 15 employees.

The 1866 law also has been used recently to broaden the definition of racial discrimination originally applied to African-Americans. In a unanimous decision, the Supreme Court ruled in 1987 that race was equated with ethnicity during the legislative debate after the Civil War, and therefore Arabs, Jews, and other ethnic groups thought of as "white" are not barred from suing under the 1866 act. The Court held that Congress intended to protect identifiable classes of persons who are subjected to intentional discrimination solely because of their ancestry or ethnic characteristics. Under the law, therefore, race involves more than just skin pigment ("Civil Rights," 1987).

EQUAL PAY FOR EQUAL WORK REGARDLESS OF SEX

Equal Pay Act of 1963

This act was passed as an amendment to the Fair Labor Standards Act (FLSA) of 1938. For those employers already subject to the FLSA the Equal Pay Act specifically prohibits sex discrimination in the payment of wages, except:

> where such payment is made pursuant to (i) a seniority system; (ii) a merit system; (iii) a system which measures earnings by quantity or quality of production, or (iv) a differential based on any other factor other than sex: *Provided,* that an employer who is paying a wage rate differential in violation of this subsection shall not, in order to comply with the provisions of this subsection, reduce the wage rate of any employee.

The Equal Pay Act, the first in the series of federal civil rights laws passed during the 1960s, is ad-

---

[2] Punitive damages are awarded in civil cases to punish or deter a defendant's conduct. They are separate from compensatory damages, which are intended to reimburse a plaintiff for injuries or harm.

ministered by the EEOC. Wages withheld in violation of its provisions are viewed as unpaid minimum wages or unpaid overtime compensation under the FLSA. Hundreds of equal pay suits were filed by aggrieved persons (predominantly women) during the 1970s and 1980s. For individual companies the price can be quite high since, as the last five lines of the law indicate, in correcting any inequity under the act, companies must ordinarily raise the lower rate. For example, at Chicago's Harris Trust, the company agreed to pay $14 million in back wages to thousands of female workers in order to settle a 12-year-old lawsuit. The women claimed that they were treated differently (female trainees were required to type whereas male trainees were not) solely because of their sex. Even before the decision, however, the bank had come a long way. In 1977, when the suit was filed, Harris had five female vice presidents. By 1989, 102 out of 380 vice presidents were female ("The Boys' Club," 1989).

Equal Pay for Jobs of Comparable Worth

When women dominate an occupational field (such as nursing or secretarial work), the rate of pay for jobs in that field tends to be lower than the pay that men receive when they are the dominant incumbents (e.g., construction, skilled trades). Is the market biased against jobs held mostly by women? Should jobs dominated by women and jobs dominated by men be paid equally if they are of "comparable" worth to an employer? Answering this question involves the knotty problem of how to make valid and accurate comparisons of the relative worth of unlike jobs. The key difference between the Equal Pay Act and comparable worth is this: The Act requires equal pay for men and women who do work that is *substantially equal.* Comparable worth would require equal pay for work of *equal value* to an employer (e.g., librarian and electrician).

Proponents argue that job evaluation schemes that assign points for the skills, responsibility, working conditions, and physical and mental effort required to perform a job are a better guide than simple reliance on the marketplace. Moreover, by focusing on the characteristics of jobs rather on than the characteristics of those who perform them, job evaluation provides an important safeguard against gender bias (Cooper and Barrett, 1984).

While it is reassuring to note that research on alternative job evaluation methods has found them generally to be reliable, to yield comparable results, and to

be free of systematic bias for or against jobs dominated by one sex, pay levels of jobs can influence judgments of job content. This means that biased market pay structures could work backward through the job evaluation process to produce relatively deflated evaluations for jobs held predominately by women without the need for any direct bias based on sex.

The crux of the issue is this: Are women underpaid for their work, or do they merely hold those jobs that are worth relatively less ("Male/Female Wage Gap," 1985)? About 20 states have enacted "comparable worth" laws that affect public employees (e.g., Minnesota), and in Canada's Ontario Province, all large private as well as public employers are covered by such a law. The state of Washington's program is typical. After several years, the program has run into difficulties. These include:

- The typing pool, once a "pink-collar ghetto," is now a better-paid, pink-collar ghetto.
- While no one has taken a pay cut, across-the-board cost-of-living increases have been cut dramatically to pay for the program.
- Men are rejecting offers of employment, and also leaving state jobs. Men now hold a minority of the state's jobs.
- Shortages are developing for skilled workers. To attract them, the state has had to grant three special pay increases (thereby fracturing the concept of comparable worth, since the concept is supposed to ignore the marketplace).
- Wages for state jobs are seriously out of line with wages for private industry jobs with whom the state competes.

The ultimate resolution of the comparable worth controversy remains to be seen, but there is an inescapable irony to the whole episode: The Equal Pay Act was passed for the express purpose of eliminating sex as a basis for the payment of wages. Comparable worth, by its very nature, *requires* that some jobs be labeled "male" and others "female." In so doing, it makes sex the fundamental consideration in the payment of wages.

Is it possible that the goals of comparable worth can be accomplished through normal labor market processes? Consider that in recent years there have been two significant achievements for women: (1) They have made dramatic inroads in jobs traditionally held by men; and (2) as women deserted such low-paying jobs as secretary and nurse, the demand for jobs held steady or increased and pay rates climbed. These are healthy trends that are likely to continue as long as aggressive enforcement of Title VII to ensure equal job opportunities for women is combined with vigorous enforcement of the Equal Pay Act. The appropriate response is to remove the barriers, not to abolish supply and demand.

EQUAL EMPLOYMENT OPPORTUNITY

The Civil Rights Act of 1964

The Civil Rights Act of 1964 is divided into several sections or titles, each dealing with a particular facet of discrimination (e.g., voting rights, public accommodations, public education). For our purposes, Title VII is particularly relevant.

Title VII (as amended by the Equal Employment Opportunity Act of 1972) has been the principal body of federal legislation in the area of fair employment. Through Title VII the Equal Employment Opportunity Commission (EEOC) was instituted to ensure compliance with Title VII by employers, employment agencies, and labor organizations. We will consider the organization and operation of the EEOC in greater detail in a following section.

Nondiscrimination on the Basis of Race, Sex, Religion, or National Origin

Employers are bound by the provisions of Section 703(a) of Title VII as amended, which states:

> It shall be an unlawful employment practice for an employer—(1) to fail or to refuse to hire or to discharge any individual or otherwise to discriminate against any individual with respect to his compensation, terms, conditions, or privileges of employment, because of such individual's race, color, religion, sex, or national origin; or (2) to limit, segregate, or classify his employees or applicants for employment in any way which would deprive or tend to deprive any individual of employment opportunities or otherwise adversely affect his status as an employee, because of such individual's race, color, religion, sex, or national origin.

Nondiscrimination in Apprenticeship Programs

Section 703(b) of Title VII states:

> It shall be an unlawful employment practice for any employer, labor organization, or joint labor-manage-

ment committee controlling apprenticeship or other training or retraining, including on-the-job training programs, to discriminate against any individual because of his race, color, religion, sex, or national origin in admission to, or employment in, any program established to provide apprenticeship or other training. A further provision of the act, Section 704(a), prohibits discrimination against an employee or applicant because he or she has opposed an unlawful employment practice or made a charge, testified, assisted, or participated in a Title VII investigation, proceeding, or hearing. Finally, Section 704(b) prohibits notices or advertisements relating to employment from indicating any preference, limitation, specification, or discrimination on any of the prohibited factors unless it is in relation to a bona fide occupational qualification (see p. 18).

Prior to 1972, Title VII was primarily aimed at private employers with 25 or more employees, labor organizations with 25 or more members, and private employment agencies. In 1973 the Equal Employment Opportunity Act expanded this coverage to: public and private employers (including state and local governments and public and private educational institutions) with 15 or more employees, labor organizations with 15 or more members, and both public and private employment agencies. These amendments provide broad coverage under Title VII, with the following exceptions: (1) private clubs, (2) places of employment connected with an Indian reservation, and (3) religious organizations (which are allowed to discriminate because of religion) (Title VII, Secs. 701[a], 702, and 703[i]). The U.S. Office of Personnel Management and the Merit Systems Protection Board, rather than the EEOC, monitor nondiscrimination and affirmative action programs of the federal government.

Suspension of Government Contracts and Back-Pay Awards

Two other provisions of the 1972 law are noteworthy. First, denial, termination, or suspension of government contracts is proscribed (without a special hearing) if an employer has and is following an affirmative action plan accepted by the federal government for the same facility within the past 12 months. Second, back-pay awards in Title VII cases are limited to 2 years *prior to the filing of a charge.* Thus, if a woman filed a Title VII charge in 1993, but the matter continued through investigation, conciliation, trial, and appeal until 1997, she might be entitled to as much as six years of back pay, from 1991 (2 years prior to the filing of her charge) to 1997 (assuming the matter was resolved in her favor).

In addition to its basic objective of protecting various minority groups against discrimination in employment, Title VII has extended the prohibition against sex discrimination to all aspects of the employment relationship. It was widely known, however, that this provision was inserted in the bill at the last minute in a vain attempt to make the bill appear ludicrous and thus to defeat it. The volume of sex discrimination complaints to the EEOC and the court decisions dealing with this aspect of discrimination have served subsequently to underscore the importance of this provision (Taylor, 1987).

Several specific exemptions to the provisions of Title VII were written into the law itself. Among these were the following.

Bona Fide Occupational Qualifications (BFOQ)

Classification or discrimination in employment according to race, religion, sex, or national origin is permissible when such qualification is a bona fide occupational qualification "reasonably necessary to the operation of that particular business or enterprise." The burden of proof rests with the employer to demonstrate this. As we shall see, however, the courts interpret BFOQs quite narrowly. Preferences of the employer, co-workers, or clients are irrelevant.

Seniority Systems

Bona fide seniority or merit systems and incentive pay systems are lawful "provided that such differences are not the result of an intention to discriminate."

Pre-Employment Inquiries

Such inquiries, for example, regarding sex and race, are permissible as long as they are not used as bases for discrimination. In addition, certain inquiries are necessary to meet the reporting requirements of the federal regulatory agencies and to ensure compliance with the law.

Testing

An employer may give or act upon any professionally developed ability test provided the test is not used as a vehicle to discriminate on the basis of race, color, reli-

gion, sex, or national origin. This issue will be examined in greater detail in a following section.

Preferential Treatment

It is unlawful to interpret Title VII as requiring the granting of preferential treatment to individuals or groups because of their race, color, religion, sex, or national origin on account of existing imbalances. Such imbalances may exist with respect to differences between the total number or percentage of similar persons employed by an employer, or admitted to or employed in any training or apprenticeship program, and the total number or percentage of such persons in any geographical area or in the available work force in any geographical area (see *Wards Cove Packing* v. *Antonio,* 1989).

Veterans' Preference Rights

These are not repealed or modified in any way by Title VII. In a 1979 ruling (*Personnel Administrator of Massachusetts* v. *Feeney,* 1979) the Supreme Court held that while veterans' preference does have an adverse impact on women's job opportunities, this was

FIGURE 2–3 The Six Exemptions to Title VII Coverage.

not caused by an *intent* to discriminate against women. Both men and women veterans receive the same preferential treatment, and male nonveterans are at the same disadvantage as female nonveterans.

National Security

When it is deemed necessary to protect the national security, discrimination (e.g., against members of the Communist Party) is permitted under Title VII. These exemptions are summarized in Figure 2–3.

Initially it appeared that these exemptions would significantly blunt the overall impact of the law. However, it soon became clear that they would be interpreted very narrowly both by the EEOC and by the courts.

AGE DISCRIMINATION IN EMPLOYMENT ACT OF 1967

Just as Title VII prohibits discrimination in employment on the basis of race, sex, religion, or national origin, employers also are mandated to provide equal employment opportunity on the basis of age. As amended in 1986, the act specifically proscribes discrimination on the basis of age for employees age 40 and over, unless the employer can demonstrate that age is a BFOQ for the job in question. In a 1985 ruling involving the forced retirement of Western Airlines flight engineers at age 60, the Supreme Court established a tough legal test that employers must meet to establish age as a BFOQ. Specifically, an employer must show that a particular age is "reasonably necessary to the normal operations of the particular business" and that "all or nearly all employees above an age lack the qualifications." Failing that, an employer must show that it is "highly impractical" to test each employee to ensure that after a certain age each individual remains qualified (Wermiel, 1985, p. 2). This law is administered by the EEOC.

A key objective of this law is to prevent financially troubled companies from singling out older employees when there are cutbacks. However, the EEOC has ruled that when there are cutbacks, older employees can waive their rights to sue under this law (e.g., in return for sweetened benefits for early retirement). Under the Older Workers Benefit Protection Act, which took effect in 1990, employees have 45 days to consider such waivers, and 7 days after signing to revoke them.

Increasingly, older workers are being asked to sign such waivers in exchange for enhanced retirement benefits. For example, at AT&T Communications, Inc., employees who signed waivers received severance pay equal to 5 percent of current pay times the number of years of service. For those without waivers, the company offered a multiplier of 3 percent.

THE IMMIGRATION REFORM AND CONTROL ACT OF 1986

This law applies to every employer in the United States, no matter how small, as well as to every employee—whether full-time, part-time, temporary, or seasonal. The act makes the enforcement of national immigration policy the job of every employer. The law requires: (1) that employers not hire or continue to employ aliens who are not legally authorized to work in the United States, and (2) that employers verify the identity and work authorization of every new employee and then sign (under penalty of perjury) a form (I-9) attesting that the employee is lawfully eligible to work in the United States. Under the law employers may not discriminate on the basis of national origin, but when two applicants are equally qualified, an employer may choose a U.S. citizen over an alien. The law also provides "amnesty rights" for illegal aliens who can show that they resided continuously in the United States from January 1982 to November 6, 1986 (the date of the law's enactment). This portion of the law granted legal status to about 1.7 million aliens who had been living in the country illegally ("Study Hints," 1988).

Penalties for noncompliance are severe. For example, failure to comply with the verification rules can result in fines ranging from $100 to $1,000 for *each* employee whose identity and work authorization have not been verified. The law also provides for criminal sanctions for employers who engage in a pattern of violations. This became obvious in 1989 when the government imposed a record fine of $580,000 against a South Carolina pillow factory accused of hiring more than 100 illegal aliens, including a 12-year-old boy. Further, the company, its owners, and nine managers were indicted by a federal grand jury on charges of illegally recruiting and harboring 117 illegal aliens. Such charges carry maximum prison terms of 653 years and fines totaling $5.1 million ("Alien Workers," 1989).

THE AMERICANS WITH DISABILITIES ACT OF 1990

Passed to protect the estimated 43 million Americans with disabilities, this law became effective in July 1992 for employers with 25 or more employees, and in July 1994 for employers with 15 or more employees. Persons with disabilities are protected from discrimination in employment, transportation, and public accommodation.

As a general rule, the ADA prohibits an employer from discriminating against a "qualified individual with a disability." A qualified individual is one who is able to perform the "essential" (i.e., primary) functions of a job with or without accommodation. "Disability" is a physical or mental impairment that substantially limits one or more major life activities, such as walking, talking, seeing, hearing, or learning. According to the EEOC's ADA Compliance Manual (1995) persons are protected if they currently have an impairment, have a record of such impairment, or if the employer *thinks* they have an impairment (e.g., a person with diabetes under control). Rehabilitated drug and alcohol abusers are protected, but current drug abusers may be fired. The alcoholic, in contrast, is covered and must be reasonably accommodated by being given a firm choice to rehabilitate himself or herself or face career-threatening consequences. The law also protects persons who have tested positive for the AIDS virus (Americans, 1990). Here are five major implications for employers:

1. Any factory, office, retail store, bank, hotel, or other building open to the public will have to be made accessible to those with physical disabilities (e.g., by installing ramps, elevators, telephones with amplifiers). "Expensive" will be no excuse, unless such modifications will lead an employer to suffer an "undue hardship."

2. Employers must make "reasonable accommodations" for job applicants or employees with disabilities (e.g., by restructuring job and training programs, modifying work schedules, or purchasing new equipment that is "user friendly" to blind or deaf people). Qualified job applicants (i.e., disabled individuals who can perform the essential functions of a job with or without reasonable accommodation) must be considered for employment. Practices such as the following may facilitate the process (Cascio, 1994):

   - Expressions of commitment by top management to accommodate workers with disabilities
   - Assignment of a specialist within the "EEO/Affirmative Action" section to focus on "equal access" for employees or applicants with disabilities
   - Centralizing recruiting, intake, and monitoring of hiring decisions
   - Identifying jobs or task assignments where a specific disability is not a bar to employment
   - Developing an orientation process for workers, supervisors, and co-workers with disabilities
   - Publicizing successful accommodation experiences within the organization and among outside organizations
   - Providing in-service training to all employees and managers about the firm's "equal access" policy, and how to distinguish "essential" from "marginal" job functions
   - Outreach recruitment to organizations that can refer job applicants with disabilities
   - Reevaluating accommodations on a regular basis

3. Preemployment physicals will now be permissible only if all employees are subject to them, and they cannot be given until after a conditional offer of employment is made. That is, the employment offer is made conditional upon passing of the physical examination. Further, employers are not permitted to ask about past workers' compensation claims or disabilities in general. However, after describing essential job functions, an employer can ask whether the applicant can perform the job in question. Here is an example of the difference between these two types of inquiries:

"Do you have any back problems?" clearly violates the ADA because it is not job-specific. However, the employer could state the following: "This job involves lifting equipment weighing up to 50 pounds at least once every hour of an eight-hour shift. Can you do that?"

4. Medical information on employees must be kept separate from other personal or work-related information about them.

5. Drug testing rules remain intact. An employer can still prohibit the use of alcohol and illegal drugs at the workplace and continue to give alcohol and drug tests.

Enforcement. This law is enforced according to the same procedures currently applicable to race, gender, national origin, and religious discrimination under Title VII of the Civil Rights Act of 1964. The enforcement agency is the Equal Employment Opportunity Commission (EEOC). In cases of *intentional* discrimination, individuals with disabilities may be awarded both compensatory and punitive damages up to $300,000 (depending on the size of the employer's workforce).

The Civil Rights Act of 1991

This act overturned six Supreme Court decisions issued in 1989. Here are some key provisions that are likely to have the greatest impact in the context of employment.

Monetary Damages and Jury Trials. A major effect of this Act is to expand the remedies in discrimination cases. Individuals who feel they are the victims of *intentional discrimination* based on race, gender (including sexual harassment), religion, or disability can ask for compensatory damages for pain and suffering, as well as for punitive damages, and they may demand a jury trial. In the past, only plaintiffs in age discrimination cases had the right to demand a jury.

Compensatory and punitive damages are available only from nonpublic employers (public employers are still subject to compensatory damages up to $300,000), and not for adverse impact (unintentional discrimination) cases. Moreover, they may not be awarded in an ADA case when an employer has engaged in good-faith efforts to provide a reasonable accommodation. The total amount of damages that can be awarded depends on the size of the employer's workforce:

Number of Employees	Maximum Combined Damages Per Complaint
15 to 100	$50,000
101 to 200	$100,000
201 to 500	$200,000
More than 500	$300,000

As we noted earlier, victims of intentional discrimination by race or national origin may sue under the Civil Rights Act of 1866, in which case there are no limits to compensatory and punitive damages. Note also that since intentional discrimination by reason of disability is a basis for compensatory and punitive damages (unless the employer makes a good-faith

effort to provide reasonable accommodation), the 1991 Civil Rights Act provides the sanctions for violations of the Americans with Disabilities Act of 1990.

Adverse Impact (Unintentional Discrimination) Cases. The act clarifies each party's obligation in such cases. As we noted earlier, when an adverse impact charge is made, the plaintiff must identify a specific employment practice as the cause of discrimination. If the plaintiff is successful in demonstrating adverse impact, the burden of producing evidence shifts to the employer, who must prove that the challenged practice is "job-related for the position in question and consistent with business necessity."

Protection in Foreign Countries. Protection from discrimination in employment, under Title VII of the 1964 Civil Rights Act and the Americans with Disabilities Act, is extended to U.S. citizens employed in a foreign facility owned or controlled by a U.S. company. However, the employer does not have to comply with U.S. discrimination law if doing so would violate the law of the foreign country.

Racial Harassment. As we noted earlier, the act amended the Civil Rights Act of 1866 so that workers are protected from intentional discrimination in *all* aspects of employment, not just hiring and promotion.

Challenges to Consent Decrees. Once a court order or consent decree is entered to resolve a lawsuit, nonparties to the original suit cannot challenge such enforcement actions.

Mixed-Motive Cases. In a mixed-motive case, an employment decision was based on a combination of job-related factors as well as unlawful factors, such as race, gender, religion, or disability. Under the Civil Rights Act of 1991, an employer is guilty of discrimination if it can be shown that a prohibited consideration was a motivating factor in a decision, even though other factors, which are lawful, also were used. However, if the employer can show that the same decision would have been reached even without the unlawful considerations, the court may not assess damages or require hiring, reinstatement, or promotion.

Seniority Systems. The act provides that a seniority system that intentionally discriminates against the members of a protected group can be challenged (within 180 days) at any of three points: (1) when the system is adopted, (2) when an individual becomes subject to the system, or (3) when a person is injured by the system.

"Race Norming" and Affirmative Action. The Act makes it unlawful "to adjust the scores of, use different cutoff scores for, or otherwise alter the results of employment-related tests on the basis of race, color, religion, sex, or national origin." Prior to the passage of this Act, within-group percentile scoring (so-called "race norming") had been used extensively to adjust the test scores of minority candidates to make them more comparable to those of nonminority candidates. When race norming is used, each individual's percentile score on a selection test is computed relative only to others in his or her race/ethnic group, and not relative to the scores of all examinees who took the test. However, a merged list of percentile scores (high to low) is presented to those responsible for hiring decisions.

Despite these prohibitions, another section of the Act states: "Nothing in the amendments made by this title shall be construed to affect court-ordered remedies, affirmative action, or conciliation agreements that are in accordance with the law." Although it could be argued that the Act would permit individual employers to make test-score adjustments as part of court-ordered affirmative action plans, or where a court approves a conciliation agreement, it is not yet clear that courts will interpret it so broadly (Arnold and Thiemann, 1992).

Extension to U.S. Senate and Appointed Officials. The Act extends protection from discrimination on the basis of race, color, religion, gender, national origin, age, and disability to employees of the U.S. Senate, political appointees of the President, and staff members employed by elected officials at the state level. Employees of the U.S. House of Representatives are covered by a House resolution adopted in 1988.

The Family and Medical Leave Act (FMLA) of 1993

The FMLA covers all private-sector employers with 50 or more employees, including part-timers, who work 1250 hours over a 12-month period (an average of 25 hours per week). The law gives workers up to 12 weeks' unpaid leave each year for birth, adoption, or foster care of a child within a year of the child's arrival; care for a spouse, parent, or child with a serious health condition; or the employee's own serious health condition if it prevents him or her from working. The

employer is responsible for designating an absence or leave as FMLA leave, based on information provided by the employee (FMLA, 1996). Employers can require workers to provide medical certification of such serious illnesses and can require a second medical opinion. Employers also can exempt from the FMLA key salaried employees who are among their highest paid 10 percent. For leave-takers, however, employers must maintain health insurance benefits and give the workers their previous jobs (or comparable positions) when their leaves are over. Enforcement provisions of the FMLA are administered by the U.S. Department of Labor ("Family," 1993). The overall impact of this law was softened considerably by the exemption of some of its fiercest opponents—companies with fewer than 50 employees, or 95 percent of all businesses. According to the Small Business Administration, such companies employ 27 percent of the nation's civilian workforce, or about 25 million people ("Most," 1993).

This completes the discussion of "absolute prohibitions" against discrimination. The following sections discuss nondiscrimination as a basis for eligibility for federal funds.

Executive Orders 11246, 11375, and 11478

Presidential Executive Orders in the realm of employment and discrimination are aimed specifically at federal agencies, contractors, and subcontractors. They have the force of law, even though they are issued unilaterally by the President without congressional approval, and they can be altered unilaterally as well. The requirements of these orders are parallel to those of Title VII.

In 1965, President Johnson issued Executive Order 11246, prohibiting discrimination on the basis of race, color, religion, or national origin as a condition of employment by federal agencies, contractors, and subcontractors with contracts of $10,000 or more. Those covered are required to establish and maintain an affirmative action plan in every facility of 50 or more people. Such programs include employment, upgrading, demotion, transfer, recruitment or recruitment advertising, layoff or termination, pay rates, and selection for training.

In 1967, Executive Order 11375 prohibited discrimination in employment based on sex. Executive Order 11478, issued by President Nixon in 1969, went even further, for it prohibited discrimination in employment based on all of the previous factors, plus political affiliation, marital status, or physical disability.

A 1995 Supreme Court ruling involving Adarand Constructors, Inc. created a legal limbo for the roughly 200,000 contractors covered under Executive Order 11246. The ruling specifies that racial preferences can be upheld if the government can prove a compelling interest, such as correcting past discrimination, and that the remedy is tailored narrowly. If contractors throw out their affirmative action plans, they could lose their government contracts. Under the Court's ruling, however, too aggressive a plan may trigger reverse-discrimination lawsuits (i.e., by nonminorities). Subsequent rulings by the Court should resolve this uncertainty (Crock and Galen, 1995).

Enforcement of Executive Orders. Executive Order 11246 provides considerable enforcement power, administered by the Department of Labor through its Office of Federal Contract Compliance Programs (OFCCP). Upon a finding by the OFCCP of noncompliance with the order, the Department of Justice may be advised to institute criminal proceedings, and the secretary of labor may cancel or suspend current contracts as well as the right to bid on future contracts. Needless to say, noncompliance can be *very* expensive.

The Rehabilitation Act of 1973

This act requires federal contractors (those receiving more than $2,500 in federal contracts annually) and subcontractors actively to recruit qualified people with disabilities and to use their talents to the fullest extent possible. The legal requirements are similar to those of the Americans with Disabilities Act.

The purpose of this act is to eliminate *systemic discrimination,* that is, any business practice that results in the denial of equal employment opportunity. Hence the act emphasizes "screening in" applicants, not screening them out. It is enforced by the OFCCP.

Uniformed Services Employment and Reemployment Rights Act of 1994

Regardless of the size of its organization, an employer may not deny a person initial employment, reemployment, promotion, or benefits based on that person's membership or potential membership in the armed service. To be protected, the employee must provide advance notice. Employers need not always rehire a returning service member (e.g., if the employee received a dishonorable discharge, or if changed circumstances at the workplace make reemployment impossible or unreasonable), but the burden of proof will almost always be on the employer. This law is administered by the U.S. Department of Labor.

ENFORCEMENT OF THE LAWS— REGULATORY AGENCIES

State Fair Employment Practices Commissions

Most states have nondiscrimination laws that include provisions expressing the public policy of the state, the persons to whom the law applies, and the prescribed activities of various administrative bodies. Moreover, the provisions specify unfair employment practices, procedures, and enforcement powers. Many states vest statutory enforcement powers in a state fair employment practices commission. Nationwide, there are about 100 such state and local agencies.

Equal Employment Opportunity Commission (EEOC)

The EEOC is an independent regulatory agency whose five commissioners (one of whom is chairperson) are appointed by the President and confirmed by the Senate for terms of five years. No more than three of the commissioners may be from the same political party. Like the OFCCP, the EEOC sets policy and in individual cases determines whether there is "reasonable cause" to believe that unlawful discrimination has occurred. It should be noted, however, that the courts give no legal standing to EEOC rulings on whether or not "reasonable cause" exists; each Title VII case constitutes a new proceeding.

The Equal Employment Opportunity Commission is the major regulatory agency charged with enforcing federal civil rights laws, but its 50 field offices and 732 investigators are rapidly becoming overwhelmed with cases. In fiscal 1994, for example, 158,612 cases were filed, or about 450 a day. Almost 194,000 cases were waiting to be heard, and the length of time between the filing of charges and their resolution averaged 13 months. Race, sex, disability, and age discrimination claims are most common. Among these four, sex discrimination claims are the fastest growing (Eisler, 1995).

The Complaint Process

Complaints filed with the EEOC first are deferred to a state or local fair employment practices commission, if there is one with statutory enforcement power. After

60 days, EEOC can begin its own investigation of the charges, whether or not the state agency takes action. Of course, the state or local agency may immediately re-defer to the EEOC.

In order to reduce its backlog of complaints, EEOC has changed its policy of treating all cases equally. As of 1995, a new system categorizes complaints according to priority. Top priority cases are those that more than likely involve illegal discrimination. The second category includes complaints that have some merit, but require additional investigation. The third group includes complaints that can be dismissed immediately (Sharpe, 1995).

Throughout the complaint process, however, the Commission encourages the parties to settle and to consider alternative resolution of disputes. This is consistent with the Commission's three-step approach: investigation, conciliation, and litigation. If conciliation efforts fail, court action can be taken. If the defendant is a private employer, the case is taken to the appropriate federal district court; if the defendant is a public employer, the case is referred to the Department of Justice.

In addition to processing complaints, EEOC is responsible for issuing written regulations governing compliance with Title VII. Among these are guidelines on discrimination because of pregnancy, sex, religion, and national origin; guidelines on employee selection procedures (in concert with three other federal agencies, see Appendix A); guidelines on affirmative action programs; and a policy statement on preemployment inquiries. These guidelines are not laws, although the Supreme Court (1975) has indicated that they are entitled to "great deference." While the purposes of the guidelines are more legal than scientific, violations of the guidelines will incur EEOC sanctions and possible court action.

EEOC has one other major function: information gathering. Each organization with 100 or more employees must file annually with EEOC a form (EEO-1) detailing the number of women and members of four different minority groups employed in nine different job categories from laborers to managers and officials. Specific minority groups are African-Americans; Americans of Cuban, Spanish, Puerto Rican, or Mexican origin; Orientals; and Native Americans (which in Alaska includes Eskimos and Aleuts). Through computerized analysis of EEO-1 forms, EEOC is better able to uncover broad patterns of discrimination and to attack them through class-action suits.

Office of Federal Contract Compliance Programs (OFCCP)

OFCCP, an agency of the U.S. Department of Labor, has all enforcement as well as administrative and policy-making authority for the entire contract compliance program under Executive Order 11246. That Order affects more than 200,000 employers. "Contract compliance" means that in addition to meeting quality, timeliness, and other requirements of federal contract work, contractors and subcontractors must satisfy EEO and affirmative action requirements covering all aspects of employment, including recruitment, hiring, training, pay, seniority, promotion, and even benefits (OFCCP, 1979).

Goals and Timetables

Whenever job categories include fewer women or minorities "than would reasonably be expected by their availability," the contractor must establish goals and timetables (subject to OFCCP review) for increasing their representation. Goals are distinguishable from quotas in that quotas are inflexible; goals, on the other hand, are flexible objectives that can be met in a realistic amount of time. In determining representation rates, eight criteria are suggested by the OFCCP, several of which include the population of women and minorities in the labor area surrounding the facility, the general availability of women and minorities having the requisite skills in the immediate labor area, or in an area in which the contractor can reasonably recruit, and the degree of training the contractor is reasonably able to undertake as a means of making all job classes available to women and minorities. The U.S. Department of Labor now collects data on the first four of these criteria for 385 standard metropolitan statistical areas throughout the United States.

How has the agency done? From 1992 to 1994 OFCCP conducted over 9,000 compliance reviews, completed almost 500 investigations of violations of Executive Order 11246, and debarred eight companies from bidding on future government contracts (OFCCP, 1995). From the employer's perspective, compliance reviews are costly. Thus City Utilities of Springfield, Missouri, spent $26,500 and 734 hours of employee time. The OFCCP found no evidence of discriminatory hiring practices (Leonard, 1996).

JUDICIAL INTERPRETATION—GENERAL PRINCIPLES

While the legislative and executive branches may write the law and provide for its enforcement, it is the responsibility of the judicial branch to interpret the law and to determine how it will be enforced. Since judicial interpretation is fundamentally a matter of legal judgment, this area is constantly changing. Of necessity, laws must be written in general rather than in specific form, and therefore they cannot possibly cover the contingencies of each particular case. Moreover, in any large body of law, conflicts and inconsistencies will exist as a matter of course. Finally, cultural dynamics (e.g., changes in public opinion and attitudes, new scientific findings) must be considered along with the letter of the law if justice is to be served (Seberhagen et al., 1972).

Legal interpretations define what is called **case law,** which serves as a precedent to guide, but not completely to determine, future legal decisions. A considerable body of case law pertinent to employment relationships has accumulated since 1964. The intent of this section is not to document thoroughly all employment case law, but merely to highlight significant developments in certain areas.

Testing

The 1964 Civil Rights Act clearly sanctions the use of "professionally-developed" ability tests, but it took several landmark Supreme Court cases to spell out the proper role and use of tests. The first of these was *Griggs* v. *Duke Power Company,* decided in March 1971 in favor of Griggs. It established several important general principles in employment discrimination cases:

1. African-Americans hired before a high school diploma requirement was instituted are entitled to the same promotional opportunities as whites hired at the same time. Congress did not intend by Title VII, however, to guarantee a job to every person regardless of qualifications. In short, the Act does not command that any person be hired simply because he was formerly the subject of discrimination, or because he is a member of a minority group. Discriminatory preference for any group, minority or majority, is precisely and only what Congress has proscribed (p. 425).
2. The employer bears the burden of proof that any given requirement for employment is related to job performance.
3. "Professionally-developed" tests (as defined in the Civil Rights Act of 1964) must be job related.
4. The law prohibits not only open and deliberate discrimination, but also practices that are fair in form but discriminatory in operation.
5. It is not necessary for the plaintiff to prove that the discrimination was intentional: intent is irrelevant. If the standards result in discrimination, they are unlawful.
6. Job-related tests and other measuring procedures are legal and useful.

What Congress has forbidden is giving these devices and mechanisms controlling force unless they are demonstrably a reasonable measure of job performance. . . . What Congress has commanded is that any tests used must measure the person for the job and not the person in the abstract (p. 428).

Subsequently, in *Albemarle Paper Co.* v. *Moody* (1974), the Supreme Court specified in much greater detail what "job relevance" means. In validating several tests to determine if they predicted success on the job, Albemarle focused almost exclusively on job groups near the top of the various lines of progression, while the same tests were being used to screen entry-level applicants. Such use of tests was prohibited.

Albemarle had not conducted any job analyses to demonstrate empirically that the knowledges, skills, and abilities among jobs and job families were similar. Yet tests that had been validated for only several jobs were being used as selection devices for all jobs. Such use of tests was ruled unlawful. Furthermore, in conducting the validation study, Albemarle's supervisors were instructed to compare each of their employees to every other employee and to rate one of each pair "better." Better in terms of what? The Court found such job-performance measures deficient, since "there is no way of knowing precisely what criteria of job performance the supervisors were considering."

Finally, Albemarle's validation study dealt only with job-experienced white workers; but the tests themselves were given to new job applicants, who were younger, largely inexperienced, and in many cases nonwhite.

Thus, the job relatedness of Albemarle's testing program had not been demonstrated adequately. However, the Supreme Court ruled in *Washington* v. *Davis* (1976) that a test that validly predicted police-recruit training performance, regardless of its ability to predict later job performance, was sufficiently job related to justify its continued use, despite the fact that four times as many African-Americans as whites failed the test.

Overall, in *Griggs, Moody,* and *Davis,* the Supreme Court has specified in much greater detail the appropriate standards of job relevance: adequate job analysis; relevant, reliable, and unbiased job-performance measures; and evidence that tests forecast job performance equally well for minorities and nonminorities.

To this point we have assumed that any tests used are job-related. But suppose that a written test used as the first hurdle in a selection program is not job-related *and* that it produces an "adverse impact" against African-Americans. *Adverse impact refers to a substantially different rate of selection in hiring, promotion, or other employment decision that works to the disadvantage of members of a race, sex, or ethnic group.* Suppose further that among those who pass the test, proportionately more African-Americans than whites are hired, so that the "bottom line" of hires indicates no adverse impact. This thorny issue faced the Supreme Court in *Connecticut* v. *Teal* (1982).

The Court ruled that Title VII provides rights to *individuals,* not to *groups.* Thus it is no defense to discriminate unfairly against certain individuals (e.g., African-American applicants) and then to "make up" for such treatment by treating other members of the same group favorably (that is, African-Americans who passed the test). In other words, it is no defense to argue that the bottom line indicates no adverse impact if intermediate steps in the hiring or promotion process do produce adverse impact and are not job-related.

The confidentiality of individual test scores has also been addressed. In 1979 the Supreme Court upheld the right of Detroit Edison Company to refuse to hand over to a labor union copies of aptitude tests taken by job applicants and to refuse to disclose individual employee test scores without the written consent of employees ("Justices Uphold Utility's Stand," 1979). However, a more recent decision by the Nevada Supreme Court held that employees and applicants who are subject to psychological testing as a condition of employment or continued employment are entitled to obtain their results (*Cleghorn* v. *Hess,* 1993). Employers are well advised to develop a policy on this issue that takes into account the interests of all relevant parties.

Personal History

Frequently qualification requirements involve personal background information or employment history, which may include minimum education or experience requirements, past wage garnishments, or previous arrest and conviction records. If such requirements have the effect of denying or restricting equal employment opportunity, they may violate Title VII.

This is not to imply that education or experience requirements should not be used. On the contrary, a review of 83 court cases indicated that educational requirements are most likely to be upheld when: (1) a highly technical job is at issue, one that involves risk to the safety of the public or one that requires advanced knowledge; (2) adverse impact cannot be established; and (3) evidence of criterion-related validity or an effective affirmative action program is offered as a defense (Meritt-Haston and Wexley, 1983).

Similar findings were reported in a review of 45 cases dealing with experience requirements (Arvey and McGowen, 1982). That is, experience requirements typically are upheld when there are greater economic and human risks involved with failure to perform adequately (e.g., airline pilots) or for higher-level jobs that are more complex. They typically are not upheld when they perpetuate a racial imbalance or past discrimination or when they are applied differently to different groups. Courts also tend to review experience requirements carefully for evidence of business necessity.

Arrest records, by their very nature, are not valid bases for screening candidates because in our society a person who is arrested is presumed innocent until proven guilty. It might therefore appear that conviction records are always permissible bases for applicant screening. In fact, conviction records may not be used in evaluating applicants unless the conviction is directly related to the work to be performed, for example, a person convicted of embezzlement applying for a job as a bank teller (cf. *Hyland* v. *Fukada,* 1978). Despite such decisions, it should be emphasized that personal history items are not unlawfully discriminatory per se, but their use in each instance requires that job relevance be demonstrated.

Sex Discrimination

In contrast to racial discrimination, sex discrimination often is overt (e.g., advertisements that specify "males only" or "female preferred"). Sex role stereotypes are deeply rooted in our society, with some jobs deemed totally inappropriate for members of the opposite sex. Such stereotypes are even more pronounced in many foreign cultures. In fact, Americans traveling abroad sometimes are stunned by the wide disparity between U.S. and foreign employment practices. As an example, consider the "help wanted" ad shown in Figure 2–4 that appeared in a Hong Kong newspaper:

OBEDIENT YOUNG SECRETARY

Very obedient young woman required by American Director for position as Secretary/ Personal Assistant. Must be attractive and eager to submit to authority, have good typing and filing skills and be free to travel. Knowledge of Mandarin an advantage. Most important, she should enjoy following orders without question and cheerfully accept directions. Send handwritten resume on unlined paper and recent photo to G.P.O. Box 6132, Hong Kong.

FIGURE 2–4 A Recent "Help Wanted" Ad from a Hong Kong Newspaper. How Many Objectionable Items Can You Find?

Judicial interpretation of Title VII clearly indicates that in the United States both sexes must be given equal opportunity to compete for jobs unless it can be demonstrated that sex is a bona fide occupational qualification for the job (e.g., actor, actress). Illegal sex discrimination may manifest itself in several different ways. Consider pregnancy, for example.

With regard to pregnancy, EEOC's 1979 interpretive guidelines of the Pregnancy Discrimination Act state:

> The basic principle of the Act is that women affected by pregnancy and related conditions must be treated the same as other applicants and employees on the basis of their ability or inability to work. A woman is therefore protected against such practices as being fired, or refused a job or promotion, merely because she is pregnant or has had an abortion. She usually cannot be forced to go on leave as long as she can still work. If other employees who take disability leave are entitled to get their jobs back when they are able to work again, so are women who have been unable to work because of pregnancy (1979, p. 13279).

Under the law, an employer is never *required* to give pregnant employees special treatment. If an organization provides no disability benefits or sick leave to other employees, it is not required to provide them for pregnant employees (Trotter, Zacur, and Greenwood, 1982). While the actual length of maternity leave is now an issue to be determined by the woman's and/or the company's physician, a 1987 Supreme Court decision in *California Federal Savings & Loan Association* v. *Guerra* upheld a California law that provides for up to 4 months of unpaid leave for pregnancy disability.

Economic pressures on employers may make legal action unnecessary in the future. Evidence now indicates that many employers are doing their best to accommodate pregnant women through flexible work scheduling and generous maternity leave policies (Shellenbarger, 1993). Given the number of women of childbearing age in the workforce and the fact that 85 percent of all women have children (Schwartz, 1992), combined with the fact that two out of every three people who will fill the 15 million new jobs between now and the twenty-first century will be women, there really is no other choice.

One large survey of company practices found that new mothers typically spend 1 to 3 months at home following childbirth, that job guarantees for returning mothers were provided by 35 percent of the companies, and that employers of 501 to 1,000 employees are most likely to provide full pay (Pregnancy, 1987).

Many of the issues raised in court cases as well as in complaints to the EEOC itself were incorporated into the amended Guidelines on Discrimination Because of Sex, issued by the EEOC in 1979. The guidelines state that, "the bona fide occupational exception as to sex should be interpreted narrowly." Assumptions about comparative employment characteristics of women in general (e.g., that turnover rates are higher among women than men); sex role stereotypes; or preferences of employers, clients, or customers do not warrant such an exception. Likewise, the courts have disallowed unvalidated physical requirements—minimum height and weight, lifting strength, or maximum hours that may be worked.

Sexual harassment is a form of illegal sex discrimination prohibited by Title VII. According to the EEOC's guidelines on sexual harassment in the workplace (1980), the term refers to unwelcome sexual advances, requests for sexual favors, and other verbal or physical conduct when submission to the conduct is either explicitly or implicitly a term or condition of an individual's employment, it is used as the basis for employment decisions affecting that individual, or it creates an intimidating, hostile, or offensive working environment. While many behaviors may constitute sexual harassment, there are two main types:

1. Quid pro quo (you give me this; I'll give you that),
2. Hostile work environment (an intimidating, hostile, or offensive atmosphere).

Quid pro quo harassment exists when the harassment is a *condition of employment. Hostile environment harassment* was defined by the Supreme Court in its 1986 ruling, *Meritor Savings Bank* v. *Vinson.* Vinson's boss had abused her verbally as well as sexually. However, since Vinson was making good career progress, the district court ruled that the relationship was a voluntary one having nothing to do with her continued employment or advancement. The Supreme Court disagreed, ruling that whether the relationship was "voluntary" is irrelevant. The key question was whether the sexual advances from the supervisor were "unwelcome." If so, and if they are "sufficiently severe or pervasive to be abusive, then they are illegal. This case was groundbreaking because it expanded the definition of harassment to include verbal or physical conduct that creates an intimidating, hostile, or offensive work environment or interferes with an employee's job performance.

In a 1993 case, *Harris* v. *Forklift Systems, Inc.,* the Supreme Court ruled that plaintiffs in such suits need not show psychological injury to prevail. While a victim's emotional state may be relevant, she or he need not prove extreme distress. In considering whether illegal harassment has occurred, juries must consider factors such as the frequency and severity of the harassment, whether it is physically threatening or humiliating, and whether it interferes with an employee's work performance (Barrett, 1993).

As we noted earlier, the Civil Rights Act of 1991 permits victims of sexual harassment—who previously could be awarded only missed wages—to collect a wide range of punitive damages and attorney's fees from employers who mishandled a complaint.

Preventive Actions by Employers. What can an employer do to escape liability for the sexually harassing acts of its managers or workers? An effective policy should include the following features:

- A statement from the chief executive officer that states firmly that sexual harassment will not be tolerated
- A workable definition of sexual harassment that is publicized via staff meetings, bulletin boards, handbooks, and new-employee orientation programs

- An established complaint procedure to provide a vehicle for employees to report claims of harassment to their supervisors or to a neutral third party, such as the HR department
- A clear statement of sanctions for violators and protection for those who make charges
- Prompt, confidential investigation of every claim of harassment, no matter how trivial
- Preservation of all investigative information, with records of all such complaints kept in a central location
- Training of all managers and supervisors to recognize and respond to complaints, giving them written materials outlining their responsibilities and obligations when a complaint is made
- Follow-up to determine if harassment has stopped (Sexual Harassment, 1992).

Age Discrimination

To discriminate fairly against employees over 40 years old, an employer must be able to demonstrate a "business necessity" for doing so. That is, it must be shown that age is a factor directly related to the safe and efficient operation of a business. Such was the case in *EEOC* v. *U. of Texas Health Science Center at San Antonio* (1983). A maximum age requirement of 45 years for applicants for a job as a campus police officer was upheld on the grounds that the job involved physical danger and required individuals to work a beat alone.

To establish a *prima facie* case (i.e., a body of facts presumed to be true until proven otherwise) of age discrimination, an aggrieved individual must show that:

1. He or she is within the protected age group (over 40 years of age).
2. He or she is doing satisfactory work.
3. He or she was discharged despite satisfactory work performance.
4. The position was filled by a person younger than the person replaced (*Schwager* v. *Sun Oil Co. of Pa.,* 1979).

For example, in *Cleverly* v. *Western Electric Co.* (1979), a decision to discharge an employee was contradicted by the weight of evidence in 14 years' worth of performance appraisal data. Cleverly had received satisfactory performance ratings and a steadily increasing salary during his 14 years of service to the company. When discharged, he was told that one reason for the discharge was to make way for younger engineers in the department, and his discharge occurred just 6 months prior to the vesting of his pension. The company was found guilty of age discrimination, and Cleverly was awarded back pay. Thus age, in addition to race, color, religion, sex, national origin, and disability, serves as one more factor on which an organization's nondiscrimination is judged—not by intent, but rather by results.

"English-Only" Rules—National Origin Discrimination?

Rules that require employees to speak only English in the workplace have come under fire in recent years. Employees who speak a language other than English claim that such rules are not related to the ability to do a job and have a harsh impact on them because of their national origin.

In a recent case, an employer applied an "English-only" rule while employees were on the premises of the company. Non-Spanish-speaking employees complained that they were being talked about by the plaintiff and others who spoke Spanish. The Eleventh Circuit Court of Appeals ruled in favor of the employer. The court noted that the rule in this case was job-related in that supervisors and other employees who spoke only English had a need to know what was being said in the workplace.

Employers should be careful when instituting an "English-only" rule. While it is not necessarily illegal to make fluency in English a job requirement, nor to discipline an employee for violating an "English-only" rule, employers must be able to show there is a legitimate business need for it. (Conversely, many employers would be delighted to have a worker who can speak the language of a non-English-speaking customer.) Otherwise, the employer may be subject to discrimination complaints on the basis of national origin (Carey and Seegull, 1995; *Garcia* v. *Gloor,* 1980; *Jurado* v. *Eleven-Fifty Corporation,* 1987).

Seniority

"Seniority" is a term that connotes length of employment. A "seniority system" is a scheme that, alone or in tandem with "nonseniority" criteria, allots to employees ever-improving employment rights and benefits as their relative lengths of pertinent employment increase (*California Brewers Assoc.* v. *Bryant,* 1982).

Various features of seniority systems have been challenged in the courts for many years (Gordon and Johnson, 1982). However, one of the most nettlesome issues is the impact of established seniority systems on programs designed to ensure equal employment opportunity. Employers often work hard to hire and promote members of protected groups. If layoffs become necessary, however, those individuals may be lost because of their low seniority. As a result, the employer takes a step backward in terms of workforce diversity. What is the employer to do when seniority conflicts with EEO?

The courts have been quite clear in their rulings on this issue. In two landmark decisions, *Firefighters Local Union No. 1784* v. *Stotts* (1984) (decided under Title VII) and *Wygant* v. *Jackson Board of Education* (1986) (decided under the equal protection clause of the Fourteenth Amendment), the Supreme Court ruled that an employer may not protect the jobs of recently hired African-American employees at the expense of whites who have more seniority (Greenhouse, 1984).

Voluntary modifications of seniority policies for affirmative action purposes remain proper, but where a collective bargaining agreement exists, the consent of the union is required. Moreover, in the unionized setting, courts have made it clear that the union must be a party to any decree that modifies a bona fide seniority system (Britt, 1984).

Preferential Selection

An unfortunate side effect of affirmative action programs designed to help minorities and women is that they may, in so doing, place qualified white males at a competitive disadvantage. However, social policy as embodied in Title VII emphasizes that so-called reverse discrimination (discrimination against whites and in favor of members of protected groups) is just as unacceptable as is discrimination by whites against members of protected groups (*McDonald* v. *Santa Fe Transportation Co.,* 1976).

Subsequent cases, together with the Civil Rights Act of 1991, have clarified a number of issues in this area:

1. Courts may order, and employers voluntarily may establish, affirmative action plans, including goals and timetables, to address problems of underutilization of women and minorities. Court-approved affirmative action settlements may not be reopened by individuals who were not parties to the original suit.

2. The plans need not be directed solely to identified victims of discrimination but may include general, class-wide relief.

3. While the courts will almost never approve a plan that would result in whites *losing* their jobs through lay-offs, they may sanction plans that impose limited burdens on whites in hiring and promotions (i.e., plans that postpone them).

4. Numerically-based preferential programs should not be used in every instance, and they need not be based on an actual finding of discrimination ("Replying," 1987).

Social policy, as articulated in pronouncements by Congress and the courts, clearly reflects an effort to provide a "more level playing field" that allows women, minorities, and nonminorities to compete for jobs on the basis of merit alone.

In Part I we have examined the legal and social environments within which organizations and individuals function. In order for both to function effectively, however, competent HR management is essential. In the next four chapters we shall present fundamental tools (systems analysis and decision theory) that will enable the HR specialist to develop a conceptual framework for viewing employment decisions, and methods for assessing the outcomes of such decisions.

Discussion Questions

1. Discuss three features of the 1991 Civil Rights Act that you consider most important. What impact do these features have on organizations?

2. Prepare a brief outline for the senior management of your company that illustrates the requirements and expected impact of the Family and Medical Leave Act.

3. What specific steps would you recommend to a firm in order to ensure fair treatment of persons with disabilities?

4. Prepare a brief outline of an organizational policy on sexual harassment. Be sure to include grievance, counseling, and enforcement procedures.

5. What guidance would you give to an employer who asks about rights and responsibilities in administering a testing program?

CHAPTER

3

PEOPLE, DECISIONS, AND THE SYSTEMS APPROACH

AT A GLANCE

Organizations and individuals frequently are confronted with alternative courses of action, and decisions are made when one alternative is chosen in preference to others. Since different cost consequences frequently are associated with various alternatives, principles are needed that will assist decision makers in choosing the most beneficial or most profitable alternatives. Utility theory, by forcing the decision maker to consider the costs, consequences, and anticipated payoffs of all available courses of action, provides such a vehicle.

Since the anticipated consequences of decisions must be viewed in terms of their implications for the organization as a whole, an integrative framework is needed that will afford a broad, macroperspective. Open systems theory is one such approach. Organiza-

tions are open systems, importing inputs (energy and information) from the environment, transforming inputs into outputs of goods and services, and finally exporting these back into the environment, which then provides feedback on the overall process. The topical areas of personnel psychology also can be cast into an open systems model. Thus, job analysis and evaluation, human resource planning, recruitment, initial screening, selection, initial training, placement, advanced training, and finally performance appraisal are seen as a network of sequential, interdependent decisions, with feedback loops interconnecting all phases in the process. The costs, consequences, and anticipated payoffs of alternative decision strategies can then be assessed in terms of their systemwide ramifications.

UTILITY THEORY—A WAY OF THINKING

Decisions, decisions—which applicants should be hired, who should be promoted, how much money should be allocated to research and development? Any time a person or an organization is confronted with alternative courses of action, there is a decision problem. For managers and HR specialists such problems occur daily in their work. Decisions to hire, not to hire, or to place on a waiting list are characteristic outcomes of the employment process, but how does one arrive at sound decisions that will ultimately spell success for the individual or organization affected? Principles are needed that will assist managers and individuals in making the most profitable or most beneficial choices

among products, investments, jobs, curricula, and so on. The aim in this chapter is not to present a detailed, mathematically sophisticated exposition of decision or utility theory (cf. Boudreau, 1991; Cascio, 1991; Cronbach and Gleser, 1965; Zeidner et al., 1988), but merely to arouse and to sensitize the reader to a provocative way of thinking.

Decision theory is engaging, for it insists that costs and expected consequences of decisions always be taken into account (Girschick, 1954). It stimulates the decision maker to formulate what he or she is after, as well as to anticipate the expected consequences of alternative courses of action. For example, the management of a professional football team must make a number of personnel decisions each year in the annual draft of the top college players. Size versus speed are two frequently-encountered selection criteria; present ability versus future potential are two others. In all cases the decision maker must first state clearly his or her overall objectives prior to actually making the decision, and then he or she must attempt to anticipate the expected consequences of alternative choices.

It should serve as some comfort to know that all employment decision processes can be characterized identically (Cronbach and Gleser, 1965). In the first place, there is an individual about whom a decision is required. Based on certain information about the individual (e.g., aptitude or diagnostic test results), the decision maker may elect to pursue various alternative courses of action. Let us consider a simple example. After an individual is hired for a certain job with an electronics firm, he or she may be assigned to one of three training classes. Class A is for fast learners who already have some familiarity with electronics. Those assigned to class B are slower learners who also possess a basic grasp of the subject matter. Class C individuals are those whose skills either are nonexistent (e.g., the hard-core unemployed) or are so rusty as to require some remedial work before entering class B training.

An aptitude test is given to each individual, and this diagnostic information is then processed according to some strategy or rule for arriving at decisions. For example, assuming a maximum score of 100 points on the aptitude test, the decision maker may choose the following strategy:

Test Score	Assignment
90–100	Class A
70–89	Class B
Below 70	Class C

In any given situation some strategies are better than others. Strategies are better (or worse) when evaluated against possible outcomes or consequences of decisions (payoffs). Although sometimes it is extremely difficult to assign values to outcomes, this is less of a problem in business settings since many outcomes can be expressed in economic (dollar) terms. Once this is accomplished, particular decisions or general strategies can then be compared, as Cronbach and Gleser (1965) noted:

> The unique feature of decision theory or utility theory is that it specifies evaluations by means of a payoff matrix or by conversion of the criterion to utility units. The values are thus plainly revealed and open to criticism. This is an asset rather than a defect of this system, as compared with systems where value judgments are embedded and often pass unrecognized. [p. 121]

In the previous example, individuals were assigned to training classes according to ability and experience. Alternatively, however, all individuals could have been assigned to a single training class regardless of ability or experience. Before choosing one of these strategies, let us compare them in terms of some possible outcomes.

If the trainees are assigned to different classes based on learning speed, the overall cost of the training program will be higher because additional staff and facilities are required to conduct the different classes. In all likelihood, however, this increased cost may be offset by the percentage of successful training graduates. For strategy I (differential assignment), therefore, assume a $50,000 total training cost and a 75 percent success rate among trainees. Alternatively, the overall cost of strategy II (single training class) would be lower, but the percentage of successful graduates may also be lower. For strategy II, therefore, assume the total training cost is $40,000 and that 50 percent of the trainees successfully complete the training program. Payoffs from the two strategies may now be compared:

	Total Training Cost	Percentage of Successful Grads
Strategy I— differential assignment	$50,000	75%
Strategy II— single training program	$40,000	50%
Strategy II—total payoff	+ $10,000	− 25%

At first glance, strategy II may appear cost effective. Yet in addition to producing 25 percent fewer graduates, this approach has hidden costs. In attempting to train all new hires at the same rate, the faster-than-average learners will be penalized because the training is not challenging enough for them, while the slower-than-average learners will be penalized in trying to keep up with what they perceive to be a demanding pace. The organization itself also may suffer in that the fast learners may quit (thereby increasing recruitment and selection costs), regarding the lack of challenge in training as symptomatic of the lack of challenge in full-time jobs with the organization.

In summary, utility theory provides a framework for making decisions by forcing the decision maker to define clearly his goal, to enumerate the expected consequences or possible outcomes of his decision, and to attach differing utilities or values to each. Such an approach has merit since resulting decisions are likely to rest on a foundation of sound reasoning and conscious forethought. As we shall see in Chapters 9 through 16, decision theory is an extremely useful tool for the HR specialist. Another useful tool, one that forces the decision maker to think in terms of multiple causes and multiple effects, is **systems analysis.**

Organizations as Systems

In recent years much attention has been devoted to the concept of "systems" and the use of "systems thinking" to frame and solve complex scientific and technological problems. The approach is particularly relevant to the social sciences, and it also provides an integrative framework for organization theory and management practice.

What is meant by a system? One view holds that a system is a collection of interrelated parts, unified by design, to attain one or more objectives. As managers, our objective is awareness of variables involved in executing managerial functions so that decisions will be made in light of the overall effect upon our organization and its objectives. These decisions must consider not only the organization itself, but also the larger systems (e.g., industry, environment) in which the organization operates (Luchsinger and Dock, 1982). Classical management theories viewed organizations as closed or self-contained systems whose problems could be divided into their component parts and solved. The closed system approach concentrated primarily on the internal operation of the organization (i.e., within its own boundary) and tended to ignore the outside environment.

This approach was criticized on several grounds. In concentrating solely on conditions inside the firm, management became sluggish in its response to the demands of the marketplace. A recent example of this is IBM. As it moved into the 1990s, the company underestimated the popularity of personal computers and workstations, assuming that businesses would prefer mainframe computers, and that foreign-made "clones"

of the IBM PC would not capture much market share. Such a miscalculation led to disastrous results for the company as it shed assets and over 100,000 employees. Obviously, the closed system approach does not describe organizational reality. To do so, it is necessary to take a broader functional view, a systemic perspective, in order to coordinate the various components.

The modern view of organizations, therefore, is that of open systems in continual interaction with multiple dynamic environments, providing for a continuous import of inputs (in the form of people, capital, raw material, and information) and a transformation of these into outputs, which are then exported back into these various environments to be consumed by clients or customers (see Figure 3–1). Subsequently, the environments (economic, legal, social, and political) provide feedback on the overall process (Schein, 1980).

Senge (1990) has described the process well:

> Systems thinking is a discipline for seeing wholes. It is a framework for seeing interrelationships rather than things, for seeing patterns of change rather than "snapshots." It is a set of general principles—distilled over the course of the twentieth century, spanning fields as diverse as the physical and social sciences, engineering, and management. It is also a specific set of tools and techniques. . . . during the last thirty years these tools have been applied to understand a wide range of corporate, urban, regional, economic, political, ecological, and even physiological systems. And systems thinking is a sensibility for the subtle interconnectedness that gives living systems their unique character [pp. 68–69].

The hierarchy of systems should be emphasized as well. A system comprises subsystems of a lower order and is also part of a supersystem. However, what constitutes a system or a subsystem is purely relative and largely depends on what level of abstraction or complexity one is focusing his or her analysis. As members of organizations, people are organized into groups, groups are organized into departments, departments are organized into divisions, divisions are organized into companies, and companies are part of an industry and an economy. There seems to be a need for this inclusive, almost concentric mode of organizing subsystems into larger systems and supersystems in order to coordinate activities and processes. It provides the macroview from which to visualize events or actions in one system and their effects on other related systems or on the organization as a whole (Katz and Kahn, 1978).

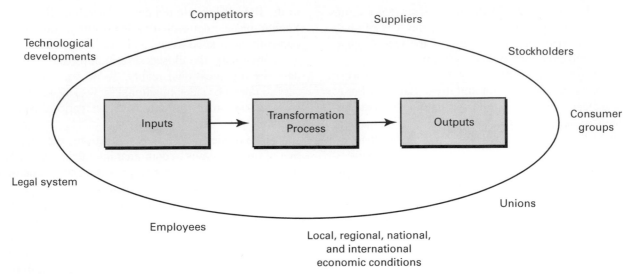

FIGURE 3–1 Organizations Are Open Systems in Continual Interaction with Multiple, Dynamic Environments.

In summary, systems theory has taken us to the edge of a new awareness—that everything is one big system with infinite, interconnected, interdependent subsystems. What we are now discovering is that managers need to *understand* systems theory, but they should resist the rational mind's instinctive desire to use it to predict and control organizational events. Organizational reality will not conform to any logical, systemic thought pattern (Banner and Gagné, 1995). Having said that, it is important to emphasize the implications that systems thinking has for organizational practice, specifically the importance of the following:

- the ability to scan and sense changes in the outside environment;
- the ability to bridge and manage critical boundaries and areas of interdependence;
- the ability to develop appropriate strategic responses.

Much of the widespread interest in corporate strategy is a product of the realization that organizations must be sensitive to what is occurring in the world beyond (Banner and Gagné, 1995; "Strategic Planning," 1996).

A SYSTEMS VIEW OF PERSONNEL PSYCHOLOGY

In order to appreciate more fully the relevance of personnel psychology to organizational effectiveness, it is useful to view the employment process as a network or

system of sequential, interdependent decisions (Bass and Barrett, 1981; Cronbach and Gleser, 1965).

Each decision is an attempt to discover what should be done with one or more individuals, and these decisions typically form a long chain. Sometimes the decision is whom to hire and whom to reject, or whom to train and whom not to train, or for which job a new hire is best suited. While the decision to reject a job applicant is usually considered final, the decision to accept an individual is really a decision to investigate him or her further. The strategy is, therefore, sequential since information gathered at one point in the overall procedure determines what, if any, information will be gathered next. This open system-decision theoretic model is shown graphically in Figure 3–2.

Although each link in the model will be described more fully in following sections, it is important to point out two general features. One, different recruitment, selection, placement, and training strategies are used for different jobs; and two, the various phases in the process are highly interdependent, as the feedback loops indicate. Consider one such feedback loop—from performance appraisal to job analysis. Suppose both supervisors and job incumbents determine that the task and personal requirements of a particular job have changed considerably from those originally determined in job analysis. Obviously, the original job analysis must be updated to reflect the newer requirements, but this may also affect the wage paid on that job. In addition, human resource planning strategies may have to be modified in order to ensure a continuous flow of qualified persons for the changed

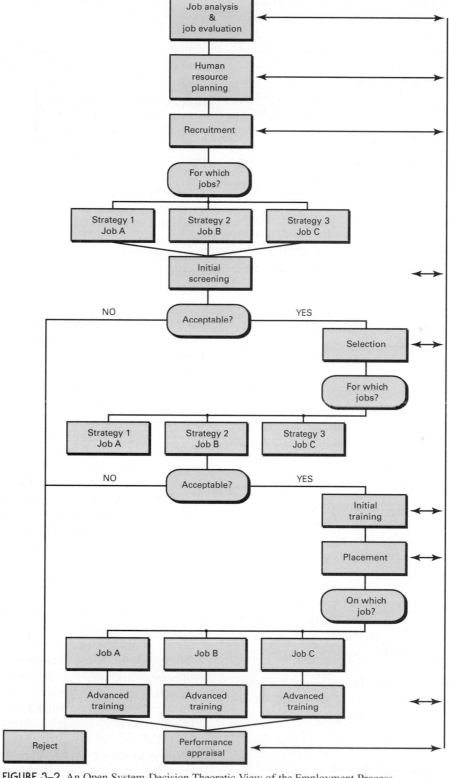

FIGURE 3–2 An Open System-Decision Theoretic View of the Employment Process.

job, different recruiting strategies may be called for in order to attract new candidates for the job, new kinds of information may be needed in order to select or promote qualified individuals, and, finally, the content of training programs for the job may have to be altered. In short, changes in one part of the system have a "reverberating" effect on all other parts of the system. Now let us examine each link in the model in greater detail.

Job Analysis and Job Evaluation

Job analysis is the fundamental building block upon which all later decisions in the employment process must rest. The process of matching the individual and the job typically begins with a detailed specification by the organization of the work to be performed, the skills needed, and the training required by the individual jobholder in order to perform the job satisfactorily.[1]

Job analysis supports many organizational activities, but one of the most basic is job evaluation. Organizations must make value judgments on the relative importance or worth of each job to the organization as a whole—that is, in terms of dollars and cents. Divisional managers are paid higher salaries than secretaries. Why is this? We may begin to answer this question by enumerating certain factors or dimensions along which the jobs differ. Responsibility for other employees is one differentiating characteristic, for example; responsibility for equipment or company resources is another.

No doubt the reader can think of many other dimensions along which the two jobs differ. When these differences are compounded across all jobs in the organization, the job evaluation process becomes a rather formidable task requiring clearly specified methods and replicable procedures that can be applied to all jobs. Alternative methods of job evaluation are currently available, but whichever method is adopted must be acceptable as well as understandable to employees, boards of directors, and other concerned groups.

Theoretically, both job analysis and job evaluation are performed independently of the particular in-

dividuals who currently happen to be performing the jobs. In theory at least, jobs and wages remain the same even though people come and go. Later on we will see that this is a rather naive assumption, but for the present such a conception is useful.

Human Resource Planning

Human resource planning (HRP) is concerned with anticipating future staffing requirements and formulating action plans to ensure that enough qualified individuals are available to meet specific staffing needs at some future time. In order to do HRP adequately, however, four conditions must be met. First, the organization must devise a talent inventory of available knowledge, abilities, skills, and experiences of present employees. Second, forecasts of internal and external human resource supply and demand must be undertaken. This requires a thorough understanding of the strategic business plans (Dyer and Holder, 1988); hence, human resource professionals must become full partners with those responsible for strategic business planning. Third, on the basis of information derived from the talent inventory and human resource supply and demand forecasts, various action plans and programs can be formulated in order to meet predicted staffing needs; such programs may include career path planning, training, transfers, promotions, or recruitment. Finally, control and evaluation procedures must be specified in order to provide feedback on the adequacy of the HRP effort. Adequate and accurate HRP is essential if organizations are to cope effectively with the radical demographic and labor market changes that are occurring throughout the 1990s. By examining the systemwide ramifications of all human resource activities, we can plan effectively, lending both direction and scope to subsequent phases in the employment process.

Recruitment

Equipped with the information derived from job analysis, job evaluation, and human resource planning, we can proceed to the next phase in the process—attracting potentially acceptable candidates to apply for the various jobs. The recruitment machinery is typically set into motion by the receipt by the HR office of a staffing requisition from a particular department. Questions such as the following often arise in recruitment. How and where should we recruit? What media or other information sources should we

---

[1] One question that has taken on added significance, especially with the increase in mechanization (the replacement of a human skill by a machine) and in automation (not only replacement of a human skill by a machine, but also automatic control and integration of a process), is whether, in fact, man should be in the system at all (Attewell and Rule, 1984).

use? Assuming the recruiting will not be done in person, what type and how much information should we include in our advertisements? How much money should we spend in order to attract qualified or qualifiable applicants?

Two basic decisions that the organization must make at this point involve the **cost of recruiting** and the **selection ratio** (Bass and Barrett, 1981; Landy, 1989). For example, the cost of recruiting a design engineer is likely to be high and may involve a nationwide effort. Furthermore, the demanding qualifications and skills required for the job imply that there will be few qualified applicants. In other words, the selection ratio, or the percentage of job applicants actually hired, will be large or unfavorable from the organization's point of view. On the other hand, a job involving small-parts assembly probably can be performed by the majority of workers. Therefore, a narrower search effort is required to attract applicants; perhaps an ad in the local newspaper will do. Given a relatively loose labor market, the probabilities are high that many potentially qualified applicants will be available. That is, because the selection ratio (the number hired relative to the number who apply) will be low or favorable, the organization can afford to be more selective.

Recruitment is of pivotal importance in the overall selection-placement process. The impression left on an applicant by company representatives or by media advertisements can significantly influence the future courses of action both of the applicant and of the organization. The author is reminded of the awkward position one company found itself in several years ago after it was pointed out that its recruiting ad read as follows: Nationally known credit firm seeks bright, energetic individual for retail sales position in local area; salary to $30,000, company car plus attractive fringe benefits package, travel 25 percent per month, previous experience desirable. Appear in person, Box D206, Miami, Fla.

Initial Screening

Given relatively favorable selection ratios and acceptable recruiting costs, the resulting applications (or applicants, should they show up in person) are then subjected to an initial screening process that is more or less intensive depending on the screening policy or strategy adopted by the organization.

As an illustration, let us consider two extreme strategies for the small-parts assembly job and the design engineer's job described earlier. Strategy I requires the setting of minimally acceptable standards. For example, no educational requirements may be set for the small-parts assembly job; only a minimum passing score on a validated aptitude test of finger dexterity is necessary. Strategy I is acceptable in cases where an individual need not have developed or perfected a particular skill at the time of hiring because the skill is expected to develop with training and practice. Such a policy may also be viewed as eminently fair by persons with disabilities (e.g., the blind worker who can probably perform small-parts assembly quickly and accurately by his finely developed sense of touch) and by minority and other culturally or environmentally disadvantaged groups.

Strategy II, on the other hand, may require the setting of very demanding qualifications initially since it is relatively more expensive to pass an applicant along to the next phase. The design engineer's job, for example, may require an advanced engineering degree plus several years' experience, as well as demonstrated research competence. The job demands a relatively intense initial screening process.

Because each stage in the employment process involves an economic cost to the organization and because the investment becomes larger and larger with each successive stage, the likely consequence of decision errors at each stage must be considered. Decision errors may be of two types: erroneous acceptances and erroneous rejections. An **erroneous acceptance** is an individual who was passed on from a preceding stage but who failed at the following stage. An **erroneous rejection,** on the other hand, is an individual who was rejected at a preceding stage, but who could have succeeded at the following stage if allowed to continue.

Different costs are attached to each of these errors, but the costs of an erroneous acceptance are immediately apparent. If an organization invests $20,000 in an applicant who subsequently fails, that $20,000 is also gone. The costs of an erroneous rejection are much less obvious and, in many cases, are not regarded as "costly" at all to the employing organization—unless the rejected applicant goes to work for a competitor and becomes a smashing success for them!

Selection

This is the central phase in the process of matching individual and job. During this phase, information is collected judgmentally (e.g., by interviews), mechanically (e.g., by written tests), or in both ways. Scorable application blanks, written or performance tests, interviews, and background and reference checks are several examples of useful data-gathering techniques. These data, however collected, must then be combined judgmentally, mechanically, or via some mixture of both methods. The resulting combination is the basis for hiring, rejecting, or placing on a waiting list every applicant who reaches the selection phase. During the selection phase, considerations of utility and cost guide the decision maker in his or her choice of information sources and method of combining data. For example, the interviewers' salaries, the time lost from production or supervision, and, finally, the very low predictive ability of the informal interview make it a rather expensive selection device. Tests, physical examinations, and credit and background investigations also are expensive, and it is imperative that decision makers weigh the economic costs of such instruments and procedures against their potential utility.

We will point out the key considerations in determining utility in Chapter 12, but it is important at this point to stress that there is not a systematic or a one-to-one relationship between the cost of a selection procedure and its subsequent utility. That is, it is not universally true that if a selection procedure costs more it is a more accurate predictor of later job performance. Many well-intentioned operating managers commonly are misled by this assumption. Procedures add genuine utility to the employment process to the extent that they enable an organization to improve its current batting average in predicting success (at an acceptable cost), however success happens to be defined in that organization. Hence, the organization must assess its present success rate, the favorableness of the selection ratio for the jobs under consideration, the predictive ability of proposed selection procedures, and the cost of adding additional predictive information; then it must weigh the alternatives and make a decision.

Placement

Applicants who reach this stage in the employment process already have been hired. They are now company employees who will begin drawing paychecks. After a relatively brief period of training the employees and exposing them to company policies and procedures, the organization faces another critical decision. On which jobs should these employees be placed? In many instances, of course, individuals are hired to fill specific jobs (so-called "one-shot" selec-

tion-testing programs). In such cases, the placement decision is made in the employment office at the time of hire; therefore, placement per se becomes a relatively unimportant part of the overall process. In other cases, the decision to hire is made first and the placement decision follows at a later time. Different rationales underlie the two types of decisions.

Hiring decisions are primarily based on **interpersonal** differences. That is, we rely on competent information derived from job analysis that certain abilities, aptitudes, or personality dimensions are required for effective job performance. Because people differ in competence along these dimensions, the observed differences provide a logical basis for staffing decisions.

A somewhat different rationale underlies placement decisions. These are fundamentally rooted in **intrapersonal** differences—that is, differences in aptitudes, abilities, temperament, or interests in a single individual. Thus, placement decisions are made on the basis of the fit between personal capabilities and characteristics and particular job requirements.

In practice, "one-shot" selection-testing programs are frequently overemphasized. Often individuals are selected not only for their abilities to perform entry-level jobs, but also in the hope that with appropriate experience and training, they will be able to assume greater responsibilities and satisfactorily perform higher-level jobs as organizational requirements and needs change. However, in order to make the best use of available personnel, job success must be estimated for all candidates with respect to all possible job assignments. For example, suppose a firm hires 40 management trainees during a 6-month period. At the completion of the training program, each trainee must be placed on one of seven possible jobs. Based on an extensive battery of tests, interviews, and interest inventories, an expected probability of success for each trainee is determined for each job. Table 3–1 presents the expected probabilities of success for four of the 40 trainees on the seven available jobs.

Given expected probabilities of success for available jobs, the problem is to optimize the total efficiency of the organization. Several strategies are available. By choosing the highest expected probability of success in each row, the *organization* benefits by choosing the best individual available. By choosing the highest expected probability of success in each column, the *individual* benefits by being placed on a job that is optimal for him or her. Sometimes the strategies conflict. For example, Jim has the highest expected probability of success for the assistant pro-

TABLE 3–1 Relative Probability of Success of Four Management Trainees on Available Jobs

Job	Anne	Bill	Sue	Jim
Asst. financial analyst	.3	.9	.6	.4
District sales supervisor	.7	.5	.4	.6
Asst. product manager	.4	.6	.3	.7
Asst. manager of employee relations	.6	.7	.5	.2
Asst. manager—new product development	.2	.5	.8	.5
Asst. manager—sales promotion	.8	.2	.4	.5
Asst. production supervisor	.5	.4	.9	.8

thought necessary to perform certain jobs may be unduly harsh or restrictive. Conversely, educational, training, or behavioral requirements may need to be added to job specifications if supervisors observe an inordinate amount of scrap or waste or an unusually large number of serious accidents. In short, jobs change and people change. Continuous rapid feedback between and among all phases in the employment process can increase considerably the fairness and accuracy of such important decisions.

Training and Development

HR specialists can increase significantly the effectiveness of the workers and managers of an organization by employing a wide range of training and development techniques. Payoffs will be significant, however, only when training techniques are chosen so as to match accurately individual and organizational needs (Goldstein and Gilliam, 1990). Most individuals have a need to feel competent (Deci, 1972; Lawler, 1969; White, 1959)—that is, to make use of their valued abilities, to realize their capabilities and potential. Training programs are designed to modify or to develop abilities, skills, attitudes, or knowledge so that employees can acquire the competence that will enable them to perform their jobs better. The gamut of training programs available ranges from basic skill training and development for the hard-core unemployed, to supervisory training for the first-line supervisors, to extensive executive development programs for top managers.

Personnel selection and placement strategies relate closely to training and development strategies. Trade-offs are likely. For example, if the organization selects individuals with minimal qualifications and skill development, then the onus of developing qualified, capable, competent employees shifts squarely onto the shoulders of the training department. On the other hand, if the organization selects only those individuals who already possess the necessary abilities and skills required to perform their jobs, then the burden of further skill development is minimal during the training phase. Given a choice between selection and training, however, the best strategy is to choose selection. Selection of high-caliber employees will enable these individuals to learn more and to learn faster from subsequent training programs than will the selection of lower-caliber employees.

Earlier we noted the importance of accurately matching training objectives with individual and job

duct manager's job, but personally Jim would probably do better as an assistant production supervisor.

The choice of an appropriate strategy is not the major stumbling block of this approach, however. The main difficulty is in estimating the expected probabilities of success with respect to available jobs. Unfortunately, such estimates frequently suffer from our inability to define and reliably measure success for each job. Moreover, situational and interpersonal factors often are more important in determining job behavior and job success than are individual factors. For these reasons, sophisticated placement strategies have not been adopted widely; however, advances in assessment and developments in job classification systems hold considerable promise for the future, as we shall see in Chapter 14.

Utility is important in the placement phase as well. Utility in this context refers to the differential payoff (to the organization as well as to the individual) of job assignments based on individual differences in aptitudes that are relevant and necessary for effective performance on the jobs under consideration.

The interdependent nature of the decisions necessary in the overall employment process is clearly evident in the placement phase. Quite possibly, established job specifications (the personal characteristics necessary for adequate job performance) may have to be revised or modified on the basis of observed job performance. Workers with disabilities (e.g., the blind, the deaf) continually amaze employers who realize that the physical or behavioral requirements they requirements. In the case of lower-level jobs, training objectives can be specified rather rigidly and defined carefully. The situation changes markedly, however, when training programs must be designed for jobs that permit considerable individual initiative and freedom (e.g., selling, research, equipment design) or jobs that require incumbents to meet and deal effectively with a variety of types and modes of information, situations, or unforeseen developments (e.g., as managers, detectives, test pilots, astronauts). The emphasis in these jobs is on developing a broad range of skills and competence in several areas in order to cope effectively with erratic job demands. Because training programs for these jobs are expensive and lengthy, initial qualifications and selection criteria are likely to be especially demanding.

Performance Appraisal

In selecting, placing, and training an individual for a specific job, an organization is essentially taking a risk in the face of uncertainty. Although most of us like to pride ourselves on being logical and rational decision makers, the fact is that we are often quite fallible. Equipped with inexhaustive, partial information about present or past behavior, we attempt to predict future job behavior. Unfortunately, it is only after employees have been performing their jobs for a reasonable length of time that we can evaluate their performance and our predictions.

In observing, evaluating, and documenting on-the-job behavior, we are essentially evaluating the degree of success attained by the individual jobholder in reaching organizational objectives. While success in some jobs can be assessed partially by objective indices (e.g., dollar volume of sales, amount of scrap and reworks), frequently judgmental appraisals of performance play a significant role.

Promotions, compensation decisions, transfers, disciplinary actions—in short, individuals' livelihoods—are extraordinarily dependent on performance appraisals. To be sure, such appraisals are of signal importance to the ultimate success and survival of a reward system based on merit. It is, therefore, ethically and morally imperative that each individual get a fair shake. If supervisory ratings are used to evaluate employee performance and if the rating instruments themselves are poorly designed, prone to bias and error, or focus on elements irrelevant or unimportant to

effective job performance, or if the raters themselves are uncooperative or untrained, then our ideal of fairness will never be realized. Fortunately, these problems can be minimized through careful attention to the development and implementation of appraisal systems, and to the thorough training of those who will use them.

In our treatment of performance appraisal in Chapter 5 we will illustrate the rating methods currently available and consider the advantages and disadvantages of each as well as the types of biases that can victimize unwary raters. We will also look at the methods used to overcome these biases.

In writing this book I have attempted to frame my ultimate objectives realistically, for it would be foolish to pretend that a single volume holds the final solution to any of these nagging employment problems. Solutions are found in concerned people—those who apply what books can only preach. Nevertheless, by urging you to consider both costs and anticipated consequences in making decisions, I hope that you will feel challenged to make better decisions and thereby to improve considerably the caliber of human resource management practice. Nowhere is systems thinking more relevant than in the HR management system of organizations (Luchsinger and Dock, 1982). As we noted earlier, the very concept of a system implies a design to attain one or more objectives. This involves a consideration of desired outcomes. In our next three chapters we will consider the special problems associated with developing reliable success criteria, that is, outcomes of the HR management process.

Discussion Questions

1. How is utility theory useful as a framework for making decisions?

2. Describe three examples of open systems. Can you think of a closed system? Why are organizations open systems?

3. Why is it useful to view the employment process as a network of sequential, interdependent decisions?

4. What is the difference between an erroneous acceptance and an erroneous rejection? Describe situations where one or the other is more serious.

5. Suppose you had to choose between "making" competent employees through training, or "buying" them through selection. Which would you choose? Why?

CHAPTER

4

CRITERIA: CONCEPTS, MEASUREMENT, AND EVALUATION

AT A GLANCE

Adequate and accurate criterion measurement is a fundamental problem in personnel psychology. Although criteria are sometimes used for predictive purposes and sometimes for evaluative purposes, in both cases they represent that which is important or desirable. Criteria are operational statements of goals or desired outcomes.

Before we can study human performance and understand it better, we must confront four problematic issues: reliability of performance, reliability of performance observation, dimensionality of performance, and modification of performance by situational characteristics. Finally, in evaluating operational criteria, we must guard against certain contaminants, such as biasing factors in ratings. In addition, operational criterion measures must be relevant, reliable, sensitive, and practical.

In general, applied psychologists are guided by two principal objectives: (1) to demonstrate the utility of their procedures and programs, and (2) to enhance their understanding of the determinants of job success. In attempting to achieve these twin objectives, sometimes composite criteria are used and sometimes multiple criteria are used. Although there has been an enduring controversy over the relative merits of each approach, we will show that the two positions differ in terms of underlying assumptions and ultimate goals. Thus, one or both may be appropriate in a given set of circumstances. In a concluding section of this chapter, we will offer several promising research designs that should prove useful in resolving the criterion dilemma and thus in advancing the field.

The development of criteria that are adequate and appropriate is at once a stumbling block and a challenge to the HR specialist. Behavioral scientists have bemoaned the "criterion problem" through the years. The term refers to the difficulties involved in the process of conceptualizing and measuring performance constructs that are multidimensional, dynamic, and appropriate for different purposes (Austin and Villanova, 1992). Yet the effectiveness and future progress of all behavioral science are fundamentally dependent upon our ability to resolve this baffling question.

The challenge is to develop theories, concepts, and measurements that will achieve the twin objectives of enhancing the utility of available procedures and programs and deepening our understanding of the psychological and behavioral processes involved in job performance. Ultimately we must strive to develop a comprehensive theory of the behavior of men and women at work.

In the early days of applied psychology, according to Jenkins (1946), most psychologists tended to accept the tacit assumption that criteria were either given of God or just to be found lying about. It is regrettable that even today we often resort to the most readily available or most expedient criteria, when with a little more effort and thought we could probably develop better criteria. Nevertheless, progress has been made, as the field has come to recognize that criterion measures are samples of a larger performance universe, and that as much effort should be devoted to understanding and validating criteria as is devoted to predictors (Campbell, McHenry, and Wise, 1990). Wallace (1965) expressed the matter aptly when he said that the answer to the question "Criteria for what?" must certainly include "for understanding" (p. 417). Let us begin by defining our terms.

DEFINITION

Various definitions of criteria exist. From one perspective criteria are standards that can be used as yardsticks for measuring employees' success or failure (Bass and Barrett, 1981; Guion, 1965; Landy, 1989). This definition is quite adequate within the context of personnel selection, placement, and performance appraisal. It is useful when prediction is involved—that is, in the establishment of a functional relationship between one variable, the predictor, and another variable, the criterion. However, there are times when we simply wish to evaluate without necessarily predicting. Suppose, for example, that the HR department is concerned with evaluating the effectiveness of a recruitment campaign aimed at attracting minority applicants. Various criteria must be used to evaluate the program adequately. The goal in this case is not prediction, but rather evaluation. One distinction between predictors and criteria is time (Mullins and Ratliff, 1979). For example, if evaluative standards such as written or performance tests are administered *before* an employment decision is made (i.e., to hire, to promote), the standards are predictors. If evaluative standards are administered *after* an employment decision has been made (i.e., to evaluate performance effectiveness), the standards are criteria.

Thus, a more comprehensive definition is required, for whether we are predicting or evaluating, a criterion represents something important or desirable. It is an operational statement of the goals or desired outcomes of the program under study (Astin, 1964). It

is an **evaluative standard** that can be used to measure a person's performance, attitude, motivation, and so forth (Blum and Naylor, 1968). Examples of some possible criteria and their uses are presented in Table 4–1, which has been modified from those given by Dunnette and Kirchner (1965) and Guion (1965). While many of these measures often would fall short as adequate criteria, each of them deserves careful study in order to develop a comprehensive sampling of job or program performance. There are several other requirements of criteria in addition to desirability and importance, but before examining them we must first consider certain conceptual dimensions.

TABLE 4–1 Possible Criteria and Their Uses

Output measures
  Units produced
  Number of items sold
  Dollar volume of sales
  Number of letters typed
  Commission earnings
  Number of candidates attracted (recruitment program)
  Readership of an advertisement

Quality measures
  Number of errors (coding, filing, bookkeeping, typing, diagnosing)
  Number of errors detected (inspector, troubleshooter, service person)
  Number of policy renewals (insurance sales)
  Number of complaints and dissatisfied persons (clients, customers, subordinates, colleagues)
  Rate of scrap, reworks, or breakage
  Cost of spoiled or rejected work

Lost time
  Number of occasions (or days) absent
  Number of times tardy
  Length and frequency of unauthorized pauses
  Employee turnover
  Number of discharges for cause
  Number of voluntary quits
  Number of transfers due to unsatisfactory performance
  Length of service

Trainability and promotability
  Time to reach standard performance
  Level of proficiency reached in a given time
  Rate of salary increase
  Number of promotions in a specified time period
  Number of times considered for promotion
  Length of time between promotions

Ratings of performance
  Ratings of personal traits or characteristics
  Ratings of behavioral expectations
  Ratings of performance in work samples

THE DOMAIN OF JOB PERFORMANCE

Performance may be defined as observable things people do that are relevant for the goals of the organization (Campbell et al., 1990). Job performance itself is multidimensional, and the behaviors that constitute performance can be scaled in terms of the level of performance they represent. It also is important to distinguish *performance* from the outcomes or results of performance, which comprise *effectiveness* (Campbell, Dunnette, Lawler, and Weick, 1970).

The term **ultimate criterion** (Thorndike, 1949) describes the full domain of performance and includes everything that ultimately defines success on the job. Such a criterion is ultimate in the sense that one cannot look beyond it for any further standard by which to judge the outcomes of performance. Since the ultimate criterion is strictly conceptual and therefore cannot be measured or observed, it embodies the notion of "true," "total," "long-term," or "ultimate worth" to the employing organization.

The ultimate criterion of a salesperson's performance must include, for example, total sales volume over the individual's entire tenure with the company; total number of new accounts brought in during the individual's career; amount of customer loyalty built up by the salesperson during his or her career; total amount of his or her influence on the morale or sales records of other company salespersons; and overall effectiveness in planning activities and calls, controlling expenses, and handling necessary reports and records. In short, an ultimate criterion is a construct that is strictly conceptual in nature.

Although the ultimate criterion is stated in broad terms that often are not susceptible to quantitative evaluation, it is an important construct because the relevance of any operational criterion measure and the factors underlying its selection are better understood if the conceptual stage is clearly and thoroughly documented (Astin, 1964).

DIMENSIONALITY OF CRITERIA

Operational measures of the conceptual criterion may vary along several dimensions. These may include a **psychological dimension** (e.g., the nurse's skill in human relationships); an **ecological dimension** (i.e., in terms of a relationship between a person and his environment such as the assembly-line worker's profi-

ciency under varying conditions of heat, noise, and light); a **physical dimension** (e.g., the physiological cost, in calories used per minute, of different types of work); or an **economic dimension** (e.g., the dollar cost of errors, scrap, and reworks). Criteria also vary along several other important dimensions, as we shall see in what follows.

Temporal Dimensionality

Once we have defined clearly our conceptual criterion, we must then specify and refine operational measures of criterion performance (i.e., the criteria actually to be used). Regardless of the operational form of the criterion measure, we must take it at some point in time. When is the best time for criterion measurement? Optimum times vary greatly from situation to situation, and conclusions therefore need to be couched in terms of when criterion measurements were taken. Far different results may occur depending on when criterion measurements are taken (Weitz, 1961), and failure to consider the temporal dimension may lead to misinterpretations.

In predicting the sales success and survival of life insurance agents, for example, ability as measured by standardized tests is significant in determining early success, but interests and personality factors play a more important role later on (Ferguson, 1960). The same is true for accountants (Bass and Barrett, 1981). Thus after two years as a staff accountant with one of the "Big 6" accounting firms, interpersonal skills with colleagues and clients are more important than pure technical expertise for continued success. In short, criterion measurements are not independent of time.

Earlier we noted that ultimate criteria embody the idea of long-term effectiveness. Ultimate criteria are not practical for day-to-day decision making or evaluation, however, because researchers and managers usually cannot afford the luxury of the time needed to gather the necessary data. Therefore, we have to use substitute criteria, immediate or intermediate (see Fig. 4–1). To be sure, all immediate and intermediate criteria are *partial* since at best they give only an approximation of the ultimate criterion (Thorndike, 1949).

Figure 4–1 lacks precision in that there is a great deal of leeway in determining when immediate criteria become intermediate criteria. Immediate criteria are near-term measures, such as test scores on the final day of training class or measurement of the rookie quarterback's performance in his first game. Interme-

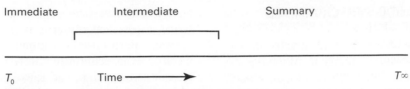

FIGURE 4-1 The Temporal Dimension of Criterion Measurement.

diate criteria are obtained at a later time, usually about 6 months after initial measurement (i.e., supervisory ratings of performance, work sample performance tests, or peer ratings of effectiveness). Summary criteria are expressed in terms of longer-term averages or totals. Summary criteria are often useful because they avoid or balance out short-term effects or trends and errors of observation and measurement. Thus, a trainee's average performance on weekly tests during 6 months of training or a student's cumulative college grade-point average is taken as the best estimate of his overall performance. Summary criteria may range from measurements taken after three months' performance, 3 to 4 years' performance, or even longer.

Temporal dimensionality is a broad concept, and in the following two sections we will consider two special cases of temporal dimensionality: static dimensionality and dynamic dimensionality.

Static Dimensionality. In a classic article Ghiselli (1956b) identified three different types of criterion dimensionality: static, dynamic, and individual dimensionality. If we observe job performance at any single point in time, we find that it is multidimensional in nature (Campbell, 1990). For example, Rush (1953) found that a number of relatively independent skills are involved in selling, such that at a given time a salesperson may be high on one performance characteristic and simultaneously low on another. Thus, the salesperson's learning aptitude (as measured by sales school grades and technical knowledge) is unrelated to objective measures of his or her achievement (such as average monthly volume of sales or percentage of quota achieved), which in turn is independent of the salesperson's general reputation (e.g., planning of work, rated potential value to the firm), which in turn is independent of his or her sales techniques (sales approaches, interest and enthusiasm, etc.). Similarly, Fleishman and Ornstein (1960) identified six component abilities in describing pilot flying performance. We could marshal an abundance of additional evidence to support the notion that job performance is multidimensional, but the important point is that the

static dimensions are those typically considered in criterion research. Frequently we take a snapshot of performance at a single point in time using a single criterion, and we assume that we have "captured" and described employee performance adequately. This is not necessarily the case, as we shall see.

Dynamic Dimensionality. Common sense suggests that as employees gain experience and "learn the ropes" on their jobs, as they more fully develop their abilities and potential, the dimensions of performance that seemed to be appropriate and valid early in their careers may be unrelated to their job performance at a later stage. Criteria might be "dynamic," changing in importance over time. In fact, dynamic criteria might assume any one of three possible forms (Barrett, Caldwell, and Alexander, 1985): (a) changes in group average performance over time, (b) changes in validity over time, and (c) changes in the rank-ordering of scores on the criterion over time. Let us examine each of these.

Traditionally criterial dynamism has been viewed as a serious conceptual and operational issue, but the research base cited to support this view was not analyzed critically until a study by Barrett et al. (1985). Consider definition (a) above, for example. Ghiselli and Haire (1960) followed the progress of a group of investment salesmen for 10 years. During this period they found a 650 percent improvement in average productivity, and still there was no evidence of leveling off! However, this increase was based only on those salesmen who survived on the job for the full 10 years; it was not true of *all* of the salesmen in the original sample. To be able to compare the productivity of the salesmen, their experience must be the same, or else it must be equalized in some manner (Ghiselli and Brown, 1955). Indeed, a considerable amount of other research evidence cited by Barrett et al. (1985) does not indicate that average productivity improves significantly over lengthy time spans.

Changes in Validity over Time. Criteria also might be dynamic if predictor validities fluctuate over time. Bass (1962) found this to be the case in a 42-month investigation of salesmen's rated performance. Scores on three ability tests as well as peer ratings on three dimensions were collected for a sample of 99 salesmen. Semiannual supervisory merit ratings served as criteria. The results show patterns of validity coefficients both for the tests and peer ratings that *appear* to fluctuate erratically over time. However, a much different conclusion is reached when the validity coefficients are tested statistically. No significant differences are found for the validities of the ability tests, and when peer ratings are used as predictors, only 16 out of 84 (roughly 20%) pairs of validity coefficients show a statistically significant difference (Barrett et al., 1985).

Researchers have suggested two hypotheses to explain why validities might change over time. One, the **changing task model,** suggests that while the relative amounts of ability possessed by individuals remain stable over time, criteria for effective performance might change in importance. Hence the validity of predictors of performance also might change. The second model, known as the **changing subjects model,** suggests that while specific abilities required for effective performance remain constant over time, each individual's level of ability changes over time, and that is why validities might fluctuate (Henry and Hulin, 1987).

Neither of the above models has received unqualified support. Indeed, proponents of the view that validity tends to decrease over time (Henry and Hulin, 1987; 1989) and proponents of the view that validity remains stable over time (Ackerman, 1989; Barrett and Alexander, 1989) agree on only one point: Initial performance tends to show some decay in its correlation with later performance. However, when only longitudinal studies are examined, it appears that validity decrements are much more common than are validity increments (Henry and Hulin, 1989). This tends to support the view that validities do fluctuate over time.

Changes in the Rank-ordering of Scores on the Criterion Over Time. To examine this definition of dynamic criteria systematically, Barrett et al. (1985) searched all issues of the *Journal of Applied Psychology* and *Personnel Psychology* for studies that reported correlations between criterion measures collected on two occasions. Of the 276 coefficients identified, only 8.7 percent were not significantly different from zero. While we cannot conclude from

these results that no change in rank-ordering has occurred, there does appear to be substantial stability in repeated criterion measurements. Subsequent research on the 6-month performance of 509 sewing machine operators found that relative performance was not stable over time (Deadrick and Madigan, 1990).

Austin, Humphreys, and Hulin (1989) criticized Barrett et al.'s (1985) use of pairwise comparisons of correlations to test for the existence of dynamic criteria. They urged the use of regression or time series analysis with individual-level criterion distributions over time. Two subsequent studies (Hofmann, Jacobs, and Baratta, 1993; Hofmann, Jacobs, and Gerras, 1992) did just that.

In both of these studies the researchers identified and tested a new perspective on the topic, a perspective focused on *individual* change patterns and differences in such patterns across individuals. Both studies (one using professional baseball players and the other using insurance sales agents) found systematic, meaningful differences in (a) intra-individual patterns of performance, and (b) in intra-individual patterns of changes in performance across individuals (see Fig. 4–2). Now the challenge is to identify factors that determine differences in intra-individual performance trajectories.

Individual Dimensionality. It is possible that individuals performing the same job may be considered equally good; yet the nature of their contributions to the organization may be quite different. Thus, different criterion dimensions should be used to evaluate them. Kingsbury (1933) recognized this problem more than 65 years ago when he said:

> Some executives are successful because they are good planners, although not successful directors. Others are splendid at coordinating and directing, but their plans and programs are defective. Few executives are equally competent in both directions. Failure to recognize and provide, in both testing and rating, for this obvious distinction is, I believe, one major reason for the unsatisfactory results of most attempts to study, rate, and test executives. Good tests of one kind of executive ability are not good tests of the other kind. [p. 123]

While in an administrative context there is only one job, it might plausibly be argued that in reality there are two. The two jobs are qualitatively different only in a psychological sense. In fact, the study of individual criterion dimensionality is a useful means of deter-

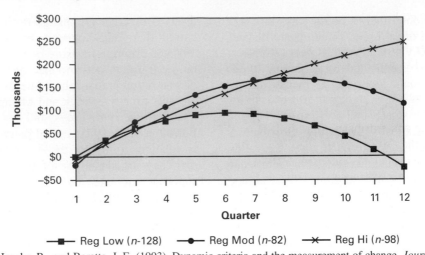

From Hofmann, D. A., Jacobs, R., and Baratta, J. E. (1993). Dynamic criteria and the measurement of change. *Journal of Applied Psychology, 78,* 194–204. Copyright 1993 by the American Psychological Association. Reprinted by permission of the publisher and the authors.

FIGURE 4–2 Regression Lines for Three Ordinary Least Squares Clusters of Insurance Agents—Low, Moderate, and High Performers— over 3 Years.

mining whether different positions in the same job are psychologically the same or different.

ESSENTIALS OF CRITERION DEVELOPMENT

Competent criterion research is one of the most pressing needs of personnel psychology today, as it has been in the past. Over 50 years ago Stuit and Wilson (1946) demonstrated that continuing attention to the development of better performance measures results in better predictions of performance. The validity of these results has not been dulled by time. In this section, therefore, we will consider certain essential requirements of criteria, point out potential pitfalls in criterion research, and sketch a logical scheme for criterion development.

At the outset it is important to set certain "chronological priorities." First we must develop and analyze criteria, for only then can we construct or select predictors to forecast relevant criteria. Far too often, unfortunately, researchers select predictors carefully, and follow this with a hasty search for "predictable criteria." To be sure, if we switch criteria, the validities of the predictors will change, but the reverse is hardly true. Pushing the argument to its logical extreme, if we use predictors with no criteria, we will never know whether or not we are selecting those individuals who are most likely to succeed. Observe the chronological priorities! At least in this process we know that the chicken comes first and then the egg follows.

Before we can study and better understand human performance, we must deal with four basic problems (Ronan and Prien, 1966; 1971). These are the problems of reliability of performance, reliability of performance observation, dimensionality of performance, and modification of performance by situational characteristics. Let us consider each in turn.

Reliability of Performance

Job performance reliability is a fundamental consideration in HR research, and its assumption is implicit in all predictive studies. Reliability in this context refers to the consistency or stability of job performance over time. Are the best (or worst) performers at Time 1 also the best (or worst) performers at Time 2? Not necessarily. Consider a series of nine studies spanning over 30 years by Rothe (summarized in Rothe, 1978). These studies specifically focused on objective measures of the reliability of performance of workers in various occupations (butter wrappers, chocolate dippers, machine operators, coil winders, welders, and foundry workers). In general, Rothe found individual output to be highly erratic and specific to the individual. Not only was the range of individual performance great, but also it was strikingly inconsistent, especially when there was no financial incentive system in operation. In one of the studies, for example, correlations of individual output over a period of 38 weeks ranged from −.03 to .91. Under an incentive plan, employee output tended to be high and consistent, with week-to-week production rates correlating above .65. Summing up all his previous work, Rothe underscored the point that the low reliability of performance could serve to mislead a researcher entirely if he or she just happened to select a period of unusually high or unusually low consistency.

What factors account for such performance variability? Thorndike (1949) identified two types of unreliability—intrinsic and extrinsic—that may serve to shed some light on the problem. **Intrinsic unreliability** is due to personal inconsistency in performance, while **extrinsic unreliability** is due to sources of variability that are external to job demands or individual behavior. Examples of the latter include variations in weather conditions (e.g., for outside construction work); unreliability due to machine downtime; or, in the case of interdependent tasks, delays in supplies, assemblies, or information. Much extrinsic unreliability is due to careless observation or poor control.

Faced with all of these potential confounding factors, what can be done? One solution is to *aggregate* (average) behavior over situations or occasions, thereby canceling out the effects of incidental, uncontrollable factors. To illustrate this Epstein (1979; 1980) conducted four studies, each of which sampled behavior on repeated occasions over a period of weeks. Data in the four studies consisted of self-ratings, ratings by others, objectively-measured behaviors, responses to personality inventories, and psychophysiological measures such as heart rate. The results provided unequivocal support for the hypothesis that *stability can be demonstrated over a wide range of variables so long as the behavior in question is averaged over a sufficient number of occurrences.* Once adequate performance reliability was obtained, evidence for validity emerged in the form of statistically significant relationships among variables.

Two further points bear emphasis. One, there is no shortcut for aggregating over occasions or people. In both cases it is necessary to sample adequately the domain over which one wishes to generalize. Two, whether aggregation is carried out within a single study or over a sample of studies, it is not a panacea. Certain systematic effects, such as gender, race, or attitudes of raters may bias an entire group of studies (Rosenthal and Rosnow, 1984). Examining large samples of studies through the techniques of meta-analysis (see Chapter 11; also Green and Hall, 1984) provides one way of detecting the existence of such variables.

It also seems logical to expect that broader levels of aggregation might be necessary in some situations than in others. Specifically, Rambo, Chomiak, and Price (1983) have shown that the reliability of performance data is a function both of task complexity and of the constancy of the work environment. These factors, along with the general effectiveness of an incentive system (if one exists), interact to create the conditions that determine the extent to which performance is consistent over time.

Rambo et al. (1983) obtained weekly production data over a three-and-a-half-year period from a group of women sewing machine operators and a group of women in folding and packaging jobs. Both groups of operators worked under a piece-rate payment plan. Median correlations in week-to-week (not day-to-day) output rates were: sewing = .94; nonsewing = .98. Among weeks separated by one year they were sewing = .69; nonsewing = .86. Finally, when output in week 1 was correlated with output in week 178, the correlations obtained were still high: sewing = .59; nonsewing = .80. These are extraordinary levels of consistency, indicating that the presence of a production-linked wage incentive, coupled with stable, narrowly routinized work tasks, will result in high levels of consistency in worker productivity. Those individuals who produced much (little) initially also tended to produce much (little) at a later time. More recent results for a sample of foundry chippers and grinders paid under an individual incentive plan over a 6-year period were generally consistent with those of the Rambo (1983) study (Vinchur et al., 1991), although there may be considerable variation in long-term reliability as a function of job content.

Reliability of Job Performance Observation

This issue is crucial in prediction since all evaluations of performance depend ultimately on observation of one sort or another, but different methods of observing performance may lead to markedly different conclusions, as was shown by Bray and Campbell (1968). In attempting to validate assessment center predictions of future sales potential, 78 men were hired as salesmen, regardless of their performance at the assessment center. Predictions then were related to field performance 6 months later. Field performance was assessed in two ways. In the first method, a trained, independent auditor accompanied each man in the field on as many visits as were necessary to determine whether he did or did not meet accepted standards in conducting his sales activities. The field reviewer was unaware of any judgments made of the candidates at the assessment center. In the second method, each individual was rated by his sales supervisor and his trainer from sales training school. Both the supervisor and the trainer also were unaware of the assessment center predictions.

While assessment center predictions correlated .51 with field-performance ratings, there were no significant relationships between assessment center predictions and either supervisors' ratings or trainers' ratings. Additionally, there were no significant relationships between the field-performance ratings and the supervisors' or trainers' ratings! The lesson to be drawn from this study is obvious: The study of reliability of performance becomes possible only when the reliability of judging performance is adequate (Ryans and Fredericksen, 1951). Unfortunately, while we know that the problem exists, little is known about how the reliability of judging performance can be improved (Borman and Hallam, 1991). We examine this issue in greater detail, including some promising new approaches, in the next chapter.

Dimensionality of Job Performance

Even the most cursory examination of personnel research reveals a great variety of **predictors** typically in use. In contrast, however, the majority of studies use only a global **criterion** measure of the job performance. Although ratings may be made of various aspects of job performance, the ratings are frequently combined into a single global score. Lent, Aurbach, and Levin (1971) demonstrated this in their analysis of 406 studies published in *Personnel Psychology.* Of the 1,506 criteria used, "Supervisors' Evaluation" was used in 879 cases. The extent to which the use of a single global criterion is characteristic of unpublished research is a matter of pure speculation, but its incidence is probably far higher than that in published research. Is it meaningful or realistic to reduce performance measurement to a single measure?

Several reviews (J. P. Campbell, 1990; Ronan and Prien, 1966, 1971) concluded that the notion of a unidimensional measure of job performance (even for lower-level jobs) is totally unrealistic. Analyses of even single measures of job performance (e.g., attitude toward the company, absenteeism) have revealed that they are much more complex than surface appearance would suggest. Despite the problems associated with global criteria, they seem to "work" quite well in most personnel selection situations. However, to the extent that one needs to solve a specific problem (e.g., too

many customer complaints about product quality), then a more specific criterion is needed. If there is more than one specific problem, then more than one specific criterion is called for (Guion, 1987).

PERFORMANCE AND SITUATIONAL CHARACTERISTICS

Most people would agree readily that individual levels of performance may be affected by conditions surrounding the performance. Yet most research investigations are conducted without regard for possible moderating effects of variables other than those measured by predictors. In the following six sections, therefore, we will examine some possible extra-individual influences.

Organizational Characteristics

Researchers have related absenteeism and turnover to a variety of environmental and organizational characteristics (Blau, 1985; Campion, 1991; Johns, 1994; McEvoy and Cascio, 1987). These include organization-wide factors (e.g., pay and promotion policies); interpersonal factors (group cohesiveness, friendship opportunities, satisfaction with peers or supervisors); job-related factors (e.g., role clarity, task repetitiveness, autonomy, and responsibility); and personal factors (e.g., age, tenure, mood, and family size). Shift-work is another frequently overlooked variable (Barton, 1994; Staines and Pleck, 1984). Clearly, organizational characteristics can have wide-ranging effects on performance.

Environmental Safety

Injuries and loss of time may also moderate job performance (Ginter, 1979). Factors such as a positive safety climate, high management commitment, and a sound safety communications program that incorporates goal setting and knowledge of results tend to increase safe behavior on the job (Reber and Wallin, 1984) and conservation of scarce resources (cf. Siero et al., 1989). These variables can be measured reliably (Zohar, 1980) and can then be related to individual performance.

Lifespace Variables

Lifespace variables measure important conditions that surround the employee both on and off the job. They describe the individual employee's interactions with organizational factors, task demands, supervision, and conditions off the job. Vicino and Bass (1978) used four lifespace variables—task challenge on first job assignment, life stability, supervisor-subordinate personality match, and immediate supervisor's success—to improve predictions of management success at Exxon. The four variables accounted for an additional 22 percent of the variance in success on the job over and above Exxon's own prediction based on aptitude and personality measures. The equivalent of a multiple *R* of .79 was obtained. Other lifespace variables such as personal orientation, career confidence, cosmopolitan versus local orientation, and job stress deserve further study (Cooke and Rousseau, 1983; Edwards and Van Harrison, 1993).

Job and Location

Schneider and Mitchel (1980) developed a comprehensive set of six behavioral job functions for the agency manager's job in the life insurance industry. Using 1,282 managers from 50 companies, they then examined the relationship of activity in these functions to five factors: origin of the agency (new versus established), type of agency (independent versus company controlled), number of agents, number of supervisors, and tenure of the agency manager. These five situational variables were chosen as correlates of managerial functions on the basis of their traditionally implied impact on managerial behavior in the life insurance industry. The most variance explained in a job function by a weighted composite of the five situational variables was 8.6 percent (general management). Thus, over 90 percent of the variance in the six agency management functions lies in sources other than the five variables used. While situational variables have been found to influence managerial job functions *across* technological boundaries, the results of this study suggest that situational characteristics also may influence managerial job functions *within* a particular technology. Performance thus depends not only on job demands, but also on other structural and contextual factors such as the policies and practices of particular companies.

Extra-Individual Differences and Sales Performance

Cravens and Woodruff (1973) recognized the need to adjust criterion standards for influences beyond a salesperson's control, and they attempted to determine the degree to which these factors explained variations in territory performance. In a multiple regression analysis using dollar volume of sales as the criterion, a curvilinear model yielded a corrected R^2 of .83, with sales experience, average market share, and performance ratings providing the major portion of explained variation. This study is noteworthy because the researchers generated a purer estimate of individual job performance by combining the effects of extra-individual influences (territory workload, market potential, company market share, and advertising effort) with two individual-difference variables (sales experience and rated sales effort).

Leadership

The effects of leadership and situational factors on morale and performance have been well documented (Hater and Bass, 1988; Kozlowski and Doherty, 1989). These studies, as well as those cited previously, demonstrate that variations in job performance are due to characteristics of individuals (age, sex, job experience, etc.), groups (Dobbins, 1985), and organizations (size, structure, management behavior, etc.). Until we can begin to partition the total variability in job performance into intra-individual and extra-individual components, we should not expect predictor variables measuring individual differences to correlate appreciably with measures of performance that are influenced by factors not under an individual's control.

STEPS IN CRITERION DEVELOPMENT

Guion (1961) outlined a five-step procedure for criterion development. It includes:

1. Analysis of job and/or organizational needs.
2. Development of measures of actual behavior relative to expected behavior as identified in job and need analysis. These measures should supplement objective measures of organizational outcomes such as turnover, absenteeism, production, and so on.
3. Identification of criterion dimensions underlying such measures by factor analysis, cluster analysis, or pattern analysis.
4. Development of reliable measures, each with high construct validity, of the elements so identified.
5. Determination of the predictive validity of each independent variable (predictor) for *each one* of the criterion measures, taking them one at a time.

In Step 2, Guion distinguishes behavior data from result-of-behavior data or organizational outcomes, and recommends that behavior data supplement result-of-behavior data. In Step 4, he advocates construct-valid measures. Construct validity is essentially a judgment that a test or other predictive device does, in fact, measure a specified attribute or construct to a significant degree, and that it can be used to promote the understanding or prediction of behavior (Messick, 1995; Landy, 1989). These two poles, **utility** (i.e., the researcher attempts to find the highest and therefore most useful validity coefficient) versus **understanding** (which focuses on construct validity), have formed part of the basis for an enduring controversy in psychology over the relative merits of the two approaches. We shall examine this in greater detail in a later section.

EVALUATING CRITERIA

Consider the following yardsticks in evaluating the usefulness of any single criterion measure.

Relevance

The principal requirement of any criterion is its judged relevance (i.e., it must be logically related to the performance domain in question). Hence, it is essential that this domain be described clearly. Professional guidelines on testing also emphasize this point: "The rationale for criterion relevance should be made explicit. It should include a description of the job in question and of the judgments used to determine relevance" (American Psychological Association, 1985, p. 60).

Much of the controversy surrounding the alleged differential prediction of tests for whites and African-Americans essentially reduces to the nature of the criteria used in different studies. For example, one study may use attendance or turnover as a criterion, while another uses a measure of job proficiency. As Bray and Moses (1972) pointed out, however:

> A well-designed study using turnover as a criterion which shows different relationships between test scores and termination for black and white groups may well be a study of practical significance. It would obviously have strong implications for the organization hiring and attempting to retain members of both groups. But when the study is said to prove differential validity of the tests, then one may object that the criterion is irrelevant. [p. 553]

Indeed, the American Psychological Association (APA) Task Force on Employment Testing of Minority Groups (1969) specifically emphasized that the most appropriate (i.e., logically relevant) criterion for evaluating tests is a direct measure of the degree of job proficiency developed by an employee after an appropriate period of time on the job (e.g., 6 months to a year). To be sure, the most relevant criterion measure will not always be the most expedient or the cheapest. A well-designed work sample test or performance appraisal system may require a great deal of ingenuity, effort, and expense to construct (cf. Borman and Hallam, 1991).

However, objective and subjective measures are not interchangeable, one for the other, as they correlate only about .39 (Bommer et al., 1995). Subjective measures should not be used as proxies for objective measures, if objective measures are the measures of interest. For example, if sales are the desired measure of performance, then organizations should not reward employees based on a supervisor's overall rating of performance. Conversely, if broadly-defined performance is the objective, then organizations should not reward employees solely on the basis of gross sales. Nevertheless, regardless of how many criteria are used, if, when considering all the dimensions of job performance, there remains an important aspect that is not being assessed, then an additional criterion measure is required.

Sensitivity or Discriminability

In order to be useful, any criterion measure also must be sensitive—that is, capable of discriminating between effective and ineffective employees. Suppose, for example, that quantity of goods produced is used as a criterion measure in a manufacturing operation. Such a criterion frequently is used inappropriately when, because of machine pacing, everyone doing a given job produces about the same number of goods. Under these circumstances there is little justification for using quantity of goods produced as a performance criterion, since the most effective workers do not differ appreciably from the least effective workers. Perhaps the amount of scrap or the number of errors made by workers would be a more sensitive indicator of real differences in job performance. Thus, the use of a particular criterion measure is warranted only if it serves to reveal discriminable differences in job performance.

It is important to point out, however, that there is no necessary association between criterion variance and criterion relevance. A criterion element *as mea-*

sured may have low variance, but the implications in terms of a different scale of measurement, such as dollars, may be considerable (e.g., industrial accident rates). In other words, the utility to the organization may not be reflected in the way the criterion is measured. This highlights the distinction between operational measures and a conceptual formulation of what is important (i.e., has high utility and relevance) to the organization (Cascio and Valenzi, 1978).

Practicality

It is important that management be informed thoroughly of the real benefits of using carefully developed criteria. Management may or may not have the expertise to appraise the soundness of a criterion measure or a series of criterion measures, but objections will almost certainly arise if record keeping and data collection for criterion measures become impractical and interfere significantly with ongoing operations. Overzealous HR researchers sometimes view organizations as ongoing laboratories existing solely for their purposes. This should not be construed as an excuse for using inadequate or irrelevant criteria. Clearly a balance must be sought, for the HR department occupies a staff role, assisting through more effective use of human resources, those who are concerned directly with achieving the organization's primary goals of profit, growth, or service. Keep criterion measurement practical!

CRITERION CONTAMINATION

When criterion measures are gathered carelessly with no checks on their worth before use either for research purposes or in the development of HR policies, they are often contaminated. Maier (1988) demonstrated this in an evaluation of the aptitude tests used to make placement decisions about military recruits. The tests were validated against hands-on job performance tests for two Marine Corps jobs, radio repairers, and auto mechanics. The job performance tests were administered by sergeants who were experienced in each specialty and who spent most of their time training and supervising junior personnel. The sergeants were not given any training on how to administer and score performance tests. In addition, they received little monitoring during the 4 months of actual data collection, and only a single administrator was used to evaluate each examinee. The data collected were filled with er-

rors, although subsequent statistical checks and corrections made the data salvageable. Did the "clean" data make a difference in the decisions made? Certainly. The original data yielded validities of 0.09 and 0.17 for the two specialties. However, after the data were "cleaned up," the validities rose to 0.49 and 0.37, thus changing the interpretation of how valid the aptitude tests actually were.

Criterion contamination occurs when the operational or actual criterion includes variance that is unrelated to the ultimate criterion. Contamination itself may be subdivided into two distinct parts, error and bias (Blum and Naylor, 1968). **Error** by definition is random variation (e.g., due to nonstandardized procedures in testing, individual fluctuations in feelings) and cannot correlate with anything except by chance alone. **Bias,** on the other hand, represents systematic criterion contamination, and it can correlate with predictor measures. Criterion bias is of great concern in HR research because its potential influence is so pervasive. In the next three sections, therefore, we will consider some of the prominent sources of criterion bias. Brogden and Taylor (1950b) offered a concise definition:

> A biasing factor may be defined as any variable, except errors of measurement and sampling error, producing a deviation of obtained criterion scores from a hypothetical "true" criterion score. [p. 161]

It should also be added that because the direction of the deviation from the true criterion score is not specified, biasing factors may serve to increase, decrease, or leave unchanged the obtained validity coefficient. Biasing factors vary widely in their distortive effect, but primarily this distortion is a function of the degree of their correlation with predictors. The magnitude of such effects must be estimated, and their influence controlled either experimentally or statistically.

Bias Due to Knowledge of Predictor Information

One of the most serious contaminants of criterion data, especially when the data are in the form of ratings, is prior knowledge of or exposure to predictor scores. In the selection of executives, for example, the assessment center method (Chapter 12) is a popular technique. If an individual's immediate superior has access to the prediction of this individual's future potential by the assessment center staff and if at a later date the superior is asked to rate the individual's performance, the supervisor's prior exposure to the assessment center prediction is likely to bias this rating. If the subordinate has been tagged as a "shooting star" by the assessment center staff and the supervisor values that judgment, he or she, too, may rate the subordinate as a "shooting star." If the supervisor views the subordinate as a rival, dislikes him or her for that reason, and wants to impede his or her progress, the assessment center report could serve as a stimulus for a *lower* rating than is deserved. In either case—spuriously high or spuriously low ratings—bias is introduced and gives an unrealistic estimate of the validity of the predictor. Because this type of bias is by definition predictor-correlated, it *looks like* the predictor is doing a better job of predicting than it actually is; yet, the effect is illusory. The rule of thumb is: *Keep predictor information away from those who must provide criterion data!*

Probably the best way to guard against this type of bias is to obtain all criterion data before any predictor data are released. Thus, in attempting to validate assessment center predictions, Bray and Grant (1966) collected data at an experimental assessment center, but these data had no bearing on subsequent promotion decisions. Eight years later the predictions were validated against a criterion of "promoted versus not promoted into middle management." By carefully shielding the predictor information from those who had responsibility for making promotion decisions, a much "cleaner" validity estimate was obtained.

Bias Due to Group Membership

An additional source of criterion bias may result from the fact that individuals belong to certain groups. In fact, sometimes explicit or implicit policies govern the hiring or promotion of these individuals. For example, some organizations tend to hire engineering graduates predominantly (or only) from certain schools. This author knows of an organization that tends to promote people internally who also receive promotions in their military reserve units!

Studies undertaken thereafter that attempt to relate these biographical characteristics to subsequent career success will necessarily be biased. The same effects also will occur when a group sets artificial limits on how much it will produce.

Bias in Ratings

Supervisory ratings, the most frequently employed criteria (Lent et al., 1971; Murphy and Cleveland, 1991), are susceptible to all the sources of bias in objective indices, as well as to others that are peculiar to subjec-

tive judgments. We shall discuss this problem in much greater detail in the next chapter, but for the present it is important to emphasize that bias in ratings may be due to spotty or inadequate observation by the rater, unequal opportunity on the part of subordinates to demonstrate proficiency, personal biases or prejudices on the part of the rater, or an inability to distinguish and reliably rate different dimensions of job performance.

Perhaps the most frequently cited biasing factor in ratings is the "halo" effect. The halo effect was pointed out originally by Thorndike (1920) on the basis of experimental evidence that some raters have a tendency to rate an individual either high or low on many factors because the rater knows (or thinks he knows) the individual to be high or low on a specific factor. In police work, for example, a supervisor may rate a patrol officer on a number of dimensions including ability to solve crimes, ability to handle domestic disputes, and skill in directing traffic. If the supervisor observed the officer perform gallantly in handling a domestic dispute, he would be making a halo error if he simply assumed that the officer must be similarly skillful at solving crimes and directing traffic. Likewise in a beauty contest, a judge would be making a halo error if he assumed that because a girl is pretty, she also must be intelligent or personable. The result of the halo effect is that ratings on the various dimensions of job performance tend to have higher intercorrelations than otherwise would be the case.

CRITERION EQUIVALENCE

If two criteria correlate highly, we may suspect halo. If they correlate perfectly after correcting both for unreliability, then they are equivalent. Criterion equivalence should not be taken lightly or assumed; it is a rarity in HR research. Strictly speaking, if two criteria are equivalent, then they contain exactly the same job elements, they are measuring precisely the same individual characteristics, and they are occupying exactly the same portion of the conceptual criterion space. Two criteria are equivalent if it doesn't make any difference which one is used.

If the correlation between criteria is less than perfect, however, the two are not equivalent. This has been demonstrated repeatedly in analyses of the relationship between performance in training and performance on the job (Ghiselli, 1966; Hartigan and Wigdor, 1989; Hunter and Hunter, 1984), as well as in learning tasks (Weitz, 1961). In analyzing criteria and using them to observe performance, one must, therefore, consider not only the *time* of measurement, but also the *type* of measurement—that is, the particular performance measures selected and the reasons for doing so. Finally, one must consider the *level* of performance measurement that represents success or failure (assuming it is necessary to dichotomize criterion performance) and attempt to estimate the effect of the chosen level of performance on the conclusions reached.

For example, suppose we are judging the performance of a group of quality control inspectors on a work sample task (a device with 10 known defects). We set our criterion cut-off at eight—that is, the identification of fewer than eight defects constitutes unsatisfactory performance. The number of "successful" inspectors may increase markedly if the criterion cutoff is lowered to five defects. Our conclusions regarding overall inspector proficiency arc likely to change as well. In sum, if we know the rules governing our criterion measures, this alone should give us more insight into the operation of our predictor measures.

The researcher may treat highly correlated criteria in several different ways. He or she may choose to drop one of the criteria, viewing it essentially as redundant information, or to keep the two criterion measures separate, reasoning that the more information collected, the better. A third strategy is to gather data relevant to both criterion measures, to convert all data to standard-score form, to compute the individual's average score, and to use this as the best estimate of his standing on the composite dimension. No matter which strategy the researcher adopts, he or she should do so only on the basis of a sound theoretical or practical rationale and should comprehend fully the implications of the chosen strategy.

COMPOSITE VERSUS MULTIPLE CRITERIA

Applied psychologists generally agree that job performance is multidimensional in nature, and that adequate measurement of job performance requires multidimensional criteria. The next question is what to do about it. Should one combine the various criterion measures into a composite score, or should one treat each criterion measure separately? If the investigator chooses to combine the elements, what rule should he or she use to do so? As with the utility versus under-

standing issue, both sides have had their share of vigorous proponents over the years. Let us consider some of the arguments.

Composite Criterion

The basic contention of Toops (1944), Thorndike (1949), Brogden and Taylor (1950a), and Nagle (1953), the strongest advocates of the composite criterion, is that the criterion should provide a yardstick or overall measure of "success" or "value to the organization" of each individual. Such a single index is indispensable in decision making and individual comparisons, and even if the criterion dimensions are treated separately in validation, they must somehow be combined into a composite when a decision is required. Although this may be (and often is) done subjectively, a quantitative weighting scheme makes objective the importance placed on each of the criterion elements.

Multiple Criteria

Advocates of multiple criteria contend that measures of demonstrably different variables should not be combined. As Cattell (1957) put it, "Ten men and two bottles of beer cannot be added to give the same total as two men and ten bottles of beer" (p. 11). Consider a study of military recruiters (Pulakos, Borman, and Hough, 1988). In measuring the effectiveness of the recruiters, it was found that selling skills, human relations skills, and organizing skills all were important and related to success. It also was found, however, that the three dimensions were unrelated to each other—that is, the recruiter with the best selling skills did not necessarily have the best human relations skills or the best organizing skills. Under these conditions, combining the measures leads to a composite that not only is ambiguous, but also is psychologically nonsensical. Guion (1961) brought the issue clearly into focus:

> The fallacy of the single criterion lies in its assumption that everything that is to be predicted is related to everything else that is to be predicted—that there is a general factor in all criteria accounting for virtually all of the important variance in behavior at work and its various consequences of value. [p. 145]

Schmidt and Kaplan (1971) subsequently pointed out that combining various criterion elements into a composite does imply that there is a single underlying dimension in job performance, but it does not, in and of itself, imply that this single underlying dimension is behavioral or psychological in nature. A composite criterion may well represent an underlying economic dimension, while at the same time being essentially meaningless from a behavioral point of view. Thus, Brogden and Taylor (1950a) argued that when all of the criteria are relevant measures of economic variables (dollars and cents), they can be combined into a composite, regardless of their intercorrelations.

Differing Assumptions

As Schmidt and Kaplan (1971) and Binning and Barrett (1989) have noted, the two positions differ in terms of: (a) the nature of the underlying constructs represented by the respective criterion measures, and (b) what they regard to be the primary purpose of the validation process itself. Let us consider the first set of assumptions. Underpinning the arguments for the composite criterion is the assumption that the criterion should represent an economic rather than a behavioral construct. The economic orientation is illustrated in Brogden and Taylor's (1950a) "dollar criterion": "The criterion should measure the overall contribution of the individual to the organization" (p. 139). Brogden and Taylor argued that overall efficiency should be measured in dollar terms by applying cost accounting concepts and procedures to the individual job behaviors of the employee. "The criterion problem centers primarily upon the quantity, quality, and cost of the finished product" (p. 141).

In contrast, advocates of multiple criteria (Dunnette, 1963; Pulakos et al., 1988) argued that the criterion should represent a behavioral or psychological construct, one that is behaviorally homogeneous. Pulakos et al. (1988) acknowledged the need to develop a composite criterion when actually making employment decisions, but they also emphasized that such composites are best formed when their components are well understood.

With regard to the goals of the validation process, advocates of the composite criterion assume that the validation process is carried out only for practical and economic reasons, and not to promote greater understanding of the psychological and behavioral processes involved in various jobs. Thus, Brogden and Taylor (1950a) clearly distinguished the end products of a given job (job products) from the job processes that lead to these end products. With regard to job processes they argued: "Such factors as skill are latent; their effect is realized in the end product. They do not

satisfy the logical requirement of an adequate criterion" (p. 141).

In contrast, the advocates of multiple criteria view increased understanding as an important goal of the validation process, along with practical and economic goals: "The goal of the search for understanding is a theory (or theories) of work behavior; theories of human behavior are cast in terms of psychological and behavioral, not economic constructs." (Schmidt and Kaplan, 1971, p. 424).

Resolving the Dilemma

Clearly there are numerous possible uses of job performance and program evaluation criteria. In general, they may be used for research purposes or operationally as an aid in managerial decision making. When criteria are used for research purposes, the emphasis is on the psychological understanding of the relationship between various predictors and separate criterion dimensions, where the dimensions themselves are behavioral in nature. When used for managerial decision-making purposes such as job assignment, promotion, capital budgeting, or evaluation of the cost-effectiveness of recruitment, training, or advertising programs, criterion dimensions must be combined into a composite, representing overall (economic) worth to the organization.

The resolution of the composite versus multiple criterion dilemma essentially depends upon the objectives of the investigator. Both methods are legitimate for their own purposes. If the goal is increased psychological understanding of predictor-criterion relationships, then the criterion elements are best kept separate. If managerial decision making is the objective, then the criterion elements should be weighted, regardless of their intercorrelations, into a composite representing an economic construct of overall worth to the organization.

Criterion measures with theoretical relevance should not replace those with practical relevance, but rather should supplement or be used along with them. The goal, therefore, is to enhance utility *and* understanding.

RESEARCH DESIGN AND CRITERION THEORY

Traditionally, personnel psychologists were guided by a simple prediction model that sought to relate performance on one or more predictors with a composite cri-

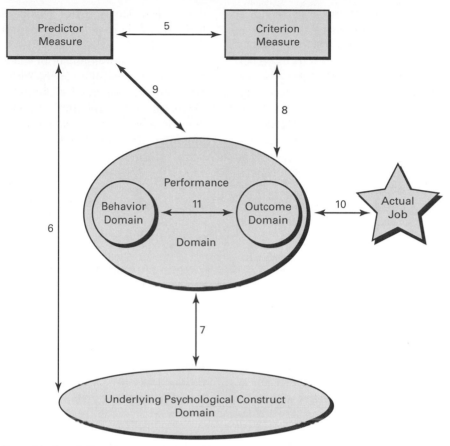

From Binning, J. F., and Barrett, G. V. (1989). Validity of personnel decisions: A conceptual analysis of the inferential and evidential bases. *Journal of Applied Psychology, 74,* 478–494. Copyright 1989 by the American Psychological Association. Reprinted by permission of the publisher and the authors.

FIGURE 4–3 A Modified Framework that Identifies the Inferences for Criterion Development.

Linkages in the figure begin with No. 5 because earlier figures in the article used Nos. 1–4 to show critical linkages in the theory-building process.

terion. Implicit intervening variables usually were neglected.

A more complete criterion model that describes the inferences required for the rigorous development of criteria was presented by Binning and Barrett (1989). The model is shown in Figure 4–3. Managers involved in employment decisions are most concerned about the extent to which assessment information will allow accurate predictions about subsequent job performance (Inference 9 in Fig. 4–3). One general approach to justifying Inference 9 would be to generate direct empirical evidence that assessment scores relate to valid measurements of job performance. Inference 5 shows this linkage, which traditionally has been the most pragmatic concern to personnel psychologists.

Indeed the term **criterion-related** has been used to denote this type of evidence. However, to have complete confidence in Inference 9, *both* Inferences 5 and 8 must be justified. That is, a predictor should be related to an operational criterion measure (Inference 5), and the operational criterion measure should be related to the performance domain it represents (Inference 8).

Performance domains are comprised of behavior-outcome units (Binning and Barrett, 1989). Outcomes (e.g., dollar volume of sales) are valued by an organization, and behaviors (e.g., selling skills) are the means to these valued ends. Thus, behaviors take on different values, depending on the value of the outcomes. This, in turn, implies that optimal description of the performance domain for a given job requires careful and complete representation of valued outcomes and the behaviors that accompany them. As we noted earlier, composite criterion models focus on outcomes, whereas multiple criterion models focus on behaviors. As Figure 4–3 shows, together they form a performance domain. This is why both are necessary and should continue to be used.

Inference 8 represents the process of criterion development. Usually it is justified by rational evidence (in the form of job analysis data) showing that all major behavioral dimensions or job outcomes have been identified and are represented in the operational criterion measure. In fact, job analysis (see Chapter 8) provides the evidential basis for justifying Inferences 7, 8, 10, and 11.

What personnel psychologists have traditionally implied by the label **construct validity** is tied to Inferences 6 and 7. That is, if it can be shown that a test (e.g., of reading comprehension) measures a specific construct (Inference 6), such as reading comprehension, that has been determined to be critical for job performance (Inference 7), then inferences about job performance from test scores (Inference 9) are, by logical implication, justified. Constructs are simply labels for behavioral regularities that underlie behavior sampled by the predictor, and, in the performance domain, by the criterion.

In the context of understanding and validating criteria, Inferences 7, 8, 10, and 11 are critical. Inference 7 is typically justified by claims, based on job analysis, that the constructs underlying performance have been identified. This process is commonly referred to as **deriving job specifications.** Inference 10, on the other hand, represents the extent to which actual job demands have been analyzed adequately, resulting in a valid description of the performance domain. This process is commonly referred to as **job description.** Finally, Inference 11 represents the extent to which the links between job behaviors and job outcomes have been verified. Again, job analysis is the process used to discover and to specify these links.

The framework shown in Figure 4–3 helps to identify possible locations for what we have referred to as the **criterion problem.** This problem results from a tendency to neglect the development of adequate evidence to support Inferences 7, 8, and 10, and fosters a very shortsighted view of the process of validating criteria. It also leads predictably to two interrelated consequences: (1) the development of criterion measures that are less rigorous psychometrically than are predictor measures, and (2) performance criteria that are less deeply or richly embedded in networks of theoretical relationships that are constructs on the predictor side. These consequences are unfortunate, for they limit the development of theories, the validation of constructs, and the generation of evidence to support important inferences about people and their behavior at work (Binning and Barrett, 1989). Conversely, the development of evidence to support the important linkages shown in Figure 4–3 will lead to better informed staffing decisions, career development decisions, and, ultimately, more effective organizations.

SUMMARY

We began by stating that the effectiveness and future progress of personnel psychology depend fundamentally upon careful, accurate criterion measurement. What is needed is a broader conceptualization of the job performance domain. We need to pay close attention to the notion of criterion relevance, which, in turn, requires prior theorizing and development of the dimensions that comprise the domain of performance. Investigators must first formulate clearly their ultimate objectives and then develop appropriate criterion measures that represent economic or behavioral constructs. Criterion measures must pass the tests of reliability, sensitivity, and practicality.

In addition, we must attempt continually to determine how dependent our conclusions are likely to be because of: (a) the particular criterion measures used, (b) the time of measurement, (c) the conditions outside the control of an individual, and (d) the distortions and biases inherent in the situation or the measuring instrument (human or otherwise). There may be many paths to success, and consequently a broader, richer schematization of job performance must be adopted. The integrated criterion model shown in Figure 4–3 represents a step in the right direction. Of one thing we can be certain: The future contribution of personnel psychology to the wiser, more efficient use of human resources will be limited sharply until we can deal successfully with the issues created by the criterion problem.

Discussion Questions

1. Why do objective measures of performance often tell an incomplete story about performance?
2. Develop some examples of immediate, intermediate,

and summary criteria for: (a) a student, (b) a judge, and (c) a professional golfer.

3. Discuss the problems that dynamic criteria pose for employment decisions.

4. How can the reliability of job performance observation be improved?

5. Describe the performance domain of a college teacher.

CHAPTER

5

PERFORMANCE APPRAISAL

AT A GLANCE

Performance appraisal is the systematic description of individual or group job-relevant strengths and weaknesses. Although technical problems (e.g., the choice of formats) and human problems (e.g., supervisory resistance, organizational politics) both plague performance appraisal, they are not insurmountable.

Performance appraisal comprises two processes, **observation** and **judgment,** both of which are subject to bias. For this reason, some have suggested that job performance be judged solely on the basis of objective indices such as production data and employment data (e.g., accidents, awards). While such data are intuitively appealing, they often measure not performance, but factors beyond an individual's control; they do not measure behavior per se, but rather the outcomes of behavior.

Because of these deficiencies, subjective criteria (e.g., supervisory ratings) are often used. However, since ratings depend on human judgment, they are subject to other kinds of biases. Each of the available methods for rating job performance attempts to reduce bias in some way, although no method is completely bias-free. Biases may be associated with raters (e.g., lack of firsthand knowledge of employee performance), ratees (e.g., gender, job tenure), the interaction of raters and ratees (e.g., race and gender), or various situational and organizational characteristics.

Bias can be reduced sharply, however, through training in both the technical and the human aspects of the rating process. Training must also address the potentially incompatible role demands of supervisors (i.e., coach and judge) during performance appraisal interviews. One especially fruitful approach for doing this is to allow subordinates more participation in the appraisal process by setting mutually agreeable goals for future performance.

Performance appraisal, the systematic description of job-relevant strengths and weaknesses within and between employees or groups, is one of the most delicate topics in HR management. Researchers are fascinated by this subject; yet their overall inability to resolve definitively the knotty technical problems of performance appraisal has led one reviewer to term it the "Achilles heel" of HR management (Heneman, 1975). Supervisors and subordinates who periodically encounter appraisal systems, either as raters or ratees, are often mistrustful of the uses of such information. They are intensely aware of the political and practical implications of the ratings and, in many cases, are

acutely ill at ease during performance appraisal interviews. Despite these shortcomings, surveys of managers from both large and small organizations consistently show that managers are unwilling to abandon performance appraisal, for they regard it as an important assessment tool (Cleveland, Murphy, and Williams, 1989; Meyer, 1991).

Many treatments of performance appraisal scarcely contain a hint of the emotional overtones, the human problems, so intimately bound up with it. Primary emphasis is placed on technical issues—for example, the advantages and disadvantages of various rating systems, sources of error, and problems of unreliability in performance observation and measurement. To be sure, these are vitally important concerns. No less important, however, are the human issues involved, for performance appraisal is not merely a technique—it is a process, a dialogue involving both people and data. In this chapter, we shall focus on both of these topics, for judgments about worker proficiency *are* made, whether implicitly or explicitly, whenever people interact in organizational settings. As HR specialists, our task is to make the formal process as meaningful and workable as present research and development will allow.

PURPOSES SERVED

In the context of human resources management, formal performance appraisals can serve several purposes:

1. They can serve as bases for employment decisions—decisions to promote outstanding performers; to terminate marginal or low performers; to train, transfer, or discipline others; and to justify merit increases (or no increases). In short, appraisal serves as a key input for administering a formal organizational reward and punishment system (Cummings, 1973).

2. Appraisals can serve as *criteria* in HR research (e.g., in test validation).

3. Appraisals can serve as *predictors* (e.g., when they are used to make promotional decisions).

4. Appraisals can help establish objectives for training programs (when they are expressed in terms of desired behaviors or outcomes rather than global personality characteristics).

5. Appraisals can provide concrete feedback to employees. In order to improve performance in the future, an employee needs to know what his or her weaknesses were in the past and how to correct them. Pointing out strengths and weaknesses is a coaching function for the supervisor; receiving meaningful feedback and acting upon it is a motivational experience for the subordinate. Thus, appraisals can serve as vehicles for personal development.

6. Appraisals can facilitate organizational diagnosis and development. Proper specification of performance levels, in addition to suggesting training needs across units and indicating necessary skills to be considered when hiring, also establishes the more general organizational requirement of ability to discriminate effective from ineffective performers. Appraisal therefore represents the beginning of a process rather than an end product (Jacobs, Kafry, and Zedeck, 1980).

REALITIES OF APPRAISAL

Independently of any organizational context, the appraisal of human performance at work confronts the appraiser with four realities (Ghorpade and Chen, 1995):

1. This activity is inevitable in all organizations, large and small, public and private, domestic and multinational. Organizations need to know if individuals are performing competently, and in the current legal climate, appraisals are essential features of an organization's defense against challenges to adverse employment actions, such as termination or layoff.

2. The conduct of appraisal is fraught with consequences for individuals (rewards, punishments) and organizations (providing appropriate rewards and punishments based on performance).

3. As job complexity increases, it becomes progressively more difficult, even for well-meaning appraisers, to assign accurate, merit-based ratings.

4. When sitting in judgment on co-workers, there is an ever-present danger of the parties being influenced by the political consequences of their actions—rewarding allies and punishing enemies or competitors (Gioia and Longenecker, 1994; Longenecker and Gioia, 1992; Longenecker, Sims, and Gioia, 1987).

BARRIERS TO EFFECTIVE APPRAISAL

Barriers to successful performance appraisal may be organizational, political, or interpersonal. Organizational barriers result when workers are held responsible for errors that may be the result of faults within the production system itself. Political barriers stem from deliberate attempts by raters to enhance or to protect their self-interests when conflicting courses of action are possible. Interpersonal barriers arise from the actual face-to-face encounter between subordinate and superior.

Organizational Barriers

According to Deming (1986), variations in performance within systems may be due to common causes or special causes. Common causes are faults that are built into the system due to prior decisions, defects in materials, flaws in the design of the system, or some other managerial shortcoming. Special causes are due to a particular event, to a particular operator, or to a subgroup within the system. Deming believes that over 90 percent of the quality problems of American industry are the result of common causes. If this is so, then judging workers according to their output may be unfair.

However, a quantitative review of the distributions of work output from 101 studies revealed that most tended to approximate normality, with the exception of machine operators, a job in which one would expect special causes to matter most (Alliger and Hosoda, 1992). These findings suggest that common causes may not be as significant a determinant of performance as Total Quality Management advocates make it out to be.

Political Barriers

Political considerations are organizational facts of life. Appraisals take place in an organizational environment that is anything but completely rational, straightforward, or dispassionate. It appears that accuracy in appraisal is less important to managers than motivating and rewarding their subordinates. Many managers will not allow excessively accurate ratings to cause problems for themselves, and they attempt to use the appraisal process to their own advantage (Longenecker et al., 1987).

Interpersonal Barriers

Interpersonal barriers also may hinder the appraisal process. Because of a lack of communication, employees may think they are being judged according to one set of standards, when their superiors actually use different ones. Furthermore, supervisors often delay or resist making face-to-face appraisals. Rather than confront substandard performers with low ratings, negative feedback, and below-average salary increases, supervisors often find it easier to "damn with faint praise" by giving average or above-average ratings to inferior performers (Benedict and Levine, 1988). Finally, some managers complain that formal performance appraisal interviews tend to interfere with the more constructive coaching relationship that should exist between superior and subordinate. They claim that appraisal interviews emphasize the superior position of the supervisor by placing him or her in the role of *judge,* thus conflicting with the supervisor's equally important roles of *teacher* and *coach* (Meyer, 1991).

This, then, is the performance appraisal dilemma: appraisal is widely accepted as a potentially useful tool but organizational, political, and interpersonal barriers often thwart its successful implementation. Much of the research on appraisals has focused on measurement issues. This is important, but HR pro-

fessionals may contribute more by improving the attitudinal and interpersonal components of performance appraisal systems as well as their technical aspects. We will begin by considering the fundamental requirements for all performance appraisal systems.

Fundamental Requirements of Appraisal Systems

In order for any appraisal system to be used successfully, it must satisfy two basic requirements. It must be *relevant* to the job(s) in question, and it must be *acceptable* both to raters and ratees. Raters must accept the importance of performance appraisal and feedback as an organizational goal, they must accept the appraisal system as an effective means for achieving that goal, and they must accept accurate performance appraisal as a personal goal (Ilgen and Barnes-Farrell, 1984). In short, diligent attention to performance appraisal must be seen as an integral part of the rater's job, not as "make-work" harassment. Probably the best way to do this is to base part of the rater's own performance appraisal on the quality of his or her ratings of subordinates.

Acceptability is a two-way street, however. From the perspective of employees, one study indicated that employees are more likely to accept an appraisal system and to believe that their performance was rated fairly and accurately if: (1) performance was evaluated frequently; (2) employees felt their supervisors were familiar with their work performance; (3) employees felt they had the opportunity to express their own feelings during appraisal interviews; and (4) new performance goals, based on the appraisals, were set during appraisal interviews (Landy, Barnes, and Murphy, 1978).

Beyond relevance and acceptability, appraisal systems should be sensitive (that is, capable of discriminating effective from ineffective performers), reliable, and practical (Cascio, 1982). Taken together, these key requirements suggest that the *process* of performance appraisal is just as important as the particular method used. With that in mind, let's consider the behavioral basis for performance appraisal.

BEHAVIORAL BASIS FOR PERFORMANCE APPRAISAL

Performance appraisal involves two distinct processes: (1) observation and (2) judgment. Observation processes are more basic, and include the detection, perception, and recall or recognition of specific behavioral events. Judgment processes include the categorization, integration, and evaluation of information (Thornton and Zorich, 1980). In practice, observation and judgment represent the last elements of a three-part sequence:

- *Job Analysis* (Describes work and personal requirements of a particular job)
- *Performance Appraisal* (Describes the job-relevant strengths and weaknesses of each individual)
- *Performance Standards* (Translate job requirements into levels of acceptable/unacceptable performance)

Job analysis identifies the components of a particular job. Our goal in performance appraisal, however, is not to make distinctions among jobs, but rather to make distinctions among people, especially among people in the same job. Performance standards provide the critical link in the process.

Ultimately, it is management's responsibility to establish performance standards: the levels of performance deemed acceptable or unacceptable for each of the job-relevant, critical areas of performance identified through job analysis. For some jobs (e.g., production or maintenance) standards can be set on the basis of engineering studies. For others, such as research, teaching, or administration, the process is considerably more subjective and is frequently a matter of manager and subordinate agreement. An example of one such set of standards is presented in Figure 5–1. Note also that standards are distinct, yet complimentary, to goals. Standards are usually constant across individuals in a given job, while goals are often determined individually or by a group (Bobko and Colella, 1994).

Performance standards are essential in all types of goods-producing and service organizations, for they help ensure consistency in supervisory judgments across individuals in the same job. Unfortunately, it is often the case that charges of unequal treatment and unfair discrimination arise in jobs where no clear performance standards exist (Cascio and Bernardin, 1981; Martin and Bartol, 1991; Nathan and Cascio, 1986). We cannot overemphasize their importance.

Performance appraisal, the last step in the sequence, represents the actual process of gathering information about individuals based on critical job requirements. Gathering job performance information is accomplished by observation. Evaluating the adequacy of individual performance is judgment.

FIGURE 5–1 Examples of Performance Standards.

Duty (from Job Description): IMPLEMENT COMPANY EEO AND AFFIRMATIVE ACTION PROGRAM

Task	*Output*	*Performance Standard*
Review unit positions and recommend potential upward mobility opportunities	Report with recommendation	*SUPERIOR*—All tasks completed well ahead of time and acceptable to management without change. Actively participates in education programs and provides positive suggestions.
Take part in and promote company program for education of employees in EEO and affirmative action principles	Program participation	Attitude is very positive as exhibited by no disscriminatory language or remarks.
Instruct and inform unit employees on EEO and affirmative action programs	Information	*SATISFACTORY*—All tasks completed by deadline with only minor changes as random occurrences. Participates in education program when asked to do so and counsels employees at their request.
Affirmative action recommendations to management on positions for unit	Recommendation	*UNACCEPTABLE*—Tasks not completed on time with changes usually necessary. Program is accepted but no or little effort to support. Comments sometimes reflect biased language. Employees seek counsel from other than supervisor.

WHO SHALL RATE?

In view of the purposes served by performance appraisal, *who* does the rating is important. In addition to being cooperative and trained in the techniques of rating, raters must have direct experience with, or first-hand knowledge of, the individual to be rated. In many jobs, individuals with varying perspectives have such firsthand knowledge. The following sections describe five of these perspectives.

Immediate Supervisor

So-called "360-degree feedback," which broadens the base of appraisals by including input from peers, subordinates, and customers, certainly increases the types and amount of information about performance that is available. Ultimately, however, the immediate supervisor is responsible for managing the overall appraisal process (Ghorpade and Chen, 1995).

While input from peers and subordinates is helpful, the supervisor is probably best able to evaluate each subordinate's performance in light of the organization's overall objectives. Since the supervisor is probably also responsible for reward (and punishment) decisions such as pay, promotion, and discipline, he or she must be able to tie effective (ineffective) performance to the employment actions taken. Inability to form such linkages between performance and punishment or reward is one of the most serious deficiencies of any appraisal system. Not surprisingly, therefore, research has shown that feedback from supervisors is more highly related to performance than that from any other source (Becker and Klimoski, 1989).

However, in jobs such as teaching, law enforcement, or sales, and in self-managed work teams, the supervisor may observe directly his or her subordinate's performance only rarely. Fortunately there are several other perspectives that can be used to provide a fuller picture of the individual's total performance.

Peer Assessment

Peer assessment actually refers to three more basic methods used by members of a well-defined group in judging each other's job performance. These include **peer nominations,** most useful for identifying persons with extremely high or low levels of KSAOs (Knowledge, Skills, Abilities, and Other Characteristics); **peer rating,** most useful for providing feedback; and **peer ranking,** best at discriminating various levels of performance from highest to lowest on each dimen-

sion. Despite the fact that two reviews of peer assessment methods reached favorable conclusions regarding the reliability, validity, and freedom from biases of this approach (Kane and Lawler, 1978; Lewin and Zwany, 1976), serious problems still remain.

Specifically, two characteristics of peer assessments appear to be related significantly and independently to user acceptance (McEvoy and Buller, 1987). Perceived friendship bias is related negatively to user acceptance, and use for developmental purposes is related positively to user acceptance. How do people react upon learning that they have been rated poorly (favorably) by their peers? Research in a controlled setting indicates that such knowledge has predictable effects on group behavior. Negative peer rating feedback produced significantly lower perceived performance of the group, plus lower cohesiveness, satisfaction, and peer ratings on a subsequent task. Positive peer rating feedback produced non-significantly higher values for these variables on a subsequent task (DeNisi, Randolph, and Blencoe, 1983).

One possible solution that might simultaneously increase feedback value and decrease the perception of friendship bias is to specify clearly (e.g., using critical incidents) the performance criteria on which peer assessments are based. Results of the peer assessment may then be used in joint employee-supervisor reviews of each employee's progress, prior to later administrative decisions concerning the employee.

Peer assessments are probably best considered as only one element in an appraisal system that includes input from all sources that have unique information or perspectives to offer. Thus the traits, behaviors, or outcomes to be assessed should be considered in the context of the groups and situations where peer assessments are to be applied. It is impossible to specify, for all situations, the kinds of characteristics that peers are able to rate best.

Appraisal by Subordinates

Subordinates offer a somewhat different perspective on a manager's performance. They know directly the extent to which a manager does or does not delegate, the extent to which he or she plans and organizes, the type of leadership style(s) he or she is most comfortable with, and how well he or she communicates. While this approach is used regularly by universities (students evaluate faculty) and sometimes by large corporations where a manager may have many subordinates, in small organizations considerable trust and openness are necessary before subordinate appraisals can pay off.

They can pay off, however, as a recent field study demonstrated. Subordinates rated their managers at two time periods 6 months apart on a 33-item behavioral observation scale that focused on areas such as the manager's commitment to quality, communications, support of subordinates, and fairness. Based on subordinates' ratings, managers whose initial level of performance was moderate or low improved modestly over the 6-month period, and this improvement could not be attributed solely to regression toward the mean. Further, both managers and their subordinates became more likely over time to indicate that the managers had an opportunity to demonstrate behaviors measured by the upward feedback instrument (Smither et al., 1995).

In general, subordinate ratings tend to have rather low correlations with self-ratings (London and Wohlers, 1991). However, subordinate ratings have been found to be valid predictors of subsequent supervisory ratings over 2-, 4-, and 7-year periods (McEvoy and Beatty, 1989). One reason for this may have been that multiple ratings on each dimension were made for each manager, and the ratings were averaged to obtain the measure for the subordinate perspective. Averaging has several advantages. First, averaged ratings are more reliable than single ratings. Second, averaging helps to ensure the anonymity of the subordinate raters. Anonymity is important; subordinates may perceive the process to be threatening since the supervisor can exert administrative controls (salary increases, promotions). In fact, when the identity of subordinates is disclosed, inflated ratings of managers' performance tend to result (Antonioni, 1994).

Any organization contemplating use of subordinate ratings should pay careful attention to the intended purpose of the ratings. Evidence indicates that ratings used for salary administration or promotion purposes may be more lenient than those used for guided self-development (Zedeck and Cascio, 1982). However, one study found the rank-order correlation between administrative-based and research-based ratings to be as high as .58 (Harris, Smith, and Champagne, 1995).

Self-Appraisal

It seems reasonable to have each individual judge his or her own job performance. On the positive side, we can see that the opportunity to participate in perfor-

mance appraisal, especially if it is combined with goal setting, should improve the individual's motivation and reduce his or her defensiveness during an appraisal interview. Research to be described later clearly supports this view. On the other hand, comparisons with appraisals by supervisors, peers, and subordinates suggest that self-appraisals tend to show more leniency, less variability, more bias, and less agreement with the judgments of others (Harris and Schaubroeck, 1988; Thornton, 1980). This seems to be the norm in Western cultures. In Taiwan, however, modesty bias (self-ratings lower than those of supervisors) has been found (Farh, Dobbins, and Cheng, 1991), but this may not be the norm in all Eastern cultures (Yu and Murphy, 1993).

To some extent, these disagreements may stem from the tendency of raters to base their ratings on different aspects of job performance or to weight facets of job performance differently. Self- and supervisors' ratings agree much more closely when both parties have a thorough knowledge of the appraisal system or process (Williams and Levy, 1992). In addition, self-ratings are less lenient when done for self-development purposes rather than for administrative purposes (Meyer, 1991).

The situation is far from hopeless, however. To improve the validity of self appraisals, carefully consider four research-based suggestions (Mabe and West, 1982; Campbell and Lee, 1988; Fox and Dinur, 1988).

1. Instead of asking individuals to rate themselves on an *absolute* scale (e.g., a scale ranging from "poor" to "average"), provide a *relative* scale that allows them to compare their performance with that of others (e.g., "below average," "average," "above average"). In addition, providing comparative information on the relative performance of co-workers promotes closer agreement between self appraisal and supervisor rating (Farh and Dobbins, 1989).

2. Provide multiple opportunities for self-appraisal, for the skill being evaluated may well be one that improves with practice.

3. Provide reassurance of confidentiality—that is, self-appraisals will not be "publicized."

4. Focus on the future—specifically on predicting future behavior.

Until the problems associated with self-appraisals can be resolved, however, they seem more appropriate for counseling and development than for employment decisions.

TABLE 5–1 Sources and Uses of Appraisal Data

	Source				
Use	Supervisor	Peers	Subordinates	Self	Clients Served
Employment decisions	X	X			X
Self-development	X	X	X	X	X
Employment research	X	X			X

Appraisal by Clients Served

A final group that may offer a different perspective on individual performance in some situations is that of clients served. In jobs that require a high degree of interaction with the public or with particular individuals (e.g., purchasing managers, suppliers, sales representatives) appraisal sometimes can be done by the "consumers" of the organization's services. While the clients served cannot be expected to identify completely with the organization's objectives, they can, nevertheless, provide useful information. Such information may affect employment decisions (promotion, transfer, need for training), but it also can be used in HR research (e.g., as a criterion in validation studies or in measuring training outcomes on the job) or as a basis for self-development activities.

In summary, there are numerous sources of appraisal information, and each provides a different perspective, a different piece of the puzzle. The various sources and their potential uses are shown in Table 5–1.

The Multi-Trait–Multi-Rater Approach

To assess the degree of inter-rater agreement within rating dimensions (convergent validity) and to assess the ability of raters to make distinctions in performance across dimensions (discriminant validity), a matrix listing dimensions as rows and raters as columns might be prepared (Lawler, 1967). As we noted earlier, however, multiple raters for the same individual may be drawn from different organizational levels, and they probably observe different facets of a ratee's job performance. Hence, across-organizational-level inter-rater agreement for ratings on all performance dimensions is not only an unduly severe expectation; it also may be erroneous.

As a more reasonable alternative, a hybrid multi-trait-multi-rater analysis may be used (see Fig. 5–2), in which raters make evaluations *only* on those dimensions that they are in good position to rate (Borman, 1974). In the hybrid analysis, within-level inter-rater agreement is taken as an index of convergent validity. The hybrid matrix provides an improved conceptual fit for analyzing performance ratings, and the probability of obtaining convergent and discriminant validity is probably higher for this method than for the multi-trait-multi-rater analysis.

Recent research indicates that data from multiple sources (e.g., self, supervisors, peers, subordinates) are desirable because they provide a complete picture of the individual's effect on others (Borman, White, and Dorsey, 1995; Wohlers and London, 1989). While contextual differences may cause raters from different levels to place different emphases on specific aspects of job performance (Motowidlo and Van Scotter, 1994), the quality of appraisals can be improved through training that focuses on, among other things, the elimination of some common judgmental biases.

JUDGMENTAL BIASES IN RATING

In the traditional view, judgmental biases result from some systematic measurement error on the part of a rater. As such, they are easier to deal with than errors that are unsystematic or random. However, each type of bias has been defined and measured in different ways in the literature. This may lead to diametrically

FIGURE 5–2 Example of a Hybrid Matrix Analysis of Performance Ratings. Level I Rates Only Traits 1–4, Level II Rates Only Traits 5–8.

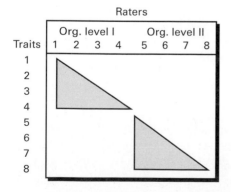

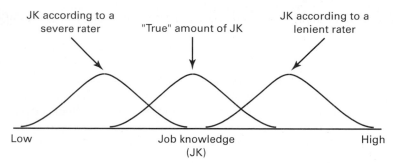

FIGURE 5–3 Distributions of Lenient and Severe Raters.

opposite conclusions, even in the same study (Saal, Downey, and Lahey, 1980). In the minds of many managers, however, these behaviors are not errors at all. Rather, they are discretionary actions that help them manage people more effectively (Longenecker et al., 1987). With these considerations in mind, let us consider some of the most commonly observed judgmental biases, along with ways of avoiding them.

Leniency and Severity

The use of ratings rests on the assumption that the human observer is capable of some degree of precision and some degree of objectivity (Guilford, 1954). His or her ratings are taken to mean something accurate about certain aspects of the person rated. "Objectivity" is the major hitch in these assumptions, and it is the one most often violated. Raters subscribe to their own sets of assumptions (that may or may not be valid), and most people have encountered raters who seemed either inordinately easy (lenient) or inordinately difficult (severe). Evidence also indicates that leniency is a stable response tendency across raters (Kane, Bernardin, Vallanova, and Peyrfitte, 1995). Graphically, the different distributions resulting from leniency and severity are shown in Figure 5–3.

Leniency and severity biases can be controlled or eliminated in several ways: (1) by allocating ratings into a forced distribution, in which ratees are apportioned according to an approximately normal distribution; or (2) by requiring supervisors to rank-order their subordinates. Firms such as IBM, Pratt-Whitney, and Grumman have done this because the extreme leniency in their ratings-based appraisal data hindered their ability to do necessary downsizing based on merit (Kane and Kane, 1993).

The idea of a normal distribution of job performance is deeply ingrained in our thinking, yet in some situations a lenient distribution may be accurate. Cascio and Valenzi (1977) found this to be the case with lenient ratings of police officer performance. An extensive, valid selection program had succeeded in weeding out most of the poorer applicants prior to appraisals of performance "on the street." Consequently, it was more proper to speak of a leniency effect, rather than a leniency bias. Even so, senior managers recognize that leniency is not to be taken lightly. Fully 77 percent of sampled Fortune 100 companies reported that lenient appraisals threaten the validity of their appraisal systems (Bretz, Milkovich, and Read, 1990).

Central Tendency

When political considerations predominate, raters may assign all their subordinates ratings that are neither too good nor too bad. They avoid using the high and low extremes of rating scales and tend to cluster all ratings about the center of all scales. "Everybody is average" is one way of expressing the central tendency bias. The unfortunate consequence, as with leniency or severity biases, is that most of the value of systematic performance appraisal is lost. The ratings fail to discriminate either within or between people, and the ratings become virtually useless as managerial decision-making aids, as predictors, as criteria, or for giving feedback. Central tendency biases can be minimized by specifying clearly what the various anchors mean. In addition, raters must be convinced of the value and potential uses of merit ratings if they are to provide meaningful information.

Halo

Halo bias (Thorndike, 1920) is perhaps the most actively-researched bias in performance appraisal. As we noted in Chapter 4, a rater who is subject to the halo bias assigns ratings on the basis of a general impression of the ratee. An individual is rated either high or low on specific factors because of the rater's general impression (good-poor) of the ratee's overall performance (Lance, LaPointe, and Stewart, 1994). According to this theory, the rater fails to distinguish among levels of performance on different performance dimensions. Ratings subject to the halo bias show spuriously high positive intercorrelations (Cooper, 1981).

A critical review of research in this area (Murphy, Jako, and Anhalt, 1993) led to three conclusions: (1) halo is not as common as believed, (2) the presence of halo does not necessarily detract from the quality of ratings, and (3) it is impossible to separate true from illusory halo in most field settings. Contrary to assumptions that have guided halo research since the 1920s, it is often difficult to determine whether halo has occurred, why it has occurred (is it due to the rater or to contextual factors unrelated to the rater's judgment), or what to do about it. Until progress can be made in each of these areas, it is not possible to develop measures of halo that are useful to the field (Murphy et al., 1993).

Up to this point we have been treating the appraisal process as an activity done by individuals. Are groups more effective in reducing response biases? One study found that groups were more effective than individuals at remembering specific behaviors over time, but that groups also demonstrated greater response bias. These results suggest that groups can be a help, but they are not a cure-all for the problems of rating accuracy (Martell and Borg, 1993).

As we noted earlier, judgmental biases may stem from a number of factors. One factor that has received considerable attention over the years has been the type of rating scale used. Each type attempts to reduce bias in some way. Although no single method is free of flaws, each has its own particular strengths and weaknesses. In the following section, we shall examine some of the most popular methods of evaluating individual job performance.

TYPES OF PERFORMANCE MEASURES

Objective Measures

Performance measures may be classified into two general types: objective and subjective. **Objective performance** measures include production data (dollar volume of sales, units produced, number of errors, amount of scrap) as well as employment data (acci-

dents, turnover, absences, tardiness). These variables directly define the goals of the organization, but as we noted in Chapter 4, they often suffer from several glaring weaknesses, the most serious of which are performance unreliability and modification of performance by situational characteristics. For example, dollar volume of sales is influenced by numerous factors beyond a particular salesperson's control—territory location, number of accounts in the territory, nature of the competition, distances between accounts, price and quality of the product, and so forth.

Our objective in performance appraisal, however, is to judge an individual's *performance,* not factors beyond his or her control. Moreover, objective measures focus not on behavior, but rather on the outcomes or results of behavior. Admittedly, there will be some degree of overlap between behavior and results, but the two are qualitatively different (Ilgen and Favero, 1985). Finally, in many jobs (e.g., those of middle managers), there simply are no good objective indices of performance, and in the case of employment data such as awards or disciplinary actions, such data are usually present in fewer than 5 percent of the cases examined (Landy, 1989). Hence, they are often useless as performance criteria.

In short, although objective measures of performance are intuitively attractive, theoretical and practical limitations often make them unsuitable. Although they can be useful when used as supplements to supervisory judgments, correlations between objective and subjective measures are often low (Bommer et al., 1995; Cascio and Valenzi, 1978; Heneman, 1986); when used as bases for employment decisions, the combinations of such measures may be weighed differently for different ethnic groups (Bass and Turner, 1973).

Subjective Measures

The disadvantages of objective measures have led researchers and managers to place major emphasis on **subjective measures** of job performance. However, since subjective measures depend upon human judgment, they are prone to certain kinds of biases we just discussed. To be useful, they must be based on a careful analysis of the behaviors viewed as necessary and important for effective job performance.

There is enormous variation in the types of subjective performance measures used by organizations. Some use a long list of elaborate rating scales; others use only a few simple scales; still others require managers to write a paragraph or two concerning the performance of each of their subordinates. In addition, subjective measures of performance may be *relative* (in which comparisons are made among a group of ratees) or *absolute* (in which a ratee is described without reference to others). The following sections provide brief descriptions of alternative formats. Interested readers may consult Bernardin and Beatty (1984), Borman (1991), or Murphy and Cleveland (1991) for more detailed information about particular methods.

RATING SYSTEMS: RELATIVE AND ABSOLUTE

Within this taxonomy, the following methods may be distinguished:

Relative	**Absolute**
Rank order	Essays
Paired comparisons	Behavior checklists
Forced distribution	Critical incidents
	Graphic rating scales

Relative Rating Systems (Employee Comparisons)

Simple ranking requires only that a rater order all ratees from highest to lowest, from "best" employee to "worst" employee. **Alternation ranking** requires that the rater initially list all ratees on a sheet of paper. From this list the rater first chooses the best ratee (#1), then the worst ratee (#n), then the second best (#2), then the second worst (#n − 1), and so forth, alternating from the top to the bottom of the list until all ratees have been ranked.

Both simple and alternation ranking implicitly require a rater to compare each ratee with every other ratee, but systematic ratee-to-ratee comparison is not a built-in feature of these methods. For this we need **paired comparisons.** The number of pairs of ratees to be compared may be calculated from the formula $[n(n − 1)]/2$. Hence if 10 individuals were being compared, $[10(9)]/2$ or 45 comparisons would be required. The rater's task is simply to choose the better of each pair, and each individual's rank is determined by counting the number of times he or she was rated superior.

Employee comparison methods are easy to explain and are helpful in making employment decisions. (For an example of this, see Siegel, 1982.) They also provide useful criterion data in validation studies, for they effectively control leniency, severity, and central tendency bias. Like other systems, however, they suffer from several weaknesses that should be recognized.

Employees usually are compared only in terms of a single overall suitability category. The rankings, therefore, lack behavioral specificity and may be subject to legal challenge. In addition, employee comparisons yield only ordinal data—data that give no indication of the relative distance between individuals. Moreover, it is often impossible to compare rankings across work groups, departments, or locations. The last two problems can be alleviated, however, by converting the ranks to normalized standard scores that form an approximately normal distribution (see Chapter 6).

A further problem stems from the tendency of employee comparison methods to reward members of an inferior group and to penalize members of a superior group. Reliability also may suffer, for when asked to rerank all individuals at a later date, the extreme high or low rankings probably will remain stable, but the rankings in the middle of the scale may shift around considerably.

Previously we discussed a final employee comparison method, the **forced distribution.** Its primary advantage is that it controls leniency, severity, and central tendency biases rather effectively. It assumes, however, that ratees conform to a normal distribution, and this may introduce a great deal of error if a group of ratees, *as a group,* is either superior or substandard. In short, rather than eliminating error, forced distributions may simply introduce a different kind of error!

Absolute Rating Systems

Absolute rating systems enable a rater to describe a ratee without making direct reference to other ratees. Perhaps the simplest absolute rating system is the **narrative essay,** in which the rater is asked to describe, in writing, an individual's strengths, weaknesses, and potential, and to make suggestions for improvement. The assumption underlying this approach is that a candid statement from a rater who is knowledgeable of a ratee's performance is just as valid as more formal and more complicated appraisal methods.

The major advantage of narrative essays (when they are done well) is that they can provide detailed feedback to ratees regarding their performance. On the other hand, essays are almost totally unstructured, and they vary widely in length and content. Comparisons across individuals, groups, or departments are virtually impossible since different essays touch on different aspects of ratee performance or personal qualifications. Finally, essays provide only *qualitative* information; yet in order for the appraisals to serve as criteria or to be compared objectively and ranked for the purpose of an employment decision, some form of rating that can be *quantified* is essential. Behavioral checklists provide one such scheme.

Behavioral Checklists

A behavioral checklist provides a rater with a series of descriptive statements of job-related behavior. His or her task is simply to indicate ("check") statements that describe the ratee in question. In this approach raters are not so much evaluators as they are reporters of job behavior. Moreover, ratings that are descriptive are likely to be higher in reliability than ratings that are evaluative (Stockford and Bissell, 1949).

To be sure, some job behaviors are more desirable than others; checklist items can, therefore, be scaled by using attitude scale construction methods. In one such method, the Likert method of **summated ratings,** a declarative statement (e.g., "she follows through on her sales") is followed by several response categories, such as "always," "very often," "fairly often," "occasionally," and "never." The rater simply checks the response category he or she feels best describes the ratee. Each response category is weighted—for example, from 5 ("always") to 1 ("never") if the statement describes desirable behavior, or vice versa if the statement describes undesirable behavior. An overall numerical rating for each individual then can be derived by summing the weights of the responses that were checked for each item, and scores for each performance dimension can be obtained by using item-analysis procedures (cf. Anastasi, 1988).

The selection of response categories for summated rating scales often is made arbitrarily, with equal intervals between scale points simply assumed. Scaled lists of adverbial modifiers of frequency and amount are available, however, together with statistically optimal 4- to 9-point scales (Bass, Cascio, and O'Connor, 1974). Scaled values also are available for categories of agreement, evaluation, and frequency

(Spector, 1976). A final issue concerns the optimal number of scale points for summated rating scales. For relatively homogeneous items, reliability increases up to 5 scale points and levels off thereafter (Lissitz and Green, 1975).

Checklists are easy to use and to understand, but it is sometimes difficult for a rater to give diagnostic feedback based on checklist ratings, for they are not cast in terms of specific behaviors. On balance, however, the many advantages of checklists probably account for their widespread popularity in organizations today.

Forced-Choice Systems

A special type of behavioral checklist is known as the forced-choice system—a technique developed specifically to reduce leniency errors and to establish objective standards of comparison between individuals (Sisson, 1948). In order to accomplish this, checklist statements are arranged in groups, from which the rater chooses statements that are most or least descriptive of the ratee. An overall rating (score) for each individual is then derived by applying a special scoring key to the rater descriptions.

Forced-choice scales are constructed according to two statistical properties of the checklist items: (1) **discriminability,** a measure of the degree to which an item differentiates effective from ineffective workers, and (2) **preference,** an index of the degree to which the quality expressed in an item is valued (i.e., is socially desirable) by people. The rationale of the forced-choice system requires that items be paired so they appear equally attractive (socially desirable) to the rater. Theoretically, then, the selection of any single item in a pair should be based solely upon the item's discriminating power, not its social desirability.

As an example, consider the following pair of items:

1. Separates opinion from fact in written reports.
2. Includes only relevant information in written reports.

Both statements are approximately equal in preference value, but only item (1) was found to discriminate effective from ineffective performers in a police department. This is the defining characteristic of the forced-choice technique: Not all equally attractive behavioral statements are equally valid.

The main advantage claimed for forced-choice scales is that a rater cannot distort a person's ratings higher or lower than is warranted since he or she has no way of knowing which statements to check in order to do so. Hence, leniency should theoretically be reduced. Their major disadvantage is rater resistance. Control is removed from the rater, who therefore cannot be sure just how he or she rated a subordinate. Finally, forced-choice forms are of little use (and may even have a negative effect) in performance appraisal interviews, for the rater is unaware of the scale values of the items he or she chooses. Since rater cooperation and acceptability are crucial determinants of the success of any appraisal system, forced-choice systems tend to be unpopular choices in many organizations.

Critical Incidents

This method of performance appraisal has generated a great deal of interest in recent years, and several variations of the basic idea are currently in use. As described by Flanagan (1954b), the critical requirements of a job are those behaviors that make a crucial difference between doing a job effectively and doing it ineffectively. **Critical incidents** are simply reports by knowledgeable observers of things employees did that were especially effective or ineffective in accomplishing parts of their jobs. Critical incidents are recorded, as they occur, for each employee by supervisors. Thus, they provide a behaviorally-based starting point for appraising performance. For example, in observing a police officer chasing an armed robbery suspect down a busy street, a supervisor recorded the following:

> June 22, Officer Mitchell withheld fire in a situation calling for the use of weapons where gunfire would endanger innocent bystanders.

These little anecdotes force attention on the situational determinants of job behavior and on ways of doing a job successfully that may be unique to the person described (individual dimensionality). The critical incidents method looks like a natural for performance appraisal interviews because supervisors can focus on actual job behavior rather than on vaguely defined traits. Performance, not personality, is being judged. Ratees receive meaningful feedback, and they can see what changes in their job behavior will be necessary in order for them to improve. In addition, when a large number of critical incidents are collected, abstracted, and categorized, they can provide a rich storehouse of information about job and organizational problems in general and are particularly well suited for establish-

ing objectives for training programs (Flanagan and Burns, 1955).

As with other approaches to performance appraisal, the critical incidents method also has drawbacks. First of all, it is time-consuming and burdensome for supervisors to record incidents for all of their subordinates on a daily or even weekly basis. Feedback may, therefore, be delayed. Doing so may actually enhance contrast effects between ratees (Maurer, Palmer, and Ashe, 1993). Nevertheless, incidents recorded in diaries allow raters to impose organization on unorganized information (DeNisi, Robbins, and Cafferty, 1989). However, in their narrative form, incidents do not readily lend themselves to quantification, which, as we noted earlier, poses problems in between-individual and between-group comparisons as well as in statistical analyses.

For these reasons two variations of the original idea have been suggested. Kirchner and Dunnette (1957b), for example, used the method to develop a behavioral checklist (using the method of summated ratings) for rating sales performance. After incidents were abstracted and classified, selected items were assembled into a checklist, for example,

Gives good service on customers' complaints

| Strongly agree | Agree | Undecided | Disagree | Strongly disagree |

A second modification has been the development of behaviorally anchored rating scales, an approach we will treat more fully in the next section.

Graphic Rating Scales

Probably the most widely used method of performance appraisal is the **graphic rating scale,** examples of which are presented in Figure 5–4. In terms of the amount of structure provided, the scales differ in three ways: (1) the degree to which the meaning of the response categories is defined, (2) the degree to which the individual who is interpreting the ratings (e.g., an HR manager or researcher) can tell clearly what response was intended, and (3) the degree to which the performance dimension being rated is defined for the rater.

On a graphic rating scale each point is defined on a continuum. Hence, in order to make meaningful distinctions in performance within dimensions, scale points must be defined unambiguously for the rater.

(a) Quality High |___|___✓___|___| Low

JOB PERFORMANCE –

LEVEL

Employee's and Supervisor's Comments and Suggestions for Making Improvement

(b) QUALITY AND QUANTITY OF WORK PERFORMED: Consider neatness and accuracy as well as volume and consistency in carrying out work assignments.

KEY TO LEVELS OF PERFORMANCE
3. COMMENDABLE
2. COMPETENT
1. NEEDS IMPROVING

Factor	OUT-STANDING	ABOVE AVERAGE	AVERAGE	BELOW AVERAGE	MARGINAL
(c) QUALITY OF WORK Caliber of work produced or accomplished compared with accepted quality standards.	◯	◯	◯	◯	◯

Comments:

(d) QUALITY OF WORK (Consider employee's thoroughness, dependability and neatness in regard to the work.)

Unsatisfactory		Satisfactory		Excellent		Outstanding	

Comments: _____

(e) QUALITY OF WORK
Accuracy and effectiveness of work. Freedom from error.

	Consistently good quality. Errors rare.		Usually good quality, few errors.		Passable work if closely supervised.		Frequent errors. Cannot be depended upon to be accurate.
5		4		3		2	1

Comments:

QUALITY OF WORK
☐ Accuracy
☐ The achievement of objectives; effectiveness
(f) ☐ Initiative and resourcefulness
☐ Neatness or work product
☐ Other _____

CHECK ITEMS   [+] Excels   [–] Unsatisfactory
               [✓] Satisfactory   [NA] Not Applicable
               [0] Needs Improvement

FIGURE 5–4 Examples of Graphic Rating Scales.

This process is called **anchoring.** Scale *a* uses qualitative end anchors only. Scale *b* includes numerical and verbal anchors, while scales *c, d,* and *f* use verbal anchors only. These anchors are almost worthless, however, since what constitutes high and low quality or "outstanding" and "unsatisfactory" is left completely up to the rater. A "commendable" for one rater may only be a "competent" for another. Scale *e* is better, for the numerical anchors are described in terms of what "quality" means in that context.

The scales also differ in the relative ease with which a person interpreting the ratings can tell exactly what response was intended by the rater. In scale *a,* for example, the particular value that the rater had in mind is a mystery. Scale *e* is less ambiguous in this respect.

Finally, the scales differ in terms of the clarity of the definition of the performance dimension in question. In terms of Figure 5–4, what does quality mean? Is quality for a nurse the same as quality for a cashier? Scales *a* and *c* offer almost no help in defining quality, scale *b* combines quantity and quality together into a single dimension (although typically they are independent), and scales *d* and *e* define quality in different terms altogether (thoroughness, dependability, and neatness versus accuracy, effectiveness, and freedom from error). Scale *f* is an improvement in the sense that, while quality is taken to represent accuracy, effectiveness, initiative, and neatness (a combination of scale *d* and *e* definitions), at least separate ratings are required for each *aspect* of quality.

An improvement over all the examples in Figure 5–4 is shown below. It is part of a graphic rating scale used to rate nurses. The response categories are defined clearly, an individual interpreting the rating can tell what response the rater intended, and the performance dimension is defined in terms that both rater and ratee understand and can agree on.

Graphic rating scales may not yield the depth of narrative essays or critical incidents, but they (1) are less time-consuming to develop and administer, (2) permit quantitative results to be determined, (3) promote consideration of more than one performance dimension, and (4) are standardized and therefore comparable across individuals. On the other hand, graphic rating scales give maximum control to the rater, thereby exercising no control over leniency, severity, central tendency, or halo. For this reason, they have been criticized. However, when simple graphic rating scales have been compared against more sophisticated forced-choice ratings, the graphic scale consistently proved just as reliable and valid (King et al., 1980) and was more acceptable to raters (Bernardin and Beatty, 1984).

Behaviorally Anchored Rating Scales

How can graphic rating scales be improved? According to Smith and Kendall (1963):

> Better ratings can be obtained, in our opinion, not by trying to trick the rater (as in forced-choice scales) but by helping him to rate. We should ask him questions which he can honestly answer about behaviors which he can observe. We should reassure him that his answers will not be misinterpreted, and we should provide a basis by which he and others can check his answers. [p. 151]

Their procedure is as follows. At an initial conference, groups of workers and/or supervisors attempt to identify and define all of the important dimensions of effective performance for a particular job. A second group then generates, for each dimension, critical incidents illustrating effective, average, and ineffective performance. A third group is then given a list of di-

---

EMERGENCY PROCEDURE AWARENESS is the knowledge an individual has of his or her DR. HEART, STAT, CODE 13, CODE D, and CODE RED responsibilities

1 2 3	4 5 6	7 8 9	10 11 12	13 14 15
Unaware or not interested	Needs additional training	Knows responsibilities and has participated in drills	Superior knowledge of responsibilities and performance during skills	Very thorough knowledge of responsibilities; able to assist in training of others

Comments: _____

_____

_____

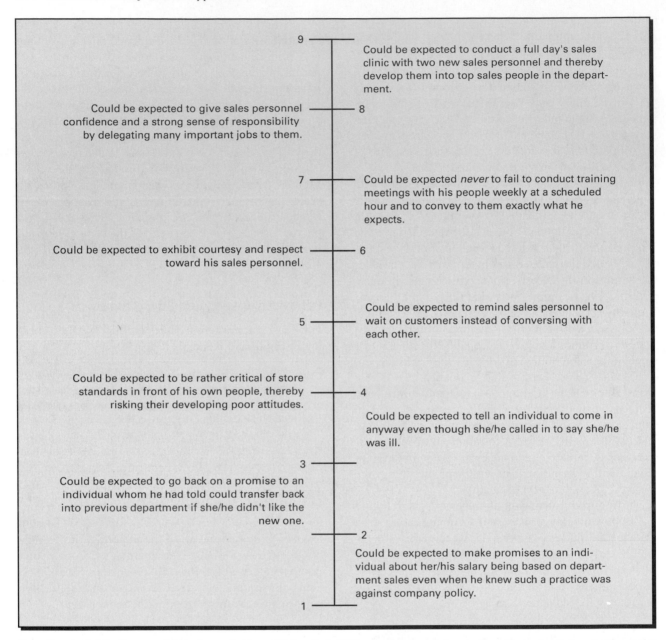

9 — Could be expected to conduct a full day's sales clinic with two new sales personnel and thereby develop them into top sales people in the department.

Could be expected to give sales personnel confidence and a strong sense of responsibility by delegating many important jobs to them. — 8

7 — Could be expected *never* to fail to conduct training meetings with his people weekly at a scheduled hour and to convey to them exactly what he expects.

Could be expected to exhibit courtesy and respect toward his sales personnel. — 6

5 — Could be expected to remind sales personnel to wait on customers instead of conversing with each other.

Could be expected to be rather critical of store standards in front of his own people, thereby risking their developing poor attitudes. — 4

Could be expected to tell an individual to come in anyway even though she/he called in to say she/he was ill.

3 —

Could be expected to go back on a promise to an individual whom he had told could transfer back into previous department if she/he didn't like the new one.

— 2

Could be expected to make promises to an individual about her/his salary being based on department sales even when he knew such a practice was against company policy.

1 —

From Campbell, J. P., Dunnette, M. D., Arvey, R. D., and Hellervik, L. V. The development and evaluation of behaviorally based rating scales. *Journal of Applied Psychology,* 1973, 57, 15–22. Copyright 1973 by the American Psychological Association. Reprinted by permission.

FIGURE 5–5 Scaled Expectations Rating Scale for the Effectiveness with which the Department Manager Supervises His or Her Sales Personnel.

mensions and their definitions, along with a randomized list of the critical incidents generated by the second group. Their task is to sort or locate incidents into the dimensions they best represent.

This procedure is known as **retranslation** since it resembles the quality control check that is used to ensure the adequacy of translations from one language into another. Material is translated into a foreign language and then retranslated back into the original by an independent translator. In the context of performance appraisal, this procedure ensures that the meaning of both the job dimensions and the behavioral incidents chosen to illustrate them is specific and clear. Incidents are eliminated if there is not clear agreement among judges (usually 60–80%) regarding the dimension to which each incident belongs. Dimensions are eliminated if incidents are not allocated to them. Conversely, dimensions may be added if many incidents are allocated to the "other" category.

Each of the items within dimensions that survived the retranslation procedure is then presented to a fourth group of judges, whose task is to place a scale value on each incident (e.g., in terms of a 7- or 9-point scale from "highly effective behavior" to "grossly ineffective behavior"). The end product looks like that in Figure 5–5.

As you can see, BARS development is a long, painstaking process that may require many individuals. Moreover, separate BARS must be developed for dissimilar jobs. Consequently, this approach may not be practical for many organizations.

How have BARS worked in practice? An enormous amount of research on BARS has been published, and much of it has been summarized by Bernardin and Beatty (1984). At the risk of oversimplification, major known effects of BARS are summarized in Table 5–2.

TABLE 5–2 Known Effects of BARS

Participation
Participation does seem to enhance the validity of ratings, but no more so for BARS than for simple graphic rating scales.

Leniency, central tendency, halo, reliability
BARS not superior to other methods (reliabilities across dimensions in published studies range from about .52 to .76).

External validity
Moderate (R^2s of .21 to .47—Shapira and Shirom, 1980) relative to the upper limits of validity in performance ratings (Borman, 1978; Weekley and Gier, 1989).

Comparisons with other formats
BARS no better or worse than other methods.

Variance in dependent variables associated with differences in rating systems
Less than 5 percent. Rating systems affect neither the level of ratings (Harris and Schaubroeck, 1988), nor subordinates' satisfaction with feedback (Russell and Goode, 1988).

Convergent/discriminant validity
Low convergent validity, extremely low discriminant validity.

Specific content of behavioral anchors
Anchors depicting behaviors observed by raters, but unrepresentative of true performance levels, produce ratings biased in the direction of the anchors (Murphy and Constans, 1987). This is unlikely to have a major impact on ratings collected in the field (Murphy and Pardaffy, 1989).

In short, there is little empirical evidence to support the superiority of BARS over other performance appraisal systems.

SUMMARY COMMENTS ON RATING FORMATS AND RATING PROCESS

For several million workers today, especially those in insurance, communications, transportation, and banking industries, being monitored on the job by a computer is a fact of life (Griffith, 1993; Kulik and Ambrose, 1993). In most jobs, though, human judgment about individual job performance is inevitable, no matter what format is used. This is the major problem with all formats.

Unless observation of ratees is extensive and representative, it is not possible for judgments to represent a ratee's true performance. Since the rater must make *inferences* about performance, the appraisal is subject to all the biases that have been linked to rating scales. Raters are free to distort their appraisals to suit their purposes. This can undo all of the painstaking work that went into scale development and probably explains why no single rating format has been shown to be superior to others.

What can be done? Both Banks and Roberson (1985) and Härtel (1993) suggest two strategies. One, build in as much structure as possible in order to minimize the amount of discretion exercised by a rater. For example, use job analysis to specify what is really relevant to effective job performance, and critical incidents to specify levels of performance effectiveness in terms of actual job behavior. Two, don't require raters to make judgments that they are not competent to make; don't tax their abilities beyond what they can do accurately. For example, for formats that require judgments of frequency, make sure that raters have had sufficient opportunity to observe ratees so that their judgments are accurate. Above all, recognize that the *process* of performance appraisal, not the *mechanics*, determines the overall effectiveness of this essential organizational activity.

FACTORS AFFECTING SUBJECTIVE APPRAISALS

Performance appraisal is a complex process that may be affected by many factors, including organizational, political, and interpersonal barriers. In this section, we

TABLE 5–3 Summary of Findings on Rater Characteristics and Rating Effectiveness

Gender
No general effect (Landy and Farr, 1980).

Race
African-American raters rate whites slightly higher than they rate African-Americans. White and African-American raters differ very little in their ratings of white ratees (Sackett and DuBois, 1991).

Age
No consistent effects (Schwab and Heneman, 1978).

Education level
Significant but extremely weak effect (Cascio and Valenzi, 1978).

Low self-confidence; increased psychological distance
More critical, negative ratings (Rothaus, Morton, and Hanson, 1965)

Interests, social insight, intelligence
No consistent effect (Zedeck and Kafry, 1977).

Accountability
Raters who are accountable for their ratings provide more accurate ratings than those who are not accountable (Mero and Motowidlo, 1995).

Job experience
Significant but weak positive effect on quality of ratings (Cascio and Valenzi, 1977).

Performance level
Effective performers tend to produce more reliable and valid ratings (Kirchner and Reisberg, 1962).

Leadership style
Supervisors who provide little structure to subordinates' work activities tend to avoid formal appraisals (Fried et al., 1992).

Organizational position
(See earlier discussion, "Who Shall Rate?")

Rater knowledge of ratee and job
Relevance of contact to the dimensions rated is critical (Lee, 1985). Ratings are less accurate when delayed rather than immediate, and when observations are based on limited data (Heneman and Wexley, 1983).

Prior expectations and information
Disconfirmation of expectations (higher or lower than expected) lowers ratings (Hogan, 1987). Prior information may bias ratings in the short run. Over time ratings reflect actual behavior (Hanges et al., 1991).

Stress
Raters under stress rely more heavily on first impressions and make fewer distinctions among performance dimensions (Srinivas and Motowidlo, 1987).

TABLE 5–4 Summary of Findings on Ratee Characteristics and Performance Ratings

Personal Characteristics

Gender
Females tend to receive lower ratings than males when they make up less than 20 percent of a work group, but higher ratings than males when they make up more than 50 percent of a work group (Sackett, DuBois, and Noe, 1991).

Race
Race of the ratee accounts for between 1 percent and 5 percent of the variance in ratings (Borman et al., 1991; Oppler et al., 1992).

Age
Older subordinates rated lower than younger subordinates (Ferris et al., 1985), by both black and white raters (Crew, 1984).

Education
No significant effects (Cascio and Valenzi, 1977).

Emotional disability
Workers with disabilities received higher ratings than warranted, but such positive bias disappears when clear standards are used (Czajka and DeNisi, 1988).

Job-Related Variables

Performance level
Actual performance level and ability have the strongest effect on ratings (Borman et al., 1991; Borman et al., 1995; Vance et al., 1983). More weight given to negative than to positive attributes of ratees (Ganzach, 1995).

Group composition
Ratings tend to be higher for satisfactory workers in groups with a large proportion of unsatisfactory workers (Grey and Kipnis, 1976), but these findings may not generalize to all occupational groups (Ivancevich, 1983).

Tenure
Although age and tenure are highly related, evidence indicates no relationship between ratings and ratee tenure, or tenure working for the same suprevisor (Ferris et al., 1985).

Job satisfaction
Knowledge of a ratee's job satisfaction may bias ratings in the same direction (+ or −) as the ratee's satisfaction (Smither, Collins, and Buda, 1989).

Personality characteristics
Both peers and supervisors rate dependability highly. However, obnoxiousness affects peer raters much more than supervisors (Borman, White, and Dorsey, 1995).

shall consider several other factors that may affect ratings: individual differences in raters and in ratees, and interactions between raters and ratees. Findings in each of these areas are summarized in Tables 5–3, 5–4, and 5–5. For each variable listed in the tables, an il-

lustrative reference is provided for those who wish to find more specific information.

As the tables demonstrate, we now know a great deal about the effects of selected individual differences variables on ratings of job performance. However, there is a great deal more that we do not know. Specifically, we know little about the cognitive processes involved in performance appraisal except that even when

TABLE 5–5 Summary of Findings on Interaction of Rater-Ratee Characteristics and Performance Ratings

Gender

In the context of merit pay and promotions, females are rated less favorably and with greater negative bias by raters who hold traditional stereotypes about women (Dobbins, Cardy, and Truxillo, 1988).

Race

Both white and African-American raters consistently assign lower ratings to African-American ratees than to white ratees. White and African-American raters differ very little in their ratings of white ratees (Sackett and DuBois, 1991; Oppler et al., 1992). Race effects may disappear when cognitive ability, education, and experience are taken into account (Waldman and Avolio, 1991).

Actual vs. perceived similarity

Actual similarity (agreement between supervisor-subordinate work-related self-descriptions) is a weak predictor of performance ratings (Wexley et al., 1980), but *perceived* similarity is a strong predictor (Turban and Jones, 1988; Wayne and Liden, 1995).

Performance attributions

Age and job performance are generally unrelated (McEvoy and Cascio, 1989).

Citizenship behaviors

Dimension ratings of ratees with high levels of citizenship behaviors show high halo effects (Werner, 1994).

presented with information about how a ratee behaves, raters seem to infer common personality characteristics that go beyond that which is warranted. Such attributions exert an independent effect on appraisals, over and above that which is attributable to actual behaviors (Krzystofiak, Cardy, and Newman, 1988). Later research has found that raters may assign ratings in a manner that is consistent with their previous attitudes toward the ratee (i.e., based on affect), and that they may use affect consistency rather than simply good or bad performance as the criterion for diagnosing performance information (Robbins and DeNisi, 1994).

This kind of research is needed to help us understand why reliable, systematic changes in ratings occur over time, as well as why ratings are consistent (Vance, Winne, and Wright, 1983). It also will help us understand underlying reasons for bias in ratings and the information processing strategies used by raters to combine evaluation data (Hobson and Gibson, 1983). Finally, it will help us to identify raters who vary in their ability to provide accurate ratings. Research findings from each of these areas can help to improve the content of rater training programs and, ultimately, the caliber of appraisals in organizations. Speaking of rater training, let us consider what is known about this process.

RATER TRAINING

The first step in the design of *any* training program is to specify objectives. In the context of rater training there are three broad objectives: (1) to improve the observational skills of raters by teaching them *what* to attend to; (2) to reduce or eliminate judgmental biases; and (3) to improve the ability of raters to communicate appraisal information in an objective, constructive manner with ratees.

Traditionally, rater training has focused on teaching raters to eliminate judgmental biases such as leniency, central tendency, halo, and contrast effects (Bernardin and Buckley, 1981). This approach assumes that certain rating distributions are more desirable than others (e.g., normal distributions, variability in ratings across dimensions for a single person). While raters may learn a new response set that results in lower average ratings (less leniency) and greater variability in ratings across dimensions (less halo) their accuracy tends to decrease (Hedge and Kavanagh, 1988; Murphy and Balzer, 1989). However, it is important to note that accuracy in appraisal has been defined in different ways by researchers and that relations among different operational definitions of accuracy are generally weak (Sulsky and Balzer, 1988). In addition, rater training programs to eliminate systematic errors typically have only short-term effects (Fay and Latham, 1982).

Of the many types of rater training programs available today, research has demonstrated reliably that frame-of-reference training (Bernardin and Buckley, 1981) is most effective at improving the accuracy of performance appraisals (Day and Sulsky, 1995). Following procedures developed by Pulakos (1984, 1986), such training proceeds as follows:

1. Participants are told that they will evaluate the performance of three ratees on three separate performance dimensions.

2. They are given rating scales and instructed to read them as the trainer reads the dimension definitions and scale anchors aloud.

3. The trainer then discusses ratee behaviors that illustrate different performance levels for each scale. The goal is to create a common performance theory (frame of reference) among raters such that they will agree on the appropriate performance dimension and effectiveness level for different behaviors.

4. Participants are shown a videotape of a practice vignette and are asked to evaluate the manager using the scales provided.

5. Ratings are then written on a blackboard and discussed by the group of participants. The trainer seeks to identify which behaviors participants used to decide on their assigned ratings, and to clarify any discrepancies among the ratings.

6. The trainer provides feedback to participants, explaining why the ratee should receive a certain rating (target score) on a given dimension.

Frame-of-reference training provides a performance-based schema to raters to help them process performance information. This schema appears to guide the encoding, storage, and retrieval of performance judgments as well as specific behavioral information (Woehr, 1994). In addition, the provision of rating standards and behavioral examples appears to be responsible for the improvements in rating accuracy. The use of target scores in performance examples and accuracy feedback on practice ratings allows raters to learn, through direct experience, how to use the different rating standards. In essence, the frame-of-reference training is a microcosm that includes an efficient model of the process by which performance-dimension standards are acquired (Stamoulis and Hauenstein, 1993).

Nevertheless, the approach described above assumes a single frame of reference for all raters. Research has shown that different raters (peers, supervisors, subordinates) demonstrate distinctly different frames of reference and that they disagree about the importance of poor performance incidents (Hauenstein and Foti, 1989). Training should highlight these differences and focus on the process by which judgments are made (Hedge and Kavanagh, 1988). Finally, the training process should identify idiosyncratic raters so their performance in training can be monitored to assess improvement.

Rater training is clearly worth the effort, and the kind of approach advocated here is especially effective in improving the accuracy of ratings for individual ratees on separate performance dimensions (Day and Sulsky, 1995). In addition, trained managers are more effective in formulating development plans for subordinates (Davis and Mount, 1984). The technical and interpersonal problems associated with performance appraisal are neither insurmountable nor inscrutable; they simply require the competent and systematic application of sound training principles.

The Wider Context of Performance Appraisal

Throughout this chapter, we have emphasized that performance appraisal systems encompass measurement issues as well as attitudinal and behavioral issues. Traditionally, we have tended to focus our research efforts on measurement issues per se; yet any measurement instrument or rating format probably has only a limited impact on performance appraisal scores (Banks and Roberson, 1985). Broader issues in performance appraisal must be addressed since appraisal outcomes are likely to represent an interaction among organizational contextual variables, rating formats, and rater motivation.

Three field studies have assessed the attitudinal implications of appraisal systems. In one of these, Ivancevich (1980), investigated the long-term impact of BARS in an organizational setting. At three measurement points over a 20-month period, 121 BARS-rated engineers reported more favorable attitudes about the system (e.g., fair, accurate, comprehensive, provides meaningful feedback), less job-related tension, and improved scheduling performance than their counterparts (128), who were rated on a trait-oriented scale. Unfortunately, since it was not possible to incorporate a true control group into the research design, we cannot say that the BARS system *caused* the improvements. Such are the problems with field research. Nevertheless these results are encouraging; hopefully they can be replicated, refined, and extended.

In another study, Mount (1983) surveyed 612 managers and 1,550 employees of a large multinational corporation to assess their satisfaction with a new performance appraisal system. It had the following features: (1) employees received at least one formal appraisal discussion per year; (2) discussions of appraisal results occurred at a time separate from discussions of salary; and (3) appraisal formats were tailored to the major pay plans of the organization, for example, clerical, sales representatives, and management.

Satisfaction differed according to the perspective of the individual. Managers saw the system as comprising more distinct components than did employees. Thus managers perceived items pertaining to company policy and to appraisal procedures (the way performance appraisal relates to other HR programs such as work planning, career planning, and salary administration) as distinct from each other. Employees perceived aspects of the system in a global way. Their satisfaction was accounted for by their overall experience with the system, the quality of the appraisal discussion, the way the forms help discuss performance, and the way the forms help to formulate development plans.

A third study examined the impact of prior expectations on ratings (Hogan, 1987). Supervisors of tellers at a large West Coast bank provided predictions about the future job performance of their new tellers. Six months later they rated the job performance of each teller. The result? Mismatches between prior expectations and later performance clearly affected the appraisals. Specifically, when a teller's actual performance disappointed *or* exceeded the supervisor's prior expectations about that performance, ratings were lower than actual performance warranted. The lesson to be learned is that it is unwise to assume that raters are faulty, but motivationally neutral, elements of the appraisal process.

This kind of knowledge is no less important than the knowledge that a new appraisal system results in less halo, leniency, and central tendency. Both types of information are meaningful and useful; both must be considered in the wider context of performance appraisal.

TABLE 5–6 Supervisory Activities Before, During, and After Appraisal
Before
Communicate frequently with subordinates about their performance.
Get training in performance appraisal.
Judge your own performance first before judging others.
Encourage subordinates to prepare for appraisal interviews.
During
Warm up and encourage subordinate participation.
Judge performance, not personality and mannerisms.
Be specific.
Be an active listener.
Avoid destructive criticism.
Set mutually agreeable goals for future improvement.
After
Communicate frequently with subordinates about their performance.
Periodically assess progress toward goals.
Make organizational rewards contingent on performance.

INFORMATION FEEDBACK: APPRAISAL AND GOAL-SETTING INTERVIEWS

One of the central purposes of performance appraisal is to serve as a personal development tool, for in order to improve, there must be some feedback regarding present performance. The facilitative effect of feedback upon future performance has been well documented (Ilgen, Fisher, and Taylor, 1979; Ilgen and Moore, 1987). Indeed, research indicates that managers should seek negative, not just positive, feedback explicitly from multiple sources (superiors, peers, and subordinates). Doing so tends to produce two desirable outcomes: (1) accuracy in detecting performance problems, and (2) favorable effectiveness ratings from the various sources of feedback (Ashford and Tsui, 1991). Responsibility for communicating such feedback from multiple sources by means of an appraisal interview often rests with the immediate supervisor (Ghorpade and Chen, 1995).

Ideally, a continuous feedback process should exist between superior and subordinate so that both may be guided. In practice, however, supervisors frequently "save up" performance-related information for a formal appraisal interview, the conduct of which is an extremely trying experience for both parties. Most supervisors resist "playing God" (playing the role of judge) and then communicating their judgments to subordinates (McGregor, 1957). Hence, the supervisor may avoid confronting uncomfortable issues, but even if he or she does, the subordinate may only deny or rationalize them in an effort to maintain self-esteem (Larson,

1989). Thus, the process is self-defeating for both parties. Fortunately this need not always be the case. Based on findings from appraisal interview research, Table 5–6 presents several activities that supervisors should engage in before, during, and after appraisal interviews. Let us briefly consider each of them.

FREQUENT COMMUNICATION. Two of the clearest results from research on the appraisal interview are that once-a-year performance appraisals are of questionable value and that coaching should be done much more frequently—particularly for poor performers or with new employees (Cederblom, 1982; Meyer, 1991). Feedback has maximum impact when it is given as close as possible to the action. If a subordinate behaves effectively, tell him or her immediately; if he behaves ineffectively, also tell him immediately. Do not file these incidents away so that they can be discussed in 6 to 9 months.

APPRAISAL TRAINING. As we noted earlier, increased emphasis should be placed on training raters to observe behavior more accurately and fairly than on providing specific illustrations of "how to" or "how not to" rate. Training managers to provide evaluative information and to give feedback should focus on managerial characteristics that are difficult to rate and on characteristics that people think are easy to rate but which generally result in disagreements. Such factors include risk-taking and development of subordinates (Wohlers and London, 1989).

JUDGE YOUR OWN PERFORMANCE FIRST. We often use ourselves as the norm or standard by which to judge others. While this tendency may be difficult to overcome, research findings in the area of interpersonal perception can help improve the process. Thus,

1. Self-protection mechanisms like denial, giving up, self-promotion, and fear of failure have a negative influence on self-awareness.

2. Knowing oneself makes it easier to see others accurately and is itself a managerial ability.

3. One's own characteristics affect the characteristics one is likely to see in others.

4. The person who accepts himself or herself is more likely to be able to see favorable aspects of other people.

5. Accuracy in perceiving others is not a single skill (Wohlers and London, 1989; Zalkind and Costello, 1962).

ENCOURAGE SUBORDINATE PREPARATION. Research conducted in a large midwestern hospital indicated that the more time employees spent prior to appraisal interviews analyzing their job duties and responsibilities, problems being encountered on the job, and the quality of their performance, the more likely they were to be satisfied with the appraisal process, motivated to improve their own performance, and actually to improve their performance (Burke, Weitzel, and Weir, 1978). To foster such preparation, (1) a BARS form could be developed for this purpose and subordinates could be encouraged or required to use it (Silverman and Wexley, 1984); (2) employees could be provided with the supervisor's review prior to the appraisal interview and encouraged to react to it in specific terms; and (3) employees could be encouraged or required to appraise their own performance on the same criteria or forms their supervisor uses (Farh, Werbel, and Bedeian, 1988).

Self-review has at least four advantages: (1) it enhances the subordinate's dignity and self-respect; (2) it places the manager into the role of counselor, not judge; (3) it is more likely to promote employee commitment to plans or goals formulated during the discussion; and (4) it is likely to be more satisfying and productive for both parties than is the more traditional manager-to-subordinate review (Meyer, 1991).

WARM UP AND ENCOURAGE PARTICIPATION. Research shows generally that the more a subordinate feels he or she participated in the interview by presenting his or her own ideas and feelings, the more likely is the subordinate to feel that the supervisor was helpful and constructive, that some current job problems were cleared up, and that future goals were set. However, these conclusions are true as long as the appraisal interview represents a low threat to the subordinate, the subordinate previously has received an appraisal interview from the superior, he or she is accustomed to participating with the superior, and he or she is knowledgeable about issues to be discussed in the interview (Cederblom, 1982).

JUDGE PERFORMANCE, NOT PERSONALITY. The more supervisors focus on the personality and mannerisms of their subordinates rather than on aspects of job-related behavior, the lower the satisfaction of both supervisor and subordinate, and the less likely the subordinate is to be motivated to improve his or her performance (Burke et al., 1978).

BE SPECIFIC. Appraisal interviews are more likely to be successful to the extent that supervisors are perceived as constructive and helpful (Russell and Goode, 1988). By being candid and specific, the supervisor offers very clear feedback to the subordinate concerning past actions. He or she also demonstrates knowledge of the subordinate's level of performance and job duties. One can be specific about positive as well as negative behaviors on a job. Data show that the acceptance and accuracy of feedback by a subordinate are strongly affected by the order in which positive or negative information is presented. Begin the appraisal interview with positive feedback associated with minor issues, then proceed to discuss feedback regarding major issues. Praise concerning minor aspects of behavior should put the individual at ease, and reduce the dysfunctional blocking effect associated with criticisms (Stone, Gueutal, and McIntosh, 1984).

BE AN ACTIVE LISTENER. Have you ever seen two people in a heated argument who are each so intent on making their own points that they have no idea what the other person is saying? That is the opposite of "active" listening, where the objective is to empathize, to stand in the other person's shoes and try to see things from her or his point of view. For example, during an interview with her boss, a member of a project team says: "I don't want to work with Sally anymore. She's lazy and snooty and complains about the rest of us not helping her as much as we should. She thinks she's above this kind of work and too good to work with the rest of us and I'm sick of being around her."

The supervisor replies, "Sally's attitude makes the work unpleasant."

By reflecting what the woman said, the supervisor is encouraging her to confront her feelings and letting her know that she understands them. Active listeners are attentive to verbal as well as nonverbal cues, and above all they accept what the other person is saying without argument or criticism. Treat each individual with the same amount of dignity and respect that you yourself demand.

AVOID DESTRUCTIVE CRITICISM. Destructive criticism is general in nature, frequently delivered in a biting, sarcastic tone, and often attributes poor performance to internal causes (e.g., lack of motivation or ability). Evidence indicates that employees are strongly predisposed to attribute performance problems to factors beyond their control (e.g., inadequate materials, equipment, instructions, or time) as a mechanism to maintain their self-esteem (Larson, 1989). Not surprisingly, therefore, destructive criticism leads to three predictable consequences: (1) it produces negative feelings among recipients and can initiate or intensify conflict among individuals, (2) it reduces the preference of recipients for handling future disagreements with the giver of the feedback in a conciliatory manner (e.g., compromise, collaboration), and (3) it has negative effects on self-set goals and feelings of self-efficacy (Baron, 1988). Needless to say, this is one type of communication that managers and others would do well to avoid.

SET MUTUALLY AGREEABLE GOALS. There are three related reasons why goal setting affects performance. First, it has a *directive* effect—that is, it focuses activity in one particular direction rather than others. Second, given that a goal is accepted, people tend to exert *effort* in proportion to the difficulty of the goal. Finally, difficult goals lead to more *persistence* (i.e., directed effort over time) than do easy goals. These three dimensions, direction (choice), effort, and persistence, are central to the motivation/appraisal process (Katzell, 1994; Latham and Wexley, 1981). Research findings from goal-setting programs in organizations can be summed up as follows: Use participation to set specific goals, for they clarify for the individual precisely what is expected. Better yet, use participation to set specific but difficult goals, for this leads to higher acceptance and performance than the setting of specific but easily achievable goals (Erez, Earley, and Hulin, 1985). These findings seem to hold across cultures, not just in the United States (Erez and Earley, 1987), and they hold for groups or teams as well as for individuals (Matsui, Kakuyama, and

Onglatco, 1987). It is the future-oriented emphasis in appraisal interviews that seems to have the most beneficial effects on subsequent performance. Top-management commitment is also crucial, as a meta-analysis of management-by-objectives programs revealed. When top-management commitment was high, the average gain in productivity was 56 percent. When commitment was low, the average gain in productivity was only 6 percent (Rodgers and Hunter, 1991).

CONTINUE TO COMMUNICATE AND ASSESS PROGRESS TOWARD GOALS REGULARLY. When coaching is a day-to-day activity, rather than a once-a-year ritual, the appraisal interview can be put in proper perspective: It merely formalizes a process that should be occurring regularly anyway. Periodic tracking of progress toward goals helps keep behavior on target, provides a better understanding of the reasons behind a given level of performance, and enhances the subordinate's commitment to effective performance.

MAKE ORGANIZATIONAL REWARDS CONTINGENT ON PERFORMANCE. Research results are clear cut on this issue. Subordinates who see a link between appraisal results and employment decisions are more likely to prepare for appraisal interviews, are more likely actively to take part in them, and are more likely to be satisfied with the appraisal system (Burke et al., 1978). Managers, in turn, are likely to get more mileage out of their appraisal systems by heeding these results.

In summary, we now have a wealth of valuable information about the appraisal process that can and should be applied in organizations. It should be built into supervisory training programs, and it should be communicated to employees in an attempt to make their working lives more satisfying and meaningful and to improve the overall quality of organizational performance.

Discussion Questions

1. Why do performance apppraisal systems often fail?

2. Under what circumstances can appraisal systems be said to "work"?

3. What kinds of unique information about performance can each of the following provide: immediate supervisor, peers, subordinates, customers?

4. What key elements would you design into a rater training program?

5. Discuss three "dos" and three "don'ts" with respect to appraisal interviews.

CHAPTER

6

MEASURING AND INTERPRETING INDIVIDUAL DIFFERENCES

AT A GLANCE

Measurement of individual differences is the heart of personnel psychology. Individual differences in physical and psychological attributes may be measured on nominal, ordinal, interval, and ratio scales. Although measurements of psychological traits are primarily nominal and ordinal in nature, they may be treated statistically as if they were interval level.

Effective decisions about people demand knowledge of their individuality, knowledge that can be gained only through measurement of individual patterns of abilities, skills, knowledge, and interests. Psychological measurement procedures are known collectively as tests, and they are systematic in three areas: content, administration, and scoring. It is cru-

cial, however, that the measures be reliable. Reliable measures are dependable, consistent, and relatively free from unsystematic errors of measurement. Since error is present to some degree in all psychological measures, test scores are most usefully considered not as exact points, but rather as bands or ranges.

Assuming the measures are valid, intelligent interpretation of individual scores requires information about the relative performance of some comparison group (a norm group) on the same measurement procedures. A major limitation of this approach, however, is that normative data provide no direct link between performance outcomes (criteria) and test scores. Fortunately, alternative approaches are available that avoid this problem.

Have you ever visited a clothing factory? One of the most striking features of a clothing factory is the vast array of clothing racks, each containing garments of different sizes. Did you ever stop to think of the physical differences among wearers of this clothing? We can visualize some of the obvious ways in which the people who ultimately wear the clothing will differ. We can see heavy people, thin people, tall people, short people, old people, young people, long hairs, short hairs, and every imaginable variant in between.

Psychology's first law is glaringly obvious: People are different. They differ not only in physical respects, but in a host of other ways as well. Consider

wearers of size 42 men's sportcoats, for example. Some will be outgoing and gregarious, others will be shy and retiring; some will be creative, others will be unimaginative; some will be well adjusted, some will be maladjusted; some will be honest, and some will be crooks. Physical and psychological variability is all around us. As scientists, our goal is to describe this variability and, through laws and theories, to understand it, to explain it, and to predict it. Measurement is one of the tools that enables us to come a little bit closer to these objectives. Once we understand the *why* of measurement, the *how*—that is, measurement techniques—becomes more meaningful (Brown, 1983).

Consider our plight if measurement did not exist. We could not describe, compare, or contrast the phenomena in the world about us. Individuals would not be able to agree on the labels or units to be attached to various physical dimensions (length, width, volume), and interpersonal communication would be hopelessly throttled. Efforts at systematic research would be doomed to failure. Talent would be shamefully wasted and the process of science would grind to a halt. Fortunately, the state of the scientific world is a bit brighter than this. Measurement does exist, but what is it? Is psychological measurement equivalent to physical measurement?

THE NATURE OF MEASUREMENT

Measurement can be defined concisely. It is the assignment of numerals to objects or events according to rules (Linn and Gronlund, 1995; Stevens, 1951). Measurement answers the question, "How much?" Suppose you are asked to judge a fishing contest. As you measure the length of each entry, the rules for assigning numbers are clear. A "ruler" is laid next to each fish, and in accordance with agreed-upon standards (inches, centimeters, feet), the length of each entry is determined rather precisely.

On the other hand, suppose you are asked to judge a sample of job applicants after interviewing each one. You are to rate each applicant's management potential on a scale from one to ten. Obviously the quality and precision of this kind of measurement are not as exact as physical measurement. Yet both procedures satisfy our original definition of measurement. In short, the definition says nothing about the *quality* of the measurement procedure, only that *somehow* numerals are assigned to objects or events. Kerlinger (1986) expressed the idea well: Measurement is a game we play with objects and numerals. Games have rules. It is, of course, important for other reasons that the rules be "good" rules, but whether the rules are "good" or "bad," the procedure is still measurement (p. 392).

Thus, the *process* of measurement, be it physical or psychological, is identical. As long as we can define a dimension (e.g., weight) or a trait (e.g., aggressiveness) to be measured, determine the measurement operations, specify the rules, and have a certain scale of units to express the measurement, the measurement of *anything* is theoretically possible.

SCALES OF MEASUREMENT

The first step in any measurement procedure is to specify the dimension or trait to be measured. Then we can develop a series of operations that will permit us to describe individuals in terms of that dimension or trait. Sometimes the variation among individuals is **qualitative,** that is, in terms of kind (gender, hair color), and in other instances it is **quantitative,** that is, in terms of frequency, amount, or degree (Ghiselli, Campbell, and Zedeck, 1981). Qualitative description is classification, whereas quantitative description is measurement.

As we shall see, there are actually four levels of measurement, not just two, and they are hierarchically related—that is, the higher-order scales meet all the assumptions of the lower-order scales plus additional assumptions characteristic of their own particular order. From lower order to higher order, from simpler to more complex, the scales are labeled **nominal, ordinal, interval,** and **ratio** (Aiken, 1994).

Nominal Measurement

This is the lowest level of measurement and represents differences in kind. Individuals are assigned or classified into qualitatively different categories. Numbers may be assigned to objects or persons, but they have no numerical meaning. They cannot be ordered or added. They are merely labels.

People frequently make use of nominal scales to systematize or catalog individuals or events. For example, individuals may be classified as for or against a certain political issue, as males or females, as college-educated or not college-educated. Athletes frequently wear numbers on their uniforms, but the numbers serve only as labels. In all these instances, the fundamental operation is **equality,** which can be written in either one of the two ways below, but not both:

$$(a = b)$$
$$\text{or} \tag{6–1}$$
$$(a \neq b),$$

All members of one class or group possess some characteristic in common that nonmembers do not possess. In addition, the classes are mutually exclusive, such that if an individual belongs to group a, he or she cannot at the same time be a member of group b.

Even though nominal measurement provides no indication of magnitude and, therefore, allows no statistical operation except counting, this classifying information, in and of itself, is useful to the HR specialist. Frequency statistics such as χ^2, percentages, and certain kinds of measures of association (contingency coefficients) can be used. In the prediction of tenure using biographical information, for example, we may be interested in the percentages of people in various categories (e.g., classified by educational level or amount of experience—less than 1 year, 1–2 years, 2–5 years, or more than 5 years) who stay or leave within some specified period of time. If reliable differences between stayers and leavers can be established, scorable application blanks can be developed and selection efforts may thereby be improved.

Ordinal Measurement

The next level of measurement, the ordinal scale, not only allows classification by category (as in a nominal scale) but also provides an indication of magnitude. The categories are rank-ordered according to greater or lesser amounts of some characteristic or dimension. Ordinal scales, therefore, satisfy the requirement of equality (Equation 6–1) as well as **transitivity** or ranking, which may be expressed as:

$$\text{If } [(a > b) \text{ and } (b > c)], \text{ then } (a > c) \qquad \textbf{(6–2)}$$

or:

$$\text{If } [(a = b) \text{ and } (b = c)], \text{ then } (a = c) \qquad \textbf{(6–3)}$$

A great deal of physical and psychological measurement satisfies the transitivity requirement. For example, in horse racing, suppose we predict the exact order of finish of three horses. We bet on horse A to win, horse B to place (second), and horse C to show (third). It is irrelevant whether horse A beats horse B by two inches or two feet, and if horse B beats horse C by *any* amount, then we know that horse A also beat horse C. We are not concerned with the distances between horses A, B, and C, only with their relative order of finish. In fact, in ordinal measurement, we can substitute many other words besides "is greater than" (>), in Equation 6–2. We can substitute "is less than" (<), "is smaller than," "is prettier than," "is more authoritarian than," and so forth.

Simple orders are far less obvious in psychological measurement. Worker A may get along quite well with worker B, and worker B with worker C, but workers A and C might fight like cats and dogs. This idea of transitivity is especially important when social psychological variables must be considered (e.g., trust, cooperation, cohesiveness).

We can perform some useful statistical operations on ordinal scales. We can compute the *median* (the score that divides the distribution into halves), *percentile ranks* (each of which represents the percentage of individuals scoring below a given individual or score point), *rank-order correlation* such as Spearman's rho and Kendall's *W* (measures of the relationship or extent of agreement between two ordered distributions), and *rank-order analysis of variance.* What we cannot do is say that a difference of a certain magnitude means the same thing at all points along the scale. For that we need interval-level measurement.

Interval Measurement

Interval scales have the properties of (1) equality (Equation 6–1), (2) transitivity, or ranking (Equations 6–2 and 6–3), and (3) **additivity,** or equal-sized units, which can be expressed as:

$$(d - a) = (c - a) + (d - c) \qquad \textbf{(6–4)}$$

Consider the measurement of length. The distance between *a* (2 inches) and *b* (5 inches) is precisely equal to the distance between *c* (12 inches) and *d* (15 inches), namely, three inches (see below).

2	5	12	15
a	*b*	*c*	*d*

The scale units (inches) are equivalent at all points along the scale. In terms of Equation 6–4:

$$(15 - 2) = (12 - 2) + (15 - 12) = 13$$

So also differences in length between *a* and *c* and between *b* and *d* are equal. We are not adding and subtracting quantities or amounts, merely intervals or distances. All that is lacking is a true zero point. The crucial operation in interval measurement is the establishment of equality of units, which in psychological measurement must be demonstrated empirically. That is, we must be able to demonstrate that a 10-point difference between two job applicants who score 87 and 97 on an aptitude test is equivalent to a 10-point difference between two other applicants who score 57 and 67. In a 100-item test, each carrying a unit weight, we would have to establish empirically that, in fact, each item measured an equivalent amount or degree of the aptitude. We will have more to say on this issue in a following section.

On an interval scale, one can compute the more commonly used statistical measures, such as central

TABLE 6–1 Characteristics of Types of Measurement Scales

Scale	Operation	Description
Nominal	Equality	Mutually exclusive categories; objects or events fall into one class only; all members of same class considered equal; categories differ qualitatively not quantitatively.
Ordinal	Equality Ranking	Idea of magnitude enters; object is larger or smaller than another (but not both); any monotonic transformation is permissible.
Interval	Equality Ranking Equal-sized units	Additivity; all units of equal size; can establish equivalent distances along scale; any linear transformation is permissible.
Ratio	Equality Ranking Equal-sized units True (absolute) Zero	True or absolute zero point can be defined; meaningful ratios can be derived.

tendency, variability, correlation, and significance tests. Interval scales have one other very useful property: One can transform scores in any linear manner by adding, subtracting, multiplying, or dividing by a constant without altering the relationships between the scores. Mathematically these relationships may be expressed as follows:

$$X' = a + bX \qquad (6\text{–}5)$$

where X' is the transformed score, a and b are constants, and X is the original score. Thus, scores on one scale may be transformed to another scale using different units by: (1) adding and/or (2) multiplying by a constant. The main advantage to be gained by transforming scores in individual differences measurement is that it allows scores on two or more tests to be compared directly in terms of a common metric.

Ratio Measurement

This is the highest level of measurement in science. In addition to equality, transitivity, and additivity, the ratio scale also has a natural or **absolute zero point** that has empirical meaning. Height, distance, weight, and the Kelvin temperature scale are all ratio scales. In measuring weight, for example, a kitchen scale has an absolute zero point, which indicates complete absence of the property.

If a scale does not have a true zero point, however, we cannot make statements about the ratio of one individual to another in terms of the amount of the property that he or she possesses or about the proportion that one individual is to another. In a track meet,

if runner A finishes the mile in 4 minutes flat, while runner B takes 6 minutes, then we can say that runner A completed the mile in two-thirds the time it took runner B to do so, and runner A ran about 33 percent faster than runner B.

On the other hand, suppose we give a group of clerical applicants a spelling test. It makes no sense to say that a person who spells every word incorrectly cannot spell any words correctly. A different sample of words would probably elicit some correct responses. Ratios or proportions in situations such as these are not meaningful because the magnitudes of such properties are measured not in terms of "distance" from an absolute zero point, but only in terms of "distance" from an arbitrary zero point (Ghiselli et al., 1981). Differences among the four types of scales are presented graphically in Table 6–1.

PSYCHOLOGICAL MEASUREMENT

Psychological measurement is principally concerned with individual differences in psychological **traits.** A trait is simply a descriptive label applied to a group of interrelated behaviors (e.g., dominance, creativity, agreeableness) that may be inherited or acquired. Based on standardized samples of individual behavior (e.g., tests, interviews), we *infer* the position or standing of the individual on the trait dimension in question.

Psychological measurement scales for the most part are nominal- or ordinal-level, although many scales and tests commonly used in behavioral measurement and research approximate interval measurement well enough for practical purposes. Strictly speaking, intelligence, aptitude, and personality test scores are ordinal-level measures. They indicate not the *amounts* of intelligence, aptitude, or personality traits of individuals, but rather their rank order with respect to the traits in question. Yet with a considerable degree of confidence we can often assume an equal interval scale, as Kerlinger (1986) noted:

> If we have, say, two or three measures of the same variables, and these measures are all substantially and linearly related, then equal intervals can be assumed. This assumption is valid because the more nearly a relation approaches linearity, the more nearly equal are the intervals of the scales. This also applies, at least to some extent, to certain psychological measures like intelligence, achievement, and aptitude tests and scales. A related argument is that many of the methods of analysis we use work quite well with most psychological scales. That is, the results we get from using scales and assuming equal intervals are quite satisfactory. [p. 402]

The argument is a pragmatic one that has been presented elsewhere (Ghiselli et al., 1981). In short, we assume an equal interval scale because this assumption works. If serious doubt exists about the tenability of this assumption, consider transforming raw scores (i.e., scores derived directly from a test, interview, or rating scale) statistically into some form of derived score scale having equal units (Rosenthal and Rosnow, 1984).

Ratio scales are virtually nonexistent in psychological measurement, although one approach that comes close is known as latent trait theory or item response theory (IRT).

Item Response Theory

This theory has received a considerable amount of attention and development in recent years (Hulin, Drasgow, and Parsons, 1983; Rogers, 1995). The general approach can be described as follows.

In contrast to classical test theory, where each examinee's score is indexed to the specific sample of items on a test, the focus in IRT is on each test item and the probability of a correct response to that item. Each item has its own item characteristic curve, which shows the relationship of the probabilities of a correct response to level of ability, that is, to examinees' positions on an underlying or latent ability continuum.

One widely used curve describing this relationship has three parameters: a difficulty parameter, a discrimination parameter (that is, the degree to which the item distinguishes high-ability examinees from low-ability examinees), and a parameter describing the probability of a correct response by examinees with extremely low levels of ability.

Some IRT approaches require the estimation of all three parameters, some use only the first two, and one model (Rasch, 1966) estimates only the difficulty parameter. All of the approaches, however, involve estimation of a "person parameter" for each examinee, that is, an estimate of latent ability, in addition to item parameters.

In theory, the parameters of an item characteristic curve do not vary across subpopulations (at least when a linear transformation is used). That is, the item parameters do not depend on the distribution of ability in a given sample. Thus item parameters obtained in one sample should match those obtained in another—even though the distributions of ability might be quite different. Ability estimates also do not vary—again, when a linear transformation is used.

A *test* characteristic curve is then found by averaging the item characteristic curves of all items in the test. The test characteristic curve shows the expected proportion of items answered correctly associated with any given level of ability (Guion and Ironson, 1983).

Perhaps the major advantage of this approach is that each examinee's ability level can be assessed quickly, without wasting his or her time on very easy problems or on an embarrassing series of very difficult problems. In view of the obvious desirability of "tailored" tests, we can expect to see much wider application of this approach in the coming years.

Another application is measurement bias. IRT allows a researcher to determine if a given item is more difficult for examinees from one group than from another when they all have the same ability. Using such methods, Drasgow (1987) showed that tests of English and mathematics usage provide equivalent measurement for Hispanic, African American, and white men and women.

A third application is "appropriateness" measurement (Drasgow and Guertler, 1987). Here we are interested in whether a test score provides a valid measure of the ability of a particular examinee. Cheating from a high-ability neighbor, alignment errors (answering, say, the tenth item in the space provided for the ninth item), unusual creativity, and language difficulties all can lead to inappropriate test scores. IRT methods provide powerful means for identifying these test scores.

CRITERIA FOR EVALUATING PSYCHOLOGICAL MEASUREMENT

Should the value of psychological measures be judged in terms of the same criteria as physical measurement? Physical measurements are evaluated in terms of the degree to which they satisfy the requirements of order, equality, and addition. In behavioral measurement the operation of addition is undefined since there seems to be no way to add physically one psychological magnitude to another to get a third, even greater in amount. Yet other, more practical criteria exist by which psychological measures may be evaluated. The purpose of psychological measures is decision making (Boudreau, 1991; Cronbach and Gleser, 1965). In selection, the decision is whether to accept or reject an applicant; in placement, which alternative course of action to pursue; in diagnosis, which remedial treatment is called for; in hypothesis testing, the accuracy of the theoretical formulation; in hypothesis building, which additional testing or other information is needed; and in evaluation, what score to assign to an individual or procedure (Brown, 1983).

Psychological measures are therefore more appropriately evaluated in terms of their social utility. The important question is not whether the psychological measures as used in a particular context are accurate or inaccurate, but rather how their predictive efficiency compares with that of other available procedures and techniques.

Frequently, HR specialists are confronted with the tasks of selecting and using psychological measurement procedures, interpreting results, and communicating the results to others. These are important tasks that frequently affect individual careers. It is essential, therefore, that HR specialists be well grounded in applied measurement concepts. Hence, we devote the remainder of this chapter, as well as the next two, to a consideration of these topics.

THE SYSTEMATIC NATURE OF MEASUREMENT PROCEDURES

A **test**[1] may be defined as a systematic procedure for measuring a sample of behavior (Brown, 1983). The

---

[1] Throughout this book the word *test* is used in the broad sense to include any psychological measurement instrument, technique, or procedure. These include, for example, written, oral, and performance tests, interviews, rating scales, assessment center exercises (i.e., situational tests), and scorable application forms. For ease of exposition, many of the examples used in the book refer specifically to written tests.

procedure is systematic in three areas: content, administration, and scoring. Item content is chosen systematically from the behavioral domain to be measured (e.g., mechanical aptitude, verbal fluency). Procedures for administration are standardized in that each time the test is given, directions for taking the test and recording the answers are identical, the same time limits pertain, and, as far as possible, distractions are minimized. Scoring is objective in that rules are specified in advance for evaluating responses. In short, procedures are systematic in order to minimize the effects of unwanted contaminants (i.e., personal and environmental variables) on test scores.

Test Selection

The results of a comprehensive job analysis should provide clues to the kinds of personal variables that are likely to be related to job success. Assuming the HR specialist has an idea about *what* should be assessed, *where* and *how* does he or she find what he is looking for? One of the most encyclopedic classification systems may be found in the *Mental Measurements Yearbooks* (Conoley and Imparra, 1994; Kramer and Conoley, 1992; and earlier editions). Tests used in education, psychology, and industry are classified into 16 broad content categories. In total, almost 2,000 English-language, commercially-published tests are referenced. The more important, widely used, new and revised tests are evaluated critically by leaders in the field of measurement. Faced with such a bewildering variety and number of tests, the need for a fairly detailed classification system is obvious.

Test Classification Methods

In selecting a test, as opposed to evaluating its technical characteristics, important factors to consider are its content, the ease with which it may be administered, the method of scoring, and the cost. One classification scheme is presented in Figure 6–1.

Content. Tests may be classified in terms of the *task* they pose for the examinee. Some tests are composed of verbal content (vocabulary, sentences) or nonverbal content (pictures, puzzles, diagrams). Examinees also may be required to manipulate objects, arrange blocks, or trace a particular pattern. These exercises are known as **performance tests.**

Tests also may be classified in terms of *process*—that is, what the examinee is asked to do. Cognitive tests measure the products of mental ability (in-

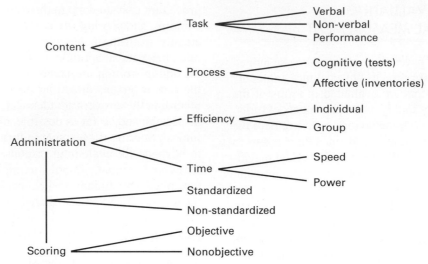

FIGURE 6-1 Methods of Classifying Tests.

tellect) and frequently are subclassified as tests of achievement and aptitude. In general, they require the performance of a task or the giving of factual information. Aptitude and achievement tests are both measures of ability, but they differ in two important ways: (1) the uniformity of prior experience assumed, and (2) the uses made of the tests (American Psychological Association, 1985). Thus achievement tests measure the effects of learning that occurred during relatively standardized sets of experiences (e.g., during an apprenticeship program or a course in computer programming). Aptitude tests, on the other hand, measure the effects of learning from the cumulative and varied experiences in daily living.

These assumptions help to determine how the tests are used. Achievement tests usually represent a final evaluation of what the individual can do at the completion of training. The focus is on present competence. Aptitude tests, on the other hand, serve to predict subsequent performance, to estimate the extent to which an individual will profit from training, or to forecast the quality of achievement in a new situation. We hasten to add, however, that no distinction between aptitude and achievement tests can be applied rigidly. Both measure the individual's *current* behavior, which inevitably reflects the influence of prior learning.

In contrast to cognitive tests, affective tests are designed to measure aspects of personality (interests, values, motives, attitudes, and temperament traits). Generally they require the reporting of feelings, beliefs, or attitudes ("I think . . . ; I feel . . . "). These self-report instruments also are referred to as **inventories,** while aptitude and achievement instruments are called tests. Tests and inventories are different, and much of the popular distrust of testing stems from a confusion of the two. Inventories reflect what the individual says he or she feels; tests measure what he or she knows or can do (Lawshe and Balma, 1966).

Administration. Tests may be classified in terms of the efficiency with which they can be administered or in terms of the time limits they impose on the examinee. Because they must be administered to one examinee at a time, individual tests are less efficient than group tests, which can be administered simultaneously to many examinees, either in paper-and-pencil format or by computer. In group testing, however, the examiner has much less opportunity to establish rapport, to obtain cooperation, and to maintain the interest of examinees. Moreover, any temporary condition that may interfere with test performance of the individual, such as illness, fatigue, anxiety, or worry, is detected less readily in group testing. These factors may represent a distinct handicap to those unaccustomed to testing, such as the disadvantaged.

In test construction, as well as in interpretation of test scores, time limits play an important role. Pure *speed* tests (e.g., number checking) consist of many easy items, but time limits are very stringent—so stringent, in fact, that no one can finish all the items. A pure *power* test, on the other hand, has a time limit generous enough to permit everyone an opportunity to attempt all the items. The difficulty of the items is steeply graded, however, and the test includes items too difficult for anyone to solve, so that no one can get a perfect score. Note that both speed and power tests are designed to prevent the achievement of perfect scores. In order to allow each person to demonstrate fully what he or she is able to accomplish, the test must have an adequate ceiling, in terms either of number of items or difficulty level. In practice, however, the distinction between speed and power is one of degree, since most tests depend on both factors in varying proportions.

Standardized and Nonstandardized Tests. Standardized tests have fixed directions for administration and scoring. These are necessary in order to compare scores made by different individuals. In the process of standardizing a test, it must be administered to a large, representative sample (usually several hundred) of individuals similar to those for whom the test ultimately is designed (e.g., children, adults, industrial trainees). This group, termed the **standardization sample,** is used to establish **norms** in order to provide a frame of reference for interpreting test scores. Norms indicate not only the average performance, but also the relative spread of scores above and below the average. Thus, it is possible to evaluate a test score in terms of the examinee's relative standing within the normative or standardization sample.

Nonstandardized tests are much more common than published, standardized tests. Typically these are classroom tests, usually constructed by a teacher or trainer in an informal manner for a single administration.

Scoring. The method of scoring a test may be objective or nonobjective. Objective scoring is particularly appropriate for employment office use because there are fixed, impersonal standards for scoring, and a computer or clerk can score the test (Schmitt et al., 1993). The amount of error introduced under these conditions is assumed to be negligible. On the other hand, the process of scoring essay tests and certain types of personality inventories (especially those employed in intensive individual examinations) may be quite subjective, and considerable "scorer variance" may be introduced. We will discuss this topic more fully in a later section.

Further Considerations

Several additional factors also need to be considered in selecting a test or other measurement procedure—namely, purpose, cost, interpretation, and face validity.

Although job analysis provides clues regarding the traits or abilities to be measured, one also must consider the purpose of the procedure—is it selection, placement, or research? Specification of purpose helps to narrow the search for an appropriate measurement procedure by indicating the format, type, and variety of scores that the procedure must supply. For example, if a mechanical aptitude test is to be used for selection or screening purposes, an instrument that provides a single overall score should suffice. On the other hand, if applicants already have been hired and the mechanical aptitude test is to be used as a diagnostic device for training or placement purposes, then we need a test that covers in some detail the various areas of mechanical aptitude and provides separate scores for each specific area.

Measurement cost is a very practical consideration. Most users operate within a budget and therefore must choose a procedure that will satisfy their cost constraints. A complete cost analysis includes direct as well as indirect costs. Direct costs may include the price of software or test booklets (some are reusable), answer sheets, scoring, and reporting services. Indirect costs (which may or may not be of consequence depending on the particular setting) may include time to prepare the test materials, examiner or interviewer time, and time for interpreting and reporting test scores. Users are well advised to make the most realistic cost estimates possible prior to committing themselves to the measurement effort. Sound advance planning can eliminate subsequent "surprises."

Managers frequently assume that since a test can be administered by almost any educated person, it also can be interpreted by almost anyone. Not so. In fact, this is one aspect of staffing that frequently is overlooked. Test interpretation includes more than a simple written or verbal reporting of test scores. Adequate interpretation requires thorough awareness of the strengths and limitations of the measurement procedure, the background of the examinee, the situation in which the procedure was applied, and the consequences that the interpretation will have on and for the examinee. Unquestionably misinterpretation of test results by untrained and incompetent persons is one of the main reasons for the dissatisfaction with psychological testing (and other measurement procedures) felt by many in our society.

A final consideration is face validity—that is, whether the measurement procedure *looks like* it is measuring the trait in question. Face validity does not refer to validity in the technical sense, but is concerned rather with establishing rapport and good public relations. In research settings, face validity may be a relatively minor concern, but when measurement procedures are being used to help make decisions about individuals (e.g., in employment situations), face validity may be an issue of signal importance because it affects the applicant's motivation and reaction to the procedure. If the content of the procedure appears irrelevant, inappropriate, or silly, the result will be poor cooperation, regardless of the technical superiority of the procedure. To be sure, if the content of the procedure is likely to affect an examinee's performance, then if at all possible, select a procedure with high face validity.

CONSISTENCY AND PREDICTIVE EFFICIENCY

In evaluating the technical characteristics of a measurement procedure—that is, its consistency and predictive efficiency—two features are of primary importance: reliability and validity. In this section we shall discuss the concept of reliability; we shall treat the concept of validity in the next chapter.

As we noted earlier, the main purpose of psychological measurement is to make decisions about individuals, but if measurement procedures are to be useful in a practical sense, they must produce dependable scores. The typical selection situation is unlike that at a shooting gallery where the customer gets 25 shots for a quarter; if he misses his target on the first shot, he still has 24 tries left. In the case of a job applicant, however, he or she usually only gets one shot. It is important, therefore, to make that shot count, to present the "truest" picture of one's abilities or personal characteristics. Yet potentially there are numerous sources of error, that is, unwanted variation (Cronbach, 1990), that can distort that "true" picture. Human behavior tends to fluctuate from time to time and from situation to situation. In addition, the measurement procedure itself contains only a sample of all possible questions and is administered at only one out of many possible times.

Our goal in psychological measurement is to minimize these sources of error—in the particular sampling of items, in the circumstances surrounding the administration of the procedure, and in the applicant—so that the "truest" picture of each applicant's abilities might emerge. In making decisions about individuals, it is imperative from an efficiency stand-

point (i.e., minimizing the number of errors) as well as from a moral/ethical standpoint (i.e., fairness to the individuals involved) that our measurement procedures be dependable, consistent, and stable—in short, as reliable as possible.

Reliability of a measurement procedure refers to its freedom from unsystematic errors of measurement. A test taker or employee may perform differently on one occasion than on another for any number of reasons. He or she may try harder, be more fatigued, more anxious, or simply more familiar with the content of questions on one test form than on another. For these and other reasons, a person's performance will not be perfectly consistent from one occasion to the next (American Psychological Association, 1985).

Such differences may be attributable to what are commonly called unsystematic errors of measurement. However, the differences are not attributable to errors of measurement if experience, training, or some other event has made the differences meaningful, or if inconsistency of response is relevant to what is being measured (for example, changes in attitudes from Time 1 to Time 2). Measurement errors reduce the reliability, and therefore the generalizability, of a person's score from a single measurement.

The critical question is the definition of error. Factors that might be considered irrelevant to the purposes of measurement (and therefore error) in one situation might be considered germane to measurement in another situation. Each of the different kinds of reliability attempts to identify and measure error in a different way, as we shall see. Theoretically, therefore, there could exist as many varieties of reliability as there are conditions affecting scores, since for any given purpose, such conditions might be irrelevant or serve to produce inconsistencies in measurement and thus be classified as error. In practice, however, the types of reliability actually computed are few.

ESTIMATION OF RELIABILITY

Since all types of reliability are concerned with the degree of consistency or agreement between two sets of independently-derived scores, the correlation coefficient (in this context termed a **reliability coefficient**) is a particularly appropriate measure of such agreement. Assuming errors of measurement occur randomly, the distribution of differences between pairs of scores for a group of individuals tested twice will be similar to the distribution of the various pairs of scores for the same individual if he or she were tested a large number of times (Brown, 1983). To the extent that each individual measured occupies the same relative position in each of the two sets of measurements, the correlation will be high; it will drop to the extent that there exist random, uncorrelated errors of measurement, which serve to alter relative positions in the two sets of measurements. It can be shown mathematically (Allen and Yen, 1979; Gulliksen, 1950) that the reliability coefficient may be interpreted directly as the percentage of total variance attributable to different sources (i.e., the coefficient of determination, r^2). For example, a reliability coefficient of .90 indicates that 90 percent of the variance in test scores is due to systematic variance in the characteristic or trait measured, and only 10 percent is due to error variance (as error is defined operationally in the method used to compute reliability). The utility of the reliability coefficient in evaluating measurement, therefore, is that it provides an estimate of the proportion of total variance that is systematic or "true" variance.

Reliability as a concept is therefore purely theoretical, wholly fashioned out of the assumption that obtained scores are composed of "true" and random error components. Yet high reliability is absolutely essential for measurement because it serves as an upper bound for validity. Only systematic variance is predictable, and theoretically a test cannot predict a criterion any better than it can predict itself.

In practice, reliability coefficients may serve one or both of two purposes: (1) to estimate the precision of a particular procedure as a measuring instrument, or (2) to estimate the consistency of performance on the procedure by the examinees. Note, however, that the second purpose of reliability includes the first. Logically it is possible to have unreliable performance by an examinee on a reliable test, but reliable examinee performance on an unreliable instrument is impossible (Wesman, 1952). These purposes can easily be seen in the various methods used to estimate reliability. Each of the methods we shall discuss—test-retest, alternate forms, internal consistency, and scorer reliability—takes into account somewhat different conditions that might produce unsystematic changes in test scores and consequently affect the test's error of measurement.

Test-Retest

The simplest and most direct estimate of reliability is obtained by administering the same form of a test (or other measurement procedure) to the same group of examinees on two different occasions. Scores from both occasions are then correlated to yield a **coefficient of stability.** The experimental procedure is as follows:

Test————————————————→**Retest**

Time > 0

In this model, error is attributed to random fluctuations in performance across occasions. Its particular relevance lies in the time interval over which the tests are administered. Since the interval may vary from a day or less to more than several years, different stability coefficients will be obtained depending on the length of the time span between testings. Thus, there is not one but theoretically an infinite number of stability coefficients for any measurement procedure. However, the magnitude of the correlations tends to show a uniform decrement over time (Cureton, 1965; Hartigan and Wigdor, 1989). When reported in a research report, a stability coefficient always should include the length of the time interval over which it was computed (e.g., Lubinski, Benbow, and Ryan, 1995). Skewed data also reduce the size of obtained reliability estimates. To overcome that problem, consider transforming the skewed data to a more symmetrical distribution before performing correlational analyses (Dunlap, Chen, and Greer, 1994).

Since the stability coefficient involves two administrations, any variable that affects the performance of some individuals on one administration and not on the other will introduce random error and, therefore, reduce reliability. Such errors may be associated with differences in administration (poor lighting or loud noises and distractions on one occasion) or with differences in the individual taking the test (e.g., due to mood, fatigue, personal problems). However, since the same test is administered on both occasions, error due to different samples of test items is not reflected in the stability coefficient.

What is the appropriate length of the time interval between administrations, and with what types of measurement procedures should the stability coefficient be used? The interval between retests should not be immediate, and only rarely should it exceed 6 months (Anastasi, 1988). In general, the retest technique is appropriate if the interval between administrations is long enough to offset the effects of practice. Although the technique is inappropriate for the large majority of psychological measures, it may be used with tests of sensory discrimination (e.g., color vision, hearing) or with psychomotor tests (e.g., eye-hand coordination), or for tests of knowledge that include the entire range of information within a restricted topic. It also is used in criterion measurement, for example, when performance is measured on different occasions.

PARALLEL (OR ALTERNATE) FORMS

Since any measurement procedure contains only a sample of the possible items from some content domain, theoretically it is possible to construct a number of parallel forms of the same procedure (each comprising the same number and difficulty of items, and each yielding nonsignificant differences in means, variances, and intercorrelations with other variables). This is shown graphically in Figure 6–2.

This procedure often circumvents the problem of the stability coefficient. With parallel forms, we seek to evaluate the consistency of scores from one form to another (alternate) form of the same procedure. The correlation between the scores obtained on the two forms (known as the **coefficient of equivalence**) is a reliability estimate. The experimental procedure is as follows:

Form A————————————→**Form B**

Time = 0

Ideally both forms would be administered simultaneously. Since this is impossible, the two forms are administered as close together in time as is practical—generally within a few days of each other.

In order to guard against order effects, half of the examinees should receive Form A followed by Form B, and the other half, Form B followed by Form A.

FIGURE 6–2 Measurement Procedures as Samples from a Content Domain.

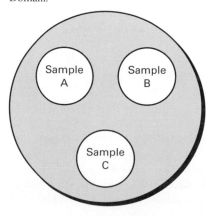

Since the two forms are administered close together in time, short-term changes in conditions of administration or in individuals cannot be eliminated entirely. Thus, a pure measure of equivalence is impossible to obtain. As with stability estimates, statements of parallel-forms reliability always should include the length of the interval between administrations as well as a description of relevant intervening experiences.

In practice, equivalence is difficult to achieve. The problem is less serious with measures of well-defined traits, such as arithmetic ability or mechanical aptitude, but it becomes a much more exacting task to develop parallel forms for measures of personality, motivation, or temperament, which are not as well defined.

In addition to reducing the possibility of cheating, parallel forms are useful in evaluating the effects of some treatment (e.g., training) on a test of achievement. Since parallel forms are merely samples of items from the same content domain, some sampling error is inevitable. This serves to lower the correlation between the forms and, in general, provides a rather conservative estimate of reliability.

Stability and Equivalence

A combination of the two methods previously discussed can be used to estimate reliability simply by lengthening the time interval between administrations. The correlation between the two sets of scores would represent a **coefficient of stability and equivalence.** The procedure is as follows:

Form A————————————→**Form B**

Time > 0

Again, to guard against order effects, half of the examinees should receive Form A followed by Form B, and the other half Form B followed by Form A. Because all the factors that operate to produce inconsistency in scores in the test-retest design, plus all the factors that operate to produce inconsistency in the parallel forms design, can operate in this design, the coefficient of stability and equivalence will provide the most rigorous test and will give the lower bound of reliability. Although parallel forms are available for a large number of measurement procedures, they are expensive and frequently quite difficult to construct. For these reasons other techniques for assessing the effect of different samples of items on reliability were introduced—the methods of internal consistency.

Internal Consistency

A measure of reliability may be derived from a single administration of a test by splitting the test statistically into two equivalent halves after it has been given, thus yielding two scores for each individual. If the test is internally consistent, then any one item or set of items should be equivalent to any other item or set of items. Using split-half methods, error variance is attributed primarily to inconsistency in content sampling. In computing split-half reliability, the first problem is how to split the test in order to obtain two halves that are equivalent in content, difficulty, means, and standard deviations. In most instances it is possible to compute two separate scores for each individual based on his or her responses to odd items and even items. However, such estimates are not really estimates of internal consistency; rather they yield spuriously high reliability estimates based on equivalence (Guion, 1965).

A preferable approach is to select randomly the items for the two halves. Random selection should balance out errors to provide equivalence for the two halves as well as varying the number of consecutive items appearing in either half. A correlation coefficient computed on the basis of the two "half" tests will provide a reliability estimate of a test only half as long as the original. For example, if a test contains 60 items, a correlation would be computed between two sets of scores, each of which contains only 30 items. This coefficient underestimates the reliability of the 60-item test since reliability tends to increase with test length. A longer test (or other measurement procedure) provides a larger sample of the content domain and tends to produce a wider range of scores, both of which have the effect of raising a reliability estimate. However, lengthening a test increases only its consistency, not its stability over time (Cureton, 1965). The relationship between reliability and test length may be shown by the Spearman-Brown prophecy formula:

$$r_{nn} = \frac{nr_{11}}{1 + (n-1)r_{11}} \qquad (6\text{--}6)$$

where r_{nn} is the estimated reliability of a test n times as long as the test available, r_{11} is the obtained reliability coefficient, and n is the number of times the test is increased (or shortened). This formula is used widely to estimate reliability by the split-half method, in which case $n = 2$—that is, the test length is doubled. Under these conditions the formula simplifies to:

$$r_{11} = \frac{2r_{1/2\ 1/2}}{1 + r_{1/2\ 1/2}} \qquad (6\text{--}7)$$

where r_{11} is the reliability of the test "corrected" to full length and $r_{1/2\ 1/2}$ is the correlation computed between scores on the two half-tests.

For example, if the correlation between total scores on the odd- and even-numbered items is .80, then the estimated reliability of the whole test is:

$$r_{11} = \frac{2(.80)}{(1 + .80)} = .89$$

A split-half reliability estimate is interpreted as a **coefficient of equivalence,** but since the two parallel forms (halves) are administered simultaneously, only errors of such a short term that they affect one item will influence reliability. Therefore, since the fewest number of contaminating factors has a chance to operate using this method, corrected split-half correlation generally yields the highest estimate of reliability.

Kuder-Richardson Reliability

Most reliability estimates indicate consistency over time or forms of a test. Techniques that involve analysis of item variances are more appropriately termed measures of internal consistency since they indicate the degree to which the various items on a test are intercorrelated. The most widely used of these methods were presented by Kuder and Richardson (1937, 1939). As in the split-half method, internal consistency is found from a single administration. While there are many possible ways to split a test into halves, Cronbach (1951) has shown that the Kuder-Richardson reliability coefficient is actually the mean of all possible half-splits. Of the several formulas derived in the original article, the most useful is their formula 20 (KR-20):

$$r_{tt} = \frac{n}{n-1}\left(\frac{\sigma_t^2 - \Sigma pq}{\sigma_t^2}\right) \qquad (6\text{--}8)$$

where r_{tt} is the reliability coefficient of the whole test, n is the number of items in the test, and σ_t^2 is the variance of the total scores on the test. The final term, Σpq, is found by computing the proportion of the group who pass (p) and do not pass (q) each item, where $q = 1 - p$. The product of p and q is then computed for each item, and these products are added for all items to yield Σpq.

To the degree that test items are unrelated to each other, KR-20 will yield a lower estimate of reliability; to the extent that test items are interrelated (internally consistent), KR-20 will yield a higher estimate of reliability. KR-20 overestimates the reliability of speed tests, however, since values of *p* and *q* can be computed only if all persons in the group attempt each item. Stability or equivalence estimates are more appropriate with speed tests.

The KR-20 formula is appropriate for tests whose items are scored as right or wrong, or according to some other all-or-none system. On some measures, however, such as personality inventories, examinees may receive a different numerical score on an item, depending on whether they check "Always," "Sometimes," "Occasionally," or "Never." In these cases, a generalized formula for computing internal consistency reliability has been derived, known as coefficient alpha (Cronbach, 1951). The formula differs from KR-20 only in one term: Σpq is replaced by $\Sigma\sigma_i^2$, the sum of the variances of item scores. That is, one first finds the variance of all examinees' scores on each item, and then adds these variances across all items. The formula for coefficient alpha is, therefore:

$$r_{tt} = \frac{n}{n-1}\left(\frac{\sigma_t^2 - \Sigma\sigma_i^2}{\sigma_t^2}\right) \quad (6\text{--}9)$$

Alpha is a sound measure of error variance, but it is affected by the number of items (more items imply higher estimates), item intercorrelations, and dimensionality. Alpha can be used to confirm the unidimensionality of a scale, or to measure the strength of a dimension once the existence of a single factor has been determined (Cortina, 1993).

Scorer Reliability

Thus far we have considered errors due to instability over time, nonequivalence of samples of items, and item heterogeneity. These are attributable either to the examinee or to the measurement procedure. Errors also may be attributable to the examiner; this is known as **scorer variance.** The problem typically is not serious with objectively scored measures. However, with nonobjective measures (e.g., observational data that involve subtle discriminations), it may be acute. With the latter there is as great a need for scorer reliability as there is for the more usual types of reliability. The reliability of ratings may be defined as the degree to which the ratings are free from error variance arising either from the ratee or from the rater (Guion, 1965).

Scorer reliability can be estimated by having a sample of tests (or ratees) independently scored (or rated) by two scorers (or raters who are familiar with ratee performance). The two scores for each ratee are then correlated as usual, to yield an estimate of scorer

reliability. In the case of dichotomous ratings (e.g., satisfactory or unsatisfactory), reliability may be estimated by determining the percentage of agreement between pairs of raters. Finally, if only one stimulus (e.g., a test, a ratee) is rated, then scorer reliability should be assessed by the standard deviation of the ratings across raters, as well as by the standard error of the mean rating and its associated confidence intervals (Schmidt and Hunter, 1989). Alternatively, an index of within-group interrater agreement (r_{wg}) has been proposed by James, Demaree, and Wolf (1993).

Note, however, that scorer reliability is not a "real" reliability coefficient since it provides no information about the measurement procedure itself. While it does contribute some evidence of reliability (since objectivity of scoring is a factor that contributes to reliability), it simply provides a statement of how much confidence we may have that two scorers (or raters) will arrive at similar scores (or ratings) for a given individual.

SUMMARY

The different kinds of reliability coefficients and their sources of error variance are presented graphically in Table 6–2.

At this point it should be obvious that there is no such thing as *the* reliability of a test. Different sources of error are accounted for in the different methods used to estimate reliability. The APA *Standards for Educational and Psychological Testing* (1985) emphasizes this point:

> Reliability coefficient is a generic term. Different reliability coefficients and estimates of components of

TABLE 6–2 Sources of Error Variance in Relation to Reliability Coefficients

Type of Reliability Coefficient	Error Variance
Test-retest	Time sampling
Alternate-form (immediate)	Content sampling
Alternate-form (delayed)	Time sampling and content sampling
Split-half	Content sampling
Kuder-Richardson and Coefficient Alpha	Content sampling and content heterogeneity
Scorer	Interscorer differences

Source: Reprinted with permission of Macmillan Publishing Company from *Psychological Testing*, 6th ed., by Anne Anastasi, p. 126. Copyright © 1988 by Dr. Anne Anastasi.

TABLE 6–3 Sources of Error Variance in Test X

From parallel form (delayed):	$1 - .75 = .25$	(time and content sampling)
From parallel form (immediate):	$1 - .85 = \underline{.15}$	(content sampling)
Difference:	.10	(time sampling)
From scorer reliability:	$1 - .94 = .06$	(interscorer difference)
Total measured error variance:	$.15 + .10 + .06 = .31$	
Systematic or "true" variance:	$1 - .31 = .69$	

measurement error can be based on various types of evidence; each type of evidence suggests a different meaning. . . . Thus the estimation of clearly labeled components of observed and error score variance is a particularly useful outcome of a reliability study, both for the test developer who wishes to improve the reliability of an instrument and for the user who wants to interpret test scores in particular circumstances with maximum understanding. [p. 19]

A simple example should serve to illustrate how the various components of total score variance may be partitioned. Suppose we have reliability estimates of equivalence and of stability and equivalence. Assume that the equivalence estimate is .85 and that the stability and equivalence estimate is .75. In addition, suppose a random sample of tests is rescored independently by a second rater, yielding a scorer reliability of .94. The various components of variance now may be partitioned as in Table 6–3.

Note that by subtracting the error variance due to content sampling alone (.15) from the error variance due to time and content sampling (.25), 10 percent of the variance can be attributed to time sampling alone. When all three components are added together—that

is, the error variance attributable to content sampling (.15), time sampling (.10), and scorer variance (.06)— the total error variance is 31 percent, leaving 69 percent of the total variance attributable to systematic sources. These proportions are presented graphically in Figure 6–3.

INTERPRETATION OF RELIABILITY

Unfortunately, there is no fixed value below which reliability is unacceptable and above which it is satisfactory. It depends on what one plans to do with the scores. Brown (1983) has expressed the matter aptly:

> Reliability is not an end in itself but rather a step on a way to a goal. That is, unless test scores are consistent, they cannot be related to other variables with any degree of confidence. Thus reliability places limits on validity, and the crucial question becomes whether a test's reliability is high enough to allow satisfactory validity. [p. 88]

Hence, the more important the decision to be reached, the greater the need for confidence in the precision of the measurement procedure and the higher the required reliability coefficient. If a procedure is to be used for comparing one individual with another, reliability should be above .90. In practice, however, many standard tests with reliabilities as low as .70 prove to be very useful, and measures with reliabilities even lower than that may be useful for research purposes. This statement needs to be tempered by considering some other factors (in addition to speed, test length, and the interval between administrations) that may influence the size of an obtained reliability coefficient.

Range of Individual Differences

While the accuracy of measurement may remain unchanged, the size of a reliability estimate will vary with the range of individual differences in the group.

FIGURE 6–3 Proportional Distribution of Error Variance and Systematic Variance.

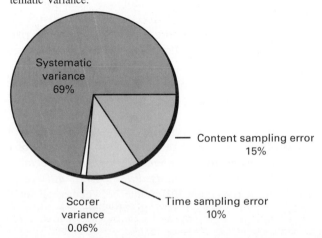

That is, as the variability of the scores increases (decreases), the correlation between them also increases (decreases).

This is an important consideration in performance measurement. Frequently the reliability of performance measures is low because of the homogeneous nature of the group in question (e.g., only individuals who are hired and stay long enough to provide performance data are included). Such underestimates serve to reduce or to attenuate validity coefficients, a fact that should be recognized.

Difficulty of the Measurement Procedure

Similar restrictions of the range of variability may result from measures that are too difficult (in which case all examinees do poorly) or too easy (in which case all examinees do extremely well). In order to maximize reliability, the level of difficulty should be such as to produce a wide range of scores, for there can be no correlation without variance.

Size and Representativeness of Sample

Although there is not necessarily a systematic relationship between the size of the sample and the size of the reliability coefficient, a reliability estimate based on a *large* number of cases will have a smaller sampling error than one based on just a *few* cases; in other words, the larger sample provides a more dependable estimate. This is shown easily when one considers the formula for the standard error of *r*:

$$\sigma_r = \frac{1 - r^2}{\sqrt{n - 1}} \qquad (6\text{--}10)$$

A reliability estimate of .70 based on a sample size of 26 yields an estimated standard error of .10; but the standard error with a sample of 101 is .05—a value only half as large as the first estimate. Not only must the sample be large, however; it also must be representative of the population for which the measurement is to be used. The reliability of a procedure designed to assess trainee performance cannot be determined adequately by administering it to experienced workers. Reliability coefficients become more meaningful the more closely the group on which the coefficient is based resembles the group about whose relative ability we need to decide.

STANDARD ERROR OF MEASUREMENT

The various kinds of reliability are important for evaluating measurement procedures, but they do not provide a direct indication of the amount of inconsistency or error to expect in an individual score. For this we need the **standard error of measurement,** a statistic expressed in test score (standard deviation) units but derived directly from the reliability coefficient. It may be expressed as:

$$\sigma_{\text{Meas}} = \sigma_x\sqrt{1 - r_{xx}} \qquad (6\text{--}11)$$

where σ_{Meas} = standard error of measurement, σ_x = the standard deviation of the distribution of obtained scores, and r_{xx} = the reliability coefficient. The standard error of measurement provides an estimate of the standard deviation of the normal distribution of scores that an individual would obtain if he or she took the test a large—in principle, an infinite—number of times. The mean of this hypothetical distribution is the individual's "true" score (Thurstone, 1931). Equation 6–11 demonstrates that the standard error of measurement increases as the reliability decreases. When r_{xx} = 1.0, there is no error in estimating an individual's true score from his or her observed score. When r_{xx} = 0.0, the error of measurement is a maximum and equal to the standard deviation of the observed scores.

The σ_{Meas} is a useful statistic because it enables us to talk about an individual's true and error scores. Given an observed score, σ_{Meas} enables us to estimate the range of score values that will, with a given probability, include the true score. In other words, we can establish confidence intervals. One also may use the σ_{Meas} to determine the amount of variability to expect upon retesting. To illustrate, assume the standard deviation of a group of observed scores is 7 and the reliability coefficient is .90. Then $\sigma_{\text{Meas}} = 7\sqrt{1 - .90} = 2.21$. Given an individual's score of 70, we can be 95 percent confident that on retesting the individual's score will be within about four points (1.96 σ_{Meas} = 1.96 × 2.21 = 4.33) of his original score and that his true score probably lies between (X_0 +/− 1.96 σ_{Meas}) or 65.67 and 74.33.

In personnel psychology the standard error of measurement is useful in three ways (Guion, 1965). First, *it can be used to determine whether the measures describing individuals differ significantly* (e.g., assuming a five-point difference between applicants, if the σ_{Meas} for the test is 6, the difference could certainly be attributed to chance). In fact, Gulliksen (1950) showed that the difference between the scores of two individuals on the same test should not be interpreted as significant unless it is equal to at least two standard errors of the difference (SED), where SED = SEM $\sqrt{2}$. Second, *it may be used to determine whether an individual measure is significantly different from some hypothetical true score.* For example, assuming a cutting score on a test is the true score, chances are two out of three that obtained scores will fall within +/− $1\sigma_{Meas}$ of the cutting score. Applicants within this range could have true scores above or below the cutting score; thus, the obtained score is "predicted" from a hypothetical true score.

A *third usage it to determine if a test discriminates differently in different groups* (e.g., high versus low ability). Assuming that the distribution of scores approaches normality and that obtained scores do not extend over the entire possible range, then σ_{Meas} will be very nearly equal for high-score levels and for low-score levels (Guilford and Fruchter, 1978). On the other hand, when subscale scores are computed, or because of peculiarities of the test itself, the test may do a better job of discriminating at one part of the score range than at another. Under these circumstances, the APA *Standards* (1985, p. 22) recommend that σ_{Meas} be reported for score levels at or near the cutscore. To do this, it is necessary to develop a scatter diagram that shows the relationship between two forms (or halves) of the same test. The standard deviations of the columns or rows at different score levels will indicate where predictions will have the greatest accuracy.

A final advantage of the σ_{Meas} is that *it forces one to think of test scores not as exact points, but rather as bands or ranges of scores.* Since measurement error is present, to some extent, in all psychological measures, such a view is both sound and proper.

GENERALIZABILITY THEORY

The discussion of reliability presented thus far is the classical or traditional approach. A more recent statistical approach, termed **generalizability theory,** conceptualizes the reliability of a test score as the precision with which that score, or sample, represents a more generalized universe value of the score (Cronbach, 1990; Cronbach, Gleser, Nanda, and Rajaratnam, 1972; Kraiger and Teachout, 1990).

In generalizability theory, observations (for example, examinees' scores on tests) are seen as samples from a universe of **admissible observations.** The universe describes the conditions under which examinees can be observed or tested that produce results that are equivalent to some specified degree. An examinee's **universe score** is defined to be the expected value of his or her observed scores over all admissible observations. The universe score is directly analogous to the true score used in classical reliability theory. Generalizability theory emphasizes that different universes exist and makes it the test publisher's responsibility to define carefully his or her universe. This definition is done in terms of **facets** or dimensions.

The use of generalizability theory involves conducting two types of research studies: a generalizability (*G*) study and a decision (*D*) study. A *G* study is done as part of the development of the measurement instrument. The main goal of the *G* study is to specify the degree to which test results are equivalent when obtained under different testing conditions. In simplified terms, a *G* study involves collecting data for examinees tested under specified conditions (that is, at various levels of specified facets), estimating variance components due to these facets and their interactions using analysis of variance, and producing coefficients of generalizability. A coefficient of generalizability is the ratio of universe-score variance to observed-score variance and is the counterpart of the reliability coefficient used in classical reliability theory. A test does not have one generalizability coefficient, but many, depending on the facets examined in the *G* study. The *G* study also provides information about how to estimate an examinee's universe score most accurately.

In a *D* study, the measurement instrument produces data to be used in making decisions or reaching conclusions, such as admitting people to programs. The information from the *G* study is used in interpreting the results of the *D* study and in reaching sound conclusions. Despite its statistical sophistication, however, generalizability theory has not replaced the classical theory of test reliability (Aiken, 1994).

INTERPRETING THE RESULTS OF MEASUREMENT PROCEDURES

In personnel psychology a knowledge of each person's individuality—his or her unique pattern of abilities, values, interests, and personality—is essential in programs designed to use human resources effectively.

Such knowledge enables us to make predictions about how individuals are likely to behave in the future. In order to interpret the results of measurement procedures intelligently, however, two kinds of information are essential: (1) evidence of validity, and (2) some information about how relevant others have performed on the same procedure. For example, Sarah is applying for admission to an industrial arts program at a local vocational school. As part of the admissions procedure she is given a mechanical aptitude test. She obtains a raw score of 48 correct responses out of a possible 68. Is this score average, above average, or below average? In and of itself, the score of 48 is meaningless because psychological measurement is relative rather than absolute. In order to interpret Sarah's score meaningfully, we need to compare her raw score to the distribution of scores of relevant others—that is, persons of approximately the same age, sex, and educational and regional background who were being tested for the same purpose. These persons make up a norm group. Theoretically there can be as many different norm groups as there are purposes for which a particular test is given and groups with different characteristics. Thus, Sarah's score of 48 may be about average when compared to her reference group, it might be distinctly above average when compared to the performance of a group of music majors, and it might represent markedly inferior performance in comparison to the performance of a group of instructor-mechanics. In short, norms must provide a relevant comparison group for the person being tested.

Immediately after the introduction of a testing or other measurement program, it may be necessary to use norms published in the test manual, but local norms (based on the scores of applicants in a specific organization or geographical area) should be prepared as soon as 100 or more cases become available. These norms should be revised from time to time as additional data accumulate (Ricks, 1971). In employment selection, local norms are especially desirable since they are more representative and fit specific organizational purposes more precisely. Local norms allow comparisons between the applicant's score and those of her immediate competitors.

Up to this point we have been referring to normative comparisons in terms of "average," "above average," or "below average." Obviously we need a more precise way of expressing each individual's position relative to the norm group. This is accomplished easily by converting raw scores into some relative measure—usually percentile ranks or standard scores. The percentile rank of a given raw score refers to the percentage of persons in the norm group who fall below it. Standard scores may be expressed either as z scores (i.e., the distance of each raw score from the mean in standard deviation units) or as some modification of the z score that eliminates negative numbers and decimal notation. A hypothetical norm table is presented in Table 6–4. The relationships between percentile ranks, standard scores, and the normal curve are presented graphically in Figure 6–4.

Note that there are no raw scores on the baseline of the curve. The baseline is presented in a generalized form, marked off in standard deviation units. For example, if the mean of a distribution of scores is 30 and if the standard deviation is 8, then +/− 1σ corresponds to 38 (30 + 8) and 22 (30 − 8) respectively. Also, since the total area under the curve represents the total distribution of scores, we can mark off subareas of the total corresponding to +/− 1, 2, 3, and 4 standard deviations. The numbers in these subareas are percentages of the total number of people. Thus, in a normal distribution of scores, roughly two-thirds (68.26%) of all cases lie between plus and minus one standard deviation. This same area also includes scores that lie above the 16th percentile (− 1σ) and below the 84th percentile (+ 1σ). In the previous example, if an individual scores 38, we may conclude that this score is 1σ above the mean and ranks at the 84th percentile of persons on whom the test was normed (provided the distribution of scores in the norm group approximates a normal curve).

Percentile ranks, while easy to compute and understand, suffer from two major limitations. First, they

TABLE 6–4 Norms for 423 Machine Tool Operator Applicants in X Company on a Test of Mechanical Comprehension		
Raw Score	*Percentile*	*z Score*
50	99	+ 2.2
46	98	+ 2.0
42	90	+ 1.3
38	84	+ 1.0
34	66	+ 0.4
30	50	+ 0.0
26	34	− 0.1
22	16	− 1.0
18	88	− 1.3
14	82	− 2.0
10	81	− 2.2

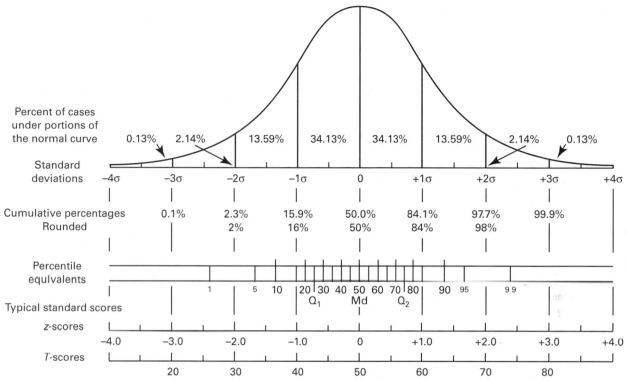

From *Test Service Bulletin*, No. 48. Princeton, N.J.: Educational Testing Service, 1955.

FIGURE 6–4 Normal Curve Chart Showing Relationships between Percentiles and Standard Scores.

are ranks and, therefore, ordinal-level measures; they cannot legitimately be added, subtracted, multiplied, or divided. Second, percentile ranks have a rectangular distribution, while test score distributions generally approximate the normal curve. Therefore, percentile units are not equivalent at all points along the scale. Note that on the percentile equivalents scale in Figure 6–4, the percentile distance between percentile ranks 5 and 10 (or 90 and 95) is distinctly greater than the distance between 45 and 50, although the numerical distances are the same. This tendency of percentile units to become progressively smaller toward the center of the scale causes special difficulties in the interpretation of change. Thus, the differences in achievement represented by a shift from 45 to 50 and from 94 to 99 are not equal on the percentile rank scale since the distance from 45 to 50 is much smaller than that from 94 to 99. In short, if you use percentiles, give greater weight to rank differences at the extremes of the scale than to those at the center.

Standard scores, on the other hand, are interval-scale measures (that by definition possess equal-size units) and, therefore, can be subjected to the common arithmetic operations. In addition, they allow direct comparison of an individual's performance on different measures. For example, as part of a selection battery, three measures with the following means and standard deviations (in a sample of applicants) are used:

	Mean	Std. Deviation
Test 1 (scorable application)	30	5
Test 2 (written test)	500	100
Test 3 (interview)	100	10

Applicant A scores 35 on Test 1, 620 on Test 2, and 105 on Test 3. What does this tell us about his or her overall performance? Assuming each of the tests possesses some validity by itself, converting each of these scores to standard score form, we find that applicant A scores $(35 - 30)/5 = +1\sigma$ on Test 1, $(620 - 500)/100 = +1.2\sigma$ on Test 2, and $(105 - 100)/10 = +.5\sigma$ on Test 3. Applicant A appears to be a good bet.

One of the disadvantages of z scores, however, is that they involve decimals and negative numbers. To avoid this, z scores may be transformed to a different scale by adding or multiplying by a constant. Although many such derived scores are commonly in use, most of them are based on z. One of the most popular is the Z scale, in which the mean and standard deviation are set equal to 50 and 10, respectively. The transformation is simply:

$$Z = 50 + 10z \qquad (6\text{--}12)$$

While Z does eliminate decimals and negative numbers, since it is a linear transformation, the shape of the transformed scores will be similar to that of the raw scores. If the distribution of the raw scores is skewed, the distribution of the transformed scores also will be skewed. This can be avoided by converting raw scores into normalized standard scores. To compute normalized standard scores, first compute percentile ranks of raw scores. Then, from a table of areas under the normal curve, locate the z score corresponding to each percentile rank. In order to get rid of decimals and negative numbers, transform the z scores into T scores by the formula:

$$T = 50 + 10z \qquad (6\text{--}13)$$

Note that the right sides of Equations 6–12 and 6–13 are identical. The only difference is that T scores are normalized standard scores, whereas z scores are simple linear transformations.

Normalized standard scores are satisfactory for most purposes since they serve to smooth out sampling errors, but all distributions should not be normalized as a matter of course. Use a normalizing transformation only when the sample is large and representative and when there is reason to believe that the deviation from normality results from defects in the measurement procedure rather than from characteristics of the sample or from other factors affecting the behavior under consideration (Anastasi, 1988). Of course, when the original distribution of scores is approximately normal, the linearly-derived scores and the normalized scores will be quite similar.

Discussion Questions

1. Why are psychological measures considered to be nominal or ordinal in nature?

2. Is it proper to speak of *the* reliability of a test? Why or why not?

3. Which methods of estimating reliability produce the highest and lowest (most conservative) estimates?

4. What does the standard error of measurement tell the HR specialist?

5. What do test norms tell us? What do they not tell us?

* * *

In the introduction to this section, we emphasized that adequate interpretation of test scores requires both normative data and validity data. Yet norms tables in and of themselves give no direct indication of validity or of the outcomes that might be associated with a particular test score. This problem is particularly acute in employment decision making where measurement procedures are used as vehicles for forecasting performance.

Methods are available for expressing raw scores in outcome terms (e.g., expectancy charts), but since such issues are directly relevant to the application and practical use of individual differences measures, we will consider them more fully in the next chapter.

VALIDATION AND USE OF INDIVIDUAL DIFFERENCES MEASURES

AT A GLANCE

Scores from measures of individual differences derive meaning only insofar as they can be related to other psychologically meaningful characteristics of behavior. The processes of gathering or evaluating the necessary data are called **validation.** Two issues are of primary concern in validation—what a test or other procedure measures and how well it measures. Validity can be assessed in several ways: by analyzing the procedure's content (content-related evidence), by relating scores on the procedure to measures of performance on some relevant criterion (predictive and concurrent designs), or by more thoroughly investigating the extent to which the procedure measures some psychological construct (construct-related evidence). In many cases, validity may generalize over time, people, situations, and criteria. The processes of cross-validation and meta-analysis are used to investigate the extent to which variation in these factors actually does affect generalizability.

Although the validity of individual differences measures is fundamental to competent HR practice, there is another, perhaps more urgent, reason why both public and private sector organizations are concerned over this issue. Legal guidelines on employee selection procedures require comprehensive, documented validity evidence for any procedure used as a basis for an employment decision if that procedure produces an adverse impact against a protected group.

RELIABILITY AND VALIDITY

Theoretically, it would be possible to develop a perfectly reliable measure whose scores were wholly uncorrelated with any other variable. Such a measure would have no practical value, nor could it be interpreted meaningfully, since its scores could be related to nothing other than scores on another administration of the same measure. It would be highly reliable, but would have no validity. Scores from individual differences measures derive meaning only insofar as they can be related to other psychologically meaningful characteristics of behavior.

Thus, high reliability is a necessary but not sufficient condition for high validity. Mathematically, it can be shown (Ghiselli et al., 1981) that:

$$r_{xy} \leq \sqrt{r_{xx}} \qquad \text{(7–1)}$$

where r_{xy} is the obtained validity coefficient (a correlation between scores on procedure X and an external criterion, Y) and r_{xx} is the reliability of the procedure. Hence, reliability serves as a limit or ceiling for validity. Conversely, validity is reduced by the unreliability in a set of measures. Some degree of unreliability, however, is unavoidably present in criteria as well as in predictors. When the reliability of the criterion is known, it is possible to correct statistically for such unreliability by the following formula:

$$r_{x_0 T_y} = \frac{r_{xy}}{\sqrt{r_{yy}}} \qquad (7\text{--}2)$$

where $r_{x_0 T_y}$ is the correlation between scores on some procedure and a perfectly reliable criterion, r_{xy} is the observed validity coefficient, and r_{yy} is the reliability of the criterion. This formula is known as the *correction for attenuation in the criterion variable only*. In personnel psychology this correction is extremely useful, for it enables us to use as criteria some measures that are highly relevant, yet unreliable. The formula allows us to evaluate an obtained validity coefficient in terms of how high it is relative to the upper bound imposed by the unreliability of the criterion.

To illustrate, assume we have obtained a validity coefficient of .50 between a test and a criterion. Assume also a criterion reliability of .30, an extremely unreliable measure. That is, only 30 percent of the variance in the criterion is systematic enough to be predictable, and the other 70 percent is attributable to error sources. Substituting these values into Equation 7–2:

$$r_{x_0 T_y} = \frac{.50}{\sqrt{.30}} = \frac{.50}{.547} = .91$$

The validity coefficient would have been .91 if the criterion had been perfectly reliable. The coefficient of determination (r^2) for this hypothetical correlation is, therefore, .83–83 percent of the total explainable variance. Let us now compare this result to the original values. The obtained validity coefficient (.50) yields a coefficient of determination of .25—that is, about 25 percent of the variance in the criterion is associated with variance in the test. This represents 83 percent (.25 is 83% of .30) of the total explainable variance. This is obviously adequate prediction within the limits of criterion unreliability.

Combined knowledge of reliability and validity makes possible practical evaluation of predictors in specific situations. While the effect of the correction for attenuation should never be a consideration when one is deciding how to evaluate a measure as it exists, such information does give the HR specialist a basis for deciding whether there is enough unexplained systematic variance in the criterion to justify a search for more and better predictors. However, if a researcher makes a correction for attenuation in the criterion, he or she should report both the corrected and uncorrected coefficients, as well as all statistics used in the correction (APA *Standards,* 1985).

One additional point is in order. Examination of the right side of Equation 7–2 will show that since the value of the criterion reliability is in the denominator, estimates of criterion reliability should be too high rather than too low since their effect is to produce more conservative corrections for attenuation. For this reason, estimates of criterion reliability based upon coefficients of equivalence and of stability are not recommended since both provide low estimates of reliability, thus yielding exaggerated estimates of probable validity.

EVIDENCE OF VALIDITY

Traditionally, validity was viewed as the extent to which a measurement procedure actually measures what it is designed to measure. Such a view is inadequate, for it implies that a procedure has only one validity, which is determined by a single study. On the contrary, a thorough knowledge of the interrelationships between scores from a particular procedure and other variables typically requires many investigations. The investigative processes of gathering or evaluating the necessary data are called **validation** (APA *Standards,* 1985). Various methods of validation revolve around two issues: (1) *what* a test or other procedure measures (i.e., the hypothesized underlying trait or construct), and (2) *how well* it measures (i.e., the relationship between scores from the procedure and some external criterion measure).

Validity is a unitary concept. There are not different "kinds" of validity, only different kinds of evidence for analyzing validity (Binning and Barrett, 1989). Although evidence of validity may be accumulated in many ways, validity always refers to the degree to which the evidence supports inferences that are made from the scores. Validity is neither a single number nor a single argument, but an inference from all of the available evidence (Guion and Gibson, 1988). It is the *inferences* regarding the specific uses of a test or other measurement procedure that are validated, not the test itself (APA *Standards,* 1985). Hence a user first must specify exactly *why* he or she intends to use a selection measure (i.e., what inferences are to be made from it). This suggests a hypothesis about the relationship between measures of human attributes and measures of work behavior, and hypothesis testing is what validation is all about (Guion, 1976).

In short, the user makes a *judgment* about the adequacy of the available evidence of validity in support of a particular instrument when used for a particular purpose. The extent to which score meaning and action implications hold across persons or population groups and across settings or contexts is a persistent empirical question. This is the main reason that validity is an evolving property and validation a continuing process (Messick, 1995).

While there are numerous procedures available for evaluating validity, the APA *Standards* (1985) use three principal strategies: **content-related evidence, criterion-related evidence** (predictive and concurrent), and **construct-related evidence.** These strategies for analyzing validity differ in terms of the kinds of inferences that may be drawn. Although they can be discussed independently, they are interrelated operationally and logically, and in the following sections we shall consider the basic concepts underlying each of them.

CONTENT-RELATED EVIDENCE

Inferences about validity based upon content-related evidence are concerned with whether or not a measurement procedure contains a fair sample of the universe of situations it is supposed to represent. Since this process involves making inferences from a sample to a population, an evaluation of content-related evidence is made in terms of the adequacy of the sampling. Such evaluation is usually a rational, judgmental process.

In employment settings we are principally concerned with making inferences about a job performance domain—an identifiable segment or aspect of the job performance universe that has been defined and about which inferences are to be made (Lawshe, 1975). Three assumptions underlie the use of content-related evidence: (1) the area of concern to the user can be conceived as a meaningful, definable universe of responses; (2) a sample can be drawn from the universe in some purposeful, meaningful fashion; and (3) the sample and the sampling process can be defined with sufficient precision to enable the user to judge how adequately the sample of performance typifies performance on the universe.

In achievement testing the universe can be identified and defined rigorously, but most jobs have several job performance domains. Most often, therefore, we identify and define operationally a job perfor-

mance domain that is only a segment of the job performance universe (e.g., a computer-based typing test administered to a secretary whose job performance universe consists of several job performance domains, only one of which is typing). The behaviors constituting job performance domains range from those behaviors that are directly observable, to those that are reportable, to those that are highly abstract.

The higher the level of abstraction, the greater is the "inferential leap" required to demonstrate validity by other than a criterion-related approach. At the "observation" end of the continuum, sound judgments by job incumbents, supervisors, or other job experts usually can be made. Content-related evidence derived from procedures such as simple proficiency tests, job knowledge tests, and work sample tests is most appropriate under these circumstances. At the "abstract" end of the continuum (e.g., inductive reasoning), construct-related evidence is appropriate.". . .within the middle range of the content-construct continuum, the distinction between content and construct should be determined functionally, in relation to the job. If the quality measured is not unduly abstract, and if it constitutes a significant aspect of the job, content validation of the test component used to measure that quality should be permitted" (*Guardians Assn. of N.Y. City Police Dept.* v. *Civil Service Comm. of City of N.Y.,* 1980, p. 47).

It is tempting to conclude from this that if a selection procedure focuses on work *products* (like typing), then content-related evidence is appropriate. If the focus is on work *processes* (like reasoning ability), then content-related evidence is not appropriate. However, even work products (like typing) are determined by work processes (like producing a sample of typed copy). Typing *ability* implies an inference about an underlying characteristic on which individuals differ. That continuum is not directly observable. Instead, we illuminate the continuum by gathering a sample of behavior that is hypothesized to vary as a function of that underlying attribute. In that sense, typing ability is no different from reasoning ability, or "strength," or memory. None of them can be observed directly (Landy, 1986).

So the question is not *if* constructs are being measured, but what *class* of constructs is being measured. Once that has been determined, procedures can be identified for examining the appropriateness of inferences based on measures of those constructs (Tenopyr, 1977; 1984). Procedures used to support inferences drawn from measures of personality constructs (like emotional stability) differ from procedures used to support inferences from measures of ability constructs (like typing ability). The distinction between a content-related strategy and a construct-related strategy is therefore a matter of degree, fundamentally because constructs underlie *all* psychological measurement.

Operationally, content-related evidence may be evaluated in terms of the extent to which members of a *Content Evaluation Panel* perceive overlap between the test and the job performance domain. The extent of overlap can be determined quantitatively (Lawshe, 1975), and the procedure is as follows.

Each member of a Content Evaluation Panel (comprising an equal number of incumbents and supervisors) is presented with a set of test items and independently indicates whether the skill (or knowledge) measured by each item is essential, useful but not essential, or not necessary to the performance of the job. Responses from all panelists are then pooled, and the number indicating "essential" for each item is determined. A Content Validity Ratio (CVR) is then determined for each item

$$\text{CVR} = \frac{n_e - N/2}{N/2} \qquad (7\text{--}3)$$

where n_e is the number of panelists indicating "essential" and N is the total number of panelists. Items are eliminated if the CVR fails to meet statistical significance (as determined from a table presented by Lawshe, 1975). The mean CVR value of the retained items (the Content Validity Index, CVI) is then computed. The CVI represents the extent to which perceived overlap exists between capability to function in a job performance domain and performance on the test under investigation.

However, since content-related evidence is concerned primarily with inferences about test *construction* rather than with inferences about test *scores*, and since by definition all validity is the accuracy of inferences about test scores, that which has been called "content validity" is really not validity at all (Tenopyr, 1977). Perhaps instead we should call it *content-oriented test development* (Guion, 1987). This is not intended to minimize its importance.

> Some would say that content validity is inferior to, or less scientifically respectable than, criterion-related validity. This view is mistaken in my opinion. Content validity is the only basic foundation for any kind of validity. If the test does not have it, the criterion measures used to validate the test must have it. And one

should never apologize for having to exercise judgment in validating a test. Data never substitute for good judgment [Ebel, 1977, p. 59].

Nevertheless, in employment situations, the use of scores from a procedure developed on the basis of content also has a predictive basis. That is, one measures performance in a domain of job activities that will be performed later. Major concern, then, should be with the *predictive* aspects of tests used for employment decisions, rather than with the descriptive aspects. Surely scores from a well-developed typing test can be used to describe a person's skill at manipulating a keyboard, but description is not our primary purpose when we use a typing test to make hiring decisions. We use the typing score to *predict* how successfully someone will perform a job involving typing (Landy, 1986).

Content-related evidence of validity is extremely important in criterion measurement. For example, quantitative indicators (e.g., CVI values or an index of profile similarity between job content and training content) can be applied meaningfully to the evaluation of job knowledge criteria or training program content. Such evidence then permits objective evaluation of the representativeness of the behavioral content of employment programs (Distefano, Pryer, and Craig, 1980; Faley and Sundstrom, 1985).

A further issue concerns fairness. Questions of fairness may arise in relation to job content domains or individual items, but they are much more likely to stem from scores or ratings of probationary performance or from bias in scoring work sample or job knowledge tests. Alternative explanations for the meaning of scores suggest hypotheses to be investigated (e.g., through policy-capturing research) using the logic of construct-related evidence. In short, disconfirmatory studies of alternative interpretations are needed (Guion, 1978). If the alternative interpretations are not disconfirmed, then there is reason to question the fairness of the test, no matter how job-related the behavioral content domain seems to be or how well it has been sampled.

In summary, although content-related evidence of validity does have its limitations, undeniably it has made a positive contribution by directing attention toward (1) improved domain sampling and job analysis procedures, (2) better behavior measurement, and (3) the role of expert judgment for confirming the fairness of sampling and scoring procedures and for determining the degree of overlap between separately-derived content domains (Dunnette and Borman, 1979).

CRITERION-RELATED EVIDENCE

Whenever measures of individual differences are used to *predict* behavior, and it is technically feasible, criterion-related evidence of validity is called for. With this approach, we test the hypothesis that test scores are related to performance on some criterion measure. In the case of content-related evidence, the criterion is expert judgment. More often, however, the criterion is a score or a rating that either is available at the time of predictor measurement or will become available at a later time. If the criterion measure is available at the same time as scores on the predictor, then concurrent evidence of validity is being assessed. In contrast, if criterion data will not become available until some time after the predictor scores are obtained, then predictive evidence of validity is being measured. Both designs involve the same paradigm, in which a relationship is established between predictor and criterion performance:

Predictor performance→Criterion performance

(Measure of relationship)

Operationally, predictive and concurrent studies may be distinguished on the basis of time. A **predictive study** is oriented toward the future and involves a time interval during which events take place (e.g., people are trained or gain experience on a job). A **concurrent study** is oriented toward the present and reflects only the status quo at a particular time.

Logically, the distinction is based not on time, but on the objectives of measurement (Anastasi, 1988). Thus, each type of validity strategy is appropriate under different circumstances. A concurrent study is relevant to measures employed for the description of existing status rather than for the prediction of future outcomes (e.g., achievement tests, tests for certification). In the employment context, the difference can be illustrated by asking "Can Laura do the job now?" (concurrent design), and "Is it likely that Laura will be able to do the job?" (predictive design).

The term **criterion-related** calls attention to the fact that the fundamental concern is with the relationship between predictor and criterion scores, not with predictor scores per se. Scores on the predictor function primarily as signs (Wernimont and Campbell, 1968) pointing to something else—criterion performance. In short, the content of the predictor measure is relatively unimportant, for it serves only as a vehicle to predict criterion performance. However, since even the simplest jobs are multidimensional in nature, theoretically, there can be as many statements of criterion-related evidence of validity as there are criteria to be predicted.

Predictive Studies

Predictive designs for obtaining evidence of criterion-related validity are the cornerstone of individual differences measurement. When the objective is to forecast behavior on the basis of scores on a predictor measure, there is simply no substitute for it. Predictive studies demonstrate in an objective, statistical manner the actual relationship between predictors and criteria in a particular situation. In this model, a procedure's ability to predict is readily apparent, but in the concurrent model, predictive ability must be inferred by the decision maker. In conducting a predictive study, the procedure is as follows:

1. Measure candidates for the job.
2. Select candidates without using the results of the measurement procedure.
3. Obtain measurements of criterion performance at some later date.
4. Assess the strength of the predictor-criterion relationship.

In planning validation research, certain issues deserve special consideration. One of these is sample size. Inadequate sample sizes are quite often the result of practical constraints on the number of available subjects, but sometimes they simply reflect a lack of rational research planning. Actually the issue of sample size is just one aspect of the more basic issue of statistical power, that is, the probability of rejecting a null hypothesis when it is, in fact, false. As Cohen (1988) has noted, in this broader perspective any statistical test of a null hypothesis may be viewed as a complex relationship among four parameters: (1) the power of the test ($1-\beta$, where beta is the probability of making a Type II error); (2) alpha, the region of rejection of the null hypothesis and whether the test is one-tailed or two-tailed (power increases as alpha increases); (3) sample size, n (power increases as n increases); and (4) the magnitude of the effect in the population or the degree of departure from the null hypothesis (power increases as the effect size increases). The four parameters are so related that when any three of them are fixed, the fourth is completely determined.

The importance of power analysis as a research planning tool is considerable, for if power turns out to be insufficient the research plans can be revised (or dropped if revisions are impossible) so that power may be increased (usually by increasing *n* and sometimes by increasing alpha). To be sure, *post hoc* power analyses, conducted after validation efforts are completed, are of doubtful utility, and frequently overestimate the average power of statistical tests (Gillett, 1994).

Alternatively, rational research planning may proceed by specifying alpha (usually .05 or .01), a desired power (e.g., .80), and an estimated population effect size.

Effect size may be estimated by examining the values obtained in related previous work; by positing some minimum population effect that would have either practical or theoretical significance; or by using conventional definitions of "small" (.10), "medium" (.30), or "large" (.50) effects, where values in parentheses are correlation coefficients. Once alpha, power, and an effect size have been specified, required sample size then can be determined, and tables are available for this purpose (Cohen, 1988).

Power analysis would present little difficulty if population effect sizes could be specified easily. In criterion-related validity studies, they frequently are overestimated, as Schmidt, Hunter, and Urry (1976) have noted, because of a failure to consider the combined effects of range restriction in both the predictor and criterion and the effect of criterion unreliability.

Thus the sample sizes necessary to produce adequate power are much larger than typically has been assumed. Hundreds or even several thousand subjects may be necessary, depending on the type and degree of range restriction (Alexander et al., 1985; Alexander et al., 1989; Raju, Edwards, and LoVerde, 1985). What can be done?

Assuming that multiple predictors are used in a validity study and that each predictor accounts for some unique criterion variance, the effect size of a linear composite of the predictors is likely to be higher than the effect size of any single predictor in the battery. Since effect size is a major determinant of statistical power (and therefore of required sample size), more criterion-related validity studies may become technically feasible if researchers base their sample size requirements on unit-weighted linear composites of predictors rather than on individual predictors (Cascio, Valenzi, and Silbey, 1978; 1980). In short, larger effect sizes mean smaller required sample sizes to achieve adequate statistical power.

Alternatively, when sample size is fixed and effect size cannot be improved, it is still possible to maintain a targeted level of statistical power by manipulating alpha, the probability of a Type I error. To establish the alpha level required to maintain statistical power, all available information (including prior information about effect sizes) should be incorporated into the planning process. Cascio and Zedeck (1983) demonstrated procedures for doing this.

If none of these strategies is feasible, get as many cases as possible, recognize that sample sizes are too small, and continue to collect data even after the initial validation study is completed. Greater confidence, practical and statistical, can be placed in repeated studies that yield the same results than in one single study based upon insufficient data.

An additional consideration is the approximate length of the time interval between the taking of the test and the collection of the criterion data. In short, when has an employee been on the job long enough to appraise his or her performance properly? Answer: when there is some evidence that the initial learning period has passed. Certainly the learning period for some jobs is far longer than for others, and training programs vary in length. For many jobs, it is reasonable to appraise employee performance approximately 6 months after the completion of training, but there is considerable variability in this figure. On jobs with short training periods and relatively little interpersonal contact, the interval may be much shorter; when the opposite conditions prevail, it may not be possible to gather reliable criterion data until a year or more has passed.

Two further considerations regarding validation samples deserve mention. The sample itself must be representative— that is, made up of individuals of the same age, education, or vocational situation as the persons for whom the predictor measure is recommended. Finally, predictive designs should use individuals who are actual job applicants and who are motivated to perform well. To be sure, motivational conditions are quite different for presently-employed individuals who are told that a test is being used only for research purposes than for job applicants for whom poor test performance means the potential loss of a job.

Concurrent Studies

Concurrent designs for obtaining evidence of criterion-related validity are useful to HR researchers in several ways. Concurrent evidence of the validity of criterion measures is particularly important. Criterion measures usually are substitutes for other more important, costly, or complex performance measures. This substitution is valuable only if (1) there is a (judged) close relationship between the more convenient or accessible measure and the more costly or complex measure, and (2) the use of the substitute measure, in fact, is more efficient, in terms of time or money, than actually collecting the more complex performance data. Certainly, concurrent evidence of validity is important in the development of performance appraisal systems; yet most often it is either not considered or simply assumed. It is also important in evaluating tests of job knowledge or achievement, trade tests, work samples, or any other measures designed to describe present performance.

With cognitive ability tests, concurrent studies often are used as substitutes for predictive studies. That is, both predictor and criterion data are gathered from present employees, and it is assumed that if workers who score high (low) on the predictor also are rated as excellent (poor) performers on the job, then the same relationships also should hold for job applicants. A review of empirical comparisons of validity estimates of cognitive ability tests using both predictive and concurrent designs indicates that, at least for these measures, the two types of designs do not yield significantly different estimates (Barrett et al., 1981; Schmitt et al., 1984). We hasten to add, however, that the concurrent design ignores the effects of motivation and job experience on ability. While the magnitude of these effects may be nonsignificant for cognitive ability tests, this is less likely to be the case with inventories (e.g., measures of interest, attitude, or personality).

Jennings (1953), for example, demonstrated empirically that individuals who are secure in their jobs, who realize that their test scores in no way will affect their job standing, and who are participating in a research study, are not motivated to the same degree as are applicants for jobs.

The effect of job experience on validity also is ignored. The author once observed a group of police officers (whose average on-the-job experience was 3 years) completing several instruments as part of a concurrent study. One of the instruments was a measure of situational judgment, and a second was a measure of attitudes toward people. It is absurd to think that presently-employed police officers who have been trained at a police academy and who have had 3 years' experience on the street will respond to a test of situational judgment or an inventory of attitudes in the same way as would applicants with no prior experience! People learn things in the course of doing a job, and events occur that may influence markedly their responses to predictor measures. Thus, validity may be enhanced or inhibited, with no way of knowing in advance the direction of such influences.

In summary, for cognitive ability tests, concurrent studies appear to provide useful estimates of validity derived from predictive studies. Although this fact has been demonstrated empirically, additional research is clearly needed to help understand the *reasons* for this equivalence. On both conceptual and practical grounds, the different validity designs are not equivalent or interchangeable across situations (Guion and Cranny, 1982). Without explicit consideration of the influence of uncontrolled variables in a given situation (e.g., range restriction, differences due to age, motivation, job experience), one cannot simply substitute a concurrent design for a predictive one.

Requirements of Criterion Measures

Any predictor measure will be no better than the criterion used to establish its validity. And, as is true for predictors, anything that introduces random error into a set of criterion scores will reduce validity. All too often, unfortunately, researchers simply *assume* that criterion measures are relevant and valid. As Guion (1987) has pointed out, these two terms are different, and it is important to distinguish between them. A job-related construct is one chosen because it represents performance or behavior on the job that is valued by an employing organization. A construct-related criterion is one chosen because of its theoretical relationship, or lack of one, to the construct to be measured. "Does it work?" is a different question from "Does it measure what we wanted to measure?" Both questions are useful, and both call for criterion-related research. For example, a judgment of acceptable construct-related evidence of validity for subjective ratings might be based on high correlations of the ratings with production data or work samples and of independence from seniority or attendance data.

It is also important that criteria be reliable. Although unreliability in the criterion can be corrected statistically, unreliability is no trifling matter. If ratings are the criteria and if supervisors are less consistent in rating some employees than in rating others, then criterion-related validity will suffer. Alternatively, if all employees are given identical ratings (e.g., "satisfactory"), then it is a case of trying to predict the unpredictable. A predictor cannot forecast differences in behavior on the job that do not exist according to supervisors!

Finally, we should beware of criterion contamination in criterion-related validity studies. It is absolutely essential that criterion data be gathered independently of predictor data and that no person who is involved in assigning criterion ratings have any knowledge of individuals' predictor scores. Brown (1979) demonstrated that failure to consider such sources of validity distortion can mislead completely researchers who are unfamiliar with the total selection and training process and with the specifics of the validity study in question.

Synthetic Validity Evidence

Small organizations have an extremely difficult problem in conducting criterion-related validity studies. Only one or, at most, several persons occupy each job in the firm, and over a period of several years only a few more may be hired. Obviously, the sample sizes available do not permit adequate predictive studies to be undertaken. The concept of synthetic validity can help overcome such difficulties. **Synthetic validity** (Balma, 1959) is the process of inferring validity in a specific situation from a systematic analysis of jobs into their elements, a determination of test validity for these elements, and a combination or synthesis of the elemental validities into a whole.

The procedure has a certain logical appeal. As we noted in Chapter 4, criteria are multidimensional and complex, and if the various dimensions of job performance are independent, each predictor in a battery may be validated against the aspect of job performance it is designed to measure. Such an analysis lends *meaning* to the predictor scores in terms of the multiple dimensions of criterion behavior.

For example, the jobs clerk, industrial products salesperson, truck driver, and teacher are different, but the teacher and salesperson probably share a basic requirement of verbal fluency; the clerk and truck driver, manual dexterity; the teacher and clerk, numerical aptitude; and the salesperson and truck driver, mechanical aptitude. Although no one test or other predictor is valid for the total jobs, tests are available to measure the more basic job aptitudes required. To determine which tests to use in selecting persons for any particular job, however, one first must analyze the job into its elements and specify common behavioral requirements across jobs. Knowing these elements, one then

can derive the particular statistical weight attached to each element (the size of the weight is a function of the importance of the element to overall job performance). When the statistical weights are combined with the test element validities, it is possible not only to determine which tests to use, but also to estimate the expected predictiveness of the tests for the job in question. Thus, it is possible to construct a "synthesized valid battery" of tests for each job. The Position Analysis Questionnaire (McCormick, Jeanneret, and Mecham, 1972), a job analysis instrument that includes generalized behaviors required in work situations, routinely makes synthetic validity predictions for each job analyzed. Predictions are based upon the General Aptitude Test Battery (12 tests that measure aptitudes in the following areas: intelligence, verbal aptitude, numerical aptitude, spatial aptitude, form perception, clerical perception, motor coordination, finger dexterity, and manual dexterity).

Research to date has demonstrated that synthetic validation is feasible (Mossholder and Arvey, 1984) and that it is legally acceptable (Trattner, 1982). In addition, Hollenbeck and Whitener (1988) showed that the order of validation and aggregation need not be fixed. That is, it is possible to aggregate across job elements and elemental performance ratings and then to assess test-job performance relationships empirically. Doing so reduces the sample sizes required for synthetic validity and may allow more small businesses to use this procedure.

OTHER FACTORS AFFECTING THE SIZE OF OBTAINED VALIDITY COEFFICIENTS

Group Differences

As we noted earlier, criterion-related evidence of validity varies with the characteristics of the group on whom the test is validated. In general, whenever a predictor is validated on a group that is more heterogeneous than the group for whom the predictor ultimately is intended, estimates of validity will be spuriously high. Suppose a test of spatial relations ability originally intended as a screening device for engineering applicants, is validated by giving it to applicants for jobs as diverse as machinists, mechanics, tool crib attendants, *and* engineers in a certain firm. This group is considerably more heterogeneous than the group for whom the test was originally intended (engineering applicants only). Consequently, there will be much variance in the test scores, and it may *look* like the test is discriminating effectively. Comparison of validity coefficients using engineering applicants only with those obtained from the more heterogeneous group will demonstrate empirically the relative amount of overestimation.

Range Restriction

Conversely, since the size of the validity coefficient is a function of two variables, a narrowing of the range either of the predictor or of the criterion will serve to lower the size of the validity coefficient (see Fig. 7–1).

In Figure 7–1 the relationship between the interview scores and the criterion data is linear, follows the elliptical shape of the bivariate normal distribution, and indicates a systematic positive relationship of about .50. Scores are restricted neither in the predictor nor in the criterion, and scores are found in nearly all the possible categories from low to high. The correlation drops considerably, however, when one considers only a limited group, such as those scores falling to the right of line *X*. When such restrictions of range occur, the points assume shapes that are not at all elliptical and indicate much lower correlations between predictors and criteria. It is tempting to conclude from this that range restriction effects on validity coefficients result from changes in the variance(s) of the variable(s). However, Alexander (1988) showed that such effects are more properly considered as nonrandom sampling that separately influences means, variances, and correlations of the variables.

Restriction can occur in the predictor when, for example, only applicants who have survived an initial screening are considered, or when measures are used for selection *prior* to validation, so that criterion data

are unavailable for low scorers who did not get hired. This is known as **direct range restriction** on the predictor. **Indirect range restriction** on the predictor occurs when an experimental predictor is administered to applicants, but is not used as a basis for selection decisions. Rather, applicants are selected in accordance with the procedure currently in use. In both cases, low scorers who are hired may become disenchanted with the job and quit before criterion data can be collected, thus further restricting the range of available scores.

The range of scores also may be narrowed by preselection. Preselection occurs, for example, when a predictive validity study is undertaken *after* a group of individuals has been hired but *before* criterion data become available for them. Estimates of the validity of the procedure will be lowered since such employees represent a superior selection of all job applicants, thus curtailing the range of predictor scores and criterion data. In short, selection at the hiring point reduces the range on the predictor variable(s), and selection on the job or during training reduces the range on the criterion variable(s). Either type of restriction has the effect of lowering estimates of validity.

In order to interpret validity coefficients properly, information on the degree of range restriction in either variable should be included. Fortunately, formulas are available that correct statistically for the various forms of range restriction (Thorndike, 1949). For example, to correct for direct range restriction on the predictor, the appropriate formula is:

$$r_u = \frac{r\dfrac{S_1}{s_1}}{\sqrt{1 - r^2 + r^2\dfrac{S_1^2}{s_1^2}}} \qquad (7\text{-}4)$$

where r_u is the estimated validity coefficient in the unrestricted sample, r is the obtained coefficient in the restricted sample, S_1 is the standard deviation of the unrestricted sample, and s_1 is the standard deviation of the restricted sample. In practice, all of the information necessary to use Equation 7–4 may not be available. However, if the validity coefficient in the restricted group and the selection ratio (proportion of applicants selected) are known, the unrestricted validity still can be estimated using tabled values prepared by Sands, Alf, and Abrahams (1978).

If restriction occurs in the criterion variable (e.g., due to turnover or transfer before criterion data could be gathered), then the appropriate formula is:

FIGURE 7–1 Effect of Range Restriction on Correlation.

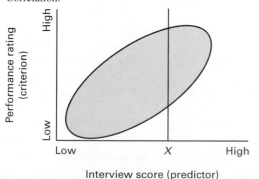

$$r_u = \sqrt{1 - \frac{s_1^2}{S_1^2}(1 - r^2)} \qquad \textbf{(7-5)}$$

where all symbols are defined as above.

In an empirical investigation of the accuracy of such statistical corrections, Lee et al. (1982) compared corrected and uncorrected estimates of validity for the Navy Basic Test Battery to the unrestricted true validity of the test. Groups of sailors were selected according to five different selection ratios. In all cases, the corrected coefficients estimated more accurately the unrestricted true validity of the test.

However, later research by Lee and Foley (1986) and Brown et al. (1988) has shown that corrected correlations tend to fluctuate considerably from test score range to test score range, with higher validity coefficients and slopes at higher predictor score ranges. Indeed, if predictor-criterion relationships are actually nonlinear, but one assumes a linear relationship, application of the correction formulas will substantially overestimate the true population correlation.

It is also worth noting that corrected correlations do not have a known sampling distribution. Since the standard error of a corrected correlation is unknown, statistical significance tests are not possible with corrected correlations (Ree et al., 1994).

Position in the Employment Process

Estimates of validity based on predictive designs may differ depending on whether a measure of individual differences is used as an initial selection device (in which case score variance is maximized) or as a final hurdle (in which case the group is more homogeneous and scores are not as likely to vary significantly).

Form of the Predictor-Criterion Relationship

Scattergrams depicting the nature of the predictor-criterion relationship always should be inspected for extreme departures from the statistical assumptions on which the computed measure of relationship is based. If an assumed type of relationship does not correctly describe the data, validity will be underestimated. The computation of the Pearson product-moment correlation coefficient assumes that both variables are normally distributed, that the relationship is linear, and that when the bivariate distribution of scores (from low to high) is divided into segments, the column variances are equal. This is called **homoscedasticity.** In less technical terms, this means that the measure predicts as well at high score ranges as at low score ranges. In practice, these assumptions often are not met. In one study (Kahneman and Ghiselli, 1962) approximately 40 percent of the validities examined were nonlinear and/or heteroscedastic. Generally, however, when scores on the two variables being related are normally distributed, they are also homoscedastic. Hence, if we can justify the normalizing of scores, we are very likely to have a relationship that is homoscedastic as well (Ghiselli, Campbell, and Zedeck, 1981).

CONSTRUCT-RELATED EVIDENCE

Neither content nor criterion-related validity strategies have as their basic objective the understanding of a trait or construct that a test measures. Yet in our quest for improved prediction, some sort of conceptual framework is required to organize and explain our data and to provide direction for further investigation. The conceptual framework specifies the meaning of the construct, distinguishes it from other constructs, and indicates how measures of the construct should relate to other variables (APA *Standards,* 1985). This is the function of **construct-related evidence of validity.** It provides the evidential basis for the interpretation of scores (Messick, 1995).

Validating inferences about a construct requires a demonstration that a test measures a specific construct that has been shown to be critical for job performance. Once this is accomplished, then inferences about job performance from test scores are justified by logical implication (Binning and Barrett, 1989). The focus is on a description of behavior that is broader and more abstract. Construct validation is not accomplished in a single study; it requires an accumulation of evidence derived from many different sources to determine the meaning of the test scores and an appraisal of their social consequences (Messick, 1995). It is, therefore, both a logical and an empirical process.

The process of construct validation begins with the formulation by the investigator of hypotheses about the characteristics of those with high scores on a particular measurement procedure, in contrast to those with low scores. Viewed in their entirety, such hypotheses form a tentative theory about the nature of the construct the test or other procedure is believed to be measuring. These hypotheses then may be used to predict how people at different score levels on the test will behave on certain other tests or in certain defined situations.

Note that in this process the measurement procedure serves as a sign (Wernimont and Campbell, 1968), clarifying the nature of the behavioral domain of interest and, thus, the essential nature of the construct. The construct (e.g., mechanical comprehension, aggression) is not defined by an isolated event, but rather by a **nomological network**—a system of interrelated concepts, propositions, and laws that relates observable characteristics to other observables, observables to theoretical constructs, or one theoretical construct to another theoretical construct (Cronbach and Meehl, 1955).

Information relevant either to the construct or to the theory surrounding the construct may be gathered from a wide variety of sources. Each can yield hypotheses that enrich the definition of a construct. Among these sources of evidence are:

1. Questioning test takers about their performance strategies or responses to particular items, or asking raters about the reasons for their ratings (APA *Standards,* 1985; Messick, 1995).

2. Analyses of the internal consistency of the measurement procedure.

3. Expert judgment that the content or behavioral domain being sampled by the procedure pertains to the construct in question. Sometimes this has led to a confusion between content and construct validities, but since content validity deals with inferences about test *construction* while construct validity involves inferences about test *scores,* content validity, at best, is one type of evidence of construct validity (Tenopyr, 1977). Thus, in one study (Schoenfeldt et al., 1976), reading behavior was measured directly from actual materials read on the job rather than through an inferential chain from various presumed indicators (e.g., a verbal ability score from an intelligence test). Test tasks and job tasks matched so well that there was little question that common constructs underlay performance on both.

4. Correlations of a new procedure (purportedly a measure of some construct) with established measures of the same construct.

5. Factor analyses of a group of procedures, demonstrating which of them share common variance and, thus, measure the same construct (e.g., Shore and Tetrick, 1991).

6. Covariance structure modeling (e.g., using LISREL) that allows testing of a measurement model that links observed variables to underlying constructs, and testing of a structural model of the relationships among constructs. Vance et al. (1989) used this approach to enhance understanding of how alternative predictors

(ability, experience, and supervisor support) relate to different types of criteria (e.g., self, supervisor, and peer ratings; work sample performance; and training success) across three categories of tasks (installation of engine parts, inspection of components, and forms completion). Such understanding might profitably be used to develop a generalizable taxonomy of tasks.

7. Ability of the scores derived from a measurement procedure to separate naturally-occurring or experimentally-contrived groups (group differentiation) or demonstrations of relationships between differences in scores and other variables on which the groups differ.

8. Demonstrations of systematic relationships between scores from a particular procedure and measures of behavior in situations where the construct of interest is thought to be an important variable. For example, a paper and pencil instrument designed to measure anxiety can be administered to a group of subjects who subsequently are put through an anxiety-arousing situation such as a final examination. The paper-and-pencil test scores are then correlated with the physiological measures of anxiety expression during the exam. A positive relationship from such an experiment would provide evidence that test scores do reflect anxiety tendencies.

9. Convergent and discriminant validation. This purpose is closely related to procedures 3 and 4. Not only should scores that purportedly measure some construct be related to scores on other measures of the same construct (convergent validation), but also they should be unrelated to scores on instruments that are not supposed to be measures of that construct (discriminant validation).

Campbell and Fiske (1959) proposed a systematic experimental procedure for analyzing convergent and discriminant validities. They pointed out that any test (or other measurement procedure) is really a trait-method unit—that is, a test measures a given trait by a single method. Therefore, since we want to know the relative contributions of trait and method variance to test scores, we must study more than one trait (e.g., dominance, affiliation) and use more than one method (e.g., peer ratings, interviews). Such studies are possible using a multi-trait-multi-method (MTMM) matrix (see Fig. 7–2).

An MTMM matrix is simply a table displaying the correlations between (a) the same trait measured by the same method, (b) different traits measured by the same method, (c) the same trait measured by different methods, and (d) different traits measured by different methods. The procedure can be used to study

		Method 1		Method 2	
	Traits	A1	B1	A2	B2
Method 1	A1	a			
	B1	b			
Method 2	A2	c			
	B2	d			

FIGURE 7–2 Example of a Multi-Trait-Multi-Method Matrix.

any number and variety of traits measured by any method. In order to obtain satisfactory evidence for the validity of a construct, the "c" correlations (convergent validities) should be larger than zero and high enough to encourage further study. In addition, the "c" correlations should be higher than the "b" and "d" correlations (i.e., show discriminant validity).

For example, if the correlation between interview (method 1) ratings of two supposedly *different* traits (e.g., assertiveness and emotional stability) is higher than the correlation between interview (method 1) ratings and written test (method 2) scores that supposedly measure the *same* trait (e.g., assertiveness), then the validity of the interview ratings as a measure of the construct "assertiveness" would be seriously questioned.

Note that in this approach, reliability is estimated by two measures of the same trait using the same method (in Fig. 7–2, the "a" correlations), while validity is defined as the extent of agreement between two measures of the same trait using different methods (in Fig. 7–2, the "c" correlations). Thus, the distinction between reliability and validity is simply a matter of degree—that is, in terms of the similarity of measurement methods.

Although the logic of this method is intuitively compelling, it does have certain limitations, principally (1) the lack of quantifiable criteria, (2) the inability to account for differential reliability, and (3) the implicit assumptions underlying the procedure (Schmitt and Stults, 1986). One such assumption is the requirement of maximally dissimilar or uncorrelated methods, since, if the correlation between methods is 0.0, then shared method variance cannot affect the assessment of shared trait variance.

When methods are correlated, however, confirmatory factor analysis should be used. Using this method, researchers can define models that propose trait or method factors (or both) a priori and then test the ability of such models to fit the data. The parameter estimates and ability of alternative models to fit the data are used to assess convergent and discriminant validity and method-halo effects. In fact, when methods are correlated, use of confirmatory factor analysis instead of the MTMM approach may actually reverse conclusions drawn in prior studies (Williams, Cote, and Buckley, 1989).

When analysis begins with multiple indicators of each Trait x Method combination, second-order or hierarchical confirmatory factor analysis (HCFA) should be used (Marsh and Hocevar, 1988). In this approach, first-order factors defined by multiple items or subscales are hypothesized for each scale, and the method and trait factors are proposed as second-order factors.

HCFA supports several important inferences about the latent structure underlying MTMM data beyond those permitted by traditional confirmatory factor analysis (Lance, Teachout, and Donnelly, 1992):

1. A satisfactory first-order factor model establishes that indicators have been assigned correctly to Trait x Method units.

2. Given a satisfactory measurement model, HCFA separates measurement error from unique systematic variance. They remain confounded in traditional confirmatory factor analyses of MTMM data.

3. HCFA permits inferences regarding the extent to which traits and measurement methods are correlated.

Illustration

A construct validation paradigm designed to study predictor-job performance linkages in the Navy recruiter's job was presented by Borman et al. (1980) and refined and extended by Pulakos, Borman, and Hough (1988). Their approach is described here since it illustrates nicely interrelationships among the sources of construct-related evidence presented earlier. Factor analyses of personality and vocational interest items that proved valid in a previous Navy recruiter test validation study yielded several factors that were interpreted as underlying constructs (e.g., selling skills, human relations skills), suggesting individual differences potentially important for success on the recruiter job. New items, selected or written to tap these constructs, along with the items found valid in the previous recruiter study, were administered to a separate sample of Navy recruiters. Peer and supervisory performance ratings also were gathered for these recruiters.

Data analyses indicated good convergent and discriminant validities in measuring many of the constructs. For about half the constructs, the addition of new items enhanced validity against the performance criteria. This approach (i.e., attempting to discover, understand, and then confirm individual differences constructs that are important for effectiveness on a job) is a workable strategy for enhancing our understanding of predictor-criterion relationships and an important contribution to personnel selection research.

CROSS-VALIDATION

Changes due to time, people, situations, and criteria make essential an independent check on the validity of any measure used for predictive purposes. This independent check is known as **cross-validation,** and it may be done in one of two ways: statistically or empirically. Statistical cross-validation (see Appendix B) involves the adjustment of the sample correlation (R) by a function of R, n (the number of cases), and p (the number of variables). The adjusted R is then used to estimate either the population correlation or the cross-validated population correlation, depending on the specific formula used.

Empirical cross-validation proceeds as follows: Collect predictor and criterion data on a validation sample, compute a validity coefficient, and derive a regression equation in order to predict criterion scores.[1] Then independently draw a second (cross-validation) sample from the same population, obtain predictor data, and calculate a predicted criterion score for each individual using the scoring scheme derived in the validation sample. Collect actual criterion data at some later time and correlate predicted performance scores with actual performance scores. The cross-validated coefficient almost always will be lower (i.e., it will shrink) because the chance factors that tend to maximize the original correlation will not operate in the cross-validation sample. Thus, the cross-validated correlation coefficient is a better estimate of the true degree of relationship.

The cross-validation sample must constitute a different sample of people independently drawn from the same population as the validation sample. This is essential; yet it is rarely done (Murphy, 1984). An investigator who, for example, derives a set of scoring weights on one sample and then uses the scoring weights to predict criterion scores for the very same group or for a subset of that same group commits the **foldback error.** That is, capitalizing on whatever chance factors were operating in the sample, the investigator merely confirms that error by folding back the items on the same sample of persons. Computation of the relationship between actual and predicted scores in such situations results in a "baloney coefficient" (Cureton, 1950).

Shrinkage in cross-validation is likely to be especially large when initial validation samples are small (and, therefore, have larger sampling errors). Shrinkage also will be large when a "shotgun" approach is used—that is, when a researcher assembles a miscellaneous set of questions with little regard to their relevance to criterion behavior and when he or she retains subsequently all items that yield significant positive or negative correlations with a criterion. Shrinkage is likely to be less when a researcher chooses items on the basis of previously-formed hypotheses derived from psychological theory or on the basis of past experience with the criterion (Anastasi, 1988). When multiple regression techniques are used, shrinkage will generally be greater as the number of predictors increases—again due to chance factors operating in the validation sample.

In many cases statistical cross-validation is preferable for three reasons. One, it is possible to use all of the information contained in a sample. This maximizes the stability of regression weights. Two, statistical correction is faster and requires less effort on the part of a researcher. Three, and most importantly, formula estimates appear to be highly accurate (Murphy, 1983).

VALIDITY GENERALIZATION

Cross-validation involves only one kind of generalization—over various samples drawn from the same population. Other kinds of generalizations are also possible—and necessary from a practical point of view. Generalizations over time are particularly noteworthy. Fluctuations over time in criterion components may cause changes in validity coefficients. Wernimont (1962) reported the following shrinkage over time for a weighted application blank originally derived by Kirchner and Dunnette (1957a): .74 (1954), .61 (1955), .38 (1956), and .07 (1957). However, a revision of both weights and variables yielded a cross-

---

[1] In the case of a single predictor, given a raw score expressed in standard score form (z_x) and a validity coefficient (r_{xy}), the individual's predicted score (z_y) should equal $r_{xy}z_x$ (cf., Appendix B). This example is only illustrative. In practice, raw score, not standard score, weights from the validation sample should be used (Dorans and Drasgow, 1980).

validation coefficient of .57. On the other hand, a personal-history-item scoring key developed on a 1933 sample of 10,111 life insurance agents, and reevaluated on a 1939 sample of 857 agents and a 1969–1971 sample of 14,738 agents, showed little loss in validity over both the 6-year and 38-year cross-validation periods (Brown, 1978). Three factors accounted for such long-term validity: scoring key confidentiality; test maintenance (e.g., adjustments in the scale values of monetary items to reflect changing dollar values); and adequate developmental sample size (10,111) and subject-to-variable ratio (421:1) in the Brown (1978) study compared to those in the Kirchner and Dunnette (1957a) study ($n = 85$; ratio = 3:1). The lesson should be obvious. Cross-validation, including rescaling and reweighting of items if necessary, should be continual (this author recommends annual), for as values change, jobs change, and people change, so also do the appropriateness and usefulness of inferences made from test scores.

One of the orthodox doctrines of personnel psychology is that employment test validities are situation-specific. This belief has been founded on the empirical fact that there is considerable variability from study to study in raw validity coefficients even when jobs and tests appear to be similar or essentially identical (Ghiselli, 1966). Thus it was assumed that empirical validation is required in each situation and that validity generalization is essentially impossible. Such an inability to generalize validities would make it impossible to develop the general principles and theories that are necessary to take the field beyond a mere technology to the status of a science (Guion, 1976). A large body of evidence now casts serious doubt on the situation-specificity doctrine.

The finding (Schmidt et al., 1976) that the typical validity study has only modest statistical power led Schmidt and Hunter (1977) to hypothesize that situation-specificity might be artifactual in nature. In developing a model to test this hypothesis they identified seven potential sources of artifactual, between-study variance in observed validity coefficients:

1. Sampling error (i.e., variance due to $N < \infty$);
2. Differences between studies in criterion reliability;
3. Differences between studies in test reliability;
4. Differences between studies in range restriction;
5. Differences between studies in amount and kind of criterion contamination and deficiency;
6. Computational, typographical, and transcription errors; and

7. Slight differences in factor structure between tests of a given type (e.g., arithmetic reasoning tests).

Situational specificity is rejected if artifacts account for 75 percent of the variance; validities are said to generalize if situational specificity is rejected or if the 90 percent credibility value (a 90% confidence interval placed around the mean test validity after taking current sample data and prior validity data into account) is positive.

The usefulness of these procedures for quantifying the between-study variability in test validities has led to a great deal of work on the methodology of validity generalization (VG) and to many studies that have used this methodology (Schmidt et al., 1985; Schmidt et al., 1993; Schmidt, Hunter, and Raju, 1988). These studies have provided disconfirming evidence of the situational-specificity doctrine. They have shown, on the basis of both published and unpublished studies, that most of the between-study variance in validity coefficients for similar jobs and a given ability is due to artifacts such as sampling error (Hedges, 1989; Koslowsky and Sagie, 1994). However, a review of all validity studies published over the 18-year period between 1964 and 1982 in the *Journal of Applied Psychology* and *Personnel Psychology* found that much unexplained variance in validity coefficients remained even after correcting for differences in sample size (Schmitt et al., 1984).

Much of the recent work on VG has been concerned with refining VG methodology and with understanding the statistical properties of the procedures themselves (e.g., Osburn and Callender, 1992). As a result, several cautions are in order.

1. The 75 percent rule may have inadequate statistical power to detect true variance in validities under certain conditions (Rasmussen and Loher, 1988; Spector and Levine, 1987). In fact when validities are bimodal, VG procedures may erroneously reject situational specificity and support generalizability (Kemery, Mossholder, and Roth, 1987). Hence there is a need to conduct VG analyses on studies with larger sample sizes (James, Demaree, Mulaik, and Mumford, 1988).

2. Since reliabilities and values for range restriction are rarely reported in validation studies, Schmidt and Hunter (1977) developed *assumed* (conservative) distributions of these properties. Although the use of rational, rather than empirical, distributions of the effects of range restriction is unlikely to change the conclusions of most VG studies (Alexander, Carson, Alliger, and Cronshaw, 1989), this is not the case with respect to reliability distributions. Specifically, if

there is reason to believe that true reliability distributions differ from those used in the Schmidt-Hunter procedures, then the 75 percent rule should be changed (higher or lower), depending on the amount of variance in the actual reliabilities. With less variance in the distribution of reliabilities, a more stringent rule for rejecting the situational specificity hypothesis should be used, especially when sample sizes are large (Paese and Switzer, 1988).

3. It is possible for the variance of the estimated true validity in the population to be negative. This makes such a statistic difficult to interpret (Thomas, 1988), and suggests that we should be cautious in interpreting the results of VG analyses.

4. Although VG procedures correct for statistical artifacts, VG cannot yield meaningful results if the studies in the analysis use methods that are fundamentally flawed (Campbell, 1986), or if the number of studies in the analysis is so small as to produce second-order sampling error (nonsystematic bias in the representativeness of the studies). Fortunately Ashworth et al. (1992) developed a procedure for determining what the mean and standard deviation of unrepresented true validities would have to be in order to pose a threat to a finding of positive VG.

5. The potential moderating effects of situations on validities are assessed in the absence of an organizational model that hypothesizes which situational variables may be important and without measuring a single situational variable. This may be addressed by making situational variables (e.g., restrictive vs. nonrestrictive organizational cultures) an integral part of generalizability analysis (James et al., 1992).

Despite these concerns, the many VG studies that now exist in the literature in applied psychology indicate that VG is a robust phenomenon. If one could correct for all seven sources of error variance identified in the Schmidt-Hunter model, the remaining variability between studies might well be zero. Perhaps the most important implication of this work is that it has called attention to the fact that the mean of several validity coefficients may be a better basis for inferring a valid relationship between predictor and criterion than any one coefficient (Society, 1987).

Nevertheless, it may well turn out that as validity generalization evidence accumulates for different occupations, researchers confronted with a new situation involving the same test type and job as those used in previous studies need not carry out a validation study of any kind. Only a job analysis is necessary to ensure that the job at hand is a member of the class of jobs on which the prior validity distribution was based. This is a Bayesian approach. Only a general job

analysis sufficient to classify jobs into broad occupational groups (e.g., clerical work) is necessary for validity generalization purposes (Schmidt, Hunter, and Pearlman, 1981). In short, it now appears possible to establish general principles and theories concerning trait-performance relationships in the world of work, enabling personnel psychology to develop beyond the stage of a technology to that of a science.

META-ANALYSIS

Work on validity generalization developed simultaneously with a class of analytical techniques termed **meta-analysis** by Glass (1976). Several authors (Green and Hall, 1984; Hunter, Schmidt, and Jackson, 1982; Rosnow and Rosenthal, 1989; Schmidt, 1992) have provided convincing arguments that the usual narrative literature review of empirical studies may arrive at erroneous conclusions because it uses qualitative rather than quantitative cumulation of results across studies. Meta-analysis is a means of quantitative cumulation that allows researchers to gain a better understanding of a phenomenon than would be available in any single study.

The methodology may be used in two ways: (1) to draw scientific conclusions (e.g., McEvoy and Cascio, 1985) and (2) to use the results of validity evidence obtained from prior studies to support the use of a test in a new situation (e.g., Hunter and Hunter, 1984). Such quantitative cumulation techniques can be applied to any area having two or more empirical studies bearing on the same relation. Generally, the procedure is as follows:

1. Calculate desired descriptive statistics across studies (e.g., the average validity coefficient).

2. Calculate the variance of this statistic across studies.

3. Subtract from #2 the amount of variance due to sampling error; this yields an estimate of the variance of r in the population.

4. Correct the mean and variance for statistical artifacts other than sampling error (e.g., measurement unreliability, restriction of range).

5. Compare the corrected standard deviation to the mean to assess the amount of potential variation in results across studies.

6. If large variation still remains (e.g., more than 25%, Sagie and Koslowsky, 1993), select moderator variables (see Chapter 12) and perform meta-analysis on subgroups (Hunter et al., 1982).

As an example, consider five studies that investigated the experimental effects of job design on turnover:

Study	1	2	3	4	5
Sample size (n)	823	95	72	46	206
Correlation (r)	.147	.155	.278	.329	.20

Step 1:

$$\bar{r} = \frac{\sum[n_i r_i]}{\sum n_i} = .171$$

Step 2:

$$S_r^2 = \frac{\sum[n_i(r_i - \bar{r}^2)^2]}{\sum n_i} = .002$$

Step 3:

$$\sigma_p^2 = S_r^2 - \sigma_e^2$$

where

$$\sigma_e^2 = \frac{K(1 - \bar{r}^2)^2}{n} = .0038$$

$$\sigma_p^2 = .002 - .0038 = -.0018$$

This implies that σ_p is approximately zero.

Step 4: Cannot be done based on the data available, but is not needed in this case anyway.

Step 5: The best estimate of the relationship in the population between job design and turnover is .171. Differences in obtained correlations across studies are due solely to sampling error.

Step 6: Not needed.

We noted earlier that meta-analysis is a class of analytical techniques. While a number of such techniques exist (e.g., Hedges and Olkin, 1985; Hunter and Schmidt, 1990; Raju et al., 1991; Rosenthal, 1991; Thomas, 1990), they differ in their conceptual and analytic foundations. More importantly, they may yield different answers to the meta-analytic questions of central tendency, variability, and prediction by moderators (Johnson, Mullen, and Salas, 1995; Law, 1992; Law, Schmidt, and Hunter, 1994a). This implies that the selection of a particular meta-analytic approach is not merely a matter of choice. Rather, be prepared to justify the choice of a particular method.

Despite its intuitive appeal, and recent statistical refinements to improve accuracy (Hufcutt and Arthur, 1995; Hunter and Schmidt, 1994; Law, Schmidt, and Hunter, 1994b) there are dangers in the indiscriminate application of meta-analysis, and they should be recognized. In fact, Bullock and Svyantek (1985) proposed a set of criteria for evaluating meta-analytic research. Meta-analysis research that meets acceptable quality standards:

1. Uses a theoretical model as the basis of the meta-analysis research and tests hypotheses from that model.
2. Identifies precisely the domain within which the hypotheses are to be tested.
3. Includes all publicly available studies in the defined content domain (not just published or easily available studies).
4. Avoids selecting studies based on criteria of methodological rigor, age of study, or publication status.
5. Publishes or makes available the final list of studies used in the analysis.
6. Selects and codes variables on theoretical grounds rather than convenience.
7. Provides detailed documentation of the coding scheme and the resolution of problems in applying the coding scheme, including estimation procedures used for missing data.
8. Uses multiple raters to apply the coding scheme and provides a rigorous assessment of interrater reliability.
9. Reports all variables analyzed in order to avoid problems of capitalizing on chance relationships in a subset of variables.
10. Publishes or makes available the data set used in the analysis.
11. Considers alternative explanations for the findings obtained.
12. Limits generalization of results to the domain specified by the research.
13. Reports study characteristics in order to understand the nature and limits of the domain actually analyzed.
14. Reports the entire study in sufficient detail to allow for direct replication.

Virtually every one of these criteria represents a "judgment call" by the researcher (Wanous, Sullivan, and Malinak, 1989). Such judgments should be described and, if possible, tested empirically. This raises a final point: To be useful, statistical methods must be used thoughtfully. Data analysis is an aid to thought, not a substitute for it (Green and Hall, 1984). Careful quantitative reviews that adhere to the criteria described above can play a useful role in furthering our understanding of organizational phenomena.

Discussion Questions

1. Explain why validity is a unitary concept.
2. Explain why construct-oriented evidence of validity is the foundation for all validity.

3. Why is cross-validation necessary?
4. What factors might affect the size of a validity coefficient?
5. Describe some of the problems associated with narrative literature reviews, and how meta-analysis might correct for these problems.

* * *

In the last two chapters we have examined applied measurement concepts that are essential to sound employment decisions. These are useful tools that will serve the HR specialist well. In the next chapter we will use these concepts to take a closer look at a topic that is widely debated in contemporary human resource management—fairness in employment decisions.

CHAPTER

8

FAIRNESS IN EMPLOYMENT DECISIONS

AT A GLANCE

When it is technically feasible, users of selection measures should investigate differences in prediction systems for racial, ethnic, and gender subgroups. Such investigations should consider possible differences in subgroup validity coefficients (differential validity), as well as possible differences in standard errors of estimate, slopes, and intercepts of subgroup regression lines (differential prediction). Theoretically, differential validity and differential prediction can assume numerous forms, but recent evidence indicates that in well-controlled studies, both occur infrequently.

However, if a measure that is valid only for one subgroup is used for all individuals regardless of group membership, then the measure may discriminate unfairly against the subgroup(s) for whom it is invalid. It is important to consider job performance along with test performance because unfair discrimination cannot be said to exist if inferior test performance by some group also is associated with inferior job performance by the same group. This issue has given rise to alternative definitions of selection fairness, each with its own assumptions and practical implications.

The ultimate resolution of the problem will probably not rest on technical grounds alone; competing values must be considered. Although some errors are inevitable in employment decisions, the crucial question is whether the use of a particular method of assessment results in less social cost than is now being paid for these errors considering all other assessment methods.

The Uniform Guidelines on Employee Selection Procedures (1978), as well as the APA *Standards* (1985), recommend that users of selection measures investigate differences in criterion-related evidence of validity for ethnic, gender, or other subsamples that can be identified when the measure is given. Investigations of differential validity should be carried out, however, only when it is technically feasible to do so—that is, when sample sizes in each subgroup are sufficient for reliable comparisons among subgroups and when relevant, unbiased criteria are available.

In fact, fairness studies are technically feasible far less often than is commonly believed. Samples of several hundred subjects *in each group* are required in order to provide adequate statistical power (Drasgow and Kang, 1984). Furthermore, it is often very difficult to verify empirically that a criterion is unbiased.

Despite the attention paid to differential validity, there is a need to consider more than differences in the validity coefficients of subgroups. We need to compare *prediction systems*, because differences in prediction systems have a more direct bearing on issues of bias in selection than do differences in correlations (Linn, 1978; Hartigan and Wigdor, 1989). Equal correlations do not necessarily imply equal standard errors of estimate, nor do they necessarily imply equal slopes or intercepts of subgroup regression equations. With these cautions in mind, we will consider first the potential forms of differential validity, then the research evidence on differential validity and differential prediction, and finally alternative definitions of selection fairness and their practical implications.

DIFFERENTIAL VALIDITY: POSSIBILITIES

In the familiar bivariate scatterplot of predictor and criterion data, each dot represents a person's score on both the predictor and the criterion (see Fig. 8–1). In this figure the dots tend to cluster in the shape of an ellipse, and since most of the dots fall in quadrants 1 and 3, with relatively few dots in quadrants 2 and 4, positive validity exists. If the relationship were negative, most of the dots would fall in quadrants 2 and 4. Since the relationship is positive, however, people with high (low) predictor scores also tend to have high (low) criterion scores. If, in the investigation of differential validity, the joint distribution of minority and nonminority predictor and criterion scores is similar throughout the scatterplot, as in Figure 8–1, no problem exists and use of the predictor should be continued.

On the other hand, if the joint distribution of predictor and criterion scores for each group is similar, but circular, as in Figure 8–2, the predictor is useless since it supplies no reliable information of a predictive nature.

The ideas for many of the following diagrams are derived from Barrett (1967) and represent various combinations of the concepts illustrated in Figure 8–1 and 8–2. Figure 8–3 is an example of a differential predictor-criterion relationship that is legal and appropriate. In this figure validity for the minority and nonminority groups is equivalent, but the minority group scores lower on the predictor and does poorer on the job (of course, the situation could be reversed).

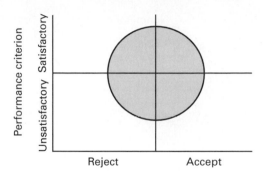

FIGURE 8–2 Zero Validity.

In this instance the very same factors that depress performance on the predictor may also serve to depress performance on the job. Thus, adverse impact (i.e., a higher selection rate for one group than for the other) is defensible in this case since minorities do poorer on what the organization considers a relevant and important measure of job success. On the other hand, government regulatory agencies probably would want evidence that the criterion was relevant, important, and not itself subject to bias. Moreover, alternative criteria that result in less of an adverse impact would have to be considered, along with the possibility that some third factor (e.g., length of service) did not cause the observed difference in job performance (Byham and Spitzer, 1971).

An additional possibility, shown in Figure 8–4, is a predictor that is valid for the combined group, but invalid for each group separately. In most cases where no validity exists for either group individually, errors in selection would result from using the predictor without validation or from failure to test for differential validity in the first place. The predictor in this case becomes solely a crude measure of the racial variable

FIGURE 8–1 Positive Validity.

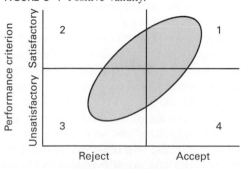

FIGURE 8–3 Valid Predictor with Adverse Impact.

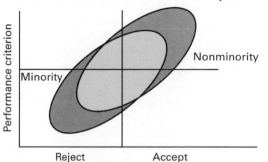

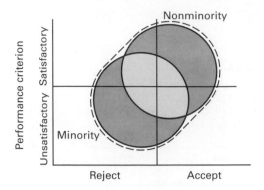

FIGURE 8–4 Valid Predictor for Entire Group; Invalid for Each Group Separately.

(Bartlett and O'Leary, 1969). This is the most clear-cut case of using selection measures to discriminate in terms of race, gender, or any other unlawful basis. Moreover, it is unethical to use a selection device that has not been validated (see Appendix A).

It also is possible to demonstrate equal validity in the two subgroups, yet have unequal predictor means or criterion means. These possibilities are presented in Figures 8–5 and 8–6.

In both of these cases, if the predictor was validated on the combined sample, the effect would be a reduction in overall validity. In Figure 8–5 if a single cut score was set for the first two groups combined, the minority group would not be as likely to be selected, even though the probability of success on the job for the two groups is essentially equal. That is, equal proportions of each group are found above the criterion cut score.

Under these conditions the most appropriate strategy is to use separate cut scores in each group

FIGURE 8–5 Equal Validity, Unequal Predictor Means.

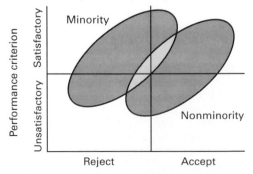

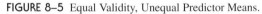

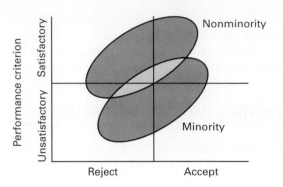

FIGURE 8–6 Equal Validity, Unequal Criterion Means.

based upon predictor performance, while the expectancy of job performance success remains equal. Thus, a Hispanic candidate with a score of 65 on an interview may have a 75 percent chance of success on the job. A white candidate with a score of 75 might have the same 75 percent probability of success on the job.

Although this situation might appear disturbing initially, remember that the predictor (the interview in this instance) is being used simply as a vehicle to forecast the likelihood of successful job performance. The primary focus is on job performance rather than on predictor performance. Even though interview scores may mean different things for different groups, as long as the expectancy of success on the job is equal for the two (or more) groups, the use of separate cut scores is justified. Indeed, the reporting of an expectancy score for each candidate is one recommendation made by a National Academy of Sciences panel with respect to the interpretation of scores on the General Aptitude Test Battery (GATB) (Hartigan and Wigdor, 1989).

Figure 8–6 depicts a situation where lowered validity also will result unless differential prediction is maintained. Although there is no significant difference in predictor performance, nonminority group members tend to perform better on the job than minority group members (or vice versa). If predictions were based on the combined sample, the result would be a systematic underprediction for nonminorities and a systematic overprediction for minorities. Thus, in this situation, the failure to use differential prediction (which would yield more accurate prediction for both groups) may only put minority persons on jobs where their probability of success is low and where their resulting performance only provides additional evidence that helps maintain prejudice (Bartlett and O'Leary, 1969). The

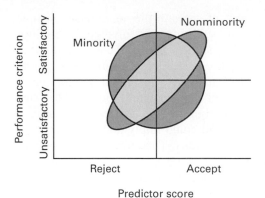

FIGURE 8–7 Equal Predictor Means, but Validity Only for the Nonminority Group.

nonminority individuals also suffer. If a test is used as a placement device, for example, since nonminority performance is systematically underpredicted, these individuals may well be placed on jobs that do not make the fullest use of their talents.

In Figure 8–7 no differences between the groups exist either on predictor or criterion scores; yet the predictor has validity only for the nonminority group. Hence, the selection measure should be used only with the nonminority group since the job performance of minorities cannot be predicted accurately. If the measure were used to select both minority and nonminority applicants, there would be no adverse impact since approximately the same proportion of applicants would be hired from each group. However, more nonminority members would succeed on the job, thereby reinforcing past stereotypes about the disadvantaged and hindering future attempts at equal employment opportunity.

In our final example (see Fig. 8–8), the two

FIGURE 8–8 Unequal Criterion Means and Validity Only for the Nonminority Group.

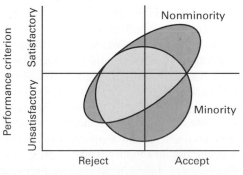

groups differ in mean criterion performance as well as in validity. The predictor might be used to select nonminority applicants, but should not be used to select minority applicants. Moreover, the cut score or decision rule used to select nonminority applicants must be derived solely from the nonminority group, *not* from the combined group. If the minority group (for whom the predictor is not valid) is included, overall validity will be lowered, as will be the overall mean criterion score. Predictions will be less accurate because the standard error of estimate will be inflated. As in the previous example, the organization should use the selection measure only for the nonminority group while continuing to search for a predictor that accurately forecasts minority job performance.

In summary, numerous possibilities exist when heterogeneous groups are combined in making predictions. The use of a single regression line, cut score, or decision rule with a heterogeneous group can lead to serious errors in prediction. When prior evidence indicates a high probability of the existence of differential validity, and when it is technically feasible to test for it, better and fairer selection is likely to result by validating separately for each identifiable subgroup. While one legitimately may question the use of race or gender as a variable in selection, the problem is really one of distinguishing between performance on the selection measure and performance on the job (Guion, 1965). If the basis for hiring is expected job performance and if differential prediction is used to improve the prediction of expected job performance rather than to discriminate on the basis of race, gender, and so on, differential prediction appears both legal and appropriate. Nevertheless, the practical implementation of this approach probably will be difficult since the fairness of any procedure that uses different standards for different groups is likely to be viewed with suspicion ("More," 1989).

DIFFERENTIAL VALIDITY: THE EVIDENCE

Let us be clear at the outset that evidence of differential validity provides information only on whether a selection device should be used to make comparisons *within* subgroups. One cannot infer evidence of unfair discrimination *between* subgroups from differences in validity alone; one also must consider mean job performance. In other words, a selection procedure may be fair and yet predict performance inaccurately, or it may discriminate unfairly and yet predict performance within a given subgroup with appreciable accuracy (Kirkpatrick, Ewen, Barrett, and Katzell, 1968).

In discussing differential validity first we must specify the criteria under which differential validity can be said to exist at all. Thus, Boehm (1972) distinguished between differential and single-group validity. Differential validity exists when: (1) there is a significant difference between the validity coefficients obtained for two ethnic groups, and (2) the correlations found in one or both of these groups are significantly different from zero. Related to but different from differential validity is single-group validity, in which a given predictor exhibits validity significantly different from zero for one group only, and there is no significant difference between the two validity coefficients.

Humphreys (1973) has pointed out that single-group validity is not equivalent to differential validity, nor can it be viewed as a means of assessing differential validity. The logic underlying this distinction is clear: To determine whether two correlations differ from each other, they must be compared directly with each other. Thus, the appropriate statistical test is a test of the null hypothesis of zero difference between the sample correlations. After allowing for sampling error in each coefficient, the task is to determine whether a difference in the samples reflects a difference in the populations. While such a procedure is correct statistically, there is a danger that in using this procedure, the power of the test of zero difference will be low because the standard error of the correlation coefficient of the (small) minority group is large (where $SE_r = f[SE_1 + SE_2]$). This makes a Type II error (i.e., not rejecting the null hypothesis when it is false) more likely. Therefore, the researcher who unwisely does not compute power (i.e., the probability of detecting a statistically significant difference when, in fact, it exists) is likely to err on the side of *too few* differences. For example, if the true validities to be compared are .50 and .30, but both are attenuated by a criterion with a reliability of .7, then even without any range restriction at all, one must have 528 persons *in each group* to yield a power of .90 at alpha = .05 (for more on this, see Trattner and O'Leary, 1980). The sample sizes typically used in any one study are therefore inadequate to provide a meaningful test of the hypothesis. However, high statistical power is possible if data are combined across studies. Such meta-analyses have been conducted, and we shall examine them shortly.

There also is a serious statistical flaw in the single-group validity paradigm. Since the number of cases in the minority sample usually is much smaller than the number of cases in the nonminority sample, the power of any statistical tests involving the minority group will be much smaller. If the nonminority coefficient is significantly different from zero while the minority coefficient is not, this could be due only to the fact that the minority sample is too small to detect the effect size as significantly different from zero in the population—and could imply nothing whatsoever about differential validity. Therefore, given widely divergent sample sizes, the employer often is forced into taking a **validator's gamble** in defending his or her employment practices; yet in the process, valid selection instruments may be rejected for minority groups.

Now let us consider research findings concerning single-group validity. Four different meta-analyses have demonstrated that evidence for single-group validity by race does not occur any more frequently in samples than would be expected solely on the basis of chance, given the complete absence of single-group validity in the population (Boehm, 1977; Katzell and Dyer, 1977; O'Connor, Wexley, and Alexander, 1975; Schmidt, Berner, and Hunter, 1973).

With respect to differential validity, the bulk of the evidence suggests that statistically significant differential validity is the exception rather than the rule (Schmidt, 1988; Schmidt and Hunter, 1981; Wigdor and Garner, 1982). In a comprehensive review and analysis of 866 black-white pairs of employment-test validity coefficients, Hunter, Schmidt, and Hunter (1979) concluded that findings of apparent differential validity in samples are produced by the operation of chance and a number of statistical artifacts. True differential validity probably does not exist. In addition, no support was found for the suggestion by Boehm (1972) and Bray and Moses (1972) that findings of validity differences by race are associated with the use of subjective criteria (ratings, rankings, etc.) and that validity differences seldom occur when more objective criteria are used.

Similar analyses of 1,337 pairs of validity coefficients from employment and educational tests for Hispanic Americans showed no evidence of differential validity (Schmidt, Pearlman, and Hunter, 1980). Researchers also have examined differential validity for males and females. Schmitt, Mellon, and Bylenga (1978) examined 6,219 pairs of validity coefficients for males and females (predominantly dealing with educational outcomes) and found that validity coefficients for females were slightly (<.05 correlation units) but significantly larger than coefficients for males. Validities for males exceeded those for females only when predictors were less cognitive in nature, such as high school experience variables. Schmitt et al. (1978) concluded: "The magnitude of the difference between male and female validities is very small and may make only trivial differences in most practical situations" (p. 150).

In a follow-up study, Schmitt, Coyle, and Mellon (1978) corrected race and gender subgroup validities for restriction of range in both predictor and criterion and then observed the effects of the corrections on differential validity. Results indicated that instances of differential validity in race or gender subgroups were not produced by subgroup differences in predictor scores, but that comparisons of male-female subgroup validities may be affected by differences in subgroup criterion scores. Schmitt et al. (1978) suggested that such findings may be due to methodological problems associated with the criteria used.

Despite these encouraging results, it is important to note that even meta-analyses generally are not technically feasible when the statistical powers of the significance tests in local validation studies are only slightly larger than the Type I error probability (alpha level) of the tests (Drasgow, 1982). Thus an examination of 31 studies of differential validity (Katzell and Dyer, 1977) revealed that the mean statistical power for detecting a true population difference in validities of 1.20 was only .26. Hence the average comparison had only a 1 in 4 chance of detecting as significant a true population difference as large as 0.20.

All is not lost, however, because differential prediction analyses have statistical powers noticeably larger than Type I error probabilities under much wider circumstances than do differential validity analyses. Hence differential prediction analyses are more appropriate for meta-analyses (Drasgow and Kang, 1984).

In summary, available research evidence indicates that the existence of single-group or differential validity in well-controlled studies is rare. Adequate controls include large enough sample sizes in each subgroup to achieve statistical power of at least .80; selection of predictors based on their logical relevance to the criterion behavior to be predicted; unbiased, relevant, and reliable criteria; and cross-validation of results. In terms of relevance, some direct measure of the degree of job skill developed by an employee after an appropriate length of time on the job (e.g., a job sample or job knowledge test) is widely held to be the most appropriate criterion in this context (Gael, Grant, and Ritchie, 1975). Failure to cross-validate results,

although a common practice (Murphy, 1984), is reprehensible; such results should not be recognized.

DIFFERENTIAL PREDICTION

The possibility of bias in selection procedures is a central issue in any discussion of EEO. As we noted earlier, these issues require a consideration of the equivalence of prediction systems for different groups. Analyses of possible differences in slopes or intercepts in subgroup regression lines result in more thorough investigations of predictive bias, since the overall regression line determines how a test is used for prediction. Lack of differential validity, in and of itself, does not assure lack of predictive bias.

When prediction systems are compared, the most frequently occurring difference (when differences occur at all) is in intercepts. Thus Bartlett, Bobko, Mosier, and Hannan (1978) examined 1,190 racial-group comparisons and found significant slope differences in about 5 percent and significant intercept differences in about 18 percent. Because these comparisons were not independent tests, it is difficult to estimate the exact probability of this occurring by chance.

Most commonly, the prediction system for the nonminority group slightly overpredicted minority group performance. That is, minorities would tend to do less well on the job than their test scores predict. Similar results also have been reported by Hartigan and Wigdor (1989). In 72 different validity studies on the GATB where there were at least 50 African-American and 50 nonminority employees (average: 87 and 166, respectively), slope differences occurred fewer than 3 percent of the time and intercept differences about 37 percent of the time. However, use of a single prediction equation for the total group of applicants would not provide predictions that were biased against African-American applicants, for they slightly overpredicted performance by African-Americans. In 220 tests each of slope and intercept differences between Hispanics and nonminority group members, about 2 percent of the slope differences and about 8 percent of the intercept differences were significant (Schmidt et al., 1980). The trend in the intercept differences was for the Hispanic intercepts to be lower (i.e., overprediction of Hispanic job performance), but firm support for this conclusion was lacking.

With respect to gender differences in performance on physical ability tests, there were no significant differences in prediction systems for males and females in the prediction of performance on outside telephone craft jobs (Reilly, Zedeck, and Tenopyr, 1979). However, considerable differences were found on both test and performance variables in the relative performances of men and women on a physical ability test for police officers (Arvey et al., 1992). If a common regression line were used for selection purposes, then the prediction of women's job performance would be systematically overpredicted.

In summary, although it is reassuring to know that differential prediction does not occur often when subgroups are compared, it has been found often enough to create concern for possible predictive bias when a common regression line is used for selection.

UNFAIR DISCRIMINATION: WHAT IS IT?

By nature and by necessity, measures of individual differences are discriminatory. This is as it should be since in employment settings random acceptance of candidates (unless the job is so easy that anyone can do it) can only lead to gross misuse of human and economic resources. To ignore individual differences is to abandon all the potential economic, societal, and personal advantages to be gained by taking into account individual patterns of abilities and varying job requirements. In short, the wisest course of action lies in the accurate matching of people and jobs.

Such an approach begins by appraising individual patterns of abilities through various types of selection measures. Such measures are *designed* to discriminate, and in order to possess adequate validity, they *must* do so. If a selection measure is valid in a particular situation, then legitimately we may attach a different behavioral meaning to high scores than we do to low scores. A valid selection measure accurately discriminates between those with high and those with low probabilities of success on the job. The crux of the matter, however, is whether the measure discriminates *unfairly*. Probably the clearest statement on this issue was made by Guion (1966): "Unfair discrimination exists when persons with equal probabilities of success on the job have unequal probabilities of being hired for the job" (p. 26).

An important principle is embodied in this definition. Investigations of unfair discrimination must consider **job performance** in addition to **predictor performance,** since a selection measure cannot be said to discriminate unfairly if inferior predictor performance by some group also is associated with inferior job performance by the same group (see Fig. 8–3). In short, the mere fact of group differences in mean scores is not a sufficient basis for a claim of unfair discrimination (Drasgow, 1987).

However, apparent but false nondiscrimination may occur when the measure of job success is itself biased in the same direction as the effects of ethnic background on predictor performance (Green, 1975). Consequently, a selection measure is unfairly discriminatory only when some specified group performs less well than a comparison group on the measure, but performs just as well as the comparison group on the job for which the selection measure is a predictor. It should be emphasized, however, that the very same factors that depress predictor performance (e.g., verbal ability, spatial relations ability) also may depress job performance. Gottfredson (1988) summarized the issue clearly:

> The vulnerability of tests is due less to their limitations for measuring important differences than it is to their very success in doing so . . . The more valid the tests are as measures of general cognitive ability, the larger the average group differences in test scores they produce. Keeping the spotlight on tests merely forestalls the real debate—how can this society justly and constructively deal with the racial-ethnic differences in ability that will be with us for some time to come? [p. 294]

SELECTION FAIRNESS

Unlike predictive bias, selection fairness is not a technical psychometric term. It is subject to different definitions in different social and political circumstances. Alternative ways of evaluating predictive bias are based on different definitions of the fairness of a selection procedure (APA *Standards,* 1985). In the sections that follow, we will examine five different definitions or "models" of selection fairness, together with their practical implications.

Regression Model

Investigations of selection fairness usually begin by subgrouping on the basis of some relevant variable (gender, race, ethnic group) since allegations of unfair discrimination generally are directed toward the members of some group (e.g., women, the disadvantaged). One approach to the investigation of selection fairness that is advocated widely is the comparison of regression slopes and intercepts for the various subgroups. This is also the definition of fairness used in the 1978 Uniform Guidelines on Employee Selection Procedures (Ledvinka, 1979). According to Cleary (1968):

> A test is biased for members of a subgroup of the population if, in the prediction of a criterion for which the test was designed, consistent nonzero errors of prediction are made for members of the subgroup. In other words, the test is biased if the criterion score predicted from the common regression line is consistently too high or too low for members of the subgroup. With this definition of bias, there may be a connotation of "unfair," particularly if the use of the test produces a prediction that is too low. If the test is used for selection, members of a subgroup may be rejected when they were capable of adequate performance. [p. 115]

Using such a regression approach (see Fig. 8–9), predictions are made by drawing a line from any predictor score on the horizontal axis up to the regression line and another line from that intersection across to the vertical axis where the estimated criterion score is indicated. Such predictions generated from a least squares regression procedure (see Appendix B) have certain characteristics: Over all persons in the sample (a) the average error in prediction is zero, and (b) the variance of the errors of prediction is a minimum. When two subgroups are compared, there are basically three possible situations (Cleary, Humphreys, Kendrick, and Wesman, 1975). In Figure 8–3, although there are two separate ellipses, one for the minority group and one for the nonminority, a single regression line may be cast for both groups. There is no need to make separate predictions for the two subgroups since the position of the regression line will be invariant for the groups whether computed separately or together.

In Figure 8–6, however, the manner in which the position of the regression line is computed clearly does make a difference. If a single regression line is cast for both groups (assuming they are equal in size), criterion scores for the nonminority group consistently will be *underpredicted,* while those of the minority group consistently will be *overpredicted.* In this situation the use of a single regression line is inappropriate, but it is the nonminority group that is affected adversely. While the slopes of the two regression lines are parallel, the intercepts are different.[1] Therefore, the same predictor score has a different predictive meaning in the two groups.

A third situation is presented in Figure 8–8. Here the slopes are not parallel, and therefore the intercepts cross. As we noted earlier, the predictor clearly is inappropriate for the minority group in this situation. When the regression lines are not parallel, the predictive validities differ and intercept differences are meaningless. Under these circumstances, once it is determined where the regression lines cross, the amount of over- or underprediction depends upon the position of a predictor score in its distribution.

When it is technically feasible to test for differential prediction using the regression model, a simple approach that is consistent conceptually with the results of the regression model may be used to communicate results of the analysis to nonstatistical audiences (Lawshe, 1983). The procedure is appropriate so long as there are nonsignificant differences in subgroup slopes (Norborg, 1984). It consists of five steps:

1. Transform predictor scores for the total sample to T-scores (P_t).
2. Transform criterion values for the total sample to T-scores (C_t).
3. Compute the *prediction error* for each member of the sample ($E_p = P_t - C_t$).
4. Compute the mean *prediction error* for the protected group and for the comparison group.
5. Examine the statistical significance of the difference between the means using a *t*-test.

There are several practical implications under a "fair" regression procedure in which separate within-group regression equations are used. The selecting in-

FIGURE 8–9 Prediction from a Single Group Regression Line.

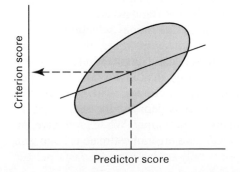

Criterion score

Predictor score

---

[1] There are several fundamental statistical requirements for such comparisons (Linn, 1973). The test for slopes is not applicable if the standard errors of estimate are significantly different, and the test for intercepts is not applicable if either the errors of estimate or the slopes are significantly different. In investigations of intercept differences, use analysis of covariance (Schmidt, Hunter, and Pearlman, 1982).

stitution, regardless of the percentage of applicants selected (i.e., the selection ratio), is assured of the selection of those applicants with the highest predicted criterion scores, while minimizing the number of erroneous acceptances. When validity is approximately equal for the minority and nonminority groups, however, and when performance differences on the criterion favor the nonminority group (e.g., Fig. 8–6), the lower-scoring minority group *as a group* is disadvantaged in inverse proportion to the validity of the selection procedure (Ledvinka, Markos, and Ladd, 1982). Moreover, for two groups with equal criterion means, if the prediction is poorer in one group than another and if only a small portion of applicants can be accepted, the selection cutoff point will be relatively higher in the group with the poorer prediction. Thus, members of the group for which prediction is poor may be penalized in the selection process (Cole, 1973). Conversely, when minority hiring levels exceed their representation in the applicant group, performance losses may be substantial, relative to strict, top-down selection (Silva and Jacobs, 1993).

Despite these potential problems the consensus seems to be that the regression model is the appropriate test for bias (Guion and Gibson, 1988). The accumulated evidence on this model is clear: Lower test scores among minorities (African-Americans and Hispanics) are accompanied by lower job performance, exactly as in the case of the majority (Schmidt, 1988).

Subjective Regression Model[2]

Darlington (1971) has argued for "culturally optimum" regression procedures in order to achieve fairness in selection. According to this model, the first step is to make a value judgment about the desirability of special selection of members of some group (racial, ethnic, etc.). If special selection of certain groups is viewed as desirable, then it is necessary to adopt some difference in criterion scores between groups that will yield equally desirable applicants from each group. For example, suppose an organization decides it is especially valuable to obtain minority group members. It might therefore decide that a minority group member's score of Y on a criterion is as desirable as a score of

---

[2] The label *subjective regression,* as well as the labels for the other procedures described below, originally were used by Cole (1973).

$Y + k$ on the criterion for nonminorities. Using a variable C, which has a value of zero for minorities and one for nonminorities, the organization then tries to maximize the new composite criterion $Y - kC$. Of course, if k is set equal to zero and no group is favored, this model becomes equivalent to the more familiar regression model.

This approach is simply an esoteric way of setting quotas (Hunter and Schmidt, 1976), since adding or subtracting a constant to the criterion is equivalent mathematically to adding or subtracting a constant to the predictor. This, in turn, is equivalent to using different cut scores for the subgroups. As Linn (1973) has noted, however, although Darlington's proposal is of theoretical interest, it seems unlikely that institutions ever will formalize the procedure and actually pick an explicit value of k. In fact, such a procedure might plausibly be viewed as reverse discrimination.

Equal-Risk Model

Guion's (1966) definition of unfair discrimination and Einhorn and Bass's (1971) model fall into this category since the same risk is taken in each group under consideration. In the Einhorn and Bass (1971) model, one examines the distribution of criterion scores about the regression line and then sets predictor cutoff points for each subgroup above which applicants have a specific minimal chance of being successful. For example, suppose an organization is willing to accept a 30 percent risk (and, therefore, a 70% chance of success) in hiring based on its predictors. Given this constraint, the predictor cutoff score is set at the point at which the criterion pass point (Y_p) is approximately one-half standard error of estimate (σ_{est}) below the predicted criterion ($\hat{Y}$), since approximately 70 percent of the cases in a normal distribution fall above minus one-half standard deviation. In terms of a standard score Z_p, $Z_p = (Y_p - \hat{Y})/\sigma_{est}$, and the probability that $\{Z > Z_p\}$ = .70.

Einhorn and Bass (1971) emphasize that it is primarily the difference in the standard errors of estimate between subgroups that determines selection fairness. As Cole (1973) has noted, however, the equal-risk model has the same practical implications as the regression model—namely, that in groups with equal criterion means, poor prediction (i.e., lower predictive validity) in one group may decrease the chances of selection of members of that group. When predictive validity is low, the standard error of estimate is large, and consequently, a higher predicted score (and predictor cutoff) is required to maintain the same one-half standard error of estimate difference between the predicted criterion and the criterion pass point.

Constant-Ratio Model

A fourth model of selection fairness has been proposed by Thorndike (1971). According to this model, a selection measure is fair only if, for any given criterion of success, the measure selects the same proportion of minority applicants that would be selected on the basis of the criterion itself or on a perfectly valid selection measure. In other words, if 40 percent of the minority group members are successful and 70 percent of the nonminority group members are successful, then the proportion of minority group members selected should match the 40:70 success ratio. In Thorndike's model, therefore, a selection measure is fair if the success ratio equals the selection ratio.

Intuitively this model is appealing since it seems unfair to accept onto a job a smaller portion of any population subgroup than could, in fact, meet the criteria of success as defined by an organization. Thus, whereas the regression and equal-risk models primarily benefit the selecting institution, the constant ratio model proposes a kind of fairness more appropriate from the applicant's viewpoint (Cole, 1973).

As Schmidt and Hunter (1974) and Hunter and Schmidt (1976) have demonstrated, however, Thorndike's model suffers from several major disadvantages. It is another form of quota setting, it yields overprediction of minority group criterion scores in most situations, and it leads to a greater incidence of placement of individuals into occupational roles for which they are psychologically unsuited. This overprediction for minorities means that certain nonminority applicants will be rejected in favor of minority applicants with lower probabilities of success on the job (reverse discrimination). Hence, the overall level of performance will decrease considerably. Moreover, this is essentially a probability-matching model; therefore, given a definition of successful criterion performance, the proportions of minority and nonminority groups chosen should correspond to the probabilities of success for individuals drawn at random from each of the two groups. If lower-scoring ethnic groups other than African-Americans, Native Americans, Spanish-surnamed individuals, and so forth, were to demand the same probability matching, and if probability matching were imposed on higher-scoring and higher-performing ethnic groups (whose chances of selection would be reduced), most of the societal benefit accruing from the use of valid selection procedures would be lost.

Conditional Probability Model

A fifth model of selection fairness advocated by Cole (1973) and Dunnette (1970) is termed a conditional probability model. The basic principle underlying this approach is that for both minority and nonminority groups whose members can achieve a satisfactory criterion score ($Y > Y_p$), there should be the same probability of selection regardless of group membership. Dunnette (1970) pointed out that traditionally organizations have been more concerned about erroneous acceptances than erroneous rejections. In the conditional probability model, unfair discrimination against a minority group occurs when, over the long run, a firm's selection decisions yield higher proportions of erroneous rejections for members of the minority group than for members of the nonminority group.

This is exactly the situation that occurs when the GATB, whose mean validity is about 0.3 (Hartigan and Wigdor, 1989; Vevea, Clements, and Hedges, 1993), is used to select minority and nonminority candidates for jobs. So long as there are average group differences in test scores, the effects of imperfect prediction will fall disproportionately on groups with lower average test scores than the nonminority group. With the GATB, African-Americans typically score about one standard deviation below whites (Hartigan and Wigdor, 1989, p. 187). However, this phenomenon is not the result of some racial or ethnic bias inherent in the test. The impact is the same for all low-scoring individuals, regardless of group identity. Not only do low scorers have a greater likelihood of being erroneously rejected, but high scorers also have a greater likelihood of being erroneously accepted (see Fig. 8–3).

As Hartigan and Wigdor's committee noted:

> At this point in our history, it is certain that use of the GATB without some sort of score adjustments would systematically screen out blacks, some of whom could have performed satisfactorily on the job. Fair test use would seem to require at the very least that the inadequacies of the technology should not fall more heavily on the social groups already burdened by the effects of past and present discrimination. [p. 260]

To reduce this problem, the committee recommended the use of within-group percentile, top-down referral. That is, a percentile score is computed for each applicant by comparing the raw score for that applicant with the scores obtained by a norm group of the same racial or ethnic identity (African-Americans, Hispanics, and all others). (This has the same effect as making the mean and variance of the test scores equivalent for all groups.) Referral is then made from the *total* group of applicants in order of percentile score.

The committee recommended that two scores be reported to employers and applicants: (1) a within-group percentile score, with the corresponding norm group identified, and (2) an expectancy score (derived from the total group percentile score) equal to the probability that an applicant will have above-average job performance. The expectancy score shows that even low scorers have a reasonable chance of success on the job and helps employers to avoid placing unwarranted weight on small differences in test scores.

The within-group percentile method (sometimes called "race-norming") has been controversial from its inception (Brown, 1994). Public and media attention peaked with the passage of the Civil Rights Act of 1991, Section 106 of which banned any form of "score adjustment" on the basis of "race, color, religion, sex, or national origin." The within-group percentile method, which adjusts scores by race and national origin, is therefore illegal.

Comparisons Among Models

The five models may be compared and contrasted by referring again to Figure 8–1. Cases falling in regions 1 and 3 represent correct decisions, cases falling in region 4 are erroneous acceptances, and those in region 2 are erroneous rejections. In the conditional probability model, the emphasis is on the proportion of applicants who are above both the criterion cutoff and the predictor cutoff. In terms of Figure 8–1 the focus is on the ratio of the number of cases in region 1 to the number of cases in regions 1 and 2 combined. If this ratio is equal for all subgroups being compared, then the selection procedure is considered fair (Linn, 1973). In the equal-risk model, the probability of success for those selected is the same for different groups when the ratio of the number of cases in region 1 to the number of cases in regions 1 and 4 combined is the same for both groups. In the constant-ratio model, a selection measure is considered fair as long as the number

of cases in region 2 equals the number of cases in region 4 (Linn, 1973). In the traditional regression model, a selection measure is considered fair as long as there is not a preponderance of individuals from one subgroup in regions 2 and 4 (when predicted from a common regression line). In the subjective regression model, however, separate criterion cutoff scores are used for the minority and nonminority groups. A selection measure is considered "culturally optimal" in this model if for each subgroup the proportion of scores in regions 2 and 4 is equal.

Sliding Bands—A New Model of Fairness

As we have seen, the concept of fairness addresses a broad set of equity issues that includes fairness of test use, freedom from bias in scoring and interpretation, and the appropriateness of the test-based constructs or rules that underlie decision making—that is, distributive justice (Messick, 1995). The sliding band model, a method for referring candidates for selection, addresses the latter consideration.

As is well known, if there is a true correlation between test scores and job performance, the use of any strategy other than strict top-down referral results in some expected loss in performance (assuming the out-of-order selection is not based on secondary criteria that are themselves correlated with performance). For some employers that are trying to increase the diversity of their workforces, this may lead to a dilemma: possible loss of some economic utility in order to accomplish broader social objectives.

The sliding band model was developed as a compromise between top-down scoring, which is likely to result in adverse impact against protected groups, and the within-group percentile method, which ignores differences in raw scores between minorities and nonminorities. It is an attempt to reconcile economic and social objectives within the framework of generally-accepted procedures for testing hypotheses about differences in individual test scores.

The sliding band method is one of a class of approaches to test use ("banding") in which individuals within a specific score range, or band, are regarded as having equivalent scores. It does not correct for very real differences in test scores that may be observed among groups; it only allows for flexibility in decision making (Cascio, Outtz, Zedeck, and Goldstein, 1991).

Banding is based on the assumption that no test is perfectly reliable; hence error is present, to some degree in all test scores. While the reliability coefficient is an index of the amount of error that is present in the test as a whole, and the standard error of measurement (SEM) allows us to establish limits for the true score of an individual who achieves a given observed score, the standard error of the difference (SED) allows us to determine whether the true scores of two individuals differ reliably from each other. In its simplest form, SED = SEM $\sqrt{2}$. Depending on the relative risk of a Type I or Type II error that an investigator is willing to tolerate, he or she may establish a confidence interval of any desired width (e.g., 95%, 90%, 68%) by using $\pm C \times$ SED, where C is the point on the normal curve that represents chance (e.g., 1.96 corresponds to the .05 level of chance). (For more on this see Zedeck et al., 1996.) Banding makes use of this psychometric information to set a cut score. For example, suppose the value of C × SED = 7 points. If the difference between the top score and any observed score is 7 points or fewer, then the scores are not considered to be reliably different from each other, whereas differences of 8 points or greater are. To illustrate, scores of 90 and 83 would not be considered to be reliably different from each other, but scores of 90 and 82 would be. The SED therefore serves as an index for testing hypotheses about ability differences among individuals.

The sliding band procedure works as follows. Beginning with the top score in a band (the score that ordinarily would be chosen first in a top-down selection procedure) a band of width, say, 1 or 2 SEDs is created. Scores that fall within the band are considered not to differ significantly from the top score in the band, within the limits of measurement error. If the scores are not reliably different from the top score (in effect they are treated as tied), then secondary criteria (e.g., experience, training, performance, or diversity-based considerations) might be used to break the ties and to determine which candidates should be referred for selection.

When the top scorer within a band is chosen, and if applicants still need to be selected, then the band slides such that the next highest scorer becomes the referent. A new band is selected by subtracting 7 points from the remaining, highest scorer. If the top scorer is not chosen, then the band cannot slide and selections must continue to be made from within the original band. This is a *minimax* strategy. That is, by proceeding in a top-down fashion, though not selecting in strict rank order, employers can minimize the

maximum loss in utility, relative to top-down selection. In fact, using a mathematical model, Siskin (1995) showed that in most situations a small loss in average performance may be expected, and that a person at the top of a band is only slightly more likely to outperform a person at the bottom of a band. These results showed generally that the social gains of banding may be greater than the economic cost.

The sliding band method has spawned a lively debate among researchers regarding its logic and consequences (Cascio, Goldstein, Outtz, and Zedeck, 1995; Cascio, Zedeck, Goldstein, and Outtz, 1995; Murphy and Myors, 1995; Sackett and Roth, 1991; Sackett and Wilk, 1994; Schmidt, 1991; Schmidt and Hunter, 1995; Zedeck, Outtz, Cascio, and Goldstein, 1991). While adverse impact may still result even when the sliding band method is used, characteristics of the applicant pool (the proportion of the applicant pool from the lower-scoring group), differences in subgroup standard deviations and means, and test reliability all combine to determine the impact of the method in any given situation (Murphy, 1994; Murphy, Osten, and Myors, 1995). Nevertheless, in its position paper on banding, the Scientific Affairs Committee of the Society for Industrial and Organizational Psychology (Report, 1994) concluded:

> The basic premise behind banding is consistent with psychometric theory. Small differences in test scores might reasonably be due to measurement error, and a case can be made on the basis of classical measurement theory for a selection system that ignores such small differences, or at least does not allow small differences in test scores to trump all other considerations in ranking individuals for hiring [p. 82] . . . There is legitimate scientific justification for the position that small differences in test scores might not imply meaningful differences in either the construct measured by the test or in future job performance [p. 85].

Finally, a ruling by the 9th Circuit Court of Appeals (*Officers for Justice* v. *Civil Service Commission of the City and County of San Francisco,* 1992) approved the use of the sliding-band procedure in a case where secondary criteria were used. The Court concluded:

> The City in concert with the union, minority job applicants, and the court finally devised a selection process which offers a facially neutral way to interpret actual scores and reduce adverse impact on mi-

nority candidates while preserving merit as the primary criterion for selection. Today we hold that the banding process is valid as a matter of constitutional and federal law [p. 9055].

SUMMARY

These six models—the traditional regression model, the subjective regression model, the equal-risk model, the constant-ratio model, the conditional probability model, and the sliding band model—illustrate that there is more than one reasonable definition of selection fairness and that the definitions have different practical and ethical implications that may conflict. Moreover, there are irreconcilable differences among various ethical positions (e.g., quotas versus unqualified individualism). Thus, the ultimate resolution of the problem probably will not rest on statistical grounds alone; competing values also must be weighed (Gottfredson, 1988; 1994; Hunter, Schmidt, and Rauschenberger, 1977; Linn, 1973).

In short, broader considerations than validity alone need to be considered. The concept of **utility** is far more inclusive, for it takes into account both the validity of a procedure and the relative importance of decisions based upon it. Utility is concerned with costs, both objective (e.g., costs of training, turnover, proficiency) and subjective (e.g., costs of undesirable job behavior, attitudinal and psychological costs of job failure or erroneous rejections). Utility is particularly relevant to selection fairness, for it forces organizations to consider carefully the cost consequences of alternative outcomes.

Utility models have been developed (Cronbach, Yalow, and Schaeffer, 1980; Gross and Su, 1975) that permit numerical estimates of the trade-off between (1) accepting more applicants from a low-scoring group whose representation one wishes to increase and (2) maximizing the quality of the work force. All are based on the idea that what is fair in a given situation depends on particular historical, contextual, and environmental variables (such as court decisions). Moreover, the rational input of responsible decision makers must be integrated with psychometric input if society's best interests are to be served.

Thus fairness reduces to a question of utilities. Although a universal, fair selection model probably will never exist, the explicit adoption of utility (or loss) values at least permits careful examination of the psychological, social, ethical, and legal implications of these values (Petersen and Novick, 1976). Equal employment opportunity sorely needs such an approach.

FAIR EMPLOYMENT AND PUBLIC POLICY

Social critics often have focused on written tests as the primary vehicles for unfair discrimination in employment, but it is important to stress that no single employment practice (such as testing) can be viewed apart from its role in the total system of employment decisions. Those who do so suffer from social myopia and, by implication, assume that if only testing can be rooted out, unfair discrimination likewise will disappear—much as the surgeon's scalpel cuts out the tumor that threatens the patient's life.

Yet unfair discrimination is a persistent infirmity that often pervades all aspects of the employment relationship. It shows itself in company recruitment practices (e.g., exhibiting passive nondiscrimination), in selection practices (e.g., requiring an advanced degree for a clerical position or using an inordinately difficult or unvalidated test for hiring or promotion), in compensation (e.g., paying lower wages to similarly qualified women or minorities than to white men for the same work), in placement (e.g., "channeling" members of certain groups into the least desirable jobs), in training and orientation (e.g., refusing to provide in-depth job training or orientation for minorities), and in performance appraisal (e.g., permitting bias in supervisory ratings). In short, unfair discrimination is hardly endemic to employment testing, although testing is certainly a visible target for public attack.

Public interest in measurement embraces three essential functions: (1) diagnosing needs (in order to implement remedial programs), (2) assessing qualifications to *do* (as in employment contexts), and (3) protecting against false credentials. Each of these functions has a long history. A sixteenth-century Spanish document requiring that tests be used to determine admission to specialized courses of study refers to each one (Casteen, 1984).

Over the past three decades we have moved from naive acceptance of tests (because they are part of the way things are), through a period of intense hostility to tests (because they are said to reflect the way things are to a degree not compatible with our social principles), to a higher acceptance of tests (because we seek salvation in a time of doubt about the quality of our schools, our workers, indeed, about ourselves) (Casteen, 1984).

Tests and other selection procedures are useful to society because society must allocate opportunities. Specialized roles must be filled. Through educational classification and employment selection, tests help determine who gains affluence and influence (Cronbach, 1990). Tests serve as instruments of public policy, and public policy must be reevaluated periodically. Indeed, each generation must think carefully about the meaning of the words "equal opportunity." Should especially rich opportunity be given to those whose homes have done least for them? What evidence about individuals should enter into selection decisions? And, once the evidence becomes available, what policies should govern how decisions are made?

To be sure, answers to questions like these are difficult; of necessity they will vary from generation to generation. But one thing is clear: Sound policy is not *for* tests or *against* tests; what really matters is how tests are *used* (Cronbach, 1990). From a public policy perspective, the Congress, the Supreme Court, the EEOC, and the OFCCP continuously have reaffirmed the substantial benefits to be derived from the informed and judicious use of staffing procedures within the framework of fair employment practices. (For more on this, see Sharf, 1988.)

Although some errors are inevitable in employment decisions, the crucial question to be asked in regard to each procedure is whether or not its use results in less social cost than is now being paid for these errors, considering all other assessment methods. After carefully reviewing all available evidence on eight alternatives to tests, Reilly and Chao (1982) concluded: "Test fairness research has, with few exceptions, supported the predictability of minority groups even though adverse impact exists . . . There is no reason to expect alternate predictors to behave differently" (p. 55). As Schmidt (1988) has pointed out, however, "alternatives" are actually misnamed. If they are valid, they should be used in combination with ability measures to maximize overall validity and utility. Thus, they are more appropriately termed "supplements," rather than "alternatives."

More recently, Maxwell and Arvey (1993) have shown that within the universe of tests that satisfy the regression model of fairness (Cleary, 1968), the most valid selection method will necessarily produce the least adverse impact. However, in cases where the job performance of minority group members is systematically overpredicted (e.g., when some cognitive ability and physical ability tests are used), then the tests do not satisfy the definition of fairness in the regression model. Thus high validity, in and of itself, does not always indicate low adverse impact.

Finally, in reviewing 50 years of public controversy over psychological testing, Cronbach (1975) concluded:

> The spokesmen for tests, then and recently, were convinced that they were improving social efficiency, not making choices about social philosophy . . . The social scientist is trained to think that he does not know all the answers. The social scientist is not trained to realize that he does not know all the questions. And that is why his social influence is not unfailingly constructive. [p. 13]

As far as the future is concerned, it is the position of this book that staffing procedures will yield better and fairer results when we can specify in detail the linkages between the personal characteristics of individuals and the requirements of jobs for which the procedures are most relevant. The inevitable result can only be a better informed, wiser use of available human resources.

Discussion Questions

1. Why are prediction systems more informative of possible group differences than correlation coefficients?

2. Summarize the available evidence on differential validity. What advice on this issue would you give to an employer?

3. When is a measure of individual differences unfairly discriminatory?

4. Compare and contrast the regression model of selection fairness to the sliding band model.

5. Discuss some of the public policy issues that surround testing.

*   *   *

In Part III we have examined applied measurement concepts that are essential to sound employment decision making. In Parts IV through VII we shall see how these concepts are applied in practice. Let us begin in Chapter 9 by considering job analysis—a topic that, as a result of legislative and judicial developments, is emerging both in importance and in emphasis.

CHAPTER 9

ANALYZING JOBS AND WORK

AT A GLANCE

From one perspective an organization may be viewed as a pattern of roles and a blueprint for their coordination. The analysis of work and roles represents such a blueprint, for individual jobs are the basic building blocks necessary to achieve broader organizational goals. The objective of job analysis is to define each job in terms of the behaviors necessary to perform it. Job analyses comprise two major elements: **job descriptions** and **job specifications.** Job specifications indicate the personal characteristics necessary to do the work, while job descriptions specify the physical and environmental characteristics of the work to be done.

Historically, job analysis methods assumed that jobs were not changed by the individuals performing them, or by time or situa-
tional factors. Thus, narrative descriptions of job activities (what gets done) were emphasized. More recent job analysis techniques recognize job dynamics and attempt to describe jobs in worker-oriented terms (how the job gets done). The latter approach not only provides a basis for establishing common behavioral requirements across jobs, but also aids in the identification of the personal qualities necessary for success in a given job. Legally and scientifically, both job- and worker-oriented approaches are acceptable, and both have helped further our understanding of the linkages between workers' personal qualities, the requirements of their jobs, and measures of organizational success.

If we were to start a brand new organization, or a new division of a larger organization, we would be faced immediately with a host of problems, several of which involve decisions about people. What are the broad goals of the new organization or division, and how should it be structured in order to achieve these goals? Since the overall work of the new organization or division is too large for any one individual to handle (e.g., jet aircraft production), how can the work be broken down into pieces (or processes) small enough (yet challenging enough) for individuals or teams? How many positions will we have to staff and what will be the nature of these positions? What abilities, skills, and personal characteristics will be required? How many individuals should we recruit? What factors (personal, social, and technical) should we be concerned with in the selection of these individuals? How should they be trained, and what criteria should we use to measure how well they have performed their jobs? Before any of these decisions can be made, we first must define the jobs in question and then discover what employee behaviors are necessary to perform the jobs. This process is known as **job analysis.**

It is difficult to overstate the importance of job analysis to employment research and administration. If thoroughly and competently conducted, job analysis provides a deeper understanding of individual jobs and their behavioral requirements and, therefore, creates a firm basis on which to make employment decisions. As the APA *Standards* (1985) note: "Job analyses pro-

Organization Design	HR Management	Work and Equipment Design	Additional Uses
Organizing Human resource planning Role definition	Job evaluation Recruitment Selection Placement Orientation Training and development Performance appraisal Promotions and transfers Career path planning Labor relations	Engineering design Job design Methods improvement Safety	Vocational guidance Rehabilitation counseling Job classification systems HR research

FIGURE 9–1 Uses of Job Analysis Information.

vide the primary basis for defining the content domain [of a job]" (p. 64).

Job analysis provides an "understanding [of] the organization's needs as they relate to the selection problem so that the researcher can formulate sound hypotheses about relationships among predictors and criteria" (Society, 1987, p. 5). Although some courts insist on extensive job analysis (e.g., as a basis for providing content-related evidence of validity), certain purposes, such as validity generalization, may not require such detail (Guion and Gibson, 1988). As can be seen in Figure 9–1, there are many uses and purposes for which job analysis information might be collected.

An organization can usefully be viewed as a pattern of roles, with job analysis providing a blueprint for the coordination of these roles (Schein, 1980). Job analysis can underpin organization structure and design by clarifying roles (patterns of expected behavior based on organizational position). Job analysis specifies employee responsibilities at all hierarchical levels—from floor sweeper to chairperson of the board—thereby avoiding job overlap and duplication of effort and promoting efficiency and harmony among individuals and departments. Job analysis is a fundamental tool that can be used in every phase of employment research and administration; in fact, job analysis is to the HR specialist what the wrench is to the plumber.

TERMINOLOGY

HR, like any other specialty area, has its own peculiar jargon, and although some of the terms are used interchangeably in everyday conversation, technically there are distinct differences among them. These differences will become apparent as we examine job analysis methods more closely. The definitions that follow generally are consistent with the terminology used by the U.S. Department of Labor (1972; 1982), McCormick (1979), and Gael (1988).

An **element** is the smallest unit into which work can be divided without analyzing separate motions, movements, and mental processes involved. Removing a saw from a tool chest prior to sawing wood for a project is an example of a job element.

A **task** is a distinct work activity carried out for a distinct purpose. Running a computer program, typing a letter, or unloading a truckload of freight are examples of tasks.

A **duty** includes a large segment of the work performed by an individual and may include any number of tasks. Examples of job duties include conducting interviews, counseling employees, and providing information to the public.

A **position** consists of one or more duties performed by a given individual in a given firm at a given time, such as clerk typist—level three. There are as many positions as there are workers.

FROM A TASK-BASED TO A PROCESS-BASED ORGANIZATION OF WORK

Traditional task-based "jobs" were packaged into clusters of similar tasks and assigned to specialist workers. Today many firms have no reason to package work that way. Instead, they are unbundling tasks into broader chunks of work that change over time. Such shifting clusters of tasks make it difficult to define a "job," at least in the traditional sense. Practices such as flex-time, job sharing, and telecommuting, not to mention temporary workers, part-timers, and consultants have compounded the definitional problem.

Today there is a detectable shift away from a task-based toward a process-based organization of work. A process is a collection of activities (such as procurement, order fulfillment, product development, or credit issuance), that takes one or more kinds of input and creates an output that is of value to a customer (Hammer and Champy, 1993). Customers may be internal or external. Individual tasks are important parts of the process, but the process itself cuts across organizational boundaries and traditional functions, such as engineering, production, marketing, and finance.

Consider credit issuance as an example. Instead of the separate jobs of credit checker and pricer, the two may be combined into one "deal structurer." Such integrated processes may cut response time and increase efficiency and productivity. Bell Atlantic created a "case team"—a group of people who have among them all of the skills necessary to handle an installation order. Members of the team—who previously were located in different departments and in different geographical areas—were brought together into a single unit and given total responsibility for installing the equipment. Such a process operates, on aver-age, ten times faster than the assembly-line version it replaces. Bell Atlantic, for example, reduced the time it takes to install a high-speed digital service link from 30 days to three (Hammer and Champy, 1993).

Employees involved in the process are responsible for ensuring that customers' requirements are met on time and with no defects, and they are empowered to experiment in ways that will cut cycle time and reduce costs. Result: less supervision is needed, while workers take on broader responsibilities and a wider purview of activities. Moreover, the kinds of activities that each worker does are likely to shift over time.

In terms of traditional job analysis, this leaves many unanswered questions and a number of challenges (Cascio, 1995b):

- What will be the future of traditional task-based descriptions of jobs and job activities? Should other types of descriptors replace task statements that describe what a worker does, to what or whom, why, and how? Will "task cluster" statements or "subprocess" statements become the basic building blocks for describing work?

- What does a job description look like in a process-based organization of work?

- Will job specifications (which identify the personal characteristics—knowledge, skills, abilities, and other characteristics—necessary to do the work) supersede job descriptions?

- Does identification of the environmental, contextual, and social dimensions of work become more important in a process-based structure?

- Will emphasis shift from describing jobs to describing roles?

While there are no clear answers to these questions as of this writing, do keep these ideas in mind as you continue reading.

A **job** is a group of positions that are similar in their significant duties, such as two or more mechanics—level two. A job, however, may only involve one position, depending on the size of the organization. For example, the local garage may employ only one mechanic—level two.

A **job family** is a group of two or more jobs that either call for similar worker characteristics or contain parallel work tasks as determined by job analysis.

An **occupation** is a group of similar jobs found in different organizations at different times—for example, electricians, machinists, and so on. A **vocation** is similar to an occupation, but the term *vocation* is more likely to be used by a worker than by an employer.

A **career** covers a sequence of positions, jobs, or occupations that one person engages in during his or her working life.

Dynamic Characteristics of Jobs

Are jobs static? Is it true that once one defines a job and specifies the behaviors necessary to perform it, the job is not changed appreciably over time by different situations or job incumbents? Actually things are a bit more complex, and in order to conduct a thorough job analysis, one must estimate, or at least take into account, the effects of factors related to change. Let's consider three major types of changes that may affect jobs.

Time-Determined Changes. Jobs that change with the seasons, such as lifeguard, ski instructor, summer-camp counselor, and so forth, fall under this heading, as do jobs that change because of technological advances. For example, computer-based word processing equipment has changed secretarial jobs radically. These types of changes in jobs are easiest to cope with in job analysis precisely because one can anticipate them ahead of time and specify appropriate behavioral requirements in advance.

Employee-Determined Changes. In some jobs, characteristics of people (abilities, skills, values, and preferences) interact with characteristics of jobs, and, thus, the jobs get redefined by the people performing them—sometimes consciously and sometimes without their full awareness. Individuals often modify the ways they behave on their jobs in light of their past training and experience, their present attitudes and beliefs, and the environmental context in which the work is performed. Strictly speaking, the job itself may not change, but in jobs that permit a wide latitude of expression, the job is frequently what the incumbent makes of it. For example, researchers, teachers, and football coaches have a great deal of freedom in the way they accomplish their jobs, whereas manufacturing technicians, precision lens grinders, and quality control inspectors are subject to more rigid procedural requirements.

The best way to take account of employee-determined changes in job analysis is to sample many employees in the same job and to identify the various

behavior patterns used successfully to perform the job. Selection then would attempt to identify employee characteristics that predict any of the acceptable behavior patterns (Dunnette, 1966).

Situation-Determined Changes. These changes are hardest to anticipate because they may stem from many different factors in the organizational environment. When a fire breaks out aboard a ship, the nature of everyone's job changes: Cooks, cabin attendants, deck hands, and officers all become firefighters. When internal conflict between groups is present in a plant, a first-level manager's job may change from supervisor to arbitrator, counselor, and problem solver. If the job is likely to involve "putting out fires," the job analyst must consider the nature of these fires. They might include elements in the physical work environment (noise, illumination, temperature), people in the work environment (co-workers, supervisors, group influences), or past trends (such as turnover rates, labor supply, recruitment, and market demand).

In the broadest sense, job analysis is concerned with analyzing any work-related information. Failure to consider the effects of potential agents of change can have a detrimental influence on all phases of the selection-placement process as well as on subsequent job performance. By taking this kind of information into account during the job analysis phase, the organization then can recruit people who are able to cope and respond successfully to changes in their jobs that inevitably will occur.

DEFINING THE JOB

Job analysis, as we have pointed out, consists of defining a job (e.g., in terms of its component tasks) and then discovering what the job calls for in terms of employee behaviors. Two elements stand out in this definition: task requirements and people requirements. In this section we will consider task requirements, and in the following section we will consider the behavioral requirements of jobs.

In many cases, the characteristics of jobs are "givens" to employees. They include, for example, the equipment used, the arrangement of the work space, the division of labor, and the procedures, methods, and standards of performance of the job. From these data, the job analyst produces a **job description** or written statement of what a worker actually does, how he or

---

CITY ARCHITECT I

NATURE OF WORK

This is professional and technical work in the preparation of architectural plans, designs, and specifications for a variety of municipal or public works building projects and facilities.

MINIMUM QUALIFICATIONS

Education and experience

Graduation from an accredited college or university with a specialization in architecture or architectural engineering or equal.

Knowledges, Abilities, and Skills

Considerable knowledge of the principles and practices of architecture; ability to make structural and related mathematical computations and make recommendations on architectural problems; ability to design moderately difficult architectural projects; ability to interpret local building codes and zoning regulations; ability to secure good working relationships with private contractors and employees; ability to train and supervise the work of technical and other subordinates in a manner conducive to full performance; ability to express ideas clearly and concisely, orally and in writing; skill in the use of architectural instruments and equipment.

ILLUSTRATION OF DUTIES

Prepares or assists in the preparation of architectural plans and designs all types of building projects constructed by the City, including fire stations, park and recreation buildings, office buildings, warehouses, and similar structures; prepares or supervises the preparation of final working drawings including architectural drawings, such as site plans, foundations, floor plans, elevations, section details, diagrams, and schedules rendering general features and scale details; prepares or supervises some of the engineering calculations, drawings and plans for mechanical details, such as plumbing, air-conditioning phases, and lighting features; writes construction standards and project specifications; prepares sketches including plans, elevations, site plans, and renderings and makes reports on feasibility and cost for proposed City work; writes specifications for all aspects of architectural projects including structural, mechanical, electrical, and air-conditioning work; confers with engineering personnel engaged in the preparation of structural plans for a building, making recommendations and suggestions as to materials, construction, and necessary adjustments in architectural designs to fit structural requirements; inspects construction in the field by checking for conformity with plans and material specifications; inspects existing structures to determine need for alterations or improvements and prepares drawings for such changes; performs related work as required.

SUPERVISION RECEIVED

General and specific assignments are received and work is performed according to prescribed methods and procedures with allowance for some independence in judgment in accomplishing the assignments.

SUPERVISION EXERCISED

Usually limited to supervision of technical assistants in any phase.

FIGURE 9–2 A Typical Job Description.

she does it, and why. This information can then be used to determine the competencies (knowledge, skills, abilities, and other characteristics) required to perform the job.

Elements of a job description may include:

1. *Job title*—for bookkeeping purposes within the firm as well as to facilitate reporting to government agencies.

2. *Job activities and procedures*—descriptions of tasks performed, materials used, machinery operated, for-

mal interactions with other workers, nature and extent of supervision given or received.

3. *Working conditions and physical environment*—heat, lighting, noise level, indoor/outdoor, physical location, hazardous conditions, and so on.

4. *Social environment*—for example, information on the number of individuals in the workgroup and the amount of interpersonal interaction required in order to perform the job.

5. *Conditions of employment*—including, for example, a

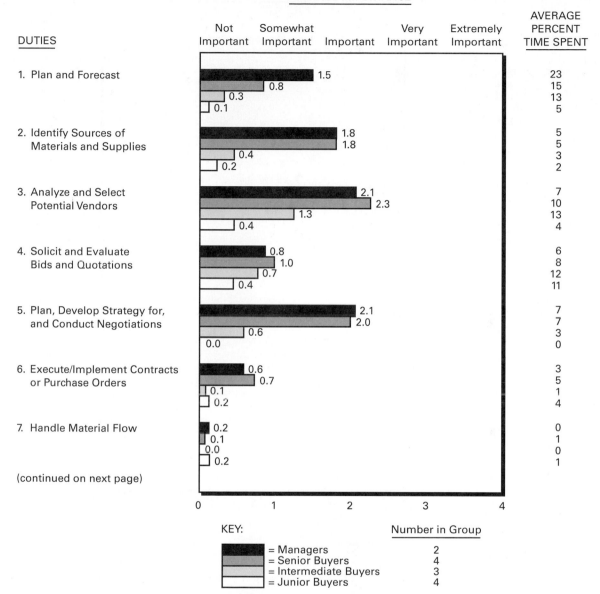

Source: From Micro-OAQ sample report formats and selection capabilities. Copyright 1986, Control Data Business Advisors, Inc. All rights reserved.

FIGURE 9–3 Example of the Duties Analysis Report, Showing Average Importance and Time Spent for Four Levels of Buyers.

description of the hours of work, wage structure, method of payment, benefits, place of the job in the formal organization, and opportunities for promotion and transfer. (An example of a job description for architect I is presented in Figure 9–2.)

Job descriptions can facilitate such processes as staffing, job evaluation, and performance appraisal,

but it is important to remember that they are narrative, written descriptions of jobs as currently constituted. They do not take job dynamics into account—a fact that is especially noticeable in job descriptions of executive or managerial positions where incumbents have a great deal of discretion in deciding what to do, and how to do it.

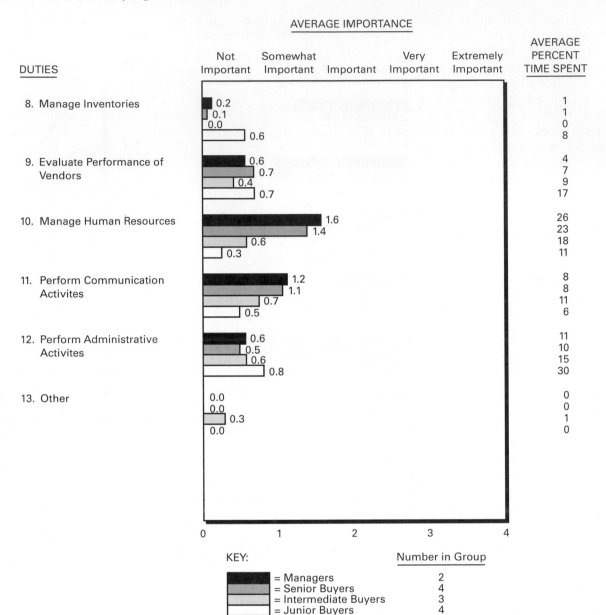

FIGURE 9–3 (Continued)

A Quantified Procedure for Obtaining Job Descriptions

Job descriptions need not always be written. For example, Control Data Business Advisors (1985) developed an Occupational Analysis Questionnaire (OAQ), a checklist of duties, tasks, and competencies for various occupations. Thus the OAQ for software jobs is organized into 19 duties comprising 310 tasks and 105 competencies. The duty "Provide User/Customer Technical Support," for example, includes the following tasks:

1. Provide "Hot Line" or telephone assistance to users/customers in solving software problems.

2. Provide software technical support to "walk-in" users/customers.

3. Provide on-site technical support to the user/customer during the software-installation process.

Job incumbents complete the OAQ. They determine whether each task is relevant to their work, and, if so, indicate on a nine-point rating scale the relative amount of time they spend on that task. Data from the OAQ are computer-scored, and written or graphic reports are generated. A profile of the job duties of four levels of buyers is shown in Figure 9–3. The resulting job descriptions then can be used in the kinds of programs shown in Figure 9–1.

JOB SPECIFICATIONS

Job specifications are the competencies, the personal characteristics deemed necessary to perform a job. For example, keen vision (usually (20/20 uncorrected) is *required* of astronauts and test pilots.

In many jobs, however, job specifications are not rigid and inflexible; they serve only as guidelines for recruitment, selection, and placement. Job specifications depend on the level of performance deemed acceptable and the degree to which some abilities can be substituted for others. For example, in one investigation of power sewing machine operators, it was thought that good eyesight was necessary to sew sheets until research demonstrated that manual dexterity was far more important. The operators could sew sheets just as well with their eyes closed! This illustrates an important point: Some individuals may be restricted from certain jobs because the job specifications (often known as job requirements) are inflexible, artificially high, or invalid. For this reason, job specifications should indicate *minimally acceptable* standards for selection and later performance.

The Nature of Job Specifications

As we have seen, the objective of job specifications is to determine the personal characteristics (including such factors as educational background, experience, or vocational training) that are valid for screening, selection, and placement. How are these specifications set? One approach is known as "Threshold Traits Analysis" (TTA) (Lopez, Kesselman, and Lopez, 1981). The trait-oriented approach seeks to identify the human attributes that predispose individuals to perform well on various types of jobs. To the extent that trait-relevant incumbents of various occupations outperform non-trait-relevant incumbents on standardized measures of ability, then greater confidence can be placed in the capability of the trait approach to identify the personal characteristics related to success on various jobs. This approach is based on construct-related evidence of validity, and it was used by Lopez et al. (1981) to validate TTA—work that began in the 1950s.

The process begins by describing and illustrating the TTA method to a group of about 15 immediate supervisors. Working independently, each supervisor then determines the *relevance* for effective job performance of each of 33 carefully-defined traits (see Fig. 9–4). If the required level is zero, then the trait is regarded as irrelevant.

For traits determined to be relevant, each supervisor next determines the *unique level* of the trait. Trait level refers to the intensity or complexity of the trait, and it is rated on a numerical rating scale that is anchored by standardized verbal descriptions. Individual ratings are then averaged to produce a list of relevant traits, along with their levels and weights in the overall performance mix. TTA takes about one hour per job to complete.

In terms of equal employment opportunity, TTA has some clear advantages. Since the method yields an array of traits required for job performance, applicants can be evaluated for more than one job at a time. Weaknesses of an applicant on one trait, based on the results of a single selection instrument, need not signal automatic rejection. Instead, an employer can evaluate other strengths that offset this weakness, or provide remedial training to remedy the deficiency. The TTA method assumes that both job and individual effectiveness are multidimensional (Lopez et al., 1981).

VALIDITY OF JOB ANALYSIS INFORMATION

Job descriptions are valid to the extent that they represent accurately job content, environment, and conditions of employment. Job specifications are valid to the extent that persons possessing the personal characteristics believed necessary for successful job performance in fact *do* perform more effectively on their jobs than persons lacking such personal characteristics.

In terms of accuracy, research indicates that the amount of job descriptive information available to raters has a significant effect on job analysis accuracy. Raters with more detailed job information are consistently more accurate than those given only a job title. Moreover, data provided by relatively job-naive raters show little convergent validity with data provided by job content experts (Harvey and Lozada-Larsen, 1988).

AREA	JOB FUNCTIONS		TRAIT	DESCRIPTION – CAN:
PHYSICAL	Physical Exertion →		1. Strength	Lift, pull or push physical objects.
			2. Stamina	Expend physical energy for long periods.
	Bodily Activity →		3. Agility	React quickly; has dexterity, coordination.
	Sensory Inputs →		4. Vision	See details and colors of objects.
			5. Hearing	Recognize sound, tone and pitch.
MENTAL	Vigilance and Attention →		6. Perception	Observe and differentiate details.
			7. Concentration	Attend to details amid distraction.
			8. Memory	Retain and recall ideas.
	Information Processing →		9. Comprehension	Understand spoken and written ideas.
			10. Problem-solving	Reason and analyze abstract information.
			11. Creativity	Produce new ideas and products.
LEARNED	Quantitative Computation →		12. Numerical Computation	Solve arithmetic and numerical problems.
	Communications →		13. Oral Expression	Speak clearly and effectively.
			14. Written Expression	Write clearly and effectively.
	Action Selection and Projection →		15. Planning	Project a course of action.
			16. Decision-making	Choose a course of action.
	Application of Information and Skill →		17. Craft Knowledge	Apply specialized information.
			18. Craft Skill	Perform a complex set of activities.
MOTIVATIONAL	Unprogrammed →		19. Adaptability – Change	Adjust to interruptions and changes.
	Cycled →		20. Adaptability – Repetition	Adjust to repetitive activities.
	Stressful ——— Working		21. Adaptability – Pressure	Adjust to critical and demanding work.
	Secluded ——— Conditions		22. Adaptability – Isolation	Work alone or with little personal contact.
	Unpleasant →		23. Adaptability – Discomfort	Work in hot, cold, noisy work places.
	Dangerous →		24. Adaptability – Hazards	Work in dangerous situations.
	Absence of Direct Supervision →		25. Control – Dependability	Work with minimum of supervision.
	Presence of Difficulties →		26. Control – Perseverance	Stick to a task until completed.
	Unstructured Conditions →		27. Control – Initiative	Act on own, take charge when needed.
	Access to Valuables →		28. Control – Integrity	Observe regular ethical and moral codes.
	Limited Mobility →		29. Control – Aspirations	Limit desire for promotion.
SOCIAL	Interpersonal Contact →		30. Personal Appearance	Meet appropriate standards of dress.
			31. Tolerance	Deal with people in tense situations.
			32. Influence	Get people to cooperate.
			33. Cooperation	Work as a member of a team.

THRESHOLD TRAITS ANALYSIS

Source: From Lopez, F. M., Kesselman, G. A., and Lopez, F. E. An empirical test of a trait-oriented job analysis technique. *Personnel Psychology*, 1981, 34, p. 484.

FIGURE 9–4 List of Threshold Traits Analysis System Job Functions, Corresponding Traits, and Abbreviated Trait Definitions.

To assess the meaningfulness of inferences drawn from job analysis information, an "indirect validity" approach might be used (McCormick, 1959). **Indirect validity** is the extrapolation or extension of validity from one situation to another. It hinges on the analysis of job characteristics and the subsequent identification of common denominators among jobs. Thus, to the extent that job analysis information in one job is valid, job analysis information in a similar job may be validated indirectly if a number of similar job and environmental characteristics can be identified, for example, by comparing profiles. It appears that the dimensions on which jobs are profiled are not crucial, as long as the profiles bear some relationship to the ultimate purpose for which the clustering is intended (e.g., improved selection, placement, training) (McCormick, Jeanneret, and Mecham, 1972). Four types of job characteristics might lend themselves to indirect validity analysis:

1. Overall nature of the job—that is, gross, general attributes.
2. Ratings of the human traits required for successful job performance.
3. Job-oriented elements—elements that describe *what the worker accomplishes;* for example, "lays bricks," "takes dictation."
4. Worker-oriented elements—elements that express *what the worker does* to accomplish the end results of his actions, such as sensing, decision making, manipulating.

Historically, job analysis procedures have involved a descriptive approach, with job duties and responsibilities typically described in a narrative essay format (see Fig. 9–2). Obviously, this information is not easily put into quantifiable terms, which is a basic requirement for indirect validity studies. For this reason, the use of task checklists (rated in terms of frequency, importance, or relative time spent) holds great promise. Similar jobs then may be grouped using statistical techniques such as factor analysis or cluster analysis. Before we address these topics, however, let us examine more closely how such information may be obtained.

OBTAINING JOB INFORMATION

Numerous methods exist for describing jobs, although they differ widely in the assumptions they make about jobs, in breadth of coverage, and in precision. Some are job-oriented and some are worker-oriented, but each method has its own particular set of advantages and disadvantages. For purposes of exposition we present the various methods separately, but sound practice dictates that several methods be used to complement each other so the end product represents a valid and comprehensive picture of job duties, responsibilities, and behaviors.

Direct Observation and Job Performance

Observation of job incumbents or actual performance of the job by the analyst are two methods of gathering job information. Data then may be recorded in a narrative format or on some type of checklist or worksheet such as that shown in Figure 9–5. Both methods assume that jobs are relatively static—that is, that they remain constant over time and are not changed appreciably by different job incumbents or different situations. Job observation is appropriate for jobs that require a great deal of manual, standardized, short-cycle activities, and job performance is appropriate for jobs that the job analyst can learn readily.

Observations should include a representative sample of job behaviors. For example, the activity "copes with emergencies" may be crucial to effective nursing performance; yet a continuous 8-hour observation of the activities of a group of staff nurses tending to the needs of a dozen sleepy postoperative patients may reveal little in the way of a valid picture of job requirements.

Furthermore, the job analyst must take care to be unobtrusive in his or her observations, lest the measuring process per se distort what is being measured (Webb et al., 1981). This does not imply that the analyst should *hide* from the worker and remain out of sight, but it does imply that the analyst should not get in the way. Consider the following incident, which actually happened.

While riding along in a police patrol car as part of a job analysis of police officers, an analyst and an officer were chatting away when a call came over the radio regarding a robbery in progress. Upon arriving at the scene the analyst and the officer both jumped out of the patrol car, but in the process the overzealous analyst managed to position himself between the robbers and the police. Although the robbers were apprehended later, they used the analyst as a decoy to make their getaway from the scene of the crime.

Observation and job performance are inappropriate for jobs that require a great deal of mental ac-

---

JOB ANALYSIS WORKSHEET

NAME OF EMPLOYEE	DATE:
CLASSIFICATION:	ANALYST:
DEPARTMENT:	DIVISION:
LENGTH OF TIME IN JOB:	LENGTH OF TIME WITH ORGANIZATION:

A description of what the classification duties currently are and what is actually needed to do the job. No indications need be made of experiences, abilities, or training acquired after employment.

1. General summary of job (primary duties):
2. Job tasks (tasks with X in front indicate observed duties; use actual examples, indicate frequency, consequences of error (0-10), difficulty (0-10), training received, supervision).
3. How detailed are assignments? Describe the form work comes in, decisions that have been made, and what still needs to be done with the work.
4. Relation to others in position:
5. Higher positions job prepares one for:
6. Equivalent positions:
7. Tools, machinery, aids:
8. Physical activity: (climbing, lifting, walking, standing, operating heavy equipment, etc.)
9. (Observe) Hazards, or unusual working conditions:
10. (Supervisor-Dept. Head) Qualifications: (competency needed)
11. (Supervisor-Dept. Head) Knowledge, skills, abilities required to do the job:
12. (Supervisor-Dept. Head) Special requirements, licenses, etc.:
13. Clarification of employee written specs, if any:
14. Contacts (inside/outside organization):
15. Supervisory responsibility, if any:

FIGURE 9–5 Job Analysis Worksheet (condensed).

tivity and concentration such as those of lawyer, computer programmer, or design engineer, but there are thousands of jobs for which these methods are perfectly appropriate. A technique known as functional job analysis (FJA) often is used to record observed tasks (Fine, 1989). FJA attempts to identify exactly what the worker *does* in the job as well as the results of the worker's behavior, that is, *what gets done.* An example of an FJA worksheet summarizing a job analyst's observations of a firefighter performing salvage and overhaul operations in response to an emergency call is shown in Figure 9–6. Let us consider the various sections of the worksheet.

Duties are general areas of responsibility. Tasks describe what gets done. Under *What,* two pieces of information are required: "Performs What Action" (i.e., describe what the worker did, using an action verb), and "To Whom or to What?" (i.e., describe the object of the verb). *Why* forces the analyst to consider the purpose of the worker's action ("To Produce or Achieve What?"). *How* requires the analyst to describe the tools, equipment, or work aids used to accomplish the task and, in addition, to specify the nature and source of instructions. This section also indicates whether the task is *prescribed* (e.g., by a superior or departmental procedures) or left to the worker's discretion.

Worker Functions describe the orientation and level of worker activity with Data, People, and Things. All jobs involve workers to some extent with information or ideas (data), with clients, co-workers, superiors, and so on (people), and with machines or equipment (things). The percentages listed under Data, People, and Things indicate the relative amount of involvement (orientation) with each of these functions. Numbers indicate the level of complexity, according to scales developed by the U.S. Department of Labor, as follows:

DATA	PEOPLE	THINGS
0 Synthesize	0 Mentor	0 Set up
1 Coordinate	1 Negotiate	1 Precision work
2 Analyze	2 Instruct	2 Operate, control
3 Compile	3 Supervise	3 Drive, operate
4 Compute	4 Divert	4 Manipulate
5 Copy	5 Persuade	5 Tend
6 Compare	6 Speak-Signal	6 Feed
	7 Serve	7 Handle
	8 Take instruction	

Of course each of these terms is defined more fully for the analyst, but the important thing to note is that since the level and orientation measures can be applied to all

Position, series: Firefighter
Duty: Response to emergency dispatches
Task Statement: Performing salvage and overhaul

	WHAT?		*WHY?*	*HOW?*		*WORKER FUNCTIONS* Orientation and Level		
	Performs What Action? (action verb)	*To Whom or To What?* (object of verb)	*To Produce or Achieve What?*	*Using What Tools, Equipment, or Work Aids?*	*Upon What Instructions?*	*Data*	*People*	*Things*
1.	Piles and covers	Furniture, clothing, and other valuables	In order to protect material from fire and water damage	Salvage covers	Prescribed content: a. Company officer b. Departmental procedure Discretionary content: a. As to the best location for preventing damage to materials	10% 2	10% 8	80% 7
2.	Examines	Walls, ceilings, floors, and furniture	In order to locate and extinguish secondary fire sources	Pike pole, charged hose line, nozzle, portable power saw, axe	Prescribed content: a. Company officer b. Departmental procedure Discretionary content: a. As to the area examined for secondary fire sources b. As to the tools used for locating secondary fire sources	50% 2	10% 8	40% 4
3.	Carries	Smoldering mattresses and furniture from buildings	In order to reduce fire and smoke damage to buildings and their contents	Crowbar	Prescribed content: a. Company officer b. Departmental procedure Discretionary content: a. As to whether article or material needs to be removed from building	20% 2	10% 8	70% 7

FIGURE 9–6 Behavior Observation Worksheet in Functional Job Analysis Terms.

tasks, and therefore to all jobs, the worker function scales provide a way of comparing all tasks and all jobs on a common basis.

Information derived from FJA can be used for purposes other than job description per se. It can provide the basis for developing job-related performance standards (Olson et al., 1981), and it can be used in job design efforts. Both Campion (1989) and Rousseau (1982) found that job codes dealing with "data" and "people" were related to perceptions of task characteristics such as autonomy, variety, and task significance. Those dealing with "things" contributed little to job perceptions. This kind of research on the impact of personal and organizational factors on job analysis methods is welcome and needed. As we shall see, it is becoming more popular.

Interview

The interview is probably the most commonly used technique for establishing the tasks, duties, and behaviors necessary both for standardized or nonstandardized activities and for physical as well as mental work. Because the worker acts as his or her own observer in the interview, he or she can report activities and behaviors that would not often be observed, as well as those activities that occur over long time spans. Moreover, because of his or her thorough knowledge of the job, the worker can report information that might not be available to the analyst from any other source. Viewing the interview as a "conversation with a purpose," however, makes it obvious that the success of this technique depends partly on the skill of the interviewer.

Thorough advance planning and training of the analyst in interview techniques should precede the actual interviewing, and for reasons of reliability and efficiency, the analyst should follow a patterned interview form that covers systematically the material to be gathered during the interview. As a guide, questions used by interviewers may be checked for their appropriateness against the following criteria (McCormick, 1979):

- The question should be related to the purpose of the analysis.
- The wording should be clear and unambiguous.
- The question should not "lead" the respondent; that is, it should not imply that a specific answer is desired.
- The question should not be "loaded" in the sense that one form of response might be considered to be more socially desirable than another.
- The question should not ask for knowledge or information the interviewee doesn't have.
- There should be no personal or intimate material that the interviewee might resent. (p. 36)

Workers often look upon interviewers with some suspicion and, understandably, they are wary of divulging information about their jobs. For this reason the analyst must provide a comfortable atmosphere where the worker or team feels free to discuss job duties and responsibilities.

The major stumbling block with the interviewing technique is distortion of information, whether this is due to outright falsification or to honest misunderstanding. For example, if the worker knows (or thinks) that the results of the job analysis may influence wages, he or she may exaggerate certain responsibilities and minimize others. Hence, interviews may require time and a good deal of adroit questioning in order to elicit valid information.

As a check on the information provided by a single job incumbent, it is wise to interview several incumbents as well as immediate supervisors who know the jobs well. Both high- and low-performing incumbents and supervisors tend to provide similar information (Conley and Sackett, 1987), as do members of different demographic subgroups (Schmitt and Cohen, 1989). However, this may be true only for simple, as opposed to complex, jobs (Mullins and Kimbrough, 1988). Multiple interviews allow researchers to take into account dynamic job factors due to time, people, and situations. This is only a partial solution to the problem, however, for often it is difficult to piece together results from several dissimilar interviews into a comprehensive picture. For this reason, consider using additional information-gathering techniques to supplement and refine interviewing results.

SME Panels

Panels of six to ten subject matter experts (SMEs) are often convened for different purposes in job analysis: (1) to develop information on tasks or competencies to be used in constructing job analysis questionnaires, and (2) in test development to establish linkages between tasks and competencies, competencies and test items, and tasks and test items. The total group of SMEs usually represents about a 10–20 percent sample of job incumbents and supervisors, representative of the race, gender, location, shift, and assignment composition of the entire group of incumbents. Evidence indicates, however, that the most important demographic variable in SME groups is experience (Landy and Vasey, 1991). Failure to include a broad cross-section of experience in a sample of SMEs could lead to distorted ratings. However, representative panels of SMEs provide results very similar to those obtained from broad surveys of respondents in the field (Tannenbaum and Wesley, 1993).

SMEs are encouraged to discuss issues and to resolve disagreements openly. For example, to promote discussion of competencies, panel members might be asked questions such as the following:

- Think of workers you know who are better than anyone else at (a particular task). Why do they do so well?

- If you were going to assign a worker to perform (a particular task) what kinds of competencies or personal characteristics would you want this person to have?

- What do you expect workers to learn in training that would make them effective at the tasks?

- Think of good workers *and* poor workers. What competencies distinguish one from the other?

If the task for SMEs is to establish linkages for test development purposes, quality-control statistics should be computed to ensure that the judgments or work products of the SMEs are meaningful (Hughes and Prien, 1989). For example, questionnaires might include repeat items and "carelessness" items (those that are inappropriate for the job under study). A high level of interrater agreement, and, for individual SMEs, a near-zero endorsement of "carelessness" items, are important checks on the meaningfulness of the data.

Questionnaires

Questionnaires usually are standardized and provide either for checking items that apply to a job or for rating items in terms of their relevance to the job in question. In general, they are cheaper and quicker to administer than other job analysis methods, and sometimes they can be completed at the respondent's leisure, thereby avoiding lost production time. In addition, when there are many workers in each job, questionnaires provide a breadth of coverage that would be exorbitantly expensive and time-consuming to obtain by any other method.

There are problems with this method, however. Questionnaires are often time-consuming and expensive to develop, and ambiguities or misunderstandings that might have been clarified in an interview are likely to go uncorrected. Similarly, it may be difficult to follow up and augment information obtained in the questionnaires. In addition, the rapport that might have been obtained in the course of face-to-face contact is impossible to achieve with an impersonal instrument. This may have adverse effects on respondent cooperation and motivation. On the other hand, the structured questionnaire approach probably has the greatest potential for quantifying job analysis information, which can then be processed by computer.

Task inventories and checklists are questionnaires that are used to collect information about a particular job or occupation. The job analyst completes a list of tasks or job activities either by checking or rating each item as it relates to the job in question in terms of the importance of the item, frequency with which the task is performed, judged difficulty, time to learn, or relationship to overall performance. Although these data are adaptable for computer analysis, checklists tend to ignore the sequencing of tasks or their relationships to other jobs. Thus, an overall perspective of the total job is extremely difficult to obtain with checklist information alone.

However, if one purpose of a task inventory is to assess the relative *importance* of each job task, then a unit-weighted, additive composite of ratings of task criticality, difficulty of learning the task, and relative time spent may provide the best prediction of average task importance across SMEs (Sanchez and Fraser, 1992).

THE POSITION ANALYSIS QUESTIONNAIRE (PAQ)

Since task inventories basically are job-oriented and make static assumptions about jobs, behavioral implications are difficult to establish. In contrast to this, worker-oriented information describes *how* a job gets done and is more concerned with generalized worker behaviors. One instrument that is based on statistical analyses of primarily worker-oriented job elements and lends itself to quantitative statistical analysis is the Position Analysis Questionnaire (PAQ), developed by McCormick, Jeanneret, and Mecham (1972). The PAQ consists of 194 items or job elements that fall into the following categories: information input (where and how the worker gets the information he or she uses for a job); mental processes (the reasoning, planning, decision making, and so forth involved in a job); work output (the physical activities the worker performs and the tools or devices he or she uses); relationships with other persons; and job context (physical and social contexts in which the work is performed). The individual items provide either for checking a job element

RELATIONSHIPS WITH OTHER PERSONS

This section deals with different aspects of interaction between people involved in various kinds of work.

Code	Importance to This Job (1)
DNA	Does not apply
1	Very minor
2	Low
3	Average
4	High
5	Extreme

4.1 Communications

Rate the following in terms of how *important* the activity is to the completion of the job. Some jobs may involve several or all of the items in this section.

4.1.1 Oral (communicating by speaking)

99 | 1 _____ Advising (dealing with individuals in order to counsel and/or guide them with regard to problems that may be resolved by legal, financial, scientific, technical, clinical, spiritual, and/or other professional principles)

100 | 1 _____ Negotiating (dealing with others in order to reach an agreement or solution, for example, labor bargaining, diplomatic relations, etc.)

101 | 1 _____ Persuading (dealing with others in order to influence them toward some action or point of view, for example, selling, political campaigning, etc.)

102 | 1 _____ Instructing (the teaching of knowledge or skills, in either an informal or a formal manner, to others, for example a public school teacher, a journeyman teaching an apprentice, etc.)

103 | 1 _____ Interviewing (conducting interviews directed toward some specific objective, for example, interviewing job applicants, census taking, etc.)

Source: E. J. McCormick, P. R. Jeanneret, and R. C. Mecham, Position Analysis Questionnaire, copyright © 1969 by Purdue Research Foundation, West Lafayette, Indiana 47907. Reprinted with permission.

FIGURE 9–7 Sample Items from the PAQ.

if it applies, or for rating it on an appropriate rating scale such as importance, time, or difficulty (see Fig. 9–7).

The average item reliability of the PAQ is a very respectable .80. Similar results emerged with a German form of the PAQ (Frieling, Kannheiser, and Lindberg, 1974).

Personal and organizational factors seem to have little impact on PAQ results. In a controlled study, similar profiles resulted, regardless of whether the analyst was male or female, whether the incumbent portrayed his or her job as interesting or uninteresting, or whether a considerable amount of information or less information about a job was presented (Arvey et al., 1982). However, as has been found using other job analysis methods, PAQ ratings from expert and job-naive raters are not equivalent (DeNisi, Cornelius, and

Blencoe, 1987). There simply are no shortcuts when using the PAQ. For example, one study found near-zero convergence of results based on the rating of each PAQ job dimension as a whole, compared to rating a number of items for each dimension and then combining them (Butler and Harvey, 1988).

McCormick et al. (1972) believe that structured, worker-oriented job analysis instruments hold considerable potential for establishing the common denominators that are required to link different jobs, and that must form the basis for indirect or synthetic validity studies. Thus:

. . . the kinds of common denominators one would seek are those of a worker-oriented nature, since they offer some possibility of serving as bridges or common denominators between and among jobs of very different technologies. One cannot possibly relate

10. Number Facility

This ability involves the degree to which adding, subtracting, multiplying, or dividing can be done quickly and correctly. These procedures can be steps in other operations like finding percents and taking square roots.

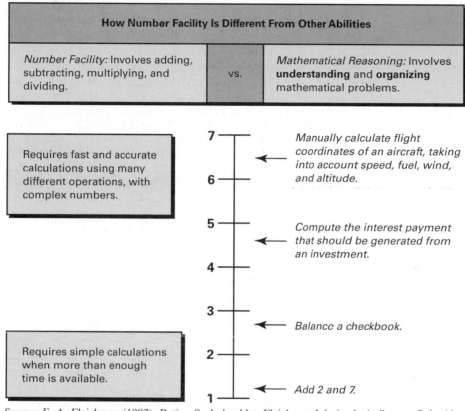

How Number Facility Is Different From Other Abilities		
Number Facility: Involves adding, subtracting, multiplying, and dividing.	vs.	*Mathematical Reasoning:* Involves **understanding** and **organizing** mathematical problems.

Requires fast and accurate calculations using many different operations, with complex numbers.

7 — *Manually calculate flight coordinates of an aircraft, taking into account speed, fuel, wind, and altitude.*

6 —

5 — *Compute the interest payment that should be generated from an investment.*

4 —

3 — *Balance a checkbook.*

Requires simple calculations when more than enough time is available.

2 —

1 — *Add 2 and 7.*

Source: E. A. Fleishman (1992). Rating Scale booklet, Fleishman Job Analysis Survey. Palo Alto, CA: Consulting Psychologists Press. Used with permission.

FIGURE 9–8 Rating Scale for Cognitive Ability No. 10, "Number Facility," in the F-JAS.

butchering, baking, and candlestick-making strictly in these technological terms; their communalities (if any) might well be revealed if they were analyzed in terms of the more generalized human behaviors involved, that is, in terms of worker-oriented elements [p. 348].

Despite these claims, research seems to indicate that much of the content of the PAQ is more suited for use with blue-collar manufacturing jobs than it is for professional, managerial, or some technical jobs (Cornelius, DeNisi, and Blencoe, 1984; DeNisi et al., 1987). The PAQ also is subject to two further limitations. First, since it does not describe specific work activities, *behavioral* similarities in jobs may mask genuine *task* differences between them—for example, a police officer's profile is quite similar to a housewife's (according to Arvey and Begalla, 1975) because of the troubleshooting, emergency-handling orientation required in both jobs. A second problem with the PAQ is readability, for

it requires a college-graduate reading level in order to comprehend the items (Ash and Edgell, 1975). Hence, the PAQ should not be given to job incumbents and supervisors unless their jobs require educational levels substantially higher than 10 to 12 years.

In an effort to make the worker-oriented approach more widely applicable, the Job Element Inventory (JEI) was developed. The JEI is a 153-item, structured questionnaire modeled after the PAQ, but with a much lower reading level (10th grade). Controlled research shows that JEI factors closely parallel those of the PAQ (Harvey et al., 1988).

Fleishman Job Analysis Survey (F-JAS)

The F-JAS (Fleishman, 1975; 1992; Fleishman and Reilly, 1992a) is one of the most thoroughly researched approaches to job analysis. Its objective is to

10. Number Facility

Definition: Number facility is the ability to add, subtract, multiply, divide, and manipulate numbers quickly and accurately. It is required for steps in other operations, such as finding percentages and taking square roots. This ability does not involve understanding or organizing mathematical problems.

Tasks: Number facility is involved in filling out income tax returns, keeping track of financial accounts, computing interest payments, adding up a restaurant bill, and balancing a checkbook.

Jobs: Jobs that require high levels of number facility include those of an accountant, audit clerk, bookkeeper, cashier, and teller.

Test Examples: Tests of number facility usually require subjects to quickly perform numerical operations such as addition or subtraction. Tests of this type require subjects to either provide the correct answer or choose the correct answer from multiple-choice items.

> *Guilford-Zimmerman Aptitude Survey: Numerical Operations*
> Consulting Psychologists Press
>
> This is a paper-pencil, multiple-choice test including simple problems of addition, subtraction, and multiplication. The results yield C-scale, centile, and T-scale norms for college groups. Eight minutes are allowed to complete the test. It has been used with accountants, sales persons, and many types of clerical workers.
>
> *Employee Aptitude Survey Test #2—Numerical Ability (EAS #2)*
> Psychological Services, Inc.
>
> This 75-item, paper-pencil, multiple-choice test assesses addition, subtraction, multiplication, and division skills. Ten minutes are allowed to complete the test. It has been used to select and place executives, supervisors, engineers, accountants, sales, and clerical workers.

Source: E. A. Fleishman and M. E. Reilly, *Handbook of human abilities* (1992). Palo Alto, CA: Consulting Psychologists Press. Used with permission.

FIGURE 9–9 Portion of the *Handbook of human abilities* Entry for "Number Facility" in the F-JAS.

describe jobs in terms of the abilities required to perform them. The ability-requirements taxonomy is intended to reflect the fewest independent ability categories that describe performance in the widest variety of tasks. Areas covered by the taxonomy include 21 cognitive abilities (e.g., oral comprehension, number facility), 10 psychomotor abilities (e.g., reaction time, finger dexterity), 9 physical abilities (e.g., gross body coordination, stamina), and 12 sensory/perceptual abilities (e.g., depth perception, hearing sensitivity). In addition, 9 interactive/social abilities (e.g., persuasion, social sensitivity) and 11 knowledges/skills abilities (e.g., mechanical knowledge, driving) are currently under development. Rating scales that define each ability, distinguish it from related abilities, and provide examples of tasks that require different levels of the ability facilitate a common understanding among raters. Figure 9–8 is an example of one such scale, cognitive ability No. 10, "Number Facility."

Inter-rater reliabilities for the scales are generally in the mid-.80s, and there is considerable construct and predictive evidence of validity in a variety of studies to support the meaningfulness of the scales (Fleishman and Reilly, 1992a). In addition, a *Handbook of Human Abilities* (Fleishman and Reilly, 1992b) integrates across the full range of human abilities, definitions of abilities with information about the kinds of tasks and jobs that require each ability, and

published tests that can be used to measure each ability. Figure 9–9 shows a portion of the *Handbook* entry for "Number Facility."

CRITICAL INCIDENTS

This is the same method we discussed in connection with performance appraisal (Chapter 5). The critical incidents approach involves the collection of a series of anecdotes of job behavior (collected from supervisors, employees, or others familiar with the job) that describe especially good or especially poor job performance. The method has value for typically it yields both static and dynamic dimensions of jobs. Each anecdote describes: (1) what led up to the incident and the context in which it occurred; (2) exactly what the individual did that was so effective or ineffective; (3) the perceived consequences of this behavior; and (4) whether or not such consequences were actually within the control of the employee.

Typically, the job analysts gather a broad sampling of observations of a large number of employees doing their jobs; depending on the nature of the job, hundreds or even thousands of incidents may be required to cover adequately the behavioral domain. Analysts then categorize incidents according to the job dimensions they represent, and assemble them into a checklist format. In their entirety, the incidents provide a composite picture of the behavioral requirements of a job.

OTHER SOURCES

Several other sources of job information are available and may serve as useful supplements to the methods already described. An examination of training materials (such as training manuals, standard operating procedures, or blueprints of equipment used) may reveal what skills, abilities, and behaviors are required for successfully learning to do the work and operating essential equipment. Technical conferences composed of experts selected for their broad knowledge and experience, or diaries in which job incumbents record their work tasks day by day, also may prove useful.

Emerging Multi-Method Approaches

As a result of advances in computer technology and wider use of sophisticated quantitative methods, new systems of job analysis are emerging. They share such common characteristics as:

- They use multidimensional perspectives on the source of job information, type of data analyzed, and response-scale formats.
- They are designed to support concurrently multiple applications in human resource management.
- They use structured questionnaires that are completed by incumbents, supervisors, and other subject matter experts.
- They employ user-friendly computer systems that perform complex statistical analyses and provide graphics-quality reports for ease of data interpretation.

These emerging procedures can efficiently analyze a geographically-dispersed work force, track and document rapidly-changing job content, and cost less per employee for large organizations. One such method, called JobScope, is used by Nationwide Insurance Companies. As a result of improved accuracy in job evaluation, the system is saving the company more than $60,000 in salary and benefits *each year.* The company recouped the entire cost of developing JobScope during its first 2 years of operation and is using it as the basis for developing an integrated HR system (Page and Van De Voort, 1989).

Future-Oriented Job Analyses

There are times when organizations want information concerning specific skill and ability requirements for jobs or positions that do not yet exist. Examples include new technology or hardware that is expected to be in operation 3–5 years in the future, new plant start-ups with unusual approaches to the organization of work (e.g., Sony's use of manufacturing "cells" of three workers to assemble components; Volvo's use of team-based automobile assembly), or the reconfiguration of existing jobs into a process-based structure of work (e.g., credit issuance, procurement).

One approach for dealing with such situations was developed by Arvey, Salas, and Gialluca (1992). Using the results of a job analysis inventory that included assessment of task and skill-ability characteristics, they first developed a matrix of correlations between tasks and skills-abilities. Then, assuming different numbers of tasks might be available to decision makers to describe the requirements of future jobs, Arvey et al. used the set of tasks in a multiple regression analysis to forecast which skills-abilities would be necessary in the future job. Then they cross-validated these decision outcomes with a different sample of raters.

While such predictions can represent useful forecasting information to decision makers, the validity of such an approach rests on two assumptions: (1) the covariance relationships among tasks and skills-abilities remain stable over time, and (2) the tasks and skills-abilities included in the data base include the same kinds of skills and abilities to be forecasted.

JOB ANALYSIS FOR MANAGERIAL JOBS

Performing an accurate job analysis for any job is not an easy task, but managerial jobs compound the problems. Different activities occupy the manager's time, such as planning and organizing work or settling disputes among subordinates. Person-determined changes are obvious when two managers at the same level and functional specialty are given similar administrative responsibilities for achieving organizational objectives, but they use different methods in order to do so. Finally, situation-determined changes also affect managerial jobs in different functional areas, on different hierarchical levels, and in different geographical regions and organizations. Marketing managers encounter different situational contingencies from finance or research and development managers, and first-level managers in the various functional areas typically encounter situations different from middle or top managers.

Since managerial jobs differ to such an extent and are subject to all three agents of change, the need is great to identify and measure the fundamental dimensions along which they differ. Initially, we must identify what managers actually do on their jobs in order to perform them effectively (i.e., their central activities), and then we must specify behavioral differences in jobs due to time, person, and situational changes.

Approaches to the Study of Managerial Work

In general, there are two approaches to the study of managerial work: the "behavioral-content" approach and the "work-activities" approach (Whitely, 1985). The behavioral content approach seeks answers to the question, "What common behaviors do managers engage in as they carry out their responsibilities?" In contrast, the work activities approach asks, "What common activities or processes (e.g., duration of activities, mode of communications, mode of contacts) are found among managerial jobs?" Both kinds of information are important for succession planning, career development, performance definition and appraisal, managerial motivation, and reward administration (Campbell et al., 1970; Stewart, 1982).

Behavioral-content Approach. Researchers examining the behavioral content of managerial work have relied on the questionnaire as a major method of data collection. Thus, Tornow and Pinto (1976) developed a 197-item Management Position Description Questionnaire (MPDQ) for objectively describing managerial positions in terms of their responsibilities, restrictions, demands, and activities (see Fig. 9–10). The mean item reliability of the MPDQ is .83, and the items describe 13 independent job factors. The MPDQ provides a behaviorally meaningful taxonomy for describing, comparing, classifying, and evaluating executive positions in terms of their content.

In an attempt to summarize the many empirical studies of manager performance, Borman and Brush (1993) collected 26 sets of dimensions from both published and unpublished studies. The 26 sets of dimensions included 187 managerial performance dimensions. Twenty-five industrial psychologists experienced in research on managers then independently sorted the 187 dimensions into categories based on similarity of content. The resulting categories were factor analyzed to yield 18 "mega-dimensions":

1. Planning and organizing
2. Guiding, directing, and motivating subordinates, and providing feedback
3. Training, coaching, and developing subordinates
4. Communicating effectively and keeping others informed
5. Representing the organization to customers and the public
6. Technical proficiency
7. Administration and paperwork
8. Maintaining good working relationships
9. Coordinating subordinates and other resources to get the job done
10. Decision making/problem solving
11. Staffing
12. Persisting to reach goals
13. Handling crises and stress
14. Organizational commitment
15. Monitoring and controlling resources
16. Delegating
17. Selling/influencing
18. Collecting and interpreting data

These "mega-dimensions," derived from data generated in many organizations and across a variety of management jobs, may be useful as a benchmark set of categories against which to compare the dimensions emerging from studies of managerial performance for individual jobs or in individual organizations (Borman and Brush, 1993). For example, the mega-dimensions agree quite closely with the MPDQ dimensions derived in a single but diverse company.

Work-activities Approach. Unfortunately, our fallible memories make it difficult to obtain accurate estimates of work activities such as activity duration or communication mode through standard questionnaire methods. Hence the work activities approach uses diaries, time-sampling, interviews, and observation (McCall, Morrison, and Hannan, 1978) in an effort to develop an accurate cumulative record of the duration of each activity. But diaries and observation do not lend themselves to gathering information on behavioral content. So the strength of the behavioral content approach is the weakness of the work activities approach, and vice versa. The two approaches

Directions:

STEP 1—SIGNIFICANCE

Indicate how significant each activity is to your position by entering a number between 0 and 4 in the column next to it. Remember to consider both its **importance** in light of all the other position activities and **frequency** of occurrence.

0—Definitely not a part of the position.
1—Minor significance to the position.
2—Moderate significance to the position.
3—Substantial significance to the position.
4—Crucial significance to the position.

Dimension: Controlling

STEP 2—COMMENTS

Use this space to clarify or comment on any aspects of **Controlling** that you feel are not adequately covered by the questions.

_____
_____
_____
_____
_____
_____
_____
_____

The Duties Of This Position Require You To:

1. Review proposed plans for adequacy and consistency with corporate policies/objectives.
2. Track and adjust activities to ensure that objectives/commitments are met in a timely fashion.
3. Develop milestones, due dates, and responsibilities for projects, plans, and activities.
4. Monitor product quality and/or service effectiveness.
5. Develop evaluation criteria to measure the progress and effectiveness of a unit.
6. Evaluate and document the effectiveness of plans, projects, and/or operations upon their completion.
7. Analyze at least monthly the effectiveness of operations.
8. Analyze operating performance reports.

9. Track expenditures to budget/forecast and determine how to make the best use of funds.
10. Review and revise expense allocations.
11. Control quality of manufactured products/services.
12. Monitor subordinates' progress toward the objectives of the unit.
13. Monitor the progress of geographically separate units and adjust activities as necessary to meet organizational goals.
14. Monitor inventory levels and ratios.
15. Monitor customer services indices.
16. Monitor conformance with Affirmative Action/Equal Employment Opportunity commitments.
17. Interpret and enforce safety and security regulations.

Source: Copyright 1984, Control Data Business Advisors, Inc. All rights reserved.
FIGURE 9–10. Sample Items from the Management Position Description Questionnaire.

complement each other. How much overlap is there in terms of the results obtained from the two methods?

Whitely (1985) used both approaches to study the work of 70 managers from three organizations: a chemical processing company, a hospital, and a bank. Cross-tabulation of the managers according to their cluster membership in each of the two approaches revealed only a moderate convergence of findings from the behavioral content and work activities methods. These results serve as a warning not to overgeneralize based on similarities in managerial work behavior, for managerial jobs differ in terms of demands, constraints, and choices (Stewart, 1982). The challenge now is to discover the linkages between managers' personal qualities, behavioral requirements of their jobs, and measures of organizational success.

A study by Dowell and Wexley (1978) provided some insight into these linkages. They developed a Supervisor Task Description Questionnaire incorporating 100 work activities of first-line supervisors. These activities described seven job dimensions: Working with Subordinates, Organizing Work of Subordinates, Work Planning and Scheduling, Maintaining Efficient/Quality Production, Maintaining Safe/Clean Work Areas, Maintaining Equipment and Machinery, and Compiling Records and Reports.

Responses from 251 first-line supervisors in 40 plants yielded few differences in the supervisors' jobs regardless of technology or function. These results imply that with the exception of the technical knowledge that may be required in a first-level supervisory position, organizations should be able to develop selection, training, and performance appraisal systems for first-line supervisors that can be applied generally throughout the organization.

OCCUPATIONAL INFORMATION

As a result of the many job analyses performed in all kinds of goods-producing and service organizations, a massive collection of occupational information exists. One of the best-known sources of standardized occupational information is the Dictionary of Occupational Titles (DOT), issued by the U.S. Department of Labor. The present fourth edition of the DOT appeared in 1977, and a supplement to the fourth edition appeared in 1986. It includes standardized, comprehensive descriptions of job duties and related information for over 20,000 military and civilian occupations covering nearly all jobs in the U.S. economy. Occupations are grouped into a systematic occupational classification structure based on the interrelationships of job tasks and requirements.

There are six parts to each occupational definition (see Fig. 9–11):

1. Occupational code number (nine digits)
2. Occupational title
3. Industry designation
4. Alternate titles (if any)
5. Body of the definition: (a) Lead statement, (b) Task element statements, and (c) "May" items
6. Undefined related titles (if any)

The nine-digit occupational code number is particularly important since the full nine digits provide each occupation with a unique code suitable for computerized operations, especially when used in conjunction with the *Handbook of Occupational Keywords* (also issued by the Department of Labor). In the example shown in Figure 9–11, the code number

FIGURE 9–11 Parts of an Occupational Definition from the *Dictionary of Occupational Titles.*

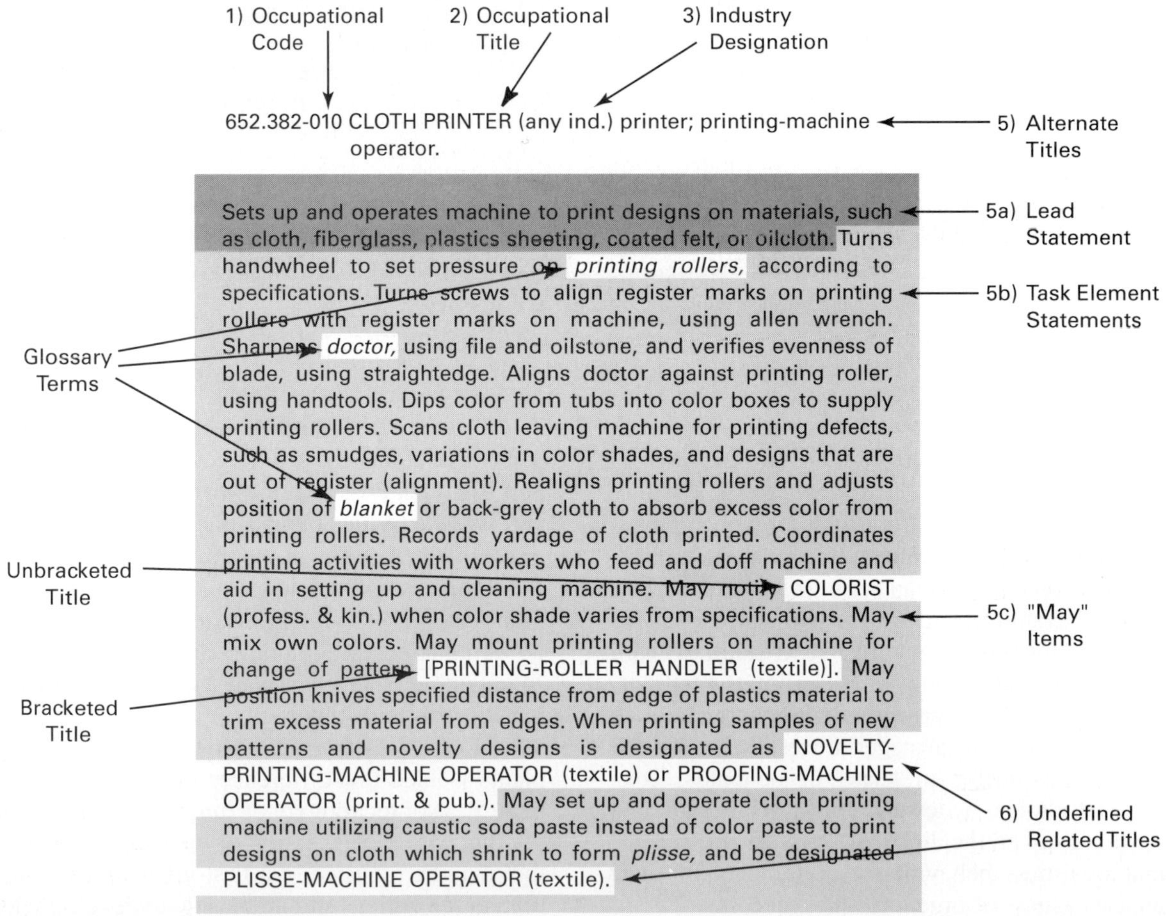

652.382.010 defines the occupation "cloth printer." The first digit indicates the major occupational category (machine trades occupations), the second digit the division within that category (printing occupations), and the third digit the specific occupational group within the division (printing machine operations).

The middle three digits of the DOT occupational code are the worker functions ratings (in relation to data, people, and things) resulting from functional job analysis. The three digits 382 in our example indicate that the worker is "compiling" in relation to data, "taking instructions-helping" in relation to people, and "operating-controlling" in relation to things. The last three digits of the code indicate the alphabetical order of titles within six-digit code groups. They uniquely identify each occupation, for although a number of occupations can have the same first six digits, no two can have the same nine digits. If a six-digit code applies only to one occupational title, the final three digits assigned are always 010 (as in Fig. 9–11).

Another valuable source of occupational information, especially for vocational guidance, is the *Occupational Outlook Handbook*, issued every 2 years by the U.S. Department of Labor. For over 300 occupations and 35 major industries, the *Handbook* describes in both words and pictures what workers do on their jobs, the training and education required, advancement possibilities, employment outlook, earnings and working conditions, and where to go for further career information. For ease of use, each job in the *Handbook* is also cross-referenced to the DOT.

The DOT serves several useful purposes. First, the reader can become familiar with the vast array of jobs in general and with the appropriate terminology in each job. Second, he or she can gain information about the activities and trade requirements of relatively standardized jobs, as the DOT categorizes them according to task similarities. Thus, it becomes possible to identify potential transfer and promotional patterns within particular occupational specialties.

An analysis of the test-retest reliabilities of DOT ratings showed them generally to be excellent, indicating that the ratings were done with great care (Cain and Green, 1983). Most of the scales had reliabilities above .70, although ratings for service jobs generally were less reliable than ratings for manufacturing jobs. Analyses of the internal consistency reliability of DOT scales found most of them to exceed .80, with a tendency for the broader, more abstract scales to have higher reliabilities than the scales representing more concrete job characteristics, such as physical demands (Geyer et al., 1989). Reasons for such high reliability include the use of pooled, independent job analysis judgments, extensive training of job analysts, and careful reviews of raw data for questionable results. These are hallmarks of competent research practice in personnel psychology.

O*NET—OCCUPATIONAL INFORMATION NETWORK

O*NET is the Department of Labor's new, automated replacement for the DOT. Replacement is necessary because occupational information has become too massive and too dynamic to rely on the DOT's traditional collection, publication, and distribution methods. Businesses, workers, educators, and policy makers require valid information about present and future jobs and about labor force skills and abilities. O*NET accomplishes this using electronic gateways such as the World Wide Web and the Internet.

O*NET includes a variety of cross-job descriptors, arranged in a hierarchy, that enable users to organize job-specific information into broad, empirically-based occupational clusters. The descriptors include, for example, experience requirements (training, licensure), worker requirements (basic and cross-functional skills, general knowledge, education), worker characteristics (abilities, interests, work styles), occupational requirements (generalized work activities, organizational context, work conditions), occupation-specific (knowledges, skills, tasks, machines, tools), and occupation characteristics (labor market information, occupational outlook, wages). This occupational information system allows users to create multiple "windows" to respond to a variety of needs. O*NET is expected to be fully operational by 1999.

INTERRELATIONSHIPS AMONG JOBS

The general problem of how to group jobs together for purposes of cooperative validation, validity generalization, and administering performance appraisal, promotional, or career planning systems has a long history (Harvey, 1991). Researchers classify jobs to facilitate description, prediction, and understanding. Jobs may be grouped based on the abilities required to do them, task characteristics, behavior description, or behavior requirements (Fleishman and Mumford, 1991).

Conventional wisdom holds that job classifications are idiosyncratic, unstable, and somewhat subjective summary descriptors (Pearlman, 1980). Certainly classifications may vary as a function of purpose (selection or training versus human factors in machine design) or analytical procedures used to develop the classification system. For example, one can look for *differences* among jobs; this would be the analysis of variance or multivariate analysis of variance approach. Alternatively, one can look for *similarities* among jobs; this is the objective of cluster analysis or Q-type factor analysis (Colihan and Burger, 1995; Zedeck and Cascio, 1984). However, when task and ability requirement data were used independently to describe 152 jobs in a broad cross-section of occupational fields, each type of indicator yielded similar occupational classifications (Hartman, Mumford, and Mueller, 1992).

To be sure, the practical significance of differences among jobs and among alternative possible job-family configurations is likely to vary according to the objective for which the job-family system has been designed (Pearlman, 1980; Harvey, 1986). There are circumstances, for example, where one may conclude that a brain surgeon is like a belly dancer—after all, both jobs involve fine motor movements! However, results from several studies (Cornelius, Schmidt, and Carron, 1984; Sackett et al., 1981) suggest that when the focus is on combining jobs for purposes of validity generalization, broad-content types of job analyses are appropriate, and therefore detailed task analyses are unnecessary. It is important to stress, however, that global job analysis procedures do not provide sufficient information for other purposes within HRM, such as the construction of work sample or job knowledge tests, performance appraisal feedback, or the development of career ladders (Harvey, 1986).

In addition, there is danger in assuming that all jobs within a classification are similar, because evidence indicates that they may differ in important, practical ways (Stutzman, 1983). Job-grouping studies should first focus on specific jobs and on understanding the differences among them and then group them into classifications when the need arises.

In summary, the question of grouping jobs is still principally a subjective, not a statistical, problem. Statistical analysis can provide useful information for such decisions, but cannot be used as the sole input. Job classification is an active, evolving area as the search continues for reliable and valid clusters of jobs and occupations that have real behavioral meaning. Indeed, this is what is required if applied psychology is to keep pace with the growing complexities of the workplace. Job analysis is a fundamental tool of the HR specialist. Once the job activities and personal requirements of each job have been specified, organizations can enhance their effectiveness if they plan judiciously for the use of available human resources. In the next chapter we will consider this topic in greater detail.

Discussion Questions

1. Describe the implications for traditional job analysis as some firms move from a task-based to a process-based organization of work.

2. Consider the job of an accountant. How is that job affected by time-, employee-, and situation-determined changes?

3. Develop an outline for a job analysis workshop with a panel of subject matter experts.

4. Discuss some of the special problems associated with conducting future-oriented job analyses.

5. In analyzing a managerial job, what kind of information might the behavioral content approach provide that the work activities approach does not, and vice versa?

CHAPTER

10

STRATEGIC HUMAN RESOURCE PLANNING

AT A GLANCE

People are among our nation's most critical resources; yet systematic approaches to HR planning, forecasting, and action programs designed to provide trained people to fill needs for particular skills are still evolving at the national as well as at the enterprise level.

HR planning systems include several specific, interrelated activities. **Talent inventories** provide a means of assessing current resources (skills, abilities, promotional potential, assignment histories, etc.). **Forecasts of HR supply and demand** enable planners to predict employment requirements (numbers, skills mix). Together, talent inventories and forecasts help to determine HR objectives and policies that provide operational meaning and direction for **action plans** in many different areas, including recruitment, selection, placement, career management and performance appraisal, as well as numerous training activities. Finally, **control and evaluation procedures** provide feedback to the HR planning system and monitor the degree of attainment of HR goals and objectives.

Ultimate success in HR planning depends on several factors: the degree of integration of HR planning with strategic planning activities, the quality of the data bases used to produce the talent inventory and forecasts of HR supply and demand, the caliber of the action programs established to achieve HR objectives, and, finally, the organization's ability to implement the programs. The net effect should be a wiser, more efficient use of human resources.

The judicious use of human resources is a perpetual problem in our society. Specific examples of HR problems that are also top management problems are:

- Finding the specialized technical talent needed to staff specific programs of planned business expansion (e.g., in the semiconductor industry see Chan, 1996).

- Finding seasoned managers to manage new and expanding operations, including those with the capability eventually to assume senior management positions.

- Developing competent, equitable HR management practices that will ensure compliance with EEO requirements and thus avoid the potentially large settlement costs of discrimination suits.

- Devising equitable, workable layoff policies that will not compromise the accumulated seniority rights of employees.

- Improving productivity, especially among managerial and technical employees.

- Managing career development opportunities to attract, motivate, and retain an effective pool of talented people over long periods of time.

To a considerable extent, emphasis on improved HR practice has arisen in response to two factors: (1) a strong desire on the part of many top managers to restore the competitive position of their companies in an increasingly challenging global marketplace; and (2) recognition of the crucial role of people as the United

States moves further into the complex and changing new world of a high-technology, service-based economy.

Despite these encouraging signs, it appears that while most U.S. companies engage in some form of long-range business planning to assess periodically their basic missions and objectives, very few actually are practicing strategic HR management today.

Organizations will not have succeeded in fully using their human resources until they can answer the following questions:

1. What talents, abilities, and skills are available within the organization today?

2. Who are the people we can dependably build on for tomorrow?

3. How are we blending the talent available with the organization's needs?

4. What are the qualitative as well as quantitative HR demands of our growth plan? (Finkle and Jones, 1970, p. 3)

In this chapter we shall first describe the HR planning process, emphasizing its linkage to strategic business planning, and then take a closer look at each element in the process including the talent inventory, forecasts of HR needs, action plans, and control and evaluation procedures.

WHAT IS HUMAN RESOURCE PLANNING (HRP)?

HRP basically is a two-step process, as shown in Figure 10–1. Primary emphasis is on anticipating and responding to *needs* emerging within and outside the organization to determine priorities and to allocate resources where they can do the most good.

The analysis of needs leads to the *planning of programs* to be conducted. Activities and programs, in turn, relate directly to current and anticipated issues and must be evaluated in terms of needs, costs, and expected benefits.

In short, HRP reflects three areas of primary concern to management:

1. *Needs forecasting:* improved planning and control over staffing and organizational requirements, based on analysis of conditions.

2. *Performance management:* improving the performance of individuals, teams, and the organization as a whole.

3. *Career management:* activities to select, assign, develop, and otherwise manage individual careers in an organization.

The important linkage, therefore, is between the broad range of external and organizational factors on the one hand, and specific HR programs on the other. In this way, recruitment, development, compensation, performance management, and other activities become integral parts of a dynamic process.

Although HRP means different things to different people, general agreement exists on its ultimate objective—namely, the wisest, most effective use of scarce or abundant talent in the interest of the individual and the organization. Thus, we may define HR planning broadly as *an effort to anticipate future business and environmental demands on an organization and to meet the HR requirements dictated by these conditions.* This general view of HRP suggests several specific, interrelated activities that together comprise an HRP system. They include:

1. *Talent inventory*—to assess current resources (skills, abilities, and potential) and analyze current use of employees.

2. *Human resource forecast*—to predict future HR requirements (numbers, skills mix, internal versus external labor supply).

3. *Action plans*—to enlarge the pool of qualified individuals by recruitment, selection, training, placement, transfer, promotion, development, and compensation.

4. *Control and evaluation*—to provide closed-loop feedback to the rest of the system and to monitor the degree of attainment of HR goals and objectives.

Linking HR Planning to Strategic Planning

Planning is the very heart of management, for it helps managers reduce the uncertainty of the future and thereby do a better job of coping with the future. Hence, a fundamental reason for planning is that *planning leads to success*—not all the time, but studies show consistently that planners outperform nonplanners (Miller and Cardinal, 1994). A second reason for planning is that it gives managers and organizations a sense of being in control of their fate, rather than leaving their fate to chance. Hence, *planning helps organizations do a better job of coping with change*—technological, social, regulatory, and environmental.

A third reason for planning is that it *requires managers to define the organization's objectives* and thus provides context, meaning, and direction for employees' work. By ensuring that all employees are

1. Needs Forecasting

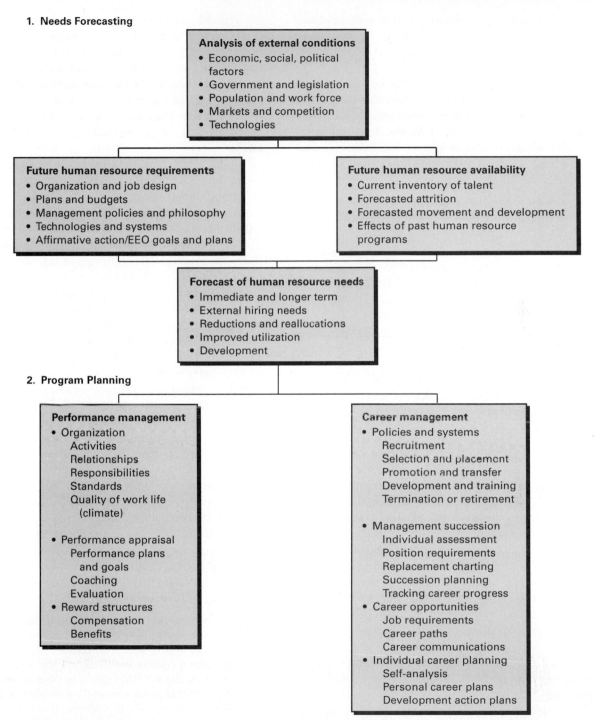

Source: J. W. Walker, *Human resource planning.* New York: McGraw-Hill, 1980, p. 11. Reprinted by permission of McGraw-Hill Book Company.

FIGURE 10–1 The Human Resource Planning Process.

aware of overall goals—*why* they are doing what they are doing—employees can tie more effectively *what* they are doing to the organization's overall objectives (Pearce and Robinson, 1989). A great deal of research indicates that the process of defining objectives leads to better employee performance and satisfaction.

A final reason for planning is that *without objectives effective control is impossible.* "If you don't know where you are going, any road will get you there."

Strategic planning is not about how to position products and businesses within an industry. Rather, it's about changing industry rules or creating tomorrow's industries, much as Wal-Mart Stores, Inc., did in retailing or Charles Schwab did in the brokerage and mutual-fund businesses (Prahalad and Hamel, 1994). It includes the following processes:

- *Defining company philosophy*—why does the business exist, what unique contribution does it make, what business should the company be in?
- *Formulating company and divisional statements of identity, purpose, and objectives.*
- *Evaluating the company's strengths and weaknesses* in order to identify the factors that may enhance or limit the choice of any future courses of action.
- *Determining the organization design* (structure, processes, interrelationships) appropriate for managing the company's chosen business.
- *Developing appropriate strategies for achieving objectives* (e.g., time-based points of measurement), including qualitative and quantitative subgoals.
- *Devising programs to implement the strategies.*

Strategic planning is different from shorter-range operational or tactical planning. Strategic planning decisions involve substantial commitments of resources, resulting either in a fundamental change in the direction of a business or a change in the speed of its development along the path it is traveling. Each step in the process may involve considerable data collection, analysis, and iterative management reviews. Thus a company making components for computers may, after reviewing its product line or subsidiary businesses, decide to divest its chemical products subsidiary since it no longer fits the company's overall objectives and long-range business plans. Strategic planning decisions may result in new business acquisitions, new capital investments, or new management approaches.

Human resource (HR) strategy parallels and facilitates implementation of the strategic business plan. HR strategy is the set of priorities a firm uses to align its resources, policies, and programs with its strategic business plan (Craft, 1988). It requires a focus on planned major changes in the business and on critical issues such as the following: What are the HR implications of the proposed business strategies? What are the possible external constraints and requirements? What are the implications for management practices, management development, and management succession? What can be done in the short term to prepare for longer-term needs? In this approach to the strategic management of human resources, a firm's business strategy and its HR strategy are interdependent (Lengnick-Hall and Lengnick-Hall, 1988; Schuler, 1992; 1993).

There are three general types of linkages between these processes. As shown in Figure 10–2, they are input linkages, decision-inclusion linkages, and review-reaction linkages. These are interdependent rather than mutually exclusive, as we noted above.

The purpose of **input linkages** is to provide or insert meaningful HR information into the strategic planning process either before or during the planning activity. **Decision-inclusion linkages** involve HR professionals either directly or indirectly in the strategic planning process. For example, at Marriott Corporation, the HR vice-president reports directly to the president and CEO, while each divisional HR manager reports directly to that division's general manager. HR managers attend decision-making sessions to raise HR issues and to note HR implications of company plans.

Review-reaction linkages afford HR managers the opportunity to respond to a proposed or final strategic business plan. In some cases their task is to assess the HR feasibility and desirability of the plan, and sometimes they may even have "sign-off" authority. For example, at IBM HR managers are required to approve strategic plans before they can be implemented. If disagreements arise, IBM has a procedure for resolving the dispute at progressively higher organizational levels (Craft, 1988).

What is the role of HR executives in all of this? According to Dyer and Holder (1988):

> [They] exercise leadership in all matters concerning HR strategy and policy. They constantly search for ways in which their organizations might achieve or enhance a competitive advantage through better people management. They question the wisdom of business strategies that appear risky because of potential HR problems. When strategic business directions change, they take the lead in evaluating the continued relevance of broad HR strategies and in making any necessary changes [pp. 1–32].

In practical terms, strategic HRM means getting everybody from the top of the organization to the bottom doing things to implement the strategy of the business effectively. It means assessing the entire system

STRATEGIC HRM IN ACTION: HOW AT&T GLOBAL BUSINESS COMMUNICATIONS SYSTEMS (GBCS) LINKS ITS PEOPLE TO ITS BUSINESS STRATEGY

GBCS (Lucent Technologies, Inc. as of October, 1996) was formed in 1992, through a merger of two AT&T business units. Senior management's first order of business was to develop a set of strategic business principles to reflect management's view of how to achieve its business objectives, to guide day-to-day actions, and to link employees with the needs of the business. Six strategic principles emerged:

1. Make people a key priority
2. Win customers for life
3. Use the total quality management approach to run the business
4. Profitably grow by being the leader in customer-led applications of technology
5. Rapidly and profitably globalize the business
6. Be the best value supplier.

To communicate its new philosophy, management developed a "GBCS Pyramid," as shown in Figure 10–3. Each element has a precise meaning.

- **Vision**—The purpose of the organization: "To be your partner of choice—dedicated to quality, committed to your success."

- **Mission**—A broad plan of action for what the organization wants to do: "To be the worldwide leader in providing the highest quality business communications products, services, and solutions."

- **Values**—Guides to decision making that represent how the organization and its people (referred to as "associates") treat customers, suppliers, and each other: respect for individuals, dedication to helping customers, highest standards of integrity, innovation, teamwork, accountability, and excellence in all activities.

- **Objectives**—identification of the key drivers of success and their interrelationships. Most such objectives start by focusing on customer or shareholder value. However, to reflect management's belief that its people (associates) are its only sustainable competitive advantage, GBCS begins with "associate value." Associate value is achieved by ensuring that all associates have the competencies to do their jobs effectively, to satisfy customers, and to find satisfaction in their daily work lives and careers. Customer value is achieved by ensuring that customers receive superior products, services, and solutions to their business needs. Together, associate value and customer value generate profitable growth for GBCS and increase value for its shareholders.

- **Strategic and tactical business plans**—the strategic plan establishes a 3-5-year direction for the business. Tactical business plans, generally fashioned around a shorter time frame, define the actions and objectives needed to achieve the long-term strategic goals.

- **People**—the power of the pyramid is based on the employees (associates) who are the foundation for supporting all other elements.

- **Business processes and management systems**—These two quality-related planks, shown vertically on the right side of the pyramid, touch all other building blocks. All associates are involved in the GBCS management system. Through formal training and learning experiences, process management teams and natural work teams use a common set of quality tools and standards for continuous improvement.

Management saw the pyramid as a focal point for transforming the business, but at the same time it also realized that any talk about "vision," "mission," and "strategy" is nothing more than rhetoric unless the employees learn to *live* a new way of doing business. A major challenge, then, was to link the HR strategy, mission, and initiatives to the needs of the business.

The solution, developed from external benchmarking studies, focus groups, surveys, training classes, interviews with senior managers, and input from various consultants, was the HR Strategy and Planning Model, shown in Figure 10–4.

The left-hand column lists the strategic business principles discussed earlier. As shown by the arrows, these principles lead to six HR strategic imperatives—*those actions that are absolutely necessary for GBCS to achieve its business goals.* The imperatives, in turn, shape the HR mission, which is stated in the third column. To achieve the mission, HR executives determined that they would need to focus on three critical HR areas:

- Cultural change

- Rewards and recognition

- Ownership

These focus areas drive the development of HROs annual plan initiatives (shown in the right-hand column of the figure). The major initiatives center on performance management, recognition, and compensation practices, as well as communication programs. We do not describe these initiatives in more detail because our focus is on GBCS's overall approach to linking HR to business strategy, rather than on the initiatives themselves.

The final step in GBCS's overall approach was to reposition the HR function from that of "provider of basic HR services" (e.g., salary administration, staffing support) to a strategic function, one that would be seen as adding value to the entire organization. This called for new roles, new relationships, and new competencies. The chief HR officer is a key member on the senior management team with responsibility for providing leadership on strategic HR issues. To accomplish this, the GBCS HR organization is made up of six teams, which HR staff members self-nominated to join. These are:

1. Associate services team—accountable for a wide variety of support services, such as staffing, pay and benefits, organization design, recognition and reward systems, employee surveys, relocation, and HR information systems.

2. Labor planning team—partnership development between unions and management to prepare associates for the challenges of the workplace of the future— high technology and new ways of working (e.g., in self-managed work teams).

3. HR business strategy and planning team—responsible for ensuring that HR initiatives support the success of the business strategy. The HR Strategy and Planning Model shown in Figure 10–4 provides the architecture for this support.

4. Diversity planning team—ensures constant attention to full use of the company's human talent. Efforts are directed at achieving awareness, understanding, and acceptance of all associates, and at ensuring a commitment to diversity throughout GBCS.

5. Associate communications team—ensures involvement and participation from all associates by establishing multiple lines of communication with senior management. This supports a key theme in the new company culture: "All associates have the power, protection, and permission to help GBCS improve the business."

6. Education and training team—develops and delivers leadership training as well as management and technical learning experiences to GBCS associates and customers.

Summary. The overall GBCS approach can be summarized as follows: based on the set of strategic principles articulated by senior management (i.e., its game plan for competing in the marketplace), GBCS developed a management philosophy (the "GBCS Pyramid") and a blueprint for linking employees to the overall business strategy of GBCS (the HR Strategy and Planning Model). To implement the practices ("Focus Areas") called for in that model, GBCS repositioned the HR function to adopt a more strategic posture, one that would add value to GBCS. The result? An excited, challenged, and motivated HR staff and employee population. These changes resulted in significant improvements in associate satisfaction, customer satisfaction, sales revenue growth, and profitability (Plevel et al., 1994). The improvements continued over time and a change in leadership at GBCS. Four elements seemed to be critical to success: *leadership* (consistent emphasis on the people dimension of the business), *linkage* (of each HR initiative to the strategy of the business), *focus* (on specific business goals and strategy), and *communication* (two-way communication that enables associates to participate, contribute ideas, and give feedback) (Nellis and Lane, 1995).

Source: Plevel, M. J., Lane, F., Nellis, S., and Schuler, R. S. (1994, Winter). AT&T Global Business Communications Systems: Linking HR With Business Strategy. *Organizational Dynamics,* 59–71.

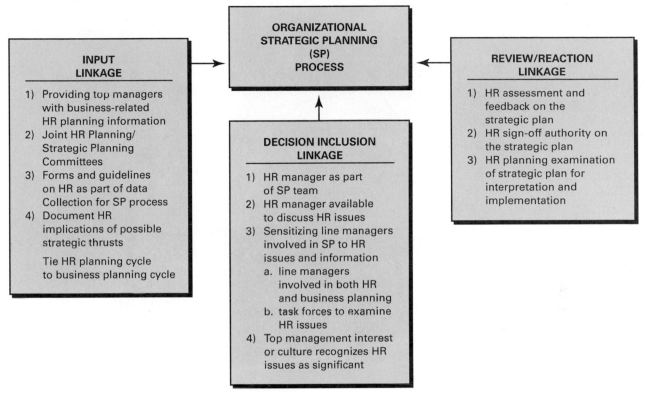

Source: J. A. Craft (1988). Human resource planning and strategy. In L. Dyer and G. W. Holder (eds.), *Human resource management: Evolving roles and responsibilities,* pp. 1–58. Washington, D.C.: Bureau of National Affairs.

FIGURE 10–2 Linkages between HR Planning and Strategic Planning.

of HR practices in terms of its ability to provide sustained competitive advantage. To provide such an advantage, employees *as a group* must pass three tests (Lado and Wilson, 1994):

1. They must add positive economic value
2. They must provide skills that are different from those of competitors
3. Their skills are not easily duplicated.

Evidence indicates quite clearly that alternative HR systems (i.e., the set of practices designed to attract, develop, and maintain human resources) have very different effects on outcomes such as turnover, productivity, and corporate financial performance (Arthur, 1994; Huselid, 1995; Sheridan, 1992). Now, in an extended example, we will see how one firm attempted to align its HR system with its general business strategy.

As the summary in the GBCS example illustrates, HR planning (which was the specific focus of teams 2, 3, and 4 above) is only one part of the broader strategic HRM effort. In the remainder of this chapter

we will examine the various components of the HRP system, as shown in Figure 10–1. As the figure shows, HRP focuses on needs forecasting and program planning. A forecast of net HR needs is the result of an analysis of future HR availability (supply) and future HR requirements (demand), tempered by an analysis of external conditions (e.g., technologies, markets, competition). With respect to future HR availability, an inventory of current talent is essential. We consider that topic next.

TALENT INVENTORIES

One of the principal requirements of an effective HRP system is a means for assessing the existing skills, abilities, career interests, and experience of the current work force. The other is a method of forecasting future needs. The two systems must complement each other, for an inventory of present workforce capabilities is not very useful unless it can be analyzed in terms of what is needed currently as well as in the future. On

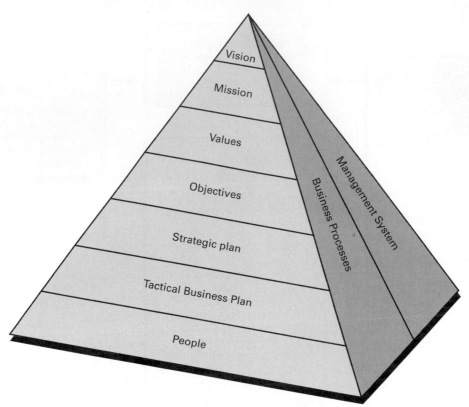

Source: M. J. Plevel, F. Lane, S. Nellis, and R. S. Schuler (1994, Winter). AT&T Global Business Communications Systems: Linking HR With Business Strategy. *Organizational Dynamics,* p. 62.
FIGURE 10–3 The GBCS Pyramid.

the other hand, a forecast of future needs is not very meaningful unless it can be analyzed in terms of the capabilities, interests, and development plans of the current work force. It makes little sense to spend large sums of money on elaborate recruitment programs if in-house talent can meet projected needs. Prior to actual data collection, therefore, certain fundamental questions must be addressed:

1. Who should be included in the inventory?
2. What specific pieces of information must be included for each individual?
3. How can this information best be obtained?
4. What is the most effective way to record such information?
5. How can inventory results be reported to top management?
6. How often must this information be updated?
7. How can the security of this information be protected?

Answers to these kinds of questions will provide both direction and scope to subsequent efforts. For ex-

ample, in answering question 1, some firms have decided to include only management, technical, and professional employees. They focus specifically on staffing, training, assignment, and succession planning at lower management levels where the largest numbers of managerial, technical, and professional employees exist and where the need to identify potential is greatest. Other organizations (e.g. high-technology firms) have chosen to include all employees in the talent inventory, for assignments change frequently in some divisions and temporary task forces often are assembled for short-term projects.

Information Type

Specific information to be stored in the inventory varies across organizations and may include only name, age, company service date, education, present position, past company assignments, and an assessment of future potential. Other systems are much more elaborate and may include, in addition to this, detailed

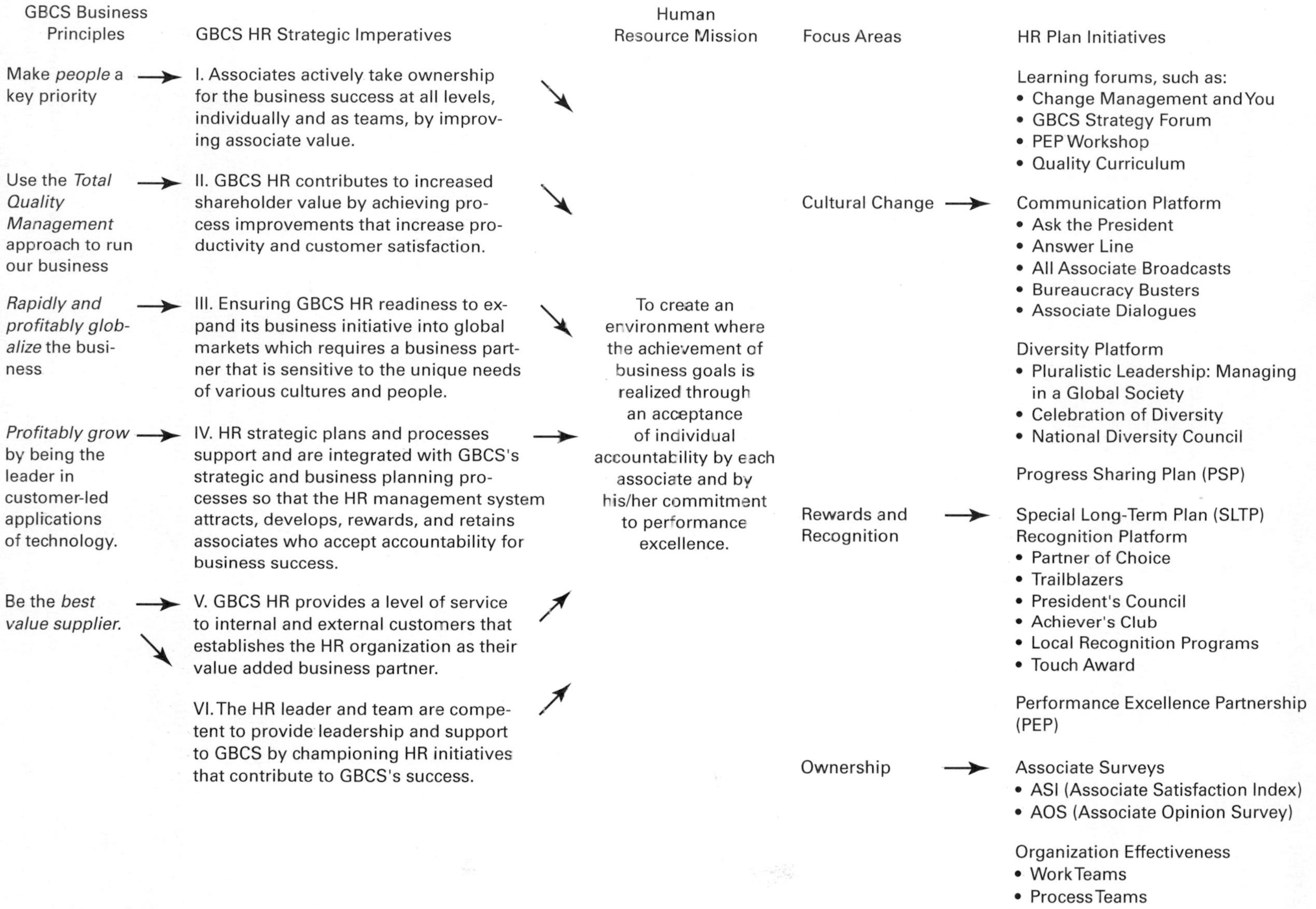

FIGURE 10—4 HR Strategy and Planning Model.

GBCS Business Principles	GBCS HR Strategic Imperatives	Human Resource Mission	Focus Areas	HR Plan Initiatives
Make *people* a key priority	I. Associates actively take ownership for the business success at all levels, individually and as teams, by improving associate value.	To create an environment where the achievement of business goals is realized through an acceptance of individual accountability by each associate and by his/her commitment to performance excellence.	Cultural Change →	Learning forums, such as: • Change Management and You • GBCS Strategy Forum • PEP Workshop • Quality Curriculum
Use the *Total Quality Management* approach to run our business	II. GBCS HR contributes to increased shareholder value by achieving process improvements that increase productivity and customer satisfaction.			Communication Platform • Ask the President • Answer Line • All Associate Broadcasts • Bureaucracy Busters • Associate Dialogues
Rapidly and profitably globalize the business	III. Ensuring GBCS HR readiness to expand its business initiative into global markets which requires a business partner that is sensitive to the unique needs of various cultures and people.			Diversity Platform • Pluralistic Leadership: Managing in a Global Society • Celebration of Diversity • National Diversity Council
Profitably grow by being the leader in customer-led applications of technology.	IV. HR strategic plans and processes support and are integrated with GBCS's strategic and business planning processes so that the HR management system attracts, develops, rewards, and retains associates who accept accountability for business success.		Rewards and Recognition →	Progress Sharing Plan (PSP) Special Long-Term Plan (SLTP) Recognition Platform • Partner of Choice • Trailblazers • President's Council • Achiever's Club • Local Recognition Programs • Touch Award
Be the *best value supplier.*	V. GBCS HR provides a level of service to internal and external customers that establishes the HR organization as their value added business partner.		Ownership →	Performance Excellence Partnership (PEP)
	VI. The HR leader and team are competent to provide leadership and support to GBCS by championing HR initiatives that contribute to GBCS's success.			Associate Surveys • ASI (Associate Satisfaction Index) • AOS (Associate Opinion Survey) Organization Effectiveness • Work Teams • Process Teams

Source: M. J. Plevel, F. Lane, S. Nellis, and R. S. Schuler (1994, Winter). AT&T Global Business Communications Systems: Linking HR With Business Strategy. *Organizational Dynamics*, p. 64.

biographical data and selection test scores, present and past company training and development activities, salary history, language skills, professional qualifications, travel attitudes and preferences, career interests and assignment preferences, and experience in foreign countries. This list is by no means exhaustive; information requirements vary with organizational needs.

Obtaining and Updating Information

Before collecting any data for a talent inventory, provide employees with a clear statement about the types of data to be collected, intended uses of the system, and privacy safeguards.

A great deal of employee-related information can probably be culled from existing employee files or from the payroll-benefits system (e.g., date of birth, education, hire date, current salary, position classification). Employees need to provide only non-redundant, new information (e.g., skills, career aspirations). Information that changes less frequently, such as licensure, certification, or educational level, can be generated by having each employee complete a standardized update form at periodic intervals (e.g., annually).

Reports

HR reports fall into three broad categories: operational reports, regulatory reports, and analytical reports.

Operational reports are used in the day-to-day management of the HR function. They include, for example, seniority lists, training reports (attendees), job vacancies (total number, number of days vacant, labor turnover reports, total accessions, new hires, quits, retirements, layoffs, transfers, promotions), and wage reports (subdivided by salary, by grade, by step). **Regulatory reports** are those required by government agencies, such as the Equal Employment Opportunity Commission and the Interstate Commerce Commission. **Analytical reports** are still used within the company but are generated less frequently. Such reports might include, for example, number of employees (subdivided by age, gender, length of service, race/ethnic group), cross-tabulations of current educational level by organization level, validity studies, attrition projections, and various types of HR research reports.

In analyzing how inventory results can be reported to top management using the proposed system, consider current reports. What additional data are needed? Which items in the current reports are superfluous? In general, reports should be tailored to include only "need to know," not "nice to know," information.

Uses

There are many possible uses for a talent inventory—for example, for the identification of candidates for promotion, assignment to special projects, transfer, and training; for organization analysis; and, of course, for human resource planning.

Talent inventories are potentially powerful tools in promoting wiser, more equitable use of human resources and more accurate HRP, but in order to realize these goals, users must know what information is contained in the inventory, how to access it, and how to interpret it. Finally, as we noted earlier, include a clear statement about employee privacy safeguards and the potential impact on employee privacy of all such in-house systems.

FORECASTING HUMAN RESOURCE SUPPLY AND DEMAND

HR forecasts are attempts to estimate future labor requirements. There are two component processes in this task: anticipating the supply of human resources, both within and without the organization at some future time period; and anticipating organizational demand for various types of employees. Consider forecasts of HR supply separately from forecasts of demand because each depends upon a different set of variables and assumptions (Walker, 1980). Internal supply forecasts tend to relate much more closely to conditions *inside* the organization, such as average rates of turnover, retirement, transfer, and new hires within job classes. Demand forecasts depend primarily on the behavior of some business factor (e.g., sales, product volume) to which HR needs can be related. In contrast to forecasts of HR supply, demand forecasts are beset with multiple uncertainties—in consumer behavior, in technology, in the general economic environment, and so forth.

Both supply and demand forecasts are of two types, estimates and projections. **Estimates** are educated guesses, based on how employees have been used in the past and plans how they will be used in the future. **Projections,** on the other hand, are mathematical extensions of HR data into the future where the data do not go. Both projections and estimates can have value, and many forecasts involve both types.

Consider two paradoxes in HR forecasts: The techniques are basically simple and easy to describe, but applying them successfully may be enormously complex and difficult. And, once the projection has been made, it may prove to be most useful when it proves to be least accurate as a vision of the future.

Here is what the latter paradox implies. Assume that a particular projection points toward a future HR problem—for example, a surplus of middle managers with comparable skills who were hired at the same time to meet a sudden expansion. The projection may be most useful if it stimulates action (e.g., appropriate training, transfer, promotion) so that the surplus never actually develops. It is useless only if the surplus develops on schedule as projected. Therein lies the value of HR forecasts: Of themselves they are little more than academic exercises, but when integrated into a total planning process, they take on special value because they enable an organization to extend the range of other phases of HRP and of planning for other functions.

External Human Resource Supply

When an organization plans to expand, recruitment and hiring of new employees may be necessary. Even when an organization is not growing, the aging of the present work force, coupled with normal attrition, makes some recruitment and selection a virtual certainty for most firms. It is wise, therefore, to examine forecasts of the external labor market for the kinds of employees that will be needed.

Several agencies regularly make projections of external labor market conditions and future occupational supply (by occupation), including the Bureau of Labor Statistics of the U.S. Department of Labor, the Engineering Manpower Commission, the National Science Foundation, the Office of Education, and the Public Health Service of the Department of Health and Human Services. The U.S. Employment Service also projects external labor supply and demand by occupation in various localities at the request of the State Employment Services.

It is important to gauge both the future supply of workers in a particular field and the future demand for these workers. Focusing only on the supply side could be seriously misleading. For example, the number of chemical engineering students scheduled to graduate from college during the next year may appear large,

and certainly adequate to meet next year's hiring needs for chemical engineers for a particular company—until one compares the aggregate demand of all companies for chemical engineering graduates with the available supply. That comparison may reveal an impending shortage and signal the need for more widespread and sophisticated recruiting efforts. Organizations are finding that they require projections of the external labor market as a starting point for their own planning, for preventing potential employee shortages from arising, and for dealing effectively with those that are to some extent unavoidable.

Internal Human Resource Supply

An organization's current work force provides a base from which to project future HR supply. Many individual items of information routinely recorded for each employee (e.g., age, gender, job title, organizational level, geographical location, training, performance ratings, and promotability) may help to determine the future supply. Perhaps the most common type of internal supply forecast is the management succession plan.

Management Succession Planning

This is the one activity that is pervasive, well accepted, and integrated with strategic business planning among firms that do HRP (Warner, 1991). In fact, succession planning is considered by many firms to be the sum and substance of HRP. Here is an overview of how several companies do it.

IBM has had such a process in place for ever 30 years, and many other firms have modeled theirs on it. The stated objective of the program is "to assure top quality and ready talent for all executive positions in the corporation worldwide." Responsibility for carrying out this process rests with line executives from division presidents up to the chief executive officer (CEO). An executive resource staff located within the corporate HR function provides staff support. Each responsible executive makes a formal presentation to a corporate policy committee consisting of the chairman, the vice-chairman, and the president. The presentation usually consists of an overall assessment of the strengths and weaknesses of the unit's executive resources, the present performance and potential of key executives and potential replacements (supplemented with pictures of the individuals involved), and rankings of all incumbents of key posi-

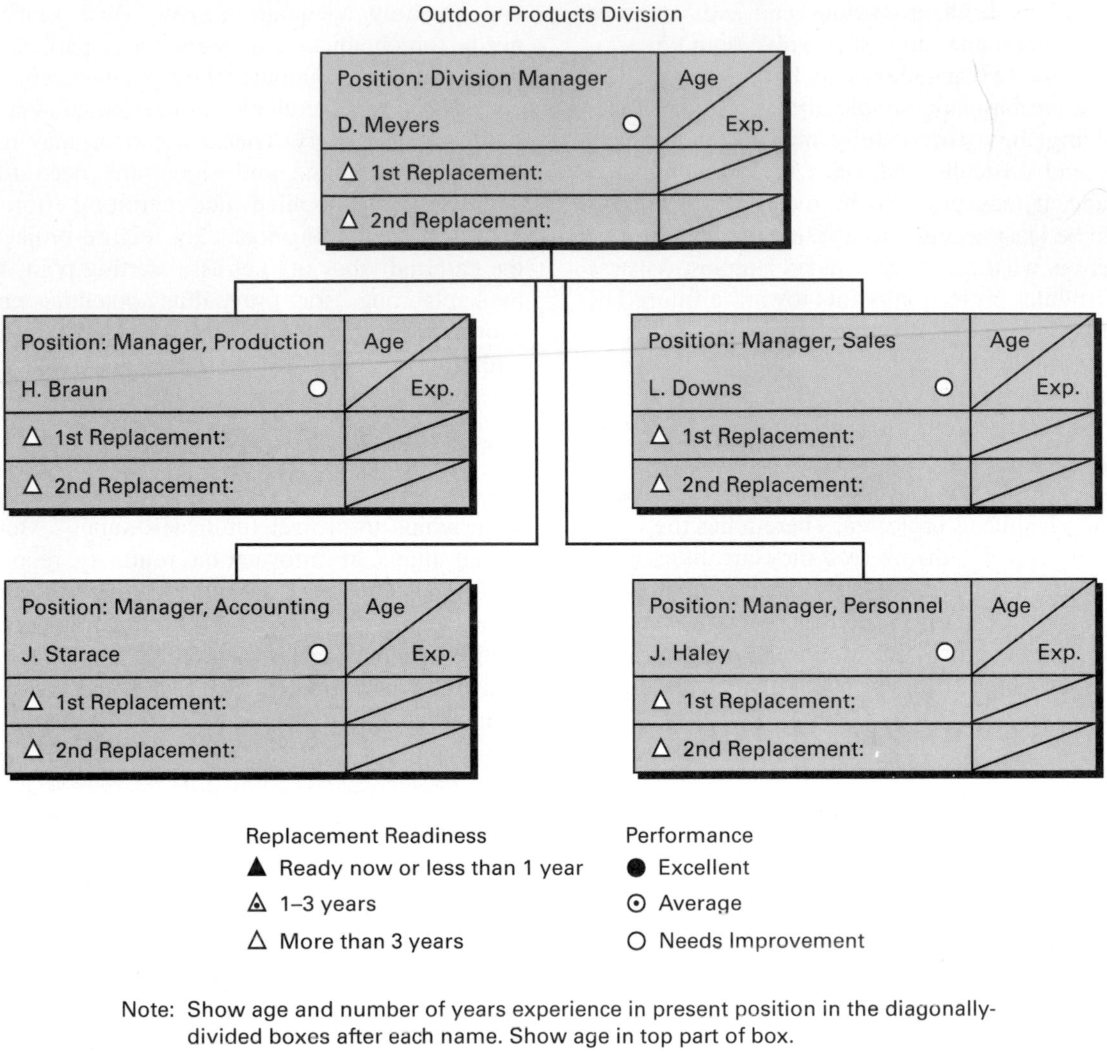

Outdoor Products Division

Position: Division Manager	Age
D. Meyers ○	Exp.
△ 1st Replacement:	
△ 2nd Replacement:	

Position: Manager, Production	Age
H. Braun ○	Exp.
△ 1st Replacement:	
△ 2nd Replacement:	

Position: Manager, Sales	Age
L. Downs ○	Exp.
△ 1st Replacement:	
△ 2nd Replacement:	

Position: Manager, Accounting	Age
J. Starace ○	Exp.
△ 1st Replacement:	
△ 2nd Replacement:	

Position: Manager, Personnel	Age
J. Haley ○	Exp.
△ 1st Replacement:	
△ 2nd Replacement:	

Replacement Readiness
▲ Ready now or less than 1 year
⧍ 1–3 years
△ More than 3 years

Performance
● Excellent
◉ Average
○ Needs Improvement

Note: Show age and number of years experience in present position in the diagonally-divided boxes after each name. Show age in top part of box.

FIGURE 10–5 Management Replacement Chart.

tions in terms of present performance and expected potential.

The policy committee reviews and critiques this information and often provides additional insights to line management on the strengths and weaknesses both of incumbents and their replacements. Sometimes the committee will even direct specific career development actions to be accomplished before the next review (Dyer and Heyer, 1984).

Security Pacific Corporation's top 100 officers must identify two successors for their jobs and develop a program for them. The chairman and president then review each executive's progress at periodic intervals. Finally, General Motors' annual appraisal of its top 5,000 managers includes a prediction regarding what job each executive will hold in 5 years and at the end of his or her career (Labor Letter, 1985).

In developing their plans, Exxon and PepsiCo rely upon a management replacement chart (Kiechel, 1984), an example of which is presented in Figure 10–5. When it comes to replacing the CEO, however, such a chart may be less useful because some companies, especially failing companies, may choose an outsider to inject change into a wide variety of organizational dimensions (Boeker and Goodstein, 1993; Miller, 1993). Over all companies, however, insiders are favored over outsiders as CEOs by a margin of nine to one (Lubatkin et al., 1989).

In the years ahead succession planning, and models used to do it, may well spread to lower levels as organizations strive to employ HRP as a means to gain competitive advantage. Yet there is danger that such models might become ends in themselves, rather than means for building more competitive organizations. When viewed as means, rather than as ends, forecasting models, and the HR plans that they suggest, tend to be presented in terms of simple, straightforward business language that leads to action plans that efficiently allocate financial and human resources (Ulrich, 1986).

HUMAN RESOURCE DEMAND

Demand forecasts are largely subjective. The most important variables and appropriate forecasting strategies must be identified in each particular organization through experimentation, experience, and testing over time against actual staffing needs. As we noted earlier, the techniques basically are easy to describe, but applying them successfully may be exceedingly complex and difficult. As an example, consider the following trend analysis procedure for forecasting HR demand (Wikstrom, 1971):

1. Find the appropriate business factor.
2. Plot the historical record of that factor in relation to employees employed.
3. Compute the productivity ratio.
4. Determine the trend.
5. Make necessary adjustments in the trend, past and future.
6. Project to the target year.

Let us elaborate each of these steps.

Predictor Selection

Selecting the proper predictor—the business factor to which HR needs will be related—is the critical first step. For a retail store, the appropriate factor might be dollar volume of sales; for a company producing steel, it might be tons of steel; for a university, it might be number of students.

To be useful, however, the predictor must satisfy at least two requirements. First, it should relate directly to the essential nature of the business so that business planning is done in terms of the factor. For example, it would make little sense for a retailer to project HR needs against units sold if it does all other planning in relation to dollar volume of sales and if frequent price changes make conversion from dollars to units difficult. The second requirement is that changes in the selected factor be proportional to required employees. For the steel company, tons of steel could be used if the number of required workers is proportional to the output of steel.

Selecting the proper business factor can be difficult, for in many organizations staffing levels required are not proportional to product volume. It may take almost as many workers to run a plant at half capacity as at full capacity, although product volume varies greatly. Further, one organization may produce many products, some of which require high labor input, while others do not. Under these circumstances, HR projections for the total organization may be misleading, and the firm must make separate projections for different products or segments of the work force (e.g., technical and nontechnical).

In order to get around the product mix problems, volumes may be converted to some factor related to dollar amounts, since sales revenue frequently is used in general business planning forecasts. The economic concept of *value added* may be appropriate here. Value added is that part of the value of products shipped actually created within a firm. Roughly it is the selling price less the cost of purchased materials and supplies. Although value added is not as easy to determine as sales revenue or inventory-adjusted revenue, it does relate much more functionally to HR requirements (Yelsey, 1982).

Thus, the selection of an appropriate predictor can be a vexing task. It requires sound judgment, thorough knowledge of the organization, and a sense of the future direction of technological change.

The Historic and Projected Relationships

Selection of an appropriate business factor is only the beginning of the projection process. What is required is a quantitative understanding of the past so that an organization can plan more accurately for the future. To be useful, one must determine the past relationship of the business factor to staffing levels accurately and estimate future levels of the business factor. The organization needs to know, for example, that it takes 237 employees to turn out 122,529 small electric appliances per year, or approximately 517 appliances per individual. This ratio—output per individual—is known as **labor productivity,** and in order to project HR requirements into the future, it is necessary to know the *rate* at which productivity is changing. It is

Year	Tons of Steel*	Productivity ratio (workers/ton)**	Human resources requirements
1984	5000	12.7	63,500
1986	5300	11.8	62,540
1988	5500	11.0	60,500
1990	5850	10.2	59,670
1992	6200	9.4	58,280
1994	6450	8.6	55,470
1996	6700	8.1	54,270
1998	7000	7.6	53,200
2000	7350	7.1	52,185
2002	7650	6.6	50,490
2004	8000	6.2	49,600
2006	8400	5.8	48,720

↑ Actual

↓ Projected

*   one hundred thousands

** effective workers per ton

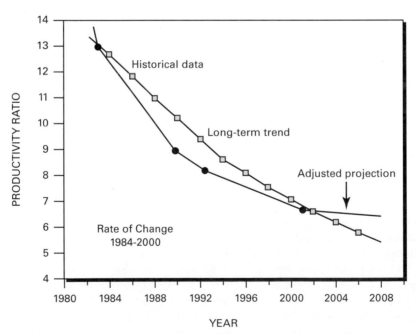

FIGURE 10–6 Hypothetical Human Resource Demand Projection.

the rate of change in this coefficient that is so important because the coefficient projected for the target year must reflect the productivity anticipated at that time.

Productivity Ratios

Productivity ratios should be computed for the previous 5 or preferably 10 years in order to determine the *average* rate of productivity change. If productivity changed significantly, it is important to identify the causes for such change (e.g., more efficient machinery, automation, economies of scale). However, productivity ratios and average rates of change must be tempered with the judgment of experienced line managers close to the scene of operations. Operating managers can help interpret the reasons for past changes in productivity and estimate the *degree* to which they will affect future projections.

Projecting Human Resource Requirements

Once an appropriate business factor has been determined and productivity ratios computed, the projection of HR needs for the target year is straightforward (see Fig. 10–6). In this figure, the projected level of the business factor (tons of steel) is multiplied by the productivity ratio (workers per ton) to arrive at the effective employees required. Adjustments to the pro-

jections for the influence of special factors (e.g., the amount of contract labor) yield a net figure for the HR demand at that time.

Integrating Supply and Demand Forecasts

If forecasts are to prove genuinely useful to managers they must result in an end product that is understandable and meaningful. Initial attempts at forecasting may result in voluminous printouts, but what is really required is a concise statement of projected staffing requirements that integrates supply and demand forecasts (see Fig. 10–7). In this figure, net HR demand at the end of each year of the 5-year forecast is compared with net HR supply for the same year. This yields a "bottom line" figure that shows an increasing deficit each year during the 5-year period. This is the kind of evidence senior managers need in order to make informed decisions regarding the future direction of HR initiatives.

Action Programs

Integrated HR supply and demand forecasts, together with talent inventories, provide support and direction for action plans and programs in many different areas, including recruitment, selection, career path planning, performance appraisal, and a host of training and development activities. Action programs inject changes into current HR systems that facilitate an organiza-

FIGURE 10–7 Integrated Human Resource Supply and Demand Forecast.

Promotion Criteria (cf. Fig 10-5): must be ready now or in less than one year and performing at an excellent level.

	1996	1997	1998	1999	2000
Demand					
Beginning in position	213	222	231	240	249
Increases (decreases)	9	9	9	9	10
Total demand (year end)	222	231	240	249	259
Supply (during year)					
Beginning in position	213	222	231	240	249
Minus promotions	(28)	(31)	(31)	(34)	(34)
Minus terminations	(12)	(12)	(13)	(13)	(13)
Minus retirements	(6)	(6)	(6)	(6)	(6)
Minus transfers	(4)	(4)	(4)	(4)	(6)
Subtotal	163	169	177	183	190
Plus promotions in	18	18	18	18	18
Total supply (year end)	181	187	195	201	208
Surplus/deficit (year end)	(41)	(44)	(45)	(48)	(51)

tion's adaptation to changing business conditions. One of the most promising action programs, and one that is becoming more popular, is career planning. It has become "big business" in organizations for the following reasons:

- Rising concern of employees for an improved quality of work life and for personal life planning.
- EEO legislation and company commitments to building a diverse work force at all levels.
- Rising educational levels of the work force, together with rising occupational aspirations.
- Slow economic growth and reduced advancement opportunities.
- Mergers, acquisitions, divestitures, rapid growth, and downsizing.

To make matters worse, baby boomers (those born between 1946 and 1964) are passing into middle life. By the year 2020, one in four workers will be between the ages of 45 and 64. Increasing longevity, coupled with the elimination of mandatory retirement at *any* age, now make it likely that older workers who stay on the job will limit promotional opportunities for younger workers.

What does this mean in terms of career management? Scarce promotions, frustrated expectations, and job-hopping—all of which lead to more stress, more burnout, and more psychological withdrawal. For a growing number of firms, therefore, career management is not an option; it's a necessity.

Career Management

Organizations have many jobs, but each individual has only one career. Consequently, it is important to make that career as fruitful and rewarding as possible. Careers develop in response to interactions with others and in relation to developing environments.

Indeed, dynamic business environments *demand* such changes (Sonnenfeld and Peiperl, 1988). Having examined its needs for future employees, the organization is in a sensible position to help the new or recently hired employee plan his or her career—not just the initial job assignment. It pays for the organization to plan actively with an individual how his or her working life—a significant part of life—will be spent because it will result in a wiser, fuller use of human potential. Likewise, it pays for the individual to plan his or her career to help maximize the personal and organizational rewards that will likely result from a bet-

ter use of his or her talents. Table 10–1 presents a summary of the key issues involved in organizational career planning, HR planning, and individual career planning.

When the individual's values and career goals mesh with the organization's needs and goals, an effective integration of the individual and the organization can occur (Quaintance, 1989). Under these ideal conditions, the individual is motivated to develop the abilities and skills necessary to take on new responsibilities in the organization, and the organization is likely to respond by providing the individual with the kinds of developmental opportunities he or she needs. On the other hand, when individual/organizational needs and goals conflict, employee dissatisfaction and poor job performance are likely to result. The literature on careers and development suggests that they often do operate in opposition (Brett and Reilly, 1988; Malos and Campion, 1995; Von Glinow et al., 1983).

Although a thorough discussion of the causes of such conflict is beyond the scope of this book, consider three contributing factors. First, and perhaps most basic, is the fact that often there are fewer positions available than there are people who desire them. In a society where most organizations are hierarchical, the inevitable result is that some people will not achieve their career goals. To the individual this may mean psychological failure; to the organization it may mean turnover and low employee motivation. However, one remedy for this problem may be to redesign lower-level jobs so that they will be more rewarding.

Second, organizations often see their development activities as a one-way process—something they do *to* the individual. Without joint planning and decision making between individual and organization, the individual has no idea of the kinds of developmental activities planned for him or her, and the organization has little information about the career aspirations of the individual. Although joint planning will not solve problems brought about by large differences in how a person's capabilities are viewed, it may prevent some of the problems caused by miscommunication.

Finally, poor assessment of the individual's capabilities and career goals (either overestimation or underestimation) by the organization frequently leads to problems for both parties. High-potential people may not get the development opportunities they need, and low-potential people may be assigned jobs they cannot handle. Both types of errors lead directly to high turnover, dissatisfaction, and feelings of frustration (Howard and Bray, 1989).

TABLE 10–1 Key Issues in Organizational Career Planning, Human Resource (HR) Planning, and Individual Career Planning

Organizational Career Planning	*Human Resource Planning*	*Individual Career Planning*
Staffing	Defining staffing needs	Developing self-awareness regarding
Strategic business planning	Defining job requirements	abilities and interests
Recruitment	Identifying relevant labor markets	Planning life and work goals
Selection	Influencing supply of talent available	Choosing a career or job
Induction and orientation	Providing realistic information to recruits	
	Validation of selection procedures	
	Socialization of new employees	
Placement	Identifying and defining career paths	Locating one's area of contribution
Defining career paths	Development and implementation of	Planning to achieve goals
Job/role planning	talent inventory	Learning how to fit into the organization
Talent inventories	Employee involvement in job/role	
	planning	
Promotion procedures	Validation of promotion procedures	
Management succession planning	Managing career progress for fast-track	
	employees	
Relocations	Controlling and managing relocations	
Growth and development	Performance appraisal and judgment of	Developing realistic assessment
	potential	of own potential, managerial skills,
		interpersonal skills
Training needs analysis	Career counseling for employees	Exploring alternatives for retraining and
Program design and development	Defining alternative approaches for	personal development within and
	meeting needs	outside the organization
Program evaluation	Considering alternative approaches for	Considering alternative career ladders
	meeting needs	within and outside the organization
Employment research	Evaluating costs, benefits, and quality of	
	programs	
Leveling off and alternatives	Designing alternative patterns of work	Late-career individual assessment of
	and rewards	interest or ability to cope with change,
Job redesign	Developing policies regarding lateral	personal abilities, interests, and
Transfers	career steps	preferences
Terminations	Developing termination policies to ensure	
	legal compliance	
Retirements	Providing retirement planning and	Letting go and retiring
	counseling	

Necessary Conditions for Career Management

While an analytical understanding of the process of career management is important (cf. London, 1983; Quaintance, 1989), the thrust of our discussion will be on the translation of theory into practice. In order to manage careers competently, three steps are required.

1. Determine how the person should behave when he or she reaches the jobs for which he or she is being prepared. An understanding of job requirements, with special emphasis on employee-determined changes, is fundamental to this process.

2. Determine whether the person has the capability to develop the kinds of behaviors that will be needed for the career plan. This implies a systematic approach to

the assessment of aptitudes (e.g., through testing or assessment center procedures).

3. Determine whether the individual wants to learn the required new behaviors and whether the career plan that the organization is considering fits the individual's own plan (Porter et al., 1975).

One additional condition is necessary for effective programs of career management; in practice, it probably should precede the others. In order to improve the career planning process, we need to collect information on the way organizations actually *do* manage careers and to understand the impact of different career tracks. To do so, we need to understand how organizations define their career paths. Let us examine this process in greater detail.

Defining Career Paths

Career path planning combines areas that previously have been regarded as individual issues—performance appraisal, development, transfer, and promotion. An initial step, however, is to identify characteristic mobility patterns (career paths) within firms. Before coaching and counseling take place, therefore, an organization first must be able to describe these paths.

Career paths are objective descriptions of sequential work experiences, as opposed to subjective, personal feelings about career progress, personal development, or satisfaction. Organizations need to move individuals along career paths in order to develop the breadth of abilities necessary to fill various levels and types of jobs. Traditionally career paths have emphasized upward mobility within a single occupation or functional area of work. The process is as follows:

1. Examine the paths followed in the past to the top "rungs of the ladders."

2. Identify entry and exit points into the career path, usually at the bottom only.

3. Define entry-level position requirements, normally in terms of educational level and specialization, experience, and years of service.

4. Identify important job experiences leading to the top "rung," and benchmark timing for reaching each "rung."

Xerox Corporation has adopted such an approach in an effort to promote diversity among its workforce at all levels of the firm (Sessa, 1992). One feature of the company's approach is a systematic examination of the backgrounds of all top executives to identify the key positions they held at lower levels—

that is, positions that get people noticed—and to set goals for getting minorities and women into these jobs. Toward that end, career paths should:

- Represent real progression possibilities, whether lateral or upward, without implied "normal" rates of progress or forced technical specialization.

- Be tentative and responsive to changes in job content, work priorities, organization patterns, and management needs.

- Be flexible, to take into consideration the compensating qualities of a particular individual, managers, subordinates, or others influencing the way work is performed.

- Specify skills, knowledge, and other specific attributes required to function effectively in each position along the paths, and not merely educational credentials or work experience, which may preclude some capable performers from career opportunities (Walker, 1980).

The emphasis in defining career paths is upon change, and on providing individuals with the tools they need to cope effectively with change. Career management is most effective when it is tied closely to business strategy. Once underway, however, such strategies must be reviewed periodically, evaluated, and perhaps altered. This is the function of control and evaluation—the topic we turn to next.

CONTROL AND EVALUATION

Control and evaluation are necessary features of any planning system, but organizationwide success in achieving HR goals will not occur through disjointed efforts. Since HRP activities override functional boundaries, broader system controls are necessary to monitor performance. Expect change. The function of control and evaluation is to guide the HRP activities through time, identifying the causes of deviations from the plan.

Goals and objectives are fundamental to this process to serve as yardsticks in measuring performance. Qualitative as well as quantitative standards may be necessary in HRP, although quantitative standards are preferable since numbers make the control and evaluation process more objective, and it becomes possible to measure deviations from desired performance more precisely. Such would be the case if a particular HR objective were to reduce the attrition rate of clerks in the first year after hire from the present 30 percent to 15 percent within 3 years. At the end of the third year, the evaluation process is simplified considerably because the initial objective was stated clearly with respect to the time period of evaluation (3 years) and expected percentage improvement (15%).

On the other hand, certain objectives, such as the quality of an early retirement program or the quality of women and minorities in management, may be harder to quantify. One strategy is to specify sub-objectives. For example, a sub-objective of a plan to improve the quality of supervision may include participation by each supervisor in a two-week training program. Evaluation at Time 2 may include a comparison of the number of employee grievances, requests for transfer, or productivity measures at Time 1 with the number at Time 2. Although other factors also may account for observed differences, usually they can be controlled by using appropriate experimental designs (see Chapter 16). Difficulty in establishing adequate and accurate criteria does not eliminate the HR planner's responsibility to evaluate programs.

Monitoring Performance

Effective control systems include periodic sampling and measurement of performance. In a space vehicle, for example, computer guidance systems continually track the flight path of the vehicle, and provide negative feedback in order to maintain the desired flight path. This is necessary in order to achieve the ultimate objective of the mission. An analogous tracking system should be part of any HRP system. In long-range planning efforts, it is important to establish and monitor shorter-run intermediate objectives in order to serve as benchmarks on the path to more remote goals. The short-run objectives allow the planner to monitor performance through time and to take corrective action before the ultimate success of longer-range goals is jeopardized.

Numerous monitoring procedures are commonly in use: examination of the costs of current practices (e.g., turnover costs, breakeven/payback for new hires); employee and management perceptions of results (e.g., by survey feedback procedures, audits of organizational climate); and measurement and analysis of costs and variations in costs under alternative decision alternatives (e.g., analysis of costs of recruiting versus internal development of current employees).

In the area of career performance, one may compare plots of salary and performance progress of individual managers against organizational norms by age,

experience, and job levels. Employees and their superiors can identify reasons for inadequate performance and they can initiate plans for improvement. It is also possible to identify and praise superior performers, and to counsel ineffective performers to reverse the trend.

Taking Corrective Action

If observed performance deviates significantly from desired performance, corrective action is necessary. First, however, one must identify the *causes* for such deviation. Problems are likely to be found in one (or both) of two places. Either objectives and performance standards are unrealistic (and therefore require revision), or behavior does not match the standards. In the former case, forecasts of impending HR shortages or surpluses may have been inaccurate. For example, suppose a 2-year forecast indicates that the current supply of engineers is adequate to meet future needs, and therefore no new engineering hires are needed for the next 2 years. Unforeseen changes in the external environment (e.g., a huge contract) may require alterations in this directive.

Alternatively, it may be necessary to modify behavior in order to meet performance standards, perhaps through training if employees lack the skills to perform their jobs competently, and perhaps by making rewards contingent on performance if incentive programs are inadequate. Finally, individual counseling or discipline may be called for. If discipline is used, it must be supported by the authority system and conform to organizational policy. Be explicit about the reasons for the disciplinary action, and how behavior should change so that the employee can be rewarded in the future.

Summary of the Evaluation Process

Walker (1974) outlined a four-stage evaluation procedure for HRP.

1. Make HRP objectives consistent with the organization's objectives.
2. Examine the various HRP policies and programs, including all aspects of forecasting and information systems.
3. Compare current practices with HR objectives and organizational needs.
4. Apply specific evaluation techniques and tools.

Here's how IBM applies these principles.

CONTROL AND EVALUATION OF HR PLANNING AT IBM

Each year line managers within each IBM division are responsible for developing "commitment plans." Such plans include quarter-by-quarter projections of sales volumes, revenues, and costs, plus action plans designed to carry out targeted business strategies. The role of HR in the process spans five activities: (1) deciding on the kinds of HR information the operating divisions should submit and the time frames for doing so; (2) preparing (with divisional managers) divisional HR plans; (3) assessing divisional business and HR plans; (4) developing corporate HR plans; and (5) evaluating selected actions against plans, and feeding back results to line managers, who have the authority and responsibility to exercise control (Dyer and Heyer, 1984).

The overall process requires that divisional managers commit to meaningful employee numbers in areas such as staffing levels, hiring, overtime, relocations, and EEO. This simply cannot be done without giving careful consideration to the HR implications of IBM's business plans, plus its HR strategies, policies, and programs. Thus HRP and business planning are interdependent (Dyer and Heyer, 1984). There is a high degree of commitment to quality in the plans because the extensive tracking process that occurs provides frequent feedback, not only on performance in a number of areas, but also on the quality of the data originally put forth.

Time Horizon

A general principle in HRP activities is that specificity of plans will vary with the length of the planning period. A 5- or 10-year statement of HR requirements need not be as detailed as next month's staffing plan. Here are two rules for establishing the length of planning periods. One, the planning period should provide the organization with adequate time to make necessary adjustments to potential problems and needs as revealed by the HR forecast. For most firms, 5 years provides enough lead time for recruitment and development of managerial, professional, and technical employees. This time frame permits a gradual adjustment to future conditions that really are not all that distant.

Two, the length of the planning period should relate to other major planning activities of the firm (Vetter, 1967). It is necessary to integrate and coordinate future plans in order to ensure overall planning effectiveness. For example, it is difficult to evaluate the impact of the HR plan on sales unless both types of plans relate to the same time period.

Exceptions will occur, however, when an HR problem requires a longer lead time for solution than is allowed by the normal planning period. One example is when long-term HR plans must be made on the basis of the organization's long-term plans (entering a new field or new market), or when large numbers of

employees are expected to retire after the normal planning period. Under these circumstances, forecasts and plans of HR needs may be projected 10 years or more into the future. As might be expected, longer-range plans are general, flexible, and contain a large margin for error.

Hence, organizations tend to have a variety of HR plans spanning different time periods. Distant time periods provide a horizon for setting objectives and general planning, as well as the necessary lead time to realize objectives. Shorter time periods (e.g., 1 year) are used to achieve immediate, short-term objectives and to serve as benchmarks for evaluating current performance against the longer-range plans. However, if substantial changes occur either in organizational objectives or in the environment, HR plans also will need to be updated to reflect current needs more accurately. Otherwise, HR plans typically are updated annually, with another year being added to the forecast. Thus, with each passing year, the long-range plan comes slowly into focus.

Responsibility for HR Planning

Whether responsibility for HRP resides formally in a planning unit located in the HR or industrial relations function or whether it is done by a corporate unit, it is a basic responsibility of every line manager in the organization. The line manager ultimately is responsible for integrating HR management functions, which include planning, supervision, performance appraisal, and job assignment. The role of the HR department is to *help* line managers manage effectively by providing tools, information, training, and support. Analysts may provide basic planning assumptions (e.g., sales or volume assumptions for some future time period) to all operating units periodically, but the individual manager must formulate his or her own HR plans that are consistent with these assumptions. Successively higher organizational units then may review the plans of individual managers and finally aggregate them into an overall HR plan.

In summary, we plan in order to reduce the uncertainty of the future. We do not have an infinite supply of any resource (people, capital, or materials), and it is important not only that we anticipate the future, but also that we actively try to influence it. Ultimate

success in HRP rests on the quality of the action programs established to achieve HR objectives and on the organization's ability to implement these programs. Managing HR problems according to plan can be difficult, but it is a lot easier than trying to manage them with no plan at all.

Discussion Questions

1. Describe the two phases of HRP.

2. Apply the two-phase approach to a hospital setting. What determines specific HR needs in various areas? What programs might you suggest to meet such needs?

3. Why is career management especially necessary in a downsizing environment?

4. Why are forecasts of HR demand more uncertain that HR supply?

5. Discuss the relationship of HRP to strategic HR management.

* * *

Systems thinking and applied measurement concepts, together with job analysis and HRP, provide the necessary foundation for sound employment decisions. In Parts V through VII we shall see how organizations apply these concepts in practice. Let us begin in Chapter 11 by considering the important processes of recruitment and initial screening.

CHAPTER
11
RECRUITMENT

AT A GLANCE

Organizations periodically recruit in order to add to, maintain, or readjust their work forces in accordance with HR requirements. Sound prior planning is a critical phase in the recruiting process. In planning for recruitment, one must establish HR plans; specify time, cost, and staff requirements; analyze sources; and determine and validate job requirements and employment standards. In the operations phase, it is important to consider both internal and external labor markets, though internal sources usually have priority. Finally, the success of the recruitment effort must be evaluated through cost and quality analyses. Evaluation strategies vary from the simple (e.g., cost per hire) to the complex (e.g., linear programming, PERT). Such information then provides closed-loop feedback to the planning of the next recruitment effort.

All organizations periodically recruit to add to, maintain, or readjust their total work forces in accordance with HR requirements. Organizations as open systems demand this dynamic equilibrium for their maintenance, survival, and growth. The logic of recruitment calls for sound HR planning systems (talent inventories, forecasts of HR supply and demand, action plans, and control and evaluative procedures) to serve as a base from which to launch recruiting efforts. This will be evident as we begin to examine the operational aspects of the recruitment function.

In this chapter, our objective is to describe how organizations search for prospective employees, and influence them to apply for available jobs. Accordingly, we will consider recruitment planning, operations, and evaluation, and include organizational examples to illustrate current practices.

RECRUITMENT PLANNING

Recruitment is frequently treated as if it were a one-way process—that is, organizations searching for prospective employees. This approach may be viewed as a **prospecting** theory of recruitment. In practice, however, prospective employees seek out organizations just as organizations seek out prospective employees. This view, termed a **mating** theory of recruitment, appears more realistic. Recruitment success (from the organization's perspective) and job search success (from the applicant's perspective) both depend on timing. If organizations are recruiting at the same time that applicants are searching for jobs, then conditions are ripe for the two to meet.

In order for organizations and applicants actually to meet, however, three other conditions must be satisfied. There must be a common communication medium (e.g., the organization advertises in a trade journal read by the job seeker), the job seeker must perceive a match between his or her personal characteristics and stated job requirements, and the job seeker must be motivated to apply for the job. Recruitment planning must address these issues.

The process of recruitment planning begins with a clear specification of HR needs (numbers, skills mix, levels) and the time frame within which such requirements must be met. This is particularly relevant to the setting of workforce diversity goals and timetables.

TABLE 11-1		African-American and Female Work Force Utilization Analysis for Managerial Jobs							
		% Available in Labor Market		*Number Presently in Job Group*		*Ultimate Goal*		*Utilization*	
Job Group	*Total Employees*	*African-Americans*	*Females*	*African-Americans*	*Females*	*African-Americans*	*Females*	*African-Americans*	*Females*
Managers	300	0.15	0.20	60	40	45	60	−15	+20

Labor force availability and internal work force representation of women and minorities are critical factors in this process. Although labor force availability of women and minorities is difficult to assess accurately, a market research technique known as trade-off analysis has been used successfully by AT&T for this purpose (Ritchie and Beardsley, 1978).

Table 11–1 examines only the job group "managers," although similar analyses must be done for eight other categories of workers specified by EEOC. Note that 300 managers are presently employed, of whom 60 are African-American and 40 are female. Researchers estimate that 15 percent of the available labor market for managers is African-American and 20 percent female. Therefore, for work force representation to reach parity with labor market representation, the organization needs 0.15 × 300, or 45, African-Americans and 0.20 × 300, or 60, females. However, African-Americans are presently being overutilized in this job category (45 − 60 = −15), while females are being underutilized (60 − 40 = +20). Thus our ultimate recruitment goal is to hire 20 more female managers to reach parity with the available labor force.

The next step is to project a timetable for reaching this ultimate goal based on expected job vacancies. If an HR forecast by job group is available the problem is straightforward, but the basic procedure in all cases is to look at what has occurred in a job group over the past several years in terms of new hires, promotions, and transfers. This provides an index of what to expect in the coming year. Employers also should examine applicant flow and internal availability to determine how many of these expected vacancies can reasonably be filled with females who are already "on board."

The effective use of "in-house" talent should come first. If an organization undertakes external recruitment efforts without considering the desires, capabilities, and potential of present employees (e.g., the 15 overutilized African-American managers in Table 11–1), it may incur both short- and long-run costs. In the short run, morale may degenerate; in the long run, an organization with a reputation for consistent neglect of in-house talent may find it difficult to attract new employees and to retain experienced ones. This is why soundly conceived action plans (that incorporate developmental and training needs for each employee), promotability indexes, and replacement charts are so important. No less important are control and evaluation procedures that provide closed loop feedback on the overall operating effectiveness of the entire HR planning system.

Primed with a comprehensive HR plan for the various segments of the work force (e.g., entry-level, managerial, professional, and technical), recruitment planning may begin.[1] To do this, three key parameters must be estimated: the time, the money, and the staff necessary to achieve a given hiring rate. The basic statistic needed to estimate these parameters is the *number of leads needed to generate a given number of hires in a given time.* Certainly the easiest way to derive this figure is on the basis of prior recruitment experience. If accurate records exist regarding yield ratios and time lapse data, there is no problem, since it is possible to determine trends and to generate reliable predictions (assuming labor market conditions are comparable). **Yield ratios** are the ratios of leads to invites, invites to interviews, interviews (and other selection instruments) to offers, and offers to hires obtained over some specified time period (e.g., 6 months or a year). **Time-lapse data** provide the average intervals between events, such as between the extension of an offer to a candidate, acceptance, and addition to the payroll.

If no experience data exist, then it is necessary to establish some "best guesses" or hypotheses and to monitor performance as the operational recruitment program unfolds. For the moment, however, suppose

---

[1] Much of the material in this section is drawn from the excellent treatment by Roger H. Hawk in *The Recruitment Function,* © 1967 by the American Management Association, Inc.

FIGURE 11-1 Recruiting Yield Pyramid—Engineering Candidates, ABC Engineering Consultants.

ABC Engineering Consultants is contemplating opening two new offices and needs 100 additional engineers in the next 6 months. Fortunately, ABC has expanded in the past, and on that basis it is able to make predictions like this:

> With technical candidates we must extend offers to two candidates to gain one acceptance, or an offer-to-acceptance ratio of 2:1. If we need 100 engineers, we'll have to extend 200 offers. Further, if the interview-to-offer ratio has been 3:2, then we must conduct 300 interviews, and since the invites-to-interview ratio is 4:3, then we must invite as many as 400 candidates. Finally, if contacts or leads required to find suitable candidates to invite are in a 6:1 proportion, then we must make 2,400 contacts. A recruiting yield pyramid for these data is presented in Figure 11-1.

Actual data from a survey of more than 500 companies revealed the following average yield ratios: 7 percent of incoming resumes were routed to hiring managers (a 14:1 ratio), 26 percent of these were invited to interview, and 40 percent of the interviewees received job offers. Not surprisingly, nontechnical positions generated twice as many acceptances (82%) as technical positions (41%) (Lord, 1989).

Additional information, critical to effective recruitment planning, can be derived from time-lapse data. For ABC Engineering Consultants, past experience may show that the interval from receipt of a résumé to invitation averages 4 days. If the candidate is still available, he or she will be interviewed 5 days later. ABC extends offers, on the average, 3 days after interviews, and within a week after that the candidate

either accepts or rejects the offer. If the candidate accepts, he or she reports to work, on the average, 3 weeks from the date of acceptance. Therefore, if ABC begins today, the best estimate is that it will be 40 days before the first new employee is added to the payroll. With this information, it becomes possible to describe the "length" of the recruitment pipeline and to fit recruiting plans to it. Figure 11–2 presents a simple time-lapse chart for these data. All of this assumes that intervals between events in the pipeline proceed as planned. In fact, longitudinal research indicates that candidates, especially high-quality ones, perceive delays in the timing of recruitment events very negatively, and these delays often cost companies job acceptances (Rynes, Bretz, and Gerhart, 1991).

The information on timing can then be integrated into staffing graphs or weekly activity charts, showing the production of leads, invitations, interviews, offers, acceptances, and reports. A 6-month staffing graph for ABC Engineering Consultants, based on the data presented earlier, is presented in Figure 11–3.

Note, however, that these yield ratios and time-lapse data are only appropriate for ABC's engineers.

FIGURE 11–2 Time-lapse Data for Recruitment of Engineers.

Average number of days from:

Résumé to invitation	4
Invitation to interview	5
Interview to offer	3
Offer to acceptance	7
Acceptance to report for work	21

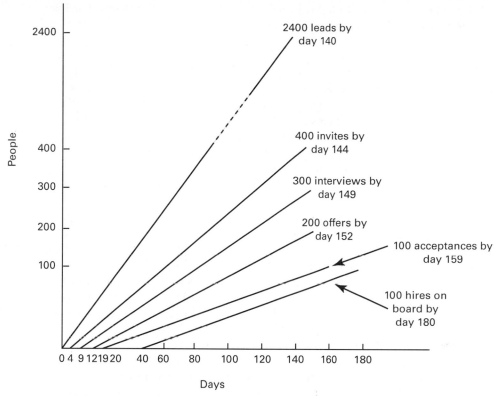

FIGURE 11–3 Staffing Graph, Engineering Candidates, ABC Engineering Consultants.

Although time frames differ from job to job and industry to industry, 3 months from the receipt of a requisition to the new employee's start date is considered an acceptable time period for recruiting a journey-level professional (Lord, 1989). Of course, the time period also depends on labor market conditions. A **labor market** is a geographical area within which the forces of supply (people looking for work) interact with the forces of demand (employers looking for people) and, thereby, determine the price of labor. However, since the geographical areas over which employers extend their recruiting efforts depend partly on the type of job being filled, it is impossible to define the boundaries of a local labor market in any clear-cut manner (Reynolds et al., 1986). If the supply of suitable workers in a particular labor market is high relative to available jobs, then the price of labor generally will be cheaper. On the other hand, if the supply is limited (e.g., suppose ABC needs certain types of engineering specialists who are unavailable locally), then it must widen the search and investigate additional labor markets in order to realize required yield ratios.

Of course, time-lapse data may have to be revised to account for the change in labor market conditions, and the price of labor generally will also rise. Recruitment is fairly simple for a small manufacturing firm in a well-populated rural area. But large, high-technology firms with global markets face far different recruitment challenges (Farish, 1989).

Staffing Requirements and Cost Analyses

Since experienced professional/technical recruiters generally produce about 50 new hires per year, then ABC will require approximately 4 full-time recruiters to meet its staffing requirements for 100 engineers in the next 6 months. ABC would need to do similar analyses before undertaking a recruitment effort for nontechnical people.

So far, we have been able to estimate ABC's recruiting time and staffing requirements on the basis of its previous recruiting experience. However, we must consider several other parameters before the planning process is complete. The most important of these, as one might expect, is cost. Before making cost estimates, however, let us go back and assume that an organization has no prior recruiting experience (or that the necessary data were not recorded). The development of working hypotheses about yield ratios is considerably more complex under these conditions, though far from impossible.

The external labor market must be analyzed by source, along with analyses of demand for similar types of people by competitors. In addition, the entire civic environment must be evaluated in order to do a "company advantage study." Numerous items must be appraised, including geographic factors (climate, recreation), location of the firm, cost of living, availability of housing, proximity to shopping centers, public and parochial schools, and so forth.

In sum, an organization should capitalize on any special factors that are likely to attract candidates (e.g., company image and reputation). Such information will prove useful when developing future recruiting strategy and when gathering baseline data for estimates of recruiting yield. It also becomes possible to generate testable hypotheses about the company's competitive position relative to published or otherwise available data on recruiting performance when these plus and minus factors are taken into account.

Yield ratios and time-lapse data are invaluable for estimating recruiting staff and time requirements. Recruitment planning is not complete, however, until the costs of alternative recruitment strategies have been estimated. Expenditures by source must be analyzed carefully in advance in order to avoid any subsequent "surprises." In short, analysis of costs is one of the most important considerations in determining where, when, and how to approach the recruiting marketplace.

At the most general level, determine the gross cost-per-hire by dividing the total cost of recruiting (TCOR) by the number of individuals hired (NH):

$$\text{Gross Cost-Per-Hire} = \text{TCOR/NH} \quad \textbf{(11–1)}$$

Data from past experience usually provide the inputs to Equation 11–1. Although this simple statistic is useful as a first step, it falls far short of the cost information necessary for thorough advance planning and later evaluation of the recruiting effort. In particular, the following cost estimates are essential:

1. *Staff costs*—salaries, benefits, and overtime premiums.
2. *Operational costs*—telephone and fax; recruiting staff travel and living expenses, professional fees and services (agency fees, consultant fees, etc.); advertising expenses (radio and TV, newspapers, technical journals, ads for field trips, etc.); medical expenses for pre-employment physical examinations; information

services (brochures describing the company and its environment); and supplies, material, and postage.
3. *Overhead*—rental expenses for temporary facilities, office furniture, equipment, and so on.

Source Analysis

Analysis of recruiting sources facilitates effective planning. Three types of analyses are required: cost-per-hire, time-lapse from candidate identification to hire, and source yield. The most expensive sources generally are private employment agencies and executive search firms, since agency fees may constitute as much as 35 percent of an individual's first-year salary (Lord, 1989). The next most expensive sources are field trips, for both advertising expenses and recruiters' travel and living expenses are incurred. Less expensive are advertising responses, write-ins, and company transfers and promotions. Employee referrals and walk-ins are the cheapest sources of candidates.

Time-lapse studies of recruiting sources are especially useful for planning purposes, since the time from initial contact to report on board varies across sources. In the case of college recruiting, for example, a steady flow of new employees is impossible, since reporting dates typically coincide closely with graduation, regardless of when the initial contact was made.

For those sources capable of producing a steady flow, however, employee referrals and walk-ins usually show the shortest delay from initial contact to report (Hawk, 1967). Field trips and company transfers generally produce longer delays, while agency referrals and ads usually are the slowest sources. In the case of agencies, for example, an intermediary is involved, the candidate must provide advance notice to his or her present employer, and, in some cases where agencies do not maintain close contact with their clients, candidates are no longer active. As in so many other areas of endeavor, "He [i.e., the organization] who hesitates is lost." Competition for top candidates is intense; the organization whose recruiting section functions smoothly and is capable of responding swiftly has the greatest likelihood of landing high-potential people.

The third index of source performance is source yield (i.e., the ratio of the number of candidates generated from a particular source to hires from that source). This information is especially valuable for determining how effectively time is being spent in a particular market. While no ranking of source yields would have validity across all types of organizations and all labor markets, collect and evaluate such information periodically along with cost and time-lapse data. Only then can an organization establish its own value ranking of the various sources and select those sources that will provide the right kinds of candidates at the lowest cost and in the shortest possible time.

We are almost ready to begin recruiting operations at this point. Recruiting efficiency can be heightened considerably, however, once employment requirements are defined thoroughly in advance. This is an essential step for both technical and nontechnical jobs. Recruiters must be familiar with the job descriptions of available jobs; they must understand (and, if possible, have direct experience with) the work to be performed. Research has shown clearly that characteristics of organizations and jobs (e.g., location, pay, opportunity to learn, challenging, interesting work) have a greater influence on the likelihood of job acceptance by candidates than do characteristics of the recruiter (Barber and Roehling, 1993; Rynes, 1991; Taylor and Bergmann, 1987).

Nevertheless, at the first stage of recruitment, characteristics of recruiters (personable, informative, competent) do *affect* the perceptions of candidates about job attributes, regard for the company, and likelihood of joining the company. Neither the job function (HR versus line management) nor the gender of the recruiter seems to make much difference to candidates (Harris and Fink, 1987; Maurer et al., 1992). However, perceived similarity and interpersonal attraction do seem to affect female recruiters in a manner that favors male applicants. Still, subjective qualifications (e.g., ability to express ideas and demonstrated initiative) have the greatest influence on interview outcomes (Graves and Powell, 1995).

Planning is now complete. We have established HR plans; specified time, cost, and staff requirements; analyzed sources; and determined and validated job requirements and employment standards. Now we are ready to begin recruiting operations.

OPERATIONS

The first step in recruiting operations is to examine internal sources for qualified or qualifiable candidates. This is especially true of large, decentralized organizations that are likely to maintain comprehensive talent inventories with detailed information on each employee. Needless to say, it is essential to update the inventory periodically to reflect changes in employee skills, educational and training achievements, job title, and so forth.

Regardless of organizational size, however, promotion-from-within policies must be supported by a managerial philosophy that permits employees to consider available opportunities for transfer or promotion. Candidates may be identified either by talent inventory search or by responding to in-house postings of available jobs. On the other hand, organizations often turn to external sources to fill entry-level jobs, jobs created by expansion, and jobs whose specifications cannot be met by present employees.

External Sources for Recruiting Applicants

A wide variety of external recruiting sources is available, with the choice of source(s) contingent upon specific hiring requirements and source analysis results. Although we shall not consider each source in detail, available sources include:

1. *Advertising*—newspapers (classified and display), technical and professional journals, direct mail, television, the Internet, and (in some cases) outdoor advertising.
2. *Employment agencies*—federal and state agencies, private agencies, executive search firms, management consulting firms, and agencies specializing in temporary help.
3. *Educational institutions*—technical and trade schools, colleges and universities, co-op work/study programs, and alumni placement offices.
4. *Professional organizations*—technical society meetings and conventions (regional and national) and society placement services.
5. *Military*—out-processing centers and placement services administered by regional and national retired officer associations.
6. *Labor unions*
7. *Career fairs*
8. *Outplacement firms*
9. *Walk-ins*
10. *Write-ins*
11. *Intracompany transfers and company retirees*
12. *Employee referrals*

To illustrate how companies try to gain a competitive advantage over their rivals in university recruiting for managerial candidates, consider the following examples.

HOW MICRON TECHNOLOGY, UNISYS, AND BRISTOL-MYERS SQUIBB FIND TOP STUDENTS

Restructurings, downsizings, and layoffs typify the experience of many companies in the 1990s. Hence, campus recruitment is a tough sell these days. Micron Technology, a 6,200-employee manufacturer of semiconductors and computer memory products in Boise, Idaho, hasn't had a layoff in 10 years. Hence the company's entrepreneurial spirit that encourages independent career growth is a big selling point. Unisys, located in Blue Bell, Pennsylvania, has had layoffs and students often ask about that. According to the company's program director for worldwide recruiting, "Anytime there are layoffs involved, people tend to remember the negatives. We show job candidates that Unisys is a company in transition. We have experienced layoffs, but that has been in one division of the company. Unisys' growth in worldwide information services has been phenomenal" (Leonard, 1995, p. 62).

In order to get itself noticed by MBA students at some of the best schools in the country, Bristol-Myers Squibb took a different tack. It distributed an interactive computer diskette that conveyed its recruitment message. That message includes information about the company, about positions available at the com-

pany, and case histories of Squibb managers, specifically, case histories of difficult business problems faced by recent MBAs who worked for Squibb. After describing a problem, the diskette provides several options for solving it. Viewers are asked which solution they would choose. Subsequently they are told which option actually was chosen and why.

Squibb chose to use these interactive quizzes so that viewers would get involved in the recruitment information it provided. In designing the diskette, Squibb provided a menu so that MBAs could access the information they were interested in and skip the rest. To set itself apart from other companies, Squibb injected humor into its "otherwise information-laden message."

Was the recruitment diskette effective? Based on follow-up research, Squibb found that 33 percent of those who received the diskette viewed it once, 29 percent viewed it twice, and 18 percent viewed it three times or more (Koch, 1990). As this example shows, employers are becoming more sophisticated in deciding where, when, and how to approach markets they have targeted.

These sources may be classified as formal (institutionalized search methods such as employment agencies, advertising, labor unions) or informal (e.g., walk-ins, write-ins, employee referrals). In terms of the most popular sources used by employers, evidence indicates that:

- Candidates at all occupational levels use informal contacts widely and effectively;
- Use of the public employment service declines as required job skills increase;
- The internal market is a major recruitment method except for entry-level, unskilled, and semiskilled workers;
- Larger firms are the most frequent users of walk-ins, write-ins, and the internal market (Bureau of National Affairs, 1988).

However, for recruiting minority workers, a study of over 20,000 applicants in a major insurance company revealed that female and African-American applicants consistently used formal recruitment sources rather than informal ones (Kirnan, Farley, and Geisinger, 1989). Informal sources such as employee referrals can work to the employer's advantage if the work force is comprised of members from different gender, racial, and ethnic groups. Indeed, company testimonials by present minority employees are probably the strongest magnet for attracting outside minority candidates and encouraging them to apply for jobs.

Employee referrals are extremely popular today. Commonly the companies offer a cash or merchandise bonus when a current employee refers a successful candidate. The Apple Bank for Savings, located in New York City, is typical. Current employees who re-

RECRUITING FOR DIVERSITY

For organizations that wish to increase the diversity of their work forces, the first (and most difficult) step is to determine their needs, goals, and target populations. What do you want your diversity program to accomplish? Then take steps such as the following (Overman, 1994):

- Determine the focus of the program and prioritize needs.
- Make initial contacts and gather information from community support and other external recruitment and training organizations.
- Develop one or more results-oriented programs. What actions will you take, who will be involved, how and when will you accomplished these actions?
- Invite program representatives to tour your organization, visit with staff members, and learn about employment opportunities and the organization's requirements for success.

- Select a diversity of organizational contacts and recruiters for outreach and support, including employees outside the HR department.
- Get top management approval and support. Train managers to value diversity in the workplace.
- Develop procedures for monitoring and follow-up; make revisions as needed to accomplish objectives.

As an aid in this process, consider using an outreach directory, such as the *Outreach And Recruitment Directory: A Resource For Diversity-Related Recruitment Needs* (1995). The directory is available as a hardcover book or as software, and the database can be sorted by a variety of factors, such as job type, location, target population, or specific types of organizations—e.g., those specific to women.

---

cruit new workers receive $250 after the recruits have remained with the bank for three months and an additional $250 when the recruits have been employed for one year. The employee who recruits the new worker also must remain with the bank to receive the payment. The bank hires about 50 percent of the candidates referred by current employees (Amante, 1989). High-technology firms are a bit more generous. Cognos Corp., a maker of business-intelligence tools, offers $4,000 to employees who refer new hires; other companies pay as much as $10,000 for referrals (Chan, 1996).

Which sources yield the highest numbers of qualified candidates? The fact is, most applicants use more than one recruitment source to learn about jobs. Hence designation of "the" recruitment source they used is misleading, for it ignores the combined effect of multiple sources. In fact, the accumulated evidence

RECRUITING IN CYBERSPACE

The interconnected network of computers known as the Internet allows users to exchange electronic mail, transfer computer files, search data bases, and communicate keyboard-to-keyboard with other on-line users. That gives organizations the opportunity to place classified ads, receive résumés, and to market themselves as the employer of choice in their industries.

Public bulletin boards where individuals and organizations can place ads on the Internet have been around for years. The drawback is that listings are dropped after 1 or 2 weeks. However, with the Online Career Center (OCC), a nonprofit organization supported by companies such as Hallmark, GTE, AT&T, MCI, Apple, and Kraft, users can search the résumé data base and to post an unlimited number of ads on line for as long as they wish—free of charge.

In the 2 years of its existence, more than 3,000 companies have used OCC. You can connect directly to the OCC data base through Gopher at gopher.msen.com (Overman, 1995).

How is the yield from Net-based recruitment? At Hewlett-Packard, fully one-third of the résumés it receives arrive by fax or E-mail. In 1996, it received over 20,000 résumés via the Net. Says HP's corporate staffing manager, "From my perspective, the Web is the future of recruiting" (Baig, 1996).

on the relationship between recruitment sources, turnover, and job performance suggests that such relationships are quite weak (Williams, Labig, and Stone, 1993). For example, a study of 10 different recruitment sources used by more than 20,000 applicants for the job of insurance agent showed that recruiting source explained 5 percent of the variation in applicant quality, 1 percent of the variation in the survival of new hires, and none of the variation in commissions (Kirnan et al., 1989). In light of these results, consider the following advice:

> Regardless of the recruitment sources used to generate an applicant population, and regardless of the differences in applicants across recruitment sources, once a final applicant pool has been generated, organizations can maximize the payoff from their selection systems by ignoring recruitment sources and using a [valid] predictor-based selection strategy [Williams et al., 1993, p. 171].

Managing Recruiting Operations

A well-coordinated administrative system for recording and controlling applicant flow is essential to effective recruitment operations and subsequent evaluation. In addition, such controls are essential if the organization is to meet its legal, ethical, and public relations responsibilities. Keep at least five types of records:

1. Incoming applications and résumés.
2. Activity at important points in the recruiting "pipeline" for each candidate (e.g., invitations, interviews, offers, acceptances/rejections, reports onto payroll).
3. Acknowledgments and "no interest" letters for each candidate.
4. Offers and acceptances relative to open staffing requisitions.
5. Records of closed cases.

In order to perform these activities accurately and in a timely manner, more and more firms are turning to computers for help. Automated employment tracking and control systems are available at affordable prices, from about $1,000 to $10,000 depending on the range and volume of recruitment needs (Lord, 1989). Here is how a typical system works.

The date of receipt and other pertinent information first are extracted from each incoming résumé, and assignment is made to a recruiter. Each step in the recruiting pipeline is recorded for each candidate by date of action. Each recruiter then receives a list of his or her assigned files with the current action recorded for each applicant. At the same time, a master active list and pipeline count are generated. Offers and acceptances are recorded against open staffing requisitions, and each recruiter routinely communicates with the system to update the file and keep records current. Time-lapse data and yield ratios, together with analyses of source and recruiter efficiency, can be generated regularly. In addition to cutting recruiting costs in large organizations, such a system permits enhanced control and evaluation of the overall recruitment effort.

MEASUREMENT, EVALUATION, AND CONTROL

Thorough recruitment planning simplifies later evaluation of the recruitment effort considerably. Early hypotheses regarding cost and quality can be measured against actual operating results. Critical trade-offs between cost and quality can be made intelligently on the basis of empirical data, not haphazardly on the basis of hunch or intuition. Perform cost and quality analyses regularly. These include:

- Cost of operations
- Cost-per-hire
- Cost-per-hire by source
- Total résumé inputs
- Résumé inputs by source
- Quality of résumés by source

HOW MOTOROLA TRACKS RÉSUMÉS

Motorola's Land Mobile Products Division must track hundreds of résumés that arrive each week in response to ads the company places for electrical engineers, managers, and corporate executives. The résumés arrive via regular mail, fax, and e-mail. Before Motorola turned to an innovative scanning system and document management program (known as PageKeeper), most résumés had to be keyed in to allow for word searches. Now, after a quick review for relevancy, résumés received on paper can be scanned, and those received electronically ported directly into PageKeeper. How has the new system worked? It has helped reduce Motorola's average time for bringing on a new employee (i.e., the recruitment pipeline) from 6 months to 46 days (Sheley, 1995).

- Source yield and source efficiency
- Time-lapse between recruiting stages by source
- Time-lapse between recruiting stages by acceptance versus rejection
- Geographical sources of candidates
- Individual recruiter activity
- Individual recruiter efficiency
- Acceptance/offer ratio
- Offer/interview ratio
- Interview/invitation ratio
- Invitation/résumé input ratio
- Biographical data analyses against acceptance/rejection data
- Analysis of post-visit and rejection questionnaires
- Analysis of reasons for acceptance and termination
- Analysis of post-reporting-date follow-up interviews
- Placement test scores on hires versus rejections
- Placement test scores versus observed performance
- Salary offered-acceptance versus rejections
- Salary versus age, year of first degree, and total work experience

As an example, consider that for exempt employees (i.e., exempt from the overtime provisions of the Fair Labor Standards Act) hiring costs averaged $7,839 over companies of all sizes (Sheley, 1995). Consider presenting the results of these analyses graphically for ease of interpretation and communication. That well-worn maxim "A picture is worth a thousand words" is especially valid in this context. The individual recruiter can analyze his or her own performance, and senior managers can track cost and hiring trends. Such information helps to determine future needs and strategies.

Formal procedures for translating recruitment-related differences in sources and costs into optimum dollar-valued payoffs from recruitment/selection activities are now available (Boudreau and Rynes, 1985; Law and Myors, 1993; Martin and Raju, 1992). Future research on recruitment effectiveness should incorporate this more meaningful framework.

As is true of other organizational subsystems, a highly coordinated, systemic view of the recruiting process is indispensable.

Position Point-Factor Analysis

Position Point-Factor Analysis (Dennis, 1985) is a checklist of 15 key factors that can be used to measure recruitment results (see Fig. 11–4). The points assigned to each factor reflect the relative expenditures of time and effort required to fill a given exempt-level position. However, different recruitment circumstances might well require revision in factors or in points assigned. Thus an 11-point position *should* require more time and effort than a 6-point position.

This approach can be used in two important ways: (1) to establish the workloads of recruitment staff, and (2) to measure the effectiveness of the recruitment staff. Although Position Point-Factor Analysis weighs explicitly the types and the number of positions to be filled, it is not the end of recruitment evaluation, only the beginning. Follow-up studies that consider the long-term performance of employees also are necessary.

Job Search from the Applicant's Perspective

How do individuals identify, investigate, and decide among job opportunities? In one study researchers collected longitudinal data on the actual search behaviors

Factor	Point Value
1. Salary level of position	
Below $30,000	+1
$30,000–59,900	+2
$60,000–99,900	+3
$100,000 plus	+4
2. Time frame within which positions must be filled (from official beginning of a search to the extension of an offer)	
30–60 days	+5
61–90 days	+3
91–120 days	+1
Over 120 days	+0
3. Position is confidential	+3
4. Position must be filled internally	+2
5. Duties are not clearly defined	+2
6. Reporting relationships (position and/or people) are not clearly defined	+2
7. Position is technically complex and/or rare in marketplace	+2
8. Marketplace competition for position is keen	+2
9. Position is located in a unit with less-than-positive reputation	+1
10. No advertising may be done	+3
11. No agency fees may be paid	+3
12. No relocation expenses may be paid	+1
13. No housing purchase assistance may be made	+1
14. Selection process involves interviews by more than the human resource department and the manager to whom the position reports (per level above this manager)	+1
15. More than one slot for a position needs to be filled	+1

Source: From D. L. Dennis, "Evaluating corporate recruitment efforts." Reprinted from the January 1985 issue of *Personnel Administrator,* copyright 1985, The American Society for Personnel Administration, 606 N. Washington Street, Alexandria, Va. 22314.

FIGURE 11–4 Position Point-Factor Analysis Checklist.

of 186 college and vocational-technical school graduates at three different time periods: (1) early in their search (2–8 months prior to graduation), (2) at graduation, and (3) and again at 3 months following graduation for those who remained unemployed. Results showed that individuals tend to follow a sequential model: first they search broadly to develop a pool of potential jobs, then they examine jobs within that pool in detail, and they reopen the search only if the initial pool does not lead to an acceptable job offer (Barber, Daly, Giannantonio, and Phillips, 1994).

Once invited for interviews, candidates sometimes encounter interviews that focus on recruitment per se (i.e., conveying information about the company and about the jobs to be filled). Alternatively, candidates may encounter dual-purpose interviews whose objective is recruitment as well as selection. Which is more effective? Longitudinal research found that applicants acquired and retained more information from recruitment-only interviews. However, applicants were more likely to persist in pursuing the job when they encountered recruitment-selection interviews (Barber, Hollenbeck, Tower, and Phillips, 1994).

How do organizational characteristics influence applicants' attraction to firms? To a certain extent it depends on the self-esteem and need for achievement (nAch) of applicants. While applicants in general were more attracted to firms that were decentralized and based pay on performance, applicants with low self-esteem were more attracted to large, decentralized firms than were those whose self-esteem was high. Applicants high in nAch, who prefer responsibility for performance outcomes and like to receive feedback, were more attracted to firms that rewarded performance rather than seniority. However, high nAch indi-

---

HOW NOT TO FIND A NEW JOB

Consider the following scenario, which has happened all too frequently over the last decade (as a result of mergers, restructurings, and downsizings) and is expected to occur often this decade as economic conditions change ("No Letup," 1995). You are a mid-level executive, well-regarded, well-paid, and seemingly well-established in your chosen field. Then—whammo!—a change in business strategy or a change in economic conditions results in your layoff from the firm you hoped to retire from. What do you do? How do you go about finding another job? According to management consultants and executive recruiters the following are some of the key things *not* to do (Rigdon, 1992):

- Don't panic—a search takes time, even for well-qualified middle- and upper-level managers. Seven months to a year is not unusual. Be prepared to wait it out.
- Don't be bitter—bitterness makes it harder to begin to search; it also turns off potential employers.
- Don't kid yourself—do a thorough self-appraisal of your strengths and weaknesses, your likes and dislikes about jobs and organizations. Face up to what has has happened, decide if you want to switch fields, figure out where you and your family want to live, and don't delay the search itself for long.
- Don't drift—develop a plan, target companies, and go after them relentlessly. Realize that your job is to find a new job. Cast a wide net; consider industries other than your own.
- Don't be lazy—the heart of a good job hunt is re-

search. Use reference books, public filings, and annual reports when drawing up a list of target companies. If negotiations get serious, talk to a range of insiders and knowledgeable outsiders to learn about politics and practices. You don't want to wind up in a worse fix than the one you left.

- Don't be shy or overeager—since personal contacts are the most effective means to land a job, pull out all the stops to get the word out that you are available. At the same time, resist the temptation to accept the first job that comes along. Unless it's absolutely right for you, the chances of making a mistake are quite high.
- Don't ignore your family—some executives are embarrassed and don't tell their families what's going on. A better approach, experts say, is to bring the family into the process and deal with them honestly.
- Don't lie—experts are unanimous on this point. Don't lie and don't stretch a point—either in résumés or in interviews. Be willing to address failures as well as strengths. Discuss openly and fully what went wrong at the old job.
- Don't jump the gun on salary—always let the potential employer bring this subject up first, but once it surfaces, thoroughly explore all aspects of your future compensation and benefits package.

Those who have been through the trauma of job loss and the challenge of finding a job often describe the entire process as a wrenching, stressful one. Avoiding the mistakes shown above can ensure that finding a new job need not take any longer than necessary.

---

viduals tended to have less attraction to organizations in general (Turban and Keon, 1993).

Realistic Job Previews

One final line of research deserves mention. Numerous investigations have studied the effect of a realistic job preview (RJP) on job acceptance, job satisfaction, and turnover. Results have been inconsistent across organizational settings and realistic preview techniques. In general, however, they demonstrate that when the naive expectations of job applicants are lowered to

match organizational reality, job acceptance rates may be lower and job performance is unaffected, but job satisfaction and job survival tend to be higher for those who receive a realistic job preview (Wanous, 1977).

A meta-analysis of 15 RJP experiments with a combined sample size of 5,250 subjects revealed that RJPs can be expected to lead to a 9 percent reduction, on average, in job turnover (McEvoy and Cascio, 1985). However, this effect is moderated to some extent by job complexity. Smaller reductions in turnover can be expected in low-complexity jobs than in high-complexity jobs.

There is a substantial debate about how RJPs work. At the level of the individual job applicant, RJPs are likely to have the greatest impact when the applicant:

1. Can be selective about accepting a job offer;
2. Has unrealistic job expectations;
3. Would have difficulty coping with job demands without the RJP (Breaugh, 1983; 1992).

Longitudinal research shows that RJPs should be *balanced* in their orientation. That is, they should be conducted to enhance overly pessimistic expectations and to reduce overly optimistic expectations. Doing so helps to bolster the applicant's perceptions of the organization as caring, trustworthy, and honest (Meglino et al., 1988). In addition, develop an RJP even when there is no turnover problem (i.e., proactively rather than reactively), employ an audiovisual medium, and, where possible, show actual job incumbents (Wanous, 1989).

Intrinsic rather than extrinsic job factors seem most in need of a realistic job preview. Recruiters find it much easier to communicate factual material than to articulate subtle, intrinsic aspects of organizational climate. Yet intrinsic factors are typically more potent contributors to overall job satisfaction than are extrinsic factors (Kacmar and Ferris, 1989). Those responsible for recruitment training and operations would do well to heed these results.

Discussion Questions

1. Describe three key issues to consider in recruitment planning.

2. Discuss the advantages and disadvantages of recruiting in cyberspace.

3. Outline the components of a diversity-based recruitment effort.

4. Identify five recommendations you would provide to a friend who asks your advice in finding a job.

5. Develop a realistic job preview for a prospective city bus driver.

CHAPTER
12
INITIAL SCREENING

AT A GLANCE

When selection is done sequentially, the earlier stages often are called **screening,** with the term **selection** being reserved for the more intensive final stages. Screening also may be used to designate any rapid, rough selection process, even when not followed by further selection procedures (Anastasi, 1988). This chapter will focus on some of the most widely used initial screening methods, including recommendations and reference checks, personal history data, biographical information, drug screening, honesty tests, evaluations of training and experience, and employment interviews. The rationale underlying all of these methods (with the exception of certain interview approaches) is that past behavior is the best predictor of future behavior. All can be valuable selection tools.

RECOMMENDATIONS AND REFERENCE CHECKS

Most initial screening methods are based on the *applicant's* statement of what he or she did in the past. However, recommendations and reference checks rely on the opinions of relevant *others* to help evaluate what and how well the applicant did in the past. Many prospective users ask a very practical question, namely, "Are recommendations and reference checks worth the amount of time and money it costs to process and consider them?" In general, four kinds of information are obtainable: (1) employment and educational history (including confirmation of degree and class standing or grade point average); (2) evaluation of the applicant's character, personality, and interpersonal competence; (3) evaluation of the applicant's job performance ability; and (4) willingness to rehire.

In order for a recommendation to make a meaningful contribution to the screening/selection process, however, it must satisfy certain preconditions. The recommender must have had an adequate opportunity to observe the applicant in job-relevant situations, he

or she must be competent to make such an evaluation, he or she must be willing to be open and candid, and he or she must express the evaluation so that the potential employer can interpret it in the manner intended (McCormick and Ilgen, 1985). Although the value of recommendations can be impaired by deficiencies in any one or more of the four preconditions, unwillingness to be candid is probably most serious.

Some people consider written recommendations to be of little value. To a certain extent, this opinion is justified, since the research evidence available indicates that the average validity of recommendations is .14 (Reilly and Chao, 1982). One of the biggest problems is that such recommendations rarely include unfavorable information and, therefore, do not discriminate among candidates.

However, to the extent that the truth of any unfavorable information cannot be demonstrated, and it harms the reputation of the individual in question, providers of references may be guilty of defamation in their written (libel) or oral (slander) communications (Ryan and Lasek, 1991).

The fact is, decisions *are* made on the basis of letters of recommendation. If such letters are to be meaningful, they should contain the following information (Knouse, 1987):

1. Degree of writer familiarity with the candidate—time known and time observed per week.

2. Degree of writer familiarity with the job in question. To help the writer make this judgment, the reader should supply to the writer a description of the job in question.

3. Specific examples of performance—goals, task difficulty, work environment, and extent of cooperation from co-workers.

4. Individuals or groups to whom the candidate is compared.

Records and reference checks are the most frequently used methods to screen outside candidates for all types and levels of jobs (Bureau of National Affairs, 1988). Unfortunately many employers believe that records and reference checks are not permissible under the law. This is not true. In fact, employers may do the following: seek information about applicants; interpret and use that information during selection; and share the results of reference checking with another employer (Sewell, 1981). In fact, employers may be found guilty of negligent hiring if they *should have known* at the time of hire about the unfitness of an applicant (e.g., prior job-related convictions, propensity for violence) that subsequently causes harm to an individual (Gregory, 1988; Ryan and Lasek, 1991). In other words, failure to check closely enough could lead to legal liability for an employer.

Reference checking is a valuable screening tool. A meta-analysis of reference checking studies (Hunter and Hunter, 1984) revealed an average validity of .26. To be most useful, however, reference checks should be:

- *Consistent*—if an item is grounds for denial of a job to one person, it should be the same for any other person who applies.

- *Relevant*—stick to items of information that really distinguish effective from ineffective employees.

- *Written*—to support the ultimate hiring decision made.

- *Based on public records*—such as court records, workers' compensation, or bankruptcy proceedings (Ryan and Lasek, 1991; Sewell, 1981).

"Sweetening" of résumés is not uncommon. One study reported that 20 to 25 percent of all résumés and job applications include at least one major fabrication (LoPresto et al., 1986). Hence, although some sources may provide only sketchy information for fear of violating some legal or ethical constraint, they can, nevertheless, provide valuable information. Few organizations are willing to abandon altogether the practice of recommendation and reference checking, despite all the shortcomings. One need only listen to a grateful manager thanking the HR department for the good ref-

---

HOW TO GET USEFUL INFORMATION FROM A REFERENCE CHECK

In today's environment of caution, many supervisors are hesitant to provide information about a former employee, especially over the telephone. To encourage them, consider doing the following:

1. Take the supervisor out of the judgmental past and into the role of an evaluator of a candidate's abilities.

2. Remove the perception of potential liability for judging a former subordinate's performance by asking for advice on how best to manage the person to bring out his or her abilities.

Questions such as the following might be helpful (Falcone, 1995):

- We're a mortgage banking firm in an intense growth mode. The phones don't stop ringing, the paperwork is endless, and we're considering Mary for a position in our customer service unit dealing with our most demanding customers. Is that an environment in which she would excel?

- Some people constantly look for ways to reinvent their jobs and assume responsibilities beyond the basic job description. Others adhere strictly to their job duties and "don't do windows," so to speak. Can you tell me where Ed fits on that continuum?

erence checking that "saved" him from making a bad offer to understand why.

PERSONAL HISTORY DATA

Selection and placement decisions often can be improved when personal history data (typically found in application blanks or biographical inventories) are considered along with other relevant information. We shall discuss these sources in the next two sections.

Undoubtedly one of the most widely used selection procedures is the application blank. Like tests, application blanks can be used to sample past or present behavior briefly but reliably. Studies of the application blanks used by 200 organizations indicated that questions generally focused on information that was job-related and necessary for the employment decision (Lowell and DeLoach, 1982; Miller, 1980). However, over 95 percent of the applications included one or more legally indefensible questions. To avoid potential problems, consider omitting any question that:

- Might lead to an adverse impact against members of protected groups.
- Does not appear job-related or related to a bona fide occupational qualification.
- Might constitute an invasion of privacy (Bahnsen, 1996).

What can applicants do when confronted by a question that they believe is irrelevant or an invasion of privacy? Some may choose not to respond. However, research indicates that employers tend to view such nonresponse as an attempt to conceal facts that would reflect poorly on an applicant. Hence applicants (especially those who have nothing to hide) are ill-advised not to respond (Stone and Stone, 1987).

Psychometric principles can be used to quantify responses or observations, and the resulting numbers can be subjected to reliability and validity analyses in the same manner as are test scores. Statistical analyses of such group data are extremely useful in specifying the personal characteristics indicative of later job success. Furthermore, the scoring of application blanks (as well as interviews) capitalizes on the three hallmarks of progress in selection: standardization, quantification, and understanding (England, 1971).

A priori one might suspect that certain aspects of an individual's total background (e.g., age, years of education, previous occupations) should be related to later job success in a specific position. The weighted application blank (WAB) technique provides a means of identifying *which* of these aspects reliably distinguish groups of effective and ineffective employees. Weights are assigned in accordance with the predictive power of each item, so that a total score can be derived for each individual. A cutoff score then can be established which, if used in selection, will eliminate the maximum number of potentially unsuccessful candidates. Hence, one use of the WAB is as a rapid screening device, but it may also be used in combination with other data to improve selection and placement decisions. The technique is appropriate in any organization having a relatively large number of employees doing similar kinds of work and for whom adequate records are available. It is particularly valuable for use with positions requiring long and costly training, where turnover is abnormally high, or where large numbers of applicants are seeking a few positions (England, 1971).

Weighting procedures are simple and straightforward (Owens, 1976), but once weights have been developed in this manner, it is absolutely *essential* that they be cross-validated. Since WAB procedures represent raw empiricism in the extreme, many of the observed differences in weights may not reflect true differences, but only chance fluctuations. If realistic cost estimates can be assigned to recruitment, the weighted application blank, the ordinary selection procedure, induction, and training, then it is possible to compute an estimate of the payoff, in dollars, that may be expected to result from implementation of the WAB (Sands, 1973).

Biographical Information Blanks (BIBs)

The BIB is similar to the weighted application blank. Like the WAB, it is a self-report instrument, although items are exclusively in a multiple-choice format, typically it includes a larger sample of items and frequently it includes items that are not normally covered in a WAB. Glennon, Albright, and Owens (1966), and more recently, Mitchell (1994) have published comprehensive catalogs of life history items covering various aspects of the applicant's past (e.g., early life experiences, hobbies, health, social relations) as well as present values, attitudes, interests, opinions, and preferences. Although primary emphasis is on past behavior as a predictor of future behavior, BIBs frequently rely also on present behavior to predict future behavior. Usually BIBs are developed specifically to predict success in a particular type of work. One of the reasons why they are so successful is because often they contain all the elements of consequence to the criterion (Asher, 1972). The mechanics of BIB development and item weighting are essentially the same as those used for WABs (Mumford and Owens, 1987; Mumford and Stokes, 1992).

Accuracy of Application Blank and Biographical Data

While falsification is possible in WAB and BIB data (Kluger and Colella, 1993), it is less likely to the extent that information can be verified. Although one investigation did find falsification (Goldstein, 1971), three other studies found substantial agreement between worker claims and records of previous employers (*rs* ranging from .90 to .98) (Keating, Paterson, and Stone, 1950; Mosel and Cozan 1952; and Cascio, 1975). In addition, a test-retest analysis of responses to a biodata form over a 5-year period revealed substantial agreement (Shaffer, Saunders, and Owens, 1986). Although biodata items can be faked (Becker and Colquitt, 1992), more objective and verifiable items are less amenable to faking, as are option-keyed items (Kluger, Reilly, and Russell, 1991). With the latter strategy, each item response option (alternative) is analyzed separately and contributes to the score only if it correlates significantly with the criterion. Finally, faking is less likely if applicants are warned of the presence of a lie scale (Kluger and Colella, 1993; Schrader and Osburn, 1977), and if biodata are used in a nonevaluative, classification context (Fleishman, 1988).

Opinions vary regarding exactly what items should be classified as biographical, since biographical items may vary along a number of dimensions, for example, verifiable-unverifiable; historical-futuristic; actual behavior—hypothetical behavior; first-hand—second-hand; external-internal; specific-general; invasive-noninvasive (see Table 12–1). Nevertheless, the core attribute of biodata items is that they pertain to

---

TABLE 12–1 A Taxonomy of Biographical Items

Historical	**Future or hypothetical**
How old were you when you got your first paying job?	What position do you think you will be holding in 10 years?
	What would you do if another person screamed at you in public?
External	**Internal**
Did you ever get fired from a job?	What is your attitude toward friends who smoke marijuana?
Objective	**Subjective**
How many hours did you study for your real-estate license test?	Would you describe yourself as shy?
	How adventurous are you compared to your co-workers?
First-hand	**Second-hand**
How punctual are you about coming to work?	How would your teachers describe your punctuality?
Discrete	**Summative**
At what age did you get your driver's license?	How many hours do you study during an average week?
Verifiable	**Nonverifiable**
What was your grade point average in college?	How many servings of fresh vegetables do you eat every day?
Were you ever suspended from your Little League team?	
Controllable	**Noncontrollable**
How many tries did it take you to pass the CPA exam?	How many brothers and sisters do you have?
Equal access	**Nonequal access**
Were you ever class president?	Were you captain of the football team?
Job relevant	**Not job relevant**
How many units of cereal did you sell during the last calendar year?	Are you proficient at crossword puzzles?
Noninvasive	**Invasive**
Were you on the tennis team in college?	How many young children do you have at home?

Source: Mael, F. A. (1991). A Conceptual Rationale for the Domain and Attributes of Biodata Items. *Personnel Psychology,* 44, p. 773.

historical events that may have shaped a person's behavior and identity (Mael, 1991).

Some have advocated that only historical and verifiable experiences, events, or situations should be classified as biographical items. Using this approach, most items on an application blank would be considered biographical (e.g., rank in high school graduating class, work history). On the other hand, if only historical, verifiable items are included on a BIB, then questions such as the following would not be asked, "Did you ever build a model airplane that flew?" Cureton (see Henry, 1965, p. 113) commented that this single item, although it cannot easily be verified for an individual, was almost as good a predictor of success in flight training during World War II as the entire Air Force Battery.

Validity of Application Blank and Biographical Data

Properly cross-validated WABs and BIBs have been developed for many occupations, including life insurance agents; law enforcement officers; service station managers; sales clerks; unskilled, clerical, office, production, and management employees; engineers; architects; research scientists; and Army officers. Criteria include turnover (by far the most common), absenteeism, rate of salary increase, performance ratings, number of publications, success in training, creativity ratings, sales volume, credit risk, and employee theft.

Evidence indicates that the accuracy of personal history data as predictors of future work behavior is superb. Thus Reilly and Chao (1982) reviewed 58 studies that used biographical information as a predictor. Over all criteria and over all occupations, the average validity was 0.35. A subsequent meta-analysis of 44 such studies revealed an average validity of 0.37 (Hunter and Hunter, 1984). As an illustration of the predictive power of these types of data, consider a study that used a true predictive validity design. Biographical items from the same inventory accurately forecast self-reports of both job and career success over a wide variety of occupations. They accounted for 10 percent of the variance in job success and 24 percent of the variance in career success (Childs and Klimoski, 1986).

Personal history data also broaden our understanding of what does and does not contribute to effective job performance. An examination of discriminating item responses can tell a great deal about what kinds of employees remain on a job and what kinds do not, what kinds sell much insurance and what kinds sell little, or what kinds are promoted slowly and what kinds are promoted rapidly. Insights obtained in this fashion may serve anyone from the initial interviewer to the manager who formulates employment policy [Owens, 1976, p. 612].

A caution is in order, however. Commonly biodata keys are developed on samples of job incumbents; it is tempting to assume that the results generalize to applicants. However, a large-scale field study that used more than 2,200 incumbents and 2,700 applicants found that 20 percent or fewer of the items that were valid in the incumbent sample were also valid in the applicant sample. Clearly, motivation and job experience differ in the two samples. The implication: match incumbent and applicant samples as closely as possible, and do not assume that predictive and concurrent validities are similar for the derivation and validation of BIB scoring keys (Stokes, Hogan, and Snell, 1993).

Adverse Impact and Selection Bias

Since the passage of Title VII of the 1964 Civil Rights Act, personal history items have come under intense legal scrutiny. While not unfairly discriminatory per se, it is legitimate to include such items in the selection process only if one can show that (a) they are job-related, and (b) they do not unfairly discriminate against either minority or nonminority subgroups.

In one study, Cascio (1976a) reported cross-validated validity coefficients of .58 (minorities) and .56 (nonminorities) for female clerical employees against a tenure criterion. When separate expectancy charts were constructed for the two groups, no significant differences in WAB scores for minorities or nonminorities on either predictor or criterion measures were found. Hence, the same scoring key could be used for both groups.

What Do Biodata Mean?

Criterion-related validity is not the only consideration in establishing job relatedness. Items that bear no rational relationship to the job in question (e.g., "applicant does not wear eyeglasses" as a predictor of credit risk or theft) are unlikely to be acceptable to courts or regulatory agencies, especially if WAB total scores produce adverse impact against a protected group.

A more prudent and reasonable approach (Mitchell, 1989; Pace and Schoenfeldt, 1977) is to use job analysis information to deduce hypotheses concerning success on the job under study and to seek from existing, previously-researched sources, either items or factors that address these hypotheses. Essentially we are asking, "What do biodata mean"? Thus in a study of recruiters' interpretations of biodata items from résumés and application forms, Brown and Campion (1994) found that recruiters deduced language and math abilities from education-related items, physical ability from sports-related items, leadership and interpersonal attributes from items that reflected previous experience in positions of authority and participation in activities of a social nature. Nearly all items were thought to tell something about a candidate's motivation. The next step is to identify hypotheses about the relationship of such abilities or attributes to success on the job in question. This approach has the twin advantages of enhancing both the utility of selection procedures and our understanding of how and why they work (cf., Mael and Ashforth, 1995). Moreover, it is probably the *only* legally defensible approach for the use of personal history data in employment selection.

Drug Screening

Drug screening tests that began in the military and spread to the sports world are now becoming common in employment (Tepper, 1994). Critics charge that such screening violates an individual's right to privacy and that the tests are frequently inaccurate (Morgan, 1989). They do concede, however, that employees in jobs where public safety is crucial—such as nuclear power plant operators—should be screened for drug use. In fact, perceptions of the extent to which different jobs might involve danger to the worker, to co-workers, or to the public relate strongly to the acceptability of drug testing (Murphy, Thornton, and Prue, 1991).

Do the results of such tests forecast certain aspects of later job performance? In the largest reported study of its kind, the U.S. Postal Service took urine samples from 5,465 job applicants. It never used the results to make hiring decisions and did not tell local managers of the findings. When the data were examined 6 months to a year later, workers who had tested positively prior to employment were absent 41 percent more often and were fired 38 percent more often. There were no differences in turnover between those who tested positively and those who did not. These results held up even after adjustment for factors such as

age, gender, and race. As a result, the Postal Service is now implementing preemployment drug testing nationwide (Wessel, 1989).

Is such drug screening legal? In two rulings in 1989, the Supreme Court upheld (1) the constitutionality of the government regulations that require railroad crews involved in accidents to submit to prompt urinalysis and blood tests, and (2) urine tests for U.S. Customs Service employees seeking drug-enforcement posts. The extent to which such rulings will be limited to safety-sensitive positions has yet to be clarified by the court. Nevertheless, an employer has a legal right to ensure that employees perform their jobs competently and that no employee endangers the safety of other workers. So if illegal drug use, on or off the job, may reduce job performance and endanger co-workers, the employer has adequate legal grounds for conducting drug tests.

To avoid legal challenge, consider instituting the following commonsense procedures:

1. Inform all employees and job applicants, in writing, of the company's policy regarding drug use.
2. Include the drug policy and the possibility of testing in all employment contracts.
3. Present the program in a medical and safety context, namely, that drug screening will help to improve the health of employees and also help to ensure a safer workplace.
4. If drug screening will be used with employees as well as job applicants, tell employees in advance that drug testing will be a routine part of their employment. (Angarola, 1985).

To enhance perceptions of procedural justice, employers should provide advance notice of drug tests, preserve the right to appeal, emphasize that drug testing is a means to enhance workplace safety, attempt to minimize invasiveness, and train supervisors (Tepper, 1994; Konovsky and Cropanzano, 1991). In addition, use employee assistance programs rather than discharge when drug use is detected (Stone and Kotch, 1989).

Honesty Tests

Paper-and-pencil honesty testing is a multi-million-dollar industry, especially since the use of polygraphs in employment settings has been severely curtailed (see below). Written honesty tests (also known as integrity tests) fall into two major categories: **overt integrity tests** and **personality-oriented measures.**

Overt integrity tests typically include two sections. One deals with attitudes toward theft and other forms of dishonesty (e.g., beliefs about the frequency and extent of employee theft, punitiveness toward theft, perceived ease of theft, and endorsement about common rationalizations about theft). The other deals with admissions of theft and other illegal activities (e.g., dollar amount stolen in the last year, drug use, gambling).

Personality-based measures are not designed as measures of honesty per se, but rather as predictors of a wide variety of counterproductive behaviors, such as substance abuse, insubordination, absenteeism, bogus workers' compensation claims, and various forms of passive aggression. For example, the Reliability Scale of the Hogan Personnel Selection Series (Hogan and Hogan, 1989) is designed to measure a construct called "organizational delinquency." It includes items dealing with hostility toward authority, thrill-seeking, conscientiousness, and social insensitivity.

Do honesty (or integrity) tests work? Yes, as several reviews have found (Camara and Schneider, 1994; Ones, Viswesvaran, and Schmidt, 1993). Ones et al. conducted a meta-analysis of 665 validity coefficients that used 576,460 test takers. The average validity of the tests, when used to predict supervisory ratings of performance, was .41. Results for overt and personality-based tests were similar. However, the average validity of overt tests for predicting theft per se (.13) was much lower. Nevertheless, Bernardin and Cooke (1993) found that scores on two overt integrity tests successfully predicted detected theft (validity = .28) for convenience store employees. For personality-based tests, there were no validity estimates available for the prediction of theft alone. Finally, since there was no correlation between race, gender, or age and integrity test scores (Bernardin and Cooke, 1993), such tests might well be used in combination with general mental ability test scores to comprise a general selection procedure.

Despite these encouraging findings, at least three key issues have yet to be resolved (Lilienfeld, Alliger, and Mitchell, 1995): (1) there are almost no data regarding the types of classification errors made by these measures; (2) while fakability or impression management has been observed on honesty tests (Cunningham et al., 1994), many such tests do not contain lie scales to detect response distortion; and (3) many writers in the field apply the same language and logic to integrity testing as to ability testing. Yet there is an important difference: While it is possible for an individual with poor moral behavior to "go straight," it is

certainly less likely that an individual who has demonstrated a lack of intelligence will "go smart." If they are honest about their past, therefore, reformed individuals with a criminal past may be "locked into" low scores on integrity tests (and therefore be subject to classification error). Thus the broad validation evidence that is often acceptable for cognitive ability tests may not hold up in the public policy domain for integrity tests.

Polygraph Tests

In the employment context, the use of polygraph tests has been severely restricted by a federal law passed in 1988. This law, the Employee Polygraph Protection Act, prohibits private employers (except firms providing security services and those manufacturing controlled substances) from requiring or requesting preemployment polygraph exams. Polygraph exams of current employees are permitted only under very restricted circumstances.

Although much of the public debate over the polygraph focuses on ethical problems, at the heart of the controversy is validity—the relatively simple question of whether physiological measures actually can assess truthfulness and deception (Saxe, Dougherty, and Cross, 1985). The most comprehensive analysis of the scientific evidence on this issue is contained in a report by the U.S. Congress, Office of Technology Assessment (1983). Here is a brief summary of its findings:

> A number of approaches to inferring truth or deceptiveness have been developed based on physiological measurement. The type of approach used depends on the situation [criminal vs. employment]. Unfortunately, none of these approaches is foolproof. Whether a person is correctly identified as being truthful or deceptive depends largely on the skill of the examiner and on a number of characteristics and behaviors of the examinee. Neither available data nor theoretical analysis indicates that polygraph tests function as claimed by their proponents. Substantial numbers of both truthful and deceptive individuals may be misidentified through use of polygraph tests, and the tests can be "beaten" [Saxe et al., 1985, p. 355].

Evaluation of Training and Experience

Judgmental evaluations of the previous work experience and training of job applicants, as presented on resumes and job applications, is a common part of initial screening. Sometimes evaluation is purely subjective and informal, and sometimes it is accomplished in a formal manner according to a standardized method. An empirical comparison of four such methods indicated that the "behavioral consistency" method showed the highest mean true validity (.45) (McDaniel et al., 1988). This method requires applicants to describe their major achievements in several job-related areas. These areas are behavioral dimensions rated by supervisors as showing maximal differences between superior and minimally acceptable performers. The applicant's achievement statements are then evaluated using anchored rating scales. The anchors are achievement descriptors whose values along a behavioral dimension have been determined reliably by subject matter experts.

A similar approach to the evaluation of training and experience, one most appropriate for selecting professionals, is the "accomplishment record" (AR) method (Hough, 1984). A comment frequently heard from professionals is "My record speaks for itself." The AR is an objective method for evaluating those records. It is a type of biodata/maximum performance/self-report instrument that appears to tap a component of an individual's history that is not measured by typical biographical inventories. It correlates essentially zero with aptitude test scores, honors, grades, and prior activities and interests.

Development of the AR begins with the collection of critical incidents to identify important dimensions of job performance. Then rating principles and scales are developed for rating an individual's set of job-relevant achievements. The method yields (1) complete definitions of the important dimensions of the job; (2) summary principles that highlight key characteristics to look for when determining the level of achievement demonstrated by an accomplishment; (3) actual examples of accomplishments that job experts agree represent various levels of achievement; and (4) numerical equivalents that allow the accomplishments to be translated into quantitative indexes of achievement.

When the AR was applied in a sample of 329 attorneys, the reliability of the overall performance ratings was a respectable 0.82, and the AR demonstrated a validity of 0.25. Moreover, the method appears to be fair for females, minorities, and white males.

What about academic qualifications? They tend not to affect managers' hiring recommendations, as compared to work experience, and they could have a negative effect. For candidates with poor work experience, having higher academic qualifications seems to

reduce their chances of being hired (Singer and Bruhns, 1991). These findings were supported by a national survey of 3,000 employers by the U.S. Census Bureau. The most important characteristics employers said they considered in hiring were attitude, communications skills, and previous work experience. The least important were academic performance (grades), school reputation, and teacher recommendations (Applebome, 1995).

EMPLOYMENT INTERVIEWS

Use of the interview in selection today is almost universal. Perhaps this is so because in the employment context the interview serves as much more than just a selection device. The interview is a communication process whereby the applicant learns more about the job and the organization and begins to develop some realistic expectations about both.

When an organization accepts an applicant, it typically negotiates terms of employment during an interview. If it rejects an applicant the interviewer performs an important public relations function, for it is essential that the rejected applicant leave with a favorable impression of the organization and its employees. For example, several studies (Phillips and Dipboye, 1989; Schmitt and Coyle, 1976) found that perceptions of the interpersonal skills of the interviewer, as well as his or her skills in listening, recruiting, and conveying information about the company and the job the applicant would hold, affected the applicant's evaluations of the interviewer and the company. However, the likelihood of accepting a job, should one be offered, was still mostly unaffected by the interviewer's behavior (Powell, 1991).

As a selection device the interview performs two vital functions: It can fill information gaps (e.g., regarding incomplete or questionable application blank responses) in other selection devices (Tucker and Rowe, 1977), and it can be used to assess factors that can be measured only via face-to-face interaction (e.g., appearance, speech, poise, and interpersonal competence). Is the applicant likely to "fit in" and get along with others in the organization, or be a source of conflict? Where can his or her talents be used most effectively? Interview impressions and perceptions can help to answer these kinds of questions.

Since few employers are willing to hire applicants they have never seen, it is imperative that we do all we can to make the interview as effective a selection technique as possible. In this section, we will consider some of the research on interviewing and offer suggestions for improving the process.

Accuracy of Interview Information

In contrast to application blanks, distortion of interview information is more probable (Weiss and Dawis, 1960; Weiss et al., 1961), the general tendency being to upgrade rather than downgrade prior work experience. But suppose the interviewer is a computer? According to Martin and Nagao (1989), candidates tend to report their grade point averages and scholastic aptitude test scores more accurately to computers than in face-to-face interviews. Perhaps this is due to the "big brother" effect. That is, because responses are on a computer rather than on paper, they may seem more subject to instant checking and verification through other computer data bases. To avoid potential embarrassment, applicants may be more likely to provide truthful responses. However, Martin and Nagao's study also placed an important boundary condition on computer interviews: There was much greater resentment by individuals competing for high-status positions than for low-status positions when they had to respond to a computer rather than to a live interviewer.

Research indicates that people generally behave on the job in a manner consistent with what they previously said they would do in response to hypothetical situations presented in a preemployment interview. However, the same research found that there was no correlation between what people *said* they had done in the past, and supervisor or peer observations of their current performance (Latham and Saari, 1984).

Reliability and Validity

An early meta-analysis of only 10 validity coefficients that were not corrected for range restriction yielded a validity of .14 for interviewer predictions of supervisory ratings (Hunter and Hunter, 1984). Four subsequent meta-analyses that did correct for range restriction and that used larger samples of studies reported much more encouraging results. Thus Wiersner and Cronshaw (1988) found a mean corrected validity of .47 across 150 interview validity studies involving all types of criteria. McDaniel et al. (1994) analyzed 245 coefficients derived from 86,311 individuals and found a mean corrected validity of .37 for job performance criteria. However, validities were higher when criteria were collected for research purposes (mean = .47) than for administrative decision making (.36).

Marchese and Muchinsky (1993) reported a mean corrected validity of .38 across 31 studies. The fourth study (Huffcutt and Arthur, 1994) analyzed 114 interview validity coefficients from 84 published and unpublished references, exclusively involving entry-level jobs and supervisory rating criteria. When corrected for criterion unreliability and range restriction, the mean validity across all 114 studies was .37. In general, therefore, the results of these studies agree quite closely.

A different meta-analysis of 111 inter-rater reliability coefficients and 49 internal consistency reliability estimates (coefficient alphas) derived from employment interviews revealed overall means of .70 for interrater reliability, and .39 for internal consistency reliability (Conway, Jako, and Goodman, 1995). These results imply that the upper limits of validity are .67 for highly structured interviews and .34 for unstructured interviews, and that the major reason for low validities is not the criteria used but rather low reliability. Hence the best way to improve validity is to improve the structure of the interview (discussed below).

As Hakel (1989) has noted, interviewing is a difficult cognitive and social task. Managing a smooth social exchange while simultaneously processing information about an applicant makes interviewing uniquely difficult among all managerial tasks. Research continues to focus on the processes of interpersonal perception between applicant and interviewer and on decision making. As a result, we now know a great deal more about what goes on in the interview and about how to improve the process.

At the very least, we should expect interviewers to be able to form opinions only about traits and characteristics that are overtly manifest in the interview (or that can be inferred from the applicant's behavior), and not about traits and characteristics that typically would become manifest only over a period of time—traits such as creativity, dependability, and honesty. In the following sections we will examine what is known about the interview process, and about ways to enhance the effectiveness and utility of the selection interview.

Factors Affecting the Decision-Making Process

First Impressions. An early series of studies conducted at McGill University over a 10-year period (Webster, 1964; 1982) found that early interview impressions play a dominant role in final decisions (accept/reject). These early impressions establish a bias in the interviewer (not usually reversed) that colors all subsequent interviewer-applicant interaction. (Early impressions were crystallized after a mean interviewing time of only 4 minutes!) Moreover, the interview is primarily a search for negative information. For example, just one unfavorable impression was followed by a reject decision 90 percent of the time. Positive information was given much less weight in the final decision (Bolster and Springbett, 1961).

Expectancies. Dipboye (1982; 1992) specified a model of self-fulfilling prophecy to explain the impact of first impressions. Both cognitive and behavioral biases mediate the effects of preinterview impressions (based on letters of reference or applications) on the evaluations of applicants. Behavioral biases involve interviewers' behaving in ways that confirm their first impressions of applicants (e.g., showing positive or negative regard for applicants). Cognitive biases occur if interviewers distort information to support first impressions, or use selective attention and recall of information. This sequence of behavioral and cognitive biases produces a self-fulfilling prophecy.

Consider how an interviewer given positive information described one applicant:

> Alert, enthusiastic, responsible, well-educated, intelligent, can express himself well, organized, well-rounded, can converse well, hard worker, reliable, fairly experienced, and generally capable of handling himself well.

On the basis of negative preinterview information, another interviewer described the same applicant as:

> Nervous, quick to object to the interviewer's assumptions, and doesn't have enough self-confidence [Dipboye, Stramler, and Fontanelle, 1984, p. 567].

Content-coding of actual employment interviews found that favorable first impressions were followed by the use of confirmatory behavior, such as positive regard for the applicant, "selling" the company, providing job information to applicants, while gathering less information from them, more confident and effective applicant behavior, and better rapport of applicants with interviewers (Dougherty et al., 1994). These findings support the existence of the confirmatory bias produced by first impressions.

Another aspect of expectancies concerns test score or biodata score information available prior to the interview. A study of 577 actual candidates for the

position of life insurance sales agents found that interview ratings predicted the hiring decision and survival on the job best for applicants with low passing scores on the biodata test and poorest for applicants with high passing scores (Dalessio and Silverhart, 1994). Apparently interviewers had such faith in the validity of the test scores that if an applicant scored well, they gave little weight to the interview, but when the applicant scored poorly, they gave more weight to performance in the interview and made better distinctions among candidates.

Verbal Cues. As part of the same series of studies at McGill, Anderson (1960) found that in those interviews where the interviewer did a lot more of the talking, and there was less silence, the applicant was more likely to be hired.

Other research has shown that the length of the interview depends much more on the quality of the applicant (interviewers take more time to decide when dealing with a high-quality applicant) and on the expected length of the interview. The longer the expected length of the interview, the longer it takes to reach a decision (Tullar et al., 1979).

Nonverbal Cues. Several studies have examined the impact of nonverbal cues on impression formation and decision making in the interview. Although Imada and Hakel (1977) found that positive nonverbal cues (e.g., greater eye contact, smiling, attentive posture, smaller interpersonal distance) produced consistently favorable ratings, later studies have helped to clarify these findings. The ability of a candidate to respond concisely, to answer questions fully, to state personal opinions when relevant, and to keep to the subject at hand appears to be more crucial in obtaining a favorable employment decision (Parsons and Liden, 1984; Rasmussen, 1984). High levels of nonverbal behavior tend to have more positive effects than low levels only when the verbal content of the interview is good. When verbal content is poor, high nonverbal behavior results in lower ratings.

Stereotypes. Returning to the McGill studies, perhaps the most important finding of all was that interviewers tend to develop their own stereotype of a good applicant and proceed to accept those who match their stereotype (Rowe, 1963; Webster, 1964). Later research has supported these findings. To the extent that the stereotypes are negative, deviate from the perception of what is needed for the job, or translate into different expectations or standards of evaluation for minorities, stereotypes may have the effect of lowering interviewers' evaluations, even when candidates are equally qualified for the job (Arvey, 1979).

Use of Criteria. Additional research has examined the decision processes of effective and ineffective interviewers in a policy-capturing framework (Graves and Karren, 1992). It appears that effective interviewers may be better able than less effective interviewers to identify job-relevant criteria in evaluating applicants. Moreover, effective interviewers are likely to be more aware of their own decision processes, enabling them to apply consistently the criteria they believe are important.

Effects of Structure

Structure refers to the degree of discretion an interviewer is allowed in conducting an interview. Operationally, two dimensions of structure affect the degree of discretion: the standardization of interview questions and response scoring (Huffcutt and Arthur, 1994). The impact of structure on validity is clear-cut. Interviews must be structured (i.e., the interviewer follows a set procedure) rather than unstructured (i.e., no set procedure; interviewer merely follows the applicant's lead) in order to generate information that will enable interviewers to agree with each other (Campion et al., 1988; 1994; Latham and Saari, 1984) and to predict job performance (Conway et al., 1995; McDaniel et al. 1994). Structured interviews provide essentially the same level of validity as cognitive ability tests (Huffcutt and Arthur, 1994). When interviews are structured, interviewers know what to ask for (thereby providing a more consistent sample of behavior across applicants) and what to do with the information they receive (thereby helping them rate better).

Form of Structured Interview Questions

Attempts to structure the interview and to ask job-relevant questions have focused on the use of two different types of interview questions, experience-based and situational (Pulakos and Schmitt, 1995). Questions in an experience-based interview are past-oriented; they ask applicants to relate what they did in past jobs or life situations that is relevant to the job in question (Janz, 1982; Motowidlo et al., 1992). The underlying assumption is that the best predictor of future performance is past performance in similar situations. Experience-based questions are of the "Tell me about a time when . . ." variety.

By contrast, situational questions (Latham et al., 1980; Maurer and Fay, 1988; Weekley and Gier, 1987) ask job applicants to imagine a set of circumstances and then indicate how they would respond in that situation. Hence the questions are future-oriented. Situational interview questions are of the "What would you do if . . ." variety.

Both experience-based and situational questions are based on a job analysis that uses the critical incidents method (cf., Chapter 9). The incidents then are turned into interview questions. Two or more interviewers independently rate each answer on a five-point Likert-type scale (see Chapter 5). To facilitate objective scoring, job experts develop behavioral statements that are used to illustrate 1, 3, and 5 answers. Table 12–2 illustrates the difference between these two types of questions.

In one comparison of the relative effectiveness of these two approaches, Campion et al. (1994) reported that the correlation between ratings of experience-based and situational items was .73, and that inter-rater reliabilities were similar—.94 (situational items) and .97 (experience-based items). The validity for experience-based items (.51) was higher than for situational items (.39), but not significantly higher. Moreover, the experience-based interview added to the prediction of job performance beyond that afforded by the situational interview, but the reverse was not true. Both question types added to the validity of a battery of cognitive ability tests.

In another comparison under tightly-controlled experimental conditions, only the experience-based interview showed a significant relationship with performance (.32) for a professional job, and it added incrementally to cognitive ability in explaining variance in performance ratings. Importantly, the experience-based interview was equally predictive for minority and nonminority subgroups, and there were very small mean differences between the groups for both the interview and the supervisory ratings (Pulakos and Schmitt, 1995).

Effect of Interviewer Experience

Although it has been hypothesized that interviewers with the same amount of experience will evaluate an applicant similarly (Rowe, 1960), empirical results do not support this hypothesis. Carlson (1967) found that when interviewers with the same experience evaluated the same recruits, they agreed with each other to no greater extent than did interviewers with differing ex-

TABLE 12–2 Examples of Experience-Based and Situational Interview Items Designed to Assess Conflict Resolution and Collaborative Problem-Solving Skills

Situational item: Suppose you had an idea for a change in work procedure to enhance quality, but there was a problem in that some members of your work team were against any type of change. What would you do in this situation?

(5) Excellent answer (top third of candidates)—Explain the change and try to show the benefits. Discuss it openly in a meeting.

(3) Good answer (middle third)—Ask them why they are against change. Try to convince them.

(1) Marginal answer (bottom third)—Tell the supervisor.

Experience-based item: What is the biggest difference of opinion you ever had with a co-worker? How did it get resolved?

(5) Excellent answer (top third of candidates)—We looked into the situation, found the problem, and resolved the difference. Had an honest conversation with the person.

(3) Good answer (middle third)—Compromised. Resolved the problem by taking turns, or I explained the problem (my side) carefully.

(1) Marginal answer (bottom third)—I got mad and told the co-worker off, or we got the supervisor to resolve the problem, or I never have differences with anyone.

Source: Campion, M. A., Campion, J. E., and Hudson, J. P., Jr. (1994). Structured interviewing: A note on incremental validity and alternative question types. *Journal of Applied Psychology, 79,* p. 999.

periences. Apparently interviewers benefit very little from day-to-day interviewing experience since the conditions necessary for learning (i.e., training and feedback) are not present in the interviewer's everyday job situation. Experienced interviewers who never learn how to conduct good interviews will simply perpetuate their poor skills over time (Jacobs and Baratta, 1989).

Contrast Effects

Several studies have found that if an interviewer evaluates a candidate who is just average after evaluating three or four very unfavorable candidates in a row, he or she tends to evaluate the average candidate very favorably. When interviewers evaluate more than one candidate at a time, they tend to use other candidates as a standard. Whom they rate favorably, then, depends partly on with whom the candidate is compared (Hakel, Ohnesorge, and Dunnette, 1970; Heneman et al., 1975; Landy and Bates, 1973).

These effects are remarkably tenacious. Wexley, Sanders, and Yukl (1973) found that despite attempts to reduce contrast effects by means of a warning (lecture) and/or anchoring procedure (comparing applicants to a preset standard), subjects continued to make this error. Only an intensive workshop (which combined practical observation and rating experience with immediate feedback) led to a significant behavior change. Similar results were reported in a later study by Latham, Wexley, and Pursell (1975). In contrast to subjects in group discussion or control groups, only those who participated in the intensive workshop did

not commit contrast, halo, similarity, or first impression errors 6 months after training.

Effect of Personal Factors

In contrast to earlier findings, recent research has not found a strong bias in favor of either sex (McDonald and Hakel, 1985). Findings regarding physical attractiveness indicate that attractiveness is only an advantage in jobs where attractiveness per se is relevant. However, being unattractive appears never to be an advantage (Beehr and Gilmore, 1982). Nor does being obese, although the bias is especially strong against women. Furthermore, overweight applicants were no more likely to be hired for a position involving minimal public contact than they were for a job requiring extensive public contact (Pingitore et al., 1994).

A related issue concerns the possible impact of pleasant artificial scents (perfume or cologne) on ratings in an employment interview. Research done in a controlled setting found that females assigned higher ratings to applicants when they used artificial scents than when they did not, whereas the opposite was true for males. These results may be due to differences in the ability of males and females to "filter out" irrelevant aspects of applicants' grooming or appearance (Baron, 1983).

Race, Age, and Disability

Contrary to the *a priori* assumption that the interview is a prime vehicle for discriminating against African-Americans and older workers, available evidence indicates that this is not the case (Arvey, 1979; McDonald and Hakel, 1985). While interviewer-applicant race similarity has a small effect on interview ratings, adding structure tends to minimize same-race bias, as does the inclusion of at least one different-race interviewer in a panel (Lin et al., 1992). With respect to age, interviewers probably have more job-related information available, which minimizes the need to use age as a primary factor in recommendations for hire. Finally, evidence available from four studies indicates that workers with disabilities are not evaluated any differently from able-bodied ones (Rose and Brief, 1979). These findings are encouraging.

Ability to Recall Information

A very practical question concerns the ability of interviewers to recall what an applicant said during an interview. Here is how researchers examined this question in one study (Carlson et al., 1971).

Prior to viewing a 20-minute videotaped selection interview, the researchers gave 40 managers an interview guide, pencils, and paper, and told the managers to perform as if *they* were conducting the interview. Following the interview the managers took a 20-question test, based on factual information. Some managers missed none, while others missed as many as 15 out of 20 items. The average number was 10 wrong.

In a short, 20-minute interview, half the managers could not report accurately on the information produced during the interview! On the other hand, those managers who had been following the interview guide and taking notes were quite accurate on the test. Those who were least accurate in their recollections assumed the interview was generally favorable and rated the candidate higher in all areas and with less variability. They adopted a halo strategy. Those managers who knew the facts rated the candidate lower and recognized intra-individual differences. Hence, the more accurate interviewers used an individual differences strategy.

None of the managers in this study was given an opportunity to preview an application form prior to the interview. Would that have made a difference? Other research indicates that the answer is no (Dipboye, Fontanelle, and Garner, 1984). When it comes to recalling information *after* the interview, there seems to be no substitute for note-taking *during* the interview. Other memory aids include mentally reconstructing

the context of the interview and retrieving information from different starting points (Mantwill et al., 1995).

Needed Improvements

Emphasis on employment interview research within a person-perception framework should continue. The interviewer's job is to develop accurate perceptions of applicants and to evaluate those perceptions in light of job requirements. Learning more about how those perceptions are formed, what affects their development, and what psychological processes best explain their development are important questions that deserve increased attention. However, we need to determine whether any of these process variables affect the validity, and ultimately the utility, of the interview (Zedeck and Cascio, 1984). We should begin by building upon our present knowledge to make improvements in selection interview technology. Here are eight research-based suggestions for improving the interview process.

1. Link interview questions tightly to job analysis results, and ensure that behaviors and skills observed in the interview are similar to those required on the job. Use a variety of types of questions, including situational questions, questions on job knowledge that is important to job performance, job sample or simulation questions, and questions regarding background (e.g., experience, education) and "willingness" (e.g., shift work, travel).

2. Ask the same questions of each candidate, because standardizing interview questions has a dramatic effect on the psychometric properties of interview ratings. Consider using the following six steps when conducting a structured interview: (1) open the interview, explaining its purpose and structure (i.e., that you will be asking a set of questions that pertain to the applicant's past job behavior, and what he or she would do in a number of job-relevant situations, and encourage the candidate to ask questions); (2) preview the job; (3) ask questions about minimum qualifications (e.g., for an airline, willingness to work nights and holidays); (4) ask experience-based questions ("Tell me about a time when . . ."); (5) ask situational questions ("What would you do if . . .?"); (6) close the interview by giving the applicant an opportunity to ask questions or volunteer information he or she thinks is important, and explain what happens next (and when) in the selection process.

3. Anchor the rating scales for scoring answers with examples and illustrations. Doing so helps to enhance consistency across interviews and objectivity in judging candidates.

4. Whether structured or unstructured, interview panels are no more valid than are individual interviews (Mc-Daniel et al. 1994). As we have seen, however, mixed-race panels may help to reduce the similar-to-me bias that individual interviewers might introduce.

5. Combine ratings mechanically (e.g., by averaging or summing them), rather than subjectively (Conway et al., 1995).

6. Provide a well-designed and properly-evaluated training program to communicate this information to interviewers, along with techniques for structuring the interview (e.g., a structured interview guide, standardized rating forms) to minimize the amount of irrelevant information. As part of their training, give interviewers the opportunity to practice interviewing with minorities or persons with disabilities. This may increase the ability of interviewers to relate.

7. Document the job analysis and interview development procedures, candidate responses and scores, evidence of content or criterion-related validity, and adverse impact analyses in accordance with testing guidelines.

8. Institute a planned system of feedback to interviewers to let them know who succeeds and who fails and to keep them up-to-date on changing job requirements and success patterns.

There are no shortcuts to reliable and valid measurement. Careful attention to detail and careful "mapping" of the interview situation to the job situation are necessary, both legally and ethically, if the interview is to continue to be used for selection purposes.

Discussion Questions

1. How can an organization improve the usefulness of recommendations and reference checks?

2. As CEO of a large retailer, you are considering using drug testing to screen new hires. What elements should you include in developing a policy on this issue?

3. In an employment interview the interviewer asks you a question that you believe is an invasion of privacy. What would you do?

4. Employers today generally assign greater weight to experience than to academic qualifications. Why do you think this is so? Should it be so?

5. Your boss asks you to develop a training program for employment interviewers. How will you proceed? What will be the elements of your program, and how will you tell if it is working?

CHAPTER

13

DECISION MAKING
FOR SELECTION

AT A GLANCE

Selection of individuals to fill available jobs only becomes meaningful when there are more applicants than jobs. Personnel selection decisions are concerned with the assignment of individuals to courses of action (e.g., accept/reject) whose outcomes are important to the organizations or individuals involved. The classical validity approach to personnel selection places primary emphasis on measurement accuracy and predictive efficiency. Simple or multiple regression, a statistical technique that enables a decision maker to forecast each individual's criterion status based on predictor information, is the basic prediction model in this approach. Multiple regression is compensatory, however, and assumes that low scores on one predictor can be offset by high scores on another. In some situations (e.g., pilot selection), such assumptions are untenable, and, therefore, other selection models, such as multiple cutoff or multiple hurdles, must be used.

The classical validity approach to selection has been criticized sharply, for it ignores certain external parameters of the situation that largely determine the overall worth of a selection instrument. In addition, the classical validity approach makes unwarranted utility assumptions and fails to consider the systemic nature of the selection process.

Decision theory, a more recent approach to selection, attempts to overcome these deficiencies. Decision theory acknowledges the importance of psychometric criteria in evaluating measurement and prediction, but in addition, it recognizes that the outcomes of prediction are of primary importance to individuals and organizations in our society. These outcomes must, therefore, be evaluated in terms of their consequences for individuals and organizations (i.e., in terms of their utility). In considering the cost consequences of alternative selection strategies, one also must consider the impact of selection on recruitment, induction, and training. Fortunately, decision-oriented, systemic selection models are now available that enable the decision maker to evaluate the payoff—in dollars—expected to result from the implementation of a proposed selection program.

PERSONNEL SELECTION IN PERSPECTIVE

If variability in physical and psychological characteristics were not so pervasive a phenomenon, there would be little need for selection of people to fill various jobs. Without variability among individuals in abilities, aptitudes, interests, and personality traits, we would forecast identical levels of job performance for all job applicants. Likewise, if there were 10 job openings available and only 10 suitably qualified applicants, selection again would not be a significant issue since all 10 applicants must be hired. Selection only becomes a relevant concern, then, when there are more qualified applicants than there are positions to be filled, for selection implies choice and choice means exclusion.

In personnel selection, decisions are made about individuals. Such decisions are concerned with the assignment of individuals to treatments or courses of action (e.g., accept/reject) whose outcomes are important to the institutions or individuals involved (Cronbach and Gleser, 1965). Since decision makers cannot know with absolute certainty the outcomes of any assignment, one must predict outcomes in advance on the basis of available information. This is a two-step procedure: *measurement* (i.e., *collecting* data such as tests or other assessment procedures that are relevant to job performance) and *prediction* (i.e., *combining* these data in such a way as to enable the decision maker to minimize predictive error in forecasting job performance) (Wiggins, 1973).

Traditionally, personnel selection programs have attempted to maximize the accuracy of measurement and the efficiency of prediction, issues we considered in Chapters 6 and 7. Decision theory, while not downgrading the importance of psychometric criteria in evaluating measurement and prediction, recognizes that the *outcomes* of predictions are of primary importance to individuals and organizations in our society. From this perspective, then, measurement and prediction are simply technical components of a system designed to make *decisions* about the assignment of individuals to jobs or treatments (Boudreau, 1991). Decision outcomes must, therefore, be evaluated in terms of their consequences for individuals and organizations (i.e., in terms of their utility). In short, traditional selection programs emphasize measurement accuracy and predictive efficiency as final goals. In the contemporary view these conditions merely set the stage for the decision problem.

In this chapter, we will consider first the traditional, or classical, validity approach to personnel selection and the several models it comprises. Next, we will examine the role of moderator and suppressor variables in this framework. Finally, we will consider decision theory and utility analysis and present alternative models that use this approach to formulate optimal recruiting-selection strategies. Our overall aim is to arouse and sensitize the reader to thinking in terms of *utility*. Such a perspective is useful for dealing with a wide range of employment decisions and for viewing organizations as open systems.

TRADITIONAL APPROACH TO PERSONNEL SELECTION

As we noted earlier, individual differences provide the basic rationale for selection. To be sure, the goal of the selection process is to capitalize on individual differences in order to select those persons who possess the greatest amount of particular characteristics judged important for job success.

Figure 13–1 illustrates the selection model underlying this approach. Since we described the elements of the model in previous chapters, we will present them only in outline form here. We will present operational examples of the model in Chapter 14. Note that job analysis is the cornerstone of the entire selection process. On the basis of this information, researchers select one or more sensitive, relevant, and reliable criteria. At the same time, they select one or more predictors (e.g., measures of aptitude, ability, interest) that presumably bear some relationship to the criterion or criteria to be predicted. Educated guesses notwithstanding, choose predictors on the basis of competent job analysis information, for such information provides clues about the type(s) of predictor(s) most likely to forecast criterion performance accurately. Once predictor measures have been selected, they are then administered to all job applicants. Such measures are *not* used in making selection decisions at this time, however; one simply files the results away and selects applicants on the basis of whatever procedures or methods are currently being used.

The rationale for not using the scores on the new predictor immediately is unequivocal from a scientific point of view. Yet management, concerned with the costs of developing and administering predictor measures, often understandably wants to use the scores without delay as a basis for selection. However, if the scores are used immediately, the organization will never know how those individuals who were not selected would have performed on the job. That is, if we simply *presume* that all persons with high (low) predictor scores will perform well (poorly) on the job without evidence to support this presumption, and if we subsequently select only those with high predictor scores, we will never be able to assess the job performance of those with low scores. It is entirely possible that the unselected group might have been superior performers relative to the selected group—an outcome we could not know for sure unless we gave these individuals the chance.

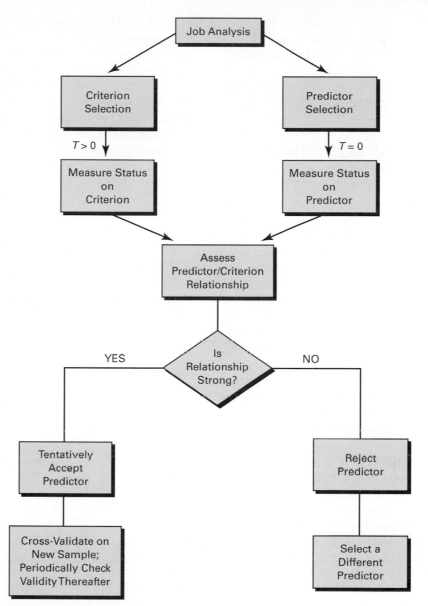

FIGURE 13–1 Traditional Model of the Personnel Selection Process.

Hence, we measure criterion status at some later time ($T > 0$ in Fig. 13–1)—the familiar predictive validity paradigm. Once criterion and predictor measures are available, then it becomes possible to assess the form and strength of their relationship. To be sure, job-success prediction is not possible unless one can establish a systematic relationship between predictor and criterion. The stronger the relationship, the more accurate the prediction. If a researcher cannot show that a predictor is job-related, he or she must discard it; but if the researcher can demonstrate a significant rela-

tionship, then he or she accepts the predictor *tentatively,* pending the outcome of a cross-validation study on a different sample of job applicants, none of whom were members of the original sample. It is important to recheck the validity or job relatedness of the predictor periodically (e.g., annually) thereafter. Subsequently, if a once-valid predictor no longer relates to a job performance criterion (assuming the criterion itself remains valid), discontinue using it and seek a new predictor. Then repeat entire procedure.

In personnel selection the name of the game is

prediction, for more accurate predictions result in greater cost savings (monetary as well as social). Researchers often use linear models to develop predictions, and they seem well-suited to this purpose. In the next section we shall examine various types of linear models and highlight their extraordinary flexibility.

EFFICIENCY OF LINEAR MODELS IN JOB SUCCESS PREDICTION

The statistical techniques of simple and multiple linear regression are based on the general linear model ($y = a + bx$) (cf. Appendix B). Linear models are extremely robust, and decision makers use them in a variety of contexts. Consider the typical interview situation, for example. Here the interviewer selectively reacts to various pieces of information (cues) elicited from the applicant. In arriving at his or her decision, the interviewer subjectively weights the various cues into a composite in order to forecast job success. Multiple linear regression encompasses the same process, albeit in more formal mathematical terms. Linear models range from those that use least squares regression procedures to derive optimal weights, to those that use subjective or intuitive weights, to those that apply unit weights.

In a comprehensive review of linear models in decision making, Dawes and Corrigan (1974) concluded that a wide range of decision-making contexts have structural characteristics that make linear models appropriate. In fact, in some contexts linear models are so appropriate that those with randomly-chosen weights outperform expert judges! Consider unit weighting schemes, for example.

Unit Weighting

Unit weighting (in which all predictors are weighted by 1.0) does extremely well in a variety of contexts. In fact, it is commonly accepted that items forming a scale should be given unit weights (Wainer, 1978; Wang and Stanley, 1970). Unit weighting also is appropriate when populations change from time to time (Lawshe and Schucker, 1959; Trattner, 1963) or when predictors are combined into a composite to boost effect size (and therefore statistical power) in criterion-related validity studies (Cascio, Valenzi, and Silbey, 1978; 1980). These studies all demonstrate that unit weighting does just as well as optimal weighting when the weights are applied to a new sample. Furthermore,

Schmidt (1971) has shown that when the ratio of subjects to predictors is below a critical sample size, the use of regression weights rather than unit weights could result in a loss of predictive power—that is, a reduction in the size of obtained correlations.

Critical sample sizes vary with the number of predictors. In the absence of suppressor variables (see below), a sample of 40 individuals is required to ensure no loss of predictive power from the use of regression techniques when just 2 predictors are used. With 6 predictors, this figure increases to 105, and if 10 predictors are used, a sample of about 194 is required before regression weights become superior to unit weights. This conclusion holds even when cross-validation is performed on samples from the same (theoretical) population. Einhorn and Hogarth (1975) have noted several other advantages of unit weighting schemes: (1) they are not estimated from the data and, therefore, do not "consume" degrees of freedom; (2) they are "estimated" without error (i.e., they have no standard errors); and (3) they cannot reverse the "true" relative weights of the variables.

Nevertheless, if it is technically feasible to use regression weights, the loss in predictive accuracy from the use of equal weights may be considerable. For example, if an interview (average validity of .14) is given equal weight with an ability composite (average validity of .53) instead of its regression weight, the validity of the combination (at most .47, Hunter and Hunter, 1984) will be lower than the validity of the best single predictor!

MODERATOR VARIABLES

In applied psychological research and practice, differential predictability often is observed. Differential predictability exists when the relationship between a predictor and a criterion (r_{x_1y}) varies as a function of classification on some third variable, x_2 (Fredericksen and Melville, 1954). In such situations, x_2 has been termed a **moderator variable** (Saunders, 1956). For example, if different patterns of scores predict job success for males and females, then gender is a moderator variable.

Figure 13–2 illustrates this situation. Scatterplot [1] illustrates a general predictor/criterion relationship of about .50. Note, however, that [1] represents the scores of a single heterogeneous group. When the groups are plotted separately, sharply divergent patterns of predictability emerge for the two groups. The

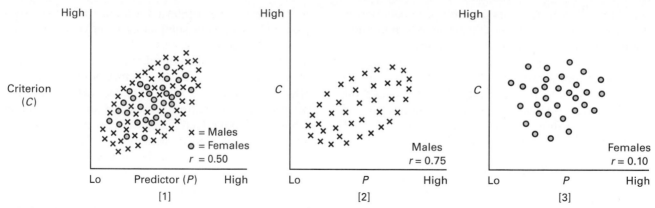

FIGURE 13–2 Scatterplots Illustrating the Effect of Gender as a Moderator Variable.

predictor is particularly appropriate for males ($r =$ .75), yet inappropriate for females (.10); therefore, it should not be used to predict the job performance of female applicants.

Moderator variables (e.g., gender, age, education) need not bear any direct relationship either to the predictor or to the criterion. Although they do not increase the size of obtained relationships between predictors and criteria, they "moderate" or enhance these relationships (i.e., they *identify subgroups* for whom selection measures are most useful). Consequently, they often have been referred to as "predictors of predictability."

Several moderator variable search strategies are available (cf. Arnold, 1984; Stone and Hollenbeck, 1984a; 1989), but all are fraught with difficulties (Cronbach, 1987). One of the biggest problems with moderators is that their utility rarely is assessed. In order to do this,

> the exact manner in which the moderator is to be used in prediction must be specified and applied to a cross-validation sample. When a particular percentage of individuals is to be selected it must be demonstrated that selecting that group on the combined basis of their moderator and test score provides a group superior to a group selected on the basis of test scores alone. Additionally, in a cross-validation sample, the hit rate using the moderator technique must be compared with the hit rate of a multiple regression prediction equation that includes the moderator as a conventional predictor variable [Abrahams and Alf, 1972, p. 250].

A further difficulty is sample size, since adequate statistical power in moderator research requires very large sample sizes in *each* group. For example, when one population correlation is .30 and the other is

.50, the reliability of both variables is .70, and there is no range restriction, 686 persons in *each* group are required to attain a power of .80 (Schmidt and Hunter, 1978). Moderated multiple regression is the most frequently used technique for identifying moderators, but it is plagued with power-related problems (Aguinis, 1995).

Meta-analysis has been proposed as one way to deal with this issue, but as several studies have shown (Kemery et al., 1989; Sackett et al., 1986) there are limits to what meta-analysis can do. It cannot consistently detect even moderate true differences in effect sizes across subgroups when the number of studies included in the meta-analysis is small (e.g., fewer than six) or when sample sizes are small. In such cases, statistical power may be quite low. Hence researchers may draw erroneous conclusions. Indeed, when the number of cases in each group differs greatly, inferences of no moderating effect may have more to do with low statistical power than with the absence of a moderating effect (Aguinis, 1995; Stone-Romero, Alliger, and Aguinis, 1994). Mistakenly concluding that no moderators exist (a Type II error) may lead to the conclusion that relations among the variables of interest are well understood and that no further research is needed. On the other hand, a Type I error may lead to an inappropriate conclusion that a moderator exists. However, as total sample sizes increase, subsequent analyses may correct these errors (Stone-Romero and Anderson, 1994). Finally, even when the proper large-sample research is done, moderators that appear plausible and important a priori may be shown to be nonexistent or trivial in magnitude (La Rocco and Jones, 1978).

Perhaps a more promising approach is subgrouping (Owens, 1978; Owens and Schoenfeldt, 1979;

Fleishman, 1988), or the use of multiple moderators to construct profiles of scores. Clustering or subgrouping similar profiles enhances our understanding of the kinds of people for whom a given device predicts or fails to predict a criterion. This kind of holistic research is likely to be more effective in the long run than continued searches for single moderators whose effects may be illusory or trivial in magnitude.

SUPPRESSOR VARIABLES

In a general sense, suppressor variables are related to moderator variables in that they can affect a given predictor/criterion relationship, even though such variables bear little or no direct relationship to the criterion itself. However, they *do* bear a significant relationship to the predictor. In order to appreciate how suppressor variables function, we need to reconsider our basic prediction model—multiple regression. As we note in Appendix B, the prediction of criterion status is likely to be high when each of the predictor variables ($x_1, x_2, \ldots x_n$) is highly related to the criterion, yet unrelated to the other predictor variables in the regression equation (i.e., $r_{x_1 x_2} = 0$). Under these conditions each predictor is validly predicting a unique portion of criterion variance with a minimum of overlap with the other predictors (see Fig. B–5).

In practice, this laudable goal is seldom realized with more than four or five predictors. Horst (1941) was the first to point out that variables that have exactly the *opposite* characteristics of conventional predictors may act to produce marked increments in the size of multiple R. He called such variables **suppressor variables,** for they are characterized by a lack of association with the criterion ($r_{Ys} = 0$) and high intercorrelation with one or more other predictors (see Fig. 13–3). In computing regression weights (w) for P_1 and P_2 using least squares procedures, the suppressor variable (P_2) receives a *negative* weight (i.e., $\hat{y} = w_1 P_1 -$

$w_2 P_2$); hence, the irrelevant variance in P_2 is "suppressed" by literally subtracting its effects out of the regression equation.

As an example, consider a strategy proposed to identify and eliminate halo from performance ratings (Henik and Tzelgov, 1985). Assume that p is a rating scale of some specific performance and g is a rating scale of general effectiveness designed to capture halo error. Both are used to predict a specific criterion c (e.g., score on a job knowledge test). In terms of a multiple regression model:

$$c = W_p p + W_g g$$

The Ws are the optimal least-squares weights of the two predictors p and g. When g is a classical suppressor, that is, when it has no correlation with the criterion c and a positive correlation with the other predictor, p, then g will contribute to the prediction of c only through the subtraction of the irrelevant (halo) variance from the specific performance variable p.

In practice, suppression effects of modest magnitude are sometimes found in complex models, particularly those that include aggregate data, where the variables are sums or averages of many observations. Under these conditions, where small error variance exists, R^2s are likely to approach 1.0 (Cohen and Cohen, 1983).

However, since the only function suppressor variables serve is to remove redundancy in measurement (Tenopyr, 1977), it is often possible to achieve a comparable predictive gain by using a more conventional variable as an additional predictor. Consequently, the utility of suppressor variables in prediction remains to be demonstrated.

ALTERNATIVE PREDICTION MODELS

Although the multiple regression approach constitutes the basic prediction model, its use in any particular situation requires that its assumptions, advantages, and disadvantages be weighed against those of alternative models. Different employment decisions might well result, depending upon the particular strategy chosen. In this section, therefore, we first will summarize the advantages and disadvantages of the multiple regression model, and then compare and contrast two alternative models to it—**multiple cutoff** and **multiple hurdle.** Although still other prediction strategies exist (e.g., profile matching, actuarial prediction), space constraints preclude their elaboration here.

FIGURE 13–3 Operation of a Suppressor Variable.

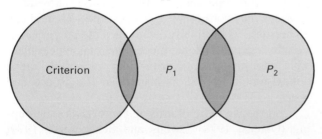

Multiple-Regression Approach

In addition to the statistical assumptions necessary for the appropriate use of the multiple-regression model, one additional assumption is required. Given predictors $X_1, X_2, X_3, \ldots X_n$, the particular values of these predictors will vary widely across individuals, although the statistical weightings of each of the predictors will remain constant. Hence, it is possible for individuals with widely different configurations of predictor scores to obtain identical predicted criterion scores. The model is, therefore, *compensatory* and assumes that high scores on one predictor can substitute or compensate for low scores on another predictor. All individuals in the sample then may be rank-ordered according to their predicted criterion scores.

If it is reasonable to assume linearity, trait additivity, and compensatory interaction among predictors in a given situation, and if the sample size is large enough, then the advantages of the multiple-regression model are considerable. In addition to minimizing errors in prediction, the model combines the predictors optimally so as to yield the most efficient estimate of criterion status. Moreover, the model is extremely flexible in two ways. Mathematically (although such embellishments are beyond the scope of this chapter) the regression model can be modified to handle nominal data, nonlinear relationships, and both linear and nonlinear interactions (cf. Cohen and Cohen, 1983). Moreover, regression equations for each of a number of jobs can be generated using either the same predictors (weighted differently) or different predictors (cf. Chapter 15). However, when the assumptions of multiple regression are untenable, then a different strategy is called for—such as a multiple-cutoff approach.

Multiple-Cutoff Approach

In some selection situations, proficiency on one predictor *cannot* compensate for deficiency on another. Consider the prediction of pilot success, for example. Regardless of his or her standing on any other characteristics important for pilot success, if the applicant is functionally blind, he cannot be selected. In short, when some *minimal* level of proficiency on one or more variables is crucial for job success and when no substitution is allowed, a simple or multiple-cutoff approach is appropriate. Selection then is made from the group of applicants who meet or exceed the required cutoffs on all predictors. Failure on any one predictor disqualifies the applicant from further consideration.

Since the multiple-cutoff approach is *noncompensatory* by definition, it assumes curvilinearity in predictor-criterion relationships. Although a minimal level of visual acuity is necessary for pilot success, increasing levels of visual acuity do not necessarily mean that the individual will be a correspondingly better pilot. Curvilinear relationships can be handled within a multiple-regression framework, but in practice the multiple-cutoff and multiple-regression approaches frequently lead to different decisions even when approximately equal proportions of applicants are selected by each method (see Fig. 13–4).

In Figure 13–4 predictors X_1 and X_2 intercorrelate about .40. Both are independent variables, used jointly to predict a criterion, Y, which is not shown. Note that the multiple-regression cutoff is *not* the same as the regression line. It simply represents the minimum score necessary to qualify for selection. First, let us look at the similar decisions resulting from the two procedures. Regardless of which procedure is chosen, all individuals in area A always will be accepted, and all individuals in area R always will be rejected. Those who will be treated differently depending on the particular model chosen are in areas C, B, and D. If multiple regression is used, then those individuals in areas C and D will be accepted, and those in area B will be rejected. Exactly the opposite decisions will be made if the multiple-cutoff model is used: those in areas C and D will be rejected and those in area B will be accepted.

In practice, the issue essentially boils down to the relative desirability of the individuals in areas C, B, and D. Psychometrically, Lord (1962) has shown that the solution is primarily a function of the reliabilities of the predictors X_1 and X_2. To be sure, the multiple-cutoff model easily could be made less conservative by lowering the cutoff scores. But what rationale guides the selection of an appropriate cutoff score?

Setting a Cutoff. In general, no satisfactory solution has yet been developed for setting optimal cutoff scores in a multiple-cutoff model (cf. Buck, 1977). In a simple cutoff system (one predictor) either the Angoff method (Angoff, 1971), the expectancy chart approach (see below), or Thorndike's "predicted yield" policy (1949) may be used. With the latter strategy, given a knowledge of the number of positions available during some future time period (say, 6 months), the number of applicants to be expected during that time, and the expected distribution of their predictor scores (based on reliable local norms), then

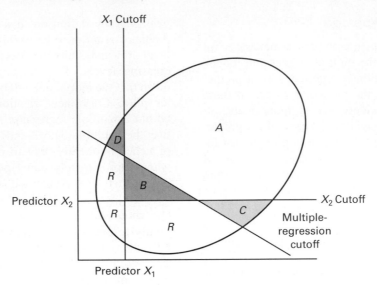

Source: Adapted from R. L. Thorndike, *AAF Aviation Psychology Research Program Reports,* No. 3. Washington, D.C.: GPO, 1947.

FIGURE 13–4 Geometric Comparison of Decisions Made by Multiple-Regression and Multiple-Cutoff Models When Approximately Equal Proportions Are Selected by Either Method.

a cutoff score may be set. For example, if a firm will need 50 secretaries in the next year and anticipates about 250 secretarial applicants during that time, then the selection ratio (50/250) is equal to .20.

Note that in this example the term "selection ratio" refers to a population parameter representing the proportion of successful applicants. More specifically, it represents the proportion of individuals in the population scoring above some cutoff score. It is equivalent to the hiring rate (a sample description) only to the extent that examinees can be considered a random sample from the applicant population (Alexander et al., 1983).

To continue with our original example, if the hiring rate does equal the selection ratio, then approximately 80 percent of the applicants will be rejected. If an aptitude test is given as part of the selection procedure, then a score at the 80th percentile on the local norms plus or minus one standard error of measurement should suffice as an acceptable cutoff score.

As the *Principles for the Validation and Use of Personnel Selection Procedures* (Society, 1987) note:

> Cutoff or other critical scores may be set as high or as low as the purposes of the organization require, if they are based on valid predictors. . . . Consequently, selecting from the top scorers on down is almost always

the most beneficial procedure from the standpoint of the organization if there is an appropriate amount of variance in the predictor [p. 32].

One review of the legal and psychometric literature on cutoff scores offered the following guidelines:

- It is unrealistic to expect that there is a single "best" method of setting cutoff scores for all situations.
- Begin with a job analysis that identifies relative levels of proficiency on critical knowledge, skills, abilities, or other characteristics.
- The validity and job relatedness of the assessment procedure are critical considerations.
- How a test is used (criterion- or norm-referenced) affects the selection and meaning of a cutoff score.
- When possible, examine data on the actual relation of test scores to outcome measures of job performance.
- Set cutoff scores high enough to ensure that minimum standards of job performance are met.
- Cutoff scores should be consistent with normal expectations of proficiency within the workforce (Cascio et al., 1988).

Angoff Method. In this approach, expert judges rate each item in terms of the probability that a barely or minimally competent person would answer the item correctly. The probabilities (or proportions) are then averaged for each item across judges to yield item cutoff scores, and item cutoff scores are summed to yield a test cutoff score. The method is easy to administer, it is as reliable as other judgmental methods for setting cutoff scores, and it has intuitive appeal because expert judges (rather than a consultant) use their knowledge and experience to help determine minimum performance standards. Not surprisingly, therefore, the Angoff method has become the favored judgmental method for setting cutoff scores on employment tests (Cascio et al., 1988; Maurer and Alexander, 1992). To produce optimal results from this method, however, choose judges carefully based on their knowledge of the job and the competencies needed to perform it. Then train them to develop a common conceptual framework of a minimally competent person (Maurer et al., 1991; Maurer and Alexander, 1992). Finally, recognize that if a test consists of items that most of the judges can answer correctly, then judges may make higher Angoff judgments when provided with answers to test items. The result may be a test with a higher cutoff score than that obtained when judges are not provided with answers (Hudson and J. E. Campion, 1994).

Expectancy Charts. Such charts are frequently used to illustrate visually the impact of cutoff scores on future hiring decisions. **Expectancy charts** depict the likelihood of successful criterion performance to be expected from any given level of predictor scores. Figure 13–5 depicts one such chart, an *institutional* expectancy chart.

In essence, the chart provides an answer to the question, "Given a selection ratio of .20, .40, .60, etc.,

what proportion of successful employees can be expected if the future is like the past?" Such an approach is useful in attempting to set cutoff scores for future hiring programs. Likewise, we can draw *individual* expectancy charts that illustrate the likelihood of successful criterion performance for an individual whose score falls within a specified range on the predictor distribution.

Expectancy charts are computed directly from raw data and need not be limited to the one-variable or composite-variable case (cf. Wesman, 1966) or to discontinuous predictors (Lawshe and Bolda, 1958; Lawshe et al., 1958). Computational procedures for developing empirical expectancies are straightforward, and theoretical expectancy charts are also available (Lawshe and Balma, 1966). In fact, when the correlation coefficient is used to summarize the degree of predictor-criterion relationship, expectancy charts are a useful way of illustrating the effect of the validity coefficient on future hiring decisions. When a test has only modest validity for predicting job performance, score differences that appear large will correspond to modest scores on the expectancy distribution, reflecting the modest predictability of job performance from test score information (Hartigan and Wigdor, 1989).

Is there one best way to proceed in the multiple-predictor situation? Perhaps a combination of the multiple-regression and multiple-cutoff approaches is optimal. Multiple-cutoff methods might be used initially to select individuals on those variables where certain minimum levels of ability are mandatory. Following this, multiple-regression methods then may be used with the remaining predictors to forecast criterion status. What we have just described is a multiple-

FIGURE 13–5 Institutional Expectancy Chart Illustrating the Likelihood of Successful Criterion Performance at Different Levels of Predictor Scores.

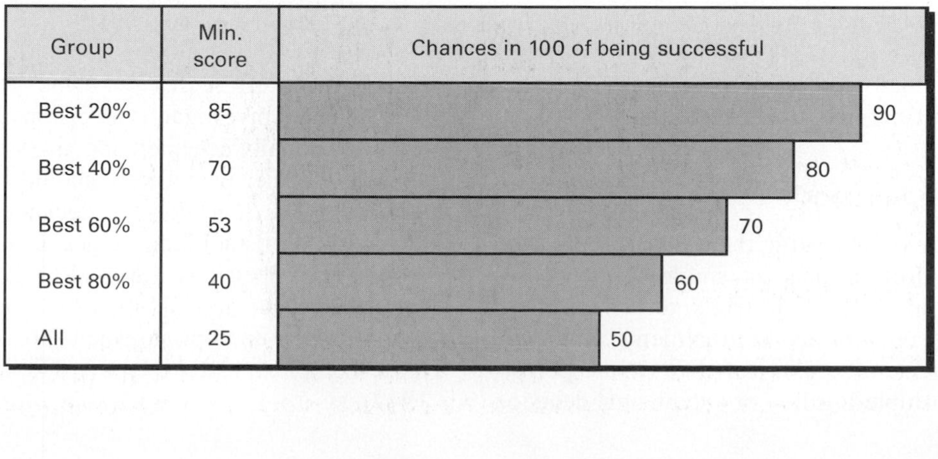

Group	Min. score	Chances in 100 of being successful
Best 20%	85	90
Best 40%	70	80
Best 60%	53	70
Best 80%	40	60
All	25	50

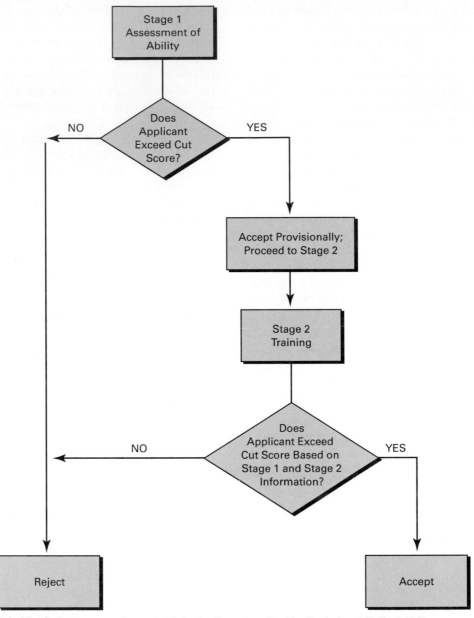

FIGURE 13–6 Two-stage Sequential Selection Procedure Used by Hanisch and Hulin (1994).

hurdle or sequential approach to selection, and we shall consider it further in the next section.

Multiple-Hurdle Approach

Thus far we have been treating the multiple-regression and multiple-cutoff models as single-stage (nonsequential) decision strategies in which terminal or final assignments of individuals to treatments are made (e.g., accept/reject) regardless of their future performance. In multiple-hurdle or sequential-decision strategies, cutoff scores on some predictor may be used to make investigatory decisions. Applicants then are provisionally accepted and assessed further to determine whether or not they should be accepted permanently. The investigatory decisions may continue through several additional stages of subsequent testing before final decisions are made regarding all applicants (Cronbach and Gleser, 1965). Such an approach is particularly appropriate when subsequent training is long, complex, and expensive (Reilly and Manese, 1979).

Hanisch and Hulin (1994) used a two-stage, sequential selection procedure in a complex experimental simulation of an air intercept and controller's task (AIC) that was developed to conduct research on the tasks and job of an air traffic controller. The procedure is shown in Figure 13–6. Assessments of ability occur in Stage 1 because this information is relatively inexpensive to obtain. Applicants who reach the cutoff score on the ability measures progress to Stage 2; the others are rejected. Final selection decisions are then based on Stage 1 and Stage 2 information. Stage 2 information normally would be more expensive to obtain than ability measures, but the information is obtained from a smaller, prescreened group, thereby reducing the cost relative to obtaining Stage 2 information from all applicants. Hanisch and Hulin (1994) examined the validity of training as second-stage information *beyond* ability in the prediction of task performance.

Across 12 blocks of AIC trials, the training-performance measure added an average of an additional 13 percent to the variance accounted for by the ability measures. Training-performance measures accounted for an additional 32 percent of the variance in total AIC task performance after ability was entered first in a hierarchical regression analysis. These results are significant both in practical and statistical terms. They document both the importance of ability in predicting performance, and the even greater importance of training performance on similar tasks. However, in order to evaluate the *utility* of training as second-stage information in sequential selection decisions, it is necessary to compute the incremental costs and the incremental validity of training (Hanisch and Hulin, 1994).

Although it is certainly in the organization's (as well as the individual's) best interest to reach a final decision as early as possible, such decisions must be as accurate as available information will permit. Often we must pay a price (such as the cost of training) for more accurate decisions. Optimal decisions could be made by selecting on the criterion itself (e.g., actual air traffic controller performance); yet the time, expense, and safety considerations involved make such an approach impossible to implement.

EVALUATING SELECTION EFFICIENCY

Employment decision makers frequently are confronted with the task of evaluating the relative efficiencies of several possible predictors. In essence, the problem reduces to a comparison of random or average choice with that obtained by selecting with some measuring instrument. Such an index should indicate directly the proportion of maximum savings actually obtained with the use of a selection measure, where the maximum saving is that obtained by selecting on the criterion itself (e.g., actual job performance). Random selection should, therefore, yield a predictive efficiency index of zero. If half the total possible savings were produced by using the predictor, then the index should be .5, and if a third of the total possible savings were produced, the index should equal .33.

Brogden (1946a) showed that if criterion performance is expressed in standard (z) score units, then:

$$r_{xy} = \frac{\Sigma \bar{z}_y}{\Sigma z_{y'}} \qquad (13-1)$$

That is, over all individuals, r represents the ratio of the average criterion score made by persons selected on the basis of their predictor scores ($\Sigma \bar{z}_y$) to the average criterion score made by selecting the same number of persons on the basis of their criterion scores ($\Sigma z_{y'}$). Equation 13–1 holds as long as the predictor and criterion are continuous and identical in distribution form, the regression of the criterion on the predictor is linear, and the selection ratio is held constant.

As an illustration, suppose a firm wants to hire 25 persons for a certain job and must choose the best 25 from 100 applicants. Ideally, the firm would hire all 100 for a period of time, collect job performance data, and retain the best 25. The average job performance score of the 25 so selected would obviously be the highest obtainable by any possible combination of 25 of the 100 original workers. Since such a procedure is usually out of the question, we administer a selection measure and select the 25 highest scorers.

Equation 13–1 indicates that the validity coefficient may be interpreted as the ratio of the average job performance of the 25 persons selected by the predictor to the average performance of the 25 who would have been selected had actual job performance been used as a basis for selection. Hence, a predictor with a validity of .50 can be expected to produce 50 percent of the gain that would result from selecting on the basis of the criterion itself. If individuals could be selected on the basis of the criterion itself (and this would save an organization $100,000 a year over random selection), then a selection measure with a validity of .50 would save $50,000 per year. In short, variation in the efficiency of a selection instrument is properly interpreted as a direct linear function of its validity.

SUMMARY OF THE CLASSICAL VALIDITY APPROACH

The general objective of the classical validity approach can be expressed concisely: The best selection battery is the one that yields the highest multiple R between predicted and actual criterion scores. This will minimize selection errors. Total emphasis is, therefore, placed on measurement and prediction.

This approach has been criticized sharply, for it ignores certain external parameters of the situation that largely determine the overall worth of a selection instrument. We shall first review these limitations and then consider an alternative selection model based on decision theory.

Several limitations of the traditional correlation model may reduce its overall value or utility. Taylor and Russell (1939) pointed out that utility depends not only on the validity of a selection measure, but also on two other parameters: the **selection ratio** (the ratio of the number of available job openings to the total number of available applicants) and the **base rate** (the proportion of persons judged successful using current selection procedures). They published a series of tables illustrating the interaction of these three parameters on the **success ratio** (the proportion of selected applicants who subsequently are judged successful). The success ratio, then, serves as an operational measure of the value or utility of the selection measure. In addition to ignoring the effects of the selection ratio (SR) and the base rate (BR), the classical validity approach makes

unwarranted utility assumptions and also fails to consider the systemic nature of the selection process.

The Selection Ratio

Whenever a quota exists on the total number of applicants that may be accepted, the selection ratio becomes a major concern. As the SR approaches 1.0 (all applicants must be selected), it becomes *high* or unfavorable from the organization's perspective. Conversely, as the SR approaches zero, it becomes *low* or favorable, and, therefore, the organization can afford to be selective. Figure 13–7 illustrates the wide-ranging effect the SR may exert on a predictor with a given validity. In each case, X_c represents a cutoff score on the predictor. As can be seen in Figure 13–7, even predictors with very low validities can be useful if the SR is low and if an organization needs to choose only the "cream of the crop." For example, given an SR of .10, a validity of .15, and a BR of .50, the success ratio is .61.[1] If the validity in this situation is .30, then the success ratio jumps to .71; if the validity is .60, then the success ratio becomes .90—a 40 percent improvement over the base rate! Conversely, given high selection ratios, a predictor must possess substantial validity before the success ratio increases significantly. For example, given a BR of .50 and an SR of .90, the maximum possible success ratio (with a validity of 1.0) is only .56.

It might, thus, appear that given a particular validity and BR, it is always best to decrease the SR (i.e., be more selective). However, the optimal strategy is

---

[1] These figures and those that follow are derived from the Taylor and Russell (1939) tables.

FIGURE 13–7 Effect of Varying Selection Ratios on a Predictor with a Given Validity.

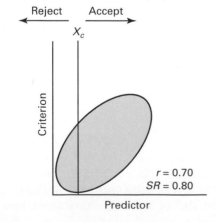

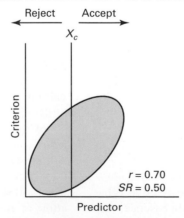

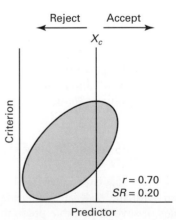

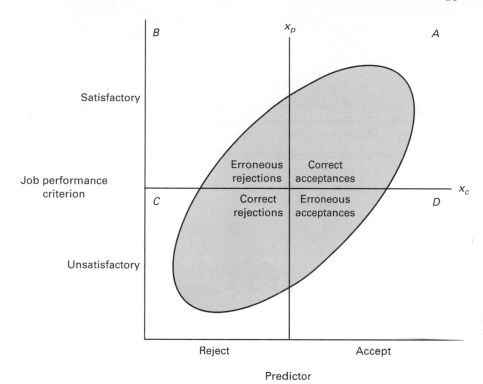

FIGURE 13–8 Selection Decision-Outcome Combinations.

not this simple (Law and Myors, 1993; Sands, 1973). When the HR manager must achieve a certain quota of satisfactory individuals, lowering the SR means that more recruiting is necessary. This strategy may or may not be cost-effective. If staffing requirements are *not* fixed or if the recruiting effort can be expanded, then the SR itself becomes flexible. Under these conditions, the problem becomes one of determining an **optimal cutoff score** on the predictor battery that will yield the desired distribution of outcomes of prediction. This is precisely what the predicted yield and expectancy chart methods do.

When predictor scores are plotted against criterion scores, the result is frequently a scattergram similar to the one in Figure 13–8. Raising the cutoff score (X_p) decreases the probability of erroneous acceptances, but it simultaneously increases the probability of erroneous rejections. Lowering the cutoff score has exactly the opposite effect. Several authors (Cronbach and Gleser, 1965; Ghiselli et al., 1981; Gordon and Leighty, 1988) have developed a simple procedure for setting a cutoff score when the objective is to minimize both kinds of errors. If the frequency distributions of the two groups are plotted separately along the same baseline, the optimum cutoff score for distinguishing between the two groups will occur at the

point where the two distributions intersect (see Fig. 13–9).

However, as we have seen, to set a cutoff score based on the *level* of job performance deemed minimally acceptable, the Angoff method is most popular. Procedures using utility concepts and Bayesian decision theory also have been suggested (Chuang, Chen, and Novick, 1981), but we do not consider them here, since in most practical situations decision makers are not free to vary SRs.

The Base Rate

In a classic article Meehl and Rosen (1955) pointed out the importance of base rates in evaluating the worth of a selection measure. In order to be of any use in selection, the measure must demonstrate *incremental* validity (Sechrest, 1963; Murphy, 1987) by improving on the BR. That is, the selection measure must result in more correct decisions than could be made without using it. As Figure 13–10 demonstrates, the higher the BR, the more difficult it is for a selection measure to improve upon it.

In each case x_c represents the minimum criterion standard (criterion cutoff score) necessary for success. Obviously, the BR in a selection situation can be

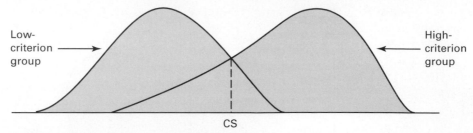

FIGURE 13–9 Procedure for Setting an Optimal Cutoff Score When the Objective Is to Minimize *Both* Erroneous Acceptances and Erroneous Rejections.

changed by raising or lowering this minimum standard on the criterion. Figure 13–10 illustrates that given a BR of .80, it would be difficult for *any* selection measure to improve on this figure. In fact, when the BR is .80, a validity of .45 is required in order to produce an improvement of even 10 percent over base rate prediction. This is also true at very low BRs where the objective is to predict failure (as would be the case, for example, in the psychiatric screening of job applicants). Given a BR of .20 and a validity of .45, the success ratio is .30—once again representing only a 10 percent increment in correct decisions.

Selection measures are most useful, however, when BRs are about .50. This is because the variance of a dichotomous variable is equal to p times q, where p and q are the proportions of successes and failures, respectively. The variance is a maximum when $p = q = 0.50$. Other things being equal, the greater the variance, the greater the potential relationship with the predictor. As the BR departs radically in either direction from .50 the benefit of an additional predictor becomes questionable, especially in view of the costs involved in gathering the additional information.

The lesson is obvious: Applications of selection measures to situations with markedly different SRs or BRs can result in quite different predictive outcomes and cost-benefit ratios. When it is not possible to gain significant incremental validity by adding a predictor, then do not use the predictor since it cannot improve on classification of persons by the base rate.

Utility Assumptions

Consider the four decision-outcome combinations in Figure 13–8. The classical validity approach, in attempting to maximize multiple R (and, thereby, minimize the number of erroneous acceptances and rejections), does not specifically take into account the varying utilities to the organization of each of the four possible outcomes. Implicitly, the classical validity approach treats both kinds of decision errors as equally costly; yet in most practical selection situations organizations attach different utilities to these outcomes. For example, it is much more serious to accept an airline pilot erroneously than it is to reject one erroneously. Most organizations are not even concerned with erroneous rejections, except as it costs money to process applications, administer tests, and so forth. On the other hand, many professional athletic teams spend lavish amounts of money on recruiting, coaching, and evaluating prospective players so as "not to let a good one get away."

The classical validity approach is deficient to the extent that it emphasizes measurement and prediction

FIGURE 13–10 Effect of Varying Base Rates on a Predictor with a Given Validity.

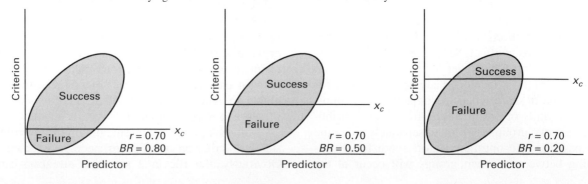

rather than the outcomes of decisions. Clearly the task of the decision maker in selection is to combine a priori predictions with the values placed on alternative outcomes in such a way as to maximize the purpose of the sponsoring organization.

Systems Approach

By focusing only on selection, the classical validity approach neglects the implications of selection decisions for the rest of the HR system. Such an observation is not new. Several authors (Dudek, 1963; Dunnette, 1962; Uhlaner, 1960; Wallace, 1965) have noted that an optimal selection strategy may not be optimal for other employment functions such as recruiting and training. In addition, other factors such as the cost of the selection procedure, the loss resulting from error, and the organization's ability to evaluate success must be considered. When an organization focuses solely on selection, to the exclusion of other related functions, the performance effectiveness of the overall HR system may suffer considerably.

In short, any selection procedure must be evaluated in terms of its total benefits to the organization. Thus, Boudreau and Berger (1985) developed a utility model that can be used to assess the interactions among employee acquisitions and employee separations. Such a model provides an important link between staffing utility and traditional research on employee separations and turnover.

DECISION-MAKING ACCURACY

Throughout this chapter we have emphasized that selection measures are useful to the extent that they help make decisions. It would seem, then, that one way to evaluate the usefulness of any predictor is in terms of the proportion of correct decisions made when the predictor is used as the basis for decision making. The model is straightforward (see Fig. 13–8), requiring only that the decision recommended by the predictor be classified into two or more mutually exclusive categories, that the criterion data be classified similarly, and that the two sets of data be compared.

One index of decision-making accuracy is the proportion of total decisions made that are correct decisions. In terms of Figure 13–8 such a proportion may be computed as follows:

$$PC_{TOT} = \frac{A + C}{A + B + C + D} \qquad (13\text{–}2)$$

where PC_{TOT} is the proportion of total decisions that are correct and *A, B, C,* and *D* are the numbers of individuals in each cell of Figure 13–8.

Note that Equation 13–2 takes into account all decisions that are made. In this sense, it is comparable to a predictive validity coefficient wherein all applicants are considered. In addition, observe that cells *B* and *D* (erroneous rejections and erroneous acceptances) are both weighted equally. In practice, as we noted earlier, some differential weighting of these categories (e.g., in terms of dollar costs) usually occurs. We will address this issue further in our discussion of utility.

In many selection situations, erroneous acceptances are viewed as far more serious than erroneous rejections. The HR manager generally is more concerned about the success or failure of those persons who are hired than about those who are not. In short, the organization derives no benefit from rejected applicants. Therefore, a more appropriate index of decision-making accuracy is the proportion of "accept" decisions that are correct decisions:

$$PC_{ACC} = \frac{A}{A + D} \qquad (13\text{–}3)$$

where PC_{ACC} is the proportion of those accepted who later turn out to be satisfactory and *A* and *D* represent the total number accepted who are satisfactory and unsatisfactory, respectively. When the goal of selection is to maximize the proportion of individuals selected who will be successful, Equation 13–3 applies.

Evaluation of the Decision-Theory Approach

In previous sections we have examined the effect of the BR, the SR, and the cutoff score on outcomes. The main advantage of the decision-theory approach to selection is that it addresses these parameters and compels the decision maker to consider explicitly the kinds of judgments he or she has to make. For example, if erroneous acceptances are a major concern, then the predictor cutoff score may be raised. Of course, this means that a larger number of erroneous rejections will result and the selection ratio must be made more favorable, but the mechanics of this approach thrust such awareness on the decision maker. While the validity coefficient provides an index of predictor-criterion association throughout the entire range of scores, the decision theory approach is more concerned with the effectiveness of a chosen cutoff score in making a certain type of decision. From a practical perspective, numbers of correct and incorrect decisions are far more meaningful and more useful in evaluating predictive accuracy than are correlational results. In addition, the decision-theory paradigm is simple to apply, to communicate, and to understand.

The decision-theory approach has been criticized, however, because errors of measurement are not considered in setting cutoff scores. Therefore, some people will be treated unjustly—especially those whose scores fall just below the cutoff score. This criticism is really directed at the way the cutoffs are used (i.e., the decision strategy) rather than at the decision-theory approach per se. As we noted earlier, the proper role of selection measures is as tools in the decision-making process. Cutoff scores need not (and should not) be regarded as absolute. Rather, they should be considered in a relative sense (with the standard error of measurement providing bands or confidence limits around the cutoff), to be weighted along with other information in order to reach a final decision. In short, we are advocating a sequential decision strategy in selection, where feasible.

Despite its advantages, tabulation of the number of "hits" and "misses" is appropriate only if we are predicting *attributes* (e.g., stayers vs. leavers, successes vs. failures in a training program), not *measurements* (such as performance ratings or sales). When we are predicting measurements, we must work in terms of *by how much,* on the average, we have missed the mark. How much better are our predictions, how much have we reduced the errors that would have been observed had we not used the information available? We compare the average deviation between fact and prediction with the average of the errors we would make without using such knowledge as a basis for prediction (Guilford and Fruchter, 1978). The *standard error of estimate* (see Appendix B) is the statistic that tells us this. However, even knowing the relative frequency of occurrence of various outcomes does not enable the decision maker to evaluate the worth of the predictor unless he or she can specify the utilities associated with each of the various outcomes.

EVALUATING UTILITIES

Operating executives justifiably demand estimates of expected costs and benefits of HR programs. Unfortunately, few HR programs actually are evaluated in these terms, although techniques for doing so have been available for years (Brogden, 1949; Cronbach and Gleser, 1965; Sands, 1973). More often selection or promotion systems are evaluated solely in correlational terms—that is, in terms of a validity coefficient. Despite the fact that the validity coefficient alone has been shown to be an incomplete index of the value of a selection device as other parameters in the situation change, few published studies incorporate more accurate estimates of expected payoffs. However, as HR costs continue to consume larger and larger proportions of the cost of doing business, we may expect to see increased pressure on HR executives to justify new or continuing programs of employee selection. This involves a consideration of the relative utilities to the organization of alternative selection strategies.

The utility of a selection device is the degree to which its use improves the quality of the individuals selected beyond what would have occurred had that device not been used (Blum and Naylor, 1968). Quality, in turn, may be defined in terms of (1) the proportion of individuals in the selected group who are considered "successful," (2) the average standard score on the criterion for the selected group, or (3) the dollar payoff to the organization resulting from the use of a particular selection procedure. Earlier we described the Taylor-Russell (1939) utility model. In this section we present a summary and critique of two additional utility models, the Naylor and Shine (1965) model and the Brogden (1946a; 1949), Cronbach, and Gleser (1965) model, together with appropriate uses of each.

The Naylor-Shine Model

In contrast to the Taylor-Russell utility model, the Naylor-Shine (1965) approach assumes a linear relationship between validity and utility. This relationship holds at all selection ratios. That is, given any arbitrarily defined cutoff on a selection measure, the higher the validity, the greater the increase in average criterion score for the selected group over that observed for the total group (Mean Criterion Score of Selectees minus Mean Criterion Score of Total Group). Thus, the Naylor-Shine index of utility is defined in terms of the increase in average criterion score to be expected from the use of a selection measure with a given validity and selection ratio. Like Taylor and Russell, Naylor and Shine assume that the new predictor will simply be added to the current selection battery. Under these circumstances, the validity coefficient should be based on the concurrent validity model. Unlike Taylor and Russell, however, use of the Naylor-Shine model does not require that researchers dichotomize employees into "satisfactory" and "unsatisfactory" groups by specifying an arbitrary cutoff on the criterion dimension that represents "minimally acceptable performance." Thus, this utility model requires less information.

The basic equation underlying the Naylor-Shine model is:

$$\bar{Z}_{yi} = r_{xy}\frac{\lambda_i}{\phi_i} \qquad (13\text{-}4)$$

where $\bar{Z}_{yi}$ is the mean criterion score (in standard score units) of all cases above the predictor cutoff; r_{xy} is the validity coefficient; λ_i is the ordinate or height of the normal distribution at the predictor cutoff, $\bar{Z}_{xi}$ (expressed in standard-score units); and ϕ_i is the selection ratio. Equation 13–4 applies whether r_{xy} is a zero-order correlation coefficient or a multiple-regression coefficient.

Using Equation 13–4 as a basic building block, Naylor and Shine (1965) present a series of tables (reproduced in Cascio, 1991) that specify, for each selection ratio, the standard (predictor) score corresponding to that selection ratio, the ordinate of the normal curve at that point, and the quotient $\frac{\lambda_i}{\phi_i}$. The table can be used to answer several important questions: (1) Given a specified selection ratio, what will be the average performance level of those selected? (2) Given a desired selection ratio, what will $\bar{Z}_{yi}$ be? and (3) Given a desired improvement in the average criterion score of those selected, what selection ratio and/or predictor cutoff value (in standard-score units) should be used?

This model is most appropriate when it is not possible to express differences in criterion performance in dollar terms, but one can assume that the function relating payoff (i.e., performance under some treatment) to predictor score is linear. For example, in the prediction of labor turnover (expressed as a percentage) based on scores from a predictor that demonstrates some validity (e.g., a weighted application blank), if percentages are expressed as standard scores, then it is possible to assess the expected decrease in the percentage of turnover as a function of variation in the selection ratio (the predictor cutoff score). If appropriate cost accounting procedures are used to calculate actual turnover costs (cf. Cascio, 1991), expected savings resulting from reduced turnover can be estimated.

The Naylor-Shine utility index appears more applicable in general than the Taylor-Russell index, because in many, if not most cases, given valid selection procedures, one would expect an increase in average criterion performance as the organization becomes

more selective in deciding whom to accept. However, neither of these models formally integrates the concept of cost of selection or dollars gained or lost into the utility index. Both simply imply that larger differences in the percentage of successful employees (Taylor-Russell) or larger increases in average criterion score (Naylor-Shine) will yield larger benefits to the employer in terms of dollars saved.

The Brogden-Cronbach-Gleser Model

Both Brogden (1946a; 1949) and Cronbach and Gleser (1965) arrived at the same conclusions regarding the effects of the validity coefficient, the selection ratio, the cost of selection, and variability in criterion scores on utility in fixed treatment selection. The only assumption required to use this model is that the relationship between test scores and job performance is linear, that is, the higher the test score, the higher the job performance, and vice versa. This assumption is justified in almost all circumstances (Cesare et al., 1994; Coward and Sackett, 1990). If we assume further that test scores are normally distributed, then the average test score of those selected ($\bar{Z}_x$) is λ/SR, where SR = selection ratio and λ = the height of the standard normal curve at the point of cut corresponding to SR.

When these assumptions are met, both Brogden (1949) and Cronbach and Gleser (1965) have shown that the net gain in utility from selecting N persons in fixed treatment selection is as follows:

$$\Delta U = (N)(T)(SD_y)(r_{xy})(\bar{Z}_x) - (N)(C_y) \quad (13\text{-}5)$$

where:

ΔU = the increase in average dollar-valued payoff resulting from use of a test or other selection procedure (x) instead of selecting randomly.

T = the expected tenure of the selected group.

r_{xy} = the correlation of the selection procedure with the job performance measure (scaled in dollars) in the group of all applicants that has been screened by any procedure that is presently in use and will continue to be used.

SD_y = the standard deviation of dollar-valued job performance in the (prescreened) applicant group.

$\bar{Z}_x$ = the average standard predictor score of the selected group, and

C = the cost of testing one applicant.

TABLE 13–1	Summary of the Utility Indexes, Data Requirements, and Assumptions of the Taylor-Russell, Naylor-Shine, and Brogden-Cronbach-Gleser Utility Models		
Model	*Utility Index*	*Data Requirements*	*Distinctive Assumptions*
Taylor-Russell (1939)	Increase in percentage successful in selected group	Validity, base rate, selection ratio	All selectees classified either as successful or unsuccessful. Equal criterion performance by all members of each group; cost of selection = $0.
Naylor-Shine (1965)	Increase in mean criterion score of selected group	Validity, selection ratio	
Brogden-Cronbach-Gleser (1965)	Increase in dollar payoff of selected group	Validity, selection ratio, criterion standard deviation in dollars	Validity linearly related to utility; cost of selection = $0.
			Validity linearly related to utility; cost of selection ≠ $0; criterion performance evaluated in dollars.

Note: All three models assume a validity coefficient based on present employees (concurrent validity).

Source: W. F. Cascio, Responding to the demand for accountability: A critical analysis of three utility models. *Organizational Behavior and Human Performance,* 1980, *25,* 32–45. Used by permission.

Note that in this expression, (SD_y) (r_{xy}) is the slope of the payoff function relating expected payoff to score. An increase in validity leads to an increase in slope, but as Equation 13–5 demonstrates, slope also depends on the dispersion of criterion scores. For any one treatment, SD_y is constant and indicates both the magnitude and practical significance of individual differences in payoff. Thus a selection procedure with r_{xy} = .25 and SD_y = $10,000 for one selection decision is just as useful as a procedure with r_{xy} = .50 and SD_y = $5,000 for some other decision (holding other parameters constant). Even procedures with low validity can still be useful when SD_y is large. Table 13–1 presents a summary of these three models.

Further Developments of the Brogden-Cronbach-Gleser Model

There have been technical modifications of the model (Raju, Burke, and Maurer, 1995), including the ability to treat recruitment and selection costs separately (Martin and Raju, 1992; Law and Myors, 1993). In the following sections, however, we discuss three other key developments in this model: (1) development of alternative methods for estimating SD_y; (2) integration of this selection utility model with capital budgeting models; and (3) assessments of the relative gain or loss in utility resulting from alternative selection strategies. Briefly let's consider each of these.

Alternative Methods of Estimating SD_y

A major stumbling block to wider use of this model has been the determination of the standard deviation of job performance in dollars. At least four procedures are now available for estimating this parameter, and in the following sections we present references that interested readers may consult for more detailed information.

- **The 40-Percent-of-Average-Salary-Rule:** Schmidt and Hunter (1983), but see also Hunter, Schmidt, and Judiesch (1990), who demonstrated that this figure covaries with job complexity (the information processing requirements of jobs).

- **Schmidt-Hunter Global Estimation Procedure:** Schmidt, Hunter, McKenzie, and Muldrow (1979); refinements of the procedure can be found in Burke and Frederick (1984; 1986).

- **Cascio-Ramos Estimate of Performance in Dollars (CREPID):** Cascio and Ramos (1986); refinements of this procedure have also been proposed (Edwards et al., 1988; Orr et al., 1989).

- **System Effectiveness Technique:** Eaton, Wing, and Mitchell (1985).

More than a dozen studies have compared results using alternative methods for estimating SD_y. However, in the absence of a meaningful external criterion, one is left with little basis for choosing one method over another (Greer and Cascio, 1987). Differences among SD_y estimates using different methods are often less that 50 percent, and may be less than $5,000 in many cases (Boudreau, 1991). However, it may be that all subjective methods underestimate the true value of SD_y. Using a unique set of field data, Becker and Huselid (1992) estimated SD_y directly. SD_y values ranged from 74 to 100 percent of mean salary—considerably greater than the 40 to 70 percent found in subjective estimates. One reason for this is that when subjective methods are used, supervisors interpret the dollar value of output in terms of wages or salaries, rather than in terms of sales revenue. However, supervisory estimates of the variability of output as a percentage of mean output (SD_p) are more accurate (Judiesch, et al., 1992). While it is tempting to call for more research on SD_y measurement, another stream of research concerned with "break-even analysis" suggests that this may not be fruitful.

Break-even Analysis. Break-even values are those at which the HRM program's benefits equal ("are even with") the program's costs. Any parameter values that exceed the break-even value will produce positive utility. Boudreau (1991) computed break-even values for 42 studies that had estimated SD_y. Without exception, the break-even values fell at or below 60 percent of the estimated value of SD_y. In many cases, the break-even value was less than 1 percent of the estimated value of SD_y. However, as Weekley et al. (1985) noted, even though the break-even value might be low when comparing implementing versus not implementing an HRM program, comparing HRM programs to other organizational investments might produce decision situations where differences in SD_y estimates do affect the ultimate decision. Research that incorporates those kinds of contextual variables (as well as others described below) might be beneficial.

Integration of Selection Utility with Capital Budgeting Models

It can be shown that selection utility models are remarkably similar to capital budgeting models that are well established in the field of finance (Cronshaw and Alexander, 1985). In both cases a projected stream of future returns is estimated and the costs associated with the selection program are subtracted from this stream of returns to yield expected net returns on utility. That is:

$$\text{Utility} = \text{Returns} - \text{Costs.}$$

However, while HR professionals consider the net dollar returns from a selection process to represent the end product of the evaluation process, capital budgeting theory considers forecasting of the dollar benefits and costs to be only the first step in the estimation of the project's utility or usefulness. What this implies is that a high net dollar return on a selection program may not produce maximum benefits for the firm. From the firm's perspective, only those projects should be undertaken that increase the market value of the firm even if the projects do not yield the highest absolute dollar returns (Brealey and Myers, 1996).

In general, there are three limitations that constrain the effectiveness of the Brogden-Cronbach-Gleser utility model for representing the benefits of selection programs within the larger firm, and that lead to overly optimistic estimates of payoffs (Cronshaw and Alexander, 1985):

1. The model does not take into account the time value of money, that is, the discount rate.

2. The model ignores the concept of risk.

3. It ignores the impact of taxation on payoffs. That is, any incremental income generated as a result of a selection program may be taxed at prevailing corporate tax rates. This is why after-tax cash returns to an investment are often used for purposes of capital budgeting. Selection utility estimates that ignore the effect of taxation may produce overly optimistic estimates of the benefits accruing to a selection program.

Although the application of capital budgeting methods to HR programs has not been endorsed universally (cf. Hunter et al., 1988), there is a theory-driven rationale for using such methods. They facilitate the comparison of competing proposals for the use of an organization's resources, whether the proposal is for the construction of a new plant or to train new employees. To make a valid comparison, both proposals must be presented in the same terms—terms that measure the benefit of the program for the organization as a whole—and in terms of the basic objectives of the organization (Cascio and Morris, 1990; Cronshaw and Alexander, 1991).

HR researchers have not totally ignored these considerations. For example, Boudreau (1983a; 1983b) developed modifications of Equation 13–5 that consider these economic factors, as well as the implications of applying selection programs for more than one year for successive groups of applicants. Returns from valid selection therefore accrue to overlapping applicant groups with varying tenure in the organization.

To be sure, the accuracy of the output from utility equations depends upon the (admittedly fallible) input data. Nevertheless, the important lesson to be learned from this analysis is that it is more advantageous and more realistic from the HR manager's perspective to consider a cash outlay for a human resource intervention as a long-term *investment,* not just as a short-term operating cost.

Assessment of the Relative Gains or Losses from Alternative Selection Strategies

Utility has been expressed in a variety of metrics, including: productivity increases, reductions in labor costs, reductions in the numbers of employees needed to perform at a given level of output, and levels of financial return. For example, Schmidt et al. (1979) used Equation 13–5 to estimate the impact of a valid test (the Programmer Aptitude Test) on productivity if it were used to select new computer programmers for one year in the federal government. Estimated productivity increases were presented for a variety of SRs and differences in validity between the new test and a previous procedure. For example, given an SR of .20, a difference in validity between the old and new selection procedures of .46, 618 new hires annually, a per-person cost of testing of $10, and an average tenure of 9.69 years for computer programmers, Schmidt et al. (1979) showed that the average gain in productivity *per selectee* is $64,725 spread out over the 9.69 years. In short, millions of dollars in lost productivity can be saved by using valid selection procedures just in this one occupation.

Two other studies investigated the impact of assessment centers on management performance (Cascio and Silbey, 1979; Cascio and Ramos, 1986). In the latter study, the payoff associated with first-level management assessment, given that 1,116 managers were selected and that their average tenure at first level was 4.4 years, was over $13 million. This represents about $12,000 in improved performance per manager over 4.4 years, or about $2,700 per year in improved job performance.

In another study, Hunter and Hunter (1984) concluded that in the case of federal entry-level jobs, substitution of a less valid predictor for the most valid ones (ability and work sample test) would result in productivity losses costing from $3.12 billion (job tryout) to $15.89 billion per year (age). Hiring on the basis of ability alone has a utility of $15.61 billion per year, but it affects minority groups adversely.

Unfortunately, none of these studies incorporated adjustments for the economic factors of discounting, variable costs, and taxes. Doing so may have produced estimates of net payoffs that were as much as 70 percent smaller (Boudreau, 1991; 1988). However, in examining the payoffs derived from the validity of clerical selection procedures, where the validities were derived from alternative validity generalization methods, Burke and Doran (1989) did incorporate adjustments for economic factors. They found that regardless of the validity generalization estimation method used, the change in utility associated with moving from the organization's current selection procedure to an alternative procedure was still sizable.

All of these utility estimates assume that selection is accomplished in a top-down fashion, beginning with the highest scoring applicant. Any other strategy (e.g., banding) will decrease the maximum gain that could be realized and result in an opportunity cost to the employer (Schmidt, Mack, and Hunter, 1984). How is utility affected when banding is used? Siskin (1995) showed that in most situations the use of banding may produce a small loss in the average performance that may be expected, and that a person at the top of the band is only slightly more likely to outperform a person at the bottom of the band. In some cases, therefore, decision makers may view the social gains of banding to outweigh its economic cost.

Adjustments in Payoffs

At this point, one might be tempted to conclude that if top-down hiring is used, the dollar gains in performance will almost always be as high as predicted. Is this realistic? Probably not. In practice, some offers are declined, and lower-scoring candidates must be accepted in place of higher-scoring candidates who decline initial offers. Hence the average ability of those *actually* selected almost always will be lower than the average ability of those who receive the initial offers. Consequently the actual increase in utility associated with valid selection generally will be lower than that which would be obtained if all offers were accepted.

Murphy (1986) presented formulas for calculating the average ability of those actually selected when the proportion of initial offers accepted is less than 100 percent. He showed that, under realistic circumstances, utility formulas currently used could overestimate gains by 30 to 80 percent. Tight versus loose la-

TABLE 13–2 Some Key Factors that Affect Economic Payoffs from Selection Programs

Generally Increase Payoffs	Generally Decrease Payoffs	May Increase or Decrease Payoffs
Low selection ratios	High selection ratios	Changes in the definition of the criterion construct
Multiple employee cohorts	Discounting	
Start-up costs[a]	Variable costs (materials + wages)	Changes in validity
Employee tenure	Taxes	Changes in the variability of job performance
Loose labor markets	Tight labor markets	
	Time lags to fully competent performance	
	Unreliability in performance across time periods	
	Recruitment costs	

[a] Start-up costs decrease payoffs in the period incurred, but they act to increase payoffs therafter, because only recurring costs remain.

Source: W. F. Cascio, (1993). Assessing the utility of selection decisions: Theoretical and practical considerations. In N. Schmitt and W. C. Borman (Eds.), *Personnel selection in organizations* (p. 330). San Francisco: Jossey-Bass.

bor markets provide one explanation for variability in the quality of applicants who accept job offers (Becker, 1989). In fact, a number of factors might affect the estimated payoffs from selection programs (Cascio, 1993). Table 13–2 is a summary of them. Incorporating such factors into the decision-making process should make utility estimates more realistic.

Overestimates or not, the utility figures associated with valid selection programs are far higher than most people would suspect, yet our inability to demonstrate such gains in the past is one of the reasons why decision makers mistakenly have emphasized the *cost* of these procedures. In most instances such costs are trivial, relative to the gains to be realized. Based on the findings presented here, emphasis on costs rather than on benefits should no longer be the case.

The Strategic Context of Personnel Selection

While certain generic economic objectives are common to all private-sector firms (profit maximization, cost minimization), strategic opportunities are not, and they do not occur within firms in a uniform, predictable way (Ansoff, 1988). As strategic objectives (e.g., economic survival, growth in market share) vary, so also must the "alignment" of labor, capital, and equipment resources. As strategic goals change over time, assessment of the relative contribution of a selection system is likely also to change. The Brogden-Cronbach-Gleser approach is deficient to the extent that it ignores the strategic context of selection decisions, and it assumes that validity and SD_y are constant over time, when, in fact, they probably vary (Russell,

Colella, and Bobko, 1993). As Becker and Huselid (1992) noted, even if the effect of employee performance on organizational output is relatively stable over time, product market changes that are beyond the control of employees will affect the economic value of their contribution to the organization.

To be more useful to decision makers, therefore, utility models should be able to provide answers to the following questions (Russell et al., 1993):

- Given all other factors besides the selection system (e.g., capitalization, availability of raw materials) what is the expected level of performance generated by a manager (ΔU per selectee)?

- How much of a gain in performance can we expect from a new performance system (ΔU for a single cohort)?

- Are the levels of performance expected with or without the selection system adequate to meet the firm's strategic needs (ΔU computed over existing cohorts and also expected new cohorts of employees)?

- Is the incremental increase in performance expected from selection instrument "A" greater than that expected from instrument "B"?

Russell et al. (1993) presented modifications of the traditional utility equation (13–5) to reflect changing contributions of the selection system over time (validity and SD_y), and changes in what is important to strategic HR decision makers (strategic needs). Doing so yields a more realistic view of how firms benefit from personnel selection. It may also overcome some of the skepticism that operating managers understandably express toward "raw" (unmodified) estimates of the economic value of valid selection procedures (Latham and Whyte, 1994).

SUMMARY

The classical validity approach to employee selection emphasizes measurement accuracy and predictive efficiency. Within this framework, multiple-regression (which may be modified to incorporate moderator or suppressor variables) and unit-weighting schemes (compensatory linear models) are used to forecast job success. In some situations, however, compensatory models are inappropriate, and thus noncompensatory models (such as multiple cutoff or multiple hurdles) must be used.

The classical validity approach is incomplete, for it ignores the effects of the selection ratio and base rate, makes unwarranted utility assumptions, and fails to consider the systemic nature of the selection process. Decision theory, which forces the decision maker to consider the utility of alternative selection strategies, has been proposed as a more suitable alternative.

Within this framework, the Taylor-Russell, Naylor-Shine, and Brogden-Cronbach-Gleser utility models can provide useful planning information to help managers make better informed and wiser HR decisions.

Discussion Questions

1. Critique the classical validity approach to employee selection.
2. What is the difference between a moderator and a suppressor variable?
3. Describe the circumstances under which sequential selection strategies might be superior to single-stage strategies.
4. How might an expectancy chart be useful to a decision maker?
5. Cite two examples to illustrate how the selection ratio and base rate affect judgments about the usefulness of a predictor.

*   *   *

This chapter has dealt largely with statistical and conceptual issues in employee selection. Chapter 14 will consider available methods plus some of the very practical problems associated with selecting individuals whose responsibility is to manage the physical, capital, and human resources of an organization, namely, managers.

CHAPTER
14

MANAGERIAL SELECTION

AT A GLANCE

Managerial selection is a topic that deserves separate treatment because of the unique problems associated with describing the components of managerial effectiveness and developing behaviorally-based predictor measures to forecast managerial effectiveness accurately. A wide assortment of data collection techniques is currently available—cognitive ability tests, objective personality and interest inventories, leadership ability tests, projective devices, personal history data, and peer ratings—each demonstrating varying degrees of predictive success in particular situations.

More recently, emphasis has shifted to the development of situational tests or "work samples" of actual managerial behavior, such as the in-basket, the leaderless group discussion, and the business game. Situational tests have been well accepted because of their face and content validity, their flexibility, and their demonstrated ability to forecast success over a variety of managerial levels and in different organizational settings.

Both situational tests and paper-and-pencil tests can be integrated into one method—the assessment center. The assessment center is a behaviorally-based selection procedure that incorporates multiple assessments and multiple ratings by trained line managers of various behavioral dimensions that represent the job in question. The method is not free of problems, but it has proven reliable, valid, and fair to minority as well as non-minority candidates. These qualities probably account for its growing popularity as a managerial selection technique.

Although the *model* of predictive validity still serves as the guiding principle in managerial selection, the special problems associated with the choice of predictors, criterion measurements, and the many practical difficulties encountered in conducting rigorous research in this area deserve special emphasis. Results from several studies suggest that *different* abilities are necessary for success at the various levels within management (Fondas, 1992). Therefore, just as success in an entry-level position may reveal little of a predictive nature regarding success as a first-line supervisor (since the job requirements of the two positions are so radically different), success as a first-line supervisor may reveal little about success as a third- or fourth-level manager. In addition, since the organizational pyramid narrows considerably as we go up the managerial ladder, the *sample sizes* required for rigorous research are virtually impossible to obtain at higher managerial levels. Finally, applicant *preselection* poses problems with severe restriction of range. That is, the full range of abilities frequently is not represented since by the time applicants are considered for managerial positions, they already have been highly screened and, therefore, comprise a rather homogeneous group.

In view of these difficulties, it is appropriate to examine managerial selection in some detail. Hence, we shall first consider the criterion problem for managers; then, critically examine the various judgmental and statistical approaches to managerial selection, noting their advantages, disadvantages, and track records; and, finally, consider one approach, the assessment center, in more detail.

CRITERIA OF MANAGERIAL SUCCESS

Both objective and subjective indicators frequently are used to measure managerial effectiveness. Conceptually, effective management can be defined in terms of organizational outcomes. In particular, Campbell et al. (1970) view the effective manager as an *optimizer* who uses both internal and external resources (human, material, and financial) in order to sustain, over the long term, the unit for which the manager bears some degree of responsibility.

The primary emphasis in this definition is on managerial *actions or behaviors* judged relevant and important for optimizing resources. This judgment only can be rendered on rational grounds; therefore, informed, expert opinion is needed to specify the full range of managerial behaviors relevant to the conceptual criterion. The process begins with a careful specification of the total domain of the manager's job responsibilities (cf. Chapter 10), along with statements of critical behaviors believed necessary for the best use of available resources. The criterion measure itself must encompass a series of observations of the manager's actual job behavior by individuals capable of judging the manager's effectiveness in accomplishing all the things judged necessary, sufficient, and important for doing his or her job (Campbell et al., 1970). The overall aim is to determine psychologically meaningful dimensions of effective executive performance. It is only by knowing these that we can achieve a fuller understanding of the complex web of interrelationships existing between various types of job behaviors and organizational performance or outcome measures (e.g., promotion rates, productivity indexes).

Since many managerial prediction studies have used objective, global, or administrative criteria (e.g., Hinrichs, 1978; Ritchie and Moses, 1983), let us pause to examine them critically. First, the good news. Global measures, such as supervisory rankings of total managerial effectiveness, salary, or organizational level (statistically corrected for age or length of time in the organization) have several advantages. In the case of ranking, since each supervisor usually ranks no

more than about 10 subordinate managers, test-retest and inter-rater reliabilities tend to be high. In addition, such rankings probably encompass a broad sampling of behaviors over time, and the manager himself or herself probably is being judged rather than organizational factors beyond his or her control. Finally, the manager is compared directly to his or her peers; this standard of comparison is appropriate since all probably are responsible for optimizing similar amounts of resources.

On the other hand, overall measures or ratings of success include multiple factors (Dunnette, 1963b; Hanser, Arabian, and Wise, 1985). Hence, such measures often serve to obscure more than they reveal about the behavioral bases for managerial success. We cannot know with certainty what portion of a global rating or administrative criterion (such as level changes or salary) is based on actual job behaviors and what portion is due to other factors such as luck, education, "having a guardian angel at the top," political savvy, and so forth. Such measures suffer both from deficiency and contamination—that is, they measure only a small portion of the variance due to individual managerial behavior, and variations in these measures depend on many job-irrelevant factors that are not under the direct control of the manager.

In short, global or administrative criteria tell us where a manager *is* on the "success" continuum, but almost nothing about *how he or she got there.* Since behaviors relevant to managerial success change over time (Korman, 1968), as well as by purpose or function in relationship to the survival of the whole organization (Carroll and Gillen, 1987), the need is great to develop psychologically meaningful dimensions of managerial effectiveness in order to discover the linkages between managerial behavior patterns and managerial success.

What is required, of course, is a behaviorally-based performance measure that will permit a systematic recording of observations across the entire domain of desired managerial job behaviors (Campbell et al., 1970). Yet in practice, these requirements are honored more in the breach than in the observance. Potential sources of error and contamination are rampant (Tsui and Ohlott, 1988). These include inadequate sampling of the job behavior domain, lack of knowledge or lack of cooperation by the raters, differing expectations and perceptions of raters (peers, subordinates, and superiors), changes in the job or job environment, and changes in the manager's behavior (cf. Chapter 5). Fortunately, we now have available the scale development methods and training methodology to eliminate many of these sources of error, but the translation of such knowledge into everyday organizational practice is a slow, painstaking process.

In summarizing the managerial criterion problem, we hasten to point out that global estimates of managerial success certainly have proven useful in many validation studies (Meyer, 1987). However, they contribute little to our understanding of the wide varieties of job behaviors indicative of managerial effectiveness. For example, in industrial organizations, managers inevitably are judged by the profitability of their respective units, yet as Likert (1967) has demonstrated, there are many factors over and above the actions of the individual manager that affect the profit picture of his or her unit. While we are not advocating the abandonment of global criteria, consider supplementing them with systematic observations and recordings of behavior so that a richer, fuller understanding of the multiple paths to managerial success might emerge. It is also important to note that from the individual manager's perspective, the variables that lead to objective career success (e.g., pay, number of promotions) often are quite different from those that lead to subjective career success (job and career satisfaction). While ambition, along with the quality and quantity of education predict objective career success, accomplishments and organization success predict subjective career success (Judge et al., 1995).

Does Context Matter?

Management selection decisions take place in the context of both organizational (e.g., culture, technology, financial health) and environmental (e.g., internal and external labor markets, competition, legal requirements) conditions. Such contextual factors may explain differences in HR practices across organizations (Schuler and Jackson, 1989), and especially with respect to the selection of general managers (Guthrie and Olian, 1991). Thus under unstable industry conditions, knowledge and skills acquired over time in a single organization may be viewed as less relevant than diverse experience outside the organization. Conversely, a cost-leadership strategic orientation is associated with a tendency to recruit insiders who know the business and the organization. The lesson? There needs to be a fit between the kinds of attributes decision makers pay attention to in selection, the business strategy of the organization, and the environmental conditions in which it operates. Keep this in mind as

you read about the many selection methods described in this chapter.

APPROACHES TO MANAGERIAL SELECTION

Let us now approach the managerial selection problem from the prediction side. Following a taxonomy developed by Meehl (1954), we shall distinguish between methods of prediction and various types of instruments used. Predictions are *mechanical* (or statistical) if individuals are assessed on some instrument(s), if they are assigned scores based on that assessment, and if the scores subsequently are correlated with a criterion measure. Most ability tests, objective personality inventories, biographical data, and certain adaptations of the interview permit the assignment of scores for predictive purposes. Alternatively, predictions are *judgmental* or clinical if a set of scores or impressions must be combined subjectively in order to forecast criterion status. Assessment interviews and observations of behavior clearly fall within this category.

However, the dichotomy between judgmental and mechanical *prediction* (data combination) does not tell the whole story. Data *collection* also may be judgmental (i.e., the data collected differ from applicant to applicant at the discretion of the collector) or mechanical (i.e., rules are prespecified so that no subjective judgment need be involved). This leads to six different prediction strategies (see Table 14–1). It is important to maintain this additional distinction in order to ensure more informed or complete comparisons between judgmental and mechanical modes of measurement *and* prediction (Sawyer, 1966).

In the **pure clinical strategy,** data are collected *and* combined judgmentally. For example, predictions of success may be based solely on an interview conducted without using any objective information. Subsequently, the interviewer may write down his or her impressions and prediction in an open-ended fashion.

Alternatively, data may be collected judgmentally (e.g., via interview or observation). However, in combining the data, the decision maker summarizes his or her impression on a standardized rating form according to prespecified categories of behavior. This is **behavior,** or **trait, rating.**

Even if data are collected mechanically, however, they still may be combined judgmentally. For example, a candidate is given an objective personality inventory (e.g., the California Psychological Inven-

TABLE 14-1 Strategies of Data Collection and Combination

Mode of Data Collection	Mode of Data Combination	
	Judgmental	Mechanical
Judgmental	1. Pure clinical	2. Behavior trait rating
Mechanical	3. Profile	4. Pure statistical interpretation
Both	5. Clinical composite	6. Mechanical composite

Source: Adapted from J. Sawyer, Measurement *and* prediction, clinical *and* statistical. *Psychological Bulletin*, 1966, *66*, 178–200. Copyright 1966 by the American Psychological Association. Reprinted by permission.

tory), which, when scored, yields a pattern or "profile" of scores. Subsequently, a decision maker interprets the candidate's profile without ever having interviewed or observed him or her. This strategy is termed **profile interpretation.**

On the other hand, data may be collected *and* combined mechanically (e.g., by using statistical equations or scoring systems). This **pure statistical strrategy** frequently is used in the collection and interpretation of scorable application blanks, BIBs, or test batteries.

In the **clinical composite strategy,** data are collected *both* judgmentally (e.g., through interviews and observations) and mechanically (e.g., through tests and BIBs), but combined judgmentally. This is perhaps the most common managerial selection strategy, in which all information is integrated either by one or several decision makers to develop a composite picture and behavioral prediction of a candidate.

Finally, data may be collected judgmentally and mechanically but combined in a mechanical fashion (i.e., according to prespecified rules, such as a multiple regression equation) for deriving behavioral predictions from all available data. This is a **mechanical composite.**

Recognizing the several prediction strategies available, let us now consider the types of instruments most often used in making such predictions. Following this, we shall return to the classification scheme in Table 14–1 and examine the relative accuracy of the different strategies.

INSTRUMENTS OF PREDICTION

Cognitive Ability Tests

At the outset, it is important to distinguish once again between *tests* (which do have correct and incorrect answers) and *inventories* (which do not). In the case of

tests, the magnitude of the total score can be interpreted to indicate greater or lesser amounts of ability. In this category we consider, for example, measures of general intelligence; verbal, nonverbal, numerical and spatial relations ability; perceptual speed and accuracy; inductive reasoning; and mechanical knowledge and/or comprehension. Rather than review the voluminous studies available, we will summarize the findings of relevant reviews and report only the most relevant studies.

After reviewing hundreds of studies conducted between 1919 and 1972, Ghiselli (1966; 1973) reported that managerial success has been forecast most accurately by tests of general intellectual ability and general perceptual ability. (The correlations range between .25 and .30). However, when these correlations were corrected statistically for criterion unreliability and for range restriction, the validity of tests of general intellectual ability increased to .53 and those for general perceptual ability increased to .43 (Hunter and Hunter, 1984). The fact is, general cognitive ability is a powerful predictor of job performance (McHenry et al., 1990; Ree et al., 1994). It has a strong effect on job knowledge, and it contributes to individuals being given the *opportunity* to acquire supervisory experience (Borman et al., 1993).

Grimsley and Jarrett (1973, 1975) used a matched-group, concurrent-validity design to determine the extent to which cognitive ability test scores and self-description inventory scores obtained during preemployment assessment distinguished top from middle managers. They used a matched-group design in order to control two moderator variables (age and education), which they presumed to be related both to test performance and to managerial achievement. Hence, each of 50 top managers was paired with one of 50 middle managers, matched by age and field of undergraduate college education. Classification as a top or middle manager (the success criterion) was based on the level of managerial responsibility attained in any company by which the subject had been employed prior to assessment. This design also has another advantage: Contrary to the usual concurrent validity study, these data were not gathered under *research* conditions, but rather under *employment* conditions, from motivated job applicants.

Of the 10 mental ability measures used (those comprising the Employee Aptitude Survey), eight significantly distinguished the top from the middle manager group: verbal comprehension ($r = .18$), numerical ability ($r = .42$), visual speed and accuracy ($r = .41$), space visualization ($r = .31$), numerical reasoning ($r = .41$), verbal reasoning ($r = .48$), word fluency ($r = .37$), and symbolic reasoning ($r = .31$). In fact, a battery composed of just the verbal reasoning and numerical ability tests yielded a multiple R (statistically corrected for shrinkage) of .52. In comparison to male college students, for example, top and middle managers scored in the 98th and 95th percentiles, respectively, on verbal comprehension, and in the 85th and 59th percentiles, respectively, on numerical ability. These results support Ghiselli's (1963; 1973) earlier conclusion that differences in intellectual competence are related to the degree of managerial success at high levels of management. Grimsley and Jarrett (1973; 1975) also concluded that differences in test scores between top and middle managers were due to fundamental differences in cognitive ability and personality rather than to the influence of on-the-job experience.

Objective Personality and Interest Inventories

Reviews of results obtained with personality and interest measures in forecasting managerial effectiveness generally have been negative. For example, a meta-analysis of the validity of personality measures used in published research, spanning 62 validity coefficients and over 23,000 subjects, revealed an average validity of only .149 (Schmitt, Gooding, et al., 1984). A meta-analysis of studies using the Strong Interest Inventory found results that were not much more encouraging. The inventory did best when used to forecast promotion (average $r = .25$), and it did worst when used to forecast supervisors' ratings (average $r = .10$) (Hunter and Hunter, 1984).

However, at the time these studies were conducted, no well-accepted taxonomy existed for classifying personality traits. Today researchers generally agree that there are five robust factors of personality (the "Big Five") that can serve as a meaningful taxon-

omy for classifying personality attributes (Digman, 1990):

- *Extraversion*—being sociable, gregarious, assertive, talkative, and active
- *Emotional Stability*—being anxious, depressed, angry, embarrassed, emotional, worried, and insecure
- *Agreeableness*—being curious, flexible, trusting, good-natured, cooperative, forgiving, soft-hearted, and tolerant
- *Conscientiousness*—dependability (i.e., being careful, thorough, responsible, organized and planful), as well as hardworking, achievement-oriented, and persevering
- *Openness to Experience*—being imaginative, cultured, curious, original, broad-minded, intelligent, and artistically sensitive

Such a taxonomy makes it possible to determine if there exist consistent, meaningful relationships between particular personality constructs and job performance measures for different occupations. With respect to the prediction of success in management, Barrick and Mount's (1991) meta-analysis revealed the following average true correlations for the five dimensions: Extraversion (.18), Emotional Stability (.08), Agreeableness (.10), Conscientiousness (.22), and Openness to Experience (.08). For managerial jobs, therefore, Extraversion and Conscientiousness are the two best predictors of job performance. When only studies that are based on sound theoretical foundations are included, as opposed to purely empirical findings, a second meta-analysis by Tett, Jackson, and Rothstein (1991) found corrected mean validities for the "Big Five" factors that ranged from .16 for Extraversion to .33 for Agreeableness. The corrected estimate of the overall relation between personality and managerial job performance was .24. While technical factors may explain differences between the two meta-analyses (Ones et al., 1994; Tett et al., 1994), the combined results firmly support the use of personality scales in managerial selection.

One point is stressed consistently in all of the reviews, and we concur: There seems to be scant attention paid to the various situational and individual difference variables that may affect the predictability of managerial effectiveness. The actual behaviors that contribute to managerial success or failure have not been mapped out adequately. To be sure, they differ across hierarchical levels within management and across organizations. With respect to situational variables, Barrick and Mount (1993) found that the degree of autonomy in the managerial job moderates the validity of Conscientiousness, Extraversion, and Agreeableness (validity is higher for managers in jobs high in autonomy). Moreover, the use of face-valid, work-related items embedded in a work-related testing context provides a common frame of reference for all respondents. This tends to reduce error variance and to increase validity and utility (Schmit et al., 1995).

Frame of reference might also differ depending on a rater's perspective. Thus from the perspective of oneself, *personality* refers to the structures, dynamics, and processes inside a person that explain why he or she behaves in a particular way. From an observer's perspective, *personality* refers to a person's public self or social reputation (i.e., the way he or she is perceived by others, such as supervisors, co-workers, customers, friends, or family members) (Hogan, 1991). Not surprisingly, observer ratings (supervisor, co-worker, customer) of the Conscientiousness and Extraversion of 105 sales representatives predicted sales performance as well as self-ratings did. They also accounted for significant variance in the criterion beyond self-ratings alone for these two dimensions (Mount, Barrick, and Strauss, 1994).

With respect to theory-driven validation of personality measures, consider a study by Day and Silverman (1989). Using a true predictive validity design with no possibility of criterion contamination, they incorporated the Jackson Personality Research form as one predictor of success as an accountant. They hypothesized that three personality dimensions (orientation toward work, degree of ascendancy, and degree and quality of interpersonal orientation) would be related to important components of job performance, above and beyond the contribution of cognitive ability.

Work orientation was hypothesized to be important because accountants in the organization in question were required to work long hours and to complete projects on time, especially during peak months of the year. Ascendancy was hypothesized to be related negatively to performance because employees were expected to be cooperative, able to work easily with others, and deferential to partners. Interpersonal orientation was hypothesized to be especially important for those aspects of performance that require social interaction, such as client relations and cooperating with co-workers.

Results confirmed each of these hypotheses. Examining behavioral dimensions of job performance (rather than a global rating of performance) revealed that some of the highest correlations were found between personality-performance links that were theoretically most similar—such as interpersonal orientation and supervisory ratings of cooperation. In sum, choosing work-related personality measures on the basis of thorough job and organizational analyses is a fundamental element in the selection process.

In general, evidence now indicates that scores on well-developed measures of normal personality are: (1) stable over reasonably long periods of time, (2) predict important occupational outcomes, (3) do not discriminate unfairly against any ethnic or national group, (4) do not violate the terms of the Americans With Disabilities Act, and (5) should always be used in conjunction with other information designed to assess technical skills, job experience, and ability to learn (Hogan, Hogan, and Roberts, 1996).

Leadership Ability Tests

Logically one might expect measures of "leadership ability" to be more predictive of managerial success, since such measures should be directly relevant to managerial job requirements. Scales designed to measure two major constructs underlying managerial behavior, *consideration* and *initiating structure,* have been developed and used in many situations (Fleishman, 1973).

Consideration involves managerial acts oriented toward developing mutual trust, which reflects respect for subordinates' ideas and consideration of their feelings. High scores on consideration denote attitudes and opinions indicating good rapport and good two-way communication, whereas low scores indicate a more impersonal approach to interpersonal relations with group members (Fleishman and Peters, 1962).

Initiating structure reflects the extent to which an individual is likely to define and structure his or her own role and those of his or her subordinates toward goal attainment. High scores on initiating structure denote attitudes and opinions indicating highly active direction of group activities, group planning, communicating information, scheduling, trying out new ideas, and so forth.

Instruments designed to measure initiating structure and consideration (the Leadership Opinion Questionnaire, the Leader Behavior Description Questionnaire, and the Supervisory Behavior Description Questionnaire) have been in use for many years. However, evidence of their predictive validity has yet to be demonstrated, and the causal implications of initiating structure and consideration remain a mystery (Kerr and Schriesheim, 1974). Various other tests of practical judgment for supervisors or homemade management practices questionnaires have been similarly disappointing as predictors of managerial success.

Is it possible that our inability to predict the effects of hierarchical leader behaviors might be due to certain subordinate, task, or organizational characteristics that serve as "neutralizers of" or "substitutes for" hierarchical leader behaviors (Kerr and Jermier, 1978)? *Neutralizers* are variables in a leader's environment that effectively eliminate the impact of a leader's behavior on subordinate outcome variables, but do not replace the impact of such behavior with an effect of their own. *Substitutes* are special types of neutralizers that reduce a leader's ability to influence subordinates' attitudes and performance, and effectively replace the impact of a leader's behavior with one of their own. Potential neutralizers or substitutes include subordinate characteristics (e.g., their ability, experience, training, or knowledge), task characteristics (intrinsically satisfying tasks; routine, invariant tasks; task feedback), and organizational characteristics (e.g., rewards outside the leader's control, rule inflexibility, work group cohesiveness). Reliable, construct valid measures of such "Substitutes for Leadership Scales" are now available (Podsakoff and MacKenzie, 1994). If it were possible to identify factors that may moderate the effect of leader behaviors on subordinates' attitudes, behaviors, and perceptions, this would explain why some leader behaviors are effective in some situations but not in others. It is the task of future research to determine whether these sorts of moderating effects really do exist.

Projective Techniques

Let us first define our terms. According to Brown (1983):

> Projection refers to the process by which individuals' personality structure influences the ways in which they perceive, organize, and interpret their environment and experiences. When tasks or situations are highly structured their meaning usually is clear, as is the appropriate way to respond to the situation . . . projection can best be seen and measured when an individual encounters new and/or ambiguous stimuli, tasks, or situations. The implication for test construction is obvious: To study personality, one should present an individual with new and/or ambiguous stimuli and observe how he reacts and structures the situation. From his responses we can then make inferences concerning his personality structure [p. 419].

Kelly (1958) has expressed the issue concisely: An objective test is a test where the test taker tries to guess what the examiner is thinking, and a projective test is a test where the examiner tries to guess what the test taker is thinking!

In a critical review of the application of projective techniques in personnel psychology since 1940 (e.g., the Rorschach, the Thematic Apperception Test), Kinslinger (1966) concluded that the need exists "for thorough job specifications in terms of personality traits and extensive use of cross-validation studies before any practical use can be made of projective techniques in personnel psychology" (p. 134).

A more recent review reached similar conclusions. Across five studies, the average validity for projectives was only .18 (Reilly and Chao, 1982). It would be a mistake to conclude from this, however, that projectives should *never* be used, especially when they are scored in terms of dimensions relevant to "motivation to manage."

Motivation to Manage

One projective instrument that has shown potential for forecasting managerial success is the Miner Sentence Completion Scale (MSCS), a measure of motivation to manage.

The MSCS consists of 40 items, 35 of which are scored. The items form seven subscales (Authority Figures, Competitive Games, Competitive Situations, Assertive Role, Imposing Wishes, Standing Out from the Group, and Routine Administrative Functions). Definitions of these subscales are shown in Table 14–2. The central hypothesis is that there is a positive relationship between positive affect toward these areas and managerial success. Median MSCS subscale intercorrelations range from .11 to .15, and reliabilities in the .90s have been obtained repeatedly with experienced scorers (Miner, 1978a).

Validity coefficients for the MSCS have ranged as high as 0.69, and significant results have been reported in over 25 different studies (Miner, 1965; 1977; 1978a; 1978b; Miner and Smith, 1982). By any criterion used—promotion rates, grade level, choice of managerial career—more successful managers have tended to obtain higher scores, and managerial groups have scored higher on the MSCS than nonmanagerial groups (Miner and Crane, 1981).

Longitudinal data indicate that those with higher initial MSCS scores subsequently are promoted more rapidly in bureaucratic systems and that those with the

TABLE 14–2 Subscales of the Miner Sentence Completion Scale and Their Interpretation

Subscale	Interpretation of Positive Responses
Authority figures	A desire to meet managerial role requirements in terms of positive relationships with superiors.
Competitive games	A desire to engage in competition with peers involving games or sports and thus meet managerial role requirements in this regard.
Competitive situations	A desire to engage in competition with peers involving occupational or work-related activities and thus meet managerial role requirements in this regard.
Assertive role	A desire to behave in an active and assertive manner involving activities which in this society are often viewed as predominantly masculine, and thus to meet managerial role requirements.
Imposing wishes	A desire to tell others what to do and to use sanctions in influencing others, thus indicating a capacity to fulfill managerial role requirements in relationships with subordinates.
Standing out from group	A desire to assume a distinctive position of a unique and highly visible nature in a manner that is role-congruent for the managerial job.
Routine administrative functions	A desire to meet managerial role requirements regarding activities often associated with managerial work which are of a day-to-day administrative nature.

Source: J. B. Miner and N. R. Smith, Decline and stabilization of managerial motivation over a 20-year period. *Journal of Applied Psychology,* 1982, *67,* 298. Copyright 1982 by the American Psychological Association. Reprinted by permission of the author.

highest scores (especially on the subscales related to power, such as competing for resources, imposing wishes on others, and respect for authority) are likely to reach top-executive levels (Berman and Miner, 1985). In another study, 59 entrepreneurs completed the MSCS as they launched new business ventures. Five and a half years later, MSCS total scores predicted the performance of their firms (growth in number of employees, dollar volume of sales, and the entrepreneurs' yearly income) with validities in the high .40s (Miner, Smith, and Bracker, 1994). The consistency of these results is impressive, and since measures of intelligence are unrelated to scores on the MSCS, the MSCS can be a useful addition to a battery of management selection measures. Further, since the causal arrow seems to point from motivation to success, companies might be advised to include "motivation to manage" in their definitions of managerial success.

A somewhat different perspective on motivation to manage comes from a longitudinal study of the development of young managers in business. A three-and-one-half day assessment of young Bell System employees shortly after beginning their careers with the company included (among other assessment procedures) three projectives—two sentence-completion blanks and six cards from the Thematic Apperception Test (TAT) (Grant, Katkovsky, and Bray, 1967).

To determine the relative amount of influence of the projective ratings on staff judgments, the projective ratings were correlated with the assessment staff's overall prediction of each individual's management potential. The higher the correlations, the greater the influence of the projective reports on staff judgments. The ratings also were correlated with an index of salary progress shown by the candidates 7 to 9 years after the assessment. These results are presented separately for college and noncollege men in Table 14–3.

Although in general the correlations are modest, two points are worthy of note. First, the projective report variables correlating highest with staff predictions also correlate highest with management progress (i.e., the salary index). Second, motivational variables (e.g., achievement motivation, willingness to accept a leadership role) are related more closely to management progress than are more adjustment-oriented variables (e.g., optimism, general adjustment). In sum, these results suggest that projective techniques may yield useful predictions when they are interpreted according to motivations relevant to management (Grant et al., 1967).

The story does not end here, however. TAT responses for 237 managers who were still employed by the company were rescored 16 years later in terms of three motivational constructs: need for power, achievement, and affiliation (hereafter nPow, nAch, and nAff). In earlier work, McClelland and Burnham (1976) found that a distinctive motive pattern, termed the "Leadership Motive Pattern" (LMP), was related to success in management: moderate-to-high nPow, low nAff, and high activity inhibition (a constraint on the need to express power).

TABLE 14–3 Correlations of Projective Variables with Staff Judgments and Salary Progress

| | College Graduates | | Noncollege | |
| | Staff Prediction (N = 207) | Salary Progress (N = 81) | Staff Prediction (N = 148) | Salary Progress (N = 120) |
Projective Variable				
Optimism-Pessimism	.11	.01	.13	.17
General adjustment	.19	.10	.17	.19
Self-confidence	.24	.11	.29	.21
Affiliation	.07	.06	.15	.07
Work or career orientation	.21	.16	.22	.17
Leadership role	.35	.24	.38	.19
Dependence	.30	.35	.30	.23
Subordinate role	.25	.25	.29	.23
Achievement motivation	.30	.26	.40	.30

Source: D. L. Grant, W. Katkovsky, and D. W. Bray, Contributions of projective techniques to assessment of management potential. *Journal of Applied Psychology,* 1967, *51,* 226–231. Copyright 1967 by the American Psychological Association. Reprinted by permission of the author.

The theoretical explanation for the LMP is as follows. High nPow is important because it means the person is interested in the "influence game," in having an impact on others. Lower nAff is important because it enables a manager to make difficult decisions without worrying unduly about being disliked; and high self control is important because it means the person is likely to be concerned with maintaining organizational systems and following orderly procedures (McClelland, 1975).

When the rescored TAT responses were related to managerial job level 16 years later, the LMP clearly distinguished senior managers in nontechnical jobs from their less senior colleagues (McClelland and Boyatzis, 1982). In fact, progress in management after 8 and 16 years was highly correlated ($r = .75$), and the estimated correlation between the LMP and management progression was .33. This is impressive, considering all of the other factors (such as ability) that also might account for upward progression in a bureaucracy over a 16-year period.

High nAch was associated with success at lower levels of nontechnical management jobs, in which promotion depends more on individual contributions than it does at higher levels. This is consistent with the finding among first-line supervisors that nAff was related to performance and favorable subordinate attitudes, not need for power or the LMP (Cornelius and Lane, 1984). At higher levels, in which promotion depends on demonstrated ability to manage others, a high nAch is not associated with success.

Whereas high nAch seems not to be related to managerial success in a bureaucracy, it is strongly related to success as an entrepreneur (Boyatzis, 1982). As for technical managers, the LMP did not predict who was more or less likely to be promoted to higher levels of management in the company, but verbal fluency clearly did. These individuals were probably promoted for their technical competencies, among which was the ability to explain what they know. Considering these findings, along with those for the MSCS, one conclusion is that both the need for power and the willingness to exert power may be important for managerial success *only* in situations where technical expertise is not critical (Cornelius and Lane, 1984).

Two criticisms of the TAT are that it is subject to social desirability bias (Arnold and Feldman, 1981) and that it requires content analysis of each subject's written responses by a trained scorer. The Job Choice Exercise (JCE) was developed (Harrell and Stahl, 1981; Stahl and Harrell, 1982) to overcome these problems. The JCE requires a subject to make 24 decisions about the attractiveness of hypothetical jobs that are described in terms of criteria for nPow, nAch, and nAff (see Fig. 14–1).

Figure 14–1 contains one of the jobs from the JCE. The "Further Information" and "Decision B"

In this job, the likelihood that a major portion of your duties will involve —establishing and maintaining friendly relationships with others is...........................	VERY HIGH (95%)
—influencing the activities or thoughts of a number of individuals is.............................	VERY LOW (5%)
—accomplishing difficult (but feasible) goals and later receiving detailed information about your personal performance is........................	VERY HIGH (95%)

DECISION A. With the factors and associated likelihood levels shown above in mind, indicate the attractiveness of this job to you.

−5	−4	−3	−2	−1	0	+1	+2	+3	+4	+5
Very Unattractive										Very Attractive

FURTHER INFORMATION ABOUT JOB # 1. If you exert a great deal of effort to get this job, the likelihood that you will be successful is MEDIUM (50%).

DECISION B. With both the attractiveness and likelihood information presented above in mind, indicate the level of effort you would exert to get this job.

0	1	2	3	4	5	6	7	8	9	10
Zero effort to get it										Great effort to get it

Source: From M. J. Stahl and A. M. Harrell, Modeling effort decisions with behavioral decision theory: Toward an individual differences version of expectancy theory. *Organizational Behavior and Human Performance,* 1981, *27,* 303–325.

Figure 14-1 Sample Item from the Job Choice Exercise.

scales are fillers. To compute a score for each motive—nPow, nAch, and nAff—the Decision A values are regressed on the three criteria. Studies conducted with a variety of samples indicate that the JCE does, in fact, measure nPow, nAch, and nAff; that test-retest and internal consistency reliabilities range from .77 to .89; that these motives do distinguish managers from nonmanagers; that there are no differences between the sexes or races on the JCE; and that the JCE is not subject to social desirability bias. The JCE is self-administered and requires 15 to 20 minutes to complete. On top of that, it does not correlate significantly with the MSCS (Stahl, 1983; Stahl, Grigsby, and Gulati, 1985). In view of these results, the JCE merits closer attention as a research instrument and as a practical tool for selecting managers.

Personal History Data

Biographical information has been used widely in managerial selection—capitalizing on the simple fact that one of the best predictors of future behavior is past behavior. Unfortunately, as we have seen, the approach has been characterized more by raw empiricism than by theoretical formulation and rigorous testing of hypotheses. On the positive side, however, the items are nonthreatening and, therefore, are probably

not as subject to distortion as are typical personality inventories (Cascio, 1975).

One review found that across seven studies (total $N = 2,284$) where personal history data were used to forecast success in management, the average validity was a respectable .38. When used to predict sales success it was .50, and when used to predict success in science/engineering it was .41 (Reilly and Chao, 1982). Another study examined the relationship between college experiences and later managerial performance at AT&T (Howard, 1986). The choice of major (humanities, social science, business versus engineering) and extracurricular activities both validly forecast the interpersonal skills that are so critical to managerial behavior.

After reviewing the literature on actuarial studies of managerial success, Campbell et al. (1970) concluded:

What is impressive is that indicators of past successes and accomplishments can be utilized in an objective way to identify persons with differing odds of being successful over the long term in their management career. People who are already intelligent, mature, ambitious, energetic and responsible and who have a record of prior achievement when they enter an organization are in excellent positions to profit from training opportunities and from challenging organizational environments [p. 196].

Peer Assessment

In the typical peer assessment paradigm, raters are asked to predict how well a peer will do if placed in a leadership or managerial role. Such information can be enlightening, for peers typically draw on a different sample of behavioral interactions (i.e., those of an equal, non-supervisor-subordinate nature) in predicting future managerial success. Peer assessment is actually a general term for three more basic methods used by members of a well-defined group in judging each other's performance. **Peer nomination** requires each group member to designate (excluding himself or herself) a certain number of group members as being highest (lowest) on a particular dimension of performance (e.g., handling customers' problems). **Peer rating,** requires each group member to rate every other group member on several performance dimensions using, for example, some type of graphic rating scale. A final method, **peer ranking,** requires each group member to rank all the others from best to worst on one or more factors.

Reviews of over 50 studies relevant to all three methods of peer assessment (Kane and Lawler, 1978; 1980; Mumford, 1983; Schmitt, Gooding et al., 1984) found that all the methods showed adequate reliability, validity (average $r = .43$), and freedom from bias. However, the three methods appear to be applicable to somewhat different assessment needs. Peer nominations are most effective in discriminating persons with extreme (high or low) levels of knowledge, skills, or abilities from the other members of their groups. For example, peer nomination for best bet for top management responsibility correlated .32 with job advancement 5 to 10 years later (Shore et al., 1992). Peer rating is most effective in providing feedback, while peer ranking is probably best for discriminating throughout the entire range of performance on each dimension.

The reviews noted three other important issues in peer assessment:

1. *The influence of friendship.* It appears from the extensive research evidence available that effective performance probably causes friendship rather than the independent influence of friendship biasing judgments of performance. These results hold up even when peers know that their assessments will affect pay and promotion decisions.

2. *The need for cooperation in planning and design.* Peer assessments implicitly require people to consider privileged information about their peers in making their assessments. Thus they easily can infringe on areas that either will raise havoc with the group or cause resistance to making the assessments. To minimize any such adverse consequences, it is imperative that groups be intimately involved in the planning and design of the peer assessment method to be used.

3. *The required length of peer interaction.* It appears that the validity of peer nominations for predicting leadership performance develops very early in the life of a group and reaches a plateau after no more than 3 weeks for intensive groups. Useful validity develops in only a matter of days. Thus, peer nominations possibly could be used in assessment centers to identify managerial talent if the competitive atmosphere of such a context does not prove to induce excessive bias. We hasten to add, however, that in situations where peers do not interact intensively on a daily basis (e.g., life insurance agents), peer ratings are unlikely to be effective predictors for individuals with less than 6 months' experience (Mayfield, 1970; 1972).

In summary, peer assessments have considerable potential as effective predictors of managerial success, and Mumford (1983) and Lewin and Zwany (1976) have provided integrative models for future research. To be sure, as Kraut (1975) noted, the use of peer ratings among managers may merely formalize a process in which managers already engage informally.

WORK SAMPLES OF MANAGERIAL PERFORMANCE

In the classic validity model, tests typically are used as signs or indicators of predispositions to behave in certain ways rather than as samples of the characteristic behavior of individuals (Cronbach, 1990). Wernimont and Campbell (1968) have argued persuasively, however, that prediction efforts are likely to be much more fruitful if we focus on meaningful samples of behavior, rather than on signs or predispositions. Since selection measures are really surrogates or substitutes for criteria, we should be trying to obtain measures that are as similar to criteria as possible. Criteria also must be measures of behavior. Hence, it makes little sense to use a behavior sample to predict an administrative criterion (promotion, salary level, etc.) since the individual frequently does not exercise a great deal of control over such organizational outcome variables. In order to understand more fully individual behavior in organizations, work-sample measures must be related to observable job-behavior measures. Only then will we understand exactly how, and to what extent, an individual has influenced his or her success. This argument is not new (cf. Campbell et al., 1970; Dunnette, 1963; Smith and Kendall, 1963), but it deserves reemphasis.

Particularly with managers, effectiveness is likely to result from an *interaction* of individual and situational or context variables, for as we noted earlier, the effective manager is an optimizer of all the resources available to him or her. It follows, then, that a situational test or work sample whose objective is to assess the ability to do rather than the ability to know should be a more representative measure of the real life complexity of managerial jobs. In situational tests (Flanagan, 1954a):

> Situations are selected to be typical of those in which the individual's performance is to be predicted . . . [Each] situation is made sufficiently complex that it is very difficult for the persons tested to know which of their reactions are being scored and for what variables. There seems to be much informal evidence (face validity) that the person tested behaves spontaneously and naturally in these situations. . . . It is hoped that the naturalness of the situations results in more valid and typical responses than are obtained from other approaches [p. 462].

These ideas have been put into theoretical form by Asher (1972), who hypothesized that the greater the degree of point-to-point correspondence between predictor elements and criterion elements, the higher the validity. By this rationale, work sample tests that are miniature replicas of specific criterion behavior should have point-to-point relationships with the criterion. This hypothesis received strong support in a meta-analytic review of the validity of work sample tests (Schmitt, Gooding, et al., 1984). In fact, when work samples are used as a basis for promotion, their average validity is .54 (Hunter and Hunter, 1984). High validity, cost-effectiveness (Cascio and Phillips, 1979), and substantially reduced adverse impact (Brugnoli, Campion, and Basen, 1979; Schmidt et al., 1977) make work sampling an especially attractive approach to staffing. Although the development of "good" work samples is time-consuming and can be quite difficult (cf. Plumlee, 1980), monetary and social payoffs from their use may well justify the effort.

In the context of managerial selection, two types of situational tests commonly are used. In **group exercises** participants are placed in a situation in which the successful completion of a task requires interaction among the participants. In **individual exercises** participants complete a task independently. We shall discuss

three of the most popular situational tests: the Leaderless Group Discussion, the In-Basket Test, and the Business Game.

Leaderless Group Discussion (LGD)

The LGD is a disarmingly simple technique. A group of participants simply is asked to carry on a discussion about some topic for a period of time (Bass, 1954). Of course, face validity is enhanced if the discussion is about a job-related topic. No one is appointed leader. Raters do not participate in the discussion, but remain free to observe and rate the performance of each participant. For example, IBM uses an LGD in which each participant is required to make a 5-minute oral presentation of a candidate for promotion and then subsequently defend his or her candidate in a group discussion with five other participants. All roles are well-defined and structured. Seven characteristics are rated, each on a five-point scale of effectiveness: aggressiveness, persuasiveness or selling ability, oral communications, self-confidence, resistance to stress, energy level, and interpersonal contact (Wollowick and McNamara, 1969).

Reliability. Inter-rater reliabilities of the LGD generally are reasonable, averaging .83 (Bass, 1954; Tziner and Dolan, 1982). Test-retest reliabilities of .72 (median of seven studies, Bass, 1954) and .62 (Petty, 1974) have been reported. Reliabilities are likely to be enhanced, however, to the extent that LGD behaviors simply are described rather than evaluated in terms of presumed underlying personality characteristics (Bass, 1954; Flanagan, 1954a).

Validity. In terms of *job performance*, Bass (1954) reported a median correlation of .38 between LGD ratings and performance ratings of student leaders, shipyard foremen, administrative trainees, foreign service administrators, civil service administrators, and oil refinery supervisors. In terms of *training performance,* Tziner and Dolan (1982) reported an LGD validity of .24 for female officer candidates; in terms of ratings of 5-year and career *potential*, Turnage and Muchinsky (1984) found LGD validities in the low .20s; and in terms of changes in position level 3 years following the LGD, Wollowick and McNamara (1969) reported a predictive validity of 0.25. Finally, since peer ratings in the LGD correlate close to .90 or higher with observers' ratings (Kaess, Witryol, and Nolan, 1961), it is possible to administer the LGD to a large group of candidates, divide them into small groups, and have them rate each other. Gleason (1957) used such a peer rating procedure with military trainees and found that reliability and validity held up as well as when independent observers were used.

EFFECTS OF TRAINING AND EXPERIENCE. Petty (1974) showed that although LGD experience did not significantly affect performance ratings, previous training did. Individuals who received a 15-minute briefing on the history, development, rating instruments, and research relative to the LGD were rated significantly higher than untrained individuals. Kurecka et al. (1982) found similar results and showed that the training effect accounted for as much as 25 percent of criterion variance. To control for this, either all individuals trained in the LGD can be put into the same group(s) or else the effects of training can be held constant statistically. One or both of these strategies are called for in order to interpret results meaningfully and fairly.

The In-Basket Test

This is an individual situational test designed to simulate important aspects of the manager's position. Hence, different types of in-basket tests may be designed, corresponding to the different requirements of various levels of managerial jobs. The first step in in-basket development is to determine what aspects of the managerial job to measure. For example, in assessing candidates for middle-manager positions, IBM determined that the following characteristics important for middle-management success should be rated in the in-basket simulation: oral communications, planning and organizing, self-confidence, written communications, decision making, risk taking, and administrative ability (Wollowick and McNamara, 1969). On the basis of this information, problems then are created that encompass the kinds of issues the candidate is likely to face, should he or she be accepted for the job.

In general, an in-basket simulation takes the following form (Fredericksen, 1962):

It consists of the letters, memoranda, notes of incoming telephone calls, and other materials which have supposedly collected in the in-basket of an administrative officer. The subject who takes the test is given appropriate background information concerning the school, business, military unit, or whatever institution is involved. He is told that he is the new incumbent of the administrative position, and that he is to deal with the material in the in-basket. The background infor-

mation is sufficiently detailed that the subject can reasonably be expected to take action on many of the problems presented by the in-basket documents. The subject is instructed that he is not to play a role, he is not to pretend to be someone else. He is to bring to the new job his own background of knowledge and experience, his own personality, and he is to deal with the problems as though he were really the incumbent of the administrative position. He is not to say what he would do; he is actually to write letters and memoranda, prepare agenda for meetings, make notes and reminders for himself, as though he were actually on the job [p. 1].

Although the situation is relatively unstructured for the candidate, each candidate faces exactly the same complex set of problem situations. At the conclusion of the in-basket test, each candidate leaves behind a packet full of notes, memos, letters, and so on, which constitute the record of his behavior. The test then is scored (by describing, not evaluating, what the candidate did) in terms of the job-relevant characteristics enumerated at the outset. This is the major asset of the in-basket: It permits *direct* observation of individual behavior within the context of a highly job-relevant, yet standardized, problem situation.

In addition to high face validity, the in-basket also discriminates well. For example, in a middle-management training program AT&T compared the responses of management trainees to those of experienced managers (Lopez, 1966). In contrast to experienced managers, the trainees were wordier; they were less likely to take action on the basis of the importance of the problem; they saw fewer implications for the organization as a whole in the problems; they tended to make final (as opposed to investigatory) decisions and actions more frequently; they tended to resort to complete delegation, whereas experienced executives delegated with some element of control; and they were far less considerate of others than the executives were. The managers' approaches to dealing with in-basket materials later served as the basis for discussing the "appropriate" ways of dealing with such problems.

In-basket performance does predict success in training, with correlations ranging from .18 to .36 (Borman, 1982; Borman et al., 1983; Tziner and Dolan, 1982). The crucial question, of course, is that of predictive validity. Does behavior during the in-basket simulation reflect actual job behavior? Results are mixed. Turnage and Muchinsky (1984) found that while in-basket scores did forecast ratings of five-year and career potential (*rs* of 0.19 and 0.25), they did not predict job performance rankings or appraisals. On the other hand, Wollowick and McNamara (1969) reported a .32 predictive validity between in-basket scores and changes in position level for 94 middle managers 3 years later, and in a concurrent study, Brass and Oldham (1976) reported significant validities that ranged from .24 to .34 between four in-basket scoring dimensions and a composite measure of supervisory effectiveness. Moreover, since the LGD and the in-basket test share only about 20 percent of variance in common (Tziner and Dolan, 1982), in combination they are potentially powerful predictors of managerial success.

The Business Game

The business game is a "live" case. For example, in the assessment of candidates for jobs as Army recruiters, two exercises required subjects to make phone calls to assessors who role-played two different prospective recruits and then to meet for follow-up interviews with these role-playing assessors. One of the cold-call/interview exercises was with a prospective recruit unwilling to consider Army enlistment, and the other was a prospect more willing to consider joining. These two exercises predicted success in recruiter training with validities of .25 and .26 (Borman et al., 1983). A desirable feature of the business game is that intelligence, as measured by cognitive ability tests, seems to have no effect on the success of players (Dill, 1972).

A variation of the business game focuses on the effects of measuring "cognitive complexity" on managerial performance. Cognitive complexity is concerned with "how" persons think and behave. It is independent of the content of executive thought and action, and it reflects a style that is difficult to assess with paper-and-pencil instruments (Streufert, Pogash, and Piasecki 1988). Using computer-based simulations, participants assume a managerial role (e.g., county disaster-control coordinator, temporary governor of a developing country) for six one-hour task periods. The simulations present a managerial task environment that is best dealt with via a number of diverse managerial activities, including preventive action, use of strategy, planning, use and timeliness of responsive action, information search, and use of opportunism. Streufert et al. (1988) reported validities as high as .50 to .67 between objective performance measures (computer-scored simulation results) and self-reported indicators of success (a corrected measure of income at age, job level at age, number of persons supervised, and number of promotions during the last 10 years). Although the self-reports may have been subject to some self-enhancing bias, these results are sufficiently promising to warrant further investigation. Because such simulations focus on the structural style of thought and action, rather than on content and interpersonal functioning, as in assessment centers (see below), the two methods in combination may account for more variance in managerial performance than is currently the case.

Individual Assessments

Individual assessment involves one psychologist making an evaluation of an individual for purposes of HR decision making (Ryan and Sackett, 1989). Survey results show that it is a common activity among I/O psychologists, particularly for the hiring, promotion, and development of middle- and upper-level managers (Ryan and Sackett, 1987).

In making their assessments, psychologists rely heavily on four types of instruments: personal history forms, ability tests, personality and interest inventories, and interviews. The personal history form is used most often as a basis for interview questions and for additional information, *not* as a scored instrument. The following eight dimensions of behavior are assessed most often: interpersonal skills, judgment/analytical skills, organization and planning, intelligence, supervisory skills, emotional maturity, leadership, and energy/drive.

In terms of prediction strategies used, it appears that the pure statistical approach is used very infrequently, while the pure clinical and clinical composite approaches are most popular (Ryan and Sackett, 1987). Feedback is typically given orally and includes a narrative description of the individual's strengths, developmental needs, and suggestions for development. Unfortunately, however, it appears that only slightly more than one in four practitioners consistently use follow-up studies to evaluate the effectiveness of the assessment practices they use.

In a laboratory study, Ryan and Sackett (1989) found large disagreements among raters, particularly in terms of which candidates to recommend for jobs and in identifying specific strengths and weaknesses among the candidates. These results highlight both the inexactness of assessment and prediction, as well as the need for more standardization and thorough job

---

HOW MICROSOFT FINDS TOP TALENT

Ask Microsoft Chairman Bill Gates what the most important thing he did last year was, and he answers, "I hired a lot of smart people" ("How Microsoft," 1992). That doesn't just happen. The No. 1 maker of PC software visited 137 campuses last year, reviewed 120,000 résumés, conducted face-to-face interviews with 7,400 candidates—to hire 2,000 people. Those invited to headquarters in Redmond, Washington, spend a day being interviewed by at least four staffers from different parts of the organization. Among other questions, candidates are asked such off-the-wall brain teasers as: if you were to put artificial turf on all the major league ballfields, how many square yards would you need? If you were a product, how would you position yourself? Says one high-level manager: "They don't have to get the right answer. But I want to see how they go through the process. If they're good, I make the game harder" (p. 65).

---

analyses as bases for the prediction instruments chosen and the dimensions assessed.

EFFECTIVENESS OF ALTERNATIVE PREDICTION STRATEGIES

Let us now consider results reported by Sawyer (1966) in his comparison of judgmental and mechanical strategies of data collection and combination. Sawyer (1966) uncovered 49 comparisons in 45 studies of the relative efficiency of two or more of the different methods of combining assessments. He then compared the predictive accuracies (expressed either as the percentage correct classifications or as a correlation coefficient) yielded by the two strategies involved in each comparison. Two strategies were called equal when they failed to show an accuracy difference significant at the .05 level or better. As can be seen in Table 14–4, the pure clinical method was never superior to other methods with which it was compared, while the pure statistical and mechanical composite were never inferior to other methods. In short, the mechanical methods of combining predictors were superior to the judgmental methods *regardless* of the method used to collect predictor information.

There are several plausible reasons for the relative superiority of mechanical prediction strategies (Bass and Barrett, 1981; Hitt and Barr, 1989). First, accuracy of prediction may depend on appropriate weighting of predictors (which is virtually impossible to judge accurately). Second, mechanical methods can continue to incorporate additional evidence on candidates and thereby improve predictive accuracy. However, an interviewer is likely to reach a plateau beyond which he or she will be unable to continue to make

TABLE 14–4 Comparisons Among Methods of Combining Data				
		Percentage of Comparisons in Which Method Was		
Method	*Number of Comparisons*	*Superior*	*Equal*	*Inferior*
Pure clinical	8	0	50	50
Behavior rating	12	8	76	16
Profile interpretation	12	0	75	25
Pure statistical	32	31	69	0
Clinical composite	24	0	63	37
Mechanical composite	10	60	40	0

Source: J. Sawyer, Measurement *and* prediction, clinical *and* statistical. *Psychological Bulletin.* 1966, *66,* 178–200. Copyright 1966 by the American Psychological Association. Reprinted by permission of the author.

modifications in judgments as new evidence accumulates (cf. Bartlett and Green, 1966). Finally, in contrast to more objective methods, an interviewer or judge needs to guard against his or her own needs, response set, and wishes, lest they contaminate the accuracy of his or her subjective combination of information about the applicant.

What, then, is the proper role for subjective judgment? Sawyer's (1966) results suggest that judgmental methods should be used to complement mechanical methods (since they do provide rich samples of behavioral information) in collecting information about managers, but that mechanical procedures should be used to formulate optimal prediction rules. As can be seen in Table 14–4, the best strategy of all (in that it always has proven either equal to or better than competing strategies) is the mechanical composite in which information is collected *both* by mechanical and by judgmental methods but is combined mechanically.

ASSESSMENT CENTERS

The assessment center (AC) is a method, not a place. It brings together many of the instruments and techniques of managerial selection that we have been discussing in a piecemeal fashion up to this point. Using multiple assessment techniques, standardizing methods of making inferences from such techniques, and pooling the judgments of multiple assessors in rating each candidate's behavior enhances the likelihood of successfully predicting future performance considerably (Cronbach, 1990; Taft, 1959). Additional research (Byham, 1986; Schmitt, Gooding, et al., 1984; Gaugler et al., 1987) supports this hypothesis. Candidate perceptions of AC exercises as highly job-related is another advantage, for it enhances legal defensibility and organizational attractiveness (Smither et al., 1993).

Multiple assessment procedures were used first by German military psychologists during World War II. They felt that paper-and-pencil tests took too "atomistic" a view of human nature; therefore, they chose to observe a candidate's behavior in a complex situation to arrive at a "holistic" appraisal of his reactions. Building upon this work and that of the War Office Selection Board of the British Army in the early 1940s, the U.S. Office of Strategic Services used the method to select spies during World War II. Each candidate had to develop a cover story that would hide his identity during the assessment. Testing for the ability to maintain cover was crucial, and ingenious situational tests were designed to seduce candidates into breaking cover (McKinnon, 1975; OSS, 1948).

The first industrial firm to adopt this approach was AT&T in 1956 in its Management Progress Study. This longitudinal study is the largest and most comprehensive investigation of managerial career development ever undertaken. Its purpose is to attempt to understand what characteristics (cognitive, motivational, and attitudinal) are important to the career progress of young employees from the time they take their first job in the Bell system and as they continue to move into middle- and upper-management levels (Bray, Campbell, and Grant, 1974). The original sample ($N = 422$) was composed of 274 college men and 148 noncollege men assessed over several summers from 1956 to 1960. In 1965, 174 of the college men and 145 of the noncollege men still were employed with the company.

Each year (between 1956 and 1965) data were collected from the men's companies (e.g., interview with departmental colleagues, supervisors, former bosses), as well as from the men themselves (e.g., interviews, questionnaires of attitudes and expectations) to determine their progress. No information about any man's performance during assessment ever has been given to company officials. There has been no contamination of subsequent criterion data by the assessment results, and staff evaluations have had no influence on the careers of the men being studied.

Predictive Validity

By July 1965, information was available on the career progress of 125 college men and 144 noncollege men originally assessed. The criterion data included management level achieved and current salary. The predictive validities of the assessment staff's global predictions were .44 for college men and .71 for noncollege men. Of the 38 college men who were promoted to middle-management positions, 31 (82%) were identified correctly by the AC staff. Likewise 15 (75%) of the 20 noncollege men who were promoted into middle management were identified correctly. Finally, of the 72 men (both college and noncollege) who were not promoted, the AC staff correctly identified 68 (94%).

Researchers conducted a second assessment of these men 8 years after the first, and they followed the advancement of the participants over the ensuing years (Bray and Howard, 1983). Results of the two sets of

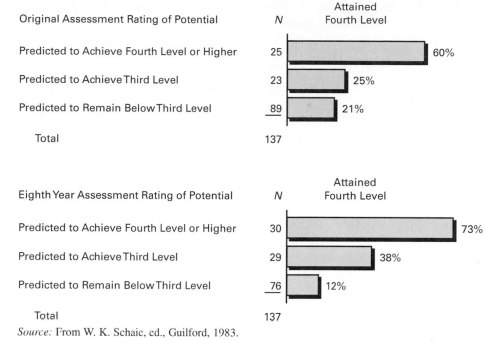

Source: From W. K. Schaie, ed., Guilford, 1983.

Figure 14–2 Ratings at Original Assessment and Eight Years Later, and Management Level Attained at Year 20. D. W. Bray and A. Howard, *Longitudinal studies of adult psychological development.*

predictions in forecasting movement over a 20-year period through the 7-level management hierarchy found in Bell operating companies are shown in Figure 14–2.

These results are impressive—so impressive that operational use of the method has spread rapidly. Currently, several thousand business, government, and nonprofit organizations worldwide use the AC method to improve the accuracy of their managerial selection decisions, to help determine individual training and development needs, and to facilitate more accurate HR planning. In view of the tremendous popularity of this approach, we will examine several aspects of AC operation (level, length, size, staff, etc.) as well as some of the research on its validity.

Level of Assessment

Since the pioneering studies by Bray and his associates at AT&T, new applications of the AC method have multiplied almost every year. There is no one best way to structure a center, and the specific design, content, administration, and cost of centers fluctuate with the target group as well as with the objectives of the center. Some firms combine assessment with training so that once development needs have been identified through the assessment process, training can be initi-

ated immediately to capitalize on employee motivation. Reviews of the predominantly successful applications of AC methodology (cf. Klimoski and Brickner, 1987) underscore the flexibility of the method and its potential for evaluating success in many different occupations.

Since it is difficult to determine supervisory skills in most nonmanagement jobs, the most common use of ACs is the identification of potential for first-level supervision (Byham, 1986). With growing regularity, however, the method is being used at higher levels of management. Here, centers focus on stimulating self-development and career planning through heightened self-knowledge. Top-level assessment focuses on long-range planning, organization design, and larger societal issues. For example, candidates for senior executive positions frequently are evaluated in simulated press conferences (Byham, 1986).

Length and Size

The length of the center typically varies with the level of candidate assessment. Centers for first-level supervisory positions often last only 1 day, while middle- and higher-management centers may last 2 or 3 days. When assessment is combined with training activities, the program may run 5 or 6 days. At present, almost all organizations that use AC methodology for selection or promotion also use it to diagnose training needs.

However, a major change in the last 15 years is the large number of firms that use AC methodology *solely* to diagnose training needs (Byham, 1971; 1986). Even in a 2-day center, however, assessors usually spend 2 additional days comparing their observations and making a final evaluation of each candidate. While some centers process only six people at a time, most process about 12. The ratio of assessors to participants also varies from about 3-to-1 to 1-to-1 (Gaugler et al., 1987).

Assessors and Their Training

Some organizations mix line managers with HR department or other staff members as assessors. Few use professional psychologists as assessors, yet cumulative evidence indicates that AC validities are higher when assessors are psychologists rather than line managers (Gaugler et al., 1987).

Substantial increases in reliabilities can be obtained as a result of training observers. In one study, for example, mean inter-rater reliabilities for untrained observers were .46 on a human relations dimension and .58 on an administrative-technical dimension. For the trained observers, however, reliabilities were .78 and .90, respectively (Richards and Jaffee, 1972). Assessors usually are trained in interviewing and feedback techniques, behavior observation, and evaluation of in-basket performance. In addition, the assessors usually go through the exercises as participants before rating others. Training may take from 2 days to several weeks depending upon the complexity of the center, the importance of the assessment decision, and the importance management attaches to assessor training.

Such variability in assessor training has led to calls for more standardization, which should include:

1. An analysis of assessor behavior;
2. The development of dimensions by which to measure assessment performance;
3. The development of training techniques to stimulate assessor behavior;
4. A method of evaluating assessor performance or competency.

Performance Feedback

The performance feedback process is crucial. Most organizations emphasize to candidates that the AC is only one portion of the assessment process. It is sim-

ply a supplement to other performance appraisal information (both supervisory and objective), and each candidate has an opportunity on the job to refute any negative insights gained from assessment. Empirically, this has been demonstrated to be the case (London and Stumpf, 1983).

What about the candidate who does poorly at the center? Organizations are justifiably concerned that turnover rates among the members of this group—many of whom represent substantial investments by the company in experience and technical expertise—will be high. Fortunately, it appears that this is not the case. Kraut and Scott (1972) reviewed the career progress of 1,086 nonmanagement candidates who had been observed at an IBM AC 1 to 6 years previously. Analysis of separation rates indicated that the proportions of low- and high-rated employees who left the company did not differ significantly.

Reliability of the Assessment Process

Inter-rater reliabilities vary across studies from a median of about .60 to over .95 (Adams and Thornton, 1989; Schmitt, 1977). Thus raters tend to appraise similar aspects of performance in candidates. In terms of temporal stability, an important question concerns the extent to which dimension ratings made by individual assessors change over time (i.e., in the course of a 6-month assignment as an assessor). Evidence on this issue was provided by Sackett and Hakel (1979), as a result of a large-scale study of 719 individuals assessed by four assessor teams at AT&T. Mean inter-rater reliabilities across teams varied from .53 to .86, with an overall mean of .69. In addition to generally high stability, there was no evidence for stable changes in assessors' or assessor teams' pattern of ratings over time.

In practice, therefore, it makes little difference whether an individual is assessed during the first or sixth month that an assessor team is working together. Despite individual differences among assessors, patterns of information usage were very similar across team consensus ratings. Thus, this study provides empirical support for one of the fundamental underpinnings of the AC method—the use of multiple assessors to offset individual biases, errors of observation or interpretation, and unreliability of individual ratings.

Standardizing an AC program so that each candidate receives relatively the same treatment is essential so that differences in performance can be attributed to differences in candidates' abilities and skills, and not to extraneous factors. Standardization concerns include, for example:

- *Exercise instructions*—provide the same information in the same manner to all candidates;
- *Time limits*—maintain them consistently to equalize opportunities for candidates to perform;
- *Assigned roles*—design and pilot test them to avoid inherently advantageous or disadvantageous positions for candidates;
- *Assessor/candidate acquaintance*—minimize it to keep biases due to previous exposure from affecting evaluations;
- *Assessor consensus discussion session*—conduct it similarly for each candidate;
- *Exercise presentation order*—use the same order so that order effects do not contaminate candidate performance.

Validity and Fairness

Applicants tend to view ACs as more face valid than cognitive ability tests, and, as a result, to be more satisfied with the selection process, the job, and the organization (Macan et al., 1994). Reviews of the predictive validity of AC ratings and subsequent promotion and performance generally have been positive. Over all types of criteria, and over 50 studies containing 107 validity coefficients, meta-analysis indicates an average validity for ACs of .37, with lower and upper bounds on the 95 percent confidence interval of .11 and .63, respectively (Gaugler et al., 1987). Yet research indicates also that AC ratings are not equally effective predictors of all types of criteria. For example, Gaugler et al. (1987) found median corrected correlations (corrected for sampling error, range restriction, and criterion unreliability) of .53 for predicting potential, but only .36 for predicting supervisors' ratings of performance.

The selection fairness of the AC method also has been demonstrated. In an extensive and well-controlled study, Huck and Bray (1976) investigated the determinants of assessment ratings for white and African-American females, as well as the relationship of the assessment dimensions to performance effectiveness 1 to 6 years after assessment. Results were extremely similar for both groups. The predictive validities of the assessment ratings and subsequent job performance ratings were .41 (whites) and .35 (African-Americans), and the predictive validities of

assessment ratings and subsequent ratings of potential for advancement were .59 (whites) and .54 (African-Americans). Regression equations for the two groups did not differ significantly. In short, African-Americans should not be assessed any differently from whites.

In a study of 4,846 women assessed at AT&T between 1963 and 1971, Moses and Boehm (1975) showed that the distribution of assessment ratings as well as the dimensions relating most strongly to subsequent management level (overall ratings, leadership, decision making, and organizing and planning) were the same for men and women. In a follow-up study, Ritchie and Moses (1983) found that AC predictions of the potential of 1,097 women managers were significantly related ($r = .42$) to their career progress 7 years later. In addition, specific dimension ratings assigned to the women were compared to those previously assigned to men in the Management Progress Study. Both were similar. These results indicate that the skills needed for a woman to advance in management are essentially the same as those needed by a man. Differences in management potential are far more likely to be attributable to differences in individuals rather than to differences in gender. Despite these encouraging findings, salary progression and geographical mobility still favor men over similarly-situated women (Stroh, Brett, and Reilly, 1992). To deal with this, firms should rely on uniform promotional processes, make promotional procedures well known to all potential applicants, and increase the accountability of decision makers (Powell and Butterfield, 1994). Managers—male or female—who want to move up should do five things well: (1) get assigned to high-visibility projects, (2) demonstrate critical skills for effective job performance, (3) attract top-level support, (4) display entrepreneurial initiative, and (5) accurately identify what the company values (Mainiero, 1994).

One final point concerning AC predictive validity studies deserves reemphasis. Assessment procedures are behaviorally-based; yet again and again they are related to organizational outcome variables (e.g., salary growth, promotion) that are all complexly determined. In order to achieve a fuller understanding of the assessment process and of exactly what aspects of managerial job behavior each assessment dimension is capable of predicting, assessment dimensions must be related to behaviorally-based, multiple criteria. Only then can we develop comprehensive psychological theories of managerial effectiveness.

Assessment Center Utility

In a field study of 600 first-level managers, Cascio and Ramos (1986) compared the utility of AC predictions to those generated from multiple interviews. Using the general utility equation (Eq. 13–5), they confirmed the findings of an earlier study (Cascio and Silbey, 1979), namely, that the cost of the procedure is incidental compared to the possible losses associated with promotion of the wrong person into a management job. Given large individual differences in job performance, use of a more valid procedure has a substantial bottom-line impact. Use of the AC to select managers instead of the multiple interview procedure resulted in an improvement in job performance of about $4,000 per year per manager (in 1997 dollars). If the average manager stays at first level for 5 years, then the net payoff per manager is over $19,000 (in 1997 dollars).

Potential Problems

A growing concern in the use of ACs is that assessment procedures may be applied carelessly or improperly. For example, content-related evidence of validity is frequently used to establish the job-relatedness of ACs. Yet as Sackett (1987) has pointed out, such a demonstration requires more than the careful construction of exercises and identification of dimensions to be rated. *How* the stimulus materials are presented to candidates (including response options) and *how* candidate responses are evaluated are also critical considerations in making judgments about content-related evidence of validity. For example, requiring candidates to write out responses to an exercise would be inappropriate if the job requires verbal responses.

Moreover, several studies (Bycio et al., 1987; Gaugler and Rudolph, 1992; Gaugler and Thornton, 1989) have shown that assessors have a limited capacity to process information and that the more complex the judgment task, the more it will be prone to cognitive biases, such as contrast effects. Thus developers of ACs should limit the cognitive demands placed on assessors, perhaps by restricting the number of dimensions that assessors are required to process. Assess broad rather than narrow qualities (e.g., interpersonal skills versus behavior flexibility).

A second potential problem, raised by Klimoski and Strickland (1977), is that a subtle criterion contamination phenomenon may inflate assessment validities when global ratings or other summary measures of effectiveness are used as criteria (e.g. salary, management level reached). This inflation will occur to the extent that assessors, supervisors, and upper-level managers share similar stereotypes of an effective manager. Hence it is possible that assessors' ratings on the various dimensions are tied closely to actual performance at the AC, but that ratings of overall potential may include a bias, either implicitly or explicitly, that enters into their judgments. Behaviorly-based ratings can *help* to clarify this issue, but it is possible that it will not be resolved definitively until studies are done in which one group from *outside an organization* provides AC ratings while another provides criterion data, with the latter not allowed access to the predictions of the former (McEvoy and Beatty, 1989).

A third problem for ACs is construct validity. Studies have found consistently that correlations between different dimensions within exercises are higher than correlations between the same dimensions across exercises (Bycio et al., 1987; Harris et al., 1993; Kleinman, 1993). When AC ratings are factor-analyzed, the solutions represent exercise factors, not dimension factors. This suggests that assessors are capturing exercise performance in their ratings, not stable personality characteristics (Joyce et al., 1994). However, when Schneider and Schmitt (1992) compared exercise form (e.g., role play, in-basket) to exercise content (design of the tasks performed in the exercise, such as superior-subordinate counseling), exercise form accounted for 16 percent of method variance, while the effect of exercise content was negligible. Form may therefore reflect a true exercise effect; that is, candidates may perform differently in one-on-one situations than in groups. This implies that it is important to model in an exercise the kinds of interpersonal relations a candidate will encounter on the job. Careful attention to these issues will ensure that the AC method is used wisely and only in situations where it makes sense to do so.

SUMMARY

Managerial selection incorporates especially knotty problems. In order to improve our understanding of the multiple paths to executive success, we need to do three things: (1) describe the components of executive success in behavioral terms; (2) develop behaviorally-based predictor measures to forecast the different aspects of managerial success (e.g., situational tests); and (3) adequately map the interrelationships between individual behaviors, managerial effectiveness (behaviorally-defined), and organizational success (objectively-defined). In the meantime, one thing is clear: A veritable kaleidoscope of managerial selection devices is available. Judicious choice and evaluation of them can result in significant improvements in the quality of managers selected.

Discussion Questions

1. Why is it difficult to predict success in management?
2. You are developing a selection process for supervisors of computer programmers. Identify the key dimensions of the job, then assemble a battery of predictors. How and why will you use each one?
3. Why might mechanical prediction strategies be superior to judgmental ones?
4. Identify and discuss three ethical issues that are relevant to ACs.
5. What are some advantages and disadvantages of work samples as predictors of success in management?

* * *

In the final chapter of Part V, we shall consider the particular problems associated with placement. This is an area that has not received a great deal of attention, but is growing in importance as organizations devote more effort to career path planning and to providing meaningful, satisfying work for all employees.

CHAPTER
15

CLASSIFICATION AND DIFFERENTIAL PLACEMENT

AT A GLANCE

Tight labor markets, increased demands for productivity, work force diversity programs, and pressure for compliance wrought by civil rights legislation have forced organizations to examine the quality of their HR management programs more closely. Effective classification and differential placement strategies are central to this effort. Selection focuses on *interpersonal* differences; classification and placement are concerned with *intrapersonal* differences as the basis for assignment to available jobs.

Alternative strategies are available for classification and placement, but the choice of an appropriate strategy depends on available candidates, as well as on the number and types of available jobs. When the number of available candidates is large relative to available jobs, only the "cream of the crop" can be selected and optimally placed. On the other hand, when many jobs are available, optimal classification and placement programs for all are possible. Placement objectives will differ, however, with different types of jobs. With *in-*

dependent jobs, where the activities of individual workers are wholly separate from those of others, the objective may be to place workers according to their highest talents, to place them so that every job is filled by a minimally qualified individual, or to place them according to a combination of these approaches. When jobs are *successive* in nature, the work done by one person depends on work previously done by someone else. The goal here is to classify individuals into homogeneous groups based on their predicted rate of production. Finally, in *coordinate,* or "team," jobs, the result is a function of group effort, and not merely the sum of individual talents. Since both technical and interpersonal issues are involved in work of this nature, the objective is to optimize overall system performance. Models are available for doing this, but the need is great for further research to provide insight and understanding into the placement process.

The past three chapters have focused on **selection.** That is, a decision to accept or reject is made for each candidate on the basis of available information. **Classification** and **placement** both differ from selection in that no one is rejected. All individuals are assigned to available "treatments" (jobs, training programs, etc.) so that individual and institutional outcomes are maximized.

Both selection and placement decisions imply prediction. In selection, a decision is based upon the prediction that the person hired will be more satisfactory than the person who is rejected. In placement, a decision is based upon the prediction that an individual will be more satisfactory in one job than in another. Although for purposes of exposition we treat selection and placement as separate processes, in practice they are often inseparable. Horst (1961) pointed out that in order to select a sample of *n* people from a larger population logically and meaningfully, some basis for selection (i.e., some criterion of "goodness") is required. Typically, the criterion is predicted job performance. Since people are being selected on the basis of predicted performance on a job or category of jobs, the placement process simultaneously is involved.

In placement, individuals are divided into two or more groups and are assigned to different treatments according to a single criterion score. For example, if all new hires are given a cognitive ability test and subsequently assigned to different training programs based upon their scores, this would be an example of **fixed-treatment placement.** A single criterion is involved (test score), the score scale is divided into segments, and persons in each successive segment of the scale are assigned to a different treatment. It is conceivable, however, that the treatments may be adapted to the persons assigned to them or that the proportion of individuals assigned to each treatment might vary. These are both examples of **adaptive-treatment placement** strategies (Cronbach and Gleser, 1965).

In contrast, classification always involves two or more criteria (Anastasi, 1988). In the classification problem, the decision maker has a number of available positions on the one hand and a number of people on the other. The task is to make the most effective matching of people and positions (Ghiselli, 1956a). Classification long has been a problem in the military. For example, the U.S. Army faces the daunting task of assigning nearly 3,000 recruits to more than 275 different kinds of jobs each week at over 60 locations (Campbell, 1990b; Schmitz, 1988). Further examples of classification problems are the assignment of new employees to training programs for different jobs or the assignment of executive trainees to jobs in production, sales, marketing, or some other functional area after completing a general training program.

THE NEED FOR A SYSTEMATIC APPROACH TO CLASSIFICATION AND PLACEMENT

In recent years, seemingly incompatible demands have aggravated HR management problems (Howard, 1995). For example, increased pressure for productivity has been coupled with growing demands for 4-day workweeks and more leisure time. High-involvement workplaces require changes in the traditional roles of managers.

To date, most HR management texts have not devoted much emphasis to classification and differential placement. This is not surprising since the conceptual, mathematical, and practical problems are exceedingly complex. Much of the research available, unfortunately, focuses on jobs in which workers function independently of each other. In today's world of work, however, the real classification and placement problems lie in jobs involving worker *interdependence*.

In this chapter, therefore, we shall examine first the potential advantages of, and major considerations involved in, placement. Next, we shall consider the various types of jobs and the placement or classification strategies appropriate to each. Our overall aim is to provide the reader with a conceptual framework and analytical tools for dealing with a wide range of classification and placement problems.

Individual Differences and Differential Placement

The fact that differential placement is practiced at all is testimony to psychology's first law: People are different. This fact leads us to assign people to jobs differentially because we believe that payoffs in expected job behavior will vary across jobs. Hence, each individual is assigned to the job that is likely to make the best use of his or her talents. The use of tests and other devices *assumes* the existence of different payoffs, so that a person who lacks the readiness or ability to profit from one assignment may be able to learn from another.

The managerial task, therefore, is to understand and capitalize on each person's individuality. Since human attributes vary along many relatively independent ability, interest, biographical, and personality dimensions, a person's individuality is viewed best as his or her unique profile of scores on a variety of measures of individual differences (Dunnette, 1966). Once we can establish this unique profile for each individual, people and jobs can be matched optimally within the constraints set by available people and available jobs. If the number of individuals is large relative to available jobs (i.e., the selection ratio is low), then only the best qualified can be selected and placed. On the other hand, when many jobs are available (e.g., in government agencies, the military, and many large organizations in the private sector), optimal classification and placement are possible.

Thus, the two key limiting factors that determine

the feasibility of classification strategies are the number of positions available and the number of individuals available to fill the positions.

Further Considerations

Individual Versus Institutional Payoffs. What is best in terms of satisfaction and productivity for the individual may not be best for the institution, and vice versa. These trade-offs can be illustrated with reference to Table 15–1, which has been modified from those presented by Dunnette (1966) and Ghiselli and Brown (1955). The data in Table 15–1 are hypothetical and assume that the predicted criterion score for each worker for each job is based on a composite of aptitude, interest, past experience, and preference. Standard scores are used so that jobs whose outcomes are expressed in different units (e.g., sales, production) may be expressed along a common scale. The task is to place each individual on one of the three jobs.

At first glance, it might appear that the objective of classification is straightforward: Assess each person's individuality and place him or her in that job for which he or she is best suited. This "vocational guidance" strategy is a laudable ideal, but it is sometimes impractical. Table 15–1 demonstrates that if this strategy were adopted, jobs 1 and 2 would be filled by unqualified workers and job 3 by a very overqualified worker. Although one might argue that most individuals would profit maximally from this strategy (in terms of increased satisfaction and a sense of self-fulfillment), one also can argue that the organization must fill available jobs with at least minimally-qualified persons.

On the other hand, in considering each person for each job, suppose our objective is to fill each job with the most qualified person for that job? One might argue that the organization would profit maximally from this "pure selection" strategy since only the "cream of the crop" will be selected. Yet a quick examination of Table 15–1 will show that this placement strategy also is impractical. Worker A would have to be a "one-man band," for he would be placed on all three jobs! Having rejected workers B and C, the organization would have to recruit additional applicants (thereby incurring greater recruitment costs), perhaps under adverse labor market conditions and tight time pressures to fill the vacant jobs. In short, in most cases it is unrealistic to expect that all available job openings can be filled by pure selection.

TABLE 15–1 Predicted Criterion Scores (in z-Score Units) for Three Applicants to Each of Three Jobs, and Assignments Made Under Three Alternative Classification Strategies

	Job 1	Job 2	Job 3	*Number of Jobs Adequately Filled*	*Number of Workers Placed According to Their Highest Talent*
Worker A	1.0	0.8	1.5		
Worker B	0.7	0.5	−0.2		
Worker C	−0.4	−0.3	−1.6		
Minimum qualification score (in z-score units)	0.9	0.0	−2.0		
Classification strategies:					
Place each according to his or her best talent (Vocational guidance)	B	C	A	1	1
Fill each job with the most qualified person (Pure selection)	A	A	A	1	1
Place workers so that all jobs are filled by those with adequate talent (Cut and fit)	A	B	C	3	0

Source: Adapted from E. E. Ghiselli and C. W. Brown, *Personnel and Industrial Psychology* (2nd ed.). New York: McGraw-Hill, 1955, p. 149. Reproduced with permission of McGraw-Hill, Inc.

Pure selection and vocational guidance strategies represent opposite ends of the placement spectrum. Pure selection seeks to maximize payoffs to the institution, whereas vocational guidance seeks to maximize payoffs to the individual. As Dunnette (1966) has noted, both strategies are impractical in their pure forms, they lead to different outcomes, and they always are incompatible. Pure selection inherently is wasteful, for it leaves many applicants unemployed and therefore underutilized. This is detrimental to the overall health and well-being of society.

Vocational guidance, in its pure form, also is unrealistic. It ignores the fact that at any particular time the number of available jobs *is* limited, and organizations must be able to fill available jobs with at least minimally-qualified workers. There is one other difficulty with this approach (Ghiselli and Brown, 1955). It presupposes that for each worker there is *one* job that he or she can perform best. Let us not be so narrow in our thinking! Most airplane pilots also can perform the jobs of flight engineer or navigator; most heavy equipment operators in the construction industry can operate bulldozers as well as dump trucks; most hotel desk clerks also can serve as cashiers. To be sure, the heavy equipment operator might fail as an airplane pilot, and the hotel desk clerk might be a disastrous bulldozer operator, but each within his or her own field of endeavor probably possesses a range of abilities that will lead to success in any of a number of related jobs.

In short, in the placement process intra-individual variability must be considered along with inter-individual variability. In view of the rapid growth in the use of cross-functional project teams and temporary task forces, plus the accelerating pace of change, organizations, of necessity, will emphasize such flexibility in their assignment policies.

An Alternative Approach. If the objective of classification and placement is not to place each individual on the job for which he or she personally is best qualified, and it is not to place the best person on each job, then what is the objective? Perhaps a combination of the two approaches is optimal. Our objective then becomes to assign individuals so that (1) all jobs are filled by at least minimally-qualified persons, and (2) individuals are placed on jobs that will make the best possible use of their talents, given available job and staffing constraints. This is the "cut-and-fit" model of E. L. Thorndike (Ghiselli, 1956a).

Guion (1965) more elegantly described it as a successive-selection technique. Jobs are ranked in order of their importance. An applicant is considered and then selected or rejected for the most important job. Ultimately, he or she is placed in the most important job for which he has the necessary qualifications. If some jobs are not filled because qualified people have been placed elsewhere, either the order of priorities or the specific placements may be adjusted.

When a cut-and-fit approach was applied to the individuals in Table 15–1, worker A was placed on job 1 because he was the only individual qualified for it and because he was overqualified for job 3. Worker B was placed on job 2 because she was most qualified for it after worker A had been placed. Furthermore, it would have been impractical to place her in accordance with her best talent (job 1) because she was not minimally qualified for job 1. Finally, worker C was placed on job 3. Worker C was not very well qualified for any of the available jobs, but job 3 is a very easy job that can be performed by more than 95 percent (-2σ) of job applicants. Worker C is minimally qualified for it.

Advantages and Disadvantages. The cut-and-fit strategy has resulted in all three jobs being filled adequately, although no individual worker has been placed according to his or her highest talent. The objective of classification that now emerges is that individuals should be assigned to available jobs in order to achieve maximum effectiveness for the organization. This goal is consistent with a utility approach to the evaluation of alternative selection strategies—namely, the strategy to be used is the one that maximizes the expected utility for the institution across all possible outcomes.

While it is true that a strategy of pure selection maximizes utility for the institution (Hunter and Hunter, 1984), this approach is not always feasible. Offers to the highest-qualified applicants sometimes will be rejected (Murphy, 1986); work-force diversity considerations sometimes dictate use of banding strategies; and when jobs differ in importance to the firm, broader societal concerns (and sometimes tax incentives) for the employment of the disadvantaged and hard-core unemployed may take precedence.

In short, use of a cut-and-fit strategy involves trade-offs. First, in order to achieve maximum benefit for the total group, the greatest talent of the individual, in many cases, must be ignored. In the extreme, complete suppression of individuality cannot be tolerated in a democratic society. This is not our objective. Our objective is to place certain types of limitations on individual action so that the individualities of the largest numbers of persons can be realized.

A second difficulty stems from the measurement of group effectiveness. Which metric(s) should be used—dollars, units produced, group morale? Clearly, group effectiveness is a multidimensional concept. There is no single scale along which payoffs can be measured in comparable units for different jobs and across situations. Likewise, there is no simple way to fit an individual into a group to optimize group effectiveness.

Relative Cost of Placement Errors.   Differential placement involves the separate prediction of success for each individual on each job. Yet jobs differ in predictability as well as in relative importance (utility), in minimum standards of performance, and in the numbers of individuals needed to perform them. Realistically we can never expect to have complete information regarding each individual's relative odds of success across all jobs. Placement decisions still must be made, despite this uncertainty. As with any other type of select/reject decision, the relative costs of erroneous acceptances and erroneous rejections must be weighed.

To be sure, the relative costs of placement errors differ across jobs. For jobs of signal importance, such as those of senior executives, the cost of an erroneous acceptance must be weighed against the cost of additional recruiting and the cost of loss to the organization of erroneous rejections. While no generally applicable "rules of thumb" can be offered, in order to appraise the issues logically and rationally decision makers at least must be able to specify the major factors to consider in their decisions.

Social and Situational Influences.   One of the reasons why classification and placement problems are so complex is that many factors combine to determine the outcomes of these decisions. In fact, the mechanistic placement model presented earlier (assess the individual, assess the requirements of available jobs, find an appropriate match) is far too simple. Often, in order to gain insight into individual behavior, we also must consider the social context within which that behavior occurs. Thus, job behavior can be affected greatly by the immediate supervisor, by co-workers, and by the overall organizational culture within which a person works.

Also important are situational factors—the kinds of patients a hospital staff must care for, the kinds of customers a salesperson must call on, the profitability picture of the firm, general economic conditions, the political milieu. All of these factors and many more, both social and situational, have a significant bearing on individual job behavior.

One way of taking these factors into account is by broadening job analyses to reflect the situational and social contexts of jobs (Bowen et al., 1991). Admittedly this adds complexity to the overall job-person assessment, but simply ignoring social and situational factors only contributes to the likelihood of placement error.

Flexibility of People and Jobs.   The mechanistic job classification model outlined earlier assumes that neither people nor jobs change. Fortunately, this assumption is false; people can change and jobs can change, though neither is completely plastic.

Certainly, people differ in their readiness and ability to profit from training; likewise, jobs differ in the amount of individual discretion they permit. In certain jobs, such as administrator, researcher, or outside salesperson, the job is principally what the incumbent makes of it. Other jobs are less flexible (e.g., production workers, automobile assembly-line workers), and people must be trained to perform them according to much more rigid specifications.

However, people differ in their preferences for jobs with high versus low structure, they differ in the extent to which they will find such jobs meaningful and personally satisfying, and they differ in their ability to profit from training for them. Likewise, jobs differ in the extent to which they can be modified, as well as in the length and difficulty of the training required to perform them. Placement specialists must consider these variances and make their decisions accordingly.

TYPES OF JOBS

Ghiselli (1951) noted that most discussions of classification and placement have ignored an important feature of the work situation—the type of job the individual is performing. We tend to focus our attention exclusively on the individual; yet in many instances, the individual does not work independently of others. Ghiselli (1951) therefore distinguished three types of jobs: independent jobs, successive jobs, and coordinate jobs. Each poses a different classification problem, as we shall see.

In many jobs, workers' contributions are largely independent. In the postal service, as well as in many outside sales jobs, for example, workers are assigned nonoverlapping territories or routes. In such situations, the activities of one worker have little bearing on the activities of other workers. This is the classification problem in its simplest form, and it is the problem for which solutions most often have been developed.

Jobs also may be successive in nature. Here, the work done by one individual depends on the work previously done by someone else. Hence, the performance of those whose activities occur late in the sequence is affected directly by those whose activities occur earlier. For example, Whyte (1955) described an operation pertaining to the spray painting of toys, where the toys were hung from moving hooks before going through a drying oven. On an experimental basis a variable-speed control was installed in the paint room. The workers in the paint room set the line running considerably faster through the paint room than it was running elsewhere. Unfortunately, the increased production of the paint room caused an excess of toys in the next process and a deficit of toys coming into the paint room. Needless to say, the experiment had to be discontinued.

Successive jobs also may refer to a hierarchy of jobs based upon different levels of the same aptitude or skill (Landy, 1989). For example, if a firm employs three classifications of machinists (machinist I, II, and III), the placement problem essentially reduces to the assignment of each individual to the appropriate labor grade. To date, classification strategies for successive jobs have received little systematic attention from researchers and practitioners alike.

Finally, classification must deal with jobs that are coordinate in nature. In coordinate or "team" jobs, the whole (i.e., the end result) is greater than the sum of its parts (i.e., individual talents). Such jobs are highly interdependent in nature, and it is difficult to identify the contributions of any single individual. Coordinate jobs abound in many different types of organizations and settings: cross-functional project teams, temporary task forces, airplane and ship crews, operating-room teams, investigatory commissions, assembly teams, athletic teams, and legal defense teams, just to name a few. The unique characteristic of coordinate jobs is that, in addition to individual capabilities, they involve (sometimes delicate) interpersonal relationships of various kinds. Personalities come into play and must be dealt with. Again, solutions to this type of classification problem have not been addressed systematically. Once the objective in classification for each of these types of jobs can be specified, however,

approximate solutions are available. Let us consider the various strategies for each type of job in greater detail.

CLASSIFICATION STRATEGIES FOR INDEPENDENT JOBS

A system for assigning individuals to independent jobs may, as we noted earlier, have any one of three objectives. The objectives may be (1) to place each person so that over all persons, the highest possible performance level will result (pure selection); (2) to place each person on the job for which he or she is best qualified (vocational guidance); or (3) to place persons on jobs so that all jobs are filled by individuals who meet at least some minimum standards of performance (cut and fit).

In attempting to achieve these objectives, four types of solutions have been proposed: nonoptimal cut-and-fit methods, mathematically optimal methods involving differential prediction, methods that classify individuals into jobs according to the discriminant function, and linear programming (Ghiselli, 1956a).

Differential prediction involves the separate prediction of success for each individual for each job and then, other things being equal, the placement of individuals on jobs so as to maximize organizational performance. Yet things are never equal in employee classification. Criteria are rarely, if ever, completely relevant or reliably measurable, testing procedures are far from perfectly valid, and individuals are less than perfectly reliable. In addition, jobs differ in importance (utility), numbers of individuals needed, and minimum standards of performance.

Given these complicating factors, Brogden (1946b) and Thorndike (1950) sought mathematically exact solutions that simultaneously will satisfy the three objectives noted earlier. None of the objectives is completely achieved, however, so that the net result is only an approximation of the optimal result and not very different from the results obtained with the much simpler cut-and-fit model. Other solutions based on linear programming (Brogden, 1954; Horst, 1956; Whitehead, Suiter, and Thorpe, 1969) or goal programming (Lee, 1972) also have been proposed.

Unfortunately these models are a bit too sophisticated for practical use in organizations. Most are based on the military assignment problem where the number of recruits selected equals the number of available positions and where all assignments can be made simultaneously. In organizations other than the military, the number of applicants usually is greater than the number of available jobs, and assignment decisions often must be made quickly, without waiting until all applicants can be considered at once. Before we discuss other assignment strategies for independent jobs, we need to consider two additional issues: the relationships among job performances and the relation of utility to validity.

Relationships Among Job Performances

Ease of classification varies directly with the degree of correlation between performances on the jobs in question (see Fig. 15–1). In example I, Figure 15–1, differential classification is difficult because the interests, abilities, and traits necessary for success on job A are very similar to those required for success on job B. In other words, performance in job A and performance in job B are related systematically, linearly, and positively. Suppose the task is to assign half the individuals to job A and the other half to job B. All individuals in quadrants 1 and 2 are predicted to succeed on job A

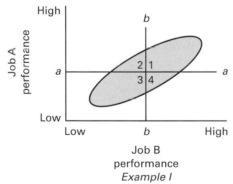

FIGURE 15–1 Example of Varying Directions of Relationships Among Jobs.

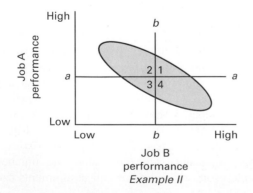

(they fall above line *aa*), and all individuals in quadrants 1 and 4 are predicted to succeed on job B (they fall to the right of line *bb*). Unfortunately, all individuals in quadrant 3 must be rejected, and all those in quadrant 1 are in demand for both jobs. Only those individuals in quadrants 2 and 4 would be assigned uniquely.

Differential classification is considerably easier when performances on two jobs are correlated negatively, as in example II. Here many more unique assignments can be made because those who are predicted to do well on job A are predicted to do poorly on job B and vice versa. Those in quadrants 1 and 2 still would be chosen for job A, those in quadrants 1 and 4 still would be chosen for job B, and those in quadrant 3 still would be rejected. However, the number of individuals in quadrants 1 and 3 is much smaller when jobs A and B are correlated negatively.

If performances on the two jobs were uncorrelated, then we would have no empirical basis for assigning individuals differentially to job A or to job B. We would do just as well to assign them randomly. Likewise, in those situations where the two jobs *are* correlated positively but individuals cannot be assigned uniquely (e.g., those in quadrant 1 in example I), they might be assigned randomly either to job A or to job B. Hence, each job would receive the same number of workers and comparable talent. This is a viable strategy assuming the jobs are equally important. But what if job A is much more important than job B? In a manufacturing operation, suppose job A persons are assigned to jobs as manufacturing technicians and job B persons to jobs loading finished product onto trucks. Clearly, it is more important to make sure that the best talent is assigned as manufacturing technicians to ensure smooth, error-free production.

In sum, the classification problem is greatly simplified when job performances are correlated negatively, when the jobs differ in importance, and when individuals show great promise for one job and much less for all others. As we noted earlier, however, this latter condition frequently is not met in practice. Nor is it common to find jobs in which performance correlates negatively (Ghiselli and Brown, 1955). On the other hand, advances in job analysis technology (cf. Chapter 9) now make it possible to determine empirically the degrees of relationship among performances in various jobs. To be sure, when the number of available jobs is large and when job classification systems are well-developed, differential assignment of people to jobs can be undertaken realistically.

Classification Versus Placement Strategies. Although placement can be done with one or more predictors, classification requires multiple predictors whose validity is determined individually against each job performance criterion. Hence, a classification battery requires a separate regression equation for each criterion (Anastasi, 1988). The least squares estimate (LSE) of performance computed for each criterion must be based on the full battery of tests in the experimental pool, and not on particular combinations of tests selected out of the total battery.

Brogden (1951) has shown that differential prediction with a battery of tests (classification) allows a much fuller use of human talent than is possible with either a single test or a composite score from a regression equation (placement). This is so because in classification problems we work with smaller selection ratios and are therefore able to assign better qualified individuals to each job. For example, suppose that out of 150 applicants, we need 15 to fill each of two jobs. If we use separate predictors (regression equations) for each job, then the selection ratio is .10 for each job. If we use one predictor (one regression equation) to select applicants for both jobs, then the selection ratio would be .20 since we would be forced to take the top 30 applicants.

Even when predictors for the two jobs are correlated highly (as in example I of Fig. 15–1) so that few unique assignments can be made, the increase in job effectiveness still is considerable when separate predictors are used. Table 15–2 illustrates this. It shows the mean criterion score (in standard or *z*-score units) of individuals selected for each of two jobs by a placement strategy (single predictor) and by a classification

strategy (two predictors, each validated against a separate job criterion).

Actually the term "predictors" may be misleading in this context (Johnson and Zeidner, 1991). Predictors do not refer to any test or test composite, but rather must be LSEs. There is one LSE of performance per job based on all tests in the experimental test pool. Thus the intercorrelation between predictors, as shown in Table 15–2, refers to the intercorrelation of two LSEs.

In the most extreme case, suppose the selection ratio for each job is .50, so that 100 percent of the workers must be assigned to one of the two jobs. If the workers were assigned randomly, the mean job performance score (in standard or *z*-score units) would be zero. Even under these conditions, however, the average job performance of those assigned can be improved by using two predictors (see the last row of Table 15–2). If the two predictors are uncorrelated, average job performance is .31 (almost a third of a standard deviation better than the chance value). As the correlation between the predictors increases, mean job performance on the two jobs decreases; but even when the two predictors are correlated highly (.80), mean job performance (.17) still exceeds the chance value. As selection ratios become more favorable, the organization benefits considerably (in terms of the overall quality of performance of individuals assigned to the two jobs) by using a classification rather than a placement strategy.

In practice, it is rare that performance scores for each of multiple jobs are available for each individual to be assigned. However, this is not an insurmountable problem. Brogden (1955) proved that the predicted

		Classification: Two Predictors Whose Intercorrelation Is				
Selection Ratio for Each Job	Placement: Single Predictor	0	.20	.40	.60	.80
5%	.88	1.03	1.02	1.01	1.00	.96
10%	.70	1.87	1.86	1.84	1.82	.79
20%	.48	1.68	1.67	1.65	1.62	.59
30%	.32	1.55	1.53	1.50	1.46	.43
40%	.18	1.42	1.41	1.37	1.34	.29
50%	.00	1.31	1.28	1.25	1.22	.17

TABLE 15–2 Mean Standard Criterion Score of Persons Placed on Two Jobs by Placement or Classification Strategies

Source: Adapted from H. E. Brogden, Increased efficiency of selection resulting from replacement of a single predictor with several differential predictors. *Educational and Psychological Measurement*, 1951, *11*, 183–196.

performance scores for each job, defined as the LSEs based on all predictors in a battery, could be substituted for the actual performance scores for these jobs without changing the expected value of the obtained mean predicted performance (standard) score. Recent extensions to this work have resulted in a set of principles known as differential assignment theory (DAT; Johnson and Zeidner, 1991). DAT is most appropriate in the context of a two-phase selection and assignment system, such as that used by the U.S. Army. Selection into the organization is first accomplished with a single composite test battery that resembles general cognitive ability (*g*); assignment is then made to specific jobs with weighted test composites tailored for each job. Note that individuals are classified from a common applicant pool to multiple jobs. In organizations outside the military, selection for multiple jobs (e.g., for an airline, ticket agents, baggage handlers, flight attendants) usually is done on the basis of independent pools of applicants.

However, when the use of DAT is justified, evidence indicates that optimal classification provides about twice as much gain in predicted performance as does the gain from selection alone (Nord and Schmitz, 1991; Scholarios, Johnson, and Zeidner, 1994).

Utility and Validity. In selection, the most desirable characteristic of a predictor is high validity—that is, a high correlation between predictor scores and actual job performance. In classification, this is not the case. Since a selection measure may have a different validity coefficient for each treatment, utility is not a simple function of any validity coefficient. However, the greater the correlation of the measure with the *differences* in payoff between treatments, the greater the utility from using the measure for placement or classification.

For example, if a cognitive ability test had a validity of .58 for job A and .56 for job B, this information would be useless for classification purposes since individuals scoring high on the test would be predicted to do well on *both* jobs. It would be impossible to predict in which job they would be more effective. Considerably more useful, however, would be an aptitude test that showed a validity of .30 for job A and .04 for job B, for the difference in validity coefficients is much greater.

Thus, utility in this context depends on two things: the power of the measure to assess a particular aptitude dimension, and the power of the aptitude dimension to predict differences in payoff (Cronbach and Gleser, 1965). In the case of jobs A and B, the information we need for differential assignment is not how much talent an individual possesses for job A and job B, but rather how much *more* talent he or she possesses for one job than for the other—that is, aptitude A *minus* aptitude B, or vice versa (Ghiselli and Brown, 1955). Absolute levels of validity for each job are, therefore, less important.

Under these conditions, the multiple-regression model based on *differential* performance takes a somewhat different form from that used in selection. For our two jobs, A and B, the regression model may be expressed as follows:

$$(y'_A - y'_B) = (b_{A1} - b_{B1})x_1 + (b_{A2} - b_{B2})x_2 + \ldots + (b_{An} - b_{Bn})x_n$$

Predictor scores are weighted by the *differences* between the regression weights for job A and those for job B. Hence, the ideal predictor in this case would have a high correlation with performance on one job and a low (or preferably negative) correlation with performance on the other. A single, multiaptitude predictor (such as a cognitive ability test) is unsuitable for classification purposes since it probably would predict success equally well in many different areas. In fact, this is the case (Gottfredson, 1986; Ree, Earles, and Teachout, 1994; Schmidt, 1988).

Since there is no rejection option in classification, the task is to develop a composite score that will indicate an individual's *relative* fitness for job A over job B. This index may be a difference score ($D = Y'_A - Y'_B$), which expresses the amount by which an individual's performance on job A is predicted to exceed his performance on job B. With this index of the expected difference in success, all individuals then may be ordered from high to low in terms of their *D* scores. If 20 percent of the individuals must be assigned to job A and the remainder to job B, then the 20 percent with highest *D* scores are assigned to job A. Variations in numbers of individuals needed for the two jobs are reflected similarly in the proportion of individuals with high *D* scores who are assigned to job A (Wiggins, 1973). Total utility may be increased by adjusting the numbers needed (when treatments are fixed in advance) or, even better, by adjusting treatments (i.e., jobs, training programs) to the persons assigned to them.

Unfortunately, the usefulness of regression equations for predicting difference scores does not generalize to situations involving more than two jobs. However, one approach that does is the use of LSEs that predict *each* criterion as the basis for making assignments. In the two-job case the predicted performance scores for each job (LSEs) are computed for each individual, and an appropriate constant is added to the job that requires more people. Each individual can then be assigned to the job that corresponds to his or her highest score. This procedure produces exactly the same assignment decisions as those made by using the regression equation to predict the difference between the two criterion scores.

Such an approach also generalizes to the assignment to three or more jobs. In the general case, an appropriate constant is added to each predicted performance score to reflect the numbers of individuals desired. Then the individual is assigned to the job that corresponds to his or her highest adjusted score. An additional feature of this method that makes it administratively attractive is that it incorporates a decision rule to reject either a prescribed number of applicants or all applicants with less than the required predicted performance score (Johnson and Zeidner, 1991).

Discriminant Analysis

Since employee classification involves the differential assignment of persons to jobs, discriminant analysis might appear well-suited to the task. **Discriminant analysis** is a statistical procedure whose aim is to distinguish maximally between groups on the basis of multivariate information that is combined in a linear fashion. In our case, the groups under consideration are groups of individuals performing the same job. On the basis of test scores and other predictor information, a new hire would be placed into the group (or job class) that he or she resembles most closely.

Discriminant analysis attempts to do this by forming linear combinations of the predictor variables. These "discriminant functions" take the following form:

$$D_i = d_{i1}Z_1 + d_{i2}Z_2 + \ldots + d_{iv}Z_u$$

where D_i is the individual's score on discriminant function i (i.e., job class i), the ds are weighting coefficients (standard partial regression weights), and the Zs are the standardized values of the v discriminating variables used in the analysis. The maximum number of discriminant functions that can be derived will be the smaller of two numbers: the number of groups minus one or the number of variables.

Once the functions are derived, we can pursue the two objectives of this technique: analysis and classification (Jackson, 1983). As an analytical tool, discriminant analysis is useful for interpreting the meaning of data (i.e., for studying and understanding the group differences); our primary concern here, however, is with classification.

Classification is achieved through the use of a series of classification functions, one for each group. Thus, if there are five groups (available jobs or job classes), each new hire will have five scores. Under the assumption of a multivariate normal distribution, the classification scores can be converted into probabilities of group membership, and the new hire then is assigned to the group for which he or she has the highest probability of membership.

Discriminant analysis was applied to two measures of personal values to distinguish employees in management from those not in management and to distinguish employees with higher levels of self-perceived success from those with lower levels (Munson and Posner, 1980). When applied to a cross-validation sample, each measure demonstrated an acceptable level of concurrent validity in correctly classifying employees into management-nonmanagement and high-low self-perceived success groups. Although the concurrent design of this study does not enable us to say that, for example, value profile scores of job applicants will predict membership in a group of managers or nonmanagers or predict success levels, these results should be investigated using a predictive design so that cause and effect statements can be made.

Discriminant analysis is a tempting classification method, except that all individuals in a given group (or job category) are treated similarly. That is, the technique assumes that all individuals in a given group perform at the same level, and it considers group membership as the only criterion.

In screening applicants who already have chosen to enter a particular job, the best selection will be achieved by choosing those who are predicted to perform best. However, when alternative job assignments are available, it is not appropriate to assume that applicants will prefer the job in which they are predicted to be most successful. That is, a person may decline a job because she is likely to be too *successful* ("too good for that job"), as well as because she may be *unsuccessful* at it.

Although group membership is the primary consideration in classification, this information can be supplemented by incorporating a prediction of success in the group, that is, by combining discriminant analysis with regression analysis (Cohen and Cohen, 1983;

Rulon et al., 1967). Doing so allows an HR adviser to consider employee choices along with requirements for particular levels of performance in the jobs in question.

CLASSIFICATION STRATEGIES FOR SUCCESSIVE OR COORDINATE JOBS

Successive Jobs

Of the two types of successive jobs described earlier—namely, those based on a hierarchy of skill levels and those related in a functional sequence—the former are considerably easier to deal with. When the same aptitude or skill is relevant for each job, and when jobs are distinguished on the basis of the level of the aptitude or skill required, the absolute level of validity of the predictors is most important. The higher the validity, the more accurately individuals can be classified. If individuals are hired on the basis of skill levels (e.g., machinist I, II, or III), then selection and placement probably will be combined into a single process. Persons will be selected and placed according to their demonstrated ability to perform at a certain level of proficiency. Alternatively, the individual may have been *selected* because he or she exceeds some minimal level of aptitude for a certain job (e.g., computer programming), but then subsequently is *placed* into one of several ability-graded training classes (e.g., fast, slow, average) on the basis of aptitude level. In both of these instances, a highly valid predictor will measure more accurately the relevant aptitude or skill.

The absolute level of validity also is important when jobs are sequential in nature. Here, the optimal strategy is to classify individuals into homogeneous groups based on their predicted rate of production (Landy, 1989). In the toy-painting operation cited earlier, instead of installing a variable speed control at one point along the line (the spray-painting room), a more appropriate strategy would be to set up several assembly lines operating at different speeds. Admittedly such a strategy would be impractical in many situations. When rate of output can be controlled, however, it makes much more sense to establish separate groups, each generating the same rate of output, than to force a single heterogeneous group to work at the pace of the slowest worker in the group. Individuals would be selected on the basis of predicted raw criterion scores (rather than standardized criterion scores) so that the speed of production of all group members is uniform. It is important that the jobs be approximately equal in predictability, however, and that the absolute levels of validity be roughly equivalent.

Differential validity is an important concern in successive jobs, not for assigning workers to appropriate work groups *but rather for assigning them to specific jobs within work groups*. Thus, in the toy-painting operation, once an individual is assigned to the "fast" group, differential validity is important for deciding whether he or she should be placed in toy assembly, toy painting, or toy packaging.

Coordinate Jobs

The result of team, or coordinate, jobs is a function of group effort and not simply the sum of individual talents. In a project involving members of a design engineering group and a production group (e.g., the design and production of a new automobile model), the quality of the overall product will suffer if the work of either group is unsatisfactory. In addition to technical competence, the interpersonal "chemistry" must be right among team members. Classification assumes its most complex form here, and, in the last analysis, team jobs must be evaluated in terms of overall system performance. Therefore, systems prediction models are needed whose objective is to optimize the overall performance of the system (or team, in this case).

There are several historical antecedents for such models of team formation. For example, Crawford (1947) hypothesized that the most effective teams (World War II bomber crews) would be comprised of persons with similar interest and personality characteristics and roughly complementary air crew aptitudes. The effectiveness of well-matched crews (in terms of abilities, age, geographical region, etc.) then was compared to the effectiveness of poorly-matched crews. Of the well-matched crews, 83 percent were judged to be effective team groups (i.e., technically competent and interpersonally compatible), while only 47 percent of the poorly-matched crews were judged effective. Likewise, Van Zelst (1952) reported that sociometrically-selected work teams of carpenters and bricklayers not only found their co-workers and jobs more rewarding, but also produced a 5 percent saving in total production cost. The workers all were well-acquainted with each other's personalities and skills, and simply nominated (in order of preference) three co-workers as their partners.

Subsequently, Owens (1968, 1971, 1976) advanced a developmental-integrative model based on the premise that past behavior is the best predictor of future behavior. Using scored autobiographical data (biodata), this model sorts individuals into subgroups so that each subgroup will display internally similar patterns of prior experience. The meaningfulness of the subgrouping then may be determined by identifying systematically the behaviors that correlate with subgroup membership. If distinctive behavior is associated with subgroup membership, we then may identify an individual to be assessed, match his or her biodata profile with the subgroup profile it resembles most closely, and predict the typical behavior of the subgroup for the individual. Hence, knowing an individual's biodata profile, we can predict his probable pattern of test scores, academic achievements, vocational interests, type of work, style of performance, rate of advancement, probable hobbies, and recreational activities—in short, much of his or her behavioral repertoire.

There is now strong support for the validity of this model. A comprehensive review of 44 separate experimental and field studies found that approximately 80 percent of the results were positive. That is, they indicated statistically significant differences in subgroup behavior (Owens and Schoenfeldt, 1979). By exten-

sion, if one who assigns individuals to biodata subgroups or families also assigns jobs to comparable families or subgroups, then the affinity of the biodata families to the job families can be examined in terms of an overall systems performance model. In fact, Schoenfeldt (1974) developed and validated such an assessment-classification model (see Fig. 15–2).

According to Schoenfeldt (1974), individual assessment, or the inventory of psychological capabilities the individual brings to the job market, has two aspects. The first involves the use of standard predictors found to be valid for the jobs in question, and the second involves implementation of the approach described by Owens (1968, 1971, 1976). Moreover, in the same way individuals are placed into subgroups homogeneous with respect to past behavior, jobs also can be classified into families homogeneous with respect to their behavioral and human attribute requirements (see Chapter 9). The assessment-classification procedure then uses discriminant analysis to determine the probability of success and satisfaction in a particular job family, given that the individual is a member of a particular life-history subgroup. The ultimate objective is to predict the job success and satisfaction of a new individual whose subgroup is known and who is

FIGURE 15–2 The Assessment-Classification Model of Human Resource Utilization.

Source: From L. F. Schoenfeldt, Utilization of manpower: Development and evaluation of an assessment-classification model for matching individuals with jobs. *Journal of Applied Psychology,* 1974, *59,* 583–595. Copyright © 1974 by the American Psychological Association. Reprinted by permission of the author.

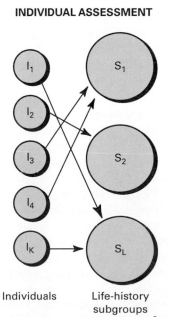
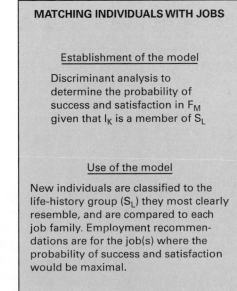
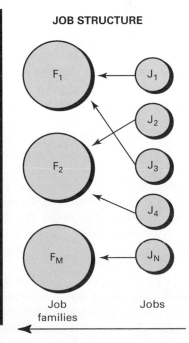

INDIVIDUAL ASSESSMENT

Individuals   Life-history subgroups

MATCHING INDIVIDUALS WITH JOBS

Establishment of the model

Discriminant analysis to determine the probability of success and satisfaction in F_M given that I_K is a member of S_L

Use of the model

New individuals are classified to the life-history group (S_L) they most clearly resemble, and are compared to each job family. Employment recommendations are for the job(s) where the probability of success and satisfaction would be maximal.

JOB STRUCTURE

Job families   Jobs

to be assigned to a job belonging to one of the job families.

Schoenfeldt (1974) applied the assessment-classification model in a college situation over a 4-year period. More than 1,900 males and females were involved in the study. He constructed a profile for each individual on the basis of responses to an extensive biographical inventory, and then grouped the profiles into "families" using a clustering procedure developed by Ward and Hook (1963). In addition, each subject had completed a battery of standard cognitive, interest, and personality measures during his or her freshman year and had been involved in several field studies (e.g., leadership, over- vs. under-achievement). All subgroups clearly were distinguishable with respect to this additional information. More importantly, with respect to five educational criteria (arts-science vs. applied studies, grade point average, etc.) and in terms of curricular paths walked, as measured 4 years later, the subgroups differed significantly. These results then were cross-validated on a new sample surveyed 2 years after the first sample, and they held up remarkably well.

Appraisal of the Assessment-Classification Model. Both cross-sectional and longitudinal studies support the validity of the model (Fleishman, 1988; Lautenschlager and Shaffer, 1987; Neiner and Owens, 1982, 1985). However, two qualifications are necessary. One, job choices among men and women in their early to mid-twenties are so unstable that trying to predict job entry is like trying to hit a moving target (Neiner and Owens, 1985). Because career stability tends to increase with age, the prediction of job entry may be more successful within an older, and more vocationally mature, population.

Two, the biodata subgroups tend to decline in similarity over time. That is, they display larger *within-group* variation and smaller *between-group* variation on variables measured at successive points in time (Davis, 1984). This is not surprising since as biodata subgroup members are exposed to a variety of new experiences over time, their paths should diverge. This suggests a need to revise the classification of individuals into new biographical subgroups as new experiences impact to change their interests, values, attitudes, and perceptions.

As we noted earlier, utility in classification is not a simple function of any single validity coefficient. Rather, utility is a function of the ability of a measure to forecast *differences* in payoff between treatments.

In fact, for reasons of validity as well as for ethical professional practice, the American Psychological Association's *Standards for Educational and Psychological Testing* (1985) require users of assessment procedures to provide evidence of differential prediction before undertaking classification in an employment setting. This is precisely the advantage of using biodata factors in classification: They tend to be uncorrelated, so whatever validity they possess tends to be differential validity (Owens and Schoenfeldt, 1979).

The significance of the model itself is twofold (Schoenfeldt, 1974). First, it is an approach to the use of human talent that promises to improve the fit between individuals and jobs, and thereby helps to optimize overall system performance. In addition, since the model considers both intellective and nonintellective dimensions, it appears to be in harmony with the trend of governmental regulations regarding validation (i.e., placing less emphasis on credentials than on personal competence). Second, when applied regionally or to a large employer, the continuous collection of relevant data will provide feedback regarding shifts in applicant characteristics or job requirements.

In spite of its advantages, however, the assessment-classification model or others like it, such as the Cleff job-matching system (Cleff, 1977), are probably too sophisticated for widespread use in the private sector, except in the case of very large firms. In fact, the model has been applied successfully in large industrial organizations (Morrison, 1977; Brush and Owens, 1979). In the latter study, the assessment-classification model was applied to almost 2,000 nonexempt members of a U.S. oil company. Clustering on the basis of an extensive biodata inventory produced 18 subgroups of employees such that within any one subgroup background experiences and interests were similar, and between subgroups they were different. Similarly, researchers clustered job analysis data for 939 office and clerical jobs into 19 job families. They found significant relationships between biodata subgroups and descriptive criteria (gender, education) and between biodata subgroups and industrial criteria (turnover, performance ratings, EEO job classification).

In addition to providing useful information for such areas as job description and classification, employee selection, career development, and HR planning, use of the model for employee classification should decrease turnover by increasing satisfaction with a particular job or occupation and by developing internal group cohesion resulting from common backgrounds and interests.

Alternative Classification Strategies for Coordinate Jobs. On a much simpler level, here are two alternative procedures. The first is appropriate when a new team must be formed. Many organizations routinely ask for job and career preferences of their employees, and they store such information in their skills banks or talent inventories. If technical criteria can be met by computer search, then the initial list of potential candidates may be reduced by taking job preferences into account. All remaining individuals then may be given a work sample or situational test of the coordinate job, and the final team formed on the basis of peer preferences (sociometrically). Alternatively, a new member may have to be assigned to an intact work team, such as a self-managing group whose members have the authority to manage their own task and interpersonal processes as they carry out their work. Each prospective member still may be screened for his or her technical competence and job preferences and then, if feasible, given a job tryout and a panel interview by his prospective teammates. To be sure, these two strategies are much less rigorous than the assessment-classification model, but in many organizations they may represent the only feasible approaches to classification for coordinate jobs.

Here's how the second strategy was applied at General Foods's Topeka (Kansas) plant. Employee-selection decisions were based primarily on factors such as the candidate's history of initiative, decision-making ability, and ability to work as a team member. Fewer than 10 percent of the applicants were chosen, and the entire selection process included five separate screening interviews plus extensive testing. Considerable attention was paid to orienting new team members to the "culture" of the Topeka plant and to integrating them into the existing social network (Walton, 1978).

As with independent and successive jobs, the first step is to state our objective. With coordinate jobs, the broad objective is to optimize overall system performance. "Performance" may be refined further to include, for example, maximal total productivity of all teams, minimal waste or turnover, or minimal total cost of operations. Unless these objectives can be articulated clearly, classification for coordinate jobs will continue to befuddle the HR specialist. On the other hand, if jobs are classified properly, then it is possible to specify assignment objectives and to adopt classification strategies that are consistent with the objectives.

Research has revealed two broad principles regarding team composition. One, the overall performance of a group or team strongly depends on the individual expertise of its members (Bottger and Yetton, 1987). However, it is the interdependence among team members that creates special job requirements (Klimoski and Jones, 1995). Group performance may be enhanced considerably by training individuals in how to search and evaluate information *before* they assemble in groups. Two, managers of effective work groups tend to monitor the performance of their team members regularly, and they provide frequent feedback to them (Komaki et al., 1989). In fact, as much as 35 percent of the variability in the performance outcomes of teams can be explained by the frequency of use of monitors and consequences. Organizations should therefore use these criteria as one basis for selecting and placing managers of teams.

The Other Side of the Classification Problem

To this point we have been discussing classification and placement issues as if they were something the organization does *to* the individual. Yet it also is true that individuals choose jobs and organizations that fit their personalities, that allow them to implement their self-concepts, and from which they can obtain outcomes they desire, particularly need satisfactions (Schneider, 1987). All of this assumes active involvement by individuals in the management of their careers. Based on current demographic, social, and economic trends, we can expect to see much more of this in the future (Hall and Mirvis, 1995).

We mention this issue here because from the organization's perspective, it is important to specify the dimensions of its "culture." Culture is the pattern of basic assumptions that a given group has invented, discovered, or developed in learning to cope with its problems of external adaptation and internal integration. The pattern of assumptions has worked well enough to be considered valid and, therefore, to be taught to new members as the correct way to perceive, think, and feel in relation to those problems (Schein, 1983, 1989). Organizational culture is embedded and transmitted through mechanisms such as the following:

1. Formal statements of organizational philosophy, materials used for recruitment and selection, and socialization.

2. Promotion criteria.

3. Stories, legends, and myths about key people and events.

4. What leaders pay attention to, measure, and control.

5. Implicit and possibly unconscious criteria that leaders use to determine who "fits" key slots in the organization (Schein, 1983, 1989).

What are the implications of organizational culture for employee classification and placement? One, cultures vary across organizations (O'Reilly et al., 1991); individuals will consider this information if it is available to them in their job-search process (Power and Aldag, 1985). Two, other things being equal, evidence indicates that individuals who choose jobs and organizations that are consistent with their own values, beliefs, and attitudes will be productive and satisfied employees who stay with their organizations. Thus, a study of 904 college graduates hired in six public accounting firms over a 6-year period revealed significant variation in organizational cultures among the firms (work-task values vs. respect for people and a team orientation). Variation in cultural values had significant effects on voluntary turnover rates and job performance across firms. In fact, the cultural effects were estimated to have resulted in over $6 million in extra human resource costs for firms emphasizing work-task values (Sheridan, 1992). Three, by specifying the dimensions of its culture, an organization can do a better job of matching individual talents to available jobs (Bowen et al., 1991). This kind of information is not as tangible as a validity coefficient or an expectancy chart, but to the extent that cultures are work-group specific (Wilkins and Dyer, 1988), and to the extent that classification decisions focus on intrapersonal strengths and weaknesses, then a better matching of individual talent with organizational needs is possible by taking this information into account than by assuming that it is of no account.

SUMMARY

The domain of worker classification and placement is as yet largely unexplored. This may be due to any one or more of the following reasons (Guion, 1991; Zedeck and Cascio, 1984): (1) classification procedures and designs are too complex; (2) organizations

ordinarily fill jobs; they do not ordinarily hire people and then decide where to put them; (3) hiring a "generalist" prolongs an organization's return on investment; and (4) individuals are unwilling to join organizations that do not have specific jobs in mind.

Nevertheless, failure to devote more attention to this area is to ignore an obvious fact. Our society seems to be espousing more of the classification than the selection approach to the staffing of organizational roles. We are entering an age when applicants tend to be considered for several (or many) jobs rather than one. If an individual fails to meet minimal requirements in one job, he or she may be considered for other available jobs and probably will be offered employment in one of them.

This orientation has clear implications for HR management and underscores the interrelatedness of the various phases of the employment process. Although the institution may benefit initially by saving in recruiting and selection costs (since fewer applicants must be recruited and selection may be less rigorous), more money will have to be spent on training in order to ensure that all applicants can meet minimal job requirements. In short, in the future world of work, the idea of rejection may have to be abandoned, as society strives to make all able-bodied individuals productive and to ensure the fullest use of each individual's potential.

Discussion Questions

1. Why are the pure selection and vocational guidance approaches to placement incompatible?

2. What is the difference between placement and classification?

3. Based on the information in this chapter, how would you put a team together?

4. Identify three examples of independent jobs. How might they change in the next 5 years? Will they remain independent?

5. In your view, to what extent does organizational or work-group culture affect organizational decisions to hire applicants, and applicants' decisions to choose particular organizations?

*   *   *

Chapters 16 and 17 are devoted entirely to consideration of the important issues associated with the design, implementation, and evaluation of efforts to train and develop employees. Training and development always has been an important topic in HR management. Current political, economic, and social trends suggest that it will continue to play an important role in most organizations in the foreseeable future.

CHAPTER

16

TRAINING AND DEVELOPMENT: CONSIDERATIONS IN DESIGN

AT A GLANCE

Training and development imply changes—changes in skill, knowledge, attitude, or social behavior. Although there are numerous strategies for effecting change, training and development is a common and important one.

Training and development activities are planned programs of organizational improvement, and it is important that they be planned as thoroughly as possible, for their ultimate objective is to link training content to desired job behaviors. This is a six-step process. First, conduct a comprehensive analysis of the training and development system, including its interaction with other organizational systems. Then determine training needs and specify training objectives clearly and unambiguously. The fourth step is to decompose the learning task into its structural components, and then to determine an optimum sequencing of the components. Finally, consider alternative ways of learning. Careful attention to these six steps helps to determine what is to be learned and what the substantive content of training and development should be.

Various behavioral models can help guide training and development efforts. These include the individual differences model, principles of learning, motivation theory, and behavior modeling. Each offers a systematic approach to training and development, and emphasizes a different aspect of the training process. The models can yield maximum payoff, however, only when programs are designed to match accurately targeted training needs.

Change, growth, and development are bald facts of organizational life. The maintenance of technological superiority, social harmony among diverse work groups, and organizational survival depend critically on the ability to confront and adapt to change. Over the past decade, a major change for most organizations is the composition of the work force. Other changes affect the number, types, and requirements of available jobs. These include automation; new ways of organizing work, continuing worker displacement as a function of mergers, acquisitions, and downsizing; and the shift from manufacturing to service jobs (Cascio and Zammuto, 1989; Howard, 1995). These issues have four key implications for training during the decade of the 1990s (Goldstein and Gilliam, 1990): (1) the number of unskilled and undereducated youth who will be needed for entry-level jobs; (2) increasingly sophisticated technological systems that will impose training and retraining requirements on the existing work force; (3) the need to train currently underutilized groups of minorities, women, and older workers; and (4) training needs stimulated by the internationally competitive environments of many organizations.

As an example, consider high-skills manufacturing—a movement begun in the mid-1980s by such innovative companies as Corning, Motorola, and Xerox. They replaced rote assemble-line workers with an industrial vision that requires skilled and nimble workers to think while they work—to watch inventories, to know suppliers and customers, costs and prices. In the 1990s, these practices spread so rapidly through the manufacturing sector that they are now mainstream. Companies large and small have learned the lesson that investments in training boost productivity, often at less cost than capital investments. And as big companies push suppliers and subcontractors on quality, price, and just-in-time delivery, even little shops see high skills as essential for competition ("The New Factory Worker," 1996).

In addition, as more firms move to employee involvement and teams in the workplace, there is a growing need to learn behaviors such as asking for ideas, offering help without being asked, listening and feedback skills, and recognizing and considering the ideas of others (Wellins et al., 1991).

These changes suggest a dual responsibility: The organization is responsible for providing an atmosphere that will support and encourage change, and the individual is responsible for deriving maximum benefit from the learning opportunities provided. This may involve the acquisition of new information, skills, attitudes, or patterns of social behavior through training and development.

Training and development are important managerial tools, but there are limits to what they can accomplish. Training is not necessarily the *only* alternative available for enhancing the person/job organization match, and it is narrow-minded to view it as an elixir for all performance problems. Nevertheless, the published literature on training and development (entry-level and managerial) is voluminous, and the annual training expenditures of large firms, such as Hewlett-Packard, may be as high as 5 percent of annual revenues (Labor Letter, 1988).

In view of the considerable amount of time, money, and effort devoted to these activities by organizations, we shall consider some important issues in training and development in this and the following chapter. Primarily we will emphasize the *design* of training and development programs, the *measurement* of the outcomes of these efforts, and the *interaction* of training outcomes with other organizational subsystems. We place substantially less emphasis on specific training methods and techniques.

Both training and development entail the following general properties and characteristics (Campbell et al., 1970):

1. Training and development is a learning experience.

2. It is planned by the organization.
3. It occurs after the individual has joined the organization.
4. It is intended to further the organization's goals.

Training and development activities are, therefore, planned programs of organizational improvement undertaken to bring about a relatively permanent change in employee knowledge, skills, attitudes, or social behavior.

We include the phrase "relatively permanent" in the definition to distinguish learning from performance. The distinction is principally a temporal one. Learning is a relatively permanent change in behavior that occurs as a result of practice or experience (not simple maturation). Learning is the ability to perform; it is available over a long period of time. Performance, on the other hand, refers to the *demonstration* of learning—it is observable, measurable behavior from which we *infer* learning. Performance is often a function of the individual's physical or mental state. For example, if an individual is fatigued, temporarily unmotivated, or distracted because of some environmental condition—noise, commotion, anxiety—he or she may not perform well in a given situation. The person is, therefore, unable to demonstrate all that he or she has *learned*. These conditions are more likely to affect short-run performance than long-term learning.

To be sure, a great deal of learning takes place in organizations—from peers, superiors, and subordinates. Some of this learning is planned and formally sanctioned by the organization, but much of it is serendipitous, unplanned, and informal (e.g., learning from someone who has the "inside track"). The critical aspect of our definition of training and development is that it requires that training results be defined in terms of measurable change either in individual states (knowledge, attitudes) or in individual performance (skills, social behavior). The definition is necessarily broad and includes simple programs of skill training as well as complex, systemwide programs of organization development.

TRAINING DESIGN

Characteristics of Effective Training Practice

One survey of corporate training and development practices found that four characteristics seemed to distinguish companies with the most effective training practices (Sirota et al., 1989):

- Top management is committed to training and development; training is part of the corporate culture.
- Training is tied to business strategy and objectives and is linked to bottom-line results.
- A comprehensive and systematic approach to training exists; training and retraining are done at all levels on a continuous, ongoing basis.
- There is commitment to invest the necessary resources, to provide sufficient time and money for training.

Does top management commitment really matter? Absolutely. For example, meta-analysis indicates that when management-by-objectives is implemented with high commitment from top management, productivity gains are five times higher than when commitment is low (Rodgers and Hunter, 1991). A subsequent meta-analysis found that job satisfaction increases about a third of a standard deviation when top management commitment is high, and little or not at all when top management commitment is low or moderate (Rodgers, Hunter, and Rogers, 1993).

Fundamental Requirements of Sound Training Practice

As an instrument for change, the potential of the training and development enterprise is awesome. In practice, however, this rarely occurs. The major reason for this is that often we have emphasized hardware and techniques rather than defining what is to be learned and what the substantive content of training and development should be (Campbell, 1971; 1988). One way to observe these priorities is to view training and development as a network of interrelated components. After all, training is an activity that is embedded within a larger organizational context (Quinones, 1995). Figure 16–1 shows such a model.

Program development comprises three major phrases, each of which is essential for success: a needs assessment, or *planning,* phase, an *implementation* phase, and an *evaluation phase.* In brief, the needs assessment phase serves as the foundation for the entire program, for as Figure 16–1 shows, both the training and evaluation phases depend on inputs from it. If needs assessment is incomplete, the training that actually is implemented may be far out of tune with what an organization really needs.

Having specified instructional objectives, the next task is to design the training environment in order to achieve the objectives. This is the purpose of the training and development phase—"a delicate process

that requires a blend of learning principles and media selection, based on the tasks that the trainee is eventually expected to perform" (Goldstein, 1993, p. 24). We will have more to say on this topic later in the chapter. If assessment and implementation have been done carefully, the evaluation should be straightforward. Evaluation (Chapter 17) is a twofold process that involves establishing measures of training and job performance success (criteria) and using experimental and quasi-experimental designs to determine what changes have occurred during the training and transfer process.

There are a number of different designs that can be used to assess the outcomes of training programs. To some extent, the choice of design(s) depends on the questions to be asked and the constraints operating in any given situation. The last column of Figure 16–1 lists a number of possible training goals:

1. *Training validity.* Did trainees learn anything during training?
2. *Transfer validity.* To what extent did the knowledge, skills, or abilities learned in training lead to improved performance on the job?
3. *Intra-organizational validity.* Is the performance of a new group of trainees in the same organization that developed the training program similar to the performance of the original training group?
4. *Inter-organizational validity.* Can a training program that "works" in one organization be used successfully in another organization?

These questions often result in different evaluation models or, at the very least, different forms of the same evaluation model (Goldstein, 1993; 1989). Evaluation, therefore, should provide continuous closed-loop feedback that can be used to reassess instructional needs, thereby creating input for the next stage of development. The purpose of Figure 16–1 is to provide a model that can help to organize the material in Chapters 16 and 17. Let us begin by defining what is to be learned.

Defining What Is to Be Learned

There are six steps in defining what is to be learned and what the substantive content of training and development should be:

1. Analyze the training and development subsystem and its interaction with other systems.
2. Determine training needs.
3. Specify training objectives.

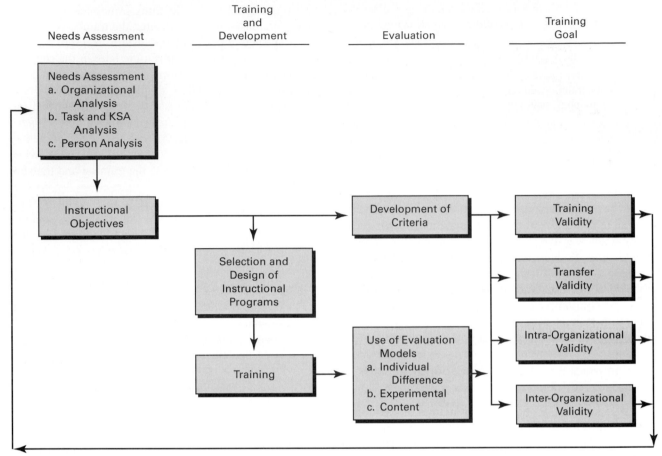

Source: From *Training in organizations: Needs assessment, development, and evaluation,* 3rd ed., by I. L. Goldstein. Copyright © 1993 by Wadsworth Inc. Reprinted by permission of Brooks/Cole Publishing Co., Pacific Grove, CA 93950.

FIGURE 16–1 A General Systems Model of the Training and Development Process.

4. Decompose the learning task into its structural components.

5. Determine an optimal sequencing of the components.

6. Consider alternative ways of learning.

Our overall goal—and we must never lose sight of it—is to link training content to desired job behaviors.

The Training and Development Subsystem

Training and development have their own inputs, throughputs, and outputs that interact with those of the larger organization. Hence, it is important to judge the relevance and importance of training needs in relation to overall organizational goals. To be most useful, training and development must complement other organizational processes, such as selection, placement, job design, and performance appraisal. Failure to do so

could produce disincentives to effective employee training. This can happen, for example, when supervisors perceive that trainers do not really understand what conditions are like on the job (and therefore supervisors do not accept the practices taught by the training program), when all levels of workers are not included in training, or when supervisors are held to normal production levels even when their subordinates are in training (Salinger, 1973).

Training and development operate in a complex organizational milieu. Failure to consider the broader organizational environment often contributes to programs that either result in no observable changes in attitudes or behavior, or, worse yet, produce negative results that do more harm than good. In particular, there are four major influences on the training and development process: the individual trainee, superiors, peers, and the formal organizational system (Allen and Sil-

---

NEW EMPLOYEE ORIENTATION AT CORNING, INC.

As a result of 2 years of development of the program and 2 years of experience with it, Corning concluded:

1. The impressions formed by new employees within their first 60 to 90 days on a job are lasting.

2. Day 1 is crucial; new employees remember it for years. It must be managed well.

3. New employees are interested in learning about the *total* organization—and how they and their unit fit into the "big" picture. This is just as important as specific information about the new employee's own job and department.

4. Give new employees major responsibility for their own orientation, through guided self-learning, but with direction and support.

5. Avoid information overload—provide it in reasonable amounts.

6. Recognize that community, family, and social ad-

justment is a critical aspect of orientation for new employees.

7. Make the immediate supervisor ultimately responsible for the success of the orientation process.

8. Thorough orientation is a "must" for productivity improvement, since it is a vital part of the total management system.

These results are exciting and provocative. They suggest that we should be at least as concerned with preparing the new employee for the social context of his or her job and for coping with the insecurities and frustrations of a new learning situation as with the development of the technical skills necessary for job performance. The payoff? After 2 years, voluntary turnover among new hires was reduced by 69 percent. In the first year the benefit-to-cost ratio was 8:1; thereafter it was 14:1 (McGarrell, 1984).

---

verzweig, 1976). The interaction among these factors was illustrated neatly in a study of new employee orientation at Corning, Inc. (see boxed insert above).

The same factors interact to some degree in all training and development activities. The individual must be capable of learning new material ("can do"), motivated to learn it ("will do"), and those individuals who exert influence over him or her must support the development effort.

Determining Training Needs

It has been said often that if you don't know where you are going, any road will get you there; *but* if you do know where you are going, you will get there sooner. This is especially true of training and development efforts. For this reason, clearly-articulated objectives are essential. Before we can do this, however, it is necessary to identify needs for individual, team, and organizational development.

Many methods have been proposed for uncovering specific training needs—that is, the components of job performance that are relevant to the organization's goals and that would benefit if they were enhanced through training (Campbell, 1988). In fact, Moore and

Dutton (1978) described 34 different procedures. All may be subsumed under the three-facet approach described in McGehee and Thayer's (1961) classic text on training. These are **organization analysis** (identification of where training is needed within the organization), **operations analysis** (identification of the content of the training), and **person analysis** (identification of who needs training, and of what kind). Each of these facets contributes *something,* but to be most fruitful conduct all three in a continuing, ongoing manner and at all three levels: at the organization level—managers who set its goals; at the operations level—managers who specify how the organization's goals are going to be achieved; and at the individual level—managers and workers who do the work and achieve those goals.

These three managerial levels are but three possible populations of individuals. In fact, needs analysis done at the policy level based on different populations is called **demographic analysis** (Latham, 1988), and it should be added to the traditional trichotomy of organization, job, and person analyses. This broader schema is shown in Figure 16–2. The following sections describe various portions of Figure 16–2 in greater detail.

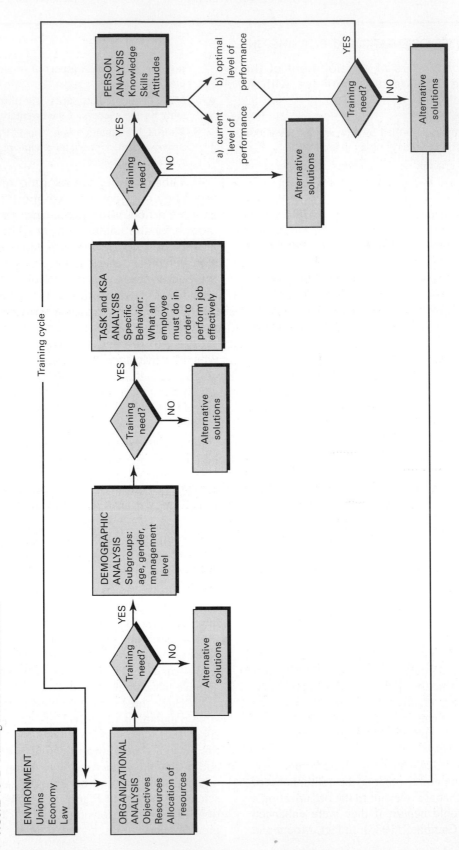

FIGURE 16–2 Training Needs Assessment Model.

Organization Analysis

The purpose of organization analysis is to link strategic planning considerations (see Chapter 10) with training needs assessment results. Another objective is to pinpoint inefficient organizational units to determine whether training is the appropriate antidote to performance problems. The important question is: "Will training produce changes in employee behavior that will contribute to the organization's goals?" If that connection cannot be made, then the training is probably not necessary.

Demographic Analysis

Demographic analysis can be helpful in determining the special needs of a particular group, such as workers over 40, women, or managers at different levels. With respect to managers, first-level supervisors identified technical training as their highest need (record-keeping, written communications), mid-level managers rated HR management courses as most relevant to their needs (e.g., leadership skills, performance appraisal), and upper managers rated conceptual courses (e.g., goal setting, planning skill) as most important for their development (Bernick, Kindley, and Pettit, 1984). Managerial level, function, and attitudes toward the usefulness of training have small but significant effects on the self-reported training needs of managers (Ford and Noe, 1987).

Demographic analysis deserves treatment in its own right because the information it provides may transcend particular jobs, even divisions of an organization. Taking this information into account lends additional perspective to the job and person analyses to follow.

Operations Analysis

Analyses of the work to be done are often included in the needs assessment process. This is an important step for two reasons. One, if the content of training programs is left to the training department, there is a real danger that the staff may not be able to identify emerging training and development needs. Seeking out the opinions of managers and subordinates close to the scene of operations decentralizes the needs assessment process and helps to counteract this tendency. Two, involvement of managers and subordinates in the needs assessment process helps build *commitment* to the training effort. As we have seen, failure to develop a commitment to training by those affected by it can have disastrous effects.

However, it would be a mistake to assume that these types of ratings are unaffected by characteristics of the raters. In fact, the breadth of experience (number of different tasks each rater has performed) and level of self-efficacy (belief in one's ability to perform competently) affect training-emphasis ratings. So also do changes in breadth of experience and self-efficacy over time (Ford et al., 1993). The implication: ensure that all raters have the experience and self-confidence to provide meaningful data.

What kinds of competencies are likely to emerge? Given the pace of change in technology and job requirements, evidence indicates that jobs of the future will require less memorizing of facts and procedures, fewer physical skills, and far more conceptual ability (Coovert, 1995). Our major concern is that training programs emphasize the development of competencies (eg., knowledge, interpersonal skills) judged important for a job. In determining training needs, we need to know *what* kind of work is performed, *how* it should be performed, and *what workers need to learn* in order to perform it properly. Use of a quantitative measure of content validity, such as the Content Validity Index described in Chapter 7, may shed some light on this problem (Ford and Wroten, 1984), particularly at lower organizational levels.

However, managerial jobs are characterized by less-prescriptive job descriptions and more room for individual initiative in achieving broad job responsibilities. Hence emphasis increasingly is being placed on individual diagnosis of training needs, self-development, and self-appraisal (McCauley et al., 1994). In addition, observations may help to identify components of managerial work that have implications for the type of training that is needed to perform managerial jobs (McCall, Lombardo, and Morrison, 1988).

Person Analysis

A key reason for identifying training needs at the level of individuals is to counter technological obsolescence. Thus Xerox used personal history items and demographic information (e.g., continuing education programs attended, years since last degree) to isolate individuals whose knowledge and skills were potentially obsolete. It then tailored training programs to the particular needs of these individuals (Morano, 1973).

One procedure that links individual or team behavior directly to training content is that of critical incidents (see Chapter 5). Critical incidents are recorded on the job as they happen, usually by the immediate supervisor. Glickman and Vallance (1958) used this method to assess the training needs of newly-commissioned naval ensigns. Over 1,000 incidents were recorded and categorized. Categories that reflected poor performance then were fed back to the training command, and changes were made in training content in an attempt to remove the causes of poor performance and enhance the causes of effective performance. Likewise, Foley (1969) determined the effective behaviors of retail sales employees by collecting critical incidents from customers. Over 2,000 incidents were collected, categorized, and made the basis for training in customer service. When behaviorally-anchored rating scales are used in performance appraisal (cf. Chapter 5) or when assessment center results are fed back to candidates, they serve the same purpose—namely, as vehicles for identifying training needs and linking them directly to individual or team behavior.

Learning Agendas. One especially fruitful approach to the identification of individual training needs is to combine behaviorally-based performance appraisals with individual learning agendas derived from self-analysis. Learning agendas should include:

1. Statements of aims—desired changes in knowledge, skills, attitudes, values, or relationships with others.
2. Definitions of areas of study, search, reflection, or testing, including lists of activities, experiences, or questions that can help achieve these aims.
3. Ideas about priorities—feelings of preference or urgency about what should be learned first.

Individuals often construct their own learning agendas, with assistance, in career planning workshops, through structured exercises, in the practice of management by objectives, or in assessment centers. The agenda then provides a focus for self-development. Individuals with similar learning agendas can be grouped together, so that training content may be adapted to their specific needs. As a result of needs assessment, it should be possible to determine what workers do, what behaviors are essential to do what they do effectively, what type of learning is necessary to acquire those behaviors, and what type of instructional content is most likely to accomplish that type of learning (Goldstein, 1989). To provide this kind of information, and in order to choose from the broad array of needs-assessment techniques available, pay careful attention to the type of information needed as input to the training process.

Training Objectives

Specification of training objectives (i.e., what is to be learned) becomes possible once training and development needs have been identified. This is *the* fundamental step in training design (Campbell, 1988). Such objectives define what the learner should be able to do after finishing the program that he or she could not do before it. Objectives are stated either in behavioral or in operational terms. Behavioral objectives refer to actions, movements, or behaviors that are observable and measurable. Each objective should describe: (1) the desired behavior, (2) the conditions under which the behavior should occur, and (3) the success criteria by which the trainee's behavior is to be judged (Mager and Pipe, 1970). For example, consider a behavioral objective for a training program for computer programmers:

> In a one-hour test at the end of the first week of training [conditions under which behavior should occur], the student will be able to list the processing steps followed by a computer in executing a software program, specifying the requirements for passage at each step [desired behavior]. All steps must be included in the correct order, and the passage requirements must match those in the textbook [success criteria].

Objectives also may be stated in operational or end-result terms. For example, it is one thing to have an objective to "lower production costs." It is quite another thing to have an objective to "lower the costs of producing Model 600 widgets 7 percent by April 30, by having operations 7, 8, and 9 done by one operator." The latter is a much more specific statement of what the objective actually is and how it will be reached. In addition, the more precise the statement, the easier it is to assess its contribution to successful operations. "To lower costs 7 percent" makes it possible to determine what changes in price or increases in profits can be anticipated as a result of combining operations 7, 8, and 9. The end result of training, of course, is the successful combination of operations, 7, 8, and 9 by a single operator.

It is important not to overemphasize the "action" component of objectives. Many of the crucial mediating factors of management performance are attitudes; yet it is difficult to demonstrate the link between attitudes and job performance (Chaiken and Stangor, 1987). This also is true of improvements in decision-making skills—another prime focus of management training. Operationally, we are interested in the characteristics of the end results or behaviors that permit us to *infer* the type of mental activity that produced them. Hence, we emphasize observable actions. If trainers were not concerned with bringing about changes in individuals or groups, they would not have to bother looking at behavior—but they do bear that responsibility and they cannot shirk it.

DECOMPOSING THE LEARNING TASK AND SEQUENCING LEARNING EXPERIENCES

Having specified training objectives, the next task is to design the training environment in order to achieve the objectives. In a classic paper, Gagné (1962) offered three psychological principles that are useful in training design:

1. Any human task may be analyzed into a set of component tasks that are quite distinct from each other in terms of the operations needed to produce them.

2. These task components are mediators of the final task performance; that is, their presence ensures positive transfer to a final performance, and their absence reduces such transfer to near zero.

3. The basic principles of training design consist of (a) identifying the component tasks of a final performance, (b) ensuring that each of these component tasks is fully achieved, and (c) arranging the total learning situation in a sequence that will ensure optimal mediational effect from one component to another (p. 88).

In this framework, "what is to be learned" is of signal importance. Successful final performance on a task depends on first attaining competence on the various subtasks that compose it. Gagné's ideas were based upon a great deal of research on skill learning in the military. For example, in putting a radar set into operation, some of the steps involved are:

1. Turn the radar set to "Stand-by" operation.
2. Connect the power cord of the TS-147.
3. Turn the power switch on.
4. Turn the test switch to the transmit position.
5. Turn the DBM dial fully counterclockwise.
6. Connect an RF cable to the RF jack on the TS-147. (Gagné, 1962, p. 83).

In training operators to put the radar set into operation, the first step is to analyze the overall task. "What is to be learned" stems directly from such an analysis: (1) the location of the appropriate buttons, switches, etc., and (2) the sequence of acts in the proper order. The component tasks bear a hierarchical relationship to each other and immediately suggest the proper sequencing for the training situation. That is, the trainee must first learn what and where the buttons and switches are (identification learning) before he or she can begin to learn the serial-order task. In short, it appears that there is a *more efficient* and a *less efficient* sequence that can be arranged for the learning of a procedural task (i.e., a task composed of at least two component tasks), and this sequence involves learning each subtask before undertaking the total task. Subsequent reviews of the empirical evidence lend considerable support to the validity of these principles (Gagné, 1967; 1977; Gagné and Briggs, 1979; Gagné and Rohwer, 1969). A similar approach may be used to design training programs that attempt to change knowledge or attitudes. Gagné's principles (1962) parallel those underlying programmed instruction. Programmed instruction requires that the trainer (or programmer) first consider what he or she wants to teach and why. The next task is to break the topic down into its component elements and then to order in sequence the learning of these elements in an optimal fashion. This is a rational, logical approach, and despite the fact that it is not possible to break down most managerial jobs into their component tasks, trainers should adopt the programmed instruction model for *every* training and development activity (Campbell et al., 1970; Campbell, 1971).

Team Training

As part of the changing nature of work, there has been an increasing emphasis on team performance. Such terms as *management teams, cross-functional project teams,* and *temporary task forces* are becoming more and more common in the parlance of organizations. A **team** is a group of individuals who are working together toward a common goal (Blum and Naylor, 1968). It is this common goal that really defines a team, and if two team members have opposite or conflicting goals, the efficiency of the total unit is likely to suffer. For example, consider the effects on a baseball team when one of the players *always* tries to hit home runs regardless of the team's situation.

Clearly, individual training cannot do the whole job; we need to address interactions among team members. This interaction is what makes team training unique—it always uses some form of simulation or real-life practice and always focuses on the interaction of team members, equipment, and work procedures (Bass, 1980). While the notion of team-based work is attractive, we hasten to add that simply placing a task (e.g., monitoring air traffic or command-and-control) within a team context may not improve overall performance (Hollenbeck et al., 1995). Nevertheless, there are many situations where teams are appropriate, and where their special training can make an important difference in performance.

In the past, there was little theoretical or empirical research on team training or on the relative effectiveness of alternative strategies (Goodman et al., 1988; Gersick, 1988). More recently, however, Cannon-Bowers et al. (1995) have developed a systematic approach to team training that focuses on skill competencies, attitude competencies, and alternative categories of teams.

While specific competencies will, of necessity, vary across categories of teams, and the tasks and environments in which they are performed, in general, a core set of skills characterizes effective teamwork. These include adaptability, shared awareness of situations, performance monitoring and feedback, leadership/team management, interpersonal skills, coordination, communication, and decision-making skills. Attitudinal skills that characterize effective teamwork include beliefs about the importance of teamwork skills, belief in placing the team's goals above those of individual members, mutual trust, and shared vision (Cannon-Bowers et al., 1995).

Teams, in turn, seem to fall into four main categories:

1. *Context-driven teams* have fairly stable membership and perform a single or a small number of tasks. Examples include surgery and other medical teams, sports teams, and air crews.

2. *Team-contingent arrangements* involve teams whose members are consistent and who must work together across a variety of tasks. Examples include self-managing work teams, management teams, quality circles, and teams that comprise functional departments.

3. *Task-contingent arrangements* are common in situations where team members perform a specific team task, but not with the same set of teammates (because of organizational policy or rapid turnover). Examples include some firefighting teams, air crews, and medical teams.

4. *Transportable team arrangements* occur when team members work on a variety of tasks and with a variety of teams. Examples include temporary task forces and project teams.

This approach has two implications for the design of team training (Cannon-Bowers et al., 1995):

- The specification of training requirements should rest on an analysis of the nature of the competencies required by the team (i.e., context-driven, team-contingent, task-contingent, or transportable). This requires a needs analysis at the level of the team.

- To specify appropriate training strategies, link competency requirements to specific training characteristics. Such strategies might include a task simulation, cross-training, role playing, a passive demonstration, or guided task practice.

Our understanding of this important area is continuing to evolve. The approach outlined above should stimulate further research, and such research is sorely needed to advance theory and to provide research-based guidance for practitioners.

BEHAVIORAL MODELS TO GUIDE TRAINING AND DEVELOPMENT EFFORTS

Once we have specified behavioral objectives, decomposed the overall task, and determined the optimum sequencing for learning subtasks, there remains one additional problem: how to acquire the appropriate responses. This is an important question to consider because different people have their own favorite ways of learning. For example, suppose Susan wants to learn a new skill, such as photography. She might begin by checking out three books on the topic from her local library. Alternately, Nancy might sign up for a photography class at a local school because she wants to experience it, not just to read about it. Finally Nicole might just begin to take pictures, experimenting in a trial-and-error fashion, until she gets the result she is looking for.

Susan, Nancy, and Nicole each prefer different learning methods. Susan prefers verbal learning, Nancy opts for kinesthetic (hands-on) learning, and Nicole chooses trial and error experiential learning. These are not the only methods; other people learn best from visual material (pictures, charts, graphs) or by modeling the behavior of others.

Often the design of a training program will incorporate as many of these modes as possible. Such a "mixed-mode" approach recognizes that no single approach is best for all training topics (e.g., skills versus attitudes) or for all people. For example, older workers can learn as well as younger ones, but they need more time, more practice, more learning by doing (Graham, 1996). Sound theoretical models are extremely useful here, for they help guide the training through the implementation phase. Let us begin by considering a model of learning based on individual differences.

Trainability and Individual Differences

Individual differences in abilities, interests, and personality play a central role in applied psychology. Variables such as prior achievement and initial skill level ("can do" factors), along with training expectations ("will do" factors), should be effective predictors of training performance. Available evidence indicates that they are (Gordon and Cohen, 1973; Robertson and Downs, 1979; 1989). In fact, general mental ability alone predicts success in training in a wide variety of jobs (Ree and Earles, 1991). So also does trainability.

Trainability refers to a person's ability to acquire the skills, knowledge, or behavior necessary to perform a job at a given level and to achieve these outcomes in a given time (Robertson and Downs, 1979). It is a combination of an individual's ability and motivation levels. A meta-analysis of 14 studies (total sample size of 2,542) showed that in most situations, work-sample trainability tests are valid predictors of training performance, more so than for job performance (Robertson and Downs, 1989).

For example, an approach called "miniature training and evaluation testing" (Siegel and Bergman, 1975; Siegel, 1983) used by the U.S. Navy focuses on the ability level of trainees to forecast trainability. It is based on the premise that a recruit who demonstrates that he or she is able to perform a sample of the tasks of a Navy job will be able to learn and to perform satisfactorily all the tasks of that job, given appropriate on-the-job training. In fact, a battery of nine training-evaluation situations derived from a job analysis of typical entry-level tasks for various naval occupations such as sailor, firefighter, and air crew member was able to improve substantially the accuracy of prediction of job performance over that obtained with standard written tests. Researchers found similar results for seven "minicourses" designed to select employees for jobs involving new technologies in the telecommunication industry (Reilly and Israelski, 1988).

While miniature training and evaluation testing focuses on ability, it is important to recognize that motivation also plays an important role in the prediction of training success (Quinones, 1995). Thus the Navy School for Divers found that a 7-item measure of trainee confidence significantly predicted graduation

---

ADAPTIVE TRAINING GOES HI-TECH

Almost 50 percent of U.S. workers use computers on the job, but studies show that only 14 percent of them are technologically skilled. To avoid the problem of having employees spend considerable time away from their normal duties in order to go to training, some firms are encouraging at-home instruction by paying employees overtime or sharing the expense of the training. Primus Marketing Associates, Inc. of Minneapolis uses a training program developed by Academic Systems that can be dialed on a user's home personal computer. Using the principles of adaptive training, the program individualizes learning by first testing users—and then offering additional material and guidance based on their responses. Trainees work at their own time and at their own pace, using interactive multimedia technology. Primus found that in addition to increasing flexibility, the interactive method produced more retention of knowledge than classroom instruction (Gupta, 1996). Other firms rely on CD-ROMs to implement their anytime, anyplace approach to training, while still others use high-definition television projected onto large theater screens in multiple locations to teach sales techniques. Trainees can grill instructors, join long-distance group discussions, and take home workbooks.

from its 10-week training program in Scuba and Deep Sea Air procedures (Ryman and Biersner, 1975). Hence it is now possible to identify reasonably accurately persons most likely to profit from training.

In order to study more precisely the behavioral transitions that occur in learning or training, however, we need to establish a behavioral baseline for each individual. Behavioral baselines result from each individual's prior history. The major advantage of this approach is that each individual's initial state serves as his own control. This procedure was used by Bass et al. (1976), for example, in a training program designed to cope with problems of race in the working environment. In order to assess changes in attitude *after* training, a behavioral baseline first was established for each of more than 2,000 subjects by having them complete a statistically-derived attitude questionnaire *prior* to training. Unfortunately, however, a great deal of training research ignores the concept of the behavioral baseline and the measurement of initial state.

Adaptive training is a logical extension of this idea (Cronbach and Snow, 1977). In adaptive training methods are varied to suit the abilities and characteristics of the trainees. In terms of training design, this suggests that we should measure the existing achievement levels of potential trainees and then tailor training content accordingly. Adaptive training is as appropriate for human relations training as it is for skill training.

Regardless of the medium used to deliver training, and regardless of its specific content, if the program is to be successful, trainers must pay careful attention to how trainees learn. Application of the classic principles of learning is essential.

PRINCIPLES OF LEARNING

If training and development are to have any long-term benefit, efficient learning, long-term retention, and positive transfer to the job situation are essential. Hence, it is not surprising that the principal theoretical basis for training in organizations has been the "learning principles" developed over the past century. While these principles may be relatively less important than other considerations, such as thorough task analysis and optimum sequencing (Gagné, 1962), we shall highlight some of them, paying special attention to their practical implementation.

Knowledge of Results (Feedback)

Information about one's attempts to improve is essential for learning to occur. Knowledge of results (KR) provides information that enables the learner to correct mistakes (as long as the learner is told *why* he or she is wrong and *how* he or she can correct the behavior in the future), and reinforcement (which makes the task more intrinsically interesting, thereby motivating the learner). KR may be intrinsic (i.e., stemming directly from the performance of the task itself) or extrinsic (i.e., administered by an outside individual). It may be qualitative ("that new ad is quite pleasing to the eye"), quantitative ("move the lever two inches down"), informative ("that new machine just arrived"), or evaluative ("you did a good job on that report—it was clear and brief").

Findings generally show that the presence of KR improves performance (Ilgen et al., 1979; Martocchio and Webster, 1992), but managers often misperceive its effects. Thus Greller (1980) found that supervisors consistently underestimated the importance subordinates attach to feedback from the task itself, comparisons to the work of others, and co-workers' comments. They overestimated the importance of formal rewards, informal assignments, and comments from the boss.

Are trainees passive recipients of KR in terms of issues such as the perception of KR, its acceptance, and psychological and behavioral reactions to it? Is there a role for trainees as monitors, seekers, and even generators of KR (Ashford and Cummings, 1983)? Recent research has provided some rather startling findings:

1. KR often results from proactive seeking, interpreting, and generating information by performers themselves (Herold and Parsons, 1985). This is more likely to occur when employees suspect the existence of a problem in their work that challenges their self-image as good, competent performers (Larson, 1989).

2. When managers attribute poor performance to lack of effort by a subordinate, they are likely to use a problem-solving approach in communicating performance feedback. However, when managers attribute poor performance to the subordinate's lack of ability, they are more likely to use a "tell and sell" approach. Only the problem-solving approach leads to changes in behavior (Dugan, 1989).

3. More KR may not always be better. A 10-month field

study of the behavioral safety performance of factory employees found that providing KR once every 2 weeks was about as good as providing it once a week (Chhokar and Wallin, 1984).

4. The impact of KR on performance is not always positive; it depends on the *type* of KR involved. Only KR that attributes prior performance to causes within the trainee's control, that explains *why* performance was effective/ineffective, and what specifically needs to be done to improve performance will be useful (Jacoby et al., 1984; Martocchio and Dulebohn, 1994).

5. To be accepted by performers as accurate, KR should include positive information first, followed by negative information (not vice versa) (Stone et al., 1984). When providing performance feedback on more than one dimension, provide it separately on all important dimensions, and allow employees the freedom to choose feedback on each dimension to reduce the possibility of redundancy and to minimize the amount of time they need to receive and evaluate feedback (Ilgen and Moore, 1987).

6. KR can help improve performance over and above the level achieved with *only* training and goal-setting. In other words, to bring about genuine improvements in performance, present training, goal-setting, and feedback as a package (Chhokar and Wallin, 1984).

7. Lastly, feedback affects group, as well as individual, performance. For example, application of performance-based feedback in a small fast-food store over a one-year period led to a 15 percent decrease in food costs and to a 193 percent increase in profits (Florin-Thuma and Boudreau, 1987). Another study, conducted in five organizational units at an Air Force Base, applied feedback for 5 months, then goal-setting for 5 months, and finally incentives for 5 months (all in an additive fashion). Results indicated that group-level feedback increased productivity an average of 50 percent over baseline, group goal-setting increased it 75 percent over baseline, and group incentives increased it 76 percent over baseline. Control group data showed no or only a slight increase over the same time period, and the level of employees either stayed the same or decreased. Work attitudes were as good or better following the interventions (Pritchard et al., 1988).

The trainee's immediate supervisor is likely to provide the most powerful KR. But if he or she does not reinforce what is learned in training, the results of training will transfer ineffectively to the job, if at all.

Transfer of Training

To a great extent, the usefulness of organizational training programs depends on the effective transfer of training—the application of behaviors learned in training to the job itself. Transfer may be positive (i.e., improve job performance), negative (i.e., hamper job performance), or neutral. It probably is the single most important consideration in training and development programs (Baldwin and Ford, 1988).

To maximize positive transfer, designers of training programs should consider doing the following:

1. Maximize the similarity between the training situation and the job situation.

2. Provide trainees as much experience as possible with the tasks, concepts, or skills being taught so that they can deal with situations that do not fit textbook examples exactly.

3. Ensure that trainees thoroughly understand the principles being taught, particularly in jobs that require the *application* of principles to solve problems, such as those of engineers, investment analysts, or systems analysts.

4. Provide a strong link between training content and job content ("What you learn in training today, you'll use on the job tomorrow").

5. In the context of team-based training (e.g., in employee involvement), transfer is maximized when teams have open, unrestricted access to information, when the membership includes diverse job functions and administrative backgrounds, and when a team has more members to draw upon to accomplish its activities. In one study, over half the variance in participant and supervisor ratings of team effectiveness could be attributed to those three design elements (Magjuka and Baldwin, 1991).

6. Ensure that what is learned in training is used and rewarded on the job. Supervisors and peers are key gatekeepers in this process (Ford et al., 1992). If immediate supervisors or peers, by their words or by their example, do not support what was learned in training, don't expect the training to have much of an impact on job performance (Tracey et al., 1995; Wexley and Latham, 1991).

The attitudes of trainees may also affect transfer (Noe, 1986). Transfer is likely to be higher when trainees: (1) are confident in using their newly-learned skills, (2) are aware of work situations where they can demonstrate their new skills, (3) perceive that both job and organizational performance will improve if they use the new skills, and (4) believe that the knowledge and skills emphasized in training are helpful in solving work-related problems. Such attitudes help the competencies learned in one training context (e.g., employee involvement training for use in quality circles) to generalize to other contexts (e.g., regular job duties) (Tesluk et al., 1995).

Self-Management to Maintain Changes in Behavior

Self-management is a novel approach to the maintenance of newly-trained behaviors. Although it was developed originally in the context of addictive behaviors (Marx, 1982), it has implications for maintaining newly-trained behaviors as well. It is a cognitive-behavioral model of self-management strategies designed to reduce the likelihood of relapse (see Fig. 16–3).

As described by Marx (1982), the first step is to make trainees aware of the relapse process itself. Training programs usually stress the positive results for participants; usually they do not make participants aware of how the training process itself is vulnerable to breakdown. Trainees then are asked to pinpoint situations that are likely to sabotage their attempts to maintain new learning. For example, in a study designed to control the abuse of sick leave (Frayne and Latham, 1987), employees listed family problems, incompatibility with supervisor or co-workers, and transportation problems as the most frequent reasons for using sick leave. Then employees were taught to self-monitor their behavior, for example, by recording (1) their own attendance, (2) the reason for missing a day of work, and (3) steps followed subsequently to get to work. Employees did this using charts and diaries.

The ability to diagnose such high-risk situations provides trainees with an early warning system, indicating when their ability to maintain new learning will be severely tested. It is not enough to anticipate high-risk circumstances in order to avoid a relapse. Employees also need coping skills. For example, if time pressure to complete a project is a high-risk situation, coping responses such as time-management skills and delegative leadership style to spread the workload may be helpful. As Figure 16–3 indicates, the presence of these skills likely will result in a feeling of mastery and a decreased probability of relapse; their absence

may lead to unproductive responses such as guilt, anxiety, and decreased self-efficacy.

In controlling sick leave, for example, trainees identified their own reinforcers (e.g., self-praise, purchasing a gift) and punishers (a disliked activity, easily self-administered, such as cleaning one's garage) to administer as a result of achieving or failing to achieve their near-term goals. Application of this system of self-management increased the self-efficacy of trainees, and their attendance was significantly higher than that of a control group. This effect held over a 12-month follow-up period (Latham and Frayne, 1989). In fact, self-management training may provide trainees who are low in self-efficacy with a skill development and maintenance program that they would not otherwise undertake due to low self-confidence (Gist et al., 1991). When combined with goal-setting (see below) it is a powerful model indeed for maintaining desired behaviors.

Reinforcement

In order for behavior to be acquired, modified, and sustained, it must be rewarded (reinforced). The principle of reinforcement also states that punishment only results in a temporary suppression of behavior and is a relatively ineffective influence on learning. Reward says to the learner, "Good, repeat what you have done"; punishment says, "Stop, you made the wrong response." Mild punishment may serve as a warning for the learner that he is getting off the track, but unless it is followed immediately by corrective feedback, punishment can be intensely frustrating.

In practice, it is difficult to apply this principle, especially the specification *prior* to training of what will function as a reward. Will it be praise from the trainer, a future promotion or salary increase, supervisory or peer commendation, or heightened feelings of self-determination and personal worth? Clearly, there are numerous sources from which rewards may originate, but, as we have seen, the most powerful rewards may be those provided by the trainee's immediate supervisor. If he or she does not reinforce what is learned in training, then the training itself will be "encapsulated" (Haire, 1964), and transfer will be minimal or negative.

Practice

For anyone learning a new skill or acquiring factual information there must be an opportunity to practice what is being learned. Practice refers to the active use

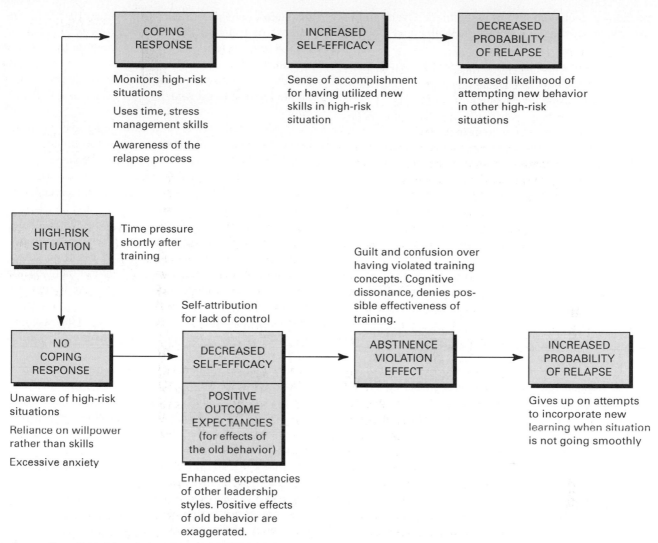

Source: From R. D. Marx, Relapse prevention for managerial training: A model for maintenance of behavior change. *Academy of Management Review,* 1982, 7, 434.

FIGURE 16–3 A Cognitive-Behavioral Model of the Relapse Process.

of training content. It has three aspects: active practice, overlearning, and the length of the practice session.

Active Practice. Particularly during skills learning (e.g., learning to operate a machine), it simply is not enough for a trainee to verbalize or to read what he or she is expected to do. Only active practice provides the internal cues that regulate motor performance. As practice continues, and given appropriate feedback, trainees discard inefficient motions and they retain the internal cues associated with smooth and precise performance. To see the end result, watch any professional athlete performing his or her specialty. Then you will appreciate why "practice makes perfect."

Overlearning. If trainees are given the opportunity to practice far beyond the point where they perform a task correctly several times, the task becomes "second nature;" they have overlearned it. For some tasks, such as those that must be performed infrequently and under great stress (e.g., the nurse who must perform CPR to save a patient's life), overlearning is critical. It is less important in jobs where workers practice their skills on a daily basis, such as auto mechanics, technicians, and assemblers. Overlearning has several advantages (Driskell, Willis, and Copper, 1992):

- It increases the length of time that trained material will be retained. The greater the degree of overlearning, the greater the retention.
- It makes learning more "reflexive," so that tasks become automatic with continued practice.
- It is effective for cognitive as well as physical tasks, but the effect is stronger for cognitive tasks.

However, without refresher training, the increase in retention due to overlearning is likely to dissipate to zero after 5–6 weeks (Driskell et al., 1992).

Length of the Practice Session. Practice may be *distributed*, involving rest intervals between sessions, or *massed,* in which practice sessions are crowded together. Although there are exceptions, most of the research evidence indicates that for the same amount of practice, learning is better when practice is distributed rather than massed (Landy, 1987). Here are two reasons why.

1. Continuous practice is fatiguing, so that individuals cannot show all that they have learned. Thus their performance is poorer than it would be if they were rested.
2. During a practice session, people usually learn both the correct performance as well as some irrelevant performances that interfere with it. But the irrelevant performances are likely to be less well practiced and so may be forgotten more rapidly between practice sessions. Performance should therefore improve if there are rest periods between practice sessions.

One exception to this rule is when people need to learn difficult conceptual material or other "thought problems." There seems to be an advantage in staying with the problem for a few massed practice sessions at first, rather than spending a day or more between sessions.

Motivation

In order actually to learn, one first must want to learn (Noe and Wilk, 1993). In practice, however, more attention usually is paid to trainees' ability to learn than to their motivation to learn, or to the interaction of ability and motivation. This is unfortunate, but understandable, since it may be easier to identify employees with high ability than those with high motivation. But what constitutes high motivation?

Motivation is a force that energizes, directs, and maintains behavior (Steers and Porter, 1975). In the context of training, this force influences enthusiasm for the training (*energizer*), keeps attention focused on training per se (*director*), and reinforces what is learned in training, even in the face of pressure back on the job to discard what has just been learned (*maintainer*).

Motivation to do well in training also is influenced by *beliefs* and perceptions of the trainee (e.g., regarding the benefits of training, and the degree of social support from managers and peers for development activity). Some of these key beliefs and perceptions are shown in Figure 16–4.

Factor I is a favorable work environment. Training is not conducted in a vacuum. If what is learned in training is to be used on the job, then it is important to anticipate the effect of the work environment on the motivation of trainees. Specifically, sufficient resources (material, financial, human) must be available to accomplish work (IA in Fig. 16–4). This includes the removal of conditions that inadvertently punish employees for attending training activities (e.g., ensuring that the trainee's work does not simply accumulate while he or she is gone). It also includes supportive interpersonal relationships with peers and supervisors (IB). Under these conditions, employees are more likely to believe that training opportunities might be useful to them in their work.

Factor II in Figure 16–4 is a belief in the soundness of the judgment by others that the trainee has strengths or weaknesses that training can improve on. Factor III is a personal belief in one's ability to master the content of the training (high self-efficacy). It is absolutely crucial to the acquisition and maintenance of competencies (Eden and Aviram, 1993; Gist et al., 1991; Mathieu, 1993; Saks, 1995). Feedback from trainers, supervisors, and peers can do much to affect this belief. Finally, Factor IV is a belief on the part of the trainee that successful completion of the program will lead to outcomes that he or she personally values (personal development, promotion, an increase in pay). Framing the context of training as an *opportunity* can enhance this belief (Martocchio, 1992).

It is possible to enhance motivation further by providing a realistic job preview of the training activity (Hicks and Klimoski, 1987), and by ensuring that employees receive realistic choices of development activities—those that they will actually have the opportunity to attend (Baldwin et al., 1991). To the extent that these factors are present, motivation to learn is likely to be high. To the extent that one or more of

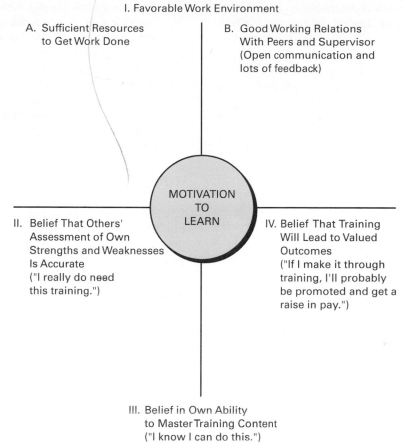

I. Favorable Work Environment

A. Sufficient Resources to Get Work Done

B. Good Working Relations With Peers and Supervisor (Open communication and lots of feedback)

MOTIVATION TO LEARN

II. Belief That Others' Assessment of Own Strengths and Weaknesses Is Accurate ("I really do need this training.")

IV. Belief That Training Will Lead to Valued Outcomes ("If I make it through training, I'll probably be promoted and get a raise in pay.")

III. Belief in Own Ability to Master Training Content ("I know I can do this.")

FIGURE 16–4 Some Factors That Affect Motivation to Perform Effectively in Training.

them is absent, a trainee may have the ability to learn, but not the motivation to do so.

While the factors shown in Figure 16–4 clearly affect trainees' motivation, so also do the *expectations* of the trainer. In fact, expectations have a way of becoming self-fulfilling prophecies, so that the higher the expectations, the better the trainees perform (and vice versa). This phenomenon of the self-fulfilling prophecy is known as the *Pygmalion effect*. It was demonstrated in one study over a 15–week combat-command course with adult trainees (Eden and Shani, 1982). Trainees of whom instructors had been induced to expect better performance scored significantly higher on objective achievement tests, showed more positive attitudes, and perceived more positive leader behavior. The Pygmalion effect has been confirmed in many studies using both male and female trainees. However, it does not appear to hold in situations where women are led (or instructed) by women (Dvir, Eden, and Banjo, 1995).

Goal-Setting

Once training is under way, motivation can be strengthened considerably by setting goals. Goal-setting has a proven track record of success in improving employee performance in a variety of settings (Locke and Latham, 1990; Locke et al., 1981). Goal-setting is founded on the premise that an individual's conscious goals or intentions regulate his or her behavior (Locke, 1968). Research findings are clear cut with respect to six issues:

1. Reviews of the literature show that goal-setting theory is among the most scientifically valid and useful theories in organizational science (Mento et al., 1987). Goal-setting effects are strongest for easy tasks and weakest for more complex tasks (Wood et al., 1987).

2. Commitment to goals by employees is a necessary condition for goal setting to work (Locke et al., 1988). Self-efficacy (a judgment about one's capability to

perform a task) affects commitment to goals, such as improving attendance (Frayne and Latham, 1987). It can be enhanced through practice, modeling, and persuasion (Bandura, 1986).

3. When tasks are complex, participation in goal-setting seems to enhance goal acceptance, particularly when employees are presented with a goal that they reject initially because it appears to be unreasonable or too difficult (Erez et al., 1985; Erez and Zidon, 1984). However, when tasks are simple, assigned goals may enhance goal acceptance, task performance, and intrinsic motivation (Shalley et al., 1987).

4. When given a choice, employees tend to choose more difficult goals if their previous goals were easy to attain, and to choose easier goals if their previous goals were difficult to attain. Thus past experience with goal-setting affects the level of goals employees choose in the future (Locke et al., 1984).

5. Once an employee accepts a goal, specific, difficult goals result in higher levels of performance than do easy goals or even a generalized goal such as "do your best" (Latham and Steele, 1983; Eden, 1988). However, this effect seems to disappear or to reverse for novel tasks that allow multiple alternative strategies (Earley et al., 1989).

6. The effects of goal-setting on performance can be enhanced further by providing information to performers about *how* to work on a task and by providing a rationale about *why* the goal and task are important (Earley, 1985).

Once employees accept goals, they keep them tenaciously, as the following study with unionized drivers of logging trucks indicates (Latham and Saari, 1982). First, the researchers conducted interviews with union business agents regarding the conditions necessary for their support of a goal-setting program. These included voluntary participation by drivers, no monetary rewards for those who attain goals, verbal praise for goal attainment as acceptable supervisory behavior (not "special treatment"), no punishment for failing to attain a goal, and no layoffs as a result of attaining goals. Then the researchers assigned goals (trips per truck to and from the logging sites) to 39 truck drivers. Results were as follows:

- Goal-setting resulted in the highest number of weekly average number of trips per truck ever obtained.
- Drivers started to use their radios to coordinate their efforts so that there always would be a truck at the logging sites when timber was ready to be loaded.
- Drivers were extremely aware of how they did. Repeatedly they bragged about attaining goals as they

came in for the evening. Some even purchased gold stars on their own and placed them beside their respective names. And, during a two-day holiday week that the truck foreman decided was too short to set goals, several drivers came into his office and demanded that goals be set.

- The study lasted 18 weeks; on the nineteenth week the company hired a consulting firm specializing in time study to implement a formal, uniform goal-setting program for all company operations. As far as the union was concerned, conditions necessary for its continued participation in the goal-setting program were no longer being met. This led to a wildcat strike.

The results of research on goal-setting are exciting. Their implications for the design of training programs are obvious: When individual trainees set explicit, difficult goals, this should lead to high motivation and commitment to the training, greater effort, and more efficient learning.

Behavior Modeling

Behavior modeling is based upon social learning theory (Bandura, 1977; 1986). In simple terms, social learning theory holds that we learn by observing others. The learning process per se requires attention, retention, the ability to reproduce what was learned, and motivation.

These principles might profitably be incorporated into a four-step "applied-learning" approach to behavior modeling (Goldstein and Sorcher, 1974):

1. *Modeling,* in which trainees watch videotapes of model persons behaving effectively in a problem situation.

2. *Role playing,* which gives trainees the opportunity to practice and rehearse the effective behaviors demonstrated by the models.

3. *Social reinforcement,* which the trainer provides to trainees in the form of praise and constructive feedback.

4. *Transfer of training,* which enables the behavior learned in training to be used effectively on the job.

Stated simply, the objective is to have people observe a model, remember what the model did, do what the model did, and, finally, use what they learned on the job (Baldwin, 1992). Sometimes the goal of behavior modeling is to enable the trainee to *reproduce* the modeled behaviors (e.g., a golf swing). However, the objective of most interpersonal- and supervisory-skills training (e.g., in problem-solving, conflict resolution) is to develop *generalizable* rules or concepts. If the goal is reproducibility, then only show positive (correct) examples of behavior. If the goal is generalization, then mix positive and negative examples (Baldwin, 1992).

Various types of retention aids can enhance modeling (Decker and Nathan, 1985; Mann and Decker, 1984): written descriptions of key behaviors (so-called "learning points"), mental rehearsal of the behaviors, and rewriting the learning points. Encourage trainees to write their own list of learning points, if they wish to do so (Hogan et al., 1986). This leads to the development of cognitive "scripts" that serve as links between cognition and behavior (Cellar and Wade, 1988).

Research also suggests that the most effective way to practice skills in a behavior-modeling program is to include a videotape replay of each rehearsal attempt, and to do so in a small group with two role players and only one or two observers (Decker, 1983). As a result of research done since the mid-1970s, the formula for behavior-modeling training now includes five components: modeling, retention processes, role playing (or behavioral rehearsal), social reinforcement, and transfer of training (Decker and Nathan, 1985).

In terms of the preferred learning styles and principles of learning we discussed earlier, behavior modeling includes most of them: conceptual learning, observational learning, practicing specific behaviors, social reinforcement, and feedback. In combination, this is a powerful training design. It has been used by a large number of firms to teach motor as well as social skills (Wexley, 1984).

Research continues to demonstrate the effectiveness of behavior modeling over other training approaches (Gist et al., 1988). In fact, a meta-analysis of 70 studies on the effectiveness of management training found that behavior modeling was among the most effective (Burke and Day, 1986). The boxed insert below presents the results of a long-term field study.

Despite these encouraging results, behavior modeling may not be suitable for everyone. Different training methods may be needed for persons with high and low self-efficacy. For example, in a study involving the use of computer software, Gist et al. (1989) found that modeling increased performance for people whose pretest self-efficacy was in the range of moderate to high. However, for those with low self-efficacy, a one-on-one tutorial was more effective.

Another potential problem surfaces when the impact of behavior modeling is evaluated in terms of its ability to produce actual behavior change back on the job (i.e., transfer). Why? In some studies (e.g., Russell et al., 1984) trainees were encouraged to use their newly acquired skills, but no formal evaluations were made, and no sanctions were levied on those who failed to comply. The result: There was no long-term behavior change. In other studies (e.g., Latham and Saari, 1979), trainees were directed and encouraged by their managers to use the new skills, and, in two cases, supervisors who refused to use them were removed from their positions. The result: Behavior changed back on the job.

In another successful transfer of skills from training to the job, employees of trained supervisors received training on identical incidents at the same time the supervisors were being trained. This was extremely important in creating an environment that encouraged the supervisors to practice and use the new behaviors (Sorcher and Spence, 1982). *Conclusion:* Although behavior modeling does produce positive trainee reactions and learning, more than modeling is

RESULTS OF BEHAVIOR MODELING TRAINING AT CHAMPION INTERNATIONAL

This program was designed to teach supervisory skills at a Champion International plywood plant in Oregon (Porras and Anderson, 1981). Four different indicators suggested positive results. One, although productivity declined immediately following the training, 6 months later it had improved by 17 percent, relative to that of a control group. Two, monthly savings of about $45,000 resulted from a reduction in the waste of raw materials. Three, supervisory behaviors, as perceived by their subordinates, improved markedly in the trained group, as compared to the control group. Four, grievances, absenteeism, and turnover decreased significantly in the trained group.

needed to produce sustained changes in behavior and performance on the job. Here are three strategies suggested by research findings (Russell et al., 1984):

1. Show supervisors why their new behaviors are more effective than their current behaviors.

2. Encourage each trainee to practice the new behavior mentally until it becomes consistent with the trainee's self-image. Then try the new behavior on the job.

3. To facilitate positive transfer, follow the training by goal-setting and reinforcement in the work setting.

SUMMARY

Each of the behavioral models we have presented—individual differences, principles of learning, motivation, and behavior modeling—offers a systematic approach to training and development. Each emphasizes a somewhat different aspect of the training process (e.g., while the individual differences model stresses trainability and the value of adaptive treatments, the behavior-modeling approach emphasizes modeling, role playing, social reinforcement, and transfer of training).

No one model is most appropriate under all circumstances, but each has much to offer those responsible for the design of training and development programs. Behavioral models can yield maximum payoff, however, only when training needs first are defined clearly. The models then can serve as guides for the design of programs that accurately match targeted training needs.

Discussion Questions

1. Transfer of training is a key issue in most organizations. What would you do to maximize it?

2. Outline a needs-assessment process to identify training needs for supermarket checkers.

3. How might behavior modeling be useful in team-based training?

4. Why do training programs tend to emphasize hardware and techniques rather than what is to be learned?

5. Top management asks you to present a briefing on the potential effects of goal-setting and feedback. What would you say?

* * *

The design of a training and development program is critical to its eventual success. No less critical, though, are implementation of the program and the measurement of outcomes resulting from it. We will consider both of these important issues in Chapter 17.

17

TRAINING AND DEVELOPMENT: IMPLEMENTATION AND THE MEASUREMENT OF OUTCOMES

AT A GLANCE

The literature on training and development techniques is massive. In general, however, the techniques comprise three categories: information-presentation techniques, simulation methods, and on-the-job training. Selection of a particular technique is likely to yield maximal payoff when designers of training follow a two-step sequence—first, specify clearly *what is to be learned; only then* choose a specific method or technique that accurately matches training requirements.

In measuring the outcomes of training and development, use multiple criteria (varying in time, type, and level), and map out and understand the interrelationships among the criteria and with other organizational variables. In addition, impose enough experimental or quasi-experimental control to allow unambiguous inferences regarding training effects.

Finally, in measuring training and development outcomes, be sure to (1) say something about the practical and theoretical significance of the results, (2) provide a logical analysis of the process and content of the training, and (3) deal with the "systems" aspects of training impact. The ultimate objective is to assess the individual and organizational utility of training efforts.

Once we define what trainees should learn and what the substantive content of training and development should be, the critical questions then become: How should we teach the content, and who should do it?

The literature on training and development techniques is massive. However, while many choices exist, evidence indicates that among U.S. companies that conduct training, fewer than one-third make any systematic effort to assess their training needs before choosing training methods (Saari et al., 1988). This implies that firms view hardware and techniques as more important than outcomes. They view (mistakenly) the identification of what trainees should learn as secondary to the choice of technique.

New training methods appear every year. Some of them are deeply rooted in theoretical models of learning and behavior change (e.g., behavior modeling, programmed instruction), others seem to be the result of trial and error, and still others (e.g., interactive multimedia, computer-based business games) seem to be more the result of technological than of theoretical developments. We will make no attempt to review specific training methods that are or have been in use. Other sources are available for this purpose (Cascio, 1998; Latham, 1988). We will only highlight some of the more popular techniques and present a set of criteria for judging the adequacy of training methods.

Training and development techniques comprise three categories (Campbell et al., 1970): information-presentation techniques, simulation methods, and on-the-job training.

Information-presentation techniques include:

1. Lectures
2. Conference methods
3. Correspondence courses
4. Motion pictures
5. Reading lists
6. Interactive multimedia (CD-ROM, video), including programmed instruction and computer-assisted instruction
7. Closed-circuit television
8. Systematic observation (closely akin to modeling)
9. T (training)-groups or sensitivity training—unstructured learning situations in which individuals meet in groups, focus on the "here and now" behavior taking place in their own group, and attempt to enhance their awareness both of themselves and of social processes
10. Laboratory education—more complete programs of training experiences, which may include (in addition to the basic T-group) short lectures, role playing, group exercises designed to illustrate problems in interpersonal or intergroup behavior, and the like. A meta-analysis of 126 studies that employed a range of techniques to change satisfaction and other attitudes revealed that laboratory education, along with team building, was most effective (Neuman et al., 1989)
11. Organization development—systematic, long-range programs of organizational improvement through action research. Action research includes (a) preliminary diagnosis, (b) data gathering from the client group, (c) data feedback to the client group, (d) data exploration by the client group, (e) action planning, and (f) action. The cycle then begins again

One of the most popular organization development methods is *survey feedback*. The process begins with a comprehensive assessment of the way the organization is currently functioning—typically via the administration of anonymous questionnaires to all employees. Researchers tabulate responses at the level of individual work groups, and for the organization as a whole. Each manager receives a summary of this information, based on the responses of his or her immediate subordinates. Then a change agent (i.e., a person skilled in the methods of applied behavioral science) meets privately with the manager-recipient to maximize his or her understanding of the survey results. Following this, the change agent attends a meeting of the manager and subordinates, the purpose of which is to examine the survey findings and to discuss implications for corrective action. The role of the change agent is to help group members better understand the survey results, to set goals, and to formulate action plans for the change effort.

Simulation methods include:

1. The case method—representative organizational situations are presented on paper, usually to groups of trainees who subsequently identify problems and offer solutions. Individuals learn from each other and receive feedback on their own performances
2. The incident method—similar to the case method, except that trainees receive only a sketchy outline of a particular incident. They have to question the trainer, and when they think they have enough information, they attempt a solution. At the end of the session, the trainer reveals all the information he or she has, and trainees compare their solution to the one based on complete information
3. Role playing—including multiple role playing, in which a large group breaks down into smaller groups and role plays the same problem within each group without a trainer. All players then reassemble and discuss with the trainer what happened in their groups
4. Programmed group exercises—simulations of experiences relevant to organizational psychology. This is a hybrid technique that incorporates many of the elements of the case study, multiple role-playing, programmed instruction, and sensitivity training. Trainees examine their responses first as individuals, then with the members of their own groups, and finally with the larger group and with the trainer
5. The task model—trainers construct a complex but easily-built physical object, and a group of trainees must duplicate it, given the proper materials. Trainees use alternative communication arrangements, and only certain trainees may view the object. Trainees discuss communication problems as they arise, and they reach solutions through group discussion
6. The in-basket technique
7. Business games
8. Assessment centers
9. Behavior modeling

On-the-job training methods are especially popular—both in basic skills training and in management training and development. Broadly conceived, they include:

1. Orientation training
2. Apprenticeships
3. On-the-job training
4. Vestibule training—duplicates exactly the materials and equipment used on the job, but takes place in an area off the production line or away from the actual job situation. The focus is exclusively on training
5. Job rotation
6. Junior executive boards. These allow promising middle-level managers to experience first-hand the problems and responsibilities faced by high-level executives in their company, thus enabling them to develop the capacity to identify and explore broad issues. Approximately a dozen young executives from diverse functions across the organization serve on the board for terms of 6 months or longer. Ordinarily the board is allowed to study any problem faced by the organization (e.g., HR policies, organization design, interdepartmental conflicts, executive compensation), and to make recommendations to the senior board of directors—the official board elected by the stockholders
7. Understudy assignments. Any organization needs to have trained people ready to assume key positions as necessary. Firms use understudy assignments for this purpose and to promote the development of "homegrown" top executives. An understudy relieves a senior executive of selected responsibilities, thereby allowing the understudy to learn certain aspects of the job and the executive's style of handling it. The benefits the trainee derives from this experience depend on the quality of the relationship with the executive, as well as on the executive's ability to teach effectively through verbal communication and behavior modeling
8. On-the-job coaching. Managers who coach employees well "model" correct behaviors, assign specific and challenging goals, and provide trainees with frequent and immediate feedback concerning their job performance. The training of managers to conduct effective coaching sessions usually incorporates a series of modeling videotapes, role-playing activities, and workbook exercises. The broad objective of such training is to increase employee motivation by giving employees more open lines of communication with their bosses, concrete feedback on areas needing improvement, positive reinforcement for what they do well, and specific goals for change. As with understudy assignments, the success of coaching depends on the quality of the boss/subordinate relationship and on the extent to which the boss is willing to share his or her experience and observations
9. Performance appraisal (see Chapter 5)

Selection of Technique

Each of the available training methods can contribute most to training programs only if it is used appropriately. Appropriate use, in this context, means rigid adherence to a two-step sequence: *first*, define what trainees are to learn, and *only then* choose a particular method that best fits these requirements. Far too often, unfortunately, trainers choose methods first and then force them to fit particular needs. This "retrofit" approach is not only wrong, but is also often extremely wasteful of organizational resources—time, people, and money. It should be banished.

In order to select a particular technique, the following checklist may prove useful. A technique is adequate to the extent that it provides the minimal conditions for effective learning to take place. To do this, a technique should:

1. Motivate the trainee to improve his or her performance;
2. Clearly illustrate desired skills;
3. Provide for the learner's active participation;
4. Provide an opportunity to practice;
5. Provide feedback on performance while the trainee learns;
6. Provide some means to reinforce the trainee while learning;
7. Be structured from simple to complex tasks;
8. Be adaptable to specific problems;
9. Enable the trainee to transfer what is learned in training to other situations.

Designers of training can apply this checklist to all proposed training techniques. If a particular technique appears to fit training requirements yet is deficient in one or more checklist areas, then either modify it to eliminate the deficiency or buttress it with another technique. Once we have selected a training method that accurately matches training requirements, the next step is to conduct the training. Although a checklist of the many logistical details involved is not appropriate here, actual implementation should not be a major stumbling block if prior planning and design have been thorough. The final step, of course, is to measure the outcomes of training and their interaction with other organizational subsystems. To this topic we now turn.

MEASURING TRAINING AND DEVELOPMENT OUTCOMES

"Evaluation" of a training program implies a dichotomous outcome (i.e., either a program has value or it does not). In practice, matters are rarely so simple, for outcomes are usually a matter of degree. To assess outcomes we need to document systematically how trainees actually behave back on their jobs, and the relevance of their behavior to the objectives of the organization (Snyder et al., 1980).

Why Measure Training Outcomes?

Evidence indicates that few companies assess the outcomes of training activities with any procedure more rigorous than participant reactions following the completion of training programs (Saari et al., 1988). This is unfortunate, because there are at least four reasons to evaluate training (Sackett and Mullen, 1993):

1. To make decisions about the future use of a training program or technique (e.g., continue, modify, eliminate);

2. To make decisions about individual trainees (e.g., certify as competent, provide additional training);

3. To contribute to a scientific understanding of the training process;

4. For political or public relations purposes (e.g., to increase the credibility and visibility of the training function by documenting success).

Beyond these basic issues, we also would like to know whether the techniques used are more efficient or more cost-effective than other available training methods. Finally, we also would like to be able to compare training with other approaches to developing workforce capability, such as improving selection procedures or redesigning jobs. To do any of this, certain elements are essential.

ESSENTIAL ELEMENTS FOR MEASURING TRAINING OUTCOMES

At the most basic level, the task of evaluation is counting—counting new customers, counting interactions, counting dollars, counting hours, and so forth. The most difficult tasks of evaluation are deciding *what* things to count and developing routine *methods* for counting them. Managers should count the things that

will provide the most useful feedback (Foote and Erfurt, 1981). The following elements are essential (Campbell et al., 1970):

1. Use of multiple criteria, not just for the sake of numbers but for the purpose of more adequately reflecting the multiple contributions of managers to the organization's goals.

2. Some attempt to study the criteria themselves—that is, their relationships with each other and with other variables. The relationship between internal and external criteria is especially important.

3. Enough experimental control to enable the causal arrow to be pointed at the training program. How much is enough will depend on the possibility of an interactive effect with the criterion measure and the susceptibility of the training program to the Hawthorne effect.

4. Provisions for saying something about the practical and theoretical significance of the results.

5. A thorough, logical analysis of the process and content of the training.

6. Some effort to deal with the "systems" aspects of training impact, that is, how training effects are altered by interaction with other organizational subsystems. For example: Are competencies learned in training strengthened or weakened by reward practices (formal or informal) in the work setting? Is the nature of the job situation such that trainees can use the skills they learned, or are other organizational changes required? Will the new skills that trainees learned hinder or facilitate the functioning of other organizational subunits? Trainers must address these issues before they can conduct any truly meaningful evaluation of training's impact.

Indeed, the effective design of training systems and the optimal prediction of training performance require that trainers examine carefully both individual and situational influences. These include characteristics of trainees (e.g., aptitude, educational preparation), course-content variables (e.g., course length, instructional quality, practice, feedback), and training-performance variables (e.g., the quality of performance, and performance counseling) (Mumford et al., 1988). The remainder of this chapter will treat each of these points more fully and provide practical illustrations of their use.

Criteria

As with any other HR program, the first step in judging the value of training is to specify multiple criteria. Although we covered the criterion problem already in

Chapter 4, it is important to emphasize that the assessment of training outcomes requires multiple criteria because training is usually directed at specific components of performance. Organizations deal with multiple objectives, and training outcomes are multidimensional. Training may contribute to movement toward some objectives and away from others at the same time (Bass, 1983). Let us examine criteria according to time, type, and level.

Time. The important question here is: When, relative to the actual conduct of the training, should we obtain criterion data? We could do so prior to, during, immediately after, or much later after the conclusion of training. To be sure, the timing of criterion measurement can make a great deal of difference in the interpretation of training's effects (Sprangers and Hoogstraten, 1989). Conclusions drawn from an analysis of changes in trainees from before to immediately after training may differ drastically from conclusions based upon the same criterion measures 6 to 12 months after training (Freeberg, 1976). Yet both measurements are important. One review of 59 studies found, for example, that the time span of measurement (the time between the first and last observations) was 1 year or less for 26 studies, 1 to 3 years for 27 studies, and more than 3 years for only six studies (Nicholas and Katz, 1985). Comparisons of short- versus long-term training effects may yield valuable information concerning the interaction of training effects with other organizational processes (norms, values, leadership styles, etc.). Finally, it is not the absolute level of behavior (e.g., number of grievances per month, number of accidents) that is crucial, but rather the *change* in behavior from the beginning of training to some time after its conclusion.

Types of Criteria. It is important to distinguish internal from external criteria. Internal criteria are those that are linked directly to performance in the training situation. Examples of internal criteria are attitude scales or objective achievement examinations designed specifically to measure what the training program is designed to teach. External criteria, on the other hand, are measures designed to assess actual changes in job behavior. For example, an organization may conduct a 2-day training program in EEO law and its implications for HR management. A written exam at the conclusion of training (designed to assess mastery of the program's content) would be an internal criterion. On the other hand, ratings by subordinates, peers, or supervisors and documented evidence re-

garding the trainees' on-the-job application of EEO principles constitute external criteria. Both internal and external criteria are necessary to evaluate the relative payoffs of training and development programs, and researchers need to understand the relationships among them in order to draw meaningful conclusions about training's effects.

Criteria also may be qualitative or quantitative. Qualitative criteria are attitudinal and perceptual measures that usually are obtained by interviews or observations of employees or by administering written instruments. Quantitative criteria include measures of the outcomes of job behavior and system performance. Employment, accounting, production, and sales records often contain these. They include outcomes such as turnover, absenteeism, dollar volume of sales, accident rates, or controllable rejects.

Both qualitative and quantitative criteria are important for a thorough understanding of training effects. Traditionally, researchers have preferred quantitative measures, except in organization development research (Nicholas, 1982; Nicholas and Katz, 1985). This may be a mistake, since there is much more to interpreting the outcomes of training than quantitative measures alone. By ignoring qualitative (process) measures, we may miss the richness of detail concerning *how* events occurred. In fact, Goldstein (1978) and Jick (1979) described studies where data would have been misinterpreted if the researchers had been unaware of the events that took place during training.

Levels of Criteria. "Levels" of criteria may refer either to organizational levels from which we collect criterion data or to the relative level of rigor we adopt in measuring training outcomes. With respect to organizational levels, information from trainers, trainees, subordinates, peers, supervisors, and the organization's policy makers (i.e., the training program's sponsors) can be extremely useful. In addition to individual sources, group sources (e.g., work units, teams, squads) can provide aggregate data regarding morale, turnover, grievances, or various cost, error, or profit measures that can be helpful in assessing training's effects.

Kirkpatrick (1977, 1983) identified four levels of rigor in the evaluation of training and development programs: reaction, learning, behavior, and results. However, it is important to note that these levels provide only a vocabulary and a rough taxonomy for criteria. Higher levels do not necessarily provide more information than lower levels do, and the levels need not be causally linked or positively intercorrelated (Alliger and Janak, 1989). In comparing two alternative training methods, for example, trainees may react more favorably to one method, even though they learn as much from either one (Bretz and Thompsett, 1992). These two levels of criteria, reaction and learning, are internal measures of training outcomes.

Reaction criteria represent the lowest level of rigor. They are simply measures of the trainee's impressions or feelings about the program. At best, researchers obtain these data by means of a written comment sheet or questionnaire administered at the end of training. At worst, the "data" consist of retrospective testimonials by a selected group of "satisfied customers." In both cases trainee reactions provide little, if any, substantive information regarding training's effects. (For instance, the questionnaire may ask: "How valuable was this program for you as a learning experience?")

Reactions moderate the relationship between training motivation and learning (Mathieu et al., 1992). The best results appear when trainees are motivated to do well *and* react positively to the training program. If they are not highly motivated at the outset, or if trainers focus solely on making the training enjoyable at the expense of developing skills, expect less-than-optimal results.

Learning criteria are multidimensional, for they may include cognitive outcomes (e.g., knowledge of procedures or strategies), skills-based outcomes, or affective outcomes (e.g., changes in attitudes or motivation) (Kraiger, Ford, and Salas, 1993). Each of these may require a different method of measurement (e.g., speed or power tests, self-reports, or targeted observations of behavior). To make results more meaningful and to rule out alternative explanations it is important to administer the measures according to some logical plan or procedure (experimental design) (e.g., before and after training as well as to a comparable control group). Numerous experimental designs are available for this purpose, and we shall consider them in a later section.

The last two levels of criteria, behavior and results, are external criteria. External criterion measures are extremely important since, as we noted in Chapter 4, there often is a low relationship between success in training and success on the job.

Behavioral criteria refer to measures of performance back on the job. The goal here is to demonstrate positive transfer between what is learned in training and what is applied on the job. This involves two steps: the first is to demonstrate behavioral changes in on-the-job behavior, and the second is to demonstrate that such changes are due specifically to training. Appropriate use of experimental or quasi-experimental designs is especially important when assessing behavioral changes since there often are alternative explanations for observed changes.

In assessing on-the-job behavioral changes, allow a reasonable period of time (e.g., at least 3 months) after the completion of training before taking measures. This is especially important for development programs that are designed to improve decision-making skills or to change attitudes or leadership styles; such programs require *at least* 3 months before their effects manifest themselves in measurable behavioral changes. To detect the changes we need carefully developed techniques for systematic observation and measurement. Examples include scripted, job-related scenarios that use empirically-derived scoring weights (Ostroff, 1991), BARS, self-reports (supplemented by reports of subordinates, peers, and supervisors), critical incidents, or various qualitative and quantitative measures of individual performance.

Results criteria provide yet another assessment of a training program's utility in terms of its contribution to organizational objectives—cost reductions, reductions in turnover, absenteeism, grievances, increases in production quality and quantity, profits, or work group morale.

Strategies for Measuring the Outcomes of Training in Terms of Results. Such measurement is not easy, but the technology to do it is available and well developed. In terms of utility analysis (see Chapter 13), the formula for assessing the outcomes of training in dollar terms (Schmidt, Hunter, and Pearlman, 1982) builds directly on the general utility formula for assessing the payoff from selection programs (Eq. 13–5):

$$\Delta U = T \times N \times d_t \times SD_y - N \times C \quad \textbf{(17–1)}$$

where:

ΔU = dollar value of the training program

T = number of years duration of the training effect on performance

N = the number of persons trained

d_t = the true difference in job performance between the average trained and untrained worker in standard *z*-score units (see Eq. 17–2)

SD_y = the variability (standard deviation) of job performance in dollars of the untrained group

C = the per-person cost of the training

NOTE 1: If the training is not held during working hours, then C should include only direct training costs. If training is held during working hours, then C should include, in addition to direct costs, all costs associated with having employees away from their jobs during the training.

NOTE 2: The term d_t is called the *effect size*. We begin with the assumption that there is no difference in job performance between trained workers (those in the experimental group) and untrained workers (those in the control group). The effect size tells us: (1) if there is a difference between the two groups, and (2), how large it is. The formula for effect size is:

$$d_t = \frac{\bar{X}_e - \bar{X}_c}{SD(\sqrt{r_{yy}})} \qquad (17\text{--}2)$$

where:

$\bar{X}_e$ = average job performance of the trained workers (those in the experimental group)

$\bar{X}_c$ = average job performance of the untrained workers (those in the control group)

SD = standard deviation of the job performance measure in the untrained group

$\sqrt{r_{yy}}$ = the reliability of the job performance measure (e.g., the degree of inter-rater agreement, expressed as a correlation coefficient)

Equation 17–2 expresses effect size in standard deviation units. To express it as a percentage change in performance (X), the formula is:

% change in $X = d_t \times 100 \times$
$$SD_{\text{pretest}}/Mean_{\text{pretest}} \qquad (17\text{--}3)$$

where $100 \times SD_{\text{pretest}}/Mean_{\text{pretest}}$ (the coefficient of variation) is the ratio of the standard deviation of pretest performance to its mean, multiplied by 100, where performance is measured on a ratio scale. Thus to change d_t into a change-in-output measure, multiply d_t by the coefficient of variation for the job in question (Sackett, 1991).

To illustrate the computation of the utility of training, suppose we wish to estimate the net payoff from a training program in supervisory skills. We develop the following information: $T = 2$ years; $N = 100$; $d_t = .31$ (Mathieu and Leonard, 1987); $SD_y = \$10,000$ (calculated by any of the methods we discussed in Chapter 13); $C = \$500$ per person. According to Equation 17–1, the net payoff from the training program is:

$$\Delta U = 2 \times 100 \times .31 \times \$10,000 - (100)(\$500)$$
$$\Delta U = \$570,000 \text{ over 2 years.}$$

Yet this figure is illusory because it fails to consider both economic and noneconomic factors that affect payoffs. For example, it fails to consider the fact that $570,000 received in 2 years is only worth $431,000 today (using the discount rate of 15 percent reported by Mathieu and Leonard, 1987). It also fails to consider the effects of variable costs and taxes (Boudreau, 1988). Finally, it looks only at a single cohort; but if training is effective, managers want to apply it to multiple cohorts. Payoffs over subsequent time periods also must consider the effects of attrition of trained employees, as well as decay in the strength of the training effect over time (Cascio, 1989). Even after taking all of these considerations into account, the monetary payoff from training and development efforts still may be substantial (Gattiker, 1995) and well worth demonstrating.

Initially, it might appear that we should hold *all* training programs accountable strictly in economic terms. However, this is a rather narrow view of the problem, for economic indexes derived from the performance of operating units often are subject to bias (e.g., turnover, market fluctuations). Measures such as unit costs are not always under the exclusive control of the manager, and the biasing influences that are present are not always obvious enough to be compensated for.

This is not to imply that results criteria should not be used to demonstrate a training program's worth; on the contrary, every effort should be made to do so. However, those responsible for assessing training outcomes should be well aware of the difficulties and limitations of results criteria. They also must consider the utility of information-gathering efforts (i.e., if the costs of trying to decide whether the program was beneficial outweigh any possible benefits, then why make the effort?). On the other hand, given the high payoff of effective management performance, the likelihood of such an occurrence is rather small. In short, don't ignore results criteria. While internal criteria demonstrate what was *learned*, external criteria demonstrate what was *transferred*. We need both types of outcomes in order to assess the overall utility of training efforts.

CLASSICAL EXPERIMENTAL DESIGN

An experimental design is a plan, an outline for conceptualizing the relations among the variables of a research study. It also implies how to control the research situation and how to analyze the data (Kerlinger, 1986).

Experimental designs can be used either with internal or external criteria. For example, researchers can collect "before" measures on-the-job before training, and collect "after" measures at the conclusion of training as well as back on the job at some time after training. Researchers use experimental designs so that they can make causal inferences. That is, by ruling out alternative plausible explanations for observed changes in the outcome of interest, we want to be able to say that training *caused* the changes.

Unfortunately, most experimental designs and most training studies do not permit the causal arrow to point unequivocally toward training as *the* explanation for observed results. To illustrate, consider a study by Boss (1979). A move to a new facility and the adoption of a new technology followed team-building sessions and organizational redesign. Subsequent studies indicated considerable improvement in terms of outcome (results) measures. Does that mean that the team-building sessions "caused" the changes in the results criteria? No, but Boss (1979) did not claim that they did. Rather, he concluded that the training programs and subsequent follow-up efforts all *contributed* to the success of the team-building effort. It was impossible to identify the unique contribution of team-building alone. In fact, Cook and Campbell (1976; 1979) suggest numerous potential contaminants or threats to valid interpretations of findings from field research. The threats may affect:

1. *Statistical conclusion validity*—conclusions about whether a presumed cause and effect covary;
2. *Internal validity*—conclusions about whether changes in one variable caused changes in another;
3. *Construct validity*—"confounding," i.e., the possibility that the operational definition of a variable implies more than one construct; or
4. *External validity*—conclusions about the extent to which results can be generalized across populations, settings, and times.

In the context of training, let us consider 12 of these threats:

1. *History*—specific events occurring between the before- and after-measurements in addition to training.
2. *Maturation*—ongoing processes within the individual, such as growing older or gaining job experience, which are a function of the passage of time.
3. *Testing*—the effect of a pretest on posttest performance.
4. *Instrumentation*—the degree to which an instrument may measure different attributes of an individual at two different points in time (e.g., parallel forms of an attitude questionnaire administered before and after training, or different raters rating behavior before and after training).
5. *Statistical regression*—changes in criterion scores resulting from selecting extreme groups on a pretest.
6. *Differential selection*—using different procedures for selecting individuals for experimental and control groups.
7. *Experimental mortality*—differential loss of respondents from various groups.
8. *Interaction of differential selection and maturation*—i.e., assuming experimental and control groups were different to begin with, the disparity between groups compounds further due to maturational changes occurring during the training period.
9. *Interaction of pretest with the experimental variable*—during the course of training, something reacts with the pretest in such a way that the pretest has a greater effect on the trained group than the untrained group.
10. *Interaction of differential selection with training*—when more than one group is trained, differential selection implies that the groups are not equivalent on the criterion variable (e.g., skill in using a computer) to begin with; therefore, they may react differently to the training.
11. *Reactive effects of the research situation*—i.e., the research design itself so changes the trainees' expectations and reactions that one cannot generalize results to future applications of the training.
12. *Multiple-treatment interference*—residual effects of previous training experiences affect trainees differently (e.g., finance managers and HR managers might not react comparably to a human relations training program because of differences in their previous training).

Table 17–1 presents examples of several experimental designs. These designs are by no means exhaustive; they merely illustrate the different kinds of

TABLE 17-1 Experimental Designs for Assessing Training and Development Outcomes

	A		B	C		D			
	After-Only (One Control Group)		*Before-After (No Control Group)*	*Before-After (One Control Group)*		*Solomon Four-Group Design Before-After (Three Control Groups)*			
	E	C	E	E	C	E	C1	C2	C3
Pretest	No	No	Yes	Yes	Yes	Yes	Yes	No	No
Training	Yes	No	Yes	Yes	No	Yes	No	Yes	No
Posttest	Yes	Yes	Yes	Yes	Yes	Yes	Yes	Yes	Yes

Note: E refers to the experimental group. *C* refers to the control group.

inferences that researchers may draw and, therefore, underline the importance of considering experimental designs *before* training.

Design A

Design A, in which neither the experimental nor the control group receives a pretest, has not been used widely in training research. This is because the concept of the pretest is deeply ingrained in the thinking of researchers, although it is not actually essential to true experimental designs (Campbell and Stanley, 1963). We hesitate to give up "knowing for sure" that experimental and control groups were, in fact, "equal" before training despite the fact that:

> the most adequate all-purpose assurance of lack of initial biases between groups is randomization. Within the limits of confidence stated by tests of significance, randomization can suffice without the pretest [Campbell and Stanley, 1963, p. 25].

Design A controls for testing as main effect and interaction, but it does not actually measure them. While such measurement is tangential to the real question of whether training did or did not produce an effect, the lack of pretest scores limits the ability to generalize since it is impossible to examine the possible interaction of training with pretest ability level. In most organizational settings, however, antecedent variables are available (e.g., job experience, age, job performance) either for "blocking" subjects (i.e., grouping subjects in pairs matched on the antecedent variable(s) and then randomly assigning one member of each pair to the experimental group and the other to the control group), or for use as covariates. Both of these strategies increase statistical precision and make posttest differences more meaningful. In short, the main advantage of Design A is that it avoids pretest bias and the "give-away" repetition of identical or highly similar material (as in attitude-change studies),

but this advantage is not without costs (Campbell and Stanley, 1963).

Design B

The defining characteristic of Design B is that it compares a group with itself. In theory, there is no better comparison since all possible variables associated with characteristics of the subjects are controlled. In practice, however, when the objective is to measure change, Design B is fraught with difficulties, for there are numerous plausible rival hypotheses that might explain changes in criterion scores. History is one. If researchers administer pre- and posttests on different days, then events in between may have caused any difference in criterion scores. While the history effect is trivial if researchers administer pre- and posttests within a 1- or 2-hour period, it becomes more and more plausible as an alternative explanation for change as the time between pre- and posttest lengthens. Aside from specific external events, various biological or psychological processes that vary systematically with time (i.e., maturation) also may account for observed differences. Hence, between pretests and posttests, trainees may have grown hungrier, more fatigued, or bored. "Changes" in criterion measures simply may reflect these differences.

In addition, the pretest itself may change that which is being measured. Hence, just the administration of an attitude questionnaire may change an individual's attitude; a manager who knows that his sales-meeting conduct is being observed and rated may change the way he behaves. In general, expect this reactive effect whenever the testing process is itself a stimulus to change rather than a passive record of behavior. The lesson is obvious: Use nonreactive measures whenever possible (cf. Webb et al., 1981; Rosenthal and Rosnow, 1984).

Instrumentation is yet a fourth uncontrolled rival

hypothesis in Design B. If different raters do pre- and posttraining observation and rating, this could account for observed differences.

A fifth potential contaminant is statistical regression (i.e., less-than-perfect pretest-posttest correlations) (Furby, 1973). This is a possibility whenever a researcher selects a group for training *because* of its extremity (e.g., all low scorers or all high scorers). Statistical regression has misled many a researcher time and again. The way it works is that lower scores on the pretest tend to be higher on the posttest, and higher scores tend to be lower on the posttest, when in fact no real change has taken place. This can deceive a researcher into concluding erroneously that a training program is effective (or ineffective). In fact, the higher and lower scores of the two groups may be due to the regression effect.

A control group allows one to "control" for the regression effect, since both the experimental and control groups have pretest and posttest scores. If the training program has had a "real" effect, then it should be apparent over and above the regression effect. That is, both groups should be affected by the same regression and other influences, other things equal. So if the groups differ in the posttest, it should be due to the training program (Kerlinger, 1986). The interaction effects (selection and maturation, testing and training, and selection and training) are likewise uncontrolled in Design B.

Despite all of the problems associated with Design B, it is still better to use it to assess change (together with a careful investigation into the plausibility of various threats) if that is the best one can do, than to do no evaluation. After all, organizations will make decisions about future training efforts with or without evaluation data (Sackett and Mullen, 1993). Moreover, if the objective is to measure individual achievement (a targeted level of performance), Design B can answer that question.

Design C

Design C (before-after measurement with a single control group) is adequate for most purposes, assuming that the experimental and control sessions are run simultaneously. The design controls history, maturation, and testing insofar as events that might produce a pretest-posttest difference for the experimental group should produce similar effects in the control group. We can control instrumentation either by assigning observers randomly to single sessions (when the number of observers is large) or by using each observer for both experimental and control sessions and ensuring that they do not know which subjects are receiving which treatments. Random assignment of individuals to treatments serves as an adequate control for regression or selection effects. Moreover, the data available for Design C enable a researcher to tell whether experimental mortality is a plausible explanation for pretest-posttest gain.

Information concerning interaction effects (involving training and some other variable) is important because, when present, interactions limit the ability to generalize results—for example, the effects of the training program may be specific only to those who have been "sensitized" by the pretest. In fact, when highly unusual test procedures (e.g., certain attitude questionnaires or personality measures) are used or when the testing procedure involves deception, surprise, stress, and the like, designs having groups that do not receive a pretest (e.g., Design A) are highly desirable, if not essential (Campbell and Stanley, 1963). In general, however, *successful replication* of pretest-posttest changes at different times and in different settings increases our ability to generalize by making interactions of training with selection, maturation, instrumentation, history, and so forth, less likely.

To compare experimental and control group results in Design C, either use analysis of covariance with pretest scores as the covariate or analyze "change" scores for each group. We shall consider the special problems associated with change scores in a following section.

Design D

The most elegant of experimental designs, the Solomon (1949) four-group design (Design D), parallels Design C except that it includes two additional control groups (lacking the pretest). C2 receives training plus a posttest; C3 receives only a posttest. In this way, one can determine both the main effect of testing and the interaction of testing with training. The four-group design allows substantial increases in the ability to generalize, and when training does produce changes in criterion performance, this effect is replicated in four different ways:

1. For the experimental group, posttest scores should be greater than pretest scores.
2. Experimental group posttest scores should be greater than C1 posttest scores.

3. C2 posttest scores should be greater than C3 posttest scores.

4. C2 posttest scores should be greater than C1 pretest scores.

If data analysis confirms these directional hypotheses, this increases substantially the strength of inferences that can be drawn on the basis of this design. Moreover, by comparing C3 posttest scores with experimental group pretest scores and C1 pretest scores, one can evaluate the combined effect of history and maturation.

Statistical analysis of the Solomon four-group design is not straightforward since there is no one statistical procedure that makes use of all the data for all four groups simultaneously.

Since all groups do not receive a pretest, the use of analysis of variance of gain scores (gain = posttest minus pretest) is out of the question. Instead, consider a simple 2×2 analysis of variance of posttest scores (Solomon, 1949):

	No Training	Training
Pretested	C_1	E
Not Pretested	C_3	C_2

Estimate training main effects from column means, estimate pretesting main effects from row means, and estimate interactions of testing with training from cell means.

Limitations of the Solomon Four-Group Design. Despite its apparent advantages, the Solomon four-group design is not without theoretical and practical problems (Bond, 1973). For example, it assumes that the simple passage of time and training experience affect all posttest scores independently. However, some interaction between these two factors is inevitable, thus jeopardizing the significance of comparisons between posttest scores for C3 and pretest scores for E and C1.

Serious practical problems also may emerge. The design requires large numbers of persons in order to represent each group adequately. For example, in order to have 30 individuals in each group, the design requires 120. This may be impractical or unrealistic in many settings. In addition, managers may disapprove of the random assignment of people to conditions. Line managers do not see their subordinates as interchangeable, like pawns on a chess board, and they often distrust randomness in experimental design.

Here is a practical example of these constraints (Sprangers and Hoogstraten, 1989). In two field studies of the impact of pretesting on posttest responses, the researchers used nonrandom assignment of 37 and 58 subjects in a Solomon four-group design. Their trade-off of low statistical power for greater experimental rigor illustrates the extreme difficulty of applying this design in field settings.

A final difficulty lies in the application of the four-group design. Solomon (1949) has suggested that after the value of the training is established using the four groups, the two control groups that did not receive training then could be trained, and two new groups could be selected to act as controls. In effect, this would replicate the entire study—but would it? Sound experimentation requires that conditions remain constant, but it is quite possible that the first training program may have changed the organization in some way, so that those who enter the second training sessions already have been influenced.

Cascio (1976b) showed this empirically in an investigation of the stability of factor structures in the measurement of attitudes. The factor structure of a survey instrument designed to provide a baseline measure of managerial attitudes toward African-Americans in the working environment did not remain constant when compared across three different samples of managers from the same company at three different time periods. During the 2-year period that the training program ran, increased societal awareness of EEO, top-management emphasis of it, and the fact that over 2,200 managers completed the training program probably altered participants' attitudes and expectations even before the training began.

Despite its limitations, when it is possible to apply the Solomon four-group design realistically, to assign subjects randomly to the four groups, and to maintain proper controls, this design controls most of the sources of invalidity that it is possible to control in one experimental design. Table 17–2 presents a summary of the sources of invalidity for Designs A through D.

Limitations of Experimental Designs

Having illustrated some of the nuances of experimental design, let us pause for a moment to place design in its proper perspective. First of all, exclusive emphasis on the design aspects of measuring training outcomes is rather narrow in scope. An experiment usually set-

TABLE 17–2 Sources of Invalidity for Experimental Designs A Through D

Design \ Sources	History	Maturation	Testing	Instrumentation	Regression	Selection	Mortality	Interaction of Selection and Maturation	Interaction of Testing and Training	Interaction of Selection and Training	Reactive Arrangements	Multiple-Treatment Interference
A. After-Only (one control)	+	+	+	+	+	+	+	+	+	?	?	
B. Before-After (no control)	−	−	−	−	?	+	+	−	−	−	?	
C. Before-After (one control)	+	+	+	+	+	+	+	+	−	?	?	
D. Before-After (three controls) Solomon Four-Group Design	+	+	+	+	+	+	+	+	+	?	?	

Note: A "+" indicates that the factor is controlled, a "−" indicates that the factor is not controlled, a "?" indicates a possible source of concern, and a blank indicates that the factor is not relevant. See text for appropriate qualifications regarding each design.

tles on a single criterion dimension, and the whole effort depends on observations of that dimension (Newstrom, 1978; Weiss and Rein, 1970). Hence, experimental designs are quite limited in the amount of information they can provide. In most practical training situations, there are several distinct outcomes of training. There is no logical reason why investigators cannot consider several criterion dimensions, but unfortunately this usually is not the case. Ideally, an experiment should be part of a continuous feedback process, rather than just an isolated event or demonstration (Snyder et al., 1980).

Second, it is important to ensure that any attempt to measure training outcomes through the use of an experimental design has adequate statistical power. Power is the probability of correctly rejecting a null

---

PRACTICAL ILLUSTRATION: A TRUE FIELD EXPERIMENT WITH A SURPRISE ENDING

The command teams of 18 logistics units in the Israel Defense Forces were assigned randomly to experimental and control conditions. Each command team included the commanding officer of the unit plus subordinate officers, both commissioned and noncommissioned. Each command team of the nine experimental units underwent an intensive 3-day team-development workshop. The null hypothesis was that the workshop had no effect on team or organizational functioning (Eden, 1985).

The experimental design provided for three different tests of the hypothesis, in ascending order of rigor. One, a "Workshop Evaluation Questionnaire," was administered to team members after the workshop to evaluate their subjective *reactions* to its effectiveness.

Two, Eden (1985) assessed the before-after perceptions of command team members in both the experimental and control groups by means of a "Team Development" questionnaire that included ratings of the team leader, subordinates, team functioning, and team efficiency. This is a true experimental design (Design C), but its major weakness is that the outcomes of interest were assessed in terms of responses from team members who personally had participated in the workshops. This might well lead to positive biases in the responses.

To overcome this problem, Eden used a third design. He selected at random about 50 subordinates representing each experimental and control unit to complete the "Survey of Organizations" both before and after the team development workshops. This instrument measures organizational functioning in terms of general management, leadership, coordination, three-way communications, peer relations, and satisfaction. Since subordinates had no knowledge of the team-development workshops and therefore no ego-involvement in them, this design represents the most internally valid test of the hypothesis. Moreover, since an average of 86 percent of the subordinates drawn from the experimental-group units completed the post-training questionnaires, as did an average of 81 percent of those representing control groups, Eden could rule out the experimental mortality effect as a threat to the internal validity of the experiment. Rejection of the null hypothesis would imply that the effects of the team-development effort really did affect the rest of the organization.

To summarize: Comparison of the command team's before-after perceptions tests whether the workshop influenced the team; comparison of the before-after perceptions of subordinates tests whether team development affected the organization. In all, 147 command-team members and 600 subordinates completed usable questionnaires.

Results. Here's the surprise: Only the weakest test of the hypothesis, the post-workshop reactions of participants, indicated that the training was effective. Neither of the two before-after comparisons detected any effects, either on the team or on the organization. Eden concluded:

The safest conclusion is that the intervention had no impact. This disconfirmation by the true experimental designs bares the frivolity of self-reported after-only perceptions of change. Rosy testimonials by . . . [trainees] may be self-serving, and their validity is therefore suspect [1985, p. 98].

hypothesis when it is false. Research indicates that the power of training evaluation designs is a complex issue, for it depends on the effect size obtained (d_t in Eq. 17–1), the reliability of the dependent measure, the correlation between pre- and posttest scores, sample size, and type of design used (Arvey et al., 1985). For example, under conditions of low reliability or low pretest-posttest correlation, or both, doubling the length of the posttest makes the posttest-only design (Design A) more powerful than the pretest-posttest design (Design C) (Maxwell et al., 1991). In fact, when it is relatively costly to bring subjects to an evaluation, and when administration costs are particularly high, posttest-only designs tend to be more powerful. In contrast, when item-development costs are high, pretest-posttest designs appear to be more powerful (Arvey et al., 1992). The median total sample size used in training evaluation research is only 43 (Arvey et al., 1985). In many cases, such small-sample (low-power) designs lead to the false conclusion that training had no effect, when in fact, use of a more powerful design would produce the opposite conclusion.

Finally, experiments often fail to focus on the real goals of an organization. For example, experimental results may indicate that job performance after treatment A is superior to performance after treatments B or C. The really important question, however, may not be whether treatment A is more effective, but rather what levels of performance we can expect from almost all trainees at an acceptable cost, and the extent to which improved performance through training "fits" the broader strategic thrust of an organization.

QUASI-EXPERIMENTAL DESIGNS

In field settings, there often are major obstacles to conducting randomized experiments. However, some less complete (i.e., quasi-experimental) designs still can provide useful data even though a true experiment is not possible. Cook and Campbell (1976; 1979) offer a number of quasi-experimental designs with the following rationale: The central purpose of an experiment is to eliminate alternative hypotheses that also might explain results. If a quasi-experimental design can help eliminate some of these rival hypotheses, then it may be worth the effort.

Because full experimental control is lacking in quasi-experiments, it is important to know which specific variables are uncontrolled in a particular design (cf. Tables 17–2, and 17–3). Investigators should, of course, design the very best experiment possible,

TABLE 17–3   Sources of Invalidity for Three Quasi-Experimental Designs

Design \ Sources	History	Maturation	Testing	Instrumentation	Regression	Selection	Mortality	Interaction of Selection and Maturation	Interaction of Testing and Training	Interaction of Selection and Training	Reactive Arrangements	Multiple-Treatment Interference
E. Time-series design Measure (M) M (Train) MMM	–	+	+	?	+	+	+	+	–		?	?
F. Nonequivalent-control-group design I. M train M II. M no train M	+	+	+	+	?	+	+	–	–		?	?
G. Institutional-cycle design Time 1 2 3 I. M (train) M (no train) M II. M (no train) M (train) M	+	–	+	+	?	–	?			+	?	+

Note: "M" means measure. A "+" indicates that the factor is controlled, a "–" indicates that the factor is not controlled, a "?" indicates a possible source of concern, and a blank indicates that the factor is not relevant.

given their circumstances, but where "full" control is not possible, then they should use the most rigorous design that *is* possible. For these reasons we present three quasi-experimental designs, together with their respective sources of invalidity, in Table 17–3.

Design E

The **time-series experiment** is especially relevant for assessing the outcomes of training and development programs. It uses a single group of individuals, and requires that criterion data be collected at several points in time, both before and after training. Criterion measures obtained before the introduction of the training experience then are compared to those obtained after training. A curve relating criterion scores to time periods may be plotted, and in order for an effect to be demonstrated, there should be a discontinuity or change in the series of measures, corresponding to the training program, that does not occur at any other point. This discontinuity may represent an abrupt change either in slope or in intercept of the curve.

Although Design E bears a superficial resemblance to Design B (both lack control groups and both use before-after measures), it is much stronger in that it provides a great deal more data on which to base conclusions about training program effects. Its most telling weakness is its failure to control for history—

that is, perhaps the discontinuity in the curve was produced not by training but rather by some more or less simultaneous organizational event. Indeed, if one cannot rule out history as an alternative plausible hypothesis, then the entire experiment loses credibility. To do so, either arrange the observational series to hold known cycles constant (e.g., weekly work cycles, seasonal variation in performance, attitude, or communication patterns), or else make it long enough to include several such cycles completely (Cook and Campbell, 1979).

Design F

Another makeshift experimental design, Design F, is the **nonequivalent-control-group design.** Although Design F appears identical to Design C (before-after measurement with one control group), there is a critical difference: In Design F individuals from a common population are not assigned randomly to the experimental and control groups. This design is common in applied settings where naturally-occurring groups must be used (e.g., work group A and work group B). Design F is especially appropriate when Designs A and C are impossible because even the addition of a nonequivalent control group makes interpretation of results much less ambiguous than in Design B, the one-group pretest-posttest design. Needless to say, the

---

PRACTICAL ILLUSTRATION: THE HAZARDS OF NONEQUIVALENT DESIGNS

This was illustrated neatly in an evaluation of a training program designed to improve the quality of group decisions by increasing the decision-making capabilities of its members. A study by Bottger and Yetton (1987) that demonstrated the effectiveness of this approach used experimental and control groups whose pretest scores differed significantly. When Ganster et al. (1991) replicated the study using a true experimental design (Design C) with random assignment of subjects to groups, the effect disappeared.

---

nonequivalent control group becomes much more effective as an experimental control as the similarity between experimental and control group pretest scores increases.

The major sources of invalidity in this design are the selection-maturation interaction and the testing-training interaction. For example, if the experimental group happens to consist of young, inexperienced workers and the control group consists of older, highly experienced workers who are tested and retested, a gain in criterion scores that appears specific to the experimental group might well be attributed to the effects of training, when, in fact, the gain would have occurred even without training.

Regression effects pose a further threat to unambiguous inferences in Design F. This is certainly the case when experimental and control groups are "matched" (which is no substitute for randomization), yet the pretest means of the two groups differ substantially. When this happens, changes in criterion scores from pretest to posttest may well be due to regression effects, not training. Despite these potential contaminants, we encourage increased use of Design F, especially in applied settings. However, be aware of potential contaminants that might make results equivocal, and attempt to control them as much as possible.

Design G

A final quasi-experimental design, appropriate for cyclical training programs, is known as the **recurrent-institutional-cycle design.** It is Design G in Table 17–3. For example, a large sales organization presented a management development program, known as the State Manager Program, every 2 months to small groups (12–15) of middle managers (state managers). The 1-week program focused on all aspects of retail sales (new product development, production, distribution, marketing, merchandising, etc.). The pro-gram was scheduled so that all state managers (approximately 110) could be trained over an 18-month period. This is precisely the type of situation for which Design G is appropriate—that is, a large number of persons will be trained, but not all at the same time. Different *cohorts* are involved. Design G is actually a combination of two (or more) before-after studies that occur at different points in time. Group I receives a pretest at Time 1, then training, and then a posttest at Time 2. At the same chronological time (Time 2), Group II receives a pretest, training, and then a posttest at Time 3. At Time 2, therefore, an experimental and a control group have, in effect, been created. One can obtain even more information (and with quasi-experimental designs, it is *always* wise to collect as much data as possible or to demonstrate the effect of training in several different ways) if it is possible to measure Group I again at Time 3 and to give Group II a pretest at Time 1. This controls the effects of history. Moreover, Time 3 data for Groups I and II and the posttests for all groups trained subsequently provide information as to how the training program is interacting with other organizational events to produce changes in the criterion measure.

Several cross-sectional comparisons are possible with the "cycle" design:

- Group I posttest scores at Time 2 can be compared with Group II posttest scores at Time 2
- Gains made in training for Group I (Time 2 posttest scores) can be compared with gains in training for Group II (Time 3 posttest scores), and
- Group II posttest scores at Time 3 can be compared with Group I posttest scores at Time 3 (i.e., gains in training versus gains [or no gains] during the no-training period).

To interpret this pattern of outcomes, all three contrasts should be statistically reliable. A chance elevation of Group II, for example, might lead to gross misinterpretations. Hence, use the design only with reliable measures and large samples (Cook and Campbell, 1979).

This design controls history and test-retest effects, but not differences in selection. One way to control for possible differences in selection, however, is to split one of the groups (assuming it is large enough) into two equated samples, one measured both before and after training and the other measured only after training:

	Time 2	Time 3	Time 4
Group II$_a$	Measure	Train	Measure
Group II$_b$		Train	Measure

Comparison of posttest scores in two carefully equated groups (Groups II$_a$ and II$_b$) is more precise than a similar comparison of posttest scores from two unequated groups (Groups I and II).

A final deficiency in the "cycle" design is the lack of adequate control for the effects of maturation. This is not a serious limitation if the training program is teaching specialized skills or competencies, but it is a plausible rival hypothesis when the objective of the training program is to change attitudes. Changes in attitude conceivably could be explained by maturational processes such as changes in job and life experiences or growing older. In order to control for this effect, give a comparable group of managers (whose age and job experience coincide with those of one of the trained groups at the time of testing) a "posttest-only" measure. To infer that training had a positive effect, posttest scores of the trained groups should be significantly greater than those of the untrained group receiving the "posttest-only" measure.

Campbell and Stanley (1963) expressed aptly the logic of all this patching and adding:

> one starts out with an inadequate design and then adds specific features to control for one or another of the recurrent sources of invalidity. The result is often an inelegant accumulation of precautionary checks, which lacks the intrinsic symmetry of the "true" experimental designs, but nonetheless approaches experimentation [p. 57].

Other quasi-experimental designs (cf. Cook and Campbell, 1976; 1979; Kerlinger, 1986), including time-series designs (cf. Armenakis and L. Smith, 1978; Komaki et al., 1977), are appropriate in specialized situations, but the three we have discussed seem well-suited to the types of problems that applied researchers are likely to encounter.

PRACTICAL ILLUSTRATION: EFFECTIVE (?) TRAINING

The following example illustrates the practical difficulties associated with implementing experimental or quasi-experimental designs. A study reported by Burnaska (1976) attempted to determine if behavior-modeling training improved the interpersonal skills of managers, and how long the effects of the training would last. Using Design A (after-only, one control group), 124 managers were assigned randomly either to the experimental or control groups. One month and 5 months after training, 25 trained observers evaluated the performance of both groups, without knowledge of the group to which each manager belonged. The observers rated typical (but not identical) situations used in training the managers. At both 1-month and 5-month intervals, the experimental group performed significantly better than the control group on tasks involving interpersonal skills.

As we noted earlier, Design A is a strong research design that controls the majority of threats to validity, with the possible exception of intra-session history. *However, this is true only of the measure taken one month after training.* There are serious threats to the validity of inferences based on measures taken 5 months after training, namely, history, instrumentation, and experimental mortality (although no mortality was mentioned).

The second part of this study attempted to determine whether or not employees perceived more behavioral changes in the trained than in the untrained managers. The researcher administered a questionnaire developed to measure employees' perceptions of managers' supervisory behavior to the subordinates of managers both in the experimental and control groups before training and 4 months after the training. Only two significant differences were found: improvement of listening skills at one location and, at another location, the ability of trained managers to establish responsibility.

The design for this part of the study is Design F (the nonequivalent-control-group design). While Design F suffers from several threats to valid inferences, notably regression and the interaction of selection with maturation, the major threat in this part of the study was subject mortality. For the experimental group, sample sizes from pretest to posttest dropped from 319 to 183. For the control group, the drop was from 137 to 91 subordinates. In this instance, failure to find significant effects for the training may well have resulted from the experimental mortality effect rather than from ineffective training. As is true of many such studies, precise cause and effect relationships remain equivocal.

THE MEASUREMENT OF CHANGE[1]

Training evaluation often focuses on measuring change—a problem that has vexed researchers for years. The problem is that difference scores that purport to represent changes in performance from Time 1 to Time 2 usually are less reliable than the scores from which they were calculated. Hence, one reason why real differences between the gains registered by trained and untrained groups are undetectable is that the difference scores are unreliable. To detect such differences, the scores must be reliable enough to reflect actual performance variance and not just error variance. Many studies use experimental, quasi-experimental, or correlational designs in an attempt to estimate experimentally-induced or naturally-occurring change, and several analytical techniques have been developed for this purpose. No single technique, however, is suitable for all research purposes.

It is particularly difficult to draw unequivocal conclusions when evaluations are based on self-report data. This is because there are three types of changes that can occur in self-reported, pre- and postintervention data (Golembiewski et al., 1976; Golembiewski and Billingsley, 1980):

- **Gamma change** is a reconceptualization of the meaning of some behavioral domain, such as customer service or team performance, usually in light of training. It may involve a shift in the perspective or frame of reference an individual uses to perceive and classify behavior.

- **Beta change** is a recalibration of a measurement scale after training. For example, after a training program, participants may view the behaviors that correspond to "above average" performance on a behaviorally-anchored rating scale that describes "skill in human relations" as expected or "average" performance.

- **Alpha change** represents a genuine change in behavior over time, relative to a constantly-calibrated measuring instrument and a constant conceptual domain.

All survey researchers run the risk of drawing the wrong conclusions unless they are able to specify what kind(s) of change their results pertain to. By definition, evidence of stable construct validity for a measurement instrument rules out gamma change. In practice, beta change occurs if a self-reported change (ΔSR, e.g., a change in expectancies from Time 1 to Time 2) is related empirically to changes in actual behavior (Δb) over the same time period. This relation is known as a "dynamic" correlation ($R_{\Delta SR, \Delta b}$). The proportion of alpha change then can be estimated as $1 - R^2_{\Delta SR, \Delta b}$ (Van de Vliert et al., 1985). Alternatively, a structural-equation approach, which includes an analysis of covariance in the latent variables underlying pre- and posttest measures, may help to distinguish these three types of change (Millsap and Hartog, 1988). Now let's consider several other approaches for measuring change.

The simplest method for estimating an individual's difference score is by means of a raw gain score. A researcher might, for example, be interested in identifying for further study those individuals who profited most (or least) from a particular course of instruction. To do this, one must obtain a pretest (X) and a posttest (Y) measure for each individual in the group. A difference score (loss or gain) for any individual then can be calculated using the formula:

$$D = Y - X \qquad (17\text{--}4)$$

However:

One can scarcely defend selecting such individuals on a raw-gain or raw-difference score, especially as these

---

[1] Those who wish may skip this section entirely without loss of continuity. Proceed directly to page 297.

scores tend to show a spurious advantage for persons low on X [Cronbach and Furby, 1970, p. 79].

Raw gain scores suffer two disadvantages: (1) they make no allowances for regression due to measurement error, and (2) they do not take into account the necessary correlation between X and Y.

A better method for estimating differences on pre- and posttest scores is to correct for measurement error in X and Y scores. Estimate an individual's "true" difference score with the following formula:

$$\hat{D}_\infty = \hat{Y}_\infty - \hat{X}_\infty \qquad (17\text{--}5)$$

where $\hat{Y}_\infty = r_{YY}Y$ and $\hat{X}_\infty = r_{XX}X$ and where r_{XX} and r_{YY} = the reliability coefficients for X and Y. This correction-for-error formula provides a better estimate of actual gain or loss, but it does not take into account the correlation between X and Y.

It is possible to obtain a more precise estimate of an individual's difference score by a regression procedure (Lord, 1963). The formula is:

$$\hat{D}_\infty = \beta_1 X + \beta_2 Y + \text{constant} \qquad (17\text{--}6)$$

where:

$$\beta_{DX.Y} = \frac{[(1 - r_{yy})(r_{xy}S_y)]/(S_x + r_{xy}^2)}{1 - r_{xy}^2}$$

and:

$$\beta_{DY.X} = \frac{[(r_{yy} - r_{xy}^2) - (1 - r_{xx})S_x r_{xy}]/S_y}{1 - r_{xy}^2}$$

This procedure takes into account both the effects of regression and the correlation between X and Y.

Cronbach and Furby (1970) carried the logic of Lord's procedure one step further and emphasized the multivariate nature of change. Even when X and Y are determined by the same operation, they often do not represent the same psychological process. Since learning or growth is multidimensional, Cronbach and Furby (1970) argued that researchers should take many measures (e.g., demographic information, data on experience) at each point in time. To leave this information out of account is to sacrifice information and possible insight. Cronbach and Furby (1970) recommended estimating *residualized gain scores* (i.e., for each posttest score, that portion of the gain that is not linearly predictable from a knowledge of the pretest score) by the formula:

$$D_\infty \bullet X_\infty = \beta_1 X + \beta_2 Y + \\ \beta_3 W + \beta_4 Z + \text{constant} \qquad (17\text{--}7)$$

where X and Y are pretest and posttest scores; W and Z are demographic, experience, and other continuous and noncontinuous variables associated with X and Y respectively; and $D_\infty \bullet X_\infty$ is the residualized gain score.

All of the techniques we have discussed provide methods for estimating true difference scores, but they fail to provide a criterion for identifying extreme individuals. For example, using Cronbach and Furby's (1970) technique, a given individual's difference score can be expressed as the difference between estimated true scores on Y and predicted true scores on Y where:

$$\hat{Y}_\infty / WXYZ = \text{estimated true final status}$$
$$\hat{Y}_\infty / \hat{W}_\infty \hat{X}_\infty = \text{predicted true final status}$$

D = difference between estimated and predicted final status. To identify extreme cases, ". . . one selects persons for whom $\hat{Y}_\infty / WXYZ$ is much larger (or smaller than $\hat{Y}_\infty / \hat{W}_\infty \hat{X}_\infty$" (Cronbach and Furby, 1970, p. 79). This estimation procedure takes into account any linkages between X and Y and between W and Z by employing partial variates, but it does not provide an objective criterion for selecting cases.

Once one identifies a suitable technique for measuring change in a particular situation, the next question is whether any given individual's change score is significantly larger (or smaller) than the group's average change score. Cascio and Kurtines (1977) developed a simple method for doing this. Their technique builds on the work of Lord (1963) and Cronbach and Furby (1970) and can be used in conjunction with all previous methods for estimating change scores (i.e., Equations 17–3 through 17–6). Ideally Equation 17–6 provides the best estimate of an individual's change score. However, in those cases where the additional information required by Equation 17–6 is unavailable, Equation 17–5 provides the next best estimate.

In addition to estimated true difference scores, the technique requires the standard error of measurement of the difference scores and a set of predefined confidence intervals. Calculate a standard error of measurement for difference scores (σ_m) as follows (Cronbach and Furby, 1970):

$$\sigma_m = \sigma\hat{D}_\infty \sqrt{1 - \rho DD'} \qquad (17\text{--}8)$$

where:

$$\rho DD' = \frac{\sigma^2 X \rho XX' + \sigma^2 Y \rho YY' - 2\sigma X \sigma Y \rho XY}{\sigma^2 X + \sigma^2 Y - 2\sigma X \sigma Y \rho XY}$$

Confidence intervals (95%, 99%) then can be established about the average true difference scores, and those individuals who score greater than M ± 1.96, or 2.58 σ_m can be considered to have registered significant change scores. Selection then can be done on the basis of visual inspection of the distribution of change scores.

Critics of experimental and quasi-experimental designs often point out that such designs make no allowance for individual differences. On this issue, Bond (1973) noted:

> The special case, or the deviant group, has always been a problem in change measurement, and the idea of a general residual gain for identifying such deviants ought to be pursued [p. 193].

Hopefully the methods we have discussed will stimulate more empirical work in this area.

STATISTICAL, PRACTICAL, AND THEORETICAL SIGNIFICANCE

As in selection, the problem of *statistical* versus *practical* significance is relevant for the assessment of training outcomes. Demonstrations of statistically significant change scores mean little in a practical sense. From that perspective, researchers must show that the effects of training *do* make a difference to organizational goals—in terms of lowered production costs, increased sales, fewer grievances, and so on. In short, external criteria are important.

A related issue concerns the relationship between practical and theoretical significance. Training practitioners frequently are content to demonstrate only that a particular program "works"—the prime concern being to sell the idea to top management or to legitimize an existing (perhaps substantial) investment in a particular development program. This is only half the story. The real test is whether the new training program is superior to previous or existing methods for accomplishing the same objectives. To show this, firms need systematic research to evaluate the effects of independent variables that are likely to affect training outcomes—for example, different training methods, depths of training, or different types of media for presenting training.

If practitioners adopt this two-pronged approach to measuring training outcomes, if they can map the effects of relevant independent variables across different populations of trainees and across different criteria (for example, by using the methods of meta-analysis discussed in Chapter 7), then the assessment takes on theoretical significance. That is, in the aggregate, the systematic contributions of various practitioners will have enriched the general body of knowledge and principles about training. Other organizations and other investigators then may use this knowledge to advantage in planning their own programs. The concept of statistical significance, while not trivial, in no sense guarantees practical or theoretical significance—the major issues in outcome measurement.

Logical Analysis

A logical analysis of the process and content of training programs can further enhance our understanding of *why* we obtained the results we did. To do this, ask a panel of experts:

1. Were the goals of the training clear both to the organization and the trainees?
2. Were the methods and content of the training really relevant to the goals?
3. Were the proposed methods actually used and the proposed content actually taught?
4. Did it appear that learning really was taking place?
5. Does the training program conflict with any other program in the organization?
6. What kinds of criteria should really be expected to show change as a result of the training? (Korb, 1956).

For every one of these questions, supplement the subjective opinions of experts with objective data. For example, to provide broader information regarding question 2, document the linkage between training content and job content. A quantitative method is now available for doing this (Bownas et al., 1985). It generates a list of tasks that receive undue emphasis in training, those that are not being trained, and those that instructors intend to train, but that graduates report being unable to perform. It proceeds as follows:

1. Identify curriculum elements in the training program.
2. Identify tasks performed on the job.
3. Obtain ratings of the emphasis given to each task in training, how well it was learned, and of its corresponding importance on the job.
4. Correlate the two sets of ratings—training emphasis

and job requirements—to arrive at an overall index of fit between training and job content.

5. Use the ratings of training effectiveness to identify tasks that appear to be over- or underemphasized in training.

Confront these kinds of questions during program planning *and* evaluation. When integrated with answers to the other issues presented earlier in this chapter, especially the "systems" aspects of training impact, then training outcomes become much more meaningful. This is the ultimate payoff of the measurement effort.

Discussion Questions

1. Discuss the advantages and disadvantages of interactive multimedia training.

2. Your boss asks you to design a study to evaluate the effects of a training class in stress reduction. How will you proceed?

3. Describe some of the key differences between experimental and quasi-experimental designs.

4. Your firm decides to train its entire population (500) of employees and managers to provide "legendary customer service." Suggest a design for evaluating the impact of such a massive training effort.

5. What additional information might a logical analysis of training outcomes provide that an experimental or quasi-experimental design does not?

*   *   *

In our next and last chapter, we shall attempt to carry our presentation one step further by examining emerging ethical issues in HR management. We shall begin by considering the nature of ethics and existing professional guidelines for ethical practice.

CHAPTER

18

ETHICAL ISSUES IN HUMAN RESOURCE MANAGEMENT

AT A GLANCE

One cannot prescribe ethical behavior by inflexible rules. Rather, it adapts and changes in response to social norms and in response to the needs and interests of those served by a profession. In the context of HR management, three areas in particular deserve special emphasis: employee privacy, testing and evaluation, and organizational research. Regarding employee privacy, some key concerns are the use and disclosure of employee records, and the monitoring of computer files and electronic mail communications. Public concern for ethical behavior in testing and evaluation centers around obligations of HR experts to their profession, to job applicants and employees, and to their employers. Employers also have ethical obligations. Finally, researchers in organizational settings, domestic or international, frequently encounter ethical dilemmas arising from role ambiguity, role conflict, and ambiguous or conflicting norms. Strategies are available for resolving these dilemmas so that an acceptable (and temporary) consensus among interested parties regarding an ethical course of action can be reached. However, the challenge of being ethical in managing people does not lie in the mechanical application of moral prescriptions. It is found in the process of creating and maintaining genuine relationships from which to address ethical dilemmas that cannot be covered by prescription.

To be ethical is to conform to moral standards or to conform to the standards of conduct of a given profession or group (*Webster's New World Dictionary,* 1974). Ethical behavior is not governed by hard-and-fast rules; it adapts and changes in response to social norms and in response to the needs and interests of those served by a profession. It represents a "continuous adjustment of interests" (Brady, 1985, p. 569). Nowhere else is this more obvious than in HR management. What was considered ethical in the 1950s and the 1960s (deep-probing selection interviews; management prescriptions of standards of dress, ideology, and life-style; refusal to let employees examine their own employment files) would be considered improper today. Accelerating concern for human rights has placed HR policies, procedures, and research practices in the public domain. Civil rights laws, discrimination suits, and union agreements have been effective instruments of social change. The resulting emphases on freedom of information and concern for individual privacy are sensitizing both employees and employers to ethical concerns.

Our intention in this last chapter is not to offer as truth a set of principles for ethical behavior in HR management. Rather, our intent is to highlight emerging ethical concerns in several important areas. We make no attempt to be comprehensive, and in fact we will limit discussion to three areas: employee privacy, testing and evaluation, and organizational research. Although we cannot prescribe the *content* of ethical behavior across all conceivable situations, we can prescribe *processes* that can lead to an acceptable (and temporary) consensus among interested parties regarding an ethical course of action. Where relevant, we will not hesitate to do so. Let us begin by defining some important terms:

- *Privacy:* The interest that employees have in controlling the use that is made of their personal information and in being able to engage in behavior free from regulation or surveillance (Piller, 1993a).
- *Confidentiality:* Information provided with the expectation that it will not be disclosed to others. Confidentiality may be established by law, by institutional rules, or by professional or scientific relationships (American Psychological Association, 1992).
- *Ethics and morality:* Behaviors about which society holds certain values (Reese and Fremouw, 1984).
- *Ethical dilemma:* In the context of organization development, any choice situation encountered by a change agent or a client system that has the potential to result in a breach of acceptable behavior (White and Wooten, 1983).
- *Ethical choice:* Considered choice among alternative courses of action where the interests of all parties have been clarified and the risks and gains have been evaluated openly and mutually (Mirvis and Seashore, 1979).
- *Ethical decisions about behavior:* Those that take account not only of one's own interests, but also equally the interests of those affected by the decision (Cullen et al., 1989).
- *Validity:* In this context, the overall degree of justification for the interpretation and use of an assessment procedure (Messick, 1980; 1995).

EMPLOYEE PRIVACY

The U.S. Constitution, along with numerous federal and state laws and executive orders, defines legally acceptable behavior in the public and private sectors of our economy. Note, however, that while illegal behaviors are by definition unethical, meeting minimal legal standards does not necessarily imply conformity to accepted guidelines of the community (Hegarty and Sims, 1978). Such legal standards have affected HR research and practice in at least three ways:

- EEO legislation, together with the interpretive guidelines of federal regulatory agencies, has emphasized the meaning and extent of unfair discrimination (e.g., with respect to racial or sexual harassment) and how it can be avoided.

- Both professional standards and federal guidelines illustrate appropriate procedures for developing and validating assessment procedures (see Appendix A). The values implied by these standards are that high-quality information should be used to make decisions about people and that HR professionals are responsible for developing procedures that result in the most accurate decisions possible.
- Twin concerns for individual privacy and freedom of information are raising new research questions and challenges. For example, does an employer have the right to search an employee's computer files or review the employee's electronic mail ("e-mail") and voice mail? How can an employer guarantee confidentiality of information and avoid invasion of privacy while providing information to those who make employment decisions?

Employees clearly are more aware of these issues, and they are willing to take legal action when they believe that their privacy rights have been violated by their employers. See the boxed insert on p. 301 for some examples.

Attention in this area centers on three main issues: the kind of information retained about individuals, how that information is used, and the extent to which it can be disclosed to others. Unfortunately, many companies are failing to safeguard the privacy of their employees. Thus a study of 126 Fortune 500 companies employing 3.7 million people found that:

- While 87 percent of the companies allow employees to look at their personnel files, only 27 percent give them access to supervisors' files, which often contain more subjective information.
- 57 percent use private investigative agencies to collect or verify information about employees, and 42 percent collect information without telling the employee.
- 38 percent have no policy covering release of data to the government; of those that do, 38 percent don't require a subpoena. Eighty percent of companies will give information to an employee's potential creditor without a subpoena, and 58 percent will give information to landlords (Solomon, 1989).

The results of a recent survey of top corporate managers of 301 businesses of all sizes and in a wide range of industries revealed another unsettling fact: fewer than one in five had a written policy regarding electronic privacy—that is, employee computer files, voice mail, electronic mail, or other networking communications. With respect to employee records contained in an HR information system, 66 percent of HR managers reported that they have unlimited access to

---

PRACTICAL APPLICATION: DO EMPLOYEES HAVE A RIGHT TO ELECTRONIC PRIVACY?

When Alana Shoars arrived for work at Epson America, Inc. one morning, she discovered her supervisor reading and printing out electronic mail messages between other employees. Ms. Shoars was appalled. When she had trained employees to use the computerized system, she told them their mail was private. Now a company manager was violating that trust.

When she questioned the practice, Ms. Shoars says she was told to mind her own business. A day later, she was fired for insubordination. Then she filed a $1 million lawsuit for wrongful termination. Although she soon found a job as e-mail administrator at another firm, she still bristles about Epson: "You don't read other people's mail, just as you don't listen to their phone conversations. Right is right, and wrong is wrong."

Michael Simmons, chief information officer at the Bank of Boston, disagrees completely. "If the corporation owns the equipment and pays for the network, that asset belongs to the company, and it has a right to look and see if people are using it for purposes other than running the business." The court agreed with this logic. Ms. Shoars lost. In another case, a supervisor at a Nissan subsidiary in California discovered e-mail between two female subordinates poking fun at his sexual prowess. When he fired them, the women sued and lost. The judge ruled (as in the Epson case) that the company had the right to read the e-mail because it owned and operated the equipment (McMorris, 1995).

---

such information, while 52 percent of executives do (Piller, 1993b).

Safeguarding Employee Privacy

To establish a privacy-protection policy, here are some general recommendations:

1. Set up guidelines and policies on requests for various types of data, on methods of obtaining the data, on retention and dissemination of information, on employee or third-party access to information, on the release of information about former employees, and on mishandling of information.

2. Inform employees of these information-handling policies.

3. Become thoroughly familiar with state and federal laws regarding privacy.

4. Establish a policy that states specifically that employees or prospective employees cannot waive their rights to privacy.

5. Establish a policy that any manager or nonmanager who violates these privacy principles will be subject to discipline or termination ("A Model," 1993).

Fair Information Practice in the Information Age

The Electronic Communications Privacy Act of 1986 prohibits "outside" interception of electronic mail by a third party—the government, the police, or an individual—without proper authorization (such as a search warrant). Information sent on public networks, such as Compuserve and MCI Mail, to which individuals and companies subscribe, is therefore protected. However, the law does not cover "inside" interception, and, in fact, no absolute privacy exists in a computer system, even for bosses. They may view employees on closed-circuit TV; tap their phones, e-mail, and network communications; and rummage through their computer files with or without employee knowledge or consent 24 hours a day (Elmer-Dewitt, 1993). Safeguards to protect personal privacy are more important than ever. Here are some suggestions.

First, *periodically and systematically, employers should review their HR record-keeping practices.* This review should consider the following:

- The number and types of records an organization maintains on employees, former employees, and applicants;

- The items maintained in each record;

- The uses made of information in each type of record;

- The uses of information within the organization;

- The disclosures made to parties outside the organization;

- The extent to which individuals are aware and informed of the uses and disclosures of information about them in the records department.

Indeed, research has shown that an individual's perceived control over the uses of information after its disclosure is the single most important variable affecting perceptions of invasion of privacy (Fusilier and Hoyer, 1980).

After reviewing their current practices, *employers should articulate, communicate, and implement fair information practice policies* by the following means:

- Limit the collection of information about individuals to that which is relevant to specific decisions;
- Inform individuals of the uses to be made of such information;
- Inform individuals as to the types of information being maintained about them;
- Adopt reasonable procedures for ensuring accuracy, timeliness, and completeness of information about individuals. The objective is to preserve the integrity of the information collected (Mitsch, 1983);
- Permit individuals to see, copy, correct, or amend records about themselves;
- Limit the internal use of records, for example, by implementing security measures such as physical security, system audit trails, passwords, read/write authentication routines, or encrypting data (Mitsch, 1983);
- Limit external disclosures of information, particularly those made without the individual's authorization;
- Provide for regular reviews of compliance with articulated fair-information-practice policies.

While the public in general, as well as peers and subordinates, tend to give executives low marks for honesty and ethical behavior (Clymer, 1985; Hager, 1991; Morgan, 1993), companies that have taken the kinds of measures described above, such as IBM, Bank of America, AT&T, Cummins Engine, Avis, and TRW, report that they have not been overly costly, produced burdensome traffic in access demands, or reduced the general quality of their HR decisions. Furthermore, they receive strong employee approval for their policies when they ask about them on company attitude surveys. By matching words with deeds, companies such as these are weaving their concerns for employee privacy into the very fabric of their corporate cultures. As one CEO commented:

> You can't just write a code and hang it up on the wall . . . you have to keep reminding people what you stand for. Unless you stress that—especially with the

emphasis in a corporation on making profits—it's not always clear to people which way management wants them to go. If more corporations would do this across America, we would raise the trust of the man-in-the-street that's been lost by business, government and all institutions [McDonnell, in Williams, 1985, p. 1F].

Management's failure to match its actions to its words may be one reason why many lower-level employees are cynical about ethics codes. On the other hand, such codes help managers and employees to identify (1) issues that their organizations believe are ethically pertinent, and (2) criteria for understanding, weighing, and resolving them. Hence they can help employees to answer two questions, "What should I do?" and "How shall I do it?" (Cullen et al., 1989). We will have more to say about ethics codes in a following section.

Employee Searches and Other Workplace Investigations

Thus far we have been dealing with *information* privacy, but the *physical* privacy of employees is no less important. The issue of employee searches in the workplace involves a careful balancing of the employer's right to manage its business and to implement reasonable work rules and standards against the privacy rights and interests of employees. One review of precedents in constitutional law, tort law, and statutory/labor law suggested the following guidelines for employers (Nobile, 1985):

1. Base the search and seizure policy upon legitimate employer interests, such as prevention of theft, drinking on company property, and use, possession, or sale of illegal drugs on company property. Most employees view reasons such as these as reasonable.

2. Include all types of searches (personal office, locker, etc.). Advise employees that the offices and lockers are the property of the company issued for the convenience of employees, that the company has a master key, and that they may be inspected at any time. This will help to preclude an employee's claim of discriminatory treatment or invasion of privacy. Such searches (without a warrant) are permissible, according to a federal court, if they are work-related and reasonable under the circumstances (Rich, 1995).

3. Provide adequate notice to employees (and labor unions, if appropriate) before implementing the policy.

4. Instruct those responsible for conducting the actual searches not to touch any employee, or if this is not possible, to limit touching to effects and pockets. This

will provide a defense against an employee's claim of assault and battery.

5. When an employee is suspected of theft, conduct the search away from other employees and on company time.

When conducting a search ensure that it is performed in a dignified and reasonable manner, with due regard for each employee's rights to due process.

Workplace investigations often involve the observation of an employee. There are only five ways that an employer can do this legally: electronic (photographic or video images), stationary (e.g., an investigator in a van watching an exit door), moving (following an employee on foot or in a vehicle), undercover operatives, and investigative interviews (Vigneau, 1995). Each carries risks.

For example, tape recordings or photos are off limits in areas where there is a reasonable expectation of privacy, such as a restroom or a home. To do otherwise is to violate privacy rights. Use undercover operatives as a last resort (e.g., at an open construction site or an open loading dock). Employees will probably react extremely negatively if they discover a "spy" in the workplace.

Investigative interviews should be voluntary. To be effective, make the employee comfortable, provide access to a phone, and allow the employee to take a break on request. Offer the employee the opportunity to call or be represented by an attorney, and be willing to conduct the interview with one present. The outcome should be a sworn written as well as a recorded statement made in the presence of a company representative. The employee's written statement should include an explanation of what happened and how he or she was treated. The recording preserves the true nature of the interview and its integrity (Vigneau, 1995). Now let's consider some ethical issues associated with testing and evaluation.

TESTING AND EVALUATION

HR decisions to select, to promote, to train, or to transfer are often major events in individuals' careers. Frequently these decisions are made with the aid of tests, interviews, situational exercises, performance appraisals, and other techniques developed by HR experts, often industrial/organizational psychologists. The experts, or psychologists, must be concerned with questions of fairness, propriety, and individual rights

as well as with other ethical issues. In fact, as London and Bray (1980) have pointed out, HR experts and psychologists have obligations to their profession, to job applicants and employees, and to their employers. Employers also have ethical obligations. We will consider each of these sets of obligations shortly, but first let us describe existing standards of ethical practice.

Among the social and behavioral science disciplines, psychologists have the most richly developed and documented ethical guidelines, as well as institutionalized agencies for surveillance of practice and resolution of public complaints. These include the *Ethical Principles of Psychologists and Code of Conduct* (American Psychological Association, 1992), *Ethical Conflicts in Psychology* (American Psychological Association, 1995), the *Standards for Educational and Psychological Testing* (see Chapters 6 and 7), and *Principles for the Validation and Use of Employment Selection Procedures* (3rd ed., 1987—see Appendix A).

Another document, developed by a task force of researchers and practitioners of assessment-center methodology, is the *Standards and Ethical Considerations for Assessment Center Operations* (Task Force, 1979). These standards specify minimally acceptable practices in training assessors, informing participants about what to expect, and using assessment-center data. Other ethical issues deal with the relevance of assessment-center exercises to what is being predicted, how individuals are selected to attend a center, and the rights of participants. Lastly, the Academy of Management (1995) has published a code of ethical conduct for its members. It covers five major areas: student relationships; the advancement of managerial knowledge; the Academy of Management and the larger professional environment; managers and the practice of management; and the world community.

While the details of any particular set of standards are beyond the scope of this chapter, let us consider briefly the ethical obligations we noted earlier. Many of the ideas in this section came from London and Bray (1980), Messick (1995), and the sets of Standards listed above.

Obligations to One's Profession

Psychologists are expected to abide by the standards and principles for ethical practice set forth by the APA. HR experts who are not psychologists often belong to professional organizations (e.g., the Society for Human Resource Management, the Academy of Management) and are expected to follow many of the same standards. Such standards generally include keeping informed of advances in the field, reporting unethical practices, and increasing colleagues' sensitivity to ethical issues.

Keeping up with advances implies continuing education, being open to new procedures, and remaining abreast of federal, state, and local regulations relevant to research and practice. Knowledge of unethical behavior poses especially knotty problems when a fellow professional is involved. The *Ethical Principles of Psychologists* (1992) advises that efforts be made to rectify the unethical conduct directly with the individual in question. Failing that, the next step is to bring the unethical activities to the attention of appropriate authorities such as state licensing boards, or APA ethics committees. While the peer review process for all professions has been criticized as being lax and ineffective, at the very least peer review makes accountability to one's colleagues a continuing presence in professional practice (Theaman, 1984).

Increasing colleagues' sensitivity to ethical practices may diminish unethical behavior and increase the likelihood that it will be reported. Research indicates that individuals can be conditioned to behave unethically (i.e., if they are rewarded for it) especially under increased competition, but that the threat of punishment has a counter-balancing influence (Hegarty and Sims, 1978; Jansen and Von Glinow, 1985). More importantly, when an informal or formal organization policy that favors ethical behavior is present, ethical behavior tends to increase (Hegarty and Sims, 1979). As an example, let's consider the phenomenon of whistle-blowing.

Whistle-Blowing—Who Does It and Why?

Research involving almost 8,600 employees of 22 agencies and departments of the federal government revealed that those who had observed alleged wrongdoing were more likely to "blow the whistle" if they: (1) were employed by organizations perceived by others to be responsive to complaints, (2) held professional positions, (3) had positive reactions to their work, (4) had long service, (5) were recently recognized for good performance, (6) were male (though race was unrelated to whistle-blowing), and (7) were

members of large work groups (Miceli and Near, 1988).

These findings are consistent with other research that has punctured the myth that whistle-blowers are social misfits. A study of nearly 100 people who reported wrongdoing in public- and private-sector organizations found that the average whistle-blower was a 47-year-old family man who was employed for 7 years before exposing his company's misdeeds (Farnsworth, 1987).

Some may question the motivation underlying whistle-blowing, but one review concluded that it is a form of prosocial behavior, that is, positive social behavior that is intended to benefit other persons (Dozier and Miceli, 1985). In short, it appears that individual ethical behavior is influenced not only by the consequences of the behavior (reinforcement), but also by the work environment prior to its occurrence.

The Future of Whistle-Blowing

We may see many more whistle-blowers coming forward in the future, even though research indicates that they can expect retaliation, financial loss, and high emotional and physical stress (Miceli and Near, 1992). Why? Increased legal protection is one reason. Some 40 states (and the federal government) now protect the jobs of workers who report—or who simply intend to report—when their companies break the law (Near and Miceli, 1995).

A second reason is the prospect of substantial financial gain for exposing wrongdoing by contractors of the federal government. As a result of amendments in 1986 to the federal False Claims Act of 1863, private citizens may sue a contractor for fraud on the government's behalf and share up to 30 percent of whatever financial recovery the government makes as a result of the charges. In one case, for example, the government recovered $14.3 million from one of its contractors, Industrial Tectonics of Dexter, Michigan. The former Tectonics employee who filed the civil lawsuit laying out evidence of overcharging won a $1.4 million reward (Stevenson, 1989).

Although critics of the new amendments claim that the law has created a modern class of bounty hunters, made up largely of disgruntled or well-meaning but ill-informed employees, proponents argue that the law has brought forward whistle-blowers in relatively high management positions who have access to detailed contract documentation. Since there is little evidence that fraud, waste, and abuse are declining, expect the number of whistle-blowers to increase in the future.

To deal with this, firms such as Hughes Tool Co., First Interstate Bank of California, and the National Aeronautics and Space Administration have developed programs to encourage valid internal whistle-blowing. Since the most important factor in an individual's decision to blow the whistle is his or her belief that something will be done to correct the problem, these firms encourage their managers to show that the company will do something in response to a complaint (Miceli and Near, 1994). If the complaint is valid, correcting the problem and showing employees that it has been corrected sends a powerful message. Conversely, if no action is warranted, it is important to explain to employees why management has chosen not to act.

Obligations to Those Who Are Evaluated

In the making of career decisions about individuals, issues of accuracy and equality of opportunity are critical. Beyond these, ethical principles include the following:

- Guarding against invasion of privacy
- Guaranteeing confidentiality
- Obtaining employees' and applicants' informed consent before evaluation
- Respecting employees' right to know
- Imposing time limitations on data
- Minimizing erroneous acceptance and rejection decisions
- Treating employees with respect and consideration

Since we already have examined the employee privacy issue in some detail, we will focus only on areas not yet considered. Let us begin with the issue of test accuracy. If validity is the overall degree of justification for test interpretation and use, and since human and social values affect both interpretation and use, then test validity should consider those value implications in the overall judgment. One of the key questions is, "Should the test be used for that purpose?" There are few prescriptions for how to proceed here, but one recommendation is to contrast the potential social consequences of the proposed testing with the potential social consequences of alternative procedures and even of procedures antagonistic to testing (such as not testing at all). Such a strategy draws attention to vulnerabilities in the proposed use, and exposes its value assumptions to open debate.

Should individuals be denied access to a test because prior knowledge of test items may decrease the test's validity? Yes, if the results are used in making decisions about them; no, if the results do not affect them in any way. "Truth in testing" legislation in New York and California requires that college and graduate school entrance tests and correct answers be made public within 30 days after the results are distributed. It also requires testing services to provide a graded answer sheet to students who request it. Someday other laws may affect employment. While the APA *Standards* (1985) do not require that test items be made public, they do make clear that the individual whose future is affected by a career decision is among those with a "right to know" the test results used to make the decision. Such interpretations should describe in simple language what the test covers, what the scores mean, common misinterpretations of test scores, and how the scores will be used.

How old must data be before they are removed from employee files? One guideline is to remove all evaluative information that has not been used for HR decisions, especially if it has been updated. When data *have* been used for HR decisions, before destroying them it is desirable to determine their likely usefulness for making future predictions and for serving as evidence of the rationale for prior decisions. Such data should not be destroyed indiscriminately.

Take care also to minimize erroneous-rejection and erroneous-acceptance decisions. One way to minimize erroneous-rejection decisions is to provide a reasonable opportunity for retesting and reconsideration (APA *Standards*), even to the extent of considering alternative routes to qualification (possibly by an on-the-job trial period or a trial period in on-the-job training if these strategies are feasible). Erroneous acceptances simply may reflect a lack of proper job training. Where remedial assistance is not effective, consider a change in job assignment (with special training or relevant job experience in preparation for career advancement).

A further concern is that employees be treated ethically both during and after evaluation. The most effective way to ensure such ethical treatment is to standardize procedures. Standard procedures should include personal and considerate treatment, a clear explanation of the evaluation process, and direct and honest answers to examinees' questions.

Obligations to Employers

Ethical issues in this area go beyond the basic design and administration of decision-making procedures. They include:

- Conveying accurate expectations for evaluation procedures
- Ensuring high-quality information for HR decisions
- Periodic review of the accuracy of decision-making procedures
- Respecting the employer's proprietary rights
- Balancing the vested interests of the employer with government regulations, with commitment to the profession, and with the rights of those evaluated for HR decisions

Accurate information (as conveyed through test manuals and research investigations) regarding the costs and benefits of a proposed assessment procedure or training program, together with the rationale for decision criteria (e.g., cutoff scores) and their likely effects, is the responsibility of the HR expert. He or she also is ethically bound to provide reliable, valid, and fair data, within the limits of the resources (time, support, money) provided by the employer. The following case illustrates this principle (Committee, 1982).

A small government agency located in a fiscally conservative community hired an industrial/organizational psychologist to prepare six promotional exams for police and firefighters over a period of only 18 months. Since the first exam had to be administered in only 5 months, there was little time for documentation. There was no relevant reference material at the agency, no additional staff resources beyond limited clerical services, and no adequate job analysis data for any of the jobs. Attempts to conduct a job analysis for the purpose of test development failed because the employees involved feared that the results would be used to downgrade their jobs. Department heads had great concern over the security of the test items and therefore refused to allow internal employees to be involved in the writing of the test items, pretesting them, or reviewing the final test.

In view of these constraints, it was difficult for the I/O psychologist to upgrade the quality of the employment tests, as required by professional and legal standards. He described the limitations of his services to the agency management. He tried to educate his agency on professional and legal requirements and convinced the agency to have two consultants carry out components of two promotional exams. Further, he successfully promoted the use of two selection devices, an assessment center and a job-related oral examination, that reduced the adverse impact on minority group applicants.

Through the I/O psychologist's efforts, the promotional exams for police and firefighters became more job-related than they were before he was hired. Considering the limited budgetary and human resources available to the small jurisdiction, he was delivering the best possible professional services he could while trying to make necessary changes in the system.

Another ethical issue arises when HR professionals are constrained from conducting research because the results may in some way be detrimental to their employer (e.g., they may be discoverable in a future lawsuit). The dilemma becomes especially acute if the HR professional believes that this hinders proper practice. It is his or her responsibility to resolve the issue, either by following the employer's wishes, by persuading the employer to do otherwise, or by changing jobs. Balancing obligations to the employer, to the profession, and to those evaluated for HR decisions is difficult. The *Ethical Standards of Psychologists* (1992) advises first to attempt to effect change by constructive action within the organization before disclosing confidential information to others. Thus, maintaining ethical standards is most important, though the need to support the integrity, reputation, and proprietary rights of the host organization is recognized.

Obligations of Employers

Executives should adhere to the same standards as psychologists and other HR professionals when setting organizational policies regarding HR decisions. Furthermore, policymakers must recognize and safeguard the ethical obligations of psychologists and other HR professionals to their profession and to the employees of the organization. This requires establishing an organizational climate that is conducive to ethical practice.

Roughly 84 percent of U.S. businesses now have ethics codes (Walter, 1995a). For example, one firm states: "The requirement that we operate within the law is just the beginning of ethical disciplines we must accept and follow." Another has established a corporate ethics committee that serves as the final authority with regard to the company's policies on business con-

PRACTICAL APPLICATION: HOW JOHNSON & JOHNSON'S ETHICS CODE SAVED THE TYLENOL BRAND

Johnson & Johnson has had such a code (which it calls a "credo") since the 1940s. To update it, the company does "credo challenges" every two years—with extensive employee involvement. The company puts the interests of the public and its customers first, followed by its employees, and stockholders. This is not new; it was first articulated by General Johnson, a World War II veteran who firmly believed the role of business was to serve society.

Here's how Jim Burke, Chairman of Johnson & Johnson from 1976 to 1989, described how the firm reacted after it heard that seven people had died from using its Tylenol product.

" . . . there was no doubt in anybody's mind what we had to do. (Pull the product.) All over the world, hundreds of people made decisions on the fly—and nobody fouled up. Everybody did it the way it needed to be done because they all had it clear in their minds and knew we were there to protect the public. It [the company's ethics code] turned out to be an extraordinary document in terms of helping us handle that situation—and save the Tylenol brand. It also reemphasized that the best way to succeed is to follow the credo's ideas. The credo is a living document" (Walter, 1995a, p. 88).

duct. The boxed insert above shows how one such code helped guide company practice.

At the very least, companies should communicate their policies on ethics clearly, and take corrective action when policies are violated. Perhaps the most important implication of these policies is that creative solutions are necessary to solve HR problems and to resolve ethical dilemmas in this area. Here's an example.

ETHICAL ISSUES IN ORGANIZATIONAL RESEARCH

In field settings researchers encounter social systems comprising people who hold positions in a hierarchy and who also have relationships with consumers, government, unions, and other public institutions. Researchers cannot single-handedly manage the ethical

PRACTICAL APPLICATION: DUN & BRADSTREET'S FRAMEWORK FOR IDENTIFYING AND RESOLVING ETHICAL ISSUES

The Dun & Bradstreet Corp. recognizes that its employees sometimes encounter ethical dilemmas in their day-to-day work. To help resolve them, the company advises employees to ask themselves six key questions (Walter, 1995b):

1. Why is this bothering me? (Am I genuinely perplexed, or am I afraid to do what I know is right?)

2. Who else matters? (What are the implications of my decision for customers, shareholders, or other D&B associates?)

3. Is it my responsibility? (Or is it someone else's? What will happen if I don't act?)

4. What is the ethical concern? (Is there a legal obligation? What about honesty, fairness, promise-keeping, protecting the integrity of data, and avoiding harm to others?)

5. Whom can I ask for advice? (My supervisor, my associates, HR, Legal? Is there an ethics hotline?)

6. Am I being true to myself? (Is my action consistent with my basic values and personal commitments? With company values? Could I share my decision in good conscience with my family? With colleagues and customers?)

dilemmas that arise, because they are a weak force in a field of powerful ones, with only limited means for ensuring moral action or for rectifying moral lapses (Mirvis and Seashore, 1979).

In the context of organization development, management consulting, and training and development, at least five types of ethical dilemmas may arise (White and Wooten, 1983):

1. *Misrepresentation and collusion.* Misrepresentation may occur when a change agent misrepresents his or her education, experience, or skills, or when an organization misrepresents its interest, need, or goal. Collusion may result from lack of clarity regarding goals, values, needs, and methods or from loss of objectivity by assimilating the change agent into the culture of the organization.

2. *Misuse of data.* This may occur when data are distorted, deleted, or not reported either by the change agent or by the organization. For a fascinating account of great frauds in the history of science, see Broad and Wade (1982). This type of dilemma also may occur when data (e.g., concerning personality traits, career interests) are used to assess persons or groups punitively, resulting in personal, professional, or organizational harm.

3. *Manipulation and coercion.* These occur most often when employees are required to abridge their personal values or needs against their will, for example, through forced participation in a change effort such as sensitivity training.

4. *Value and goal conflict.* This occurs when there is ambiguity or conflict concerning whose values will be maximized by the change effort (the change agent's or the organization's) or whose needs will be fulfilled by meeting such goals. This can lead to a reluctance by either party to alter change strategies or to a withholding of services or needed resources.

5. *Technical ineptness.* This can occur through a lack of appropriate knowledge or skill or through an inability to evaluate effectively an intervention or to terminate an organizational-development relationship. It also may result from a reluctance to reduce client dependency or to transfer monitoring of the change effort to internal parties.

Science Versus Advocacy in Organizational Research

Organizations frequently use the expertise of university-based professionals to design various HR systems, to evaluate programs, to direct field research efforts, to serve as workshop leaders, and for other similar activities that provide opportunities to influence organizational life. Problems of distortion can arise when a researcher attempts both to extend the base of scientific knowledge in his or her discipline and to promote changes in organizational practice. This is no "ivory tower" issue, for the problem is relevant to academics as well as to practicing managers.

Many of the ideas in this section come from the excellent discussion by Yorks and Whitsett (1985). When a scientist/practitioner tries to inspire change that runs counter to conventional wisdom there is pressure to report and present data selectively. Why?

> Challenging widely accepted conventional wisdom can generate a strong need to present as convincing a case as possible, without confusing the issue with qualifications. Alternative hypotheses may become adversarial positions to be neutralized, as opposed to alternative interpretations worthy of careful scrutiny. Scientific caution is undermined as one defends prescriptions in managerial forums [Yorks and Whitsett, 1985, p. 27].

To counter pressures such as these, consider the following guidelines:

- When reporting field studies, lecturing to students, and making presentations to practicing managers, distinguish clearly between what has been observed under certain circumscribed conditions and what is being advocated as a desired state of affairs.

- Avoid use of success stories that managers can expect to duplicate rather painlessly. Doing so has led to the recurring fads that have characterized behavioral science-based management approaches, followed by the inevitable and often unfortunate discrediting of a given approach. This discrediting almost is inevitable when managerial action is based on generalizations from highly specific social situations.

- Respect the limitations of data obtained from a single study. Behavioral-science propositions are strongest when they are derived from many situations and they are analyzed by a number of independent scholars.

- Do not allow advocacy of certain techniques or organizational policies to masquerade as science, not because such statements do not stimulate useful debate among managers, but because scientific pretensions confuse the issues involved and make it difficult to separate myth from scientific principles. Ultimately, this frustrates the goals both of science and of practice. Managers get tired of hearing still more claims of "scientific conclusions" about how to manage.

What do these guidelines imply?

> Hunch and bias provide no basis for decisions, only controlled research and substantiated theory will do. "I don't know" thus becomes not only an acceptable

answer to a question, but in many cases a highly valued one [Miner, 1978, p. 70].

In our final section we will examine a conceptual scheme and proposed means to investigate ethical issues in organizational research. First, however, we need to provide some background.

Strategies for Addressing Ethical Issues in Organizational Research

Organizations may be viewed as *role systems,* that is, sets of relations among people that are maintained, in part, by the expectations people have for one another. When communicated, these expectations specify the behavior of organization members and their rights and responsibilities with respect to others in their role system. This implies that when social scientists, as members of one role system, begin a research effort with organization members, who are members of another, it is important to anticipate, diagnose, and treat ethical problems in light of this intersection of role systems. Problems must be resolved through mutual collaboration and appeal to common goals. Ethical dilemmas arise as a result of **role ambiguity** (uncertainty about what the occupant of a particular role is supposed to do), **role conflict** (the simultaneous occurrence of two or more role expectations such that compliance with one makes compliance with the other more difficult), and **ambiguous,** or **conflicting, norms** (standards of behavior).

Table 18–1 presents a summary of strategies for resolving such ethical dilemmas. Column 1 of the table provides examples of typical sources of role ambiguity, role conflict, and ambiguous or conflicting norms encountered in organizational research. Column 2 describes strategies for dealing with each of the Column 1 dilemmas. While the implementation of these strategies may seem excessively legalistic and rigid, agreements negotiated at the start and throughout research projects serve to affirm ethical norms binding on all parties. These ethical norms include, for example, those pertaining to protection of participants' welfare, preservation of scientific interests, avoidance of coercion, and minimization of risk. Such agreements emphasize that the achievement of ethical solutions to operating problems is plainly a matter of concern to all parties, not only a matter of the researcher's judgment.

Column 3 of Table 18–1 describes the ethical and social norms that operate to reduce the adverse consequences of ethical dilemmas and at the same time facilitate the achievement of research objectives with a reasonable balance of risk and benefit. Such widely shared norms include, for example, freedom, self-determination, democracy, due process, and equity. So while roles serve to distinguish the various parties involved in a research effort, shared norms embody general expectations and serve to bind the parties together. In some contexts, however, one set of ethical norms may conflict with another. This can occur, for example, when full and accurate reporting of research to the scientific community might pose an undue risk to the individual welfare of participants (Reese and Fremouw, 1984; Wilson and Donnerstein, 1976). In such cases the researcher bears the responsibility of invoking the additional norm that the conflict be confronted openly, fully, and honestly. While all parties' values may not be honored in its resolution, they should be represented (Baumrind, 1985; Cullen et al., 1989). In short, the conflict should be settled by reason and reciprocity rather than by the preemptive use of power or the selfish reversion to personal whim (Mirvis and Seashore, 1979).

Research Issues in an International Context

When researchers collect data across national borders, they sometimes face conflicts between home- and host-country ethics. In all cases, the interests of participants in the research process take precedence. It is the researcher's responsibility to understand these interests from the perspective of the participant, and to respect them in all aspects of the research process. Such interests include: participants' familiarity with the research process, their political and religious views, and their cultural values. Each of these may have an impact on participants' understanding of the nature of the research. It also may be necessary to devote considerably more time and effort to debrief participants when they are not familiar with research, or where their political, religious, or cultural values might influence their interpretation of a researcher's motives (Punnett and Shenkar, 1996). The boxed insert on p. 311 is an example from Shenkar (1994).

In short, consider the local implications of any research effort. To get a fuller understanding of these implications, it may help to conduct small focus groups with potential subjects, or with local academics. Doing so will help a foreign researcher to understand ethical issues from a local perspective, and to balance these with the requirements of his or her home-country culture.

TABLE 18-1 Strategies for Addressing Ethical Dilemmas in Organizational Research

Source	Strategy	Ethical Norm
Role ambiguity		Anticipating coercion or cooptation of or by uninvolved parties, researcher, participants, and stakeholders; examining risks and benefits; identifying personal, professional, scientific, organizational, jobholder, and stakeholder interests
Regarding which persons or groups are part of the research	Creating an in-house research group composed of all parties implicated directly or indirectly in the study	
Regarding the researcher's role	Communicating clearly, explicitly, and by example the intended role; clarifying the intended role; clarifying the intended means and ends; examining potential unintended consequences; providing for informed participation	
Regarding the participants' roles	Clarifying role responsibilities and rights; providing for informed consent and voluntary participation; establishing procedures to ensure anonymity, confidentiality, job security, and entitlements; providing for redress of grievances and unilateral termination of the research	
Regarding the stakeholders' roles	Clarifying role responsibilities and rights; establishing procedures to ensure participants' anonymity, confidentiality, job security, and entitlements	
Role conflict		Avoiding coercion of or by uninvolved parties, researcher, participants, and stakeholders; acting with knowledge of risks and benefits; representing personal, professional, scientific, organizational, jobholder, and stakeholder interests through collaborative effort and commitment to ethical basis of the research
Between researcher and participants, between researcher and stakeholders, within researcher	Creating and building role relations, providing for joint examination of intended means and ends and potential unintended consequences, establishing procedures for resolution of conflict through joint effort within established ethical norms	
Between participants, between stakeholders, between participants and stakeholders, within participant or stakeholder	Organizing full role system, providing for collaborative examination of intended means and ends and potential unintended consequences, establishing procedures for resolution of conflict through collaborative effort within established ethical norms	
Ambiguous or conflicting norms		Establishing ethical basis of research
Within or between researcher, participants, and stakeholders	Clarifying ethical norms for research, providing for collaborative examination of unclear or incompatible norms, establishing procedures for resolution of value conflicts through collaborative effort	

Source: P. H. Mirvis and S. E. Seashore. Being ethical in organizational research. *American Psychologist*, 1979, *34*, 777. Copyright 1979 by the American Psychological Association. Reprinted by permission of the authors.

PRACTICAL EXAMPLE: ETHICAL ISSUES IN CROSS-NATIONAL RESEARCH

Chinese respondents are more at risk than subjects in other countries, especially when the researchers are foreigners. Despite a decade of reforms, contact with foreigners can be a significant liability. Information that in the West would be considered ordinary may be regarded in China as classified and potentially harmful to national interest. Respondents are more closely supervised than in other nations, and what they say or write is more likely to be distorted or taken out of context and used against them. Sanctions against offenders are also much more significant. Ethical concerns are therefore of paramount importance.

Discussion Questions

1. You work for an advertising agency. Develop a privacy protection policy for electronic- and voice-mail communications.

2. How can an organization develop a policy that actually encourages whistle-blowers to come forward?

3. As a CEO, do you see any potential disadvantages in developing a code of ethics and personal conduct for your company?

4. Discuss the ethical obligations of an employer to job candidates.

5. What kinds of ethical dilemmas might arise in conducting domestic and cross-border research in organizations? How might you deal with them?

*   *   *

Ethical choices are rarely easy. The challenge of being ethical in managing human resources does not lie in the mechanical application of moral prescriptions, but rather in the process of creating and maintaining genuine relationships from which to address ethical dilemmas that cannot be covered by prescription.

SCIENTIFIC AND LEGAL GUIDELINES ON EMPLOYEE SELECTION PROCEDURES—CHECKLISTS FOR COMPLIANCE

Both scientific and legal guidelines for selecting employees are available to HR professionals. The purpose of this Appendix is to present both sets of guidelines in the form of questions to be answered. Obviously the relevance of each question will vary with the context in which it is asked. Taken together, both sets of guidelines represent key issues to address in any selection situation, and more broadly, with respect to any HR decision.

SCIENTIFIC GUIDELINES—SUMMARY CHECKLIST[1]

Premise

When any selection procedure is used, it is used at least with the implicit assumption that some important aspect of behavior on the job (including performance in training, advancement, or other organizationally-pertinent behavior, as well as quality or quantity of job performance) can be predicted from numerical scores on that selection procedure. The essential principle in the evaluation of any selection procedure is that evidence be accumulated to support an inference of job-relatedness (p. 1).

OBJECTIVES, JOB ANALYSIS

1. Is there a clear statement of purpose (objective) of the assessment or validation, based on an understanding of the needs of the organization and of its present and prospective employees?
2. Has there been a systematic examination of the job

and the context in which it is performed (i.e., a job analysis)?
3. Does the job analysis specify the descriptors or units of analysis (tasks, behaviors, etc.)?
4. Does the job analysis provide job information appropriate to the purpose or objective of the research?

CRITERION-RELATED STRATEGY

Feasibility

1. Is the job in question reasonably stable and not in some rapid period of evolution?
2. Is it possible to obtain or develop a relevant, reasonably reliable, and uncontaminated criterion measure(s)?
3. Is it possible to do the research on a sample that is reasonably representative of the population of people and jobs to which the results are to be generalized?
4. Does the study have adequate (e.g., .80) statistical power, that is, probability of detecting a significant predictor-criterion relationship in a sample if such a relationship does, in fact, exist?
5. Has the researcher identified the design characteristics required for excellence in validation (e.g., appropriate samples, need for, and feasibility of statistical controls, corrections, or analyses; numbers of cases)? Given the situational constraints faced by the researcher, is criterion-related validity feasible?

DESIGN AND CONDUCT OF TECHNICALLY-FEASIBLE CRITERION-RELATED STUDIES

I. Criterion Development

1. Are criteria related to the purposes of the study?
2. Do all criteria represent important work behaviors or

---

[1] *Source:* Based on materials found in Principles for the Validation and Use of Personnel Selection Procedures (3rd ed.), Society for Industrial-Organizational Psychology, Inc., College Park, Md.: Author, 1987. For more information on checklist items, consult the subject index.

work outputs on the job or in job-related training, as indicated by a job analysis?

3. Do adequate safeguards exist to reduce the possibility of bias or other criterion contamination?

4. If evidence recommends that several criteria be combined to obtain a single variate, is there a rationale to support the rules of combination?

5. Has criterion reliability been estimated?

6. Are criterion measures highly reliable?

II. Choice of Predictors

1. Is there an empirical, logical, or theoretical foundation for each predictor variable chosen?

2. Is the choice of trial predictors based on relevant research rather than on personal interest, familiarity, or expediency?

3. Other things equal, are more objective predictors preferred over those that rely on subjective judgment?

4. If subjective judgment is used in weighting and summarizing predictor data, are these judgments or decisions recognized as additional predictors?

III. Choice of Sample

1. Is the sample for a validation study representative of the applicant population?

2. Is the sample upon which the research is based large enough to provide adequate statistical power?

3. Are unusual findings (e.g., suppressor or moderator effects, nonlinear regression, post hoc hypotheses in multivariate studies, differential weightings of highly correlated variables) supported by extremely large samples or replication?

4. If data from separate samples are combined, are both jobs and workers similar on variables that research has shown to affect validity?

IV. Procedural Considerations

1. Is validation research directed to entry-level jobs, immediate promotions, or jobs likely to be attained?

2. Have alternate criterion-related research methods been considered if they offer a sound rationale (e.g., cooperative research on an industry-wide basis)?

3. Have procedures for test administration and scoring in validation research been set forth clearly? Are they consistent with the standardization plan for operational use?

4. Is there at least presumptive evidence for the validity of a predictor prior to its operational use?

5. Operationally, are predictor data collected independently of criterion measures?

V. Data Analysis

1. Has the method of analysis been chosen with due consideration for the characteristics of the data and the assumptions involved in the development of the method?

2. Has the type of statistical analysis to be used been considered during the planning of the research?

3. Does the data analysis provide information about the magnitude and statistical significance of a predictor-criterion relationship?

4. Have the relative risks of Type I and Type II errors been considered?

5. Does the analysis provide information about the nature and strength of the predictor-criterion relationship and how it might be used in prediction (e.g., group-specific regression slopes, expectancy charts)?

6. Have adjustments been made for range restriction and/or criterion unreliability, if appropriate, in order to obtain an unbiased estimate of the validity of the predictor in the population in which it will be used?

7. If predictors are to be used in combination, has careful consideration been given to the method used to combine them (e.g., linearly, by summing scores on different tests; or nonlinearly, using multiple cutoffs)?

8. Have appropriate safeguards been applied (e.g., use of cross-validation or shrinkage formulas) to guard against overestimates of validity resulting from capitalization on chance?

9. Have the results of the present criterion-related validity study been interpreted against the background of previous relevant research literature?

10. Has there been an assessment of the practical value or utility of the selection procedure?

11. Has all keypunching, coding, and computational work been checked carefully and thoroughly to ensure that data are free from clerical error?

CONTENT-ORIENTED STRATEGIES

1. Has each job content domain been defined completely and described thoroughly in terms of what it does and does not include?

2. Does the specificity-generality of the content of the selection procedure reflect the extent to which the job is likely to change as a result of organizational needs, technology, equipment, and work assignments?

3. Where appropriate, have special circumstances been considered in defining job content domains (e.g., different locations of seldom-used symbols on different typewriter keyboards)?

4. Has each content domain been defined in terms of tasks, activities, or responsibilities *or* specific knowledge, job skills, or abilities necessary for effective behavior in the domain?

5. Is justification for the measurement and use of broad psychological traits (such as empathy, dominance, leadership aptitude) based on empirical data rather than on content sampling alone?

6. Is each content domain defined in terms of the knowledge, skills, and abilities an employee is expected to have without training or job experience?

7. Is the job content domain restricted to critical or frequent activities or to prerequisite knowledge, skills, or abilities?

8. Do the results of sampling a job content domain for the purpose of constructing or choosing a selection procedure indicate that elements of the procedure include the major elements of the defined domain?

9. Has the selection procedure been subjected to pretesting and analysis in terms of the means, variances, and intercorrelations of its parts?

10. If replacement parts are necessary, do the replacement parts reflect the same area of the content domain as those parts that were eliminated?

11. Is there enough redundancy in measurement (sufficient intercorrelation among various parts of the selection procedure) to provide adequate reliability of measurement?

12. If a work sample is used, have extraneous factors (such as scoring variability, small sample sizes, variability in equipment) been controlled so reliability is adequate for individual prediction?

13. Have scoring keys for content-oriented tests been checked for accuracy? For answers keyed as correct, are they correct under all reasonably-expected job-relevant circumstances?

14. Does the interpretation of the content-oriented selection procedure reflect the measurement properties of the procedure? That is, persons are ranked if the procedure is reliable and provides adequate discrimination in the score ranges involved; a *critical score* is used if examinees are expected to get nearly all items correct.

15. Are all persons used in any aspect of the development or choice of selection procedures defined on the basis of content sampling clearly qualified?

CONSTRUCT APPLICATIONS

1. Is the construct for a particular test embedded in a conceptual framework, no matter how imperfect? Does the conceptual framework specify the meaning of the construct, distinguish it from other constructs, and indicate how measures of the construct should relate to other variables?

2. Is there evidence that the test adequately measures the construct under consideration?

3. Has the process of compiling construct-related evidence for test validity begun with test development? Has it continued until the pattern of empirical relationships between test scores and other variables indicates clearly the meaning of the test scores?

4. Is there a clear conceptual rationale for the linkage between the construct and the work to be done?

VALIDITY GENERALIZATION

1. Does cumulative evidence demonstrate either (a) that situational differences have little or no effect on operational (or true) validities, or (b) that true validities of measures of the construct or of the predictor type have acceptably low probabilities of falling below specified values in new settings?

2. Have researchers fully reported the rules they used to categorize jobs, tests, criteria, and other characteristics of their studies? Have they reported the reliability of the coding schemes used to categorize these variables?

3. Are citations to the reports that contributed to the meta-analytic results available?

4. If the cumulative validity evidence indicates generalizability of validity for a selection procedure only for particular kinds of jobs or job families, and if validity generalization results are relied upon for jobs in new settings or organizations, are the following conditions met?

(a) Is the selection procedure to be used a measure of the trait, ability, or construct studied? Is it a representative sample of the type of selection procedure included in the validity generalization study?

(b) Is the job in the new setting similar to the job, or

a member of the same job family, included in the validity generalization study?

IMPLEMENTATION

Research Reports and Procedures Manuals

1. Do all reports of validation research include the name of the author and date of the study, a statement of the problem, a job description, a description of the criterion measures, and the rationale behind their use?

2. Do the reports describe the research sample, the selection procedures used, the relationship of the selection procedures to job duties, and identification and results of related studies?

3. Are all summary data available that bear on the conclusions drawn by the researcher and on his or her recommendations?

4. Have all research findings that might qualify the conclusions or the generalizability of results been reported?

5. Is all informational material developed for users or examinees accurate, complete for its purposes, and written in language that is not misleading?

6. Are research reports and procedures manuals reviewed periodically and revised as needed?

7. Do research reports and procedures manuals help readers make correct interpretations of data and warn readers against common misuses of information?

8. Are any special qualifications required to administer, score, or interpret a selection procedure clearly stated in the research report or procedures manual?

9. Are any claims made for any selection procedure supported in the documentation with appropriate research evidence?

10. Does the procedures manual for persons who administer selection measures specify clearly the procedures to be followed and emphasize the necessity for standardization of administration, scoring, and interpretation?

11. Are scoring or scaling procedures presented in the procedures manual with as much detail and clarity as possible?

12. Are the samples, measures of central tendency, and variability described in any normative interpretation of scores such as centiles or expectancies of success?

13. Has any derived scale used for reporting scores (e.g., Z, T) been described carefully in the research report or procedures manual?

14. Has validity evidence been built on a foundation of systematic procedures rather than on assumptions generalized from promotional literature or testimonial statements?

USE OF RESEARCH RESULTS

1. Did the research recommend specific methods of score interpretation to the user?

2. Is the recommended use consistent with the procedures by which validity was established?

3. Are any computer-based test interpretations validated using the principles outlined in this document?

4. If critical scores are established, are they based on a reasonable rationale (e.g., estimated cost-benefit ratio, selection ratio, success ratio)?

5. Has this rationale for critical-score determination been communicated clearly to users?

6. Is it technically feasible to reconsider (by retesting or reevaluation) candidates for employment?

7. Have systematic procedures been established for checking the validity of selection procedures in use?

8. Are all persons within the organization who have responsibilities related to the use of employment tests and related predictors qualified through appropriate training to carry out their responsibilities?

9. In choosing, administering, and interpreting selection procedures, have appropriate measures been taken to avoid even the appearance of bias or discriminatory practice?

10. Have the researchers recommended procedures to ensure periodic audit of selection procedure use (i.e., departures from established procedures, incorporation of new research findings or social criticisms)?

11. Have the researchers (or outside scoring services) recommended procedures that will assure clerical accuracy in scoring, checking, coding, or recording selection-procedure results?

12. If a finding of differential prediction is observed, has the researcher made a recommendation for dealing with it (e.g., conducting further research, replacing the selection procedure, or using it operationally in a uniform manner)?

13. Are adequate safeguards available to ensure the security both of test and nontest (e.g., reference checks) predictors?

14. Are implementation procedures designed to safeguard the validity of the selection procedures (i.e., no public disclosure of test content, uniform prior information given to candidates)?

15. In making interpretations of scores is there room for judgment, especially when situational variables (e.g., uncommon distractions, sensory or physical disability in a candidate) might introduce error?

16. Are all records of scores kept in terms of raw scores?

17. Have employment files been purged of data rendered potentially invalid by new experience, aging, maturation, and so on, or by changes in jobs or organizations?

18. When reporting results, are reports presented in terms likely to be interpreted correctly by persons at that level of knowledge?

19. Have measures been taken to ensure that scores will not be reported to persons who may be asked later to provide criterion ratings for validation?

20. In order to prevent misinterpretation of scores intended for use in the context of employment, are derived-score forms such as IQs or grade-equivalents avoided?

21. Are selection procedures administered only to *bona fide* job candidates?

A "yes" answer to each question in the checklist, while an ideal to strive for, is somewhat unrealistic to expect. This raises the question of relative stringency in adhering to the individual principles.

> The importance of a principle depends primarily on the consequences of failure to satisfy it. . . . Will selection errors result in physical, psychological, or economic injury to people? Will the safety or operating efficiency of the organization be impaired because of selection errors? If so then the principles may have to be followed more rigorously than in less crucial situations [p. 4].

LEGAL GUIDELINES ON EMPLOYEE SELECTION PROCEDURES[2]

1. Adverse Impact

A. Records Relating to Adverse Impact

1. What is the race, sex, or ethnic group of each applicant or candidate who has applied for, or is eligible for, consideration for each job? Sec. 4B, 15A

2. How are data gathered for those who appear in person? Sec. 4B

3. How are data gathered for those who do not appear in person? Sec. 4B

4. What are the operational definitions of "hires," "promoted" or "otherwise selected," and "applicant" or "candidate" used for computing the selection rate? Sec. 16R

5. Where records of race, sex, or ethnic background are kept on a sample, how is the sample selected? Sec. 4A

6. For a user with more than 100 employees, what, for the past year, is the adverse impact of the selection procedures for groups that constitute more than 2 percent of the labor force or applicable work force? Sec. 15A(2)(a)

B. Special Record-Keeping Provisions

1. Is the user exempted from keeping records on a race or ethnic group because it constitutes less than 2 percent of the labor force? Sec. 15A(1)

2. Does the user, by virtue of having fewer than 100 employees, qualify for simplified record-keeping procedures? Sec. 15A(1)

3. Where adverse impact has been eliminated, what is the adverse impact for the two succeeding years? Sec. 15A(2)(b)

C. Four-Fifths Rule

1. What is the distribution by race, sex, and ethnic group of applicants, candidates and those hired or promoted for each job for the period in question? Sec. 4B

2. Is the selection rate of any racial, ethnic, or sex group less than four-fifths of that of the group with the highest rate? Sec. 4D

3. Where the total selection process has an adverse impact, what is the adverse impact of the components? Sec. 15A(2)(a)

D. Adverse Impact When User Meets Four-Fifths Rule

1. Does a statistically-significant difference in selection rate have a practically-significant impact on the employment of members of a race, sex, or ethnic group, even when it does not meet the four-fifths rule? Sec. 4D

2. Is the sample of candidates for promotion used in determining adverse impact restricted by prior selection on a selection procedure that is the same as, similar to, or correlated with, the procedure in question? Sec. 4C

3. Is the selection procedure a significant factor in the continuation of discriminatory assignments? Sec. 4C(1)

---

[2] This *Zetetic For Testers II,* © Richard S. Barrett, 1978, is used with the author's permission. Checklist items are keyed to sections in the Uniform Guidelines on Employee Selection Procedures (1978).

4. Does the weight of court decisions or administrative interpretations hold that the selection procedure is not job-related? Sec. 4C(2)

5. What data are there in the literature or available unpublished sources that bear on the differences in test scores of candidates from different races, sexes, or ethnic groups? Sec. 4D

E. Qualifying Circumstances Relating to Adverse Impact

1. What procedures are used to recruit minorities and women, and what was their effect on the applicant population? Sec. 4D

2. How does the user's general, long-term posture toward fair employment affect the conclusions regarding adverse impact? Sec. 4E

3. What safeguards are adopted to assure that recorded information of sex, race, or ethnic background is not used adversely against protected minorities and women? Sec. 4B

2. Validation

A. General Information Regarding Validity

1. What is the purpose of the selection procedure? Sec. 15B(2), 15B(10), 15C(2), 15C(7), 15D(2), 15D(9)

2. What is the rationale for the choice of the validation strategy that is used? Sec. 5A, B, C, 14B(1), 14C(1), 14D(1)

3. How is it determined that specific jobs are included or excluded from the study? Sec. 14B(1), 14C(1), 14D(2), 15B(3), 15D(4)

4. What are the existing selection procedures, and how are they used? Sec. 15B(2), 15C(2), 15D(2)

5. What reasons are advanced, if any, that a criterion-related validity study is not technically feasible? Sec. 14B(1)

6. What reasons are advanced, if any, that a test cannot, or need not, be validated? Sec. 15A(3)(v)

7. Does the user have, or has the user had since the Civil Rights Act applied to the user, records of data that can be or could have been used as predictors or criteria for a criterion-related validity study? Sec. 14B(1)

8. What has been done to change an informal or unscored selection procedure to one which is formal, scored, and quantifiable? Sec. 6B(1)

B. Identifying Information

1. What are the names and addresses of the contact person or of the researchers who prepared any report on the selection procedure that is used in establishing its job-relatedness? Sec. 15B(12), 15C(8), 15D(12)

2. What are the locations and dates of the validity study(ies)? Sec. 15B(1), 15C(1), 15D(1)

3. For each published selection procedure, manual, and technical report, what is the name, author, publisher, date of publication or revision, or form? Sec. 15B(1), 15C(4), 15D(6)

4. What is the content and format of each unpublished selection procedure? Sec. 15B(1), 15C(4), 15D(6)

C. Job Analysis

1. What job-analysis procedure is used? Sec. 14A, 14B(2), 14C(2), 14D(2), 15B(3), 15C(3), 15D(4)

2. When and for what purposes was the job analysis prepared and last revised? Sec. 14A, 14B(2), 14C(2), 14D(2), 15B(3), 15C(3), 15D(4)

3. How does the job analysis describe the work behaviors, their relative frequency, criticality or importance, level of complexity, or the consequences of error? Sec. 14A, 14B(2), 14C(2), 14D(2), 15B(3), 15C(3), 15D(4)

4. How are the relative frequency, criticality or importance, level of complexity, and the consequences of error in job performance determined? Sec. 14A, 14B(2), 14C(2), 14D(2), 15B(3), 15C(3), 15D(4)

D. Professional Control

1. What professional control is exercised to assure the completeness and accuracy of the collection of the data? Sec. 5E, 15B(13), 15C(9), 15D(10)

2. What professional control is exercised to assure the accuracy of the data analyses? Sec. 5E, 15B(13), 15C(9), 15D(10)

3. Was the analysis planned before examination of the data? If not, what changes were made, and why? Sec. 15B(8)

3. Criterion-Related Validity

A. Sample

1. What is the definition of the population to which the study is to be generalized, and how is the sample drawn from it? Sec. 14B(4), 15B(6)

2. How does the departure, if any, from a random sample of applicants or candidates affect the interpretation of the results? Sec. 14B(4), 15B(6)

3. If any members of the population are excluded from the sample, what is the reason for their exclusion? Sec. 14B(4), 15B(6)

4. If any data on any members of the sample were eliminated after they were collected, what is the reason for their being eliminated, and how does their omission affect the conclusions? Sec. 14B(4), 15B(6), 15B(13)

5. What are the pertinent demographic data on the sample such as age, sex, education, training, experience, race, national origin, or native language? Sec. 14B(4), 15B(6)

6. Is the sample used in the validation study representative of the candidates for the job in age, sex, education, training, job experience, motivation, and test-taking experience, or other pertinent characteristics? Sec. 14B(4), 15B(6)

7. Where samples are combined, what evidence is there that the work performed and the composition of the samples are comparable? Sec. 14B(4)

B. Criterion Measures

1. What is measured by each criterion? Sec. 14B, 15B(5)

2. How was criterion performance observed, recorded, and quantified? Sec. 15B(5)

3. What forms were used for each criterion measure? Sec. 14B(3), 15B(5)

4. What instructions are given to those who provide the criterion data, and how is it established that the instructions are followed? Sec. 14B(3), 15B(5)

5. Where an overall measure or a measure of an aspect of work performance is used, what steps were taken to make sure that it measures relevant work behaviors or work outcomes, and not irrelevant information? Sec. 14B(3), 15B(5)

6. Where several criteria are combined into one overall measure, what is the rationale behind the procedure for combination? Sec. 15B(5)

7. Where measures of success in training are used as the criterion, what showing is there of the relevance of the training to performance of the work, and of the relationship of performance on the training measures to work performance? Sec. 14B(3), 15B(5)

8. How is opportunity bias taken into account in the use and interpretation of objective measures? Sec. 14B(3), 15B(5)

9. Where measures other than those of job performance are used, such as tenure, regularity of attendance, error rate, and training time, what is the utility of predicting performance on these measures? Sec. 14B(3), 15B(5)

10. Where a paper and pencil test is used as a criterion, how is its relevance established? Sec. 14B(3), 15B(5)

11. Where criterion measures are couched in terms that tend to define the subject matter covered by the test, what is the job-relatedness of the measures? Sec. 14B(3), 15B(5)

12. What precautions are taken to make sure that judgments of employee adequacy are not contaminated by knowledge of performance on selection procedures? Sec. 14B(3), 15B(5)

13. What are the data bearing on leniency, halo, and reliability of measures of job performance? Sec. 15B(5), 15B(8)

C. Fairness of Criterion Measures

1. What steps are taken to eliminate or take into account possible distortion in performance measures as the result of conscious or unconscious bias on the part of raters against persons of any race, sex, or ethnic group? Sec. 14B(2), 15B(5)

2. Do minorities and women have equivalent assignments, materials, and quality control standards? Sec. 14B(2), 15B(5)

3. Do minorities and women have equal job experience and access to training or help from supervisors? Sec. 14B(2), 15B(5)

4. What comparison is made of rating results, broken down by race, sex, or ethnic group of raters and race, sex, or ethnic group of the workers who are rated? Sec. 15B(11)

D. Results

1. What methods are used for analyzing the data? Sec. 14B(5), 15B(8)

2. What are the validity coefficients for all comparisons between predictors and criteria for all major subgroups? What is the number of cases and significance level associated with each validity coefficient? Sec. 14B(5), 15B(8)

3. For each measure of the selection procedure or criterion, what is the mean and standard deviation for each major group? What is the reliability and standard error of measurement? Sec. 14B(5), 15B(8)

4. When statistics other than the Pearson Product-Moment Correlation Coefficient (or its derivatives) or expectancy tables or charts are used, what is the reason that they are preferred? Sec. 14B(5)

5. Are validity coefficients and weights verified on the basis of a cross-validation study when one is called for? Sec. 14B(7)

6. How much benefit would accrue to the employer if it were possible to select those who score highest on the performance measure and how much actually accrues through the use of the selection procedure? Sec. 15B(10)

7. What does item analysis show about the difficulty of the items, the effectiveness of distractors (answers keyed as incorrect), and the relation between the items and the test or between the items and the criterion? Sec. 15B(5), 15C(5)

E. Corrections and Categorization

1. Where a validity coefficient is corrected for restriction in range of the selection procedure, how is the restriction in range established? Are there any reasons why its use might overestimate the validity? Sec. 15B(8)

2. Where a validity coefficient is corrected for unreliability of the criterion, what is the rationale behind the choice of the reliability measure used? Are there any reasons why its use might overestimate the validity? Sec. 15B(8)

3. What are the levels of significance based on uncorrected correlation coefficients? Sec. 15B(8)

4. Where continuous data are categorized, and particularly where they are dichotomized, what is the rationale for the categorization? Sec. 15B(8)

F. Concurrent Validity

1. Where concurrent validity is used, how does the researcher take into account the effect of training or experience that might influence performance of the research subjects on the selection procedure? Sec. 14B(2), 14B(4), 15B(5)

2. Where concurrent validity is used, what account is taken of those persons who were considered for employment but not hired, or if hired, who left the job before their work performance was measured as part of the research study? Sec. 14B(4), 15B(6)

G. Prediction of Performance on Higher-Level Jobs

1. Where proficiency on the higher-level job is used as a criterion, are the knowledges, skills, and abilities developed by training and experience on that job? Sec. 5I

2. Where proficiency on the higher-level job is used as a criterion, do a majority of the employees advance to the higher-level job in fewer than 5 years? Sec. 5I

H. Fairness

1. How is fairness defined? Sec. 14B(8), 15B(8)

2. How is the fairness of the selection procedure established? Sec. 14B(8), 15B(8)

3. What steps are taken to eliminate unfairness in performance measurements and what is the evidence that they were successful? Sec. 14B(8), 15B(8)

4. Where the performance on a selection procedure is relatively poorer for minorities or women than their performance on the job, how is the selection procedure modified to eliminate the disparity? Sec. 14B(8), 15B(8)

4. Content Validity

A. Relevance of a Content-Validity Strategy

1. Are the applicants or candidates expected to be trained or experienced in the work? Sec. 14C(1)

2. Are the knowledges, skills, or abilities measured by the selection procedure learned on the job? Sec. 14C(1)

3. Does the selection procedure require inferences about the psychological processes involved? Sec. 14C(1)

B. Relation Between Selection Procedure and Work Behaviors

1. Is the selection procedure a representative sample of work behaviors? Sec. 14C(1), 14C(2)

2. How is it shown that the behaviors demonstrated in the selection procedure are representative of the behaviors required by the work? Sec. 14C(4)

3. Does the selection procedure produce an observable work product? Sec. 14C(2)

4. How is it shown that the work product generated by the selection procedure is representative of work products generated on the job? Sec. 14C(4)

5. What is the reliability of the selection procedure and how is it determined? Sec. 14C(5)

C. Knowledges, Skills, and Abilities

1. What is the operational definition of the knowledge, skill, or ability measured by the selection procedure? Sec. 14C(4)

2. How is it established that the knowledge or skill or ability measured by the test is a necessary prerequisite to successful performance? Sec. 14C(1), 14C(4)

D. Adequacy of Simulation

1. Is that part of the work content represented by each item identified so that it is possible to determine whether the behavior required by the selection procedure is a sample of the behavior required by the job? Sec. 15C(5)

2. Does the test question require a response that implies identifiable behavior? Sec. 14C(4)

3. Is the behavior identified by the keyed answer correct and appropriate to the job and the specific situation described? Sec. 14C(4)

4. Is the behavior identified by the test question accurately perceived by the test taker? Sec. 14C(4)

5. Is it likely that the actual job behavior will conform to the behavior described by the candidate's response? Sec. 14C(4)

6. Does the level of difficulty of the question correspond to the level of difficulty of the work behavior required for satisfactory performance? Sec. 14C(4)

7. Can journey workers who are performing satisfactorily pass the test? Sec. 14C(4)

E. Training

1. Is a requirement for a specified level of training, education, or experience justified on the basis of the relationship between the content of the work and of the training, education, or experience? Sec. 14C(6)

2. Where a measure of success in training is used as a selection procedure, how is it shown that the performance evaluated by the measure is a prerequisite to successful work performance? Sec. 14C(7)

5. Construct Validity

1. What is the operational definition of the construct measured by the test? Sec. 14D(2)

2. How is it determined that the constructs covered by the test underlie successful performance of frequent, important, or critical duties of the job? Sec. 14D(2)

3. What is the psychological or other reasoning underlying the test? Sec. 14D(2)

4. What is the evidence from studies conducted by the user and by other researchers, that shows that the selection procedure is validly related to the construct? Sec. 14D(3)

5. What evidence shows that the construct, as it is measured by the selection procedure, is related to work behaviors? Sec. 14D(3)

6. Validity Generalization

Where criterion-related validity studies performed elsewhere are used to show the job-relatedness of a test that has not been validated locally, what showing is there that:

1. All reasonably accessible studies useful for establishing the weight of evidence of validity are included in

the bibliography? (Copies of unpublished studies, or studies reported in journals that are not commonly available, should be described in detail or attached) Sec. 15E(1)(e)

2. The studies are reasonably current and current research methods are used? Sec. 15E(1)(e)

3. The population and the sample drawn from it, the performance measures and job behaviors and other significant variables are sufficiently similar to permit generalization? Sec. 7B(2), 7D, 8B, 15E(1)(a), 15E(1)(b), 15E(1)(c)

4. The selection procedures are fair and valid for the relevant races, sexes, or ethnic groups? Sec. 7B(1), 7B(3), 7C, 15E

5. Where validity data come from an unpublished source, does the representative of the source assert that there is no evidence from other studies that failed to demonstrate validity or that shows the test to be unfair? Sec. 15E(1)(e)

6. What sources of unpublished research who were contacted indicated a) that they had no relevant information, b) that they had relevant information but would not communicate it, c) that they communicated some or all of the relevant data? Sec. 15E(1)(e)

7. Where validity studies incorporate two or more jobs that have one or more work behaviors in common, how similar are the work behaviors, and how was the similarity established? Sec. 14D(4)(b), 15E(1)

7. Application

A. Use of Selection Procedures

1. How is each of the selection procedures used in the selection decision? Sec. 14B(6), 14C(8), 14C(9), 15B(10), 15C(7), 15D(9), 15E(1)(d)

2. Does the use made of the validated selection procedures conform to the findings of the validity study? Sec. 5G, 14B(6)

3. What is the rationale for the weight given to each element in the employment procedure, including tests, interviews, reference checks, and any other sources of information? Sec. 15B(10)

4. How is it determined that rank-ordering, if used, is appropriate for selecting employees? Sec. 14B(6), 14C(9), 15B(10), 15C(7), 15D(9)

5. How is it determined that the passing score, if used, is reasonable and consistent with normal expectations of acceptable proficiency of the work force employed on the job? Sec. 5H, 14B(6), 14C(8), 15B(10), 15C(7), 15D(9)

6. If the passing score is based on the anticipated num-

ber of openings, how is the score related to an acceptable level of job proficiency? Sec. 5H

B. Test Administration

1. Under what conditions is the test administered with respect to giving instructions, permitting practice sessions, answering procedural questions, applying time limits, and following anonymous scoring procedures? Sec. 9B

2. What precautions are made to protect the security of the test? Is there any reason to believe that the test is not secure? Sec. 12

3. What steps were taken to assure accuracy in scoring, coding, and recording test results? Sec. 9B, 15B(13), 15C(9), 15D(10)

4. What procedures are followed to assure that the significance of guessing, time limits, and other test procedures are understood? Sec. 9B

5. Are the test takers given practice, warm-up time, and instructions on the mechanics of answering questions? Sec. 9B

6. Do all candidates have equal access to test-preparation programs? Sec. 11

7. Under what conditions may candidates retake tests? Sec. 12

C. Selection Decisions

1. What are the qualifications of those who interpret the results of the selection procedure? Sec. 9B, 14B(6), 14C(8)

2. How are HR department receptionists and interviewers selected, trained, and supervised? Sec. 9B

3. What questions do interviewers ask, what records do they keep, and what decision rules do they follow in making recommendations? Sec. 15B(7), 15C(4), 15D(6)

4. What control is exercised, and what records kept, regarding the decisions of supervisors to hire or promote candidates? Sec. 15B(7), 15C(4), 15D(6)

5. What are the procedures used to combine the information collected by the selection process for making the selection decision? Sec. 15B(7), 15C(4), 15D(6)

D. Reduction of Adverse Impact

1. What adjustments are made in selection procedures to reduce adverse impact and to eliminate unfairness? Sec. 13B, 14B(8)(d)

2. Is the job designed in such a way as to eliminate unnecessary difficulties for minorities and women? Sec. 13A

3. In determining the operational use of a selection procedure, how are adverse impact and the availability of other selection procedures with less of an adverse impact taken into account? Sec. 13B

4. What investigation was made to identify procedures that serve the user's legitimate interest in efficient and trustworthy workmanship and have less adverse impact? What are the results? Sec. 3B, 15B(9)

5. Has anyone with a legitimate interest shown the user an alternative procedure that is purported to have less adverse impact? If so, what investigation has the user conducted into its appropriateness? Sec. 3B

6. Have all races, sexes, and ethnic groups of applicants or candidates been subjected to the same standards? Sec. 11

7. Where validation is not feasible, what procedures are used to establish that the selection procedures are as job-related as possible and will minimize or eliminate adverse impact? Sec. 6A, 6B

8. Is the person who scores the tests or other selection procedure directly aware of, or able to infer the sex, race, or national origin of the applicants? Sec. 9B

E. Currency, Interim Use

1. Does a user who is using a test that is not fully supported by a validity study have substantial evidence of validity, or have a study under way? Sec. 5J

2. When was the validity study last reviewed for currency of the validation strategy and changes in the labor market and job duties? Sec. 5K

AN OVERVIEW OF CORRELATION AND LINEAR REGRESSION

THE CONCEPT OF CORRELATION

The degree of relationship between any two variables (in the employment context, predictor and criterion) is simply the extent to which they vary together (covary) in a systematic fashion. The magnitude or degree to which they are related linearly is indicated by some measure of correlation, the most popular of which is the Pearson Product-Moment Correlation Coefficient, r. As a measure of relationship, r varies between ± 1.00. When r is 1.00, the two sets of scores are related perfectly and systematically to each other (see Fig. B–1).

Bivariate plots of predictor and criterion scores, as in Figure B–2, are known as **scatterplots.** In the case of an r of +1.00, high (low) predictor scores are matched perfectly by high (low) criterion scores. When r is −1.00, however, the relationship is inverse, and high (low) predictor scores are accompanied by low (high) criterion scores. In both cases, r indicates the extent to which the two sets of scores are ordered similarly. Needless to say, given the complexity of variables operating in applied settings, r's of 1.00 are the stuff of which dreams are made! If no relationship exists between the two variables, then r is 0.0, and the scatterplot is circular in shape. If r is moderate (posi-tive or negative), then the scores tend to cluster in the shape of a football or ellipse (see Fig. B-2).

Obviously, the fatter the football, the weaker the relationship, and vice versa. Note that in predicting job success, the *sign* of the correlation coefficient is not important, but the magnitude is. The greater the absolute value of r, the better the prediction of criterion performance, given a knowledge of predictor performance. In fact, the square of r indicates the percentage of criterion variance accounted for, given a knowledge of the predictor. Assuming a predictor-criterion correlation of .40, $r^2 = .16$ and indicates that 16 percent of the variance in the criterion may be determined (or explained), given a knowledge of the predictor. The statistic r^2 is known as the **coefficient of determination.**

As an overall measure of relationship, r is simply a summary statistic, like a mean. In fact, if both variables are put into standard score form

$$\frac{(x - \bar{x})}{\sigma}$$

r can be interpreted as a mean. It is simply the average of the sum of the cross-products of Z_x and Z_y:

$$r = \frac{\Sigma Z_x Z_y}{n} \qquad \textbf{(B–1)}$$

FIGURE B–1 Perfect Positive and Negative Relationships.

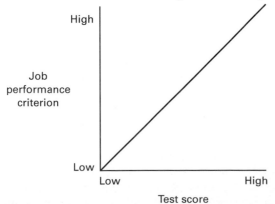
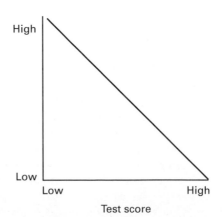

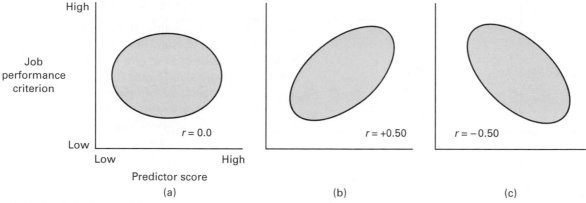

FIGURE B–2 Examples of Correlations Varying in Magnitude and Direction.

Of course, *r* is only one type of correlational measure. Sometimes the scatterplot of *x* and *y* values will indicate that the statistical assumptions necessary to interpret *r*—namely, bivariate normality, linearity, and homoscedasticity (cf. Chapter 7)—cannot be met. Under these circumstances, other, less restrictive measures of correlation may be computed (cf. Guilford and Fruchter, 1978, Chapter 14), but, like *r*, each is a measure of relationship between two variables and may be interpreted as such.

THE CONCEPT OF REGRESSION

Although correlation is a useful procedure for assessing the degree of relationship between two variables, by itself it does not allow us to *predict* one set of scores (criterion scores) from another set of scores (predictor scores). The statistical technique by which this is accomplished is known as **regression analysis,** and correlation is fundamental to its implementation.

The conceptual basis for regression analysis can be presented quite simply by examining a typical bivariate scatterplot of predictor and criterion scores, as in Figure B–2(b). The scatterplot yields several useful pieces of information. The predictor-criterion relationship obviously is positive, moderately strong (*r* = +.50), and linear. In order to predict criterion scores from predictor scores, however, we must be able to describe this relationship more specifically. Prediction becomes possible when the relationship between two variables can be described by means of an equation of the general form $y = f(x)$ read "*y* is a function of *x*." In other words, for every value of *x*, a value of *y* can be generated by carrying out appropriate mathematical operations on the value of *x*. In short, if *x* is the pre-

dictor, *y* (the criterion) can be predicted if we can specify the function *f*, which serves to relate *x* and *y*.

Perhaps the most familiar of all functional relationships is the equation for a straight line: $y = a + bx$. Since *r* always measures only the degree of linear relationship between two variables, the equation describing a straight line (the basis for the general linear model in statistical theory) is especially well-suited to our discussion. The interpretation of this equation (in this context termed a **regression line**) is straightforward. For every unit increase in *x*, there is an increase in *y* that may be determined by multiplying *x* by a regression coefficient *b* (the slope of the straight line, $\Delta y/\Delta x$, which indicates the change in *y* observed for a unit change in *x*) and adding a constant *a* (indicating the point at which the regression line crosses the *y*-axis). When this functional relationship is plotted for all individuals in the sample, the result will be a straight line or linear function, as in Figure B–3.

The goodness of fit of the regression line to the data points can be assessed by observing the extent to which actual scores fall on the regression line as opposed to falling either above it or below it. In Figure B–3, for example, note that for a predictor score of 50, we predict a job performance score of 77 for *all* individuals with predictor scores of 50. This *y*-value may be determined by extending a projection upward from the *x*-axis (predictor score) until it intersects the regression line, and then reading off the predicted *y*-value from the *y*-axis (criterion score). As Figure B–3 demonstrates, however, of those individuals with the same predictor score of 50, some score above 77 on the criterion and some score below 77. Since the correlation between predictor and criterion is less than 1.00, prediction will not be perfect, and some errors in prediction are inevitable. The regression line, there-

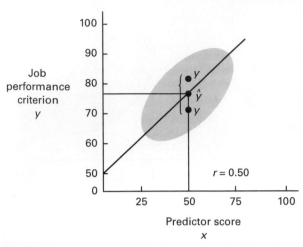

FIGURE B–3 Prediction of Job Performance from Predictor Scores.

fore, is simply a moving average or mean, which summarizes the predictor-criterion relationship at each x-value. The difference between observed (y) and predicted ($\hat{y}$) job performance scores at each x value is the amount by which the regression line prediction is in error. By extension, the *average* error in prediction from the regression equation for all individuals could be summarized by $\Sigma(y - \hat{y})/n$. But since the regression line is a moving average or mean, and since one property of a mean is that deviations above it are exactly compensated by deviations below it (thereby summing to zero), such an index of predictive accuracy is inappropriate. Hence, deviations from the regression line $(y - \hat{y})$ are squared, and the index of predictive accuracy or error variance is expressed as:

$$\sigma^2_{y \cdot x} = \Sigma(y - \hat{y})^2/n \qquad \textbf{(B–2)}$$

Note the subscripts $y \cdot x$ in Equation B–2. These are important and indicate that we are predicting y from a knowledge of x (technically we are regressing y on x). In correlation analysis, the order of the subscripts is irrelevant since we only are summarizing the degree of relationship between x and y and not attempting to predict one value from the other. That is, $r_{xy} = r_{yx}$. In regression analysis, however, $b_{y \cdot x}$ ordinarily will not be equivalent to $b_{x \cdot y}$ (unless $r_{xy} = 1.00$). Since the aim is to predict, the designation of one variable as the predictor and the other as the criterion is important; so also is the order of the subscripts. For any given problem in bivariate linear regression, therefore, there are two regression lines:

$$y = a + bx$$

and

$$x = a' + b'y$$

A logical question at this point is, "Okay, we know how to measure how accurate our regression line is, but how can we plot it so that it provides the best fit to the data points?" Statisticians generally agree that a line of best fit is one that is cast in such a way that the average error of prediction, $\Sigma(y - \hat{y})^2/n$, is a *minimum*. When this condition is satisfied, we have achieved a *least squares* solution of our regression equation ($y = a + bx$). Although in principle the number of possible values of b that will yield a linear equation is infinite, only one value will produce a line of best fit (in the least squares sense) since the average error of prediction will be minimized at that value.

How can such a value be determined? Mathematically, the optimum value of b is directly related to r:

$$b_{y \cdot x} = r_{xy} \frac{\sigma_y}{\sigma_x} \qquad \textbf{(B–3)}$$

That is, b represents the *slope* of the regression line. The slope is affected by two parameters: (1) r_{xy}, the correlation coefficient; and (2) the variability of criterion scores about their mean (σ_y), relative to the variability of predictor scores about their mean (σ_x). If both x and y are in standard (z) score form, then both σ_x and σ_y are equal to 1.0, and the slope of the regression line is equal to r_{xy}. For example, suppose Jerry scores 75 on an aptitude test whose validity with respect to a certain criterion is .50. The mean test score is 60, and the standard deviation of the test scores is 15. Therefore, Jerry's z_x score is:

$$\frac{(75 - 60)}{15} = \frac{15}{15} = +1.0$$

Since the test-criterion relationship is .50, Jerry's predicted criterion score is:

$$z_{\hat{y}} = r_{xy}z_x$$
$$z_{\hat{y}} = .50(1.0)$$
$$= +.50$$

or half a standard deviation above the mean criterion score. Since all scores are in standardized form, $a = 0$; but when x and y are in raw-score (unstandardized) form, then $a \neq 0$. The value of a may be obtained, however, by the following formula:

$$a = \bar{y} - b\bar{x} \qquad \textbf{(B–4)}$$

Assume that in Figure B–3 the regression line crosses the y-axis at a value of 50 (that is, $a = 50$). Assume also that for every unit increase in x, there is a half-unit increase in y (that is, $b = 0.5$). The regression equation ($y = a + bx$) then may be expressed as:

$$\hat{y} = 50 + 0.5x$$

For any given x value, we now have a regression equation that allows us to predict a y value corresponding to it. For example, if x were 80, then

$$\hat{y} = 50 + (.5)(80)$$
$$= 50 + 40$$
$$= 90$$

Let us pause for a moment to answer a question that probably is perplexing you by now: "If we already know the criterion scores of a group, why do we need to predict them?" The answer is that when we set out initially to determine the degree of predictor-criterion relationship, we do need both sets of scores: otherwise, we could not assess the relationship in the first place. If the relationship is strong, then we may want to use the predictor to forecast the criterion status of all new applicants for whom no criterion data exist, and we probably can do so quite accurately. Accuracy also may be increased by adding one or more predictors to our single predictor. The problem then becomes one of multiple prediction, and we shall consider it further in the next section.

PREDICTING FROM MULTIVARIATE INFORMATION

Geometrically, the amount of bivariate predictor-criterion association may be visualized in terms of Venn diagrams—that is, in terms of the amount of overlap between two circles that represent, respectively, the total variances of x and y (see Fig. B–4).

Since there still exists a fair amount of potentially predictable criterion variance, a stronger relationship (and, therefore, appreciably more accurate

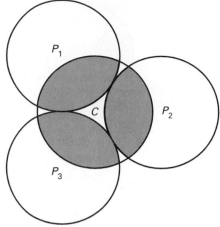

FIGURE B–5 Predictor/Criterion Covariation Given Uncorrelated Predictors.

criterion prediction) is likely to result if additional valid predictors can be found and incorporated into the regression equation (see Fig. B–5). Such a conception is much more representative of real-world job success prediction since decisions generally are made on the basis of *multiple* sources of information. This more complex state of affairs presents little problem conceptually, representing only a generalization of bivariate correlation and linear regression to the multivariate case. For a more rigorous treatment of these topics, consult any one of several excellent texts: Cohen and Cohen (1983); Kelly, Beggs, and McNeil (1969); or Kerlinger and Pedhazur (1973).

In the multivariate case, we have one dependent (criterion) variable but more than one independent (predictor) variable. Their combined relationship is called a *multiple correlation* and is symbolized by R. Likewise R^2, the coefficient of *multiple determination,* is analogous to r^2 and indicates the proportion of criterion variance that may be explained using more than one predictor. In practice, the degree to which prediction can be improved (i.e., the amount of additional criterion variance that can be accounted for) depends on several factors, the most crucial of which is the degree of intercorrelation among the predictors themselves. Compare the situation in Figure B–5 with that of Figure B–6.

When the predictors are uncorrelated, as in Figure B–5, R^2 may be computed simply by adding together the individual squared correlation coefficients, r^2:

$$R^2_{y \cdot x_1 x_2 \ldots x_n} = r^2_{x_1 y} + r^2_{x_2 y} + r^2_{x_3 y} + \cdots + r^2_{x_n y} \quad \textbf{(B–5)}$$

When the predictors are correlated with one another, however, the computation of R^2 becomes a bit more

FIGURE B–4 Bivariate Predictor/Criterion Covariation.

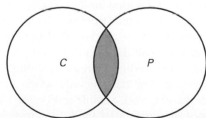

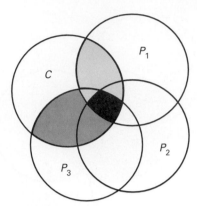

FIGURE B–6 Predictor/Criterion Correlation in the Case of Correlated Predictors.

involved. In examining Figure B–6, note that the amount of overlap between the criterion and each predictor can be partitioned into two components: (1) that which is unique to a given predictor, and (2) that which is shared with the other predictors. In computing R^2, we are concerned only with determining the amount of unique criterion variance explainable by the predictor composite. Therefore, for each predictor, that portion of predictor-criterion overlap that is shared with the other predictors must be removed. This can be accomplished (in the two-predictor case) as follows:

$$R^2_{y \cdot x_1 x_2} = \frac{r^2_{x_1 y} + r^2_{x_2 y} - 2 r_{x_1 x_2} r_{x_1 y} r_{x_2 y}}{1 - r^2_{x_1 x_2}} \quad \textbf{(B–6)}$$

Consider two extreme cases. If $r_{x_1 x_2} = 0$, then Equation B–6 reduces to Equation B–5. On the other hand, if x_1 and x_2 are perfectly correlated, then no additional criterion variance can be accounted for over and above that which is accounted for using bivariate correlation. As a general rule of thumb then, *the higher the intercorrelation between predictors, the smaller the increase in R^2 as a result of adding additional predictors to the selection battery.*

In the employment context, we are concerned primarily with generating predictions of job success (using the multiple linear-regression model), given knowledge of an individual's standing on several predictor variables. As with bivariate regression, certain statistical assumptions are necessary: linearity, homoscedasticity, and normality. In addition, it is assumed that errors are random, with a mean value of zero and a variance equal to σ^2_ε, and that any pair of errors will be independent

(i.e., the errors corresponding to two observations, y_1 and y_2, do not influence one another).

The multiple-regression model is simply an extension of the bivariate-regression model. The general form of the model is as follows:

$$y = a + b_{yx_1 \cdot x_2 \dots x_n} x_1 + b_{yx_2 \cdot x_1 \dots x_n} x_2 \\ + b_{y_n \cdot x_1 \cdot x_2 \dots n - 1} x_n \quad \textbf{(B–7)}$$

The a and b coefficients are interpreted as in bivariate regression, except that $b_{yx_1 \cdot x_2 \dots x_n}$ is the regression coefficient for the x_1 values and $b_{yx_2 \cdot x_1 \dots x_n}$ is the regression coefficient for the x_2 values. The value of $b_{yx_1 \cdot x_2 \dots x_n}$ (known as a **partial regression coeffecient**) indicates how many units y increases for every unit increase in x_1, when the effects of $x_2 \dots x_n$ have been held constant. Likewise, the value $b_{yx_2 \cdot x_1 \dots x_n}$ indicates how many units y increases for every unit increase in x_2 when the effects of $x_1 \dots x_n$ have been held constant. In short, each partial regression coefficient indicates the unique contribution of each predictor to the prediction of criterion status. As in bivariate regression, the b weights are optimal (in the least-squares sense) and guarantee the maximum possible correlation between predicted and obtained y values.

Calculation of the optimal b weights requires the simultaneous solution of a set of linear equations (known as **normal equations**) in which there are as many normal equations as there are predictors. This is a rather complex procedure, but in view of the wide availability of statistical software programs, it is less of an obstacle today than it once was. The constant a can be computed readily in the multiple-regression two-predictor case from:

$$a = \hat{y} - \bar{x}_1 b_{y1 \cdot 2} - \bar{x}_2 b_{y2 \cdot 1} \quad \textbf{(B–8)}$$

Likewise,

$$R^2 = 1 - \frac{\sigma^2_{y \cdot x_1 x_2 \dots x_n}}{\sigma^2_y}$$

and indicates the proportion of total criterion variance that is accounted for by the predictor variables.

The implementation of the multiple-regression model is straightforward, once we have derived our prediction rule (i.e., determined the optimal b weights). Assume we have data on 200 persons hired over a 6-month period in a large, expanding manufacturing operation. The data include scores on an aptitude test (x_1) and a work-sample test (x_2) as well as job performance measures after the 6-month period. After analyzing these data to determine the values $a, b_{y1\cdot2}$, and $b_{y2\cdot1}$ that best describe the relationship between predictors and criterion, suppose our multiple-regression equation assumes the following form:

$$\hat{y} = 8 + .3x_1 + .7x_2$$

This equation says that the most likely criterion score for any new applicant (assuming the applicant comes from the same population as that on whom the equation was derived) is equal to 8 plus .3 times his or her aptitude test score plus .7 times his or her work-sample score. If a new applicant scores 60 on the aptitude test and 70 on the work-sample test, his or her predicted job performance score 6 months after hire would be:

$$y = 8 + (.3)(60) + (.7)(70)$$
$$= 8 + 18 + 49$$
$$= 75$$

CROSS-VALIDATION OF REGRESSION WEIGHTS

A multiple R computed between predicted and actual criterion scores for a sample of individuals provides an *estimate* of the degree of relationship between the combination of predictor scores and the criterion measures. This particular combination of predictor scores is optimal (in the least-squares sense) for the sample on whom the weights were originally derived—an outcome guaranteed by the least-squares solution. Such a solution also capitalizes on any idiosyncrasies in the sample that favor a high multiple R. In practice, therefore, multiple R derived from a single sample is an overestimate, since if this combination of predictor weights is applied to similar samples that differ in any way from the original sample, then multiple R in the new samples almost always will be lower. This is known in statistics as the *shrinkage* problem (see Chapter 7). In short, multiple R obtained in any given sample is a biased estimate of the multiple correlation to be expected in similar samples from the same population. Consequently, multiple R must be corrected for the shrinkage expected when the regression weights are applied to the same predictors in new samples of applicants.

In general, there are two classes of procedures available for doing this: statistical and empirical. Each is appropriate under different sets of circumstances. When the population cross-validated multiple correlation (ρ) is estimated with respect to a *fixed set* of predictors (that is, predictors that have not been selected from a larger set), statistical formulas that estimate shrinkage are appropriate. Such formulas "shrink" $\hat{\rho}$ according to the extent to which the number of predictors is large relative to the size of the original sample. Cattin (1980) has shown that the following formula produces least-biased estimates:

$$\hat{\rho}_c^2 = \frac{(N - k - 3)\rho^4 + \rho^2}{(N - 2k - 2)\rho^2 + \rho} \qquad \textbf{(B–9)}$$

where:

$\hat{\rho}_c^2$ = estimated population cross-validated multiple correlation

N = number of people in the validation sample

k = number of predictors in the regression equation

ρ = population multiple correlation

ρ^4 = the square of ρ^2

If N is less than 50, the following formula should be used to estimate the squared population multiple correlation (ρ^2) in Equation B–9:

$$\rho^2 = 1 - \frac{N - 3}{N - k - 1}(1 - R^2) \times$$
$$\left[1 + \frac{2(1 - R^2)}{(N - k + 1)} + \frac{8(1 - R^2)^2}{(N - k - 1)(N - k + 3)} \right] \qquad \textbf{(B–10)}$$

where R^2 = the squared multiple-correlation coefficient obtained in the validation sample, and all other terms are as defined above.

If N is greater than 50, then a simpler formula should be used to estimate ρ^2 in Equation B–9:

$$\hat{\rho}^2 = 1 - \frac{N - 1}{N - k - 1}(1 - R^2) \qquad \textbf{(B–11)}$$

where all terms are as defined above. Equation B–11 is the well-known Wherry (1931) formula for estimating ρ^2.

Equation B–9 is appropriate assuming that ordinary least-squares estimation is used, that a fixed set of predictors is used, and that the observations used in the validation sample and the observations whose criterion values are to be predicted, come from the same population and are independent. If stepwise regression is used to eliminate predictor variables that add little to R^2, or if predictor variables are selected on the basis of high zero-order sample correlations with the criterion variable, then Equation B–9 will tend to overestimate

$\hat{\rho}_c^2$ since the predictor variables are not selected a priori. Use care in interpreting the results.

If Equation B–9 is appropriate, then no additional samples of individuals are required. Moreover, the resulting estimates are more precise because all the information is used at once, which cannot be done by cross-validation. Empirical studies of prediction from a set of fixed predictors have demonstrated that in typical selection situations, estimates of ρ based on the entire sample are more accurate than estimates from cross-validation procedures (Schmitt, Coyle, and Rauschenberger, 1977).

On the other hand, when the population from which successive samples are obtained changes from sample to sample (as in long-term studies in applied settings), shrinkage formulas are inappropriate since the best predictors in the original sample may not be the best predictors in the other samples. Consequently, an empirical check (cross-validation) is essential to obtain an estimate of ρ that would be obtained in other samples of subjects (McNemar, 1969). Cross-validation of a selected set of predictors is mandatory whether the selected variables are tests, single scales, or items.

PREDICTIVE ACCURACY OF MULTIPLE REGRESSION

The best-fitting regression line may be considered a kind of moving average or mean, but there will be some dispersion of actual criterion scores both above and below those predicted by the regression line. These scores tend to distribute themselves normally (see Fig. B–3), with the preponderance of actual criterion scores falling on or near the regression line and fewer scores falling farther away from it. A distribution of these deviations for all individuals would provide a useful index of how far off we are in predicting y from x. The wider the dispersion, the greater the error of prediction. (Conversely, the smaller the dispersion, the smaller the error of prediction.) Since the standard deviation is a convenient measure of dispersion, we can use it as an index of the extent of our errors in prediction.

What we referred to earlier (Eq. B–2) as our index of predictive accuracy $[\sigma_{y\cdot x}^2 = \Sigma(y - \hat{y})^2/n]$ is a variance, indicating the amount of variability about the regression line. The square root of this expression is a standard deviation—the standard deviation of the errors of estimate—more commonly known as the **standard error of estimate.** It can be shown (Ghiselli et al., 1981, p. 145) that

$$\sigma_{y\cdot x} = \sqrt{\Sigma(y - \hat{y})^2/n}$$

is equivalent to

$$\sigma_{y\cdot x} = \sigma_y\sqrt{1 - r_{xy}^2}$$

or in the multivariate case

$$\sigma_{y\cdot x_1 x_2} = \sigma_y\sqrt{1 - R_{y\cdot x_1 x_2}^2} \qquad \textbf{(B–12)}$$

The standard error of estimate (σ_{est}) is interpreted in the same way as any standard deviation. It is a most useful measure, for it allows us to erect confidence limits around a predicted criterion score, within which we would expect some specified percentage of actual criterion scores to fall. Thus, on the average, 68 out of 100 actual criterion scores will fall within $\pm 1\sigma_{est}$ of predicted criterion scores, and 95 out of 100 actual criterion scores will fall within $\pm 1.96\,\sigma_{est}$ of predicted criterion scores. To illustrate, suppose the standard deviation of a sample of job performance scores for recent hires is 8.2 and the multiple R between a battery of three tests and a criterion is .68. The σ_{est} for these data may be computed as follows:

$$\sigma_{est} = 8.2\sqrt{1 - .68^2}$$
$$= 6.0$$

For all applicants with predicted criterion scores of 86, for example, the limits 80 and 92 (86 ± 6.0) will contain, on the average, the actual criterion scores of 68 percent of the applicants. Likewise, the limits 74.2 and 97.8 (86 ± 1.96 σ_{est}) will contain, on the average, the actual criterion scores of 95 percent of the applicants.

Suppose $R^2 = 0$ for a given predictor-criterion relationship. Under these circumstances, the slope of the regression line is zero (i.e., it is parallel to the x-axis), and the best estimate of criterion status for every value of the predictor is equal to $\bar{y}$. In such a situation, σ_{est} equals

$$\sigma_{y\cdot x_1 x_2} = \sigma_y\sqrt{1 - R_{y\cdot x_1 x_2}^2}$$
$$\sigma_{est} = \sqrt{1 - 0}$$
$$= \sigma_y$$

Thus, even if $R^2 = 0$, criterion status for all individuals still can be predicted with $\sigma_{est} = \sigma_y$ if $\bar{y}$ is known. Therefore, σ_y serves as a baseline of predictive error from which to judge the degree of improvement in predictive accuracy by any regression equation with $R^2 > 0$. As R^2 increases, σ_{est} decreases, thereby demonstrating enhanced predictive accuracy over baseline prediction.

DECISION TREES
FOR STATISTICAL METHODS

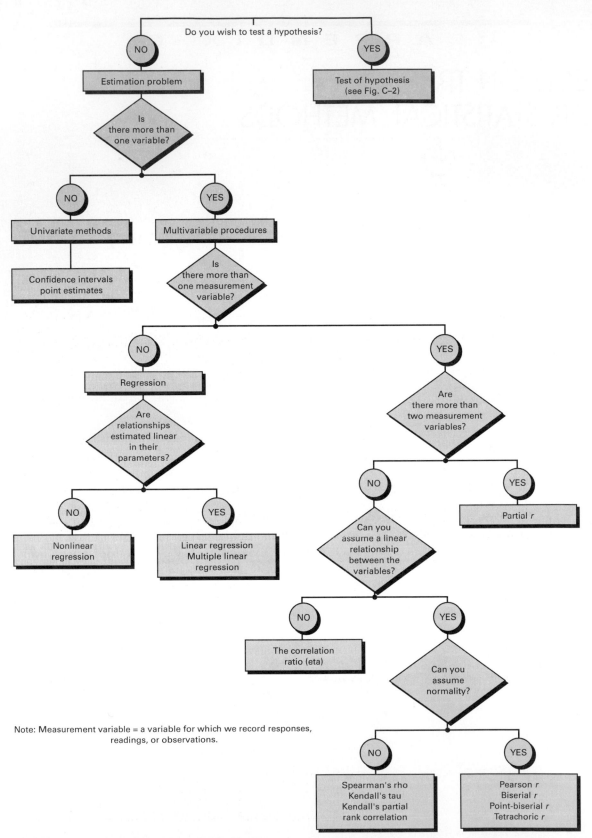

FIGURE C–1 Decision Tree for Estimation Problems.

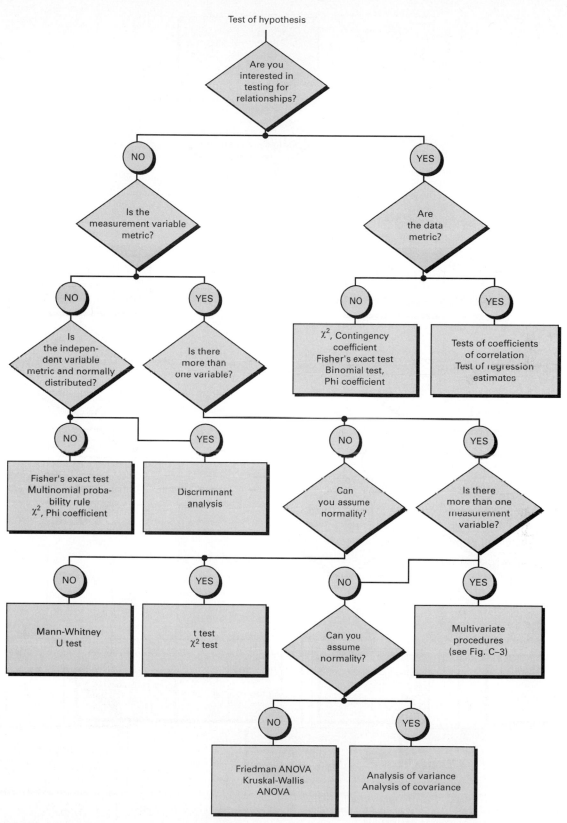

FIGURE C–2 Decision Tree for Hypothesis Testing.

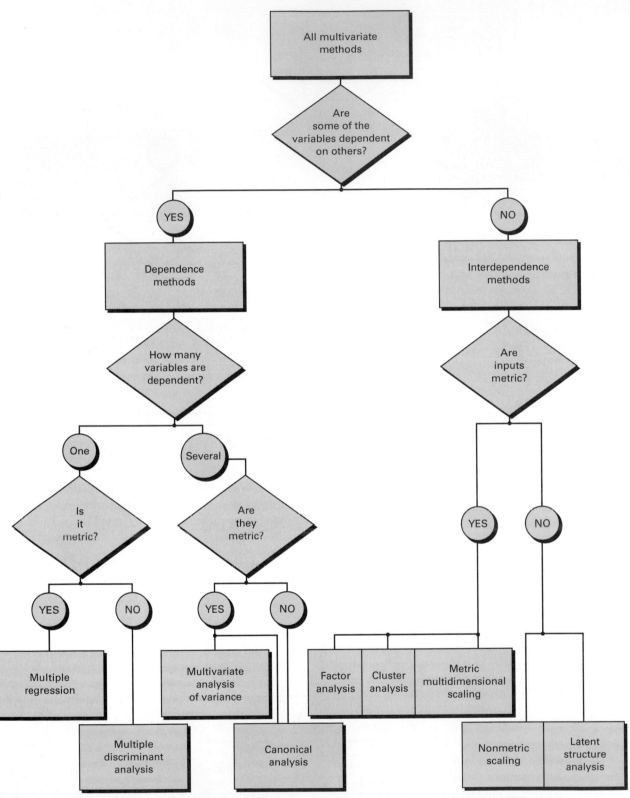

Source: Reprinted from J. N. Sheth. The multivariate revolution in marketing research. *Journal of Marketing,* 1971, *35,* 15. Published by the American Marketing Association.

FIGURE C–3 A Classification of Multivariate Methods.

REFERENCES

Abrahams, N. M., and Alf, E., Jr. (1972). Pratfalls in moderator research. *Journal of Applied Psychology* 56, 245–251.

Academy of Management. (1995). The Academy of Management code of ethical conduct. *Academy of Management Journal* 38, 573–577.

Ackerman, P. L. (1989). Within-task intercorrelations of skilled performance: Implications for predicting individual differences? (A comment on Henry and Hulin, 1987). *Journal of Applied Psychology* 74, 360–364.

Adams, S.R., and Thornton, G.C., III. (1989, October). *The assessor judgement process: A review of the reliability and validity of assessment center ratings.* Paper presented at the 1989 National Assessment Conference, Minneapolis, MN.

Aguinis, H. (1995). Statistical power problems with moderated multiple regression in management research. *Journal of Management* 21, 1141–1158.

Aiken, L. R. (1994). *Psychological testing and assessment* (8th ed.). Boston: Allyn & Bacon.

Ajzen, I., and Fishbein, M. (1977). Attitude-behavior relations: A theoretical analysis and review of empirical research. *Psychological Bulletin* 84, 888–918.

Ajzen, I., and Fishbein, M. (1980). *Understanding attitudes and predicting social behavior.* Englewood Cliffs, NJ: Prentice Hall.

Albemarle Paper Company v. *Moody.* (1975). 422 U.S. 405.

Alexander, R. A. (1988). Group homogeneity, range restriction, and range enhancement effects on correlations. *Personnel Psychology* 41, 773–777.

Alexander, R. A., Barrett, G. V., and Doverspike, D. (1983). An explication of the selection ratio and its relationship to hiring rate. *Journal of Applied Psychology* 68, 342–344.

Alexander, R. A., Carson, K. P., Alliger, G. M., and Barrett, G. V. (1985). Further consideration of the power to detect nonzero validity coefficients under range restriction. *Journal of Applied Psychology* 70, 451–460.

Alexander, R. A., Carson, K. P., Alliger, G. M., and Cronshaw, S. F. (1989). Empirical distributions of range restricted SDx in validity studies. *Journal of Applied Psychology* 74, 253–258.

Alien workers bring factory a $580,000 fine (1989, Dec. 14). *The New York Times,* p. A32.

Allen, M. J., and Yen, W. M. (1979). *Introduction to measurement theory.* Monterey, CA: Brooks/Cole.

Allen R. F., and Silverzweig, S. (1976). Group norms: Their influence on training effectiveness. In R. C. Craig (Ed.), *Training and development handbook.* New York: McGraw-Hill.

Alliger, G. M., and Hosoda, M. (1992, May). *The shape of work: The distribution of measures of work performance and implications for Total Quality Management.* Paper presented at the annual conference of the Society for Industrial and Organizational Psychology, Montreal, Canada.

Alliger, G. M., and Janak, E. A. (1989). Kirkpatrick's levels of training criteria: Thirty years later. *Personnel Psychology* 42, 331–342.

Alpander, G. G. (1980). Human resource planning in U.S. corporations. *California Management Review* 22 (Spring), 24–32.

Amante, L. (1989). Help wanted: Creative recruitment tactics. *Personnel* 66 (10), 32–36.

American Psychological Association. (1992). Ethical Principles of Psychologists and Code of Conduct. *American Psychologist* 47, 1597–1611.

American Psychological Association. (1995). *Ethical conflicts in psychology.* Washington, DC: Author.

American Psychological Association Task Force on

Employment Testing of Minority Groups. (1969). Job testing and the disadvantaged. *American Psychologist* 24, 637–650.

American Psychological Association, American Educational Research Association, and National Council on Measurement in Education (Joint Committee). (1985). *Standards for educational and psychological testing.* Washington, DC: American Psychological Association.

Americans With Disabilities Act of 1990, Public Law No. 101–336, 104 Stat. 328 (1990). Codified at 42 U.S.C., Section 12101 *et seq.*

American Tobacco Company v. *Patterson.* (1982). 102 Supreme Court Rep. 1534.

A model employment-privacy policy. (1993, July). *Macworld,* p. 121.

Anastasi, A. (1988). *Psychological testing* (6th ed.). New York: Macmillan.

Anderson, C. W. (1960). The relation between speaking times and decisions in the employment interview. *Journal of Applied Psychology* 44, 267–268.

Angarola, R. T. (1985). Drug testing in the workplace: Is it legal? *Personnel Administrator* 30 (9), 79–89.

Angoff, W. H. (1971). Scales, norms, and equivalent scores. In Thorndike, R. L. (Ed.), *Educational measurement* (pp. 508–600). Washington, DC: American Council on Education.

Ansoff, H. I. (1988). *The new corporate strategy.* New York: Wiley.

Antonioni, D. (1994). The effects of feedback accountability on upward appraisal ratings. *Personnel Psychology* 47, 349–356.

Armenakis, A., and Smith, L. (1978). A practical alternative to comparison group designs in OD evaluations: The abbreviated time series design. *Academy of Management Journal* 21, 499–507.

Applebome, P. (1995, February 20). Employers wary of school system. *New York Times,* pp. A1, A13.

Armer, P. (1970). The individual: His privacy, self-image and obsolescence. *Proceedings of the Meeting of the Panel on Science and Technology,* 11th "Science and Astronautics." U.S. House of Representatives. Washington, DC: U.S. Government Printing Office.

Arnold, D. W., and Thiemann, A. J. (1992, December). Test scoring under the Civil Rights Act of 1991. *PTC Quarterly, 8* (4), pp. 1, 2.

Arnold, H. J. (1984). Testing moderator variable hypotheses: A reply to Stone and Hollenbeck. *Organizational Behavior and Human Performance* 34, 214–224.

Arnold, H. J., and Feldman, D. C. (1981). Social desirability response bias in self-report choice situations. *Academy of Management Journal* 24, 377–385.

Arthur, J. B. (1994). Effects of human resource systems on manufacturing performance and turnover. *Academy of Management Journal* 37, 670–687.

Arvey, R. D. (1979). Unfair discrimination in the employment interview: Legal and psychological aspects. *Psychological Bulletin* 86, 736–765.

Arvey, R. D., and Begalla, M. E. (1975). Analyzing the homemaker job using the Position Analysis Questionnaire (PAQ). *Journal of Applied Psychology* 60, 513–517.

Arvey, R. D., Cole, D. A., Hazucha, J. F., and Hartanto, F. M. (1985). Statistical power of training evaluation designs. *Personnel Psychology* 38, 493–507.

Arvey, R. D., Davis, G. A., McGowen, S. L., and Dipboye, R. L. (1982). Potential sources of bias in job analytic processes. *Academy of Management Journal* 25, 618–629.

Arvey, R. D., Landon, T. E., Nutting, S. M., and Maxwell, S. E. (1992). Development of physical ability tests for police officers: A construct validation approach. *Journal of Applied Psychology* 77, 996–1009.

Arvey, R. D., Maxwell, S. E., and Salas, E. (1992). The relative power of training evaluation designs under different cost configurations. *Journal of Applied Psychology* 77, 155–160.

Arvey, R. D., and McGowen, S. L. (1982, August). *The use of experience requirements in selecting employees.* Paper presented at the annual meeting of the American Psychological Association, Washington, DC.

Arvey, R. D., Salas, E., and Gialluca, K. A. (1992). Using task inventories to forecast skills and abilities. *Human Performance* 5, 171–190.

Ash, P. (1973). Reading difficulty of merit system tests. *Proceedings of the 81st Annual Convention of the American Psychological Association* (pp. 49–50), Montreal, Canada.

Ash, R. A., and Edgell, S. L. (1975). A note on the readability of the Position Analysis Questionnaire (PAQ). *Journal of Applied Psychology* 60, 765–766.

Asher, J. J. (1972). The biographical item: Can it be improved? *Personnel Psychology* 25, 251–269.

Ashford, S. J., and Cummings, L. L. (1983). Feedback as an individual resource: Personal strategies of creating information. *Organizational Behavior and Human Performance* 32, 370–398.

Ashford, S. J., and Tsui, A. S. (1991). Self-regulation for managerial effectiveness: The role of active feedback seeking. *Academy of Management Journal* 34, 251–280.

Ashworth, S. D., Osburn, H. G., Callender, J., and Boyle, K. A. (1992). The effects of unrepresented studies on the robustness of validity generalization results. *Personnel Psychology* 45, 341–361.

Astin, A. W. (1964). Criterion-centered research. *Educational and Psychological Measurement* 24, 807–822.

Athey, T. R., and McIntyre, R. M. (1987). Effect of rater training on rater accuracy: Levels-of-processing theory and social facilitation theory perspectives. *Journal of Applied Psychology* 72, 567–572.

Attewell, P., and Rule, J. (1984). Computing and organizations: What we know and what we don't know. *Communications of the ACM* 27,1184–1192.

Austin, J. T., Humphreys, L. G., and Hulin, C. L. (1989). Another view of dynamic criteria: A critical reanalysis of Barrett, Caldwell, and Alexander. *Personnel Psychology* 42, 583–596.

Austin, J. T., and Villanova, P. (1992). The criterion problem: 1917–1992. *Journal of Applied Psychology* 77, 836–874.

Bahnsen, E. (1996, November). Questions to ask, and not ask, job applicants. *HR News*, pp. 10, 11.

Baig, E. (1996, September 30). Pounding the virtual pavement. *Business Week,* pp. 152E4, 152E5.

The Bakke ruling. (1978, June 29). *Wall Street Journal,* pp. 1, 17, 18.

Baldwin, T. T. (1992). Effects of alternative modeling strategies on outcomes of interpersonal skills training. *Journal of Applied Psychology* 77, 147–154.

Baldwin, T. T., and Ford, J. K. (1988). Transfer of training: A review and directions for future research. *Personnel Psychology* 41, 63–105.

Baldwin, T. T., Magjuka, R. J., and Loher, B. T. (1991). The perils of participation: Effects of choice of training on trainee motivation and learning. *Personnel Psychology* 44, 51–65.

Balma, J. J. (1959). The concept of synthetic validity. *Personnel Psychology* 12, 395–396.

Bandura, A. (1969). *Principles of behavior modification.* New York: Holt, Rinehart, and Winston.

Bandura, A. (1977). *Social learning theory.* Englewood Cliffs, NJ: Prentice Hall.

Bandura, A. (1986). *Social foundations of thought and action: A social cognitive theory.* Englewood Cliffs, NJ: Prentice Hall.

Banks, C. G, and Roberson, I. (1985). Performance appraisers as test developers. *Academy of Management Review* 10, 128–142.

Banks, M. H., Jackson, P. R., Stafford, E. M., and Warr, P. B. (1983). The Job Components Inventory and the analysis of jobs requiring limited skill. *Personnel Psychology* 36, 57–66.

Banner, D. K., and Gagné, T. E. (1995). *Designing effective organizations.* Thousand Oaks, CA: Sage.

Barber, A. E., Daly, C. L., Giannantonio, C. M., and Phillips, J. M. (1994). Job search activities: An examination of changes over time. *Personnel Psychology* 47, 739–766.

Barber, A. E., Hollenbeck, J. R., Tower, S. L., and Phillips, J. M. (1994). The effects of interview focus on effectiveness: A field experiment. *Journal of Applied Psychology* 79, 886–896.

Barber, A. E., and Roehling, M. V. (1993). Job postings and the decision to interview: A verbal protocol analysis. *Journal of Applied Psychology* 78, 845–856.

Barney, J. (1991). Firm resources and sustained competitive advantage. *Journal of Management* 17, 99–120.

Baron, R. A. (1983). "Sweet smell of success"? The impact of pleasant artificial scents on evaluations of job applicants. *Journal of Applied Psychology* 68, 709–713.

Baron, R. A. (1988). Negative effects of destructive criticism: Impact on conflict, self-efficacy, and task performance. *Journal of Applied Psychology* 73, 199–207.

Barrett, G. V., and Alexander, R. A. (1989). Rejoinder to Austin, Humphreys, and Hulin: Critical reanalysis of Barrett, Caldwell, and Alexander. *Personnel Psychology* 42, 597–612.

Barrett, G. V., Caldwell, M. S., and Alexander, R. A. (1985). The concept of dynamic criteria: A critical reanalysis. *Personnel Psychology* 38, 41–56.

Barrett, G. V., Phillips, J. S., and Alexander, R. A. (1981). Concurrent and predictive validity designs: A critical reanalysis. *Journal of Applied Psychology* 66, 1–6.

Barrett, P. M. (1993, November 10). Justices make it easier to prove sex harassment. *The Wall Street Journal,* pp. A3, A4.

Barrett, R. S. (1966). Influence of supervisor's requirements on ratings. *Personnel Psychology* 19, 375–387.

Barrett, R. S. (1967). Correlation diagrams for fair employment testing, (mimeo).

Barrick, M. R., and Mount, M. K. (1991). The Big Five personality dimensions and job performance: A meta-analysis. *Personnel Psychology* 44, 1–26.

Barrick, M. R., and Mount, M. K. (1993). Autonomy as a moderator of the relationships between the Big Five personality dimensions and job performance. *Journal of Applied Psychology* 78, 111–118.

Bartlett, C. J., Bobko, P., Mosier, S. B., and Hannan, R. (1978). Testing for fairness with a moderated multiple regression strategy: An alternative to differential analysis. *Personnel Psychology* 31, 233–241.

Bartlett, C. J., Bobko, P., Mosier, S. B., Hannan, R., and Green, C. G. (1966). Clinical prediction: Does one sometimes know too much? *Journal of Counseling Psychology* 13, 267–270.

Bartlett, C. J., and O'Leary, B. S. (1969). A differential prediction model to moderate the effects of heterogeneous groups in personnel selection and classification. *Personnel Psychology* 22, 1–17.

Bartol, K. M., and Martin, D. C. (1989). Effects of dependence, dependency threats, and pay secrecy on managerial pay allocations. *Journal of Applied Psychology* 74, 105–113.

Barton, J. (1994). Choosing to work at night: A moderating influence on individual tolerance to shift work. *Journal of Applied Psychology* 79, 449–454.

Bass, B. M. (1954). The leaderless group discussion. *Psychological Bulletin* 51, 465–492.

Bass, B. M. (1962). Further evidence on the dyanamic nature of criteria. *Personnel Psychology* 15, 93–97.

Bass, B. M. (1980). Team productivity and individual member competence. *Small Group Behavior* 11, 431–504.

Bass, B. M. (1983). Issues involved in relations between methodological rigor and reported outcomes in evaluations of organizational development. *Journal of Applied Psychology* 6, 197–199.

Bass, B. M. (1985). *Leadership and performance beyond expectations.* New York: Free Press.

Bass, B. M., and Barrett, G. V. (1981). *People, work, and organizations* (2nd ed.). Boston: Allyn & Bacon.

Bass, B. M., Cascio, W. F., McPherson, J. W., and Tragash, H. (1976). Prosper-training and research for increasing management awareness about affirmative action in race relations. *Academy of Management Journal* 19, 353–369.

Bass, B. M., Cascio, W. F., and O'Connor, E. J. (1974). Magnitude estimations of expressions of frequency and amount. *Journal of Applied Psychology* 59, 313–320.

Baumrind, D. (1985). Research using intentional deception: Ethical issues revisited. *American Psychologist* 40, 165–174.

Becker, B. E. (1989). The influence of labor markets on human resources utility estimates. *Personnel Psychology* 42, 531–546.

Becker, B. E., and Huselid, M. A. (1992). Direct estimates of Sd_y and the implications for utility analysis. *Journal of Applied Psychology* 77, 227–233.

Becker, T. E., and Colquitt, A. L. (1992). Potential versus actual faking of a biodata form: An analysis along several dimensions of item type. *Personnel Psychology* 45, 406.

Becker, T. E., and Klimoski, R. J. (1989). A field study of the relationship between the organizational feedback environment and performance, *Personnel Psychology* 42, 343–358.

Beehr, T. A., and Gilmore, D. C. (1982). Applicant attractiveness as a perceived job-relevant variable in selection of management trainees. *Academy of Management Journal* 25, 607–617.

Benedict, M. E., and Levine, E. L. (1988). Delay and distortion: Tacit influences on performance appraisal effectiveness. *Journal of Applied Psychology* 73, 507–514.

Berman, F. E., and Miner, J. B. (1985). Motivation to manage at the top executive level: A test of the hierarchic role-motivation theory. *Personnel Psychology* 38, 377–391.

Bernardin, H. J., and Beatty, R. W. (1984). *Performance appraisal: Assessing human behavior at work.* Boston: Kent.

Bernardin, H. J., and Buckley, M. R. (1981). A consideration of strategies in rater training. *Academy of Management Review* 6, 205–212.

Bernardin, H. J., and Cooke, D. K. (1993). Validity of an honesty test in predicting theft among convenience store employees. *Academy of Management Journal* 36, 1097–1108.

Bernick, E. L., Kindley, R., and Pettit, K. K. (1984). The structure of training courses and the effects of hierarchy. *Public Personnel Management* 13, 109–119.

Bias issue. (1978, September 21). *Wall Street Journal,* pp. 1, 33.

Binning, J. F., and Barrett, G. V. (1989). Validity of personnel decisions: A conceptual analysis of the inferential and evidential bases. *Journal of Applied Psychology* 74, 478–494.

Blau, G. J. (1985). Relationship of extrinsic, intrinsic, and demographic predictors to various types of withdrawal behaviors. *Journal of Applied Psychology* 70, 442–450.

Blum, M. L., and Naylor, J. C. (1968). *Industrial psychology, its theoretical and social foundations* (Rev. ed.). New York: Harper & Row.

Bobko, P., and Collela, A. (1994). Employee reactions to performance standards: A review and research propositions. *Personnel Psychology* 47, 1–29.

Boehm, V. R. (1972). Negro-white differences in validity of employment and training selection procedures: Summary of research evidence. *Journal of Applied Psychology* 56, 33–39.

Boehm, V. R. (1977). Differential prediction: A methodological artifact? *Journal of Applied Psychology* 62, 146–154.

Boeker, W., and Goodstein, J. (1993). Performance and successor choice: The moderating effects of governance and ownership. *Academy of Management Journal* 36, 172–186.

Bolster, B. I., and Springbett, B. M. (1961). The reaction of interviewers to favorable and unfavorable information. *Journal of Applied Psychology,* 45, 97–103.

Bommer, W. H., Johnson, J. L., Rich, G. A., Podsakoff, P. M., and Mackenzie, S. B. (1995). On the interchangeability of objective and subjective measures of employee performance: A meta-analysis. *Personnel Psychology* 48, 587–605.

Bond, N. (1973). Auditing change: The technology of measuring change. In M. D. Dunnette (Ed.), *Work and nonwork in the year 2001.* Monterey, CA: Brooks/Cole.

Borman, W. C. (1974). The rating of individuals in organizations: An alternate approach. *Organizational Behavior and Human Performance* 12, 105–124.

Borman, W. C. (1978). Exploring the upper limits of reliability and validity in job performance ratings. *Journal of Applied Psychology* 63, 135–144.

Borman, W. C. (1982). Validity of behavioral assessment for predicting military recruiter performance. *Journal of Applied Psychology* 67, 3–9.

Borman, W. C. (1991). Job behavior, performance, and effectiveness. In M. D. Dunnette and L. M. Hough (Eds.), *Handbook of industrial and organizational psychology* (2nd ed., Vol. 2, pp. 271–326). Palo Alto, CA: Consulting Psychologists Press.

Borman, W. C., and Brush, D. H. (1993). More progress toward a taxonomy of managerial performance requirements. *Human Performance* 6, 1–21.

Borman, W. C., Eaton, N. K., Bryan, D. J., and Rosse, R. (1983). Validity of Army recruiter behavioral assessment: Does the assessor make a difference? *Journal of Applied Psychology* 68, 415–419.

Borman, W. C., and Hallam, G. L. (1991). Observation accuracy for assessors of work-sample performance: Consistency across task and individual-differences correlates. *Journal of Applied Psychology* 76, 11–18.

Borman, W. C., Hanson, M. A., Oppler, S. H., Pulakos, E. D., and White, L. A. (1993). Role of early supervisory experience in supervisor performance. *Journal of Applied Psychology* 78, 443–449.

Borman, W. C., Rosse, R. L., and Abrahams, N. M. (1980). An empirical construct validity approach to studying predictor-job performance links. *Journal of Applied Psychology* 65, 662–671.

Borman, W. C., White, L. A., and Dorsey, D. W. (1995). Effects of ratee task performance and interpersonal factors on supervisor and peer performance ratings. *Journal of Applied Psychology* 80, 168–177.

Borman, W. C., White, L. A., Pulakos, E. D., and Oppler, S. H. (1991). Models of supervisory job performance ratings. *Journal of Applied Psychology* 76, 863–872.

Boss, R. W. (1979). It doesn't matter if you win or lose, unless you're losing: Organizational change in a law enforcement agency. *Journal of Applied Behavioral Science* 15, 198–220.

Bottger, P. C., and Yetton, P. W. (1987). Improving group performance by training in individual problem solving. *Journal of Applied Psychology* 72, 651–657.

Boudreau, J. W. (1983a). Economic considerations in estimating the utility of human resource productivity improvement programs. *Personnel Psychology* 36, 551–576.

Boudreau, J. W. (1983b). Effects of employee flows on utility analysis of human resource productivity improvement programs. *Journal of Applied Psychology* 68, 396–406.

Boudreau, J. W. (1988). Utility analysis. In L. Dyer (Ed.), *Human resource management: Evolving roles and responsibilities* (pp. 1-125–1-186). Washington, DC: Bureau of National Affairs.

Boudreau, J. W. (1991). Utility analysis for decisions in human resource management. In M. D. Dunnette and L. M. Hough (Eds.), *Handbook of industrial and organizational psychology* (2nd ed., Vol. 2, pp. 621–745). Palo Alto, CA: Consulting Psychologists Press.

Boudreau, J. W., and Berger, C. J. (1985). Decision-theoretic utility analysis applied to employee separations and acquisitions. *Journal of Applied Psychology* 70, 581–612.

Boudreau, J. W., and Rynes, S. L. (1985). Role of recruitment in staffing utility analysis. *Journal of Applied Psychology* 70, 354–366.

Bowen, D. E., Ledford, G. E., and Nathan, B. R. (1991). Hiring for the organization, not the job. *Academy of Management Executive* 5 (4), 35–51.

Bownas, D. A., Bosshardt, M. J., and Donnelly, L. F. (1985). A quantitative approach to evaluating training curriculum content sampling adequacy. *Personnel Psychology* 38, 117–131.

Boyatzis, R. E. (1982). *The competent manager: A model for effective performance*. New York: Wiley.

The boys' club pays its dues. (1989, January 23). *Time*, p. 47.

Brady, F. N. (1985). A Janus-headed model of ethical theory: Looking two ways at business/society issues. *Academy of Management Review* 10, 568–576.

Brass, D. J., and Oldham, G. R. (1976). Validating an in-basket test using an alternative set of leadership scoring dimensions. *Journal of Applied Psychology* 61, 652–657.

Bray, D. W., and Campbell, R. J. (1968). Selection of salesmen by means of an assessment center. *Journal of Applied Psychology* 52, 36–41.

Bray, D. W., and Grant, D. L. (1966). The assessment center in the measurement of potential for business management. *Psychological Monographs* 80, (17, Whole No. 625).

Bray, D. W., Campbell, R. J., and Grant, D. L. (1974). *Formative years in business: A long-term AT&T study of managerial lives*. New York: Wiley.

Bray, D. W., and Howard, A. (1983). *Longitudinal studies of adult psychological development*. New York: Guilford.

Bray, D. W., and Moses, J. L. (1972). Personnel selection. *Annual Review of Psychology* 23, 545–576.

Brealey, R., and Myers, S. (1996). *Principles of corporate finance* (5th ed.). New York: McGraw-Hill.

Breaugh, J. A. (1983). Realistic job previews: A critical appraisal and future research directions. *Academy of Management Review* 8, 612–619.

Breaugh, J. A. (1992). *Recruitment: Science and practice.* Boston: PWS-Kent.

Brett, J. M., and Reilly, A. H. (1988). On the road again: Predicting the job transfer decision. *Journal of Applied Psychology* 73, 614–620.

Bretz, R. D., Jr., Milkovich, G. T., and Read, W. (1990). The current state of performance appraisal research and practice: Concerns, directions, and implications. *Journal of Management* 18, 321–352.

Bretz, R. D., Jr., and Thompsett, R. E. (1992). Comparing traditional and integrative learning methods in organizational training programs. *Journal of Applied Psychology* 77, 941–951.

Brewer, M. B., and Kramer, R. M. (1985). The psychology of intergroup attitudes and behavior. *Annual Review of Psychology* 36, 219–243.

Bridges, W. (1994, September 19). The end of the job. *Fortune*, pp. 62–64, 68, 72, 74.

Britt, L. P., III. (1984). Affirmative action: Is there life after *Stotts*? *Personnel Administrator* 29, 96–100.

Broad, W., and Wade, N. (1982). *Betrayers of the truth: Fraud and deceit in the halls of science.* New York: Simon and Schuster.

Brogden, H. E. (1946a). On the interpretation of the correlation coefficient as a measure of predictive efficiency. *Journal of Educational Psychology* 37, 64–76.

Brogden, H. E. (1946b). An approach to the problem of differential prediction. *Psychometrika* 11, 139–154.

Brogden, H. E. (1949). When testing pays off. *Personnel Psychology* 2, 171–183.

Brogden, H. E. (1951). Increased efficiency of selection resulting from replacement of a single predictor with several differential predictors. *Educational and Psychological Measurement* 11, 183–196.

Brogden, H. E. (1954). A simple proof of a personnel classification theorem. *Psychometrika* 19, 205–208.

Brogden, H. E. (1955). Least squares estimates and optimal classification. *Psychometrika* 20, 249–252.

Brogden, H. E., and Taylor, E. K. (1950a). The dollar criterion—Applying the cost accounting concept to criterion construction. *Personnel Psychology* 3, 133–154.

Brogden, H. E., and Taylor, E. K. (1950b). The theory and classification of criterion bias. *Educational and Psychological Measurement* 10, 159–186.

Brown, B. K., and Campion, M. A. (1994). Biodata phenomenology: Recruiters' perceptions and use of biographical information in resume screening. *Journal of Applied Psychology* 79, 897–908.

Brown, D. C. (1994). Subgroup norming: Legitimate testing practice or reverse discrimination? *American Psychologist* 49, 927–928.

Brown, F. G. (1983). *Principles of educational and psychological testing* (3rd ed.). New York: Holt, Rinehart, and Winston.

Brown, S. H. (1978). Long-term validity of a personal history item scoring procedure. *Journal of Applied Psychology* 63, 673–676.

Brown, S. H. (1979). Validity distortions associated with a test in use. *Journal of Applied Psychology* 64, 460–462.

Brown S. H., Stout, J. D., Dalessio, A. T., and Crosby, M. M. (1988). Stability of validity indices through test score ranges. *Journal of Applied Psychology* 73, 736–742.

Brugnoli, G. A., Campion, J. E., and Basen, J. A. (1979). Racial bias in the use of work samples for personnel selection. *Journal of Applied Psychology* 64, 119–123.

Brush, D. H. and Owens, W. A. (1979). Implementation and evaluation of an assessment-classification model for manpower utilization. *Personnel Psychology* 32, 369–383.

Buck, L. S. (1977). *Guide to the setting of appropriate cutting scores for written tests: A summary of the concerns and procedures* (T. M. 77–84). Washington, DC: U.S. Office of Personnel Management, Personnel Research and Development Center.

Bullock, R. J., and Svyantek, D. J. (1985). Analyzing meta-analysis: Potential problems, an unsuccessful replication, and evaluation criteria. *Journal of Applied Psychology* 70, 108–115.

Bureau of National Affairs. (1988). *Recruiting and selection procedures* (Personnel Policies Forum, Survey No. 146). Washington, DC: Author.

Burke, M. J., and Day, R. R. (1986). A cumulative study of the effectiveness of managerial training. *Journal of Applied Psychology* 71, 232–246.

Burke, M. J., and Doran, L. I. (1989). A note on the economic utility of generalized validity coefficients in personnel selection. *Journal of Applied Psychology* 74, 171–175.

Burke, M. J., and Frederick, J. T. (1984). Two modified procedures for estimating standard deviations in utility analyses. *Journal of Applied Psychology* 69, 482–489.

Burke, M. J., and Frederick, J. T. (1986). A comparison of economic utility estimates for alternative Sd_y estimation procedures. *Journal of Applied Psychology* 71, 334–339.

Burke, R. J., Weitzel, W., and Weir, T. (1978). Characteristics of effective employee performance review and development interviews: Replication and extension. *Personnel Psychology* 31, 903–919.

Burnaska, R. F. (1976). The effects of behavior modeling training upon managers' behaviors and employees' perceptions. *Personnel Psychology* 29, 329–335.

Butler, S. K., and Harvey, R. J. (1988). A comparison of holistic versus decomposed rating of Position Analysis Questionnaire work dimensions. *Personnel Psychology* 41, 761–771.

Bycio, P., Alvares, K. M., and Hahn, J. (1987). Situational specificity in assessment center ratings: A confirmatory factor analysis. *Journal of Applied Psychology* 72, 463–474.

Byham, W. C. (1971). The assessment center as an aid in management development. *Training and Development Journal* 25, 10–22.

Byham, W. C. (1986). *Assessment centers—More than just predicting management potential.* Monograph VII. Pittsburgh, PA: Development Dimensions International.

Byham, W. C., and Spitzer, M. E. (1971). *The law and personnel testing.* New York: American Management Association.

Byrne, J. A. (1993, February 8). The virtual corporation. *Business Week,* pp. 98–103.

Cain, P. S., and Green, B. F. (1983). Reliabilities of selected ratings available from the *Dictionary of Occupational Titles. Journal of Applied Psychology* 68, 155–165.

California Brewers Association v. *Bryant.* (1982). 444 U.S. 598, p. 605.

California Federal Savings and Loan Association v. *Guerra.* (1987). 42 FEP Cases 1073.

Camara, W. J., and Schneider, D. L. (1994). Integrity tests: Facts and unresolved issues. *American Psychologist* 49, 112–119.

Campbell D. J., and Lee, C. (1988). Self-appraisal in performance evaluation: Development versus evaluation. *Academy of Management Review* 13, 302–314.

Campbell, D. T., and Fiske, D. W. (1959). Convergent and discriminant validation by the multitrait-multimethod matrix. *Psychological Bulletin* 56, 81–105.

Campbell, D. T., and Stanley, J. C. (1963). *Experimental and quasi-experimental designs for research.* Chicago: Rand McNally.

Campbell, J. P. (1967). *Cross-validation revisited.* Paper presented at the Midwestern Psychological Association, Chicago.

Campbell, J. P. (1971). Personnel training and development. *Annual Review of Psychology* 22, 565–602.

Campbell, J. P. (1986). Labs, fields, and straw issues. In Locke, E. A. (Ed.), *Generalizing from laboratory to field settings.* Lexington, MA: Lexington Books, pp. 269–279.

Campbell, J. P. (1988). Training design for performance improvement. In J. P. Campbell and R. J. Campbell (Eds.), *Productivity in organizations,* pp. 177–215. San Francisco: Jossey-Bass.

Campbell, J. P. (1990a). Modeling the performance prediction problem in industrial and organizational psychology. In M. D. Dunnette and L. M. Hough (Eds.), *Handbook of industrial and organizational psychology* (2nd ed., Vol. 1, pp. 687–782). Palo Alto, CA: Consulting Psychologists Press.

Campbell, J. P. (1990b). An overview of the Army selection and classification project (Project A). *Personnel Psychology* 43, 231–239.

Campbell, J. P., Dunnette, M. D., Arvey, R. D., and Hellervik, L. V. (1973). The development and evaluation of behaviorally based rating scales. *Journal of Applied Psychology* 57, 15–22.

Campbell, J. P., Dunnette, M. D., Lawler, E. E., III, and Weick, K. E., Jr. (1970). *Managerial behavior, performance and effectiveness.* New York: McGraw-Hill.

Campbell, J. P., McHenry, J. J., and Wise, L. L. (1990). Modeling job performance in a population of jobs. *Personnel Psychology* 43, 313–333.

Campion, M. A. (1989). Ability requirement implications of job design: An interdisciplinary perspective. *Personnel Psychology* 42, 1–24.

Campion, M. A. (1991). Meaning and measurement of turnover: Comparison of alternative measures and recommendations for research. *Journal of Applied Psychology* 76, 199–212.

Campion, M. A., Pursell, E. D., and Brown, B. K. (1988). Structured interviewing: Raising the psychometric properties of the employment interview. *Personnel Psychology* 41, 25–42.

Campion, M. A., Campion, J. E., and Hudson, J. P., Jr. (1994). Structured interviewing: A note on incremental validity and alternative question types. *Journal of Applied Psychology* 79, 998–1002.

Cannon-Bowers, J. A., Tannenbaum, S. I., Salas, E., and Volpe, C. E. (1995). Defining competencies and establishing team training requirements. In R. A. Guzzo and E. Salas (Eds.), *Team effectiveness and decision making in organizations* (pp. 333–380). San Francisco: Jossey-Bass.

Carey, J. H., and Seegull, L. R. (1995, Spring). Beware the native tongue: National origin and English-only rules. *HR Legal Report*, pp. 1–4.

Carlson, R. E. (1967). Selection interview decisions: The effect of interviewer experience, relative quota situation, and applicant sample on interviewer decisions. *Personnel Psychology* 20, 259–280.

Carlson, R. E., Thayer, P. W., Mayfield, E. C., and Peterson, D. A. (1971). Improvements in the selection interview. *Personnel Journal* 50, 268–275.

Carroll S. J., and Gillen, D. J. (1987). Are the classical management functions useful in describing managerial work? *Academy of Management Review* 12, 38–51.

Cartwright, D., and Zander, A. F. (Eds.). (1968).

Group dynamics: Research and theory (3rd ed.). New York: Harper.

Cascio, W. F. (1975). Accuracy of verifiable biographical information blank responses. *Journal of Applied Psychology* 60, 767–769.

Cascio, W. F. (1976a). Turnover, biographical data, and fair employment practice. *Journal of Applied Psychology* 61, 576–580.

Cascio, W. F. (1976b). Factor structure stability in attitude measurement. *Educational and Psychological Measurement* 36, 847–854.

Cascio, W. F. (1982). Scientific, operational, and legal imperatives of workable performance appraisal systems. *Public Personnel Management Journal* 11, 367–375.

Cascio, W. F. (1989). Using utility analysis to assess training outcomes. In I. L. Goldstein (Ed.), *Training and development in organizations* (pp. 63–88). San Francisco: Jossey-Bass.

Cascio, W. F. (1991). *Costing human resources: The financial impact of behavior in organizations* (3rd ed.). Boston: PWS-Kent.

Cascio, W. F. (1993, February). Downsizing: What do we know? What have we learned? *Academy of Management Executive* 7 (1), 95–104.

Cascio, W. F. (1993). Assessing the utility of selection decisions: Theoretical and practical considerations. In N. Schmitt and W. C. Borman (Eds.), *Personnel selection in organizations* (pp. 310–340). San Francisco: Jossey-Bass.

Cascio, W. F. (1994). The Americans With Disabilities Act of 1990 and the 1991 Civil Rights Act: Requirements for psychological practice in the workplace. In B. D. Sales and G. R. VandenBos (Eds.), *Psychology in litigation and legislation* (pp. 175–211). Washington, DC: American Psychological Association.

Cascio, W. F. (1995). Whither industrial and organizational psychology in a changing world of work? *American Psychologist* 50 (11), 928–939.

Cascio, W. F. (1998). *Managing human resources: Productivity, quality of work life, profits* (5th ed.). New York: McGraw-Hill.

Cascio, W. F., Alexander, R. A., and Barrett, G. V. (1988). Setting cutoff scores: Legal, psychometric, and professional issues and guidelines. *Personnel Psychology* 41, 1–24.

Cascio, W. F., and Awad, E. M. (1981). *Human resources management: An information systems approach.* Reston, VA: Reston.

Cascio, W. F., and Bass, B. M. (1976). The effects of role playing in a program to modify attitudes toward black employees. *Journal of Psychology* 92, 261–266.

Cascio, W. F., and Bernardin, H. J. (1981). Implications of performance appraisal litigation for personnel decisions. *Personnel Psychology* 34, 211–226.

Cascio, W. F., Goldstein, I. L., Outtz, J., and Zedeck, S. (1995). Twenty issues and answers about sliding bands. *Human Performance* 8 (3), 227–242.

Cascio, W. F., and Kurtines, W. L. (1977). A practical method for indentifying significant change scores. *Educational and Psychological Measurement* 37, 889–895.

Cascio, W. F., and Morris, J. R. (1990). A critical reanalysis of Hunter, Schmidt, and Coggin's "Problems and pitfalls in using capital budgeting and financial accounting techniques in assessing the utility of personnel programs." *Journal of Applied Psychology* 75, 410–417.

Cascio, W. F., Outtz, J., Zedeck, S., and Goldstein, I. L. (1991). Statistical implications of six methods of test score use in personnel selection. *Human Performance* 4 (4), 233–264.

Cascio, W. F., and Phillips, N. (1979). Performance testing: A rose among thorns? *Personnel Psychology* 32, 751–766.

Cascio, W. F., and Ramos, R. A. (1986). Development and application of a new method for assessing job performance in behavioral/economic terms. *Journal of Applied Psychology* 71, 20–28.

Cascio, W. F., and Silbey, V. (1979). Utility of the assessment center as a selection device. *Journal of Applied Psychology* 64, 107–118.

Cascio, W. F. and Valenzi, E. R. (1977). Behaviorally anchored rating scales: Effects of education and job experience of raters and ratees. *Journal of Applied Psychology* 62, 278–282.

Cascio, W. F., and Valenzi, E. R. (1978). Relations among criteria of police performance. *Journal of Applied Psychology* 63, 22–28.

Cascio, W. F., Valenzi, E. R., and Silbey, V. (1978). Validation and statistical power: Implications for applied research. *Journal of Applied Psychology* 63, 589–595.

Cascio, W. F., Valenzi, E. R., and Silbey, V. (1980). More on validation and statistical power. *Journal of Applied Psychology* 65, 135–138.

Cascio, W. F., and Zammuto, R. F. (1989). Societal trends and staffing policies. In W. F. Cascio (Ed.), *Human resource planning, employment, and placement* (pp. 2-1–2-33). Washington, DC: Bureau of National Affairs.

Cascio, W. F., and Zedeck, S. (1983). Open a new window in rational research planning: Adjust alpha to maximize statistical power. *Personnel Psychology* 36, 517–526.

Cascio, W. F., Zedeck, S., Goldstein, I. L., and Outtz, J. (1995). Selective science or selective interpretation? *American Psychologist* 50, 881–882.

Casteen, J. T., III. (1984). The public stake in proper test use. In C. W. Daves (Ed.), *The uses and misuses of tests.* San Francisco: Jossey-Bass.

Cattell, R. B. (1957). *Personality and motivation structure and measurement.* New York: Harcourt, Brace, & World.

Cattin, P. (1980). Estimation of the predictive power of a regression model. *Journal of Applied Psychology* 65, 407–414.

Cederblom, D. (1982). The performance appraisal interview: A review, implications, and suggestions. *Academy of Management Review* 7, 219–227.

Cellar, D. F., and Wade, K. (1988). Effect of behavioral modeling on intrinsic motivation and script-related recognition. *Journal of Applied Psychology* 73, 181–192.

Cesare, S. J., Blankenship, M. H., and Giannetto, P. W. (1994). A dual focus of Sd_y estimations: A test of the linearity assumption and multivariate application. *Human Performance* 7, 235–253.

Chaiken, S., and Stangor, C. (1987). Attitudes and attitude change. *Annual Review of Psychology* 38, 573–630.

Chan, S. (1996, August 9). In frenzy to recruit, high-tech concerns try gimmicks, songs. *The Wall Street Journal,* pp. B1, B3.

Chandler, R. E. (1964). *Validity, reliability, baloney, and a little mustard.* Paper presented at the Midwestern Psychological Association, Chicago.

Chaney, F. B., and Teal, K. S. (1967). Improving inspector performance through training and visual aids. *Journal of Applied Psychology* 51, 311–315.

Chesler, D. J. (1948). Reliability and comparability of different job evaluation systems. *Journal of Applied Psychology* 32, 465–475.

Chhokar, J. S., and Wallin, J. A. (1984). A field study of the effect of feedback frequency on performance. *Journal of Applied Psychology* 69, 524–530.

Childs, A., and Klimoski, R. J. (1986). Successfully predicting career success: An application of the biographical inventory. *Journal of Applied Psychology* 71, 3–8.

Chuang, D. T., Chen, J. J., and Novick, M. R. (1981). Theory and practice for the use of cut-scores for personnel decisions. *Journal of Educational Statistics* 6, 129–152.

Civil Rights Act of 1991, Public Law No. 102-166, 105 Stat. 1071 (1991). Codified as amended at 42 U.S.C., Section 1981, 2000e *et seq.*

Civil rights statutes extended to Arabs, Jews. (1987, May 19). *Daily Labor Report,* pp. 2, A-6.

Cleary, T. A. (1968). Test bias: Prediction of grades of negro and white students in integrated colleges. *Journal of Educational Measurement* 5, 115–124.

Cleary, T. A., Humphreys, L. G., Kendrick, S. A., and Wesman, A. (1975). Educational uses of tests with disadvantaged students. *American Psychologist* 30, 15–41.

Cleff, S. H. (1977). *The Cleff job matching system.* Princeton, NJ: Human Technology.

Cleghorn v. *Hess.* (1993, June 9). No. 22426, Nevada Supreme Court.

Cleveland, J. N., Murphy, K. R., and Williams, R. E. (1989). Multiple uses of performance appraisal: Prevalence and correlates. *Journal of Applied Psychology* 74, 130–135.

Cleverly v. *Western Electric Co.* (8th Cir. 1979). 594 F.2d 638.

Clymer, A. (1985, June 9). Low marks for executive honesty. *The New York Times,* pp. 1F, 6F.

Cohen, J. (1977). *Statistical power analysis for the behavioral sciences* (Rev. ed.). New York: Academic Press.

Cohen, J. (1988). *Statistical power analysis* (2nd ed.). Hillsdale, NJ: Erlbaum.

Cohen, J., and Cohen, P. (1983). *Applied multiple regression/correlation for the behavioral sciences* (2nd ed.). Hillsdale, NJ: Erlbaum.

Cole, N. S. (1973). Bias in selection. *Journal of Educational Measurement* 10, 237–255.

Colihan, J., and Burger, G. K. (1995). Constructing job families: An analysis of quantitative techniques used for grouping jobs. *Personnel Psychology* 48, 563–586.

Committee on Professional Standards. (1982). Casebook for providers of psychological services. *American Psychologist* 37, 698–701.

Comparable worth—New problems. (1991, October). *Mountain States Employers Council Bulletin,* p. 2.

Conley, P. R., and Sackett, P. R. (1987). Effects of using high- versus low-performing job incumbents as sources of job-analysis information. *Journal of Applied Psychology* 72, 434–437.

Connecticut v. *Teal.* (1982) 457 U.S. 440.

Conoley, J. C., and Imparra, J. C. (Eds.). (1994). *The supplement to the eleventh mental measurements yearbook.* Lincoln, NE: University of Nebraska Press.

Control Data Business Advisors. (1985). *Micro-OAQ sample report formats and selection capabilities.* Minneapolis: Control Data Corporation.

Conway, J. M., Jako, R. A., and Goodman, D. F. (1995). A meta-analysis of interrater and internal consistency reliability of selection interviews. *Journal of Applied Psychology* 80, 565–579.

Cook, S. W., and Selltiz, C. (1964). A multiple-indicator approach to attitude measurement. *Psychological Bulletin* 62, 36–55.

Cook, T. D., and Campbell, D. T. (1976). The design and conduct of quasi-experiments and true experiments in field settings. In M. D. Dunnette (Ed.), *Handbook of industrial and organizational psychology.* Chicago: Rand McNally.

Cook, T. D., and Campbell, D. T. (1979). *Quasi-experimentation: Design and analysis issues for field settings.* Chicago: Rand McNally.

Cooke, R. A., and Rousseau, D. M. (1983). Relationship of life events and personal orientations to symptoms of strain. *Journal of Applied Psychology* 68, 446–458.

Cooper, E. A., and Barrett, G. V. (1984). Equal pay and gender: Implications of court cases for personnel practices. *Academy of Management Review* 9, 84–94.

Cooper, W. H. (1981). Ubiquitous halo. *Psychological Bulletin* 90, 218–244.

Coovert, M. D. (1995). Technological changes in office jobs: What we know and what we can expect. In A. Howard (Ed.), *The changing nature of work* (pp. 175–208). San Francisco: Jossey-Bass.

Cornelius, E. T., DeNisi, A. S., and Blencoe, A. G. (1984). Expert and naive raters using the PAQ: Does it matter? *Personnel Psychology* 37, 453–464.

Cornelius, E. T., and Lane, F. B. (1984). The power motive and managerial succession a professionally oriented service industry organization. *Journal of Applied Psychology* 69, 32–39.

Cornelius, E. T., Schmidt, F. L., and Carron, T. J. (1984). Job classification approaches and the implementation of validity generalization results. *Personnel Psychology* 37, 247–260.

Cortina, J. M. (1993). What is coefficient alpha? An examination of theory and applications. *Journal of Applied Psychology* 78, 98–104.

Coward, W. M., and Sackett, P. R. (1990). Linearity of ability-performance relationships: A reconfirmation. *Journal of Applied Psychology* 75, 297–300.

Craft, J. A. (1988). Human resource planning and strategy. In L. Dyer and G. W. Holder (Eds.), *Human resource management: Evolving roles and responsibilities* (pp. 1-47–1-87). Washington, DC: Bureau of National Affairs.

Cravens, D. W., and Woodruff, R. B. (1973). An approach for determining criteria of sales performance. *Journal of Applied Psychology* 57, 242–247.

Crawford, M. P. (1947). *Psychological research on operational training in the continental Air Forces.* (Research Report No. 16). Army Air Forces Aviation Psychology program.

Crew, J. C. (1984). Age stereotypes as a function of race. *Academy of Management Journal* 27, 431–435.

Crock, S., and Galen, M. (1995, June 26). 'A thunderous impact' on equal opportunity. *Business Week,* p. 37.

Cronbach, L. J. (1951). Coefficient alpha and the internal structure of tests. *Psychometrika* 16, 297–334.

Cronbach, L. J. (1975). Five decades of public controversy over mental testing. *American Psychologist* 30, 1–14.

Cronbach, L. J. (1987). Statistical tests for moderator variables: Flaws in analyses recently proposed. *Psychological Bulletin* 102, 414–417.

Cronbach, L. J. (1990). *Essentials of psychological testing* (5th ed.). New York: HarperCollins.

Cronbach, L. J., and Furby, L. (1970). How should we measure "change"—or should we? *Psychological Bulletin* 74, 68–80.

Cronbach, L. J., and Gleser, G. C. (1965). *Psychological tests and personnel decisions* (2nd ed.). Urbana, IL: University of Illinois Press.

Cronbach, L. J., Gleser, G. C., Nanda, H., and Rajaratnam, N. (1972). *The dependability of behavioral measurements: Theory of generalizability for scores and profiles.* New York: Wiley.

Cronbach, L. J., and Meehl, P. E. (1955). Construct validity in psychological tests. *Psychological Bulletin* 52, 281–302.

Cronbach. L. J., and Snow, R. E. (1977). *Aptitudes and instructional methods.* New York: Irvington.

Cronbach, L. J., Yalow, E., and Schaeffer, G. A. (1980). A mathematical structure for analyzing fairness in selection. *Personnel Psychology* 33, 693–704.

Cronshaw, S. F., and Alexander, R. A. (1985). One answer to the demand for accountability: Selection utility as an investment decision. *Organizational Behavior and Human Decision Processes* 35, 102–118.

Cronshaw, S. F., and Alexander, R. A. (1991). Why capital budgeting techniques are suited for assessing the utility of personnel programs: A reply to Hunter, Schmidt, and Coggin (1988). *Journal of Applied Psychology* 76, 454–457.

Cullen, J. B., Victor, B., and Stephens, C. (1989). An ethical weather report: Assessing the organization's ethical climate. *Organizational Dynamics* 18, 50–62.

Cummings, L. L. (1973). A field experimental study of the effects of two performance appraisal systems. *Personnel Psychology* 26, 489–502.

Cunningham, M. R., Wong, D. T., and Barbee, A. P. (1994). Self-presentation dynamics on overt integrity tests: Experimental studies of the Reid Report. *Journal of Applied Psychology* 79, 643–658.

Cureton, E. E. (1950). Validity, reliability, and baloney. *Educational and Psychological Measurement* 10, 94–96.

Cureton, E. E. (1965). Reliability and validity: Basic assumptions and experimental designs. *Educational and Psychological Measurement* 25, 327–346.

Czajka, J. M., and DeNisi, A. S. (1988). Effects of emotional disability and clear performance standards on performance ratings. *Academy of Management Journal* 31, 393–404.

Dalessio, A. T., and Silverhart, T. A. (1994). Combining biodata test and interview information: Predicting decisions and performance criteria. *Personnel Psychology* 47, 303–315.

Darlington, R. B. (1968). Multiple regression in psychological research and practice. *Psychological Bulletin* 69, 161–182.

Darlington, R. B. (1971). Another look at "culture fairness." *Journal of Educational Measurement* 8, 71–82.

Davis, B. L., and Mount, M. K. (1984). Effectiveness of performance appraisal training using computer-assisted instruction and behavior modeling. *Personnel Psychology* 37, 439–452.

Davis, K. R., Jr. (1984). A longitudinal analysis of biographical subgroups using Owens' developmental-integrative model. *Personnel Psychology* 37, 1–14.

Dawes, R. M., and Corrigan, B. (1974). Linear models in decision making. *Psychological Bulletin* 81, 95–106.

Day, D. V., and Silverman, S. B. (1989). Personality and job performance: Evidence of incremental validity. *Personnel Psychology* 42, 25–36.

Day, D. V., and Sulsky, L. M. (1995). Effects of frame-of-reference training and information configuration on memory organization and rating accuracy. *Journal of Applied Psychology* 80, 158–167.

Deadrick, D. L., and Madigan, R. M. (1990). Dynamic criteria revisited: A longitudinal study of performance stability and predictive validity. *Personnel Psychology* 43, 717–744.

Deci, E. L. (1972). Work, who does not like it and why. *Psychology Today* 6, 57–58, 92.

Decker, P. J. (1983). The effects of rehearsal group size and video feedback in behavior modeling training. *Personnel Psychology* 36, 763–773.

Decker, P. J., and Nathan, B. R. (1985). *Behavior modeling training: Principles and applications.* New York: Praeger.

Decker, R. H. (1988, August). Eleven ways to stamp out the potential for sexual harassment. *The American School Board Journal,* pp. 28, 29.

Deming, W. E. (1986). *Out of the crisis.* Cambridge, MA: Center for Advanced Engineering Study, Massachusetts Institute of Technology.

DeNisi, A. S., Cornelius, E. T., III, and Blencoe, A. G. (1987). Further investigation of common knowledge effects on job analysis ratings. *Journal of Applied Psychology* 72, 262–268.

DeNisi, A. S., Randolph, W. A., and Blencoe, A. G. (1983). Potential problems with peer ratings. *Academy of Management Journal* 26, 457–464.

DeNisi A. S., Robbins, T., and Cafferty, T. P. (1989). Organization of information used for performance appraisals: Role of diary-keeping. *Journal of Applied Psychology* 74, 124–129.

Dennis, D. L. (1985). Evaluating corporate recruitment efforts. *Personnel Administrator* 30 (1), 21–26.

Digman, J. M. (1990). Personality structure: Emergence of the five-factor model. *Annual Review of Psychology* 41, 417–440.

Dill, W. R. (1972). What management games do best. In E. L. Deci, B. V. H. Gilmer, and H. W. Karn

(Eds.), *Readings in industrial and organizational psychology.* New York: McGraw-Hill.

Dipboye, R. L. (1982). Self-fulfilling prophecies in the selection-recruitment interview. *Academy of Management Review 7,* 579–586.

Dipboye, R. L. (1992). *Selection interviews: Process perspectives.* Cincinnati: South-Western.

Dipboye, R. L., Fontenelle, G. A., and Garner, K. (1984). Effects of previewing the application on interview process and outcomes. *Journal of Applied Psychology 69,* 118–128.

Dipboye, R. L., Stramler, C. S., and Fontenelle, G. A. (1984). The effects of the application on recall of information from the interview. *Academy of Management Journal 27,* 561–575.

Distefano, M. K., Pryer, M., and Craig, S. H. (1980). Job-relatedness of a posttraining job knowledge criterion used to assess validity and test fairness. *Personnel Psychology 33,* 785–793.

Dobbins, G. H. (1985). Effects of gender on leaders' responses to poor performers: An attributional interpretation. *Academy of Management Journal 28,* 587–598.

Dobbins, G. H., Cardy, R. L., and Truxillo, D. M. (1988). The effects of purpose of appraisal and individual differences in stereotypes of women on sex differences in performance ratings: A laboratory and field study. *Journal of Applied Psychology 73,* 551–558.

Dorans, N. J., and Drasgow, F. (1980). A note on cross-validating prediction equations. *Journal of Applied Psychology 65,* 728–730.

Dougherty, T. W., Turban, D. B., and Callender, J. C. (1994). Confirming first impressions in the employment interview: A field study of interviewer behavior. *Journal of Applied Psychology 79,* 659–665.

Dowell, B. E., and Wexley, K. N. (1978). Development of a work behavior taxonomy for first-line supervisors. *Journal of Applied Psychology 63,* 563–572.

Dozier, J. B., and Miceli, M. P. (1985). Potential predictors of whistle-blowing: A prosocial behavior perspective. *Academy of Management Review 10,* 823–836.

Draper, N. R., and Smith, H. (1966). *Applied regression analysis.* New York: Wiley.

Drasgow, F. (1982). Biased test items and differential validity. *Psychological Bulletin, 92,* 526–531.

Drasgow, F. (1987). Study of the measurement bias of two standardized psychological tests. *Journal of Applied Psychology 72,* 19–29.

Drasgow, F., and Guertler, E. (1987). A decision-theoretic approach to the use of appropriateness measurement for detecting invalid test and scale scores. *Journal of Applied Psychology 72,* 10–18.

Drasgow, F., and Kang, T. (1984). Statistical power of differential validity and differential prediction analyses for detecting measurement nonequivalence. *Journal of Applied Psychology 69,* 498–508.

Driskell, J. E., Willis, R. P., and Copper, C. (1992). Effect of overlearning on retention. *Journal of Applied Psychology 77,* 615–622.

Dubno, P. (1985). Attitudes toward women executives: A longitudinal approach. *Academy of Management Journal 28,* 235–239.

Dudek, E. E. (1963). Personnel selection. In P. R. Farnsworth, O. McNemar, and Q. McNemar (Eds.), *Annual Review of Psychology 14,* 261–284.

Dugan, K. W. (1989). Ability and effort attributions: Do they affect how managers communicate performance feedback information? *Academy of Management Journal 32,* 87–114.

Dunlap, W. P., Chen, R., and Greer, T. (1994). Skew reduces test-retest reliability. *Journal of Applied Psychology 79,* 310–313.

Dunlop, J. T. (1958). *Industrial relations systems.* New York: Holt.

Dunnette, M. D. (1962). Personnel management. In P. R. Farnsworth, O. McNemar, and Q. McNemar (Eds.), *Annual Review of Psychology 13,* 285–314.

Dunnette, M. D. (1963a). A note on *the* criterion. *Journal of Applied Psychology 47,* 251–253.

Dunnette, M. D. (1963b). A modified model for test validation and selection research. *Journal of Applied Psychology 47,* 317–332.

Dunnette, M. D. (1966). *Personnel selection and placement.* Belmont, CA: Wadsworth.

Dunnette, M. D. (1970). *Personnel selection and job placement of the disadvantaged: Problems, issues, and suggestions* (Technical Report No. 4001). Minneapolis, University of Minnesota, Center for Research in Organizational Performance and Human Effectiveness.

Dunnette, M. D. (1971). Multiple assessment procedures in identifying and developing managerial talent. In P. McReynolds (Ed.), *Advances in psychological assessment* (Vol. 2). Palo Alto: Science and Behavior Books.

Dunnette, M. D., and Borman, W. S. (1979). Personnel selection and classification systems. *Annual Review of Psychology* 30, 477–525.

Dunnette, M. D., and Kirchner, W. K. (1965). *Psychology applied to industry.* New York: Meredith.

Dvir, T., Eden, D., and Banjo, M. L. (1995). Self-fulfilling prophecy and gender: Can women be Pygmalion and Galatea? *Journal of Applied Psychology* 80, 253–270.

Dyer, L., and Heyer, N. O. (1984). Human resource planning at IBM. *Human Resource Planning* 7, 111–121.

Dyer, L., and Holder, G. W. (1988). A strategic perspective of human resource management. In L. Dyer and G. W. Holder (Eds.), *Human resource management: Evolving roles and responsibilities* (pp. 1-1–1-46). Washington, DC: Bureau of National Affairs.

Dyer, L., Schwab, D. P., and Fossum, J. A. (1978, January). Impacts of pay on employee behavior and attitudes: An update. *The Personnel Administrator,* pp. 51–58.

Earley, P. C. (1985). Influence of information, choice, and task complexity upon goal acceptance, performance, and personal goals. *Journal of Applied Psychology* 70, 481–491.

Earley, P. C., Connolly, T., and Ekegren, G. (1989). Goals, strategy development, and task performance: Some limits on the efficacy of goal setting. *Journal of Applied Psychology* 74, 24–33.

Eaton, N. K., Wing, H., and Mitchell, K. J. (1985). Alternate methods of estimating the dollar value of performance. *Personnel Psychology* 38, 27–40.

Ebel, R. L. (1977). Comments on some problems of employment testing. *Personnel Psychology* 30, 55–68.

Eberhardt, B. J., and Muchinsky, P. M. (1982). An empirical investigation of the factor stability of Owens' biographical questionnaire. *Journal of Applied Psychology* 67, 138–145.

Eden, D. (1985). Team development: A true field experiment at three levels of rigor. *Journal of Applied Psychology* 70, 94–100.

Eden, D. (1988). Pygmalion, goal setting, and expectancy: Compatible ways to boost productivity. *Academy of Management Review* 13, 639–652.

Eden, D., and Aviram, A. (1993). Self-efficacy training to speed reemployment: Helping people to help themselves. *Journal of Applied Psychology* 78, 352–360.

Eden, D., and Shani, A. B. (1982). Pygmalion goes to boot camp: Expectancy, leadership, and trainee performance. *Journal of Applied Psychology* 67, 194–199.

Edwards, J. E., Frederick, J. T., and Burke, M. J. (1988). Efficacy of modified CREPID Sd_ys on the basis of archival organizational data. *Journal of Applied Psychology* 73, 529–535.

Edwards, J. R., and Van Harrison, R. (1993). Job demands and worker health: Three-dimensional reexamination of the relationship between person-environment fit and strain. *Journal of Applied Psychology* 78, 628–648.

EEOC v. *University of Texas Health Science Center at San Antonio.* (5th Cir. 1983) 1110 F.2d 1091.

Einhorn, H. J., and Bass, A. R. (1971). Methodological considerations relevant to discrimination in employment testing. *Psychological Bulletin* 75, 261–269.

Einhorn, H. J., and Hogarth, R. M. (1975). Unit weighting schemes for decision making. *Organizational Behavior and Human Performance* 13, 171–192.

Eisler, P. (1995, August 15). Waiting for justice: Workplace discrimination claims hit record. *USA Today,* pp. 1A, 2A, 10A.

Elmer-Dewitt, P. (1993, January 18). Who's reading your screen? *Time,* p. 46.

England, G. W. (1971). *Development and use of weighted application blanks* (Rev. ed.). Minneapolis: Unversity of Minnesota Industrial Relations Center.

Epperson, L. L. (1975). The dynamics of factor comparison/point evaluation. *Public Personnel Management,* January-February, 38–48.

Epstein, A. (1985, January 26). Employers responsible in sex-harassment cases. *Denver Post,* p. 3A.

Epstein S. (1979). The stability of behavior: I. On predicting most of the people much of the time. *Journal of Personality and Social Psychology* 37, 1097–1126.

Epstein, S. (1980). The stability of behavior: II. Implications for psychological research. *American Psychologist* 35, 790–806.

Equal Employment Opportunity Commission (1979). Affirmative action guidelines. 44 FR 4421–4424.

Equal Employment Opportunity Commission (1980). Guidelines on sexual harassment in the workplace. 45 FR 74676–74677.

Equal Employment Opportunity Commission (1979, March 9). Pregnancy Discrimination Act: Adoption of interim interpretive guidelines, questions, and answers. 44 FR 13277–13281.

Erez, M., and Earley, P. C. (1987). Comparative analysis of goal-setting strategies across cultures. *Journal of Applied Psychology* 72, 658–665.

Erez, M., Earley, P. C., and Hulin, C. L. (1985). The impact of goal acceptance and performance: A two-step model. *Academy of Management Journal* 28, 50–66.

Erez, M., and Zidon, I. (1984). Effect of goal acceptance on the relationship of goal difficulty to performance. *Journal of Applied Psychology* 69, 69–78.

Falcone, P. (1995). Getting employers to open up on a reference check. *HR Magazine* 40 (7), 58–63.

Faley, R. H., and Sundstrom, E. (1985). Content representativeness: An empirical method of evaluation. *Journal of Applied Psychology* 70, 567–571.

Fallows, J. (1980, September). American industry—What ails it, how to save it. *The Atlantic Monthly,* pp. 35–50.

Family and Medical Leave Act—The Regulations. (1993, August). *Bulletin,* Mountain States Employers Council, Inc., Denver.

Farh, J. L., and Dobbins, G. H. (1989). Effects of comparative performance information on the accuracy of self-ratings and agreement between self- and supervisor ratings. *Journal of Applied Psychology* 74, 606–610.

Farh, J. L., Dobbins, G. H., and Cheng, B. S. (1991). Cultural relativity in action: A comparison of self-ratings made by Chinese and U.S. workers. *Personnel Psychology* 44, 129–147.

Farh, J. L., Werbel, J. D., and Bedeian, A. G. (1988). An empirical investigation of self-appraisal-based performance evaluation. *Personnel Psychology,* 41, 141–156.

Farish, P. (1989). Recruitment sources. In W. F. Cascio (Ed.), *Human resource planning, employment, and placement* (pp. 2-103–2-134). Washington, DC: Bureau of National Affairs.

Farnsworth, C. H. (1987, February 22). Survey of whistle-blowers finds retaliation but few regrets. *New York Times,* p. 22.

Fay, C. H., and Latham, G. P. (1982). Effects of training and rating scales on rating errors. *Personnel Psychology* 35, 105–116.

Ferguson, L. W. (1960). Ability, interest, and aptitude. *Journal of Applied Psychology* 44, 126–131.

Ferris, G. R., Yates, V. L., Gilmore, D. C., and Rowland, K. M. (1985). The influence of subordinate age on performance ratings and causal attributions. *Psychology* 38, 545–557.

Fiedler, F. E. (1965). Engineer the job to fit the manager. *Harvard Business Review* 43, 115–122.

Fiedler, F. E. (1967). *A theory of leadership effectiveness.* New York: McGraw-Hill.

Fine, S. A. (1989). *Functional job analysis scales: A desk aid.* Milwaukee, WI: Sidney A. Fine.

Fine, S. A., and Wiley, W. W. (1971). An introduction to functional job analysis: Methods for manpower analysis (Monograph No. 4). Kalamazoo, MI: W. E. Upjohn Institute. Rand McNally.

Finkle, R. B., and Jones, W. S. (1970). *Assessing corporate talent, a key to managerial manpower planning.* New York: Wiley-Interscience.

Firefighters Local Union No 1784 v. *Stotts.* (1984). 467 U.S. 661.

Flanagan, J. C. (1951). Defining the requirements of the executive's job. *Personnel* 28, 8–35.

Flanagan, J. C. (1954a). Some considerations in the development of situational tests. *Personnel Psychology* 7, 461–464.

Flanagan, J. C. (1954b). The critical incident technique. *Psychological Bulletin* 51, 327–358.

Flanagan, J. C., and Burns, R. K. (1955). The employee performance record: A new appraisal and development tool. *Harvard Business Review* 33, 95–102.

Fleishman, E. A. (1973). Twenty years of consideration and structure. In E. A. Fleishman and J. G. Hunt (Eds.), *Current developments in the study of leadership.* Carbondale, IL: Southern Illinois University Press.

Fleishman, E. A. (1975). Toward a taxonomy of human performance. *American Psychologist* 30, 1127–1149.

Fleishman, E. A. (1988). Some new frontiers in personnel selection research. *Personnel Psychology* 42, 679–701.

Fleishman, E. A. (1992). *Rating scale booklet: F-JAS.* Palo Alto, CA: Consulting Psychologists Press.

Fleishman, E. A., and Mumford, M. D. (1991). Evaluating classifications of job behavior: A construct validation of the ability requirement scales. *Personnel Psychology* 44, 523–575.

Fleishman, E. A., and Ornstein, G. N. (1960). An analysis of pilot flying performance in terms of component abilities. *Journal of Applied Psychology* 44, 146–155.

Fleishman, E. A., and Peters, D. A. (1962). Interpersonal values, leadership attitudes, and managerial "success." *Personnel Psychology* 15, 127–143.

Fleishman, E. A., and Reilly, M. E. (1992a). *Administrator's guide: F-JAS.* Palo Alto, CA: Consulting Psychologists Press.

Fleishman, E. A., and Reilly, M. E. (1992b). *Handbook of human abilities.* Palo Alto, CA: Consulting Psychologists Press.

Florin-Thuma, B. C., and Boudreau, J. W. (1987). Performance feedback utility in a small organization: Effects on organizational outcomes and managerial decision processes. *Personnel Psychology* 40, 693–713.

FMLA—The supervisor's role. (1996, August). *Bulletin.* Denver: Mountain States Employers Council, Inc., p.1.

Foley, J. D., Jr. (1969). Determining training needs of department store sales personnel. *Training and Development Journal* 23, 24–27.

Fondas, N. (1992, Summer). A behavioral job description for managers. *Organizational Dynamics* 47–58.

Foote, A., and Erfurt, J. (1981, September-October). Evaluating an employee assistance program. *EAP Digest,* pp. 14–25.

Ford, J. K., and Noe, R. A. (1987). Self-assessed training needs: The effects of attitudes toward training, managerial level, and function. *Personnel Psychology* 40, 39–53.

Ford, J. K., Quinones, M. A., Sego, D. J., and Sorra, J. S. (1992). Factors affecting the opportunity to perform trained tasks on the job. *Personnel Psychology* 45, 511–527.

Ford, J. K., Smith, E. M., Sego, D. J., and Quinones, M. A. (1993). Impact of task experience and individual factors on training-emphasis ratings. *Journal of Applied Psychology* 78, 583–590.

Ford, J. K., and Wroten, S. P. (1984). Introducing new methods for conducting training evaluation and for linking training evaluation to program redesign. *Personnel Psychology* 37, 651–656.

Fox, S., and Dinur, Y. (1988). Validity of self-assessment: A field evaluation. *Personnel Psychology* 41, 581–592.

Frayne, C. A., and Latham, G. P. (1987). The application of social learning theory to employee self-management of attendance. *Journal of Applied Psychology* 72, 387–392.

Fredericksen, N. (1962). Factors in in-basket performance. *Psychological Monographs* 76 (22 Whole No. 541).

Fredericksen, N., and Melville, S. D. (1954). Differential predictability in the use of test scores. *Educational and Psychological Measurement* 14, 647–656.

Freeberg, N. E. (1976). Criterion measures for youth-work training programs: The development of relevant performance dimensions. *Journal of Applied Psychology* 61, 537–545.

Fried, Y., Tiegs, R. B., and Bellamy, A. R. (1992). Personal and interpersonal predictors of supervisors' avoidance of evaluating subordinates. *Journal of Applied Psychology* 77, 462–468.

Friedman, A. (1972). Attacking discrimination through the Thirteenth Amendment. *Cleveland State Law Review* 21, 165–178.

Frieling, E., Kannheiser, W., and Lindberg, R. (1974). Some results with the German form of the Position Analysis Questionnaire (PAQ). *Journal of Applied Psychology* 59, 741–747.

Furby, L. (1973). Interpreting regression toward the mean in developmental research. *Developmental Psychology* 8, 172–179.

Furnco Construction Corp. v. *Waters.* (1978). 438 U.S. 567.

Fusilier, M. R., and Hoyer, W. D. (1980). Variables affecting perceptions of invasion of privacy in a personnel selection situation. *Journal of Applied Psychology* 65, 623–626.

Gael, S. (Ed.). (1988). *The job analysis handbook for business, industry, and government.* New York: Wiley.

Gael, S., Grant, D. L., and Ritchie, R. J. (1975). Employment test validation for minority and nonminority clerks with work sample criteria. *Journal of Applied Psychology* 60, 420–426.

Gagné, R. M. (1962). Military training and principles of learning. *American Psychologist* 18, 83–91.

Gagné, R. M. (Ed.). (1967). *Learning and individual differences.* Columbus, OH: Merrill.

Gagné, R. M. (1977). *Conditions of learning* (3rd ed.). New York: Holt, Rinehart, and Winston.

Gagné, R. M., and Briggs, L. J. (1979). *Principles of instructional design* (2nd ed.). New York: Holt, Rinehart, and Winston.

Gagné, R. M. and Rohwer, W. D., Jr. (1969). Instructional psychology. *Annual Review of Psychology* 20, 381–418.

Ganster, D. C., Williams, S., and Poppler, P. (1991). Does training in problem solving improve the quality of group decisions? *Journal of Applied Psychology* 76, 479–483.

Ganzach, Y. (1995). Negativity (and positivity) in performance evaluation: Three field studies. *Journal of Applied Psychology* 80, 491–499.

Garcia, L. T., Erskine, N., Hawn, K., and Casmay, S. (1981). The effect of affirmative action on attributions about minority group members. *Journal of Personality* 49, 427–437.

Garcia v. *Gloor.* (5th Cir. 1980). 618 F.2d 264.

Gattiker, U. E. (1995). Firm and taxpayer returns from training of semiskilled employees. *Academy of Management Journal* 38, 1152–1173.

Gaugler, B. B., Rosenthal, D. B., Thornton, G. C., III, and Bentson, C. (1987). Meta-analysis of assessment center validity. *Journal of Applied Psychology* 72, 493–511.

Gaugler, B. B., and Rudolph, A. S. (1992). The influence of assessee performance variation on assessors' judgments. *Personnel Psychology* 45, 77–98.

Gaugler, B. B., and Thornton, G. C., III. (1989). Number of assessment center dimensions as a determinant of assessor accuracy *Journal of Applied Psychology* 74, 611–618.

Gersick, C. J. G. (1988). Time and transition in work teams: Toward a new model of group development. *Academy of Management Journal* 31, 9–41.

Geyer, P. D., Hice, J., Hawk, J., Boese, R., and Brannon, Y. (1989). Reliabilities of ratings available from the *Dictionary of Occupational Titles. Personnel Psychology* 42, 547–560.

Ghiselli, E. E. (1951). New ideas in industrial psychology. *Journal of Applied Psychology* 35, 229–235.

Ghiselli, E. E. (1956a). The placement of workers: Concepts and problems. *Personnel Psychology* 9, 1–16.

Ghiselli, E. E. (1963). Managerial talent. *American Psychologist* 8, 631–642.

Ghiselli, E. E. (1966). *The validity of occupational aptitude tests.* New York: Wiley.

Ghiselli, E. E. (1973). The validity of aptitude tests in personnel selection. *Personnel Psychology* 26, 461–477.

Ghiselli, E. E., and Brown, C. W. (1955). *Personnel and industrial psychology* (2nd ed.). New York: McGraw-Hill.

Ghiselli, E. E., Campbell, J. P. and Zedeck, S. (1981). *Measurement theory for the behavioral sciences.* San Francisco: Freeman.

Ghiselli, E. E., and Haire, M. (1960). The validation of selection tests in the light of the dyanamic nature of criteria. *Personnel Psychology* 13, 225–231.

Ghorpade, J., and Chen, M. M. (1995). Creating quality-driven performance appraisal systems. *Academy of Management Executive* 9 (1), 32–39.

Giese, W. (1987, June 15). Pulse of the USA: World of work. *USA Today*, pp. 1, 2.

Gillett, R. (1994). Post-hoc power analysis. *Journal of Applied Psychology* 79, 783–785.

Ginter, E. M. (1979, May). Communications and cost-benefit aspects of employee safety. *Management Accounting,* pp. 24–26, 32.

Gioia, D. A., and Longenecker, C. O., (1994, Winter). Delving into the dark side: The politics of executive appraisal. *Organizational Dynamics*, pp. 47–58.

Girschick, M. A. (1954). An elementary review of statistical decision theory. *Review of Educational Research* 24, 448–466.

Gist, M., Rosen, B., and Schwoerer, C. (1988). The influence of training method and trainee age on the acquisition of computer skills. *Personnel Psychology* 40, 255–265.

Gist, M. E., Schwoerer, C., and Rosen, B. (1989). Effects of alternative training methods on self-efficacy and performance in computer software training. *Journal of Applied Psychology* 74, 884–891.

Gist, M. E., Stevens, C. K., and Bavetta, A. G. (1991). Effects of self-efficacy and post-training intervention on the acquisition and maintenance of complex interpersonal skills. *Personnel Psychology* 44, 837–861.

Glaser, R. (1967). Some implications of previous work on learning and individual differences. In R. M. Gagné (Ed.), *Learning and individual differences.* Columbus, OH: Merrill.

Glass, G. V. (1976, November). Primary, secondary, and meta-analysis of research. *Educational Research,* pp. 3–8.

Gleason, W. J. (1957). Predicting army leadership ability by modified leaderless group discussion. *Journal of Applied Psychology* 41, 231–235.

Glennon, J. R., Albright, L. E., and Owens, W. A. (1966). *A catalog of life history items.* Greensboro, NC: The Richardson Foundation.

Glickman, A. S., and Vallance, T. R. (1958). Curriculum assessment with critical incidents. *Journal of Applied Psychology* 42, 329–335.

Goldstein, A. P., and Sorcher, M. (1974). *Changing supervisor behavior.* New York: Pergamon.

Goldstein, I. L. (1971). The application blank: How honest are the responses? *Journal of Applied Psychology* 55, 491–492.

Goldstein, I. L. (1974). *Training: Program development and evaluation.* Monterey, CA: Brooks/Cole.

Goldstein, I. L. (1978). The pursuit of validity in the evaluation of training programs. *Human Factors* 20, 131–144.

Goldstein, I. L. (1993). *Training in organizations: Needs assessment, development, and evaluation* (3rd ed.). Monterey, CA: Brooks/Cole.

Goldstein, I. L. and Associates. (1989). *Training and development in organizations.* San Francisco: Jossey-Bass.

Goldstein, I. L., and Gilliam, P. (1990). Training system issues in the year 2000. *American Psychologist* 45, 134–143.

Golembiewski, R. T., and Billingsley, K. R. (1980). Measuring change in OD panel designs: A response to critics. *Academy of Management Review* 5, 97–103.

Golembiewski, R. T., Billingsley, K. R., and Yeager, S. (1976). Measuring change and persistence in human affairs: Types of change generated by OD designs. *Journal of Applied Behavioral Science* 12, 133–157.

Goodman, P. S., Devadas, R., and Hughson, T. L. G. (1988). Groups and productivity: Analyzing the effectiveness of self-managing teams. In J. P. Campbell and R. J. Campbell (Eds.), *Productivity in Organizations* (pp. 295–327). San Francisco: Jossey-Bass.

Gomersall, E. R., and Myers, M. S. (1966). Breakthrough in on-the-job training. *Harvard Business Review* 44, 62–72.

Gomez-Mejia, L. R., and Balkin, D. B. (1992). *Compensation, organizational strategy, and firm performance.* Cincinnati, OH: South-Western.

Gordon, H. W., and Leighty, R. (1988). Importance of specialized cognitive function in the selection of military pilots. *Journal of Applied Psychology* 73, 38–45.

Gordon, M. E., and Cohen, S. L. (1973). Training behavior as a predictor of trainability. *Personnel Psychology* 26, 261–272.

Gordon, M. E., and Johnson, W. A. (1982). Seniority: A review of its legal and scientific standing. *Personnel Psychology* 35, 255–280.

Gottfredson, L. S. (1986). Societal consequences of the *g* factor in employment. *Journal of Vocational Behavior* 29, 370–410.

Gottfredson, L. S. (1988). Reconsidering fairness: A matter of social and ethical priorities. *Journal of Vocational Behavior* 33, 293–319.

Gottfredson, L. S. (1994). The science and politics of race-norming. *American Psychologist* 49, 955–963.

Graham, S. (1996). Debunk the myths about older workers. *Safety & Health* 153 (1), 38–42.

Grant, D. L., Katkovsky, W., and Bray, D. W. (1967). Contributions of projective techniques to assessment of management potential. *Journal of Applied Psychology* 51, 226–231.

Graves, L. M., and Karren, R. J. (1992). Interviewer decision processes and effectiveness: An experimental policy-capturing investigation. *Personnel Psychology* 45, 313–340.

Graves, L. M., and Powell, G. N. (1995). The effect of sex similarity on recruiters' evaluations of actual applicants: A test of the similarity-attraction paradigm. *Personnel Psychology* 48, 85–98.

Gregory, D. L. (1988). Reducing the risk of negligence in hiring. *Employee Relations Law Journal* 14, 31–40.

Green, B. F., and Hall, J. A. (1984). Quantitative methods for literature reviews. *Annual Review of Psychology* 35, 37–53.

Green, D. R. (1975, March). *What does it mean to say a test is biased?* Paper presented at the meeting of the American Educational Research Association, Washington, DC.

Greenhouse, L. (1984, June 13). Seniority is held to outweigh race as a layoff guide. *New York Times,* pp. A1, B12.

Greer, O. L., and Cascio, W. F. (1987). Is cost accounting the answer? Comparison of two behaviorally based methods for estimating the standard deviation of performance in dollars with a cost-accounting-based approach. *Journal of Applied Psychology* 72, 588–595.

Greller, M. (1980). Evaluation of feedback sources as a function of role and organizational level. *Journal of Applied Psychology* 65, 24–27.

Grey, R. J., and Kipnis, D. (1976). Untangling the performance appraisal dilemma: The influence of perceived organizational context on evaluation processes. *Journal of Applied Psychology* 61, 329–335.

Griffith, T. L. (1993). Teaching big brother to be a team player: Computer monitoring and quality. *Academy of Management Executive* 7 (1), 73–80.

Grimsley, G., and Jarrett, H. F. (1973). The relation of managerial achievement to test measures obtained in the employment situation: Methodology and results. *Personnel Psychology* 26, 31–48.

Grimsley, G., and Jarrett, H. F. (1975). The relation of past managerial achievement to test measures obtained in the employment situation: Methodology and results—II. *Personnel Psychology* 28, 215–231.

Gross, A. L., and Su, W. (1975). Defining a "fair" or "unbiased" selection model: A question of utilities. *Journal of Applied Psychology* 60, 345–351.

Guardians Assn. of N. Y. City Police Dept. v. *Civil Service Comm. of City of N. Y.* (1980, November). *The Industrial-Organizational Psychologist,* pp. 44–49.

Guilford, J. P. (1954). *Psychometric methods* (2nd ed.). New York: McGraw-Hill.

Guilford, J. P., and Fruchter, B. (1978). *Fundamental statistics in psychology and education.* (6th ed.). New York: McGraw-Hill.

Guion, R. M. (1961). Criterion measurement and personnel judgments. *Personnel Psychology* 14, 141–149.

Guion, R. M. (1965). *Personnel testing.* New York: McGraw-Hill.

Guion, R. M. (1966). Employment tests and discriminatory hiring. *Industrial Relations* 5, 20–37.

Guion, R. M. (1976). Recruiting, selection, and job placement. In M. D. Dunnette (Ed.), *Handbook of industrial-organizational psychology.* Chicago: Rand McNally.

Guion, R. M. (1978). Scoring of content domain samples: The problem of fairness. *Journal of Applied Psychology* 63, 449–506.

Guion, R. M. (1987). Changing views for personnel selection research. *Personnel Psychology* 40, 199–213.

Guion, R. M. (1991). Personnel assessment, selection, and placement. In M. D. Dunnette and L. M. Hough (Eds.), *Handbook of industrial-organizational psychology* (2nd ed., Vol. 2, pp. 327–397). Palo Alto, CA: Consulting Psychologists Press.

Guion, R. M., and Cranny, C. J. (1982). A note on concurrent and predictive validity designs: A critical reanalysis. *Journal of Applied Psychology* 67, 239–244.

Guion, R. M., and Gibson, W. M. (1988). Personnel selection and placement. *Annual Review of Psychology* 39, 349–374.

Guion, R. M., and Ironson, G. H. (1983). Latent trait theory for organizational research. *Organizational Behavior and Human Performance* 31, 54–87.

Gulliksen, H. (1950). *Theory of mental tests.* New York: Wiley.

Gupta, U. (1996, January 3). TV seminars and CD-ROMs train workers. *The Wall Street Journal,* pp. B1, B8.

Guthrie, J. P., and Olian, J. D. (1991). Does context affect staffing decisions? The case of general managers. *Personnel Psychology* 44, 263–292.

Gwynne, S. C. (1992, September 28). The long haul. *Time,* pp. 34–38.

Hager, B. (1991, September 23). What's behind business' sudden fervor for ethics? *Business Week,* p. 65.

Haire, M. (1964). *Psychology of management* (2nd ed.). New York: McGraw-Hill.

Hakel, M. D. (1976). Some questions and comments about applied learning. *Personnel Psychology* 29, 261–363.

Hakel, M. D. (1989). Merit-based selection: Measuring the person for the job. In W. F. Cascio (Ed.), *Human resource planning, employment, and placement* (pp. 2-135–2-158). Washington, DC: Bureau of National Affairs.

Hakel, M. D., Ohnesorge, J. P., and Dunnette, M. D. (1970). Interviewer evaluations of job applicants' resumes as a function of the qualifications of the immediately-preceding applicants: An examination of contrast effects. *Journal of Applied Psychology* 54, 27–30.

Hall, D. T. and Mirvis, P. H. (1995). Careers as lifelong learning. In A. Howard (Ed.), *The changing nature of work* (pp. 323–361). San Francisco: Jossey-Bass.

Hammer, M., and Champy, J. (1993). *Reengineering the corporation.* New York: Harper Business.

Hanges, P. J., Braverman, E. P., and Rentch, J. R. (1991). Changes in raters' perceptions of subordinates: A catastrophe model. *Journal of Applied Psychology* 76, 878–888.

Hanisch, K. A., and Hulin, C. L. (1994). Two-stage sequential selection procedures using ability and training performance: Incremental validity of behavioral consistency measures. *Personnel Psychology* 47, 767–785.

Hanser, L. M., Arabian, J. M., and Wise, L. (1985, October). *Multi-dimensional performance measurement.* Paper presented at the annual meeting of the Military Testing Association, San Diego.

Harrell, A. M., and Stahl, M. J. (1981). A behavioral decision theory approach for measuring McClelland's trichotomy of needs. *Journal of Applied Psychology* 66, 242–247.

Harris, M. M., Becker, A. S., and Smith, D. E. (1993). Does the assessment center scoring method affect the cross-situational consistency of ratings? *Journal of Applied Psychology* 78, 675–678.

Harris, M. M., and Fink. L. S. (1987). A field study of applicant reactions to employment opportunities: Does the recruiter make a difference? *Personnel Psychology* 40, 765–784.

Harris, M. M., and Schaubroeck, J. (1988). A meta-analysis of self-supervisor, self-peer, and peer-supervisor ratings. *Personnel Psychology* 41, 43–62.

Harris, M. M., Smith, D. E., and Champagne, D. (1995). A field study of performance appraisal purpose: Research- versus administrative-based ratings. *Personnel Psychology* 48, 151–160.

Harris v. *Forklift Systems, Inc.,* (1993). 510 U.S. 17.

Härtel, C. E. J. (1993). Rating format research revisited: Format effectiveness and acceptability depend on rater characteristics. *Journal of Applied Psychology* 78, 212–217.

Hartigan, J. A., and Wigdor, A. K. (Eds.). (1989). *Fairness in employment testing: Validity generalization, minority issues, and the General Aptitude Test Battery.* Washington, DC: National Academy Press.

Hartman, E. A., Mumford, M. D., and Mueller, S. (1992). Validity of job classifications: An examination of alternative indicators. *Human Performance* 5, 191–211.

Harvey, R. J. (1986). Quantitative approaches to job classification: A review and critique. *Personnel Psychology* 39, 267–289.

Harvey, R. J. (1991). Job analysis. In M. D. Dunnette and L. M. Hough (Eds.), *Handbook of industrial and organizational psychology* (2nd ed., Vol. 2, pp. 71–163). Palo Alto, CA: Consulting Psychologists Press.

Harvey, R. J., Friedman, L., Hakel, M. D., and Cornelius, E. T., III. (1988). Dimensionality of the Job Element Inventory, a simplified worker-oriented job analysis questionnaire. *Journal of Applied Psychology* 73, 639–646.

Harvey, R. J., and Lozada-Larsen, S. R. (1988). Influence of amount of job descriptive information on job analysis rating accuracy. *Journal of Applied Psychology* 73, 457–461.

Hater, J. J., and Bass, B. M. (1988). Superiors' evaluations and subordinates' perceptions of transformational and transactional leadership. *Journal of Applied Psychology* 74, 695–702.

Hauenstein, N. M., and Foti, R. J. (1989). From laboratory to practice: Neglected issues in implementing frame-of-reference rater training. *Personnel Psychology* 42, 359–378.

Hawk, R. H. (1967). *The recruitment function.* New York: American Management Association.

Hedge, J. W., and Kavanagh, M. J. (1988). Improving the accuracy of performance evaluations: Comparison of three methods of performance appraiser training. *Journal of Applied Psychology* 73, 68–73.

Hedges, L. V. (1989). An unbiased correction for sampling error in validity generalization studies. *Journal of Applied Psychology* 74, 469–477.

Hedges, L. V., and Olkin, I. (1985). *Statistical methods for meta-analysis.* Orlando, FL: Academic Press.

Hegarty, W. H., and Sims, H. P., Jr. (1978). Some determinants of unethical decision behavior: An experiment. *Journal of Applied Psychology* 63, 451–457.

Hegarty, W. H., and Sims, H. P., Jr. (1979). Organizational philosophy, policies, and objectives related to unethical decision behavior: A laboratory experiment. *Journal of Applied Psychology* 64, 331–338.

Heneman, H. G., III. (1975). Research roundup. *The Personnel Administrator* 20 (6), 61.

Heneman, H. G., III. (1980). Self-assessment: A critical analysis. *Personnel Psychology* 33, 297–300.

Heneman, H. G., III., Schwab, D. P., Huett, D. L., and Ford, J. J. (1975). Interviewer validity as a function of interview structure, biographical data, and interviewee order. *Journal of Applied Psychology* 60, 748–753.

Heneman, R. L. (1986). The relationship between supervisory ratings and results-oriented measures of performance: A meta-analysis. *Personnel Psychology* 39, 811–826.

Heneman, R. L., and Wexley, K. N. (1983). The effects of time delay in rating and amount of information observed on performance rating accuracy. *Academy of Management Journal* 26, 677–686.

Henik, A., and Tzelgov, J. (1985). Control of halo error: A multiple regression approach. *Journal of Applied Psychology* 70, 577–580.

Henkoff, R. (1994, October 3). Finding, training, and keeping the best service workers. *Fortune,* pp. 110–122.

Henry, E. R. (1965). *Research conference on the use of autobiographical data as psychological predictors.* Greensboro, NC: The Richardson Foundation.

Henry, R. A., and Hulin, C. L. (1987). Stability of skilled performance across time: Some generalizations and limitations on utilities. *Journal of Applied Psychology* 72, 457–462.

Henry, R. A., and Hulin, C. L. (1989). Changing validities: Ability-performance relations and utilities. *Journal of Applied Psychology* 74, 365–367.

Herold, D. M., and Parsons, C. K. (1985). Assessing the feedback environment in work organizations: Development of the Job Feedback Survey. *Journal of Applied Psychology* 70, 290–305.

Hicks, W. D., and Klimoski, R. J. (1987). Entry into training programs and its effects on training outcomes: A field experiment. *Academy of Management Journal* 30, 542–552.

Hinrichs, J. R. (1978). An eight-year follow-up of a management assessment center. *Journal of Applied Psychology* 63 596–601.

Hitt, M. A., and Barr, S. H. (1989). Managerial selection decision models: Examination of configural cue processing. *Journal of Applied Psychology* 74, 53–61.

Hobson, C. J., and Gibson, F. W. (1983). Policy capturing as an approach to understanding and improving performance appraisal: A review of the literature. *Academy of Management Review* 8, 640–649.

Hodgson v. *First Federal Savings and Loan Association of Broward County, Florida,* (5th Cir. 1972). 455 F.2d 818.

Hoffman, D. A., Jacobs, R., and Baratta, J. E. (1993). Dynamic criteria and the measurement of change. *Journal of Applied Psychology* 78, 194–204.

Hoffman, D. A., Jacobs, R., and Gerras, S. J. (1992). Mapping individual performance over time. *Journal of Applied Psychology* 77, 185–195.

Hogan, E. A. (1987). Effects of prior expectations on performance ratings: A longitudinal study. *Academy of Management Journal* 30, 354–368.

Hogan, J., and Hogan, R. (1989). How to measure employee reliability. *Journal of Applied Psychology* 74, 273–279.

Hogan, R., Hogan, J., and Roberts, B. W. (1996). Personality measurement and employment decisions. *American Psychologist* 51, 469–477.

Hogan, P. M., Hakel, M. D., and Decker, P. J. (1986). Effects of trainee-generated versus trainer-provided rule codes on generalization in behavior-modeling training. *Journal of Applied Psychology* 71, 469–473.

Hogan, R. (1991). Personality and personality measurement. In M. D. Dunnette and L. M. Hough (Eds.), *Handbook of industrial and organizational psychology* (pp. 873–919). Palo Alto, CA: Consulting Psychologists Press.

Hoiberg, A., and Pugh, W. M. (1978). Predicting Navy effectiveness: Expectations, motivation, personality, aptitude, and background variables. *Personnel Psychology* 31, 841–852.

Hollenbeck, J. R., Ilgen, D. R., Tuttle, D. B., and Sego, D. J. (1995). Team performance on monitoring tasks: An examination of decision errors in contexts requiring sustained attention. *Journal of Applied Psychology* 80, 685–696.

Hollenbeck, J. R., and Whitener, E. M. (1988). Criterion-related validation for small sample contexts: An integrated approach to synthetic validity. *Journal of Applied Psychology* 73, 536–544.

Hollenbeck, J. R., Williams, C. R., and Klein, H. J. (1989). An empirical examination of the antecedents of commitment to difficult goals. *Journal of Applied Psychology* 74, 18–23.

Horst, P. (1941). *The prediction of personal adjustment.* New York: Social Science Research Council.

Horst, P. (1956). Multiple classification by the method of least squares. *Journal of Clinical Psychology* 12, 3–16.

Horst, P. (1961). *The logic of personnel selection.* Seattle: University of Washington Press.

Hough, L. M. (1984). Development and evaluation of the "Accomplishment Record" method of selecting and promoting professionals. *Journal of Applied Psychology* 69, 135–146.

House, R. J., and Mitchell, T. R. (1974). Path-goal theory of leadership. *Journal of Contemporary Business* 3, 81–97.

How Microsoft makes offers people can't refuse. (1992, February 24). *Business Week,* p. 65.

Howard, A. (1986). College experiences and managerial performance. *Journal of Applied Psychology* 71, 530–552.

Howard, A. (1995). Rethinking the psychology of work. In A. Howard (Ed.), *The changing nature of work* (pp. 513–555). San Francisco: Jossey-Bass.

Howard, A., and Bray, D. W. (1989). *Managerial lives in transition: Advancing age and changing times.* New York: Guilford.

Huck, J. R. (1973). Assessment centers: A review of the external and internal validities. *Personnel Psychology* 26, 191–212.

Huck, J. R., and Bray, D. W. (1976). Management assessment center evaluations and subsequent job performance of white and black females. *Personnel Psychology* 29, 13–30.

Hudson, J. P., Jr., and Campion, J. E. (1994). Hindsight bias in an application of the Angoff method for setting cutoff scores. *Journal of Applied Psychology* 79, 860–865.

Huffcutt, A. J., and Arthur, W., Jr. (1994). Hunter and Hunter (1984) revisited: Interview validity for entry-level jobs. *Journal of Applied Psychology* 79, 184–190.

Huffcutt, A. J., and Arthur, W., Jr. (1995). Development of a new outlier statistic for meta-analytic data. *Journal of Applied Psychology* 80, 327–334.

Hughes, G. L., and Prien, E. P. (1989). Evaluation of task and job skill linkage judgments used to develop test specifications. *Personnel Psychology* 42, 283–292.

Hulin, C. L., Drasgow, F., and Parsons, C. K. (1983). *Item response theory: Application to psychological measurement.* Homewood, IL: Dow Jones-Irwin.

Humphreys, L. G. (1973). Statistical definitions of test validity for minority groups. *Journal of Applied Psychology* 58, 1–4.

Hunter, J. E., and Hunter, R. F. (1984). Validity and utility of alternative predictors of job performance. *Psychological Bulletin* 96, 72–98.

Hunter, J. E., and Schmidt, F. L. (1976). Critical analysis of the statistical and ethical implications of various definitions of test bias. *Psychological Bulletin* 83, 1053–1071.

Hunter, J. E., and Schmidt, F. L. (1983). Quantifying the effects of psychological interventions on employee job performance and workforce productivity. *American Psychologist* 38, 473–478.

Hunter, J. S., and Schmidt, F. L. (1990). *Methods of meta-analysis: Correcting error and bias in research findings.* Newbury Park, CA: Sage.

Hunter, J. S., and Schmidt, F. L. (1994). Estimation of sampling error variance in the meta-analysis of correlations: Use of average correlation in the homogeneous case. *Journal of Applied Psychology* 79, 171–177.

Hunter, J. E., Schmidt, F. L., and Coggin, T. D. (1988). Problems and pitfalls in using capital budgeting and financial accounting techniques in assessing the utility of personnel programs. *Journal of Applied Psychology* 73, 522–528.

Hunter, J. E., Schmidt, F. L., and Hunter, R. (1979). Differential validity of employment tests by race: A comprehensive review and analysis. *Psychological Bulletin* 86, 721–735.

Hunter, J. E., Schmidt, F. L., and Jackson, G. B. (1982). *Meta-analysis: Cumulating research findings across studies.* Beverly Hills, CA: Sage.

Hunter, J. E., Schmidt, F. L., and Judiesch, M. K. (1990). Individual differences in output variability as a function of job complexity. *Journal of Applied Psychology* 75, 28–42.

Hunter, J. E., Schmidt, F. L., and Rauschenberger, J. M. (1977). Fairness of psychological tests: Implications of four definitions for selection utility and minority hiring. *Journal of Applied Psychology* 62, 245–260.

Huselid, M. A. (1995). The impact of human resource management practices on turnover, productivity, and corporate financial performance. *Academy of Management Journal* 38, 635–672.

Hyland v. *Fukada,* 580 F2d 977 (9th Circuit, 1978).

Ilgen, D. R., and Barnes-Farrell, J. L. (1984). *Performance planning and evaluation.* Chicago: Science Research Associates.

Ilgen, D. R., and Favero, J. L. (1985). Limits in generalization from psychological research to performance appraisal processes. *Academy of Management Review* 10, 311–321.

Ilgen, D. R., Fisher, C. D., and Taylor, M. S. (1979). Consequences of individual feedback on behavior in organizations. *Journal of Applied Psychology* 64, 349–371.

Ilgen, D. R., and Moore, C. F. (1987). Types and choices of performance feedback. *Journal of Applied Psychology* 72, 401–406.

Imada, A. S., and Hakel, M. D. (1977). Influence of nonverbal communication and rater proximity on impressions and decisions in simulated employment interviews. *Journal of Applied Psychology* 62, 295–300.

In Bakke's Wake: Kaiser Aluminum Case May Help in Clarifying Reverse-Job Bias Issue. (1978, September 21). *The Wall Street Journal*, pp. 1, 33.

Investing in people and prosperity. (May, 1994). U.S. Department of Labor, Washington, DC, p. 7.

Ironson, G. H., Guion, R. M., and Ostrander, M. (1982). Adverse impact from a psychometric perspective. *Journal of Applied Psychology* 67, 419–432.

Ivancevich, J. M. (1980). A longtitudinal study of behavioral expectation scales: Attitudes and performance. *Journal of Applied Psychology* 65, 139–146.

Ivancevich, J. M. (1983). Contrast effects in performance evaluation and reward practices. *Academy of Management Journal* 26, 465–476.

Jackson, B. B. (1983). *Multivariate data analysis: An introduction.* Homewood, IL: Irwin.

Jackson, D. J. (1978). Update on handicapped discrimination. *Personnel Journal* 57, 488–491.

Jacobs, R., and Baratta, J. E. (1989). Tools for staffing decisions: What can they do? What do they cost? In W. F. Cascio (Ed.), *Human resource planning, employment, and placement* (pp. 2-159–2-199). Washington, DC: Bureau of National Affairs.

Jacobs, R., Kafry, D., and Zedeck, S. (1980). Expectations of behaviorally anchored rating scales. *Personnel Psychology* 33, 595–640.

Jacoby, J., Mazursky, D., Troutman, T., and Kuss, A. (1984). When feedback is ignored: The disutility of outcome feedback. *Journal of Applied Psychology* 69, 531–545.

James, L. R., Demaree, R. G., Mulaik, S. A., and Mumford, M. D. (1988). Validity generalization: Rejoinder to Schmidt, Hunter, and Raju (1988). *Journal of Applied Psychology* 73, 673–678.

James, L. R., Demaree, R. G., Mulaik, S. A., and Ladd, R. T. (1992). Validity generalization in the context of situational models. *Journal of Applied Psychology* 77, 3–14.

James, L. R., Demaree, R. G., and Wolf, G. (1993). r_{ws}: An assessment of within-group interrater agreement. *Journal of Applied Psychology* 78, 306–309.

Jansen, E., and Von Glinow, M. A. (1985). Ethical ambivalence and organizational reward systems. *Academy of Management Review* 10, 814–822.

Janz, T. (1982). Initial comparisons of patterned behavior description interviews versus unstructured interviews. *Journal of Applied Psychology* 67, 577–580.

Jenkins, J. G. (1946). Validity for what? *Journal of Consulting Psychology* 10, 93–98.

Jennings, E. E. (1953). The motivation factor in testing supervisors. *Journal of Applied Psychology* 37, 168–69.

Jick, T. D. (1979). Mixing qualitative and quantitative methods: Triangulation in action. *Administrative Science Quarterly* 24, 602–611.

Johns, G. (1994). How often were you absent? A review of the use of self-reported absence data. *Journal of Applied Psychology* 79, 574–591.

Johnson, B. T., Mullen, B., and Salas, E. (1995). Comparison of three major meta-analytic approaches. *Journal of Applied Psychology* 80, 94–106.

Johnson, C. D., and Zeidner, J. (1991). *The economic benefits of predicting job performance: Vol. 2. Classification efficiency.* New York: Praeger.

Johnson v. *Railway Express Agency,* (1975). 95 S. Ct. 1716.

Jonah, B. A. (1984). Legislation and the prediction of reported seat belt use. *Journal of Applied Psychology* 69, 401–407.

Jones, E. E., and Gerard, H. B. (1967). *Foundations of social psychology*. New York: Wiley.

Jones, J. E., Jr., Murphy, W. P., and Belton, R. (1987). *Discrimination in employment* (5th ed.). St. Paul, MN: West.

Joyce, L. W., Thayer, P. W., and Pond, S. B. III. (1994). Managerial functions: An alternative to traditional assessment center dimensions? *Personnel Psychology* 47, 109–121.

Judge, T. A., Cable, D. M., Boudreau, J. W., and Bretz, R. D., Jr. (1995). An empirical investigation of the predictors of executive career success. *Personnel Psychology* 48, 485–519.

Judiesch, M. K., Schmidt, F. L., and Mount, M. K. (1992). Estimates of the dollar value of employee output in utility analyses: An empirical test of two theories. *Journal of Applied Psychology* 77, 234–250.

Justices uphold utility's stand on job testing. (1979, March 6). *Wall Street Journal*, p. 4.

Jurado v. *Eleven-Fifty Corporation*. (9th Cir. 1987). 813 F.2d 1406.

Kacmar, K. M., and Ferris, G. R. (1989). Theoretical and methodological considerations in the age-job satisfaction relationship. *Journal of Applied Psychology* 74, 201–207.

Kaess, W. A., Witryol, S. L., and Nolan, R. E. (1961). Reliability, sex differences, and validity in the leaderless group discussion technique. *Journal of Applied Psychology* 45, 345–350.

Kahneman, D., and Ghiselli, E. E. (1962). Validity and nonlinear heteroscedastic models. *Personnel Psychology* 15, 1–12.

Kane, J. S., Bernardin, H. J., Villanova, P., and Peyrefitte, J. (1995). Stability of rater leniency: Three studies. *Academy of Management Journal* 38, 1036–1051.

Kane, J. S., and Kane, K. F. (1993). Performance appraisal. In H. J. Bernardin and J. E. A. Russell (Eds.), *Human resource management: An experiential approach* (pp. 377–404). New York: McGraw-Hill.

Kane, J. S., and Lawler, E. E., III. (1978). Methods of peer assessment. *Psychological Bulletin* 85, 555–586.

Kane, J. S., and Lawler, E. E., III. (1980). In defense of peer assessment: A rebuttal to Brief's critique. *Psychological Bulletin* 88, 80–81.

Katz, D., and Kahn, R. L. (1978). *The social psychology of organizations* (2nd ed.). New York: Wiley.

Katz, H. C., Kochan, T. A., and Weber, M. R. (1985). Assessing the effects of industrial relations systems and efforts to improve the quality of working life on organizational effectiveness. *Academy of Management Journal* 28, 509–526.

Katzell, R. A. (1994). Contemporary meta-trends in industrial and organizational psychology. In H. C. Triandis, M. D. Dunnette, and L. M. Hough (Eds.), *Handbook of industrial and organizational psychology* (2nd ed., Vol. 4, pp. 1–89). Palo Alto, CA: Consulting Psychologists Press.

Katzell, R. A., and Dyer, F. J. (1977). Differential validity revived. *Journal of Applied Psychology* 62, 137–145.

Kavanaugh, M. J., MacKinney, A. C., and Wolins, L. (1970). Issues in managerial performance: Multitrait-multimethod analyses of ratings. *Psychological Bulletin* 75, 34–49.

Keating, E., Paterson, D. G., and Stone, H. C. (1950). Validity of work histories obtained by interview. *Journal of Applied Psychology* 34, 6–11.

Kelly, F. J., Beggs, D. L., and McNeil, K. A. (1969). *Research design in the behavioral sciences: multiple regression approach*. Carbondale: Southern Illinois University Press.

Kelly, G. A. (1958). The theory and technique of assessment. *Annual Review of Psychology* 9, 323–352.

Kemery, E. R., Mossholder, K. W., and Dunlap, W.P. (1989). Meta-analysis and moderator variables: A cautionary note on transportability. *Journal of Applied Psychology* 74, 168–170.

Kemery, E. R., Mossholder, K. W., and Roth, L. (1987). The power of the Schmidt and Hunter additive model of validity generalization. *Journal of Applied Psychology* 72, 30–37.

Kendrick, J. W. (1984, August 29). Productivity gains will continue. *Wall Street Journal*, p. 22.

Kerlinger, F. N. (1986). *Foundations of behavioral research* (3rd ed.). New York: Holt, Rinehart, and Winston.

Kerlinger, F. N., and Pedhazur, E. J. (1973). *Multiple regression in behavioral research.* New York: Holt, Rinehart, and Winston.

Kerr, S., and Jermier, J. M. (1978). Substitutes for leadership: Their meaning and measurement. *Organizational Behavior and Human Performance* 22, 375–403.

Kerr, S., and Schriesheim, C. (1974). Consideration, initiating structure, and organizational criteria—An update of Korman's 1966 review. *Personnel Psychology* 27, 555–568.

Kiechel, W., III. (1984, December 10). Picking your successor. *Fortune,* pp. 237–240.

Kiechel, W. III. (1993, May 17). How we will work in the year 2000. *Fortune,* pp. 38–52.

King, L. M., Hunter, J. E., and Schmidt, F. L. (1980). Halo in a multi-dimensional forced-choice performance evaluation scale. *Journal of Applied Psychology* 65, 507–516.

Kingsbury, F. A. (1933). Psychological tests for executives. *Personnel* 9, 121–133.

Kingslinger, H. J. (1966). Application of projective techniques in personnel psychology since 1940. *Psychological Bulletin* 66, 134–150.

Kirchner, W. K., and Dunnette, M. D. (1957). Applying the weighted application blank technique to a variety of office jobs. *Journal of Applied Psychology* 41, 206–208.

Kirchner, W. K., and Reisberg, D. J. (1962). Differences between better and less effective supervisors in appraisal of subordinates. *Personnel Psychology* 15, 295–302.

Kirkpatrick, D. L. (1977). Evaluating training programs: Evidence vs. proof. *Training and Development Journal* 31, 9–12.

Kirkpatrick, D. L. (1983). Four steps to measuring training effectiveness. *Personnel Administrator* 28 (11), 19–25.

Kirkpatrick, J. J., Ewen, R. B., Barrett, R. S., and Katzell, R. A. (1968). *Testing and fair employment.* New York: New York University Press.

Kirnan, J. P., Farley, J. A., and Geisinger, K. F. (1989). The relationship between recruiting source, applicant quality, and hire performance: An analysis by sex, ethnicity, and age. *Personnel Psychology* 42, 293–308.

Kleinman, M. (1993). Are rating dimensions in assessment centers transparent for participants? Consequences for criterion and construct validity. *Journal of Applied Psychology* 78, 988–993.

Klimoski, R., and Brickner, M. (1987). Why do assessment centers work? The puzzle of assessment center validity. *Personnel Psychology* 40, 243–260.

Klimoski, R., and Jones, R. G. (1995). Staffing for effective group decision making: Key issues in matching people and teams. In R. A. Guzzo and E. Salas (Eds.), *Team effectiveness and decision making in organizations* (pp. 291–332). San Francisco: Jossey-Bass.

Klimoski, R. J., and Strickland, W. J. (1977). Assessment centers—Valid or merely prescient? *Personnel Psychology* 30, 353–361.

Klimoski, R. J., and Strickland, W. J. (1981). *The comparative view of assessment centers.* Unpublished manuscript, Ohio State University, Department of Psychology.

Kluger, A. N., and Colella, A. (1993). Beyond the mean bias: The effect of warning against faking on biodata item variances. *Personnel Psychology* 46, 763–780.

Kluger, A. N., Reilly, R. R., and Russell, C. J. (1991). Faking biodata tests: Are option-keyed instruments more resistant? *Journal of Applied Psychology* 76, 889–896.

Knouse, S. B. (1987). An attribution theory approach to the letter of recommendation. *International Journal of Management* 4 (1), 5–13.

Koch, J. (1990, Winter). Desktop recruiting. *Recruitment Today* 3, p. 32–37.

Kolb, D. A., Rubin, I. M., and McIntyre, J. M. (1980). *Organizational psychology: An experiential approach* (3rd ed.). Englewood Cliffs, NJ: Prentice Hall.

Komaki, J. L., Desselles, M. L., and Bowman, E. D. (1989). Definitely not a breeze: Extending an operant model of effective supervision to teams. *Journal of Applied Psychology* 74, 522–529.

Komaki, J. L., Waddell, W. M., and Pearce, M. G. (1977). The applied behavior analysis approach and individual employees: Improving performance in two small businesses. *Organizational Behavior and Human Performance* 19, 337–352.

Konovsky, M. A., and Cropanzano, R. (1991). Perceived fairness of employee drug testing as a predictor of employee attitudes and job performance. *Journal of Applied Psychology* 76, 698–707.

Koslowsky, M., and Sagie, A. (1994). Components of artifactual variance in meta-analytic research. *Personnel Psychology* 47, 561–574.

Korb, L. D. (1956). How to measure the results of supervisory training. *Personnel* 32, 378–391.

Korman, A. K. (1966). Consideration, initiating structure, and organizational criteria: A review. *Personnel Psychology* 19, 349–363.

Korman, A. K. (1968). The prediction of managerial performance: A review. *Personnel Psychology* 21, 295–322.

Kovach, K. A., and Millspaugh, P. E. (1990). Comparable worth: Canada legislates pay equity. *The Academy of Management Executive* 4(2), 92–101.

Kozlowski, S. W. J., and Doherty, M. L. (1989). Integration of climate and leadership: Examination of a neglected issue. *Journal of Applied Psychology* 74, 546–553.

Kraiger, K., and Teachout, M. A. (1990). Generalizability theory as construct-related evidence of the validity of job performance ratings. *Human Performance* 3, 19–35.

Kraiger, K., Ford, J. K., and Salas, E. (1992). Application of cognitive, skill-based, and affective theories of learning outcomes to new methods of training evaluation. *Journal of Applied Psychology* 78, 311–328.

Kramer, J. L., and Conoley, J. C., (Eds.). (1992). *The eleventh mental measurements yearbook.* Lincoln, NE: University of Nebraska Press.

Kraut, A. I. (1969). Intellectual ability and promotional success among high-level managers. *Personnel Psychology* 22, 281–290.

Kraut, A. I. (1975). Prediction of managerial success by peer and training staff ratings. *Journal of Applied Psychology* 60, 14–19.

Kraut, A. I., and Scott, G. J. (1972). Validity of an op-

erational management assessment program. *Journal of Applied Psychology* 56, 124–129.

Kretch, D., Crutchfield, R. S., and Ballachey, E. L. (1962). *Individual in society: A textbook of social psychology.* New York: McGraw-Hill.

Krzystofiak, F., Cardy, R., and Newman, J. (1988). Implicit personality and performance appraisal: The influence of trait inferences on evaluations of behavior. *Journal of Applied Psychology* 73, 515–521.

Kuder, G. F., and Richardson, M. W. (1937). The theory of the estimation of test reliability. *Psychometrika* 2, 151–160.

Kuder, G. F., and Richardson, M. W. (1939). The calculation of test reliability coefficients based on the method of rational equivalence. *Journal of Educational Psychology* 30, 681–687.

Kulik, C. T., and Ambrose, M. L. (1993). Category-based and feature-based processes in performance appraisal: Integrating visual and computerized sources of performance data. *Journal of Applied Psychology* 78, 821–830.

Kurecka, P. M., Austin, J. M., Jr., Johnson, W., and Mendoza, J. L. (1982). Full and errant coaching effects on assigned role leaderless group discussion performance. *Personnel Psychology* 35, 805–812.

Labor Letter. (1985, June 18). *The Wall Street Journal,* p. 1.

Labor Letter. (1987, August 25). *The Wall Street Journal,* p. 1.

Labor Letter. (1988, November 22). *The Wall Street Journal,* p. 1.

Lado, A. A., and Wilson, M. C. (1994). Human resource systems and sustained competitive advantage: A competency–based perspective. *Academy of Management Review* 19, 699–727.

Lance, C. E., Teachout, M. S., and Donnelly, T. M. (1992). Specification of the criterion construct space: An application of hierarchical confirmatory factor analysis. *Journal of Applied Psychology* 77, 437–452.

Lance, C. E., LaPointe, J. A., and Stewart, A. M. (1994). A test of the context dependency of three causal models of halo rating error. *Journal of Applied Psychology* 79, 332–340.

Landy, F. J. (1986). Stamp collecting versus science: Validation as hypothesis testing. *American Psychologist* 41, 1183–1192.

Landy, F. J. (1987). *Psychology: The science of people* (2nd ed.). Englewood Cliffs, NJ: Prentice Hall.

Landy, F. J. (1989). *Psychology of work behavior* (4th ed.). Belmont, CA: Brooks/Cole.

Landy, F. J., Barnes, J. L., and Murphy, K. R. (1978). Correlates of perceived fairness and accuracy of performance evaluation. *Journal of Applied Psychology* 63, 751–754.

Landy, F. J., and Bates, F. (1973). Another look at contrast effects in the employment interview. *Journal of Applied Psychology* 58, 141–144.

Landy, F. J., and Farr, J. L. (1980). Performance rating. *Psychological Bulletin* 87, 72–107.

Landy, F. J., and Vasey, J. (1991). Job analysis: The composition of SME samples. *Personnel Psychology* 44, 27–50.

La Rocco, J. M., and Jones, A. P. (1978). Co-worker and leader support as moderators of stress-strain relationships in work situations. *Journal of Applied Psychology* 63, 629–634.

Larson, J. R., Jr. (1989). The dynamic interplay between employees' feedback-seeking strategies and supervisors' delivery of performance feedback. *Academy of Management Review* 14, 408–422.

Latham, G. P. (1988). Human resource training and development. *Annual Review of Psychology* 39, 545–582.

Latham, G. P., and Frayne, C. A. (1989). Self-management training for increasing job attendance: A follow-up and a replication. *Journal of Applied Psychology* 74, 411–416.

Latham, G. P., Mitchell, T. R., and Dossett, D. C. (1978). Importance of participative goal setting and anticipated rewards on goal difficulty and job performance. *Journal of Applied Psychology* 63, 163–171.

Latham, G. P., and Saari, L. M. (1979). Application of social–learning theory to training supervisors through behavioral modeling. *Journal of Applied Psychology* 64, 239–246.

Latham, G. P., and Saari, L. M. (1982). The importance of union acceptance for productivity improvement through goal setting. *Personnel Psychology* 35, 781–787.

Latham, G. P., and Saari, L. M. (1984). Do people do what they say? Further studies on the situational interview. *Journal of Applied Psychology* 69, 569–573.

Latham, G. P., Saari, L. M., Pursell, E. D., and Campion, M. A. (1980). The situational interview. *Journal of Applied Psychology* 65, 422–427.

Latham, G. P., and Steele, T. P. (1983). The motivational effects of participation versus goal setting on performance. *Academy of Management Journal* 26, 406–417.

Latham, G. P., and Wexley, K. N. (1981). *Increasing productivity through performance appraisal.* Reading, MA: Addison-Wesley.

Latham, G. P., Wexley, K. N., and Pursell, E. D. (1975). Training managers to minimize rating errors in the observation of behavior. *Journal of Applied Psychology* 60, 550–555.

Latham, G. P. and Whyte, G. (1994). The futility of utility analysis. *Personnel Psychology* 47, 31–46.

Latham, G. P., and Yukl, G. A. (1975). A review of research on the application of goal setting in organizations. *Academy of Management Journal* 18, 824–845.

Lautenschlager, G. J., and Shaffer, G. S. (1987). Reexamining the component stability of Owens's biographical questionnaire. *Journal of Applied Psychology* 72, 149–152.

Law, K. S. (1992). Estimation accuracy of Thomas's likelihood-based procedure of meta-analysis: A Monte Carlo simulation. *Journal of Applied Psychology* 77, 986–995.

Law, K. S., and Myors, B. (1993). Cutoff scores that maximize the total utility of a selection program: Comment on Martin and Raju's (1992) procedure. *Journal of Applied Psychology* 78, 736–740.

Law, K. S., Schmidt, F. L., and Hunter, J. E. (1994a). Nonlinearity of range corrections in meta-analysis: Test of an improved procedure. *Journal of Applied Psychology* 79, 425–438.

Law, K. S., Schmidt, F. L., and Hunter, J. E. (1994b). A test of two refinements in procedures for meta-analysis. *Journal of Applied Psychology* 79, 978–986.

Lawler, E. E., III. (1967). The multitrait-multirater approach to measuring managerial job performance. *Journal of Applied Psychology* 51, 369–381.

Lawler, E. E., III. (1969). Job design and employee motivation. *Personnel Psychology* 22, 435–436.

Lawler, E. E., III. (1971). *Pay and organizational effectiveness: A psychological view.* New York: Mc-Graw-Hill.

Lawler, E. E., III., and Suttle, J. L. (1973). Expectancy theory and job behavior. *Organizational Behavior and Human Performance* 9, 482–503.

Lawshe, C. H. (1975). A quantitative approach to content validity. *Personnel Psychology* 28, 563–575.

Lawshe, C. H. (1983). A simplified approach to the evaluation of fairness in employee selection procedures. *Personnel Psychology* 36, 601–608.

Lawshe, C. H. (1985). Inferences from personnel tests and their validities. *Journal of Applied Psychology* 70, 237–238.

Lawshe, C. H., and Balma, M. J. (1966). *Principles of personnel testing* (2nd ed.). New York: McGraw-Hill.

Lawshe, C. H., and Bolda, R. A. (1958). Expectancy charts. I. Their use and empirical development. *Personnel Psychology* 11, 353–365.

Lawshe, C. H., Bolda, R. A., Brune, R. L., and Auclair, G. (1958). Expectancy charts. II. Their theoretical development. *Personnel Psychology* 11, 545–559.

Lawshe, C. H., and Schucker, R. E. (1959). The relative efficiency of four test weighting methods in multiple prediction. *Educational and Psychological Measurement* 19, 103–114.

Ledvinka, J. (1979). The statistical definition of fairness in the federal selection guidelines and its implications for minority employment. *Personnel Psychology* 32, 551–562.

Ledvinka, J., Markos, V. H., and Ladd, R. T. (1982). Long-range impact of "fair selection" standards on minority employment. *Journal of Applied Psychology* 67, 18–36.

Lee, R., and Foley, P. P. (1986). Is the validity of a test constant through the test score range? *Journal of Applied Psychology* 71, 641–644.

Lee, R., Miller, K. J., and Graham, W. K. (1982). Corrections for restriction of range and attenuation in criterion-related validation studies. *Journal of Applied Psychology* 67, 637–639.

Lee, S. M. (1972). *Goal programming for decision analysis.* Philadelphia: Auerbach.

Leonard, B. (1995). The sell gets tough on college campuses. *HR Magazine* 40 (6), 61–63.

Lengnick-Hall, C. A., and Lengnick-Hall, M. L. (1988). Strategic human resource management: A review of the literature and a proposed typology. *Academy of Management Review* 13, 454–470.

Lent, R. H., Aurbach, H. D., and Levin, L. S. (1971). Predictors, criteria, and significant results. *Personnel Psychology* 24, 519–533.

Leonard, B. (1996, April). Affirmative action debated in hearings, conference panel. *HR News*, pp. 1, 11.

Lewin, A. Y., and Zwany, A. (1976). Peer nominations: A model, literature critique, and a paradigm for research. *Personnel Psychology* 29, 423–447.

Likert, R. (1967). *The human organization: Its management and value.* New York: McGraw-Hill.

Lilienfeld, S. O., Alliger, G., and Mitchell, K. (1995). Why integrity testing remains controversial. *American Psychologist* 50, 457–458.

Linn, R. L. (1973). Fair test use in selection. *Review of Educational Research* 43, 139–161.

Linn, R. L. (1978). Single-group validity, differential validity, and differential prediction. *Journal of Applied Psychology* 63, 507–512.

Linn, R. L., and Gronlund, N. E. (1995). *Measurement and assessment in teaching* (7th ed.). Englewood Cliffs, NJ: Prentice Hall.

Lin, T. R., Dobbins, G. H., and Farh, J. L. (1992). A field study of race and age similarity effects on interview ratings in conventional and situational interviews. *Journal of Applied Psychology* 77, 363–371.

Lissitz, R. W., and Green, S. B. (1975). Effects of the number of scale points on reliability: A Monte Carlo approach. *Journal of Applied Psychology* 60, 10–13.

Locke, E. A. (1968). Toward a theory of task motivation and incentives. *Organizational Behavior and Human Performance* 3, 157–189.

Locke, E. A., Frederick, E., Buckner, E., and Bobko, P. (1984). Effect of previously assigned goals on self-set goals and performance. *Journal of Applied Psychology* 69, 694–699.

Locke, E. A., and Latham, G. P. (1990). *A theory of goal setting and task performance.* Englewood Cliffs, NJ: Prentice Hall.

Locke, E. A., Latham, G. P., and Erez, M. (1988). The determinants of goal commitment. *Academy of Management Review* 13, 23–39.

Locke, E. A., Shaw, K. N., Saari, L. M., and Latham, G. P. (1981). Goal setting and task performance: 1969–1980. *Psychological Bulletin* 90, 125–152.

London, M. (1983). Toward a theory of career motivation. *Academy of Management Review* 8, 620–630.

London, M., and Bray, D. W. (1980). Ethical issues in testing and evaluation for personnel decisions. *American Psychologist* 35, 890–901.

London, M., and Stumpf, S. A. (1983). Effects of candidate characteristics on management promotion decisions: An experimental study. *Personnel Psychology* 36, 241–259.

London, M., and Wohlers, A. J. (1991). Agreement between subordinate and self-ratings in upward feedback. *Personnel Psychology* 44, 375–390.

Longenecker, C. O., and Gioia, D. A. (1992). The executive appraisal paradox. *Academy of Management Executive* 6 (2), 18–28.

Longenecker, C. O., Sims, H. P., and Gioia, D. A. (1987). Behind the mask: The politics of employee appraisal. *Academy of Management Executive* 1, 183–193.

Lopez, F. M., Jr. (1966). *Evaluating executive decision making* (Research Study 75). New York: American Management Association.

Lopez, F. M., Kesselman, G. A., and Lopez, F. E. (1981). An empirical test of a trait-oriented job analysis technique. *Personnel Psychology* 34, 479–502.

LoPresto, R. L., Mitcham, D. E., and Ripley, D. E. (1986). *Reference checking handbook.* Alexandria, VA: American Society for Personnel Administration.

Lord, F. M. (1962). Cutting scores and errors of measurement. *Psychometrika* 27, 19–30.

Lord, F. M. (1963). Elementary models for measuring change. In C. W. Harris (Ed.), *Problems in measuring change.* Madison: University of Wisconsin Press.

Lord, J. S. (1989). External and internal recruitment. In W. F. Cascio (Ed.), *Human resource planning, employment, and placement* (pp. 2-73–2-102). Washington, DC: Bureau of National Affairs.

Lowell, R. S., and DeLoach, J. A. (1982). Equal employment opportunity: Are you overlooking the application form? *Personnel* 59 (4), 49–55.

Lubatkin, M. H., Chung, K. H., Rogers, R. C., and Owers, J. E. (1989). Stockholder reactions to CEO changes in large corporations. *Academy of Management Journal* 32, 47–68.

Lubinski, D., Benbow, C. P., and Ryan, J. (1995). Stability of vocational interests among the intellectually gifted from adolescence to adulthood: A 15-year longitudinal study. *Journal of Applied Psychology* 80, 196–200.

Luchsinger, V. P., and Dock, V. T. (1982). *The systems approach: An introduction* (2nd ed.). Dubuque, IA: Kendall/Hunt.

Mabe, P. A., III, and West, S. G. (1982). Validity of self-evaluation of ability: A review and meta-analysis. *Journal of Applied Psychology* 67, 280–296.

Macan, T. H., Avedon, M. J., Paese, M., and Smith, D. E. (1994). The effects of applicants' reactions to cognitive ability tests and an assessment center. *Personnel Psychology* 47, 715–738.

Mael, F. A. (1991). A conceptual rationale for the domain and attributes of biodata items. *Personnel Psychology* 44, 763–792.

Mael, F. A., and Ashforth, B. E. (1995). Loyal from day one: Biodata, organizational identification, and turnover among newcomers. *Personnel Psychology* 48, 309–333.

Mager, R. F., and Pipe, P. (1970). *Analyzing performance problems.* Belmont, CA: Fearon.

Magjuka, R. J., and Baldwin, T. T. (1991). Team-based employee involvement programs: Effects of design and administration. *Personnel Psychology* 44, 793–812.

Maier, M. H. (1988). On the need for quality control in validation research. *Personnel Psychology* 41, 497–502.

Mainiero, L. A. (1994). Getting annointed for advancement: The case of executive women. *Academy of Management Executive* 8 (2), 53–67.

Mali, P. (1970). Measurement of obsolescence in engineering practitioners. *Continuing Education* 3, 59.

Malos, S. B., and, Campion, M. A. (1995). An options-based model of career mobility in professional service firms. *Academy of Management Review* 20, 611–644.

Mann, R. B. and Decker, P. J. (1984). The effect of key behavior distinctiveness on generalization and recall in behavior modeling training. *Academy of Management Journal* 27, 900–910.

Mantwill, M., Kohnken, G., and Aschermann, E. (1995). Effects of the cognitive interview on the recall of familiar and unfamiliar events. *Journal of Applied Psychology* 80, 68–78.

Marchese, M. C., and Muchinsky, P. M. (1993). The validity of the employment interview: A meta-analysis. *International Journal of Selection and Assessment* 1, 18–26.

Marsh, H. W., and Hocevar, D. (1988). A new, more powerful approach to multitrait-multimethod analyses: Application of second-order confirmatory factor analysis. *Journal of Applied Psychology* 73, 107–117.

Martell, R. F., and Borg, M. R. (1993). A comparison of the behavioral rating accuracy of groups and individuals. *Journal of Applied Psychology* 78, 43–50.

Martin, D. C., and Bartol, K. M. (1991). The legal ramifications of performance appraisal: An update. *Employee Relations Law Journal* 17 (2), 257–286.

Martin v. *Wilks.* (1989). U.S. Supreme Court, No. 87-1614.

Martin, C. L., and Nagao, D. H. (1989). Some effects of computerized interviewing on job applicant responses. *Journal of Applied Psychology* 74, 72–80.

Martin, S. L., and Raju, N. S. (1992). Determining cut-off scores that optimize utility: A recognition of recruiting costs. *Journal of Applied Psychology* 77, 15–23.

Martocchio, J. J. (1992). Microcomputer usage as an opportunity: The influence of context in employee training. *Personnel Psychology* 45, 529–552.

Martocchio, J. J., and Dulebohn, J. (1994). Performance feedback effects in training: The role of perceived controllability. *Personnel Psychology* 47, 358–373.

Martocchio, J. J., and Webster, J. (1992). Effects of feedback and cognitive playfulness on performance in microcomputer software training. *Personnel Psychology* 45, 553–578.

Marx, R. D. (1982). Relapse prevention for managerial training: A model for maintenance of behavior change. *Academy of Management Review* 7, 433–441.

Mathieu, J. E., and Leonard, R. L., Jr. (1987). Applying utility concepts to a training program in supervisory skills: A time-based approach. *Academy of Management Journal* 30, 316–335.

Mathieu, J. E., Martineau, J. W., and Tannenbaum, S. I. (1993). Individual and situational influences on the development of self-efficacy: Implications for training effectiveness. *Personnel Psychology* 46, 125–147.

Mathieu, J. E., Tannenbaum, S. I., and Salas, E. (1992). Influences of individual and situational characteristics on measures of training effectiveness. *Academy of Management Journal* 35, 828–847.

Matsui, T., Kakuyama, T., and Onglatco, M. L. U. (1987). Effects of goals and feedback on performance in groups. *Journal of Applied Psychology* 72, 407–415.

Maurer, S. D., and Fay, C. (1988). Effect of situational interviews, conventional structured interviews, and training on interview rating agreement: An experimental analysis. *Personnel Psychology* 41, 329–344.

Maurer, S. D., Howe, V., and Lee, T. W. (1992). Organizational recruiting as marketing management: An interdisciplinary study of engineering graduates. *Personnel Psychology* 45, 807–833.

Maurer, S. D., Palmer, J. K., and Ashe, D. K. (1993). Diaries, checklists, evaluations, and contrast effects in measurement of behavior. *Journal of Applied Psychology* 78, 226–231.

Maurer, T. J., and Alexander, R. A. (1992). Methods of improving employment test critical scores derived by judging test content: A review and critique. *Personnel Psychology* 45, 727–762.

Maurer, T. J., Alexander, R. A., Callahan, C. M., Bailey, J. J., and Dambrot, F. H. (1991). Methodological and psychometric issues in setting cutoff scores using the Angoff method. *Personnel Psychology* 44, 235–262.

Maxwell, S. E., and Arvey, R. D. (1993). The search for predictors with high validity and low adverse impact: Compatible or incompatible goals? *Journal of Applied Psychology* 78, 433–437.

Maxwell, S. E., Cole, D. A., Arvey, R. D., and Salas, E. (1991). A comparison of methods for increasing power in randomized between-subjects designs. *Psychological Bulletin* 110, 328–337.

Mayfield, E. C. (1970). Management selection: Buddy nominations revisited. *Personnel Psychology* 23, 377–391.

Mayfield, E. C. (1972). Value of peer nominations in predicting life insurance sales performance. *Journal of Applied Psychology* 56, 319–323.

McCall, M. W., Jr., Lombardo, M. M., and Morrison, A. M. (1988). *The lessons of experience: How successful executives develop on the job.* Lexington, MA: Lexington Books.

McCall, M. W., Jr., Morrison, A. M., and Hannan, R. L. (1978). *Studies of managerial work: Results and methods.* Center for Creative Leadership, TP-9, Greensboro, NC.

McCauley, C. D., Ruderman, M. N., Ohlott, P. J., and Morrow, J. E. (1994). Assessing the developmental components of managerial jobs. *Journal of Applied Psychology* 79, 544–560.

McClelland, D. C. (1975). *Power: The inner experience.* New York: Irvington-Halsted-Wiley.

McClelland, D. C., and Boyatzis, R. E. (1982). Leadership motive pattern and long-term success in management. *Journal of Applied Psychology* 67, 737–743.

McClelland, D. C., and Burnham, D. (1976, March-April). Power is the great motivator. *Harvard Business Review,* pp. 159–166.

McCormick, E. J. (1959). The development of processes for indirect or synthetic validity: III. Application of job analysis to indirect validity (a symposium). *Personnel Psychology* 12, 402–413.

McCormick, E. J. (1979). *Job analysis: Methods and applications.* New York: AMACON.

McCormick, E. J., and Ilgen, D. R. (1985). *Industrial and organizational psychology* (8th ed.). Englewood Cliffs, NJ: Prentice-Hall.

McCormick, E. J., Jeanneret, P. R., and Mecham, R. C. (1972). A study of job characteristics and job dimensions as based on the Position Analysis Questionnaire (PAQ). *Journal of Applied Psychology* 56, 347–368.

McCormick, E. J., Mecham, R. C., and Jeanneret, P. R. (1972). *Technical manual for the Position Analysis Questionnaire (PAQ).* West Lafayette, IN: PAQ Services.

McDaniel, M. A., Schmidt, F. L., and Hunter, J. E. (1988). A meta-analysis of the validity of methods for rating training and experience in personnel selection. *Personnel Psychology* 41, 283–314.

McDaniel, M. A., Whetzel, D. L., Schmidt, F. L., and Maurer, S. (1994). The validity of employment interviews: A comprehensive review and meta-analysis. *Journal of Applied Psychology* 79, 599–616.

McDonald v. *Santa Fe Transportation Co.* (1976). 96 U.S. 2574.

McDonald, T., and Hakel, M. D. (1985). Effects of applicant race, sex, suitability, and answers on interviewer's questioning strategy and ratings. *Personnel Psychology* 38, 321–334.

McDowell, J. D. (1985, March 3). Job loyalty: Not the virtue it seems. *The New York Times,* pp. 27–28.

McEvoy, G. M., and Beatty, R. W. (1989). Assessment centers and subordinate appraisals of managers: A seven-year examination of predictive validity. *Personnel Psychology* 42, 37–52.

McEvoy, G. M., and Buller, P. F. (1987). User acceptance of peer appraisals in an industrial setting. *Personnel Psychology* 40, 785–797.

McEvoy, G. M., and Cascio, W. F. (1985). Strategies for reducing employee turnover: A meta-analysis. *Journal of Applied Psychology* 70, 342–353.

McEvoy, G. M., and Cascio, W. F. (1987). Do good or poor performers leave? A meta-analysis of the relationship between performance and turnover. *Academy of Management Journal* 30, 744–762.

McEvoy, G. M., and Cascio, W. F. (1989). Cumulative evidence of the relationship between employee age and job performance. *Journal of Applied Psychology* 74, 11–17.

McGarrell, E. J., Jr. (1984). An orientation system that builds productivity. *Personnel Administrator* 29 (10), 75–85.

McGehee, W., and Thayer, P. W. (1961). *Training in business and industry.* New York: Wiley.

McGrath, J. E., and Kravitz, D. A. (1982). Group research. *Annual Review of Psychology* 33, 195–230.

McGregor, D. (1957). An uneasy look at performance appraisal. *Harvard Business Review* 35 (3), 89–94.

McHenry, J. J., Hough, L. M., Toquam, J. L., Hanson, M. A., and Ashworth, S. (1990). Project A validity results: The relationship between predictor and criterion domains. *Personnel Psychology* 43, 335–354.

McKinnon, D. W. (1975). Assessment centers then and now. *Assessment and Development* 2, 8–9.

McMorris, F. A. (1995, February 28). Is office voice mail private? Don't bet on it. *The Wall Street Journal,* p. B1.

Meehl, P. E. (1954). *Clinical vs. statistical prediction.* Minneapolis: University of Minnesota Press.

Meehl, P. E., and Rosen, A. (1955). Antecedent probability and the efficiency of psychometric signs, patterns, or cutting scores. *Psychological Bulletin* 52, 194–216.

Meglino, B. M., DeNisi, A. S., Youngblood, S. A., and Williams, K. J. (1988). Effects of realistic job previews: A comparison using an enhancement and a reduction preview. *Journal of Applied Psychology* 73, 259–266.

Memphis Fire Department v. *Stotts.* (June 12, 1984). U.S. Supreme Court, Decision No. 82–206.

Mento, A. J., Steele, R. P., and Karren, R. J. (1987). A meta-analytic study of the effects of goal setting on task performance: 1966–1984. *Organizational Behavior and Human Decision Processes* 39, 52–83.

Meritor Savings Bank v. *Vinson.* (1986). 477 U.S. 57.

Mero, N. P., and Motowidlo, S. J. (1995). Effects of rater accountability on the accuracy and the favorability of performance ratings. *Journal of Applied Psychology* 80, 517–524.

Merritt-Haston, R., and Wexley, K. N. (1983). Educational requirements: Legality and validity. *Personnel Psychology* 36, 743–753.

Messick, S. (1980). Test validity and the ethics of assessment. *American Psychologist* 35, 1012–1027.

Messick, S. (1995). Validity of psychological assessment. *American Psychologist* 50, 741–749.

Meyer, H. H. (1975, Winter). The pay-for-performance dilemma. *Organizational Dynamics,* pp. 39–50.

Meyer, H. H. (1987). Predicting supervisory ratings versus promotional progress in test validation studies. *Journal of Applied Psychology* 72, 696–697.

Meyer, H. H. (1991). A solution to the performance appraisal feedback enigma. *Academy of Management Executive* 5 (1), 68–76.

Miceli, M. P., and Near, J. P. (1988). Individual and situational correlates of whistle-blowing. *Personnel Psychology* 41, 267–281.

Miceli, M. P., and Near, J. P. (1992). *Blowing the whistle: The organizational and legal implications for companies and employees.* Lexington, MA: Lexington Books.

Miceli, M. P., and Near, J. P. (1994). Whistleblowing: Reaping the benefits. *Academy of Management Executive* 8 (3), 65–72.

Miller, C. C., and Cardinal, L. B. (1994). Strategic planning and firm performance: A synthesis of more than two decades of research. *Academy of Management Journal* 37, 1649–1665.

Miller, D. (1993). Some organizational consequences of CEO succession. *Academy of Management Journal* 36, 644–659.

Miller, E. C. (1980). An EEO examination of employment applications. *Personnel Administrator* 25 (3), 63–69, 81.

Millsap, R. E., and Hartog, S. B. (1988). Alpha, beta, and gamma change in evaluation research: A structural equation approach. *Journal of Applied Psychology* 73, 574–584.

Miner, J. B. (1978a). The Miner Sentence Completion Scale: A reappraisal. *Academy of Management Journal* 21, 283–294.

Miner, J. B. (1978b). Twenty years of research on role-motivation theory of managerial effectiveness. *Personnel Psychology* 31, 739–760.

Miner, J. B., and Crane, D. P. (1981). Motivation to manage and the manifestation of a managerial orientation in career planning. *Academy of Management Journal* 24, 626–633.

Miner, J. B., and Smith, N. R. (1982). Decline and stabilization of managerial motivation over a 20-year period. *Journal of Applied Psychology* 67, 297–305.

Miner, J. B., Smith, N. R., and Bracker, J. S. (1994). Role of entrepreneurial task motivation in the growth of technologically innovative firms: Interpretations from follow-up data. *Journal of Applied Psychology* 79, 627–630.

Miner, J. R. (1965). *Studies in management education.* New York: Springer.

Mirvis, P. H., and Seashore, S. E. (1979). Being ethical in organizational research. *American Psychologist* 34, 766–780.

Mitchell, T. W. (1989, October). *Are weighted application data valid and legal?* Paper presented at the National Assessment Conference, Minneapolis.

Mitchell, T. W. (1994). Catalog of biodata items. San Diego, CA: MPORT.

Mitsch, R. J. (1983). Ensuring privacy and accuracy of computerized employee records. *Personnel Administrator* 28 (9), 37–41.

Moore, M. L., and Dutton, P. (1978). Training needs analysis: Review and critique. *Academy of Management Review* 3, 532–545.

Morano, R. (1973). Determining organizational training needs. *Personnel Psychology* 26, 479–487.

More normal nonsense. (1989, July 17). *Fortune,* p. 118.

Morgan, J. P. (1989, August 20). Employee drug tests are unreliable and intrusive. *Hospitals,* p. 42.

Morgan, R. B. (1993). Self- and co-worker perceptions of ethics and their relationships to leadership and salary. *Academy of Management Journal* 36, 200–214.

Morrison, R. F. (1977). A multivariate model for the occupational placement decision. *Journal of Applied Psychology* 62, 271–277.

Mosel, J. N., and Cozan, C. W. (1952). The accuracy of application blank work histories. *Journal of Applied Psychology* 36, 365–369.

Moses, J. L., and Boehm, V. R. (1975). Relationship of assessment center performance to management progress of women. *Journal of Applied Psychology* 60, 527–529.

Mossholder, K. W. (1980). Effects of externally mediated goal setting on intrinsic motivation: A laboratory experiment. *Journal of Applied Psychology* 65, 202–210.

Mossholder, K. W., and Arvey, R. D. (1984). Synthetic validity: A conceptual and comparative review. *Journal of Applied Psychology* 69, 322–333.

Most Small Businesses Appear Prepared to Cope With New Family-Leave Rules. (1993, February 8). *The Wall Street Journal,* pp. B1, B2.

Motowidlo, S. J., Carter, G. W., Dunnette, M. D., Tippins, N., Werner, S., Burnett, J. R., and Vaughn, M. J. (1992). Studies of the structured behavioral interview. *Journal of Applied Psychology* 77, 571–587.

Motowidlo, S. J., and Van Scotter, J. R. (1994). Evidence that task performance should be distinguished from contextual performance. *Journal of Applied Psychology* 79, 475–480.

Mount, M. K. (1983). Comparison of managerial and employee satisfaction with a performance appraisal system. *Personnel Psychology* 36, 99–110.

Mount, M. K. (1984). Psychometric properties of subordinate ratings of managerial performance. *Personnel Psychology* 37, 687–702.

Mount, M. K., Barrick, M. R., and Strauss, P. (1994). Validity of observer ratings of the Big Five personality factors. *Journal of Applied Psychology* 79, 272–280.

Mount, M. K., and Thompson, D. E. (1987). Cognitive categorization and quality of performance ratings. *Journal of Applied Psychology* 72, 240–246.

Mullins, C., and Ratliff, F. R. (1979, March). *Application of a generalized development curve to problems in human assessment.* Paper presented at the U.S. Air Force Human Resources Laboratory Conference on Human Assessment, Brooks Air Force Base, Texas.

Mullins, W. C., and Kimbrough, W. W. (1988). Group composition as a determinant of job analysis outcomes. *Journal of Applied Psychology* 73, 657–664.

Mumford, M. D. (1983). Social comparison theory and the evaluation of peer evaluations: A review and some applied implications. *Personnel Psychology* 36, 867–881.

Mumford, M. D., and Owens, W. A. (1987). Methodology review: Principles, procedures, and findings in the application of background data measures. *Applied Psychological Measurement* 11, 1–31.

Mumford. M. D., and Stokes, G. S. (1992). Developmental determinants of individual action: Theory and practice in applying background measures. In M. D. Dunnette and L. M. Hough (Eds.), *Handbook of industrial and organizational psychology* (2nd ed, Vol. 3, pp. 61–138). Palo Alto, CA: Consulting Psychologists Press.

Mumford, M. D., Weeks, J. L., Harding, F. D., and Fleishman, E. A. (1988). Relations between student characteristics, course content, and training outcomes: An integrative modeling effort. *Journal of Applied Psychology* 73, 443–456.

Munson, J. M., and Posner, B. Z. (1980). Concurrent validation of two value inventories in predicting job classification and success for organizational personnel. *Journal of Applied Psychology* 65, 563–542.

Murphy, K. R. (1983). Fooling yourself with cross-validation: Single-sample designs. *Personnel Psychology* 36, 111–118.

Murphy, K. R. (1984). Cost-benefit considerations in choosing among cross-validation methods. *Personnel Psychology* 37, 15–22.

Murphy, K. R. (1986). When your top choice turns you down: Effect of rejected offers on the utility of selection tests. *Psychological Bulletin* 99, 133–138.

Murphy, K. R. (1987). Detecting infrequent deception. *Journal of Applied Psychology* 72, 611–614.

Murphy, K. R. (1994). Potential effects of banding as a function of test reliability. *Personnel Psychology* 47, 477–495.

Murphy, K. R., and Balzer, W. K. (1989). Rater errors and rating accuracy. *Journal of Applied Psychology* 74, 619–624.

Murphy, K. R., and Cleveland, J. N. (1991). *Performance appraisal: An organizational perspective.* Boston: Allyn & Bacon.

Murphy, K. R., and Constans, J. I. (1987). Behavioral anchors as a source of bias in ratings. *Journal of Applied Psychology* 72, 573–577.

Murphy, K. R., Jako, R. A., and Anhalt, R. L. (1993). Nature and consequences of halo error: A critical analysis. *Journal of Applied Psychology* 78, 218–225.

Murphy, K. R., Osten, K., and Myors, B. (1995). Modeling the effects of banding in personnel selection. *Personnel Psychology* 48, 61–84.

Murphy, K. R., and Myors, B. (1995). Evaluating the logical critique of banding. *Human Performance* 8 (3), 201.

Murphy, K. R., and Pardaffy, V. A. (1989). Bias in behaviorally anchored rating scales: Global or scale-specific? *Journal of Applied Psychology* 74, 343–346.

Murphy, K. R., Thornton, G. C., III, and Prue, K. (1991). Influence of job characteristics on the acceptability of employee drug testing. *Journal of Applied Psychology* 76, 447–453.

Nagle, B. F. (1953). Criterion development. *Personnel Psychology* 6, 271–288.

Nathan, B. R., and Cascio, W. F. (1986). Technical and legal standards for performance assessment. In R. A. Berk (Ed.), *Performance Management.* Baltimore: Johns Hopkins University Press.

Naylor, J. C., and Shine, L. C. (1965). A table for determining the increase in mean criterion score obtained by using a selection device. *Journal of Industrial Psychology* 3, 33–42.

Near, J. P., and Miceli, M. P. (1995). Effective whistle-blowing. *Academy of Management Review* 20, 679–708.

Nellis, S., and Lane, F. (1995, Spring). A second look at AT&T's Global Business Communications Systems. *Organizational Dynamics,* pp. 72–76.

Neiner, A. G., and Owens, W. A. (1982). Relationships between two sets of biodata with 7 years separation. *Journal of Applied Psychology* 67, 146–150.

Neiner, A. G., and Owens, W. A. (1985). Using biodata to predict job choice among college graduates. *Journal of Applied Psychology* 70, 127–136.

Nelan, B. W. (1992, Fall). How the world will look in 50 years. *Time* (Special Issue: Beyond the Year 2000), pp. 36–38.

Neuman, G. A., Edwards, J. E., and Raju, N. S. (1989). Organization development interventions: A meta-analysis of their effects on satisfaction and other attitudes. *Personnel Psychology* 42, 461–489.

Newstrom, J. W. (1978). Catch 22: The problems of incomplete evaluation of training. *Training and Development Journal* 32, 22–24.

Nicholas, J. M. (1982). The comparative impact of organization development on hard criteria measures. *Academy of Management Review* 7, 531–542.

Nicholas, J. M., and Katz, M. (1985). Research methods and reporting practices in organization development: A review and some guidelines. *Academy of Management Review* 10, 737–749.

1994 AMA survey on downsizing and assistance to displaced workers. New York: American Management Association.

Nobile, R. J. (1985). Employee searches in the workplace: Developing a realistic policy. *Personnel Administrator* 30 (5), 89–98.

Noe, R. A. (1986). Trainees' attributes and attitudes: Neglected influences on training effectiveness. *Academy of Management Review* 11, 736–749.

Noe, R. A., and Wilk, S. L. (1993). Investigation of the factors that influence employees' participation in development activities. *Journal of Applied Psychology* 78, 291–302.

No letup in U.S. layoffs. (1995, September 11). *Business Week,* p. 26.

Nord, R., and Schmitz, E. (1991). Estimating performance and utility effects of alternative selection and classification policies. In J. Zeidner and C. D. Johnson (Eds.), *The economic benefits of predicting job performance: Vol. 3. The gains of alternative policies.* New York: Praeger.

Norborg, J. M. (1984). A warning regarding the simplified approach to the evaluation of test fairness in employee selection procedures. *Personnel Psychology* 37, 483–486.

O'Boyle, T. F. (1985, July 11). Loyalty ebbs at many companies as employees grow disillusioned. *Wall Street Journal,* p. 29.

O'Connor, E. J., Wexley, K. N., and Alexander, R. A. (1975). Single group validity: Fact or fallacy? *Journal of Applied Psychology* 60, 352–355.

OFCCP: Making EEO and affirmative action work. (1979). Washington, DC: U.S. Department of Labor, Employment Standards Administration.

OFCCP enforcement. (1995, April). *HR News,* p. 4.

Office of Strategic Services (OSS) Assessment Staff. (1948). *Assessment of men.* New York: Rinehart.

Office of the American Workplace. (1994). *Promoting world-class workplaces.* Washington, DC: U.S. Department of Labor.

Officers for Justice v. *Civil Service Commission of the City and County of San Francisco,* (9th Cir. 1992). 979 F.2d 721. *Cert. denied.* (March 29, 1993). 61 *U.S. L. W.* 3367, 113 S. Ct. 1645.

Olson, H. C., Fine, S. A., Myers, D. C., and Jennings, M. C. (1981). The use of functional job analysis in establishing performance standards for heavy equipment operators. *Personnel Psychology* 34, 351–364.

Ones, D. S., Mount, M. K., Barrick, M. R., and Hunter, J. E. (1994). Personality and job performance: A critique of the Tett, Jackson, and Rothstein (1991) meta-analysis. *Personnel Psychology* 47, 147–156.

Ones, D. S., Viswesvaran, C., and Schmidt, F. L. (1993). Comprehensive meta-analysis of integrity test validities: Findings and implications for personnel selection and theories of job performance. *Journal of Applied Psychology* 78, 679–703.

Oppler, S. H., Campbell, J. P., Pulakos, E. D., and Borman, W. C. (1992). Three approaches to the investigation of subgroup bias in performance measurement: Review, results, and conclusions. *Journal of Applied Psychology* 77, 201–217.

O'Reilly, C. A. III, Chatman, J., and Caldwell, D. F. (1991). People and organizational culture: A profile comparison approach to assessing person-oganization fit. *Academy of Management Journal* 34, 487–516.

Orr, J. M., Sackett, P. R., and Mercer, M. (1989). The role of prescribed and nonprescribed behaviors in estimating the dollar value of performance. *Journal of Applied Psychology* 74, 34–40.

Osburn, H. G., and Callender, J. (1992). A note on the sampling variance of the mean uncorrected correlation in meta-analysis and validity generalization. *Journal of Applied Psychology* 77, 115–122.

Ostroff, C. (1991). Training effectiveness measures and scoring schemes: A comparison. *Personnel Psychology* 44, 353–374.

Outreach and recruitment directory: A resource for diversity-related recruitment needs. (1995). Columbia, MD: Berkshire Associates, Inc.

Overman, S. (1994). Best ways to go for AA, avoiding ad scams along the way. *HR Magazine* 39 (12), 60–64.

Overman, S. (1995). Cruising cyberspace for the best recruits. *HR Magazine* 40 (2), 52–55.

Owens, W. A. (1968). Toward one discipline of scientific psychology. *American Psychologist* 23, 782–785.

Owens, W. A. (1971). A quasi-actuarial prospect for individual assessment. *American Psychologist* 26, 992–999.

Owens, W. A. (1976). Background data. In M. D. Dunnette (Ed.), *Handbook of industrial and organizational psychology.* Chicago: Rand McNally.

Owens, W. A. (1978). Moderators and subgroups. *Personnel Psychology* 31, 243–247.

Owens, W. A., and Schoenfeldt, L. F. (1979). Toward a classification of persons. *Journal of Applied Psychology* 65, 569–607.

Pace, L. A., and Schoenfeldt, L. F. (1977). Legal concerns in the use of weighted applications. *Personnel Psychology* 30, 159–166.

Paese, P. W., and Switzer, F. S., III. (1988). Validity generalization and hypothetical reliability distributions: A test of the Schmidt-Hunter procedure. *Journal of Applied Psychology* 73, 273–274.

Page, R. C., and Van De Voort, D. M. (1989). Job analysis and HR planning. In W. F. Cascio (Ed.), *Human resource planning, employment, and placement* (pp. 2-34–2-72). Washington, DC: Bureau of National Affairs.

Panel reports sex disparity in engineering. (1985, December 26). *New York Times,* p. A15.

Parsons, C. K., and Liden, R. C. (1984). Interviewer perceptions of applicant qualifications: A multivariate field study of demographic characteristics and nonverbal cues. *Journal of Applied Psychology* 69, 557–568.

Pearce, J. A., II, and Robinson, R. B., Jr. (1989). *Management.* New York: Random House.

Pearlman, K. (1980). Job families: A review and discussion of their implications for personnel selection. *Psychological Bulletin* 87, 1–28.

Personnel Administrator of Mass. v. Feeney. (1979, June 5). 19 FEP cases 1377.

Peters, T., and Austin, N. (1985). *A passion for excellence.* New York: Random House.

Peters, T. J., and Waterman, R. H., Jr. (1982). *In search of excellence.* New York: Warner.

Petersen, N. S., and Novick, M. R. (1976). An evaluation of some models for culture-fair selection. *Journal of Educational Measurement* 13, 3–29.

Petty, M. M. (1974). A multivariate analysis of the effects of experience and training upon performance in a leaderless group discussion. *Personnel Psychology* 27, 271–282.

Pffefer, J. (1994). *Competitive advantage through people.* Boston: Harvard Business School Press, p. 8.

Phillips, A. P., and Dipboye, R. L. (1989). Correlational tests of predictions from a process model of the interview. *Journal of Applied Psychology* 74, 41–52.

Piller, C. (1993a, July). Privacy in peril. *Macworld,* pp. 124–130.

Piller, C. (1993b, July). Bosses with X-ray eyes. *Macworld,* pp. 118–123.

Pingitore, R., Dugoni, B. L., Tindale, R. S., and Spring, B. (1994). Bias against overweight job applicants in a simulated employment interview. *Journal of Applied Psychology* 79, 909–917.

Plevel, M. J., Lane, F., Nellis, S., and Schuler, R. S. (1994, Winter). AT&T Global Business Communications Systems: Linking HR With Business Strategy. *Organizational Dynamics,* pp. 59–71.

Plumlee, L. B. (1980, February). *A short guide to the development of work sample and performance tests* (2nd ed.). Washington, DC: U.S. Office of Personnel Management, Personnel Research and Development Center.

Podsakoff, P. M., and MacKenzie, S. B. (1994). An examination of the psychometric properties and nomological validities of some revised and reduced substitutes for leadership scales. *Journal of Applied Psychology* 79, 702–713.

Porras, J. I., and Anderson, B. (1981). Improving managerial effectiveness through modeling-based training. *Organizational Dynamics* 9 (4), 60–77.

Porter, L. W., Lawler, E. E., III, and Hackman, J. R. (1975). *Behavior in organizations.* New York: McGraw-Hill.

Powell, G. N. (1991). Applicant reactions to the initial employment interview: Exploring theoretical and methodological issues. *Personnel Psychology* 44, 67–83.

Powell, G. N., and Butterfield, D. A. (1994). Investigating the "glass ceiling" phenomenon: An empirical study of actual promotions to top management. *Academy of Management Journal* 37, 68–86.

Power, D. J., and Aldag, R. J. (1985). Soelberg's job search and choice model: A clarification, review, and critique. *Academy of Management Review* 10, 48–58.

Prahalad, C. K. and Hamel, G. (1994). *Competing for the future.* Boston: Harvard Business School Press.

Pregnancy and employment: The complete handbook on discrimination, maternity leave, and health and safety (1987). Washington, DC: Bureau of National Affairs.

Pritchard, R. D., Jones, S. D., Roth, P. L., Stuebing, K. K., and Ekeberg, S. E. (1988). Effects of group feedback, goal setting, and incentive on organizational productivity. *Journal of Applied Psychology* 73, 337–358.

Pulakos, E. D. (1984). A comparison of rater training programs: Error training and accuracy training. *Journal of Applied Psychology* 69, 581–588.

Pulakos, E. D. (1986). The development of training programs to increase accuracy with different rating tasks. *Organizational Behavior and Human Decision Processes* 38, 76–91.

Pulakos, E. D., Borman, W. C., and Hough, L. M. (1988). Test validation for scientific understanding: Two demonstrations of an approach to studying predictor-criterion linkages. *Personnel Psychology* 41, 703–716.

Pulakos, E. D., and Schmitt, N. (1995). Experience-based and situational interview questions: Studies of validity. *Personnel Psychology* 48, 289–308.

Punnett, B. J., and Shenkar, O. (1996). Ethics in international management research. In B. J. Punnett and O. Shenkar (Eds.), *Handbook for International Management Research* (pp. 145–154). Cambridge, MA: Blackwell.

Quaintance, M. K. (1989). Internal placement and career management. In W. F. Cascio (Ed.), *Human resource planning, employment, and placement* (pp. 2-200–2-235). Washington, DC: Bureau of National Affairs.

Quinones, M. A. (1995). Pretraining context effects: Training assignment as feedback. *Journal of Applied Psychology* 80, 226–238.

Raju, N. S., Burke, M. J., and Maurer, T. J. (1995). A note on direct range restriction corrections in utility analysis. *Personnel Psychology* 48, 143–149.

Raju, N. S., Burke, M. J., Normand, J., and Langlois, G. M. (1991). A new meta-analytic approach. *Journal of Applied Psychology* 76, 432–446.

Raju, N. S., Edwards, J. E., LoVerde, M. A. (1985). Corrected formulas for computing sample sizes under indirect range restriction. *Journal of Applied Psychology* 70, 565–566.

Rambo, W. W., Chomiak, A. M., and Price, J. M. (1983). Consistency of performance under stable conditions of work. *Journal of Applied Psychology* 68, 78–87.

Rasch, G. (1966). An item analysis which takes individual differences into account. *British Journal of Mathematical and Statistical Psychology* 19, 49–57.

Rasmussen, J. L., and Loher, B. T. (1988). Appropriate critical percentages for the Schmidt and Hunter meta-analysis procedure: Comparative evaluation of Type I error rate and power. *Journal of Applied Psychology* 73, 683–687.

Rasmussen, K. G., Jr. (1984). Nonverbal behavior, verbal behavior, resume credentials, and selection interview outcomes. *Journal of Applied Psychology* 69, 551–556.

Reber, R. A., and Wallin, J. A. (1984). The effects of training, goal setting, and knowledge of results on safe behavior: A component analysis. *Academy of Management Journal* 27, 544–560.

Ree, M. J., Carretta, T. R., Earles, J. A., and Albert, W. (1994). Sign changes when correcting for range restriction: A note on Pearson's and Lawley's selection formulas. *Journal of Applied Psychology* 79, 298–301.

Ree, M. J., and Earles, J. A. (1991). Predicting training success: Not much more than *g*. *Personnel Psychology* 44, 321–332.

Ree, M. J., Earles, J. A., and Teachout, M. S. (1994). Predicting job performance: Not much more than *g*. *Journal of Applied Psychology* 79, 518–524.

Reeb, M. (1976). Differential test validity for ethnic groups in the Israel Army and the effects of educational level. *Journal of Applied Psychology* 61, 253–261.

Reese, H. W., and Fremouw, W. J. (1984). Normal and normative ethics in behavioral sciences. *American Psychologist* 39, 863–876.

Reilly, R. R., and Chao, G. T. (1982). Validity and fairness of some alternative employee selection procedures. *Personnel Psychology* 35, 1–62.

Reilly, R. R., and Israelski, E. W. (1988). Development and validation of minicourses in the telecommunication industry. *Journal of Applied Psychology* 73, 721–726.

Reilly, R. R., and Manese, W. R. (1979). The validation of a minicourse for telephone company switching technicians. *Personnel Psychology* 32, 83–90.

Reilly, R. R., Zedeck, S., and Tenopyr, M. L. (1979). Validity and fairness of physical ability tests for predicting performance in craft jobs. *Journal of Applied Psychology* 64, 262–274.

Replying in the affirmative (1987, March 9). *Time,* p. 66.

Report of the Scientific Affairs Committee. (1994). An evaluation of banding methods in personnel selection. *The Industrial/Organizational Psychologist* 32 (1), 80–86.

Reynolds, L. G., Masters, S. H., and Moser, C. H. (1986). *Labor economics and labor relations* (9th ed). Englewood Cliffs, NJ: Prentice Hall.

Rich, L. L. (1995). Right to privacy in the workplace in the information age. *Colorado Lawyer* 24 (3), 539–540.

Richards, S. A., and Jaffee, C. L. (1972). Blacks supervising whites: A study of inter-racial difficulties in working together in a simulated organization. *Journal of Applied Psychology* 56, 234–240.

Ricks, J. R., Jr. (1971). *Local norms: When and why.* Test Service Bulletin No. 58. New York: The Psychological Corporation.

Rigdon, J. E. (1992, June 17). Deceptive résumés can be door openers but can become an employee's undoing. *The Wall Street Journal,* pp. B1, B7.

Ritchie, R. J., and Beardsley, V. D. (1978). A market research approach to determining local labor market availability for nonmanagement jobs. *Personnel Psychology* 31, 449–459.

Ritchie, R. J., and Moses, J. L. (1983). Assessment center correlates of women's advancement into middle management: A 7-year longitudinal analysis. *Journal of Applied Psychology* 68, 227–231.

Robertson, I., and Downs, S. (1979). Learning and the prediction of performance: Development of trainability testing in the United Kingdom. *Journal of Applied Psychology* 64, 42–50.

Robertson, I. T., and Downs, S. (1989). Work-sample tests of trainability: A meta-analysis. *Journal of Applied Psychology* 74, 402–410.

Robbins, T., and DeNisi, A. S. (1994). A closer look at interpersonal affect as a distinct influence on cognitive processing in performance evaluations. *Journal of Applied Psychology* 79, 341–353.

Rodgers, R., and Hunter, J. E. (1991). Impact of management by objectives on organizational productivity. *Journal of Applied Psychology* 76, 322–336.

Rodgers, R., Hunter, J. E., and Rogers, D. L. (1993). Influence of top management commitment on management program success. *Journal of Applied Psychology* 78, 151–155.

Rogers, T. B. (1995). *The psychological testing enterprise: An introduction.* Pacific Grove, CA: Brooks/Cole.

Ronan, W. W., and Prien, E. P. (1966). *Toward a criterion theory: A review and analysis of research and opinion.* Greensboro, NC: The Richardson Foundation.

Ronan, W. W., and Prien, E. P. (1971). *Perspectives on the measurement of human performance.* New York: Appleton-Century-Crofts.

Rose, G. L., and Brief, A. P. (1979). Effects of handicap and job characteristics on selection evaluations. *Personnel Psychology* 32, 385–392.

Rosen, B., and Jerdee, T. H. (1976). The nature of job-related age stereotypes on managerial decisions. *Journal of Applied Psychology* 61, 180–183.

Rosen, N. A. (1961). How supervise?—1943–1960. *Personnel Psychology* 49, 87–100.

Rosenthal, R. (1991). *Meta-analytic procedures for social research* (Rev. ed.). Beverly Hills, CA: Sage.

Rosenthal, R., and Rosnow, R. L. (1984). *Essentials of behavioral research: Methods and data analysis.* New York: McGraw-Hill.

Rosnow, R. L., and Rosenthal, R. (1989). Statistical procedures and the justification of knowledge in psychological science. *American Psychologist* 44, 1276–1284.

Rothaus, P., Morton, R. B., and Hanson, P. G. (1965). Performance appraisal and psychological distance. *Journal of Applied Psychology* 49, 48–54.

Rothe, H. F. (1978). Output rates among industrial employees. *Journal of Applied Psychology* 63, 40–46.

Rousseau, D. M. (1982). Job perceptions when working with data, people, and things. *Journal of Occupational Psychology* 55, 43–52.

Rowe, P. M. (1960). *Individual differences in assessment decisions.* Unpublished doctoral dissertation. McGill University, Montreal.

Rowe, P. M. (1963). Individual differences in selection decisions. *Journal of Applied Psychology* 47, 304–307.

Rulon, P. J., Tiedeman, D. V., Tatsuoka, M. M., and Langmuir, C. R. (1967). *Multivariate statistics for personnel classification.* New York: Wiley.

Rush, C. H., Jr. (1953). A factorial study of sales criteria. *Personnel Psychology* 6, 9–24.

Rusmore, J. T. (1967). *Pychological tests and fair employment: A study of employment testing in the San Francisco Bay area.* State of California Fair Employment Practice Commission, San Francisco, CA.

Russell, C. J., Colella, A., and Bobko, P. (1993). Expanding the context of utility: The strategic impact of personnel selection. *Personnel Psychology* 46, 781–801.

Russell, J. S. (1984). A review of fair employment cases in the field of training. *Personnel Psychology* 37, 261–276.

Russell, J. S., and Goode, D. L. (1988). An analysis of managers' reactions to their own performance appraisal feedback, *Journal of Applied Psychology* 73, 63–67.

Russell, J. S., Wexley, K. N., and Hunter, J. E. (1984). Questioning the effectiveness of behavior modeling training in an industrial setting. *Personnel Psychology* 37, 465–481.

Ryan, A. M., and Lasek, M. (1991). Negligent hiring and defamation: Arcas of liability related to preemployment inquiries. *Personnel Psychology* 44, 293–319.

Ryan, A. M., and Sackett, P. R. (1987). A survey of individual assessment practices by I/O psychologists. *Personnel Psychology* 40, 455–488.

Ryan, A. M., and Sackett, P. R. (1989). Exploratory study of individual assessment practices: Interrater reliability and judgments of assessor effectiveness. *Journal of Applied Psychology* 74, 568–579.

Ryans, D. G., and Fredericksen, N. (1951). Performance tests of educational achievement. In E. F. Lindquist (Ed.), *Educational measurement.* Washington, DC: American Council on Education.

Ryman, D. H., and Biersner, R. J. (1975). Attitudes predictive of diving training success. *Personnel Psychology* 28, 181–188.

Rynes, S. L. (1991). Recruitment, job choice, and post-hire consequences: A call for new research directions. In M. D. Dunnette and L. M. Hough (Eds.), *Handbook of industrial and organizational psychology* (2nd ed., Vol. 2, pp. 399–444). Palo Alto, CA: Consulting Psychologists Press.

Rynes, S. L., Bretz, R. D., and Gerhart, B. (1991). The importance of recruitment in job choice: A different way of looking. *Personnel Psychology* 44, 487–521.

Rynes, S. L, Heneman, H. G., III, and Schwab, D. P. (1980). Individual reactions to organizational recruiting: A review. *Personnel Psychology* 33, 529–542.

Rynes, S. L., and Miller, H. E. (1983). Recruiter and job influences on candidates for employment. *Journal of Applied Psychology* 68, 147–154.

Saal, F. E., Downey, R. G., and Lahey, M. A. (1980). Rating the ratings: Assessing the psychometric quality of rating data. *Psychological Bulletin* 88, 413–428.

Saari, L. M., Johnson, T. R., McLaughlin, S. D., and Zimmerle, D. M. (1988). A survey of management training and education practices in U.S. companies. *Personnel Psychology* 41, 731–743.

Sackett, P. R. (1987). Assessment centers and content validity: Some neglected issues. *Personnel Psychology* 40, 13–25.

Sackett, P. R. (1991). On interpreting measures of change due to training or other interventions: A comment on Cascio (1989, 1991). *Journal of Applied Psychology* 76, 590–591.

Sackett, P. R., Cornelius, E. T., and Carron, T. J. (1981). A comparison of global judgment vs. task-oriented approaches to job classification. *Personnel Psychology* 34, 791–804.

Sackett, P. R., and DuBois, C. L. Z. (1991). Rater-ratee race effects on performance evaluation: Challenging meta-analytic conclusions. *Journal of Applied Psychology* 76, 873–877.

Sackett, P. R., DuBois, C. L. Z., and Noe, A. W. (1991). Tokenism in performance evaluation: The effects of work group representation on male-female and white-black differences in performance ratings. *Journal of Applied Psychology* 76, 263–267.

Sackett, P. R., and Hakel, M. D. (1979). Temporal stability and individual differences in using assessment information to form overall ratings. *Organizational Behavior and Human Performance* 23, 120–137.

Sackett, P. R., Harris, M. M., and Orr, J. M. (1986). On seeking moderator variables in the meta-analysis of correlational data: A Monte Carlo investigation of statistical power and resistance to Type I error. *Journal of Applied Psychology* 71, 302–310.

Sackett, P. R., and Mullen, E. J. (1993). Beyond formal experimental design: Towards an expanded view of the training evaluation process. *Personnel Psychology* 46, 613–627.

Sackett, P. R., and Roth, L. (1991). A Monte Carlo examination of banding and rank order methods of test score use in personnel selection. *Human Performance* 4, 279–295.

Sackett, P. R., and Wilk, S. L. (1994). Within-group norming and other forms of score adjustment in pre-employment testing. *American Psychologist* 49, 929–954.

Sagie, A., and Koslowsky, M. (1993). Detecting moderators with meta-analysis: An evaluation and comparison of techniques. *Personnel Psychology* 46, 629–640.

Saks, A. M. (1995). Longitudinal field investigation of the moderating and mediating effects of self-efficacy on the relationship between training and newcomer adjustment. *Journal of Applied Psychology* 80, 211–225.

Salinger, R. D. (1973). *Disincentives to effective employee training and development.* Washington, DC: U.S. Civil Service Commission, Bureau of Training.

Sanchez, J. I., and Fraser, S. L. (1992). On the choice of scales for task analysis. *Journal of Applied Psychology* 77, 545–553.

Sands, W. A. (1973). A method for evaluating alternative recruiting-selection strategies: The CAPER model. *Journal of Applied Psychology* 57, 222–227.

Sands, W. A., Alf, E. F., Jr., and Abrahams, N. M. (1978). Correction of validity coefficients for direct restriction in range occasioned by univariate selection. *Journal of Applied Psychology* 63, 747–750.

Saunders, D. R. (1956). Moderator variables in prediction. *Educational and Psychological Measurement* 16, 209–222.

Sawyer, J. (1966). Measurement and prediction, clinical and statistical. *Psychological Bulletin* 66, 178–200.

Saxe, L., Dougherty, D., and Cross, T. (1985). The validity of polygraph testing. *American Psychologist* 40, 355–366.

Schein, E. H. (1980). *Organizational Psychology* (3rd. ed.). Englewood Cliffs, NJ: Prentice-Hall.

Schein, E. H. (1983). The role of the founder in creating organization culture. *Organization Dynamics* 11, 13–28.

Schein, E. H. (1989, Spring). Conversation with Edgar H. Schein. *Organizational Dynamics* 17, 60–76.

Schermerhorn, J. R., Jr., Hunt, J. G., and Osborn, R. N. (1994). *Managing organizational behavior* (5th ed.). New York: Wiley.

Schmidt, F. L. (1971). The relative efficiency of regression and simple unit predictor weights in applied differential psychology. *Educational and Psychological Measurement* 31, 699–714.

Schmidt, F. L. (1988). The problem of group differences in ability test scores in employment selection. *Journal of Vocational Behavior* 33, 272–292.

Schmidt, F. L. (1991). Why all banding procedures in personnel selection are logically flawed. *Human Performance* 4 (4), 265–277.

Schmidt, F. L. (1992). What do data really mean? Research findings, meta-analysis, and cumulative knowledge in psychology. *American Psychologist* 47, 1173–1181.

Schmidt, F. L., Berner, J. G., and Hunter, J. E. (1973). Racial differences in validity of employment tests: Reality or illusion? *Journal of Applied Psychology* 58, 5–6.

Schmidt, F. L., Greenthal, A. L., Hunter, J. E., Berner, J. G., and Seaton, F. W. (1977). Job sample vs. paper-and-pencil trades and technical tests: Adverse impact and examinee attitudes. *Personnel Psychology* 30, 187–197.

Schmidt, F. L., and Hunter, J. E. (1974). Racial and ethnic bias in psychological tests: Divergent implications of two definitions of test bias. *American Psychologist* 29, 1–8.

Schmidt, F. L., and Hunter, J. E. (1977). Development of a general solution to the problem of validity generalization. *Journal of Applied Psychology* 62, 529–540.

Schmidt, F. L., and Hunter, J. E. (1978). Moderator research and the law of small numbers. *Personnel Psychology* 31, 215–232.

Schmidt, F. L., and Hunter, J. E. (1981). Employment testing: Old theories and new research. *American Psychologist* 36, 1128–1137.

Schmidt, F. L., and Hunter, J. E. (1983). Individual differences in productivity: An empirical test of estimates derived from studies of selection procedure utility. *Journal of Applied Psychology* 68, 407–414.

Schmidt, F. L., and Hunter, J. E. (1989). Interrater reliability coefficients cannot be computed when only one stimulus is rated. *Journal of Applied Psychology* 74, 368–370.

Schmidt, F. L., and Hunter, J. E. (1995). The fatal internal contradiction in banding: Its statistical rationale is logically inconsistent with its operational procedures. *Human Performance* 8 (3), 203–214.

Schmidt, F. L., Hunter, J. E., McKenzie, R. C., and Muldrow, T. W. (1979). Impact of valid selection procedures on work-force productivity. *Journal of Applied Psychology* 64, 609–626.

Schmidt. F. L., Hunter, J. E., and Pearlman, K. (1981). Task differences as moderators of aptitude test validity in selection: A red herring. *Journal of Applied Psychology* 66, 166–185.

Schmidt, F. L., Hunter, J. E., and Pearlman, K. (1982). Assessing the economic impact of personnel programs on productivity. *Personnel Psychology* 35, 333–347.

Schmidt, F. L., Hunter, J. E., Pearlman, K., Hirsch, H. R., Sackett, P. R., Schmitt, N., Tenopyr, M. L., Kehoe, J., and Zedeck, S. (1985). Forty questions about validity generalization and meta-analysis with commentaries. *Personnel Psychology* 38, 697–798.

Schmidt, F. L., Hunter, J. E., and Raju, N. S. (1988). Validity generalization and situational specificity: A second look at the 75% rule and Fisher's z transformation. *Journal of Applied Psychology* 73, 665–672.

Schmidt, F. L., Hunter, J. E., and Urry, V. W. (1976). Statistical power in criterion-related validity studies. *Journal of Applied Psychology* 61, 473–485.

Schmidt, F. L., and Kaplan, L. B. (1971). Composite vs. multiple criteria: A review and resolution of the controversy. *Personnel Psychology* 24, 419–434.

Schmidt, F. L., Law, K., Hunter, J. E., Rothstein, H. R., Pearlman, K., and McDaniel, M. (1993). Refinements in validity generalization methods: Implications for the situational specificity hypothesis. *Journal of Applied Psychology* 78, 3–12.

Schmidt, F. L., Mack, M. J., and Hunter, J. E. (1984). Selection utility in the occupation of U.S. Park Ranger for three modes of test use. *Journal of Applied Psychology* 69, 490–497.

Schmidt, F. L., Pearlman, K., and Hunter, J. E. (1980). The validity and fairness of employment and educational tests for Hispanic Americans: A review and analysis. *Personnel Psychology* 33, 705–724.

Schmit, M. J., Ryan, A. M., Stierwalt, S. L., and Powell, A. B. (1995). Frame-of-reference effects on personality scale scores and criterion-related validity. *Journal of Applied Psychology* 80, 607–620.

Schmitt, N. (1977). Interrater agreement in dimensionality and combination of assessment center judgments. *Journal of Applied Psychology* 62, 171–176.

Schmitt, N., and Cohen, S. A. (1989). Internal analyses of task ratings by job incumbents. *Journal of Applied Psychology* 73, 96–104.

Schmitt, N., and Coyle, B. W. (1979). Applicant decisions in the employment interview. *Journal of Applied Psychology* 61, 184–192.

Schmitt, N., Coyle, B. W., and Mellon, P. M. (1978). Subgroup differences in predictor and criterion variances and differential validity. *Journal of Applied Psychology* 63, 667–672.

Schmitt, N., Coyle, B. W., and Rauschenberger, J. (1977). A Monte Carlo evaluation of three formula estimates of cross-validated multiple correlation. *Psychological Bulletin* 84, 751–758.

Schmitt, N., Gilliland, S. W., Landis, R. S., and Devine, D. (1993). Computer-based testing applied to selection of secretarial applicants. *Personnel Psychology* 46, 149–165.

Schmitt, N., Gooding, R. Z., Noe, R. A., and Kirsch, M. (1984). Meta-analysis of validity studies published between 1964 and 1982 and the investigation of study characteristics. *Personnel Psychology* 37, 407–422.

Schmitt, N., and Lappin, M. (1980). Race and sex as determinants of the mean and variance of performance ratings. *Journal of Applied Psychology* 65, 428–435.

Schmitt, N., Mellon, P. M., and Bylenga, C. (1978). Sex differences in validity for academic and employment criteria, and different types of predictors. *Journal of Applied Psychology* 63, 145–150.

Schmitt, N., and Stults, D. (1986). Methodology review: Analysis of multitrait-multimethod matrices. *Applied Psychological Measurement* 10, 1–22.

Schmitz, E. J. (1988). Improving personnel performance through assignment policy. In B. F. Green, Jr., H. Wing, and A. K. Wigdor (Eds.), *Linking military enlistment standards to job performance*. Washington, DC: National Academy Press.

Schneider, B. (1987). The people make the place. *Personnel Psychology* 40, 437–453.

Schneider, J., and Mitchel, J. O. (1980). Functions of life insurance agency managers and relationships with agency characteristics and managerial tenure. *Personnel Psychology* 33, 795–808.

Schneider, J. R., and Schmitt, N. (1992). An exercise design approach to understanding assessment center dimension and exercise constructs. *Journal of Applied Psychology* 77, 32–41.

Schoenfeldt, L. F. (1974). Utilization of manpower: Development and evaluation of an assessment-classification model for matching individuals with jobs. *Journal of Applied Psychology* 59, 583–595.

Schoenfeldt, L. F., Schoenfeldt, B. B., Acker, S. R., and Perlson, M. R. (1976). Content validity revisited: The development of a content-oriented test of industrial reading. *Journal of Applied Psychology* 61, 581–588.

Scholarios, D. M., Johnson, C. D., and Zeidner, J. (1994). Selecting predictors for maximizing the classification efficiency of a battery. *Journal of Applied Psychology* 79, 412–424.

Schrader, A. D., and Osburn, H. G. (1977). Biodata faking: Effects of induced subtlety and position specificity. *Personnel Psychology* 30, 395–404.

Schriesheim, J. F. (1980). The social context of leader-subordinate relations: An investigation of the effects of group cohesiveness. *Journal of Applied Psychology* 65, 183–194.

Schuler, R. S. (1992, Summer). Strategic human resources management: Linking the people with the strategic needs of the business. *Organizational Dynamics,* pp. 18-32.

Schuler, R. S. (Ed.). (1993). *Strategic human resources management: A special report from Organizational Dynamics.* New York: American Management Association.

Schuler, R. S., and Jackson, S. E. (1989). Determinants of human resource management priorities and implications for industrial relations. *Journal of Management* 15, 89–99.

Schwab, D. P., and Heneman, H. G., III. (1978). Age stereotyping in performance appraisal. *Journal of Applied Psychology* 63, 573–578.

Schwager v. *Sun Oil Co. of Pa.* (10th Cir. 1979). 591 F.2d 58.

Schwartz, F. N. (1992, March-April). Women as a business imperative. *Harvard Business Review,* pp. 105–113.

Seberhagen, L. W. (1977). Federal EEO requirements for state and local government. In S. Mussio (Ed.), *Self-administered instruction in personnel selection.* Minneapolis: Minneapolis Civil Service Commission.

Seberhagen, L. W., McCollum, M. D., and Churchill, C. D. (1972). *Legal aspects of personnel selection in the public service.* Chicago: International Personnel Management Association.

Sechrest, L. (1963). Incremental validity: A recommendation. *Educational and Psychological Measurement* 23, 153–158.

Senge, P. M. (1990). *The fifth discipline: The art and practice of the learning organization.* Garden City, NY: Doubleday.

Sessa, V. J. (1992). Managing diversity at the Xerox Corporation: Balanced workforce goals and caucus groups. In S. E. Jackson (Ed.), *Diversity in the workplace.* New York: Guilford, pp. 37–64.

Sewell, C. (1981). Pre-employment investigations: The key to security in hiring. *Personnel Journal* 60 (5), 376–379.

Sexual harassment: Preventive measures. (1992, January). *Bulletin.* Denver: Mountain States Employers Council, p. 2.

Shaffer, G. S., Saunders, V., and Owens, W. A. (1986). Additional evidence for the accuracy of biographical data: Long-term retest and observer ratings. *Personnel Psychology* 39, 791–809.

Shalley, C. E., Oldham, G. R., and Porac, J. F. (1987). Effects of goal difficulty, goal-setting method, and expected external evaluation on intrinsic motivation. *Academy of Management Journal* 30, 553–563.

Shapira, Z., and Shirom, A. (1980). New issues in the use of behaviorally anchored rating scales: Level of analysis, the effects of incident frequency, and external validation. *Journal of Applied Psychology* 65, 517–523.

Sharf, J. C. (1988). Litigating personnel measurement policy. *Journal of Vocational Behavior* 33, 235–271.

Sharpe, R. (1995, April 20). EEOC is making sweeping changes in handling cases. *The Wall Street Journal,* p. B11.

Sheley, E. (1995). High-tech recruiting methods. *HR Magazine* 40 (9), 61–64.

Shellenbarger, S. (1993, September 14). Concerns fight to be called best for moms. *The Wall Street Journal,* pp. B1, B11.

Shenkar, O. (1994, Spring/Summer). The People's Republic of China: Raising the bamboo screen through international management research. *International Studies of Management and Organizations,* pp. 9–34.

Sheridan, J. E. (1992). Organizational culture and employee retention. *Academy of Management Journal* 35, 1036–1056.

Sherif, M. (1966). *In common predicament: Social psychology of intergroup conflict and cooperation.* New York: Houghton Mifflin.

Shore, L. M., and Tetrick, L. E. (1991). A construct validity study of the Survey of Perceived Organizational Support. *Journal of Applied Psychology* 76, 637–643.

Shore, T. H., Shore, L. M., and Thornton, G. C. III. (1992). Construct validity of self- and peer evaluations of performance dimensions in an assessment center. *Journal of Applied Psychology* 77, 42–54.

Siegel, A. I. (1983). The miniature job training and evaluation approach: Additional findings. *Personnel Psychology* 36, 41–56.

Siegel, A. I., and Bergman, B. A. (1975). A job learning approach to performance prediction. *Personnel Psychology* 28, 325–339.

Siegel, L. (1982). Paired comparison evaluations of managerial effectiveness by peers and supervisors. *Personnel Psychology* 37, 703–710.

Siero, S., Boon, M., Kok, G., and Siero, F. (1989). Modification of driving behavior in a large transport organization: A field experiment. *Journal of Applied Psychology* 74, 417–423.

Silva, J. M., and Jacobs, R. R. (1993). Performance as a function of increased minority hiring. *Journal of Applied Psychology* 78, 591–601.

Silverman, S. B., and Wexley, K. N. (1984). Reaction of employees to performance appraisal interviews as a function of their participation in rating scale development. *Personnel Psychology* 37, 703–710.

Singer, M. S., and Bruhns, C. (1991). Relative effect of applicant work experience and academic qualification on selection interview decisions: A study of between-sample generalizability. *Journal of Applied Psychology* 76, 550–559.

Sirota, Alper, and Pfau, Inc. (1989). *Report to respondents: Survey of views toward corporate education and training practices.* New York: Author.

Siskin, B. R. (1995). Relation between performance and banding. *Human Performance* 8 (3), 215–226.

Sisson, D. E. (1948). Forced choice, the new Army rating. *Personnel Psychology* 1, 365–381.

Sisson, D. E. (1953). *Science and human behavior.* New York: Macmillan.

Smith, P. C., and Kendall, L. M. (1963). Retranslation of expectations: An approach to the construction of unambiguous anchors for rating scales. *Journal of Applied Psychology* 47, 149–155.

Smither, J. W., Collins, H., and Buda, R. (1989). When ratee satisfaction influences performance evaluations: A case of illusory correlation. *Journal of Applied Psychology* 74, 599–605.

Smither, J. W., London, M., Vasilopoulos, N. L., Reilly, R. R., Millsap, R., and Salvemini, N. (1995). An examination of the effects of an upward feedback program over time. *Personnel Psychology* 48, 1–34.

Smither, J. W., Reilly, R. R., Millsap, R. E., Pearlman, K., and Stoffey, R. W. (1993). Applicant reactions to selection procedures. *Personnel Psychology* 46, 49–76.

Snyder, R. A., Raben, C. S., and Farr, J. L. (1980). A model for the systematic evaluation of human resource development programs. *Academy of Management Review* 5, 431–444.

Society for Industrial and Organizational Psychology, Inc. (1987). *Principles for the validation and use of personnel selection procedures* (3rd ed.). College Park, MD: Author.

Solomon, J. (1989, April 4). As firms' personnel files grow, worker privacy falls. *The Wall Street Journal,* p. B1.

Solomon, R. L. (1949). An extension of a control group design. *Psychological Bulletin* 46, 137–150.

Sonnenfeld, J. S., and Peiperl, M. A. (1988). Staffing policy as a strategic response: A typology of career systems. *Academy of Management Review* 13, 588–600.

Sorcher, M., and Spence, R. (1982). The interface project: Behavior modeling as social technology in South Africa. *Personnel Psychology* 35, 557–581.

Spector, P. E. (1976). Choosing response categories for simulated rating scales. *Journal of Applied Psychology* 61, 374–375.

Spector, P. E., and Levine, E. L. (1987). Meta-analysis for integrating study outcomes: A Monte Carlo study of its susceptibility to Type I and Type II errors. *Journal of Applied Psychology* 72, 3–9.

Sprangers, M., and Hoogstraten, J. (1989). Pretesting effects in retrospective pretest-posttest designs. *Journal of Applied Psychology* 74, 265–272.

Srinivas, S., and Motowidlo, S. J. (1987). Effects of raters' stress on the dispersion and favorability of performance ratings. *Journal of Applied Psychology* 72, 247–251.

Stahl, M. J. (1983). Achievement, power, and managerial motivation: Selecting managerial talent with the job choice exercise. *Personnel Psychology* 36, 775–789.

Stahl, M. J., Grigsby, D. W., and Gulati, A. (1985). Comparing the Job Choice Exercise and the multiple-choice version of the Miner Sentence Completion Scale. *Journal of Applied Psychology* 70, 228–232.

Stahl, M. J., and Harrell, A. M. (1982). Evolution and validation of a behavioral decision theory measurement approach to achievement, power, and affiliation. *Journal of Applied Psychology* 67, 744–751.

Staines, G. L., and Pleck, J. H. (1984). Nonstandard work schedules and family life. *Journal of Applied Psychology* 69, 515–523.

Stamoulis, D. T., and Hauenstein, N. M. (1993). Rater training and rating accuracy: Training for dimensional accuracy versus training for ratee differentiation. *Journal of Applied Psychology* 78, 994–1003.

Steers, R. M., and Porter, L. W. (Eds.). (1975). *Motivation and work behavior.* New York: McGraw-Hill.

Steiner, D. D., and Rain, J. S. (1989). Immediate and delayed primacy and recency effects in performance evaluation. *Journal of Applied Psychology* 74, 136–142.

Stevens, S. S. (1951). Mathematics, measurement, and psychophysics. In S. S. Stevens (Ed.), *Handbook of experimental psychology.* New York: Wiley, 1–49.

Stevenson, R. W. (1989, July 10). Workers who turn in bosses use law to seek big rewards. *New York Times,* pp. 1, D3.

Stewart, R. (1982). A model for understanding managerial jobs and behavior. *Academy of Management Review* 7, 7–13.

Stockford, L., and Bissel, H. W. (1949). Factors involved in establishing a merit rating scale. *Personnel* 26, 94–116.

Stokes, G. S., Hogan, J. B., and Snell, A. F. (1993). Comparability of incumbent and applicant samples for the development of biodata keys: The influence of social desirability. *Personnel Psychology* 46, 739–762.

Stone, D. L., Gueutal, H. G., and McIntosh, B. (1984). The effects of feedback sequence and expertise of the rater on perceived feedback accuracy. *Personnel Psychology* 37, 487–506.

Stone, D. L., and Kotch, D. A. (1989). Individuals' attitudes toward organizational drug testing policies and practices. *Journal of Applied Psychology* 74, 518–521.

Stone, D. L., and Stone, E. F. (1987). Effects of missing application-blank information on personnel selection decisions: Do privacy-protection strategies bias the outcome? *Journal of Applied Psychology* 72, 452–456.

Stone, E. F., and Hollenbeck, J. R. (1984). Some issues associated with the use of moderated regression. *Organizational Behavior and Human Performance* 34, 195–213.

Stone, E. F., and Hollenbeck, J. R. (1989). Clarifying some controversial issues surrounding statistical procedures for detecting moderator variables: Empirical evidence and related matters. *Journal of Applied Psychology* 74, 3–10.

Stone-Romero, E. F., Alliger, G. M., and Aguinis, H. (1994). Type II error problems in the use of moderated multiple regression for the detection of moderating effects in dichotomous variables. *Journal of Management* 20, 167–178.

Stone-Romero, E. F., and Anderson, L. E. (1994). Relative power of moderated multiple regression and the comparison of subgroup correlation coefficients for detecting moderating effects. *Journal of Applied Psychology* 79, 354–359.

Strategic planning. (1996, August 26). *Business Week,* p. 50.

Streufert, S., Pogash, R., and Piasecki, M. (1988). Simulation-based assessment of managerial competence: Reliability and validity. *Personnel Psychology* 41, 537–557.

Stroh, L. K., Brett, J. M., and Reilly, A. H. (1992). All the right stuff: A comparison of female and male managers' career progression. *Journal of Applied Psychology* 77, 251–260.

Study hints job bias against the foreign-looking. (1988, November 20). *New York Times,* p. 27.

Stuit, D. B., and Wilson, J. T. (1946). The effect of an increasingly well defined criterion on the prediction of success at naval training school (tactical radar). *Journal of Applied Psychology* 30, 614–623.

Stutzman, T. M. (1983). Within classification job differences. *Personnel Psychology* 36, 503-516.

Sulsky, L. M., and Balzer, W. K. (1988). Meaning and measurement of performance rating accuracy: Some methodological and theoretical concerns. *Journal of Applied Psychology* 73, 497–506.

Taft, R. (1959). Multiple methods of personality assessment. *Psychological Bulletin* 56, 333–352.

Tannenbaum, R. J., and Wesley, S. (1993). Agreement between committee-based and field-based job analyses: A study in the context of licensure testing. *Journal of Applied Psychology* 78, 975–980.

Task Force on Assessment Center Standards. (1979, June). *Standards and ethical considerations for assessment center operations.* Paper presented at the VII International Congress on the Assessment Center Method, New Orleans.

Taylor, H. C., and Russell, J. T. (1939). The relationship of validity coefficients to the practical effectiveness of tests in selection. *Journal of Applied Psychology* 23, 565–578.

Taylor, M. S., and Bergmann, T. J. (1987). Organizational recruitment activities and applicants' reactions at different stages of the recruitment process. *Personnel Psychology* 40, 261–285.

Taylor, S., Jr. (1987, March 27). Court's change of course. *New York Times,* pp. A1, A17.

Teamsters v. *U.S.* (1977). 14 U.S. 7579.

Tenopyr, M. L. (1977). Content-construct confusion. *Personnel Psychology* 30, 47–54.

Tenopyr, M. L., (1984, November). *So let it be with content validity.* Paper presented at the Content Validity III Conference, Bowling Green, Ohio.

Tepper, B. J. (1994). Investigation of general and program-specific attitudes toward corporate drug-testing policies. *Journal of Applied Psychology* 79, 392–401.

Tesluk, P. E., Farr, J. L., Mathieu, J. E., and Vance, R. J. (1995). Generalization of employee involvement training to the job setting: Individual and situational effects. *Personnel Psychology* 48, 607–632.

Tett, R. P., Jackson, D. N., and Rothstein, M. (1991). Personality measures as predictors of job perfor-

mance: A meta-analytic review. *Personnel Psychology* 44, 703–742.

Tett, R. P., Jackson, D. N., Rothstein, M., and Reddon, J. R. (1994). Meta-analysis of personality-job performance relations: A reply to Ones, Mount, Barrick, and Hunter (1994). *Personnel Psychology* 47, 157–172.

The New Factory Worker. (1996, September 30). *Business Week,* pp. 59–68.

Theaman, M. (1984). The impact of peer review on professional practice. *American Psychologist* 39, 406–414.

Thomas, H. (1988). What is the interpretation of the validity generalization estimate $S_\rho^2 = S_r^2 - S_e^2$? *Journal of Applied Psychology* 73, 679–682.

Thomas, H. (1990). A likelihood-based model for validity generalization. *Journal of Applied Psychology* 75, 13–20.

Thomas, R. R., Jr. (1990, March-April). From affirmative action to affirming diversity. *Harvard Business Review,* pp. 107–117.

Thorndike, E. L. (1920). A constant error in psychological ratings. *Journal of Applied Psychology* 4, 25–29.

Thorndike, R. L. (1949). *Personnel selection: Test and measurement techniques.* New York: Wiley.

Thorndike, R. L. (1950). The problem of classification of personnel. *Psychometrika* 15, 215–235.

Thorndike, R. L. (1971). Concepts of culture fairness. *Journal of Educational Measurement* 8, 63–70.

Thornton, G. C. (1980). Psychometric properties of self-appraisals of job performance. *Personnel Psychology* 33, 263–271.

Thornton, G. C., III., and Byham, W. C. (1982). *Assessment centers and managerial performance.* New York: Academic Press.

Thornton, G. C., and Zorich, S. (1980). Training to improve observer accuracy. *Journal of Applied Psychology* 65, 351–354.

Thurstone, L. L. (1931). *The reliability and validity of tests.* Ann Arbor, MI: Edwards.

Toops, H. A. (1944). The criterion. *Educational and Psychological Measurement* 4, 271–297.

Tornow, W. W., and Pinto, P. R. (1976). The development of a managerial job taxonomy: A system for describing, classifying, and evaluating executive positions. *Journal of Applied Psychology* 61, 410–418.

Tracey, J. B., Tannenbaum, S. I., and Kavanagh, M. J. (1995). Applying trained skills on the job: The importance of the work environment. *Journal of Applied Psychology* 80, 239–252.

Trattner, M. H. (1963). A comparison of three methods for assembling an aptitude test battery. *Personnel Psychology* 16, 221–232.

Trattner, M. H. (1982). Synthetic validity and its application to the Uniform Guidelines' validation requirements. *Personnel Psychology* 35, 383–397.

Trattner, M. H., and O'Leary, B. S. (1980). Sample sizes for specified statistical power in testing for differential validity. *Journal of Applied Psychology* 65, 127–134.

Trotter, R., Zacur, S. R., and Greenwood, W. (1982). The pregnancy disability amendment: What the law provides, Part II. *Personnel Administrator* 27, 55–58.

Tsui, A. S., and Ohlott, P. (1988). Multiple assessment of managerial effectiveness: Interrater agreement and consensus in effectiveness models. *Personnel Psychology* 41, 779–803.

Tucker, D. H., and Rowe, P. M. (1977). Consulting the application form prior to the interview: An essential step in the selection process. *Journal of Applied Psychology* 62, 283–287.

Tullar, W. D., Mullins, T. W., and Caldwell, S. A. (1979). Effects of interview length and applicant quality on interview decision time. *Journal of Applied Psychology* 64, 669–674.

Turban, D. B., and Keon, T. L. (1993). Organizational attractiveness: An interactionist perspective. *Journal of Applied Psychology* 78, 184–193.

Turban, D. B., and Jones, A. P. (1988). Supervisor-subordinate similarity: Types, effects, and mechanisms. *Journal of Applied Psychology* 73, 228–234.

Turnage, J. J., and Muchinsky, P. M. (1984). A comparison of the predictive validity of assessment center evaluations versus traditional measures in forecasting supervisory job performance: Interpretive implications of criterion distortion for the assessment paradigm. *Journal of Applied Psychology* 69, 595–602.

Tziner, A., and Dolan, S. (1982). Validity of an assessment center for identifying future female officers in the military. *Journal of Applied Psychology* 67, 728–736.

Uhlaner, J. E. (1960, July). *Systems research—Opportunity and challenge for the measurement research psychologist.* Tech. Research Note 108. Washington, DC: U.S. Army Personnel Research Office.

Ulrich, D. (1986). Human resource planning as a competitive edge. *Human Resource Planning* 9 (2), 41–50.

Umstot, D. D., Bell, C. H., and Mitchell, T. R. (1976). Effects of job enrichment and task goals on satisfaction and productivity: Implications for job design. *Journal of Applied Psychology* 61, 379–394.

Uniform guidelines on employee selection procedures (1978). *Federal Register* 43, 38290–38315.

Uniformed Services Employment and Reemployment Rights Act of 1994. Public Law 103–353; H. R. 995.

U.S. Congress, Office of Technology Assessment. (1983, November). *Scientific validity of polygraph testing: A research review and evaluation* (OTA-TM-H-15). Washington, DC: Author.

U.S. Department of Labor. (1972). *Handbook for analyzing jobs.* Washington, DC: U.S. Government Printing Office.

U.S. Department of Labor. (1982). *A guide to job analysis: A "how to" publication for occupational analysts.* Washington, DC: U.S. Government Printing Office.

U.S. Department of Labor. (1986). *Dictionary of occupational titles* (4th ed. supplement). Washington, DC: U.S. Government Printing Office.

U.S. Department of Labor. (1993, August). *High-performance work practices and firm performance.* Washington, DC: U.S. Government Printing Office.

U.S. Supreme Court (1971). *Griggs* v. *Duke Power Company. United States Reports* 401, 424.

Valenzi, E. R., and Andrews, I. R. (1973). Individual differences in the decision process of employment interviewers. *Journal of Applied Psychology* 58, 49–53.

Vance, R. J., Coovert, M. D., MacCallum, R. C., and Hedge, J. W. (1989). Construct models of task performance. *Journal of Applied Psychology* 74, 447–455.

Vance, R. J., Winne, P. S., and Wright, E. S. (1983). A longitudinal examination of rater and ratee effects in performance ratings. *Personnel Psychology* 36, 609–620.

Van de Vliert, E., Huismans, S. E., and Stok, J. J. L. (1985). The criterion approach to unraveling beta and alpha change. *Academy of Management Review* 10, 269–275.

Van Zelst, R. H. (1952). Sociometrically selected work teams increase production. *Personnel Psychology* 5, 175–185.

Vetter, E. (1967). *Manpower planning for high talent personnel.* Ann Arbor: Bureau of Industrial Relations, University of Michigan.

Vevea, J. L., Clements, N. C., and Hedges, L. V. (1993). Assessing the effects of selection bias on validity data for the General Aptitude Test Battery. *Journal of Applied Psychology* 78, 981–987.

Vicino, F. C., and Bass, B. M. (1978). Lifespace variables and managerial success. *Journal of Applied Psychology* 63, 81–88.

Vigneau, J. D. (1995). To catch a thief—and other workplace investigations. *HR Magazine* 40 (1), 90–95.

Vinchur, A. J., Schippmann, J. S., Smalley, M. D., and Rothe, H. F. (1991). Productivity consistency of foundry chippers and grinders: A 6-year field study. *Journal of Applied Psychology* 76, 134–136.

Von Glinow, M. A., Driver, M. J., Brousseau, K., and Prince, J. B. (1983). The design of a career-oriented human resource system. *Academy of Management Review* 8, 23–32.

Vroom, V. H., and Yetton, P. W. (1973). *Leadership and decision making.* Pittsburgh: University of Pittsburgh Press.

Wainer, H. (1978). On the sensitivity of regression and regressors. *Psychological Bulletin* 85, 267–273.

Waldman, D. A., and Avolio, B. J. (1991). Race effects in performance evaluations: Controlling for ability, education, and experience. *Journal of Applied Psychology* 76, 897–901.

Walker, J. W. (1969). Forecasting manpower needs. *Harvard Business Review* 47, 152–164.

Walker, J. W. (1974). Evaluating the practical effectiveness of human resource planning applications. *Human Resource Management* 13, 19–27.

Walker, J. W. (1980). *Human resource planning.* New York: McGraw-Hill.

Wallace, S. R. (1965). Criteria for what? *American Psychologist* 20, 411–417.

Walter, K. (1995a). Values statements that augment corporate success. *HR Magazine,* 40 (10), 87–93.

Walter, K. (1995b). Ethics hotlines tap into more than wrongdoing. *HR Magazine,* 40 (9), 79–85.

Walton, R. E. (1978, Spring). The Topeka story: Teaching an old dog food new tricks. *The Wharton Magazine,* pp. 38–46.

Wang, M. D., and Stanley, J. C. (1970). Differential weighting: A review of methods in empirical studies. *Review of Educational Research* 40, 663–705.

Wanous, J. P. (1977). Organizational entry: Newcomers moving from outside to inside. *Psychological Bulletin* 84, 601–618.

Wanous, J. P. (1989). Installing a realistic job preview: Ten tough choices. *Personnel Psychology* 42, 117–134.

Wanous, J. P., Sullivan, S. E., and Malinak, J. (1989). The role of judgment calls in meta-analysis. *Journal of Applied Psychology* 74, 259–264.

Ward, J. H., and Hook, M. E. (1963). Application of a hierarchical grouping procedure to a problem of grouping profiles. *Educational and Psychological Measurement* 23, 69–82.

Wards Cove Packing v. *Antonio.* (1989). U.S. Supreme Court, No. 87-1387.

Warner, J. (1991, September 30). Nothing succeeds like a succession plan. *Business Week,* pp. 126, 127.

Washington v. *Davis* (1976). 96 U.S. 2574.

Wayne, S. J., and Liden, R. C. (1995). Effects of impression management on performance ratings: A longitudinal study. *Academy of Management Journal* 38, 232–260.

Webb, E. J., Campbell, D. T., Schwartz, R. D., Sechrest, L., and Grove, J. B. (1981). *Nonreactive measures in the social sciences* (2nd ed.). Boston: Houghton Mifflin.

Webb, S. L. (1984, December). Sexual harassment: Court costs rise for a persistent problem. *Management Review,* pp. 25–28.

Webster, E. C. (1982). *The employment interview: A social judgment process.* Ontario, Canada: S.I.P.

Webster, E. C. (1964). *Decision making in the employment interview.* Montreal: Eagle.

Weekley, J. A., Frank, B., O'Connor, E. J., and Peters, L. H. (1985). A comparison of three methods of estimating the standard deviation of performance in dollars. *Journal of Applied Psychology* 70, 122–126.

Weekley, J. A., and Gier, J. A. (1987). Reliability and validity of the situational interview for a sales position. *Journal of Applied Psychology* 72, 484–487.

Weekley, J. A., and Gier, J. A. (1989). Ceilings in the reliability and validity of performance ratings: The case of expert raters. *Academy of Management Journal* 32, 213–222.

Weiss, D. J., and Dawis, R. V. (1960). An objective validation of factual interview data. *Journal of Applied Psychology* 40, 381–385.

Weiss, D. J., England, G. W., and Lofquist, L. H. (1961). *Validity of work histories obtained by interview* (Minnesota Studies in Vocational Rehabilitation: No. 12). Minneapolis: University of Minnesota.

Weiss, R. S., and Rein, M. (1970). The evaluation of broad aim programs: Experimental design, its difficulties, and an alternative. *Administrative Science Quarterly* 15, 97–109.

Weitz, J. (1961). Criteria for criteria. *American Psychologist* 16, 228–231.

Wellins, R. S., Byham, W. C., and Wilson, J. M. (1991). *Empowered teams: Creating self-directed work groups that improve quality, productivity, and participation.* San Francisco: Jossey-Bass.

Wermiel, S. (1985, June 18). Justices adopt a tough test for retirement. *The Wall Street Journal,* p. 2.

Wermiel, S., and Trost, C. (1986, June 20). Justices say hostile job environment due to sex harassment violates rights. *The Wall Street Journal,* p. 2.

Werner, J. M. (1994). Dimensions that make a difference: Examining the impact of in-role and extrarole behaviors on supervisory ratings. *Journal of Applied Psychology* 79, 98–107.

Wernimont, P. F. (1962). Re-evaluation of a weighted application blank for office personnel. *Journal of Applied Psychology* 46, 417–419.

Wernimont, P. F., and Campbell, J. P. (1968). Signs, samples, and criteria. *Journal of Applied Psychology* 52, 372–376.

Wesman, A. G. (1952). *Reliability and confidence.* (Test Service Bulletin No. 44). New York: The Psychological Corporation.

Wesman, A. G. (1966). *Double-entry expectancy tables* (Test Service Bulletin No. 56). New York: The Psychological Corporation.

Wessel, D. (1989, September 7). Evidence is skimpy that drug testing works, but employers embrace practice. *Wall Street Journal,* pp. B1, B8.

Wexley, K. N. (1984). Personnel training. *Annual Review of Psychology* 35, 519–551.

Wexley, K. N., Alexander, R. A., Greenawalt, J. P., and Couch, M. A. (1980). Attitudinal congruence and similarity as related to interpersonal evaluations in manager-subordinate dyads. *Academy of Management Journal* 23, 320–330.

Wexley, K. N., and Latham, G. P. (1991). *Developing and training human resources in organizations* (2nd ed.). New York: Harper-Collins.

Wexley, K. N., Sanders, R. E., and Yukl, G. A. (1973). Training interviewers to eliminate contrast effects in employment interviews. *Journal of Applied Psychology* 57, 233–236.

White, B. H. (1972). Problems of industrial organizations in manpower planning and forecasting. In E. H. Burack and J. W. Walker (Eds.), *Manpower planning and programming.* Boston: Allyn & Bacon.

White, L. P., and Wooten, K. C. (1983). Ethical dilemmas in various stages of organizational development. *Academy of Management Review* 8, 690–697.

White, R. W. (1959). Motivation reconsidered: The concept of competence. *Psychological Bulletin* 66, 297–333.

Whitehead, R. F., Suiter, R. N., and Thorpe, R. P. (1969, August). The development of a computer-assisted distribution and assignment system for Navy enlisted personnel. *U.S. Naval Personnel Research Activity Research Report, SRR 70-1,* San Diego, CA.

Whitely, W. (1985). Managerial work behavior: An integration of results from two major approaches. *Academy of Management Journal* 28, 344–362.

Whyte, W. F. (1955). *Money and motivation.* New York: Harper.

Wiersner, W., and Cronshaw, S. (1988). A meta-analytic investigation of the impact of interview format and degree of structure on the validity of the employment interview. *Journal of Occupational Psychology* 61, 275–290.

Wigdor, A. K., and Garner, W. R. (Eds.). (1982). *Ability testing: Use, consequences, and controversies.* Washington, DC: National Academy Press.

Wiggins, J. S. (1973). *Personality and prediction: Principles of personality assessment.* Reading, MA: Addison-Wesley.

Wikstrom, W. S. (1971). *Manpower planning: Evolving systems.* (Report No. 521). New York: The Conference Board.

Wilder, D. A. (1984). Intergroup contact: The typical member and the exception to the rule. *Journal of Experimental and Social Psychology* 20, 177–194.

Wilkins, A. L., and Dyer, W. G., Jr. (1988). Toward culturally sensitive theories of culture change. *Academy of Management Review* 13, 522–533.

Williams, C. R., Labig, C. E., Jr., and Stone, T. H. (1993). Recruitment sources and posthire outcomes for job applicants and new hires: A test of two hypotheses. *Journal of Applied Psychology* 78, 163–172.

Williams, J. R., and Levy, P. E. (1992). The effects of perceived system knowledge on the agreement between self-ratings and supervisor ratings. *Personnel Psychology* 45, 835–847.

Williams, L. J., Cote, J. A., and Buckley, M. R. (1989). Lack of method variance in self-reported affect and perceptions at work: Reality or artifact? *Journal of Applied Psychology* 74, 462–468.

Williams, W. (1985, June 9). White-collar crime: Booming again. *The New York Times,* pp. F1, F6.

Wilson, D. S., and Donnerstein, E. (1976). Legal and ethical aspects of nonreactive social psychological research: An excursion into the public mind. *American Psychologist* 31, 765–773.

Woehr, D. J. (1994). Understanding frame-of-reference training: The impact of training on the recall of performance information. *Journal of Applied Psychology* 79, 525–534.

Wohlers, A. J., and London, M. (1989). Ratings of managerial characteristics: Evaluation, difficulty, co-worker agreement, and self-awareness. *Personnel Psychology* 42, 235–261.

Wollowick, H. B., and McNamara, W. J. (1969). Relationship of the components of an assessment center to management success. *Journal of Applied Psychology* 53, 348–352.

Wood, R. E., Mento, A. J., and Locke, E. A. (1987). Task complexity as a moderator of goal effects: A meta-analysis. *Journal of Applied Psychology* 72, 416–425.

Workplace of the future: A Report of the Conference on the Future of the American Workplace. U.S. Departments of Commerce and Labor, July 26, 1993, p. 15.

Wygant v. *Jackson Board of Education.* (1986). 476 U.S. 261.

Yelsey, A. (1982). Validity of human resources forecast designs. *Human Resource Planning* 5 (4), 217–224.

Yorks, L., and Whitsett, D. A. (1985). Hawthorne, Topeka, and the issue of science versus advocacy in organizational behavior. *Academy of Management Review* 10, 21–30.

Young, F. W. (1984). Scaling. *Annual Review of Psychology* 35, 55–81.

Yu, J., and Murphy, K. R. (1993). Modesty bias in self-ratings of performance: A test of the cultural relativity hypothesis. *Personnel Psychology* 46, 357–363.

Zalkind, S. S., and Costello, T. W. (1962). Perception: Some recent research and implications for administration. *Administrative Science Quarterly* 7, 218–235.

Zedeck, S., and Cascio, W. F. (1982). Performance appraisal decisions as a function of rater training and purpose of the appraisal. *Journal of Applied Psychology* 67, 752–758.

Zedeck, S., and Cascio, W. F.(1984). Psychological issues in personnel decisions. *Annual Review of Psychology* 35, 461–518.

Zedeck, S., Cascio, W. F., Goldstein, I. L., and Outtz, J. (1996). Sliding bands: An alternative to top-down selection. In R. S. Barrett (Ed.), *Fair employment strategies in human resource management* (pp. 222-234). Westport, CT: Quorum.

Zedeck, S., and Kafry, D. (1977). Capturing rater policies for processing evaluation data. *Organizational Behavior and Human Performance* 18, 269–294.

Zedeck, S., Outtz, J., Cascio, W. F., and Goldstein, I. L. (1991). Why do "testing experts" have such limited vision? *Human Performance* 4 (4), 297–308.

Zeidner, J., Johnson, C., Orlansky, J., Schmitz, E., and Nord, R. (1988, December). *The economic benefits of predicting job performance.* Alexandria, VA: Institute for Defense Analyses.

Zohar, D. (1980). Safety climate in industrial organizations: Theoretical and applied implications. *Journal of Applied Psychology* 65, 96–102.

SUBJECT INDEX

NAME INDEX